Gunkholing in South Puget Sound

A Comprehensive Cruising Guide from Kingston-Edmonds South to Olympia

with Jo Bailey & Carl Nyberg

Ⓖ **'gunk•hol•ing'** *adj* : "a quiet anchorage, as in a cove used by small yachts (Random House);" where the anchor usually sinks into soft mud, or 'gunk'— thus 'gunkholing' applies to those who engage in this low-key, relaxed style of cruising (Bailey-Nyberg).

Published by San Juan Enterprises, Inc.
Seattle, Washington

Disclaimer: The charts, tables and illustrations contained in this book are not for navigational purposes, as the charts may not be current and are not reproduced in sufficient detail for use. Selected laws require all vessels to have on board, maintain, and use appropriate navigational charts and equipment. None of the material in this book is intended to replace nor substitute, any government or other navigational charts or other government publications, including *Notice to Mariners,* for current information regarding changes, additions and deletions to existing navigational materials.

San Juan Enterprises, Inc., and the authors offer this book as a general cruising guide about the cruising area, vessel outfitting, operation, and facilities and services. Experience, hands-on training and sources of written information beyond this book are necessary to engage in cruising safely. The reader is strongly advised to make use of all these sources prior to cruising Puget Sound.

San Juan Enterprises, Inc., and the authors do not guarantee or warrant information in this book to be complete, correct or current. The authors and publisher disclaim liability and responsibility to any person or entity with respect to any loss or damage caused, or alleged to be caused, directly or indirectly, by the use and/or interpretation of any of the information contained in this book.

The reader needs to understand that under no circumstances are the authors to be held responsible for any omissions, oversights or errors. This book is about cruising in this area as we know it or believe it to be.

GUNKHOLING IN SOUTH PUGET SOUND
The Comprehensive Cruising Guide from Kingston-Edmonds South to Olympia
With Joanne "Jo" Bailey and Carl Nyberg

Published by San Juan Enterprises, Inc.
3218 Portage Bay Place East
Seattle, Washington 98102
© 1997 by Joanne I. Bailey and Carl O. Nyberg
First edition printing 1997
All rights reserved
0 9 8 7 6 5 4 3 2 1

No part of this book may be reproduced in any form, or by any electronic, mechanical or other means, including photocopying and computer scanning, recording, or by any information storage and retrieval system, without permission in writing from the publisher, except for inclusion of brief quotations in a review.

Manufactured in the United States of America
Printed in the United States of America

Final book design and layout by Sally Cox Bryan, Carl and Jo
Edited by Sally Cox Bryan and Louise Dustrude
Photographs by Joanne Bailey, unless otherwise noted
Illustrations by Carl Nyberg
Cover photograph: Mount Rainier from Penrose Point State Marine Park
Back photo: Authors Joanne and Carl, by Debi Bailey

Library of Congress Cataloging-in-Publication Data
Library of Congress Catalog Card Number: 96-68526
Bailey, Joanne and Nyberg, Carl
        Gunkholing in South Puget Sound: The Complete Guide to Cruising from Kingston-Edmonds
    South to Olympia / Joanne "Jo" Bailey and Carl Nyberg, 1st Ed. Volume #4 in Gunkholing series
        Includes bibliographical references and index
        ISBN 0-944257-02-X

        1. Outdoor recreation—Washington (State)—Puget Sound. 2. Outdoor recreation—Washington
(State)—Puget Sound—Directories. 3. Puget Sound (Wash.)—Guidebooks. 4. Marinas—Washington
(State)—Puget Sound—Guidebooks. I. Title.

**Dedicated
To You, Our Readers**

We've written this book for you seasoned or novice mariners, residents or visitors, because you're enthusiastic about cruising, sailing or paddling adventures, including exploring the explorable in South Puget Sound, and anchoring serenely at the end of the day.

Visualize as you cruise what it must have been like many years ago for those chartless, able souls who plied these unique inland waters with determination, powered only by paddle, sail and oar. We've tried to weave the historical maritime past of South Sound with present day cruising facilities, including the gunkholes we've found.   And so . . . . .

Welcome aboard!

Jo and Carl

"Nothing can be more striking than the beauty of these waters without a shoal or rock or any danger whatever for the whole length of this Internal Navigation, the finest in the world, accustomed as we are to prize that of our own country," Lt. Charles Wilkes, commander of the U.S. Naval Exploring Expedition, 1838-42.

Acknowledgments, in addition to our families, with special thanks to Sally Cox Bryan (our angel, advisor and editor), are to due the following for helping us in so many different and special ways:

John Adams, Phil & Ledjie Ballard, Mike Bass, Beau Beauchamp, Robert Beckman, John & Lauralee Brainard, Sally & Bob Bryan, Ed Brighton, Howard & Pearl Calloway; Jon Daniel, Sue Anne Sanders & the crew at Captain's Nautical; Gerry & Jackie Carlstrom, John Condon, Rich Costello, Larry Duthie, Jerry Elfendahl, Jim Ellis, John Erickson, Don & Willa Fassett, Sally Giovine-Kerr, George & Betty Hansen, Dale & Ella Marie Hawley, Jerry & Jean Home, David Kutz, Eva Pickrell Meacham, Glen Miller, Steve Ness, Paul Petrucci, Dan Precourt, Gary Proutt, Lisa Randlett, Rod Smith, Howdie Springer, Gus & Ellyn Swanson, Kathy Timmons, Dick Wagner, Buz & Gina Whitely, Bill Watts, Geoff Wilson & Debbie Bennett, Robert Wing, Leonard Ziska; special Friday Harbor friends: John & Louise Dustrude, Les & Betsy Gunther, Hugh & Joan Lawrence, Lee & Tal Sturdivant (always with a warm meal and extra room); Army Corps of Engineers, Binsford & Mort, Portland, Oregon, for gracious use of quotations from Vancouver's Discovery of Puget Sound; personnel at Hiram M. Chittenden Locks; Goodman Middle School students, Gig Harbor, for quotations from their charming book, Along the Waterfront; National Ocean & Atmospheric Administration (NOAA), Puget Sound Cruising Club, Seattle Harbor Patrol, Seattle Parks Department, Seattle Historical Maritime Society, Museum of History & Industry, Surprise Charters, U.S. Coast Guard, Washington State Parks Department, Department of Natural Resources, Department of Fisheries & Wildlife, Washington State Ferries, and so many others.

Peter Puget Begins . . . .

In the pre-dawn darkness, waves slapping gently at the planked sides of two small boats, Peter Puget and his men started their voyage of exploration.

They were leaving Bainbridge Island's southeastern shore, heading south for they knew not what. It was Sunday, May 20, 1792.

From the decks of the 96-foot long sloop-of-war *Discovery,* Captain George Vancouver had directed the exploration of the Northwest Coast of North America, authorized by the British government.

Now he instructed Lt. Puget and Sailing Master Joseph Whidbey to lead a party in the launch and cutter to examine *"that branch of the inlet leading to the south-westward; keep always the starboard or continental shore on board; which was accordingly carried into execution, at four o'clock the next morning."*

Vancouver's orders to Puget sound strange to us. Heading south from the ship, the Olympic Peninsula would be to starboard. On his return Puget failed to investigate Dalco and East Passages and Commencement Bay which would then also be to starboard.

They were about to enter the incredibly beautiful, pristine wilderness of what would eventually be known as South Puget Sound. While they were the first recorded non-Native Americans to explore the Sound, Coastal Indians had been plying the waters in their fast, lightweight, masterfully designed cedar canoes for hundreds, even thousands, of years. They knew the secrets of the Sound that Puget was searching.

The two boats with 12 men were to return by the following Thursday and report to Vancouver on *"the appearance of the Country, its Productions and Inhabitants, if varying from what we have already seen."* They had one week's supply of food.

They actually explored most of the area within the seven days. It was a pretty remarkable feat considering that there were no navigational charts, channel markers, buoys or beacons to warn of potential shoals and offshore rocks, no tide and current charts or tables to help them navigate through narrow, fast-running passages; nothing to go on except their own innate sense of the sea, wind and weather.

Puget put the area "on the map" as he, Whidbey, and botanist Archibald Menzies painstakingly surveyed, charted and detailed the shorelines, natives, flora and fauna for the first time in recorded history.

Vancouver also surveyed much of South Sound. He became anxious as the men didn't return as soon as he had hoped. He headed south on May 26 through East Passage to Ketron Island, continuing on down to Budd Inlet, returning on the fourth day. He took no credit for his part in the exploration of the area, although he did verify many of Puget's findings.

"Thus, by our joint efforts, we had completely explored every turning of this extensive inlet and to commemorate Mr. Puget's exertions, the south extremity of it I named PUGET'S SOUND," Vancouver wrote.

It was 49 years later that Charles Wilkes surveyed the same region in the *Peacock* and *Vincennes.* He used many of the charts Vancouver had drawn and named many of the places Vancouver did not.

About the Authors

Jo and Carl are both Seattle natives and their combined cruising of Puget Sound, the San Juans and British Columbia waters amounts to well over 3/4 of a century in a variety of sailboats, including Carl's 50' yawl, Winsome; 24' schooner, Condor, and assorted dories and Port Madison prams; Jo's 8' El Toro, Wee Witch; 15' sloop, Naiad; 19' sloop, Winsome, and 29' sloop, Sea Witch. They currently cruise the 35' Chris Craft sloop, Scheherazade.

Baggy Wrinkle

'bag•gy•wrink•le' *noun* **:** short lengths of old line matted together
to protect against chafing (*Piloting*, Charles F. Chapman)

⒢ Gunkholing— *"the mariners term for cruising in sheltered waters and anchoring every night"* is really a great way to cruise. Anchoring in snug little bays, adventures on the beach, hikes in nearby woods, enjoying the beauty of the natural surroundings or watching twinkling city lights from afar—the stuff of which dreams and fond memories are made.

Where to Start . . . .

Gunkholing all of Puget Sound covers too large a geographic area for one book. We debated nearly a year on where to start ***Gunkholing in Puget Sound,*** finally deciding the material warrants two volumes to do it justice.

We cover unique and challenging weather, tide and currents in all of the Sound. There are many sheltered bays and harbors where local knowledge is critical. There are historical items of importance and interest to recreational mariners, as well as vignettes of experiences in each region. It seems logical to write about cruising in Puget Sound in two volumes, rather than try to compress all this information in one book.

This volume, ***Gunkholing in South Puget Sound,*** follows and crosses the wakes of George Vancouver, Peter Puget, Joseph Whidbey, Charles Wilkes and other explorers, as they proceeded south past Kingston-Edmonds into the upper reaches of Puget Sound in search of the Northwest Passage.

For those of you heading north, take heart. We try to be omni-directional in the book whenever possible: sometimes we circumnavigate islands, or cruise around inlets in varying directions— it doesn't matter which direction you are going.

Many cruising boaters in the greater Seattle and Tacoma areas flee north when "cruising season" arrrives, without considering the great places to explore in South Puget Sound, which offers a beautiful alternative.

South We Go . . . .

To find uncrowded bays, inlets and islands of this region, sometimes following in the wakes (keel tracks) of Puget, Vancouver or Wilkes; discovering intriguing **gunkholes,** sights to see and things to do, including wonderful state marine parks, other state lands, marinas, places to launch kayaks or runabouts, get boat repairs, buy groceries or fuel, even places to eat or drink lattes.

We'll visit villages, towns and cities along the seashore. We toss in snippets of history or nautical lore as we go, including where Peter Puget spent each night during his seven-day exploration of the Sound. It's taken us much longer than his seven days—more like nearly four years— to explore (granted in greater detail) the same area.

We hope you'll have as much fun reading and cruising with this book as we had cruising and writing it. After all, that's the purpose of boating.

As Seattle-born natives, while researching this book we learned so much of our state's history, maritime and otherwise, met so many wonderful people, renewed old friendships and had great experiences that it's been a fabulous time.

Let's get on with our cruising—hunting for the best of ***Gunkholing in South Puget Sound!***

When you're in a boat, you're where you're going!

Tribute by
GLEN CARTER
FORMER MARITIME EDITOR SEATTLE TIMES

*Every once in a while a book comes along to make the reader wonder how it was done. In my 25 years of waterfront wandering and sailing in the Seattle area, I had come to take things for granted. But **Gunkholing in South Puget Sound** shows me something new on page after page.*

A mariner can repeatedly sail past an intriguing landmark, place or thing, wondering about it. The book explains a lot through people and happenings of yesteryear as well as here and now.

Surprisingly, at the same time, the narration also is helping you navigate waters, mark by mark and light by light, that you may be visiting for the first time.

This is done meticulously, taking us beyond the visually obvious. For instance, while traversing the Ballard Locks, the reader not only sees handling of lines but is learning how the system operates, spiced by interesting incidents voiced by the lockmaster.

Ever cruised through the Locks, beyond Lake Union, Portage Bay and most all 50 miles around Lake Washington? The book takes you there. And far, far southward on a gunkholing tour highlighted through the eyes and words of earliest-day explorers and settlers in ports, towns, hamlets. But meanwhile guiding you, here and now, as if aboard a vessel which periodically drops anchor for visits ashore.

The book's historical matter reaches back beyond a century—as things were then. And readers a century from now likely will learn from this book, again with interest, how things are now in South Puget Sound, noting, as we do now, that only the bays inlets, passes, tides and mountains have changed little or none over time.

Thanks to this book, we can see clearer with better comprehension and appreciation those landmarks and waters we sometimes took for granted.

Congratulations to Jo and Carl on a big job so well done.

THANKS, GLEN!

Charts, Publications & Maps
Charts

Chart Number	Date	Name	Scale	Soundings
18440	08/05/95	Puget Sound	1:150,000	Fathoms
18441	02/18/95	Puget Sound—Northern Part	1:80,000	Fathoms
18445	06/03/95	Puget Sound—Possession Sound to Olympia/Hood Canal	1:80,000	Fathoms
18446	06/16/90	Puget Sound—Apple Cove Point to Keyport, Agate Passage Inset	1:25,000 / 1:10,000	Feet / Feet
18447	08/15/92	Lake Wash. Ship Canal—Side A / Lake Washington— Side B	1:10,000 / 1:25,000	Feet / Feet
18448	10/30/93	Puget Sound—Southern Part	1:80,000	Fathoms
18449	10/29/94	Puget Sound—Seattle to Bremerton	1:25,000	Feet
18450	08/22/92	Seattle Harbor, Elliott Bay, Duwamish Water Way	1:10,000	Feet
18453	08/05/95	Tacoma Harbor	1:15,000	Feet
18456	05/20/95	Olympia Harbor and Budd Inlet	1:20,000	Feet
18457	09/02/89	Puget Sound—Hammersley Inlet to Shelton	1:10,000	Feet
18473	08/14/93	Puget Sound—Oak Bay to Shilshole Bay	1:40,000	Fathoms
18474	03/25/95	Puget Sound—Shilshole Bay to Commencement Bay	1:40,000	Fathoms

Publications

Tide Tables, West Coast of North & South America, NOAA
Tidal Current Tables, Pacific Coast of North & South America, NOAA
Tidal Current Charts, Puget Sound, Southern Part, 1973
Tidal Current Charts, Puget Sound, Northern Part, 1973
Puget Sound Public Shellfish Sites
United States Coast Pilot 7
Light List, Volume VI, Pacific Coast & Pacific Islands

Maps

Washington State Public Lands Quadrangle Map, **Seattle** 1:100,000
Washington State Public Lands Quadrangle Map, **Shelton** 1:100,000
Washington State Public Lands Quadrangle Map, **Tacoma** 1:100,000

Gunkholing in South Puget Sound
Chapters

Table of Contents

Legend

Ⓖ = GUNKHOLE   ➡ = CAUTION   ☸ = UNDERWAY   ⚓ = ANCHORING

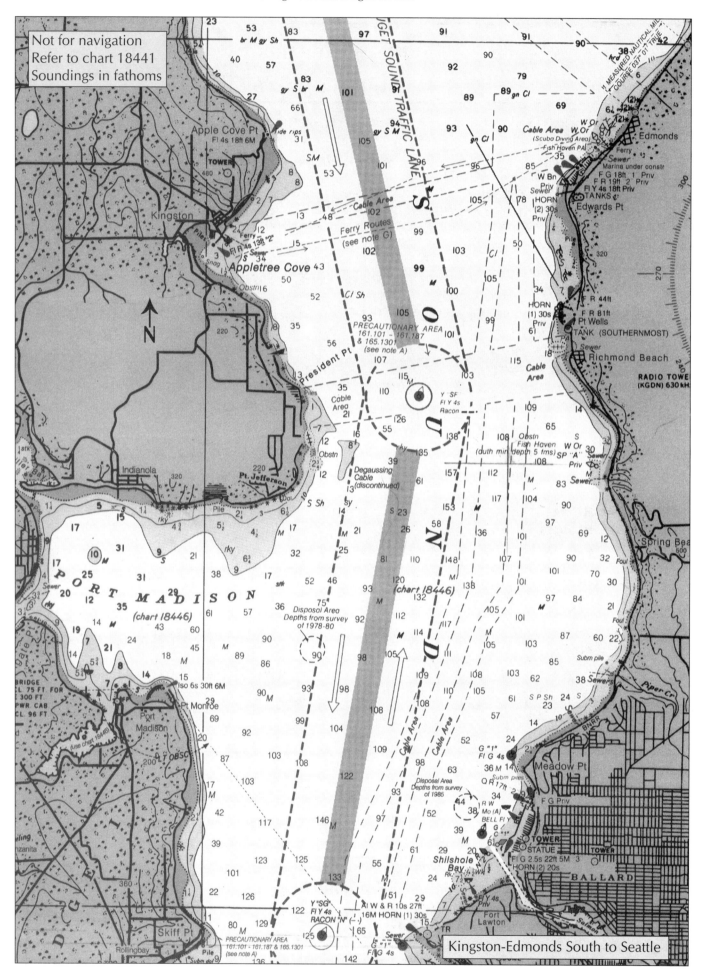

Not for navigation
Refer to chart 18441
Soundings in fathoms

Kingston-Edmonds South to Seattle

3

CHAPTER 1
From Kingston-Edmonds South to Seattle

		Charts and publications for this chapter		
Chart	**Date**	**Title**	**Scale**	**Soundings**
***18446	06/16/90	Puget Sound, Apple Cove Point to Keyport	1:25,000	Feet
** 18473	08/14/93	Oak Bay to Shilshole	1:40,000	Fathoms
* 18445	06/03/95	Puget Sound—Possession Sound to Olympia page A;	1:80,000	Fathoms
		page D, inset 11	1:10,000	Feet
18441	02/18/95	Puget Sound, Northern Part	1:80,000	Fathoms
18440	08/05/95	Puget Sound	1:150,000	Fathoms
		Tidal Current Charts, Puget Sound, Northern Part		
		Puget Sound Shellfish Sites		
		Washington State Public Lands, Quad Map—Seattle	1:100,000	

➡ *Compare charts used with the dates of the ones noted above for changes and discrepancies. Review actual charts while reading book text.*

Appletree Cove and Kingston

☸ Here we are, approaching **Appletree Cove**, home of the North Kitsap town of **Kingston** on the western shore of Puget Sound. Between here and **Edmonds** on the eastern shore is where this book starts, and proceeds south to Olympia, in this, our rediscovery of South Puget Sound.

It's a brilliant, clear, sunny, Pacific Northwest day for crossing Puget Sound on one of the most gloriously scenic passages that can be made. It's the kind of day with just the right breeze, when sun glints off the cobalt blue seas reflecting the skies, white frothy waves crest and topple into the troughs. Spectacular.

To the west, rugged, snow-tipped Olympic peaks rise beyond the forested shores. North is the flashing beacon of the Point No Point light, visible for 20 miles. Northeast, snow-capped Mount Baker dominates the horizon past the bluffs of Whidbey Island.

On the eastern rim are the Cascade Mountains, with a bit of snow visible even in late summer. Although the eastern shore is lined with thousands of homes, it often appears richly green because some trees have been left standing.

Southeast, the skyline of metropolitan Seattle and the Space Needle are ever-present reminders of the city's vitality. Even the "box it came in"—the Columbia Center—looks urbanely stylish.

Mount Rainier, the magnificent symbol of the region, looms over Puget Sound to the south, with breathtaking glory that Indians revered and early explorers praised. As native Washingtonians, we both take unashamed delight in "our" mountain.

Add to this the great likelihood of encountering Dall's porpoises joyfully diving beneath the boat as we make our way across the Sound. You will certainly see seals and may even be graced with the sight of an Orca or gray whale as they make occasional forays into the Sound.

The crossing is not always this dazzling. Sometimes it's rainy or foggy, there's too much wind or it's from the wrong direction and you wonder what you're doing out in this mess.

➡ **NOTE: Marine gas and diesel** are available at the **Ports** of **Kingston** and **Edmonds,** and at **Shilshole Marina,** for the areas covered in this chapter.

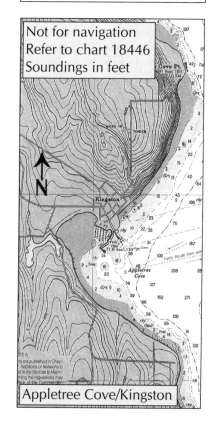

Not for navigation
Refer to chart 18446
Soundings in feet

Appletree Cove/Kingston

Capt. George Vancouver, the first recorded explorer in the area, didn't even mention Appletree Cove as he sailed past in *H.M.S. Discovery* on May 19, 1792, heading to a rendezvous at the south end of Bainbridge Island with *H.M.S. Chatham.* He missed a beautiful spot. He was too busy repairing a broken yard on one of his masts to document this part of his voyage.

Had Vancouver taken a few moments to look around as he sailed south, he would have noticed the cove with its anchorage snugged back in against an evergreen forest.

H.M.S. Discovery
96' sloop of war, replica of Vancouver's ship

Winsome

Getting There

Winsome, close-hauled and nearly rail down, with only working heads'ls and mizzen, plunged south toward Kingston in a southerly winter gale. Carl and his (then) wife Mildred were anxious to get their feverish infant, John, to the doctor in Seattle. It was the late 1940s.

About 2:30 in the morning, as the baby's temperature finally began to drop, they felt it was past time to anchor and get a little rest. Carl headed the 50 foot yawl into the relatively calm bight one mile northwest of Apple Cove Point Light.

The storm prompted him to rig a heavier anchor than the 50 pound Danforth he usually used. At the time, he thought they would be anchored only a few hours, and in the urgency to get secured, he tightened the anchor shackle pin on a 70 pound anchor.

The hook dug in and held well in 8 to 10 fathoms about 300 yards offshore. Two purse seiners were also anchored in the lee of the 300-400 foot high shoulder of land rising abruptly to the southeast and west.

In the gray light of dawn *Winsome* had not dragged anchor, although the wind was still blowing hard. When Carl "weighed" anchor the chain came up easily, too easily, sans anchor.

Repeated tugging and wave movement had unscrewed the shackle pin, which most likely fell out about the time the chain was pulled aboard. Except for the cost of the anchor, the sea had reminded Carl always to wire the anchor shackle pins. It was a gentle reminder this time–spare anchors were on board.

Kingston-bound under power, *Winsome* hit three to six foot steep chop off Apple Cove Point with a flood current against the gusting southerly. Spanning more than one wave at a time, the fore and aft decks were awash at the same time frequently as she passed through the tide rips about 0.3 mile off the point.

The 10 fathom curve is barely 100 yards off the beach at the point, but extends 0.5 mile off the beach south of the point. A wreck symbol shows on the chart 0.5 mile southwest of the Apple Cove Point Light—a grim reminder of the fate of vessels which get caught on the shoals of this lee shore.

Once past the point and tide rips the chop stretched out and *Winsome* was again dealing with one wave at a time, which diminished gradually as she powered into Appletree Cove.

After securely wiring the shackle pin on one of the spare anchors, Carl anchored *Winsome* with her nine foot draft in about three fathoms, southwest of the ferry dock, clear of the ferry maneuvering area.

He dinghied his wife and baby to the float at the ferry landing so they could take the ferry to Edmonds, where Mom and baby would meet Carl's dad who would drive them to the doctor.

John Adams, an old sailing friend, had interrupted his work day to ride to Edmonds with Carl's dad, ferry to Kingston and sail back to Seattle on the yawl with Carl. The two had sailed on their own and other's boats summer or winter, fair weather or foul, since they had been kids.

Under power they left Kingston headed for the Ballard Locks. *Winsome* was soon plunging into large seas as the two squared things away. But before they got to the foredeck to secure the anchor it decided it would rather stay back in Appletree Cove and jumped overboard. Holy cow, another reminder. First things first. Adams heard the rattling chain paying out from below and hurried topside to help winch the wayward anchor back aboard.

Anchor retrieved and secured, they hoisted the mizzen, the main storm tris'l and heads'ls. Close hauled, they had a great passage to Shilshole.

Carl's son John and mom were doing just fine, once they were home.

> ### We don't promise weather in this book!

Ⓖ As we said, we're approaching Appletree Cove, a **marginal gunkhole.** It doesn't quite meet the criteria: anchoring in a small, sheltered, quiet bay. The cove has a fairly large area that dries at low tide and now is a bit noisy at times. However, it's still a good stopover.

The approach to Appletree Cove most likely involves a course which will pass near or cross the invisible man-made **V**essel **T**raffic **S**ystem lanes—like a marine highway for fast ships, tugs and tows—the big boys. It's marked by buoys arranged as shown on the charts with approved courses for inbound and outbound vessel traffic. Before venturing into these areas we suggest reviewing the **VTS** section in the appendix, or better yet, read the U.S. Coast Guard **VTS** Manual—important information for all mariners.

Appletree Cove, Kingston and the Ferries

The highly visible ferry terminal for the two state ferries busily shuttling between Kingston and Edmonds dominates the northern shoreline of the cove with its three ferry slips, a two-story, glass-enclosed ramp for foot passengers (aka. the "habitrail") supported by a giant concrete column, and the huge holding area for waiting vehicles. There are 56 daily crossings.

Kingston's 340 yard-long riprap, rock breakwater arcs southwest from the ferry dock. It partially encircles the marina and protects it from most storms.

Fl R 4s 13ft 5M "2" Kingston Small Boat Harbor light, flashing red 4 second, with triangular red daymark on skeleton tower, 13 feet high, marks the marina entrance at the southwest end of the breakwater. Tucked between the ferry dock and the breakwater is a well-used public fishing pier.

*Kingston ferry landing,
outbound cutter*

Appletree Cove provides overnight anchorage or moorage at the guest floats behind the breakwater in the marina, to take advantage of the hospitality and services of Kingston.

⚓ **Anchoring** in the cove, a close look at Chart 18446—the soundings are in feet—shows a lot of green in Appletree Cove, much of which really does go dry at low tide. Anchor south and east of the breakwater to avoid the tide flats immediately south and west of the breakwater, and keep clear of the marina entrance and ferry maneuvering area.

Cable area comes ashore east of the ferry dock.

The cove is a good anchorage as long as we watch the weather. There is a reasonable amount of protection with some exposure to winds from the northeast through the southeast. We usually anchor in about 25 feet—depending on the tide—and so far have never dragged. The boat may roll a bit from ferry wake and other traffic. We know of three boats that were blown ashore in heavy winter northeasterlies, one sustaining major damage after pounding on the rocks south of Kingston. If it's really blowing from the northeast to southeast we consider mooring in the marina.

In **Kingston**, within a few blocks on either side of the main street are restaurants, delis, a small grocery, taverns, espresso shops, boutiques, and a marine supply store which also carries fishing gear. The historic Kingston Hotel has been revitalized into a restaurant on the main floor and an art gallery and goldsmith upstairs. They have entertainment occasionally, as does Dickinson's Restaurant adjacent to the marina. The town's taverns have darts, pool and Karaoke nights.

Public tidelands, unless otherwise noted, are state-owned. Some may be leased and posted for aquaculture or other private use. When we go ashore we take the Washington State Public Lands Quad Map, to avoid trespassing on adjacent private property.

There's just over one mile of public tidelands in the areas covered in this chapter.

Farmers Market

A shopping center about one-half mile northwest of the marina on the main highway has a major supermarket, pharmacy and variety store, post office, hardware and lumber store, banks, liquor store, restaurants and other amenities. Dentists, doctors, real estate offices, churches and other businesses are along the way.

Outdoor enthusiasts will find places for walking, jogging, bicycling, tennis, softball and basketball. Walk the beach, swim north of the ferry pier or go across the cove to Arness County Park.

Farmers market at the port's Mike Wallace Park is held every Saturday from May to October. It's jammed with fresh fruits and vegetables in season, handicrafts, jewelry, baked goods, food—even entertainment. You won't want to miss it. Be there at 9 a.m. for the best selection.

Port of Kingston is charted as #19 on 18445. Facilities are as listed except there were no marine services or repair facilities at the port in 1996.

Inside Kingston marina looking SW towards entrance past the fuel float, guest moorage at left

Port of Kingston Marina Facilities
➤ Guest slips, approximately 50
➤ Moorage rates 35 cents per foot per day
➤ 30 amp shore power $3 per day
➤ Water at each slip
➤ Fuel: gas and diesel at fuel float at head of guest float
➤ Propane sold onshore
➤ Pump-out and porta-potty dump
➤ Restrooms, showers, laundry facilities on first floor of port office building at the head of guest float
➤ Register in the second floor office
➤ Hoist launch for small boats
➤ Grid for certain emergency repairs
➤ Phone: 360-297-3545.

Kingston Marina breakwater and entrance

Marina entrance, enter close to the southwest end of the breakwater, turning right after passing marker "2." To port are signs on stakes that caution about shallow water, and tide flats that go dry.

Guest slips are on the northwest side of the long, angled float paralleling the breakwater. Tie up in any unoccupied slip—slips for larger boats are near the fuel dock at the head of the guest float. The southeast side next to the breakwater is shallow and for dinghy use only.

Arness County Park is at the very head of Appletree Cove about 700 yards west from the end of the breakwater. If anchored off or moored in Kingston, it's easy to take a small boat and visit this delightful park on the incoming tide.

Park attractions, include picnic tables, fireplaces, sani-can, beachcombing and swimming from the 400 feet of no-bank waterfront. The park is alongside a local arterial road. A culvert under the road leads into a shallow slough—a favorite swimming hole at high tide—which becomes a mud flat as the tide ebbs. The water churns in and out through the culvert with the rising and falling tides, creating small whirlpools. Kids love jumping into the salt chuck, paddling and splashing through the foaming tide changes.

Arness Park

You're on your own here—there are no lifeguards. As on most beaches, we suggest wearing shoes to avoid cut feet.

Leave the park on the ebb, before the cove goes dry. It's much easier to row out than to drag your kayak or skiff across the wide expanse of tide flats.

History: A Bit of Old Kingston

The first settlers to file for a homestead in Kingston were W.S. and Caroline Ladd in 1869. They sold their property in 1878 to a logger named Michael King who built a small bunkhouse and cookhouse in Appletree Cove. When he took off a couple of years later, he left little cedar shacks that had been occupied by out-of-work loggers, squatters and others. It was a pretty disreputable place. The righteous town folk began calling it "King's Town," perhaps as a joke.

By 1890 all land surrounding Kingston was owned by Puget Sound Mill Company of Port Gamble. Objections by town promoters were over-ridden by the company which touted Kingston as a resort, "The Monterey of Washington."

They predicted: "Excursion parties will be run this summer, and thousands of weary mortals will cast off the cankering cares of business as they wander on the shining sands strewn with curious shells, or under the shade of great alders, willows, cottonwoods, and blossoming dogwoods that line the shore ... "

It never quite panned out like that. Instead, Kingston just sort of grew like Topsy. It became a "little city by the sea," through which tourists pass from one side of Puget Sound to the other.

There's a fine book, *Little City by the Sea, Kingston Centennial,* **1890-1990**, by Harold F. Osborne. It's filled with wonderful old photos and great reminiscences and is sold in local stores.

Kingston Ferries: Past and Future

Kingston was served by the original Mosquito fleet steamers until 1923 when car ferry service began. The dock used to have "Gateway to the Olympic Peninsula" emblazoned in large letters across the overhead bracing.

Washington State Ferries plans to build a passenger-only ferry pier adjacent to the present piers to facilitate walk-on commuters. This ferry, direct to Seattle, will increase the number and directions of ferry crossings. The ferries are North Kitsap's and the Olympic Peninsula's umbilical cord to the mainland and many of the town's businesses are based on ferry traffic.

Appletree Cove was mis-named by Charles Wilkes when his expedition passed by on May 9, 1841. Seeing blossoming dogwood trees on shore, thinking they were apple trees, Wilkes named it Appletree Cove.

➥ **Caution:** During fishing season Coast Guard Rule Part 165.301 states, "Vessels engaged in fishing, including gillnet and purse seine fishing, are prohibited in ... Edmonds/Kingston ferry crossing lanes, to include the waters within 0.25 mile on either side of a straight line connecting the Edmonds and Kingston ferry landings during the hours the ferries operate."

Port of Kingston

The port's plans to build a two-lane launch ramp were approved by Kitsap county commissioners in late 1996. Included in the plans are a 200 foot float, additional parking spaces, waterfront boardwalk, beach access trail and launch facility for hand-carried boats. About 275 boats are moored permanently in the Port Marina.

Porpoise in the Sound

A new Kingston Cove Yacht Club facility is in the marina near the marina park and is one of only two or three structures at the port. Reciprocal moorage is available for visiting yacht club members at the head of the guest dock.

Edmonds Breakwater

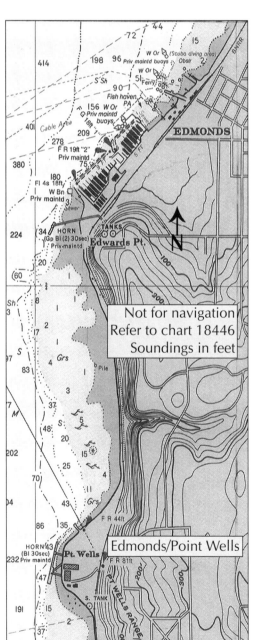

Not for navigation
Refer to chart 18446
Soundings in feet

Edmonds/Point Wells

Underway to Edmonds

✵ Four and one-half miles east across the Sound from Kingston is the city of **Edmonds.** We'll stop there and then cruise along the eastern shore to Golden Gardens and Shilshole Marina in Seattle.

Trains are seen running day and night through Edmonds and along much of the west shore of Puget Sound from Everett to Seattle, and from Tacoma to Nisqually. You can hear them rumbling even in Kingston and elsewhere as you cruise the Sound. All foot and vehicle traffic from daily ferry crossings must cross the tracks in Edmonds.

VTS lanes must be crossed going from Kingston to Edmonds.

In fog we'll check in with VTS on VHF channel 14. This passage is not the sort we enjoy making in fog even with radar; there is a lot of vessel traffic out here. What we think we see on radar is not always what we get. But as we said earlier, it can be an absolutely gorgeous crossing, given the proper weather.

Cable areas for Kingston/Edmonds are marked by the longer dashed magenta lines on the charts which define the unusual-shaped cable near Edmonds. The "cable area" shown on the chart east of the Kingston ferry landing intersects with other cable areas running north and south, and then continues east to go ashore at the north end of the Edmonds breakwater.

Ferry routes are shown as short dashed magenta lines and are easily confused with the cable area lines.

Two-way ferry traffic will be encountered head on or from astern during this crossing. Refer to "Note B" on chart 18446 cautioning mariners about the innovative and creative deviations by Washington State Ferries from the east-west courses shown on the charts.

Point Wells range markers—looking southeast toward Point Wells as we crossed from Kingston to Edmonds, we used to be able to see the range markers as we neared Edmonds. In 1996, the range lights were extinguished as they were considered no longer necesssary for safe navigation. When the markers were aligned vertically we were about one mile from the Edmonds breakwater on a course from Kingston.

Point Wells range was a useful reference for small craft, as well as large tankers arriving at the Point Wells pier.

Measured nautical mile course is about 0.5 mile north of Edmonds ferry terminal. To check the knotmeter or speed indicator, try the measured mile on a course of 37° 01' true.

Anchoring near Edmonds is not practical because of currents, ferry wakes, shoal waters, exposure to winds and seas, and cable areas. That's enough to encourage us to head for the marina.

Edmonds: Gem of Puget Sound

Approaching Edmonds the dominating features of the city are the ferry terminal, the 950 foot long fishing pier, the 700 yard long marina breakwater, the old UNOCAL fuel tanks and pier at Edwards Point, located south of the ferry terminal.

Downtown Edmonds is on the gradual slope inshore from the ferry pier—no skyscrapers here. Waterfront residential and commercial development run from north of the ferry pier south to the 220 foot elevation near Edwards Point and the more gradual rise to 400 feet about 1.5 miles to the east.

We find good supplies, services, repair facilities and guest moorage in a friendly community of business, commercial and artistic interests.

Along the waterfront are parks, shops and restaurants. A short walk uptown and there are ethnic restaurants, coffee shops, an antique mall, bookstores, historical and marine museums, art galleries, grocery stores, even a theater with first run features at a nominal price. In short, most everything you need in a small, delightful city. Just be careful crossing those train tracks.

Port of Edmonds is charted as #18 on 18445. Facilities exceed those listed.

Port of Edmonds Marina Facilities

➤ Guest moorage 1,000 feet of dock space, additional space available during summer months
➤ Moorage fees 40 cents per foot per night
➤ 20/30 amp shore power $2 per night
➤ Water on floats
➤ Fuel: gas, #2 diesel, oil products sold at the fuel float
➤ Pump-out
➤ Restrooms with showers
➤ Nearby laundry
➤ Two sling boat launchers (dual rail), 70 cents per foot round trip, boats up to 26' and 7,800 pounds
➤ Haulout of boats up to 35 tons
➤ Do-it-yourself boat yard, pressure washer
➤ Nearby repair services
➤ Fishing: gear nearby, live bait at marina, ice
➤ Nearby stores and restaurants
➤ 20 boat charter fishing fleet moors at Edmonds
➤ Permanent moorage for 800 boats; waiting list of over 500
➤ Dry storage for 200 boats with 2 self-service sling launchers
➤ Port monitors VHF Channel 69
➤ Phone: 206-774-0549

Marina entrance has only one opening near midway in the breakwater.

Fl G "1" Edmonds Small Boat Harbor entrance light, flashing green light with square white daybeacon on dolphin, is on the north breakwater entrance.

Fl R "2" Edmonds Small Boat Harbor entrance light, flashing red light with red triangular daybeacon on pedestal, is on the south breakwater entrance.

Just inside the marina entrance is a piling breakwater directly ahead on entering. Turn right and proceed to fuel float for moorage check-in. Guest slips are east of the fuel dock and in front of the administration building, or visitors may be assigned to an empty slip. Call ahead on VHF radio or telephone.

Fl Y 4s light Edmonds South Breakwater Light, flashing yellow 4 second light, is 18 feet high on the south end of the breakwater.

Waterfront Parks

Three shoreline parks and a public fishing pier line Edmonds' mile-long beach, worth a walking visit after mooring.

Edmonds Underwater State Park at Brackett's Landing is immediately north of the ferry landing, the first of its kind for scuba divers on the west coast.

Washington State Ferries warns divers to stay away from the ferry dock at all times due to the hazard of being sucked into the rotating ferry propellers.

There are no floats or piers at this park and motorized boats are not permitted in its boundaries.

Before the days of VTS lanes, we could plot a single 330° true course from Point Wells range markers which would give us a clear course past Point No Point, Double Bluff, Bush Point, and on through Admiralty Inlet to Partridge Bank and Smith Island in the east end of the Strait of Juan de Fuca.

Or, when abeam of Point Wilson, by making one course change to 281° true with Admiralty Head dead astern (adjusted to tidal current offsets), we could continue into the Pacific Ocean. With only one more appropriate course change we could make a landfall anywhere between the Aleutian Chain and French Polynesia.

If we try this today no doubt we will get a visit from the Coast Guard who might not appreciate our creative cruising method in the VTS lanes. Life is infinitely more complicated with heavy vessel traffic, but with the introduction of VTS it's also safer, and long straight courses are boring anyway.

Edmonds Marina entrance & fuel float

"Locals" by Georgia Gerber

Park attractions include 32 acres of subtidal fish habitat enhanced by the submerged wreck of a vessel that sank here in 1935. It was dedicated as a marine sanctuary in 1971 and is covered with a great variety of marine life. More fish habitats have since been sunk adding to the underwater environment.

Sea lions used to hang out on the scuba divers' rest floats. The floats were removed because the large marine mammals had become a nuisance.

The park has 1,800 feet of walkable shoreline and 27 acres on shore. There are changing rooms, showers, restrooms and an informational display.

A rock jetty and walkway are off the northern shore of the park. The jetty was completed in 1988, replacing the decayed ruins of what was Brackett's original wharf. A second park is planned just south of the ferry dock.

Olympic Beach is two hundred yards south of the ferry dock and adjacent to the port marina. It is a lovely, sandy beach honoring Edmonds residents who have become Olympic athletes.

At the south end of this beach, on broad low steps leading from sand to lawn, is a seal who flip-flopped his way up the steps. He's waiting to be greeted.

And then you see two enchanting groups in juxtaposition: a dad holding a thumb-sucking toddler on his shoulders, while a slightly older girl clings shyly to dad's legs. All three are transfixed by what they see in front of them—several large sea lions and seals in various poses.

They are **"Locals"** in bronze, by artist Georgia Gerber of Whidbey Island. Don't miss this—it's wonderful art, a gift to the city of Edmonds by the Edmonds Arts Festival and the Edmonds Arts Festival Museum in 1989.

Edmonds public fishing pier juts out into the Sound just south of Olympic Beach at the north end of the port. The pier then angles south to parallel part of the marina breakwater. Its several fish cleaning tables and benches are used by lucky anglers. This popular pier was the first public, saltwater fishing pier in the state.

The Wildlife Sanctuary Trail and Interpretive Point is inland from the marina, across the railroad tracks and south of Harbor Square. The trail has interpretive signs bordering the natural marshy area.

Edmonds Marina Beach is between the south end of the marina breakwater and Edwards Point.

The old UNOCAL Pier is several hundred feet south of the breakwater. The 4.5 acres were extensively redeveloped in 1984-85 after the Union Oil Company closed the Edmonds facility. The now permanently inactive tank farm behind and above this beach formerly stored petroleum off-loaded from tankers.

Walk the 978 feet of shoreline, fly kites or sit back and relax against a drift log. There are lawns and walkways, a kids' playground, volleyball set-up and a delightful, sandy beach, picnic areas and a free cartop launch for hand-carried boats only—no trailered boats. This is another favorite spot with scuba divers who explore around pilings of the old Union Oil tanker pier.

Sculptures at Olympic Beach

Edwards Point was named Point Edmund by Charles Wilkes, who explored Puget Sound in 1841.

Named for the explorer's son, the name was later changed to Edwards Point.

Early Steamer History

The sternwheel steamer *Gleaner* was near Richmond Beach one day in the early 1900s when a passenger train jumped the tracks. The engineer was trapped in the cab and several passengers were injured. The *Gleaner* sent a boat ashore to pick up the injured and they were taken to Seattle aboard the vessel—the fastest way to get to a hospital.

Edmonds was such a growing town that by 1910 the 185 foot steamship *Telegraph* stopped there six times daily.

By 1912 the antiquated *Telegraph,* built in Everett in 1903, was having difficulty maintaining schedules because of its frequent breakdowns.

On April 25, 1912, the steamship *Alameda* lost control and charged through the waiting room of Colman Dock in Seattle, toppling the tower into Elliott Bay. It then hit and sank the *Telegraph,* moored at the pier. Concerns about repairing the ancient *Telegraph* were over.

The 150 foot steamer *Sioux* then replaced the *Telegraph* on the Edmonds to Seattle run, while a rival company placed the steamer *Vashon* on the run between Everett, Edmonds, Seattle and Tacoma. This was not the Washington State ferry *Vashon,* but a 94 foot passenger steamer built in Dockton in 1905 and dismantled in 1930.

Weather has always played an important role in the maritime history of Edmonds. On November 10, 1911, the combination of a strong northwest gale and high tides caused damage to moored launches when they crashed into each other or into pilings, and one sank. Pilings were washed out from under several mills and the wharf was declared unsafe.

Polar Bare: Walking the beach one wintry day, we encountered a barefoot woman in her 70s. She carefully pulled off her sweat suit, folded it neatly and laid it on a log.

She then waded out into the frigid water without so much as a flinch. She swam several laps from the fishing pier at the north end of the marina to the ferry dock—a ritual she performs daily, wearing only a bathing suit.

Early Edmonds

George Brackett's canoe was forced ashore on the Edmonds beach by a sudden gust of wind in 1870, while he was intently dreaming of possible logging operations along the heavily timbered shores. The 29 year old logger was so taken with the area that in 1872 he bought 147 acres at $4.42 an acre—property which became the townsite of Edmonds. Later he was named the first postmaster and built a wharf and general store with a small stock of merchandise. The first post office was housed in this store.

Settlers began to arrive in the new community, and by 1889, Brackett had built a sawmill. In addition, there was fairly regular steamer service, a hotel, cigar factory, dance hall, drug store, shingle mill and wharf.

In 1890, the town petitioned to incorporate but lacked two of the 72 signatures needed. Entrepreneur Brackett promptly signed the names of his two oxen, Isaac and Bolivar, to the petition. Incorporation passed and Brackett was elected the first mayor. (From ***Edmonds, The Gem of Puget Sound***, by Ray V. Cloud)

Brackett's Landing

South to Shilshole

Underway again, we're heading south of Edmonds along the mainland shore.

The next guest moorage and/or supply, service and repair stop for mariners on this eastern side of the Sound is at Seattle's **Shilshole Bay Marina**. However, on the way south we pass several interesting places which divers, kayakers, beachcombers and fishing enthusiasts enjoy.

There are relics at Richmond Beach that are over 60 years old.

Just before setting the fixed center span of the Aurora Bridge in Seattle in place during its construction in the 1930s, several sailing vessels with masts too tall to pass under the nearly completed bridge were towed to the beach where they were beached and burned. These fittings are all that remain.

Meadow Point's northern portion was a shipyard until 1913. Stub pilings jutting out from the point still remain from the old piers. There are covered at high tide.

Grounding: Many years back Carl knew a fellow sailor named Schoals who managed to run aground on a shoal in this area. From then on he was fondly known as "Deep Water Schoals."

A train robbery story we enjoy has nothing to do with the water, but with the trains that we all see from the water as they rumble along the tracks:

On a September night in 1918, a masked bandit boarded a Great Northern passenger train near Mukilteo. He ordered the trainmen to break the train behind the baggage and mail cars and proceed south down the track, leaving the passenger cars behind. At gunpoint he commanded the mail clerk to hand him the registered mail. He stopped the train near Meadowdale and fled into the woods.

The engineer ran the train to Edmonds and reported the holdup before returning to pick up the rest of the cars and passengers.

⚓ Anchoring-off is permitted at most King County Parks. Pick your weather as these parks are exposed to most winds. Some of them are not accessible by land.

☸ Southwest from the Edmonds Marina passing Edwards Point we swing south after safely skirting the shoal between Points Edwards and Wells. There may be some kelp to port approaching Point Wells.

Point Wells Chevron tank farm is located about 1.3 miles south of Edwards Point. Although the lights were extinguished, Chevron attempts to maintain operation of a horn located on the pier during times of limited visibility.

The piers at Point Wells are private property and are off-limits to recreational scuba divers. Chevron officials said they service about 20 ships and barges each year which transport asphalt to the facility.

Proceeding south from Point Wells, we keep at least 0.3 mile off shore. About 0.3 mile south of here is a charted wreck which might be of interest to divers, although there is a Metro treatment facility inshore and a sewer line is near the wreck.

Many homes are along the shores as we cruise past various residential developments of Richmond Beach, the Highlands and others.

Richmond Beach (King) County Park is about 1.2 miles south of Point Wells. It has nearly 2,000 feet of shoreline and 40 acres of uplands. From offshore, we see a curving cement footpath leading up a sandy hill to cross a pedestrian bridge over the train tracks The park is low bank at its protruding point.

This is a favorite swimming and scuba diving beach, where divers often swim among some stub pilings from old docks. Iron fittings from old sailing ships have occasionally been found embedded in the sand by divers, beachcombers or others searching through tidepools.

The park has restrooms and changing rooms, a playground, picnic tables and fireplaces on the beach and in the uplands. For those who want to do a bit of walking, there's a trail at the very top of the bluff beyond a parking lot to a scenic viewpoint with a spectacular view looking far out over the Sound.

⚓ **Anchor** fairly close to shore here in calm stable weather. The charted 18 foot curve is only about 100 yards offshore.

☸ **The Trees** "fish haven" at **Boeing Creek** has no public road or land access. Chart 18446 shows the fish haven about 2.1 miles south of Point Wells, 0.2 mile offshore of the creek.

W Or "A" two white and orange striped buoys mark Boeing Creek Reef.

Depth of 30 feet is charted. However, we note the inshore east side of the charted shaded area appears to be at a marginal depth of two to 18 feet, while the offshore, southwest corner of the shaded area appears to be at a depth of about 180 feet.

We understand the charted sewer discharge in the fish haven, and a second discharge about 0.25 mile north, are not sanitary sewers.

Washington State Department of Fisheries developed and maintains this as one of their "Artificial Fishing Reefs in Puget Sound" sites for recreational anglers. (See "Fish Havens" in the appendix for details on the types of fish, locations of other artificial reefs, anchoring and more.)

The state specifically requests that mariners **not** moor to the buoys—they are not meant to hold boats.

Carkeek Park, a Seattle Park, is shown as at Pipers Creek on chart 18446. The park is about 2.1 miles south of Boeing Creek or one mile north of Meadow Point.

There's good beachcombing and swimming along the 2,000 feet of beach. Onshore are restrooms, hiking and nature trails, picnic tables and shelters, fireplaces and a softball diamond.

Currently, Seattle Park Department regulations prohibit anchoring within the city limits. Hopefully this will change. This would be a difficult place to launch a hand-carried boat as the parking lot is quite a distance from the beach.

Public tidelands of about one mile in three parcels are between Carkeek Park and Golden Gardens.

Fl G 4s "1" Meadow Point Lighted Buoy, with a four mile range, marks the point. We stay at least 0.25 mile offshore to avoid shallows as we approach.

Golden Gardens City Park, south of Meadow Point, is a jewel. There are 95 acres of land and 3,850 feet of sandy beach to enjoy, picnic tables and shelters, bathhouse, restrooms, beach-walking, swimming, bird-watching, volleyball, soccer.

We see kayaks and windsurfers launched here, and occasionally a boat anchored offshore. We can moor at Shilshole Marina and walk to Golden Gardens, since city rules just now don't allow anchoring off city parks. Some of Golden Gardens' nicest hiking trails are on the hillside east of the railroad tracks. Just walk under the railroad overpass.

Golden Gardens Park

Golden Gardens was the terminus of a Seattle trolley line at the turn of the century. It quickly became the city's most popular north end seaside park and many a family, church or company potluck picnic has been held here over the years.

Shilshole Bay Marina

Shilshole Bay Marina is south of Golden Gardens and north of the entrance to the Lake Washington Ship Canal. Shilshole is charted as #23 on 18445. Facilities are greater than listed, including fuel, boatyards, haul-out facilities and restaurants.

Shilshole is the largest marina for recreational boats in the greater Seattle area, with about 1,500 permanent slips. Its forest of white masts against the green trees of Sunset Hill above the marina is visible for miles.

Shilshole is well protected by a 4,440 foot-long rock breakwater, completed in 1961. Opened in 1960, the last expansion was completed in 1978.

A large statue of Lief Ericson oversees the entire marina a few hundred feet south of the main building.

Marina piers start with A at the south end through W at the north end. W dock accommodates vessels up to 35 feet long with beam of 9 1/2 feet.

For guest moorage or fuel we go to the Central Pier between I and J docks.

Enter marina north or south of the breakwater.

Entering from the north end:

QR, quick red Shilshole Boat Basin Light 2 is 17 feet-high with a triangular, red dayboard on a pile at the north end of the rock breakwater.

FG, fixed green Park Department Boat Ramp light,10 feet high, is on the end a breakwater north of the ramp off the east shore.

Go inside the breakwater between the red and green lights. On the shore side is a wave-break, a public fishing pier, then the launch ramp and W dock to port.

Entering from the south end:

First, locate Ballard buoy.

RW Mo (A) Ballard Bell Buoy is the most seaward buoy of all Shilshole Bay entrance buoys. It's about 0.4 mile north and west of the breakwater's south end. Follow the Shilshole Bay range to the southeast, leaving red nun buoys "2" and "4" to starboard, keep green buoy "C1" to port.

FL G 2.5s "3" Shilshole Bay Breakwater Light 3, horn (Bl (2) 20s) 22 feet high with square, green dayboard on white house, is at the south end of Shilshole breakwater.

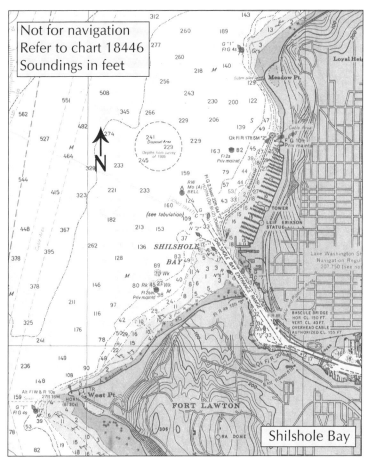

Not for navigation
Refer to chart 18446
Soundings in feet

Shilshole Bay

Shilshole north entrance with fishing pier on the right

Ballard buoy—seal condo—no longer exists as there is now a fence around the buoy to keep the sea lions and seals off. RW Mo (A)

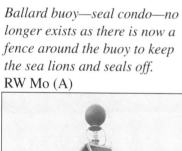

Shilshole Marina looking SW to south entrance and West Point, is an extremely busy area at the entrance to Lake Washington Ship Canal. Every size vessel goes through here, from small craft to large sea-going ships.

Fl G 2.5s "3" Shilshole rock breakwater, south end, with seals and sea lions

Shilshole Marina Facilities

➤ Guest moorage for approximately 100 to 150 boats
➤ Moorage rate 60 cents per foot per day
➤ 30 amp shore power included, water
➤ Texaco fuel on Central Pier has diesel, gas, Phone: 206-783-7555
➤ Propane at Seaview Boat Yard at head of A dock, Phone: 206-783-6550
➤ Pump-out is west of Texaco station
➤ Porta-potty dump on upper apron of Central Pier
➤ Restrooms, showers laundry in parking lot area at head of J dock
➤ Coded locks; contact attendant
➤ Small basic store on Central Pier
➤ Marina office directly inshore of Central Pier
➤ Vessels over 60 feet call ahead by phone or VHF Ch. 17
➤ Hoists available for launching or retrieving equipment
➤ 35 ton marine travel lift for boats up to 55' at Seaview Boatyard
➤ Dry storage
➤ Eddie Vine nine lane launch ramp operated by Seattle Parks
➤ Nearby restaurants, boatyard, services and repairs, marine equipment stores
➤ Other services: downtown Ballard 1.5 miles away, bus service
➤ Shilshole Marina monitors VHF Ch. 17
➤ Phone: 206-728-3006

Almost due north: Marina management tells us the main east/west piers are laid out 89°-269°; finger piers, north/south, are laid out 359°-179°, which appears to be magnetic.

Guest moorage is generally available at the marina on a first come, first served basis with no time limits. Moorage is on either side of Central Pier, east of Texaco fuel dock area. Rafting up to five vessels deep is allowed on Central Pier. J dock, directly north of Central Pier, is also available for guest moorage. These are 60 foot berths and may be shared with another vessel. Some areas on J dock are marked reserved and are not available for guest moorage.

⚓ Anchor in a large crook at the south end of the breakwater if moorages are filled. The fee will be the same as moorage.

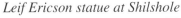
Leif Ericson statue at Shilshole

In Chapter 2 we'll go through the Hiram S. Chittenden Locks, the Lake Washington Ship Canal, and into Lake Union.

Lake Washington Ship Canal

From Puget Sound via the Lake Washington Ship Canal to Lake Washington

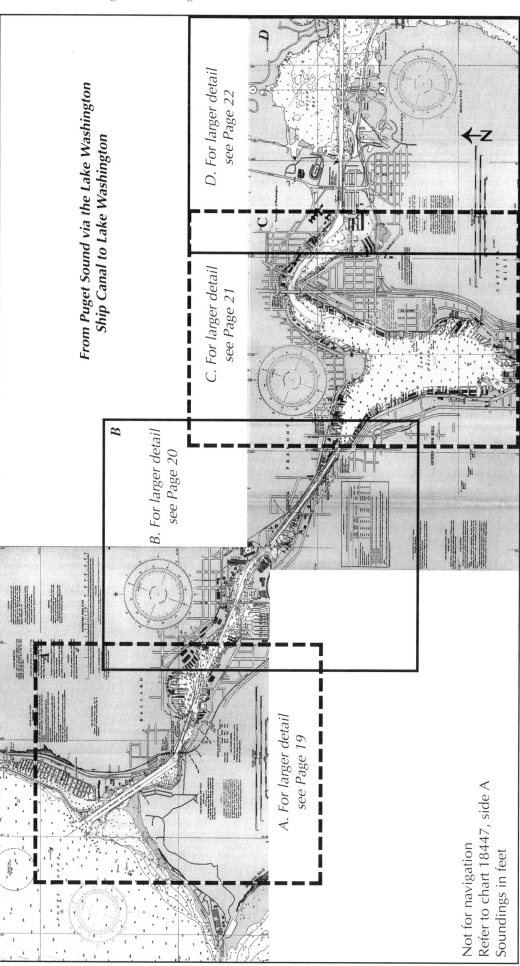

D. For larger detail see Page 22

C. For larger detail see Page 21

B. For larger detail see Page 20

A. For larger detail see Page 19

Not for navigation
Refer to chart 18447, side A
Soundings in feet

CHAPTER 2
The Lake Washington Ship Canal including the Hiram M. Chittenden Locks

Charts and publications for this chapter				
Chart	**Date**	**Title**	**Scale**	**Soundings**
18447	08/15/92	Lake Washington Ship Canal, side A	1:10,000.............Feet	

Booklet Guidelines for Boaters–US Army Corps of Engineers

➡ *Compare chart used with the dates of the one noted above for changes and discrepancies. Review actual charts while reading book text.*

Overview

Let's take a fascinating cruise through the heart of Seattle by way of the Lake Washington Ship Canal, a seven mile long waterway connecting Puget Sound with Lake Washington.

We pass through the Hiram M. Chittenden locks—which made the canal possible after construction was completed in 1916.

The two navigation locks, the culmination of the grand "Seattle Ditch," are an intriguing and popular spot for visitors, locals and, of course, mariners. They are the water elevators which move about 80,000 vessels annually between the saltwater of Puget Sound and freshwater of Lake Washington. The vessels are mostly pleasure craft, but also include fishboats, sightseeing ships, sand and gravel barges, log rafts, container ships bound for Alaska and world ports, government research vessels, fuel barges and others.

It's fascinating to watch the lock operation: vessels tying to the lock walls or each other, the gates closing, lock waters swirling and boiling about boats as they are raised or lowered; gates reopening and boats sent on their way—a sometimes waterborne melodrama. It's even more of an adventure to be aboard a boat locking through.

Depending on height of the tide and lake level, water in the locks may be raised or lowered as much as 26 feet or as little as six feet. Also at the locks are a modern fish ladder, spillway dam, a regional visitor center and formal garden with plants, shrubs and trees from around the world.

In the canal, we go under seven bridges, first through Salmon Bay with maritime businesses and commercial Fishermen's Terminal, then thru the Fremont Cut into urban Lake Union lined with shipyards, marine businesses, private moorages, houseboats, and restaurants with moorage for dining in the heart of the city. Next is Portage Bay with private moorages, two large yacht clubs and houseboats hugging the southwest shore, while the University of Washington dominates the northeast shore. The canal's last leg is through the Montlake Cut into Union Bay, with the lush Arboretum marshes along the south shore—and we reach Lake Washington.

There are as many reasons for going through the locks and canal as there are people who do it. Some boat owners moor their boats "inside" in fresh water, others commute from Puget Sound to Lake Washington or vice versa, and are regulars in the canal.

Marine facilities in the Ship Canal provide fuel, moorage, repair, supplies, services, and fills needs of the smallest and largest ships that can clear the locks.

➡ **NOTE: Marine fuel** is available at **four fuel docks** in the Lake Washington Ship Canal. (See page 35)

➡ See **"Important Things to Know Before We Go,"** before transiting the Locks and Ship Canal. See pages 31-52:
Aids to Navigation	33
Shoals & Hazards	35
Currents	35
Maneuvering	36
Canal Traffic	38
Bridges & Signals	39
Locks	42

From Lake Union, looking west into the Fremont Cut

Ballard Buoy RW Mo (A) Bell, the seal/sea lion condo. In summer 1996, a wire frame was added to keep the sea lions off the bell.

Activities such as Opening Day of Yachting, Fourth of July fireworks, Center for Wooden Boats, UW football games, Duck Dodge races, and other events, attract boaters into the lakes.

Views along the way are of shimmering Seattle skyscrapers, hundreds of geese and ducks and their babies, salmon jumping in and near the locks, an occasional bald eagle soaring over the city, Gasworks park, and shoreside universities. Seals have visited as far east as Portage Bay.

Anchoring is not allowed in the Ship Canal or in Lake Union, with only limited anchorage in Portage Bay, a topic that is under consideration by the city.

Our main interest in this book is finding gunkholes, locating public access and interesting places to visit, moor and anchor, but we realize that other information is important and include it as we find it.

Making the Passage from the Ballard Buoy to Webster Point

We're going to make a passage from Puget Sound through the locks and Ship Canal to Lake Washington, starting in Puget Sound at the Ballard buoy and ending at Webster Point in Lake Washington.

Underway, today we're approaching Shilshole; it's been a blustery lumpy day, but sails are finally furled and stopped off. Locklines are in place fore and aft and fenders rigged on both sides, letting us concentrate on our course and other traffic, which helps avoid last minute confusion or running aground.

The most important navigation aid to locate is the Ballard buoy.

• **RW Mo (A) Bell** The large red and white striped lighted Ballard buoy (Shilshole Bay Approach Lighted Bell Buoy according to Light List) is ahead, marking the west end of the one mile long entrance channel to the Ship Canal.

The forest of masts at Shilshole Bay Marina extend for nearly a mile north of the channel. At the south edge of the channel a bluff rises crowned with residential development, and two houses appear imbedded into the bluff at the shoreline.

Caution: There is a no wake, seven knot speed limit throughout the entire Lake Washington Ship Canal.

• **Q R 20 ft and Iso R 6s 81 ft. 2 entrance range lights.** When these range lights near the BNRR Bridge are lined up one above the other, we're roughly in the channel.

• **G C "1" R N "2"** Green can and red nun buoys mark the edge of the five fathom depth curve at the northwestern end of the dredged channel. It narrows from about 150 yards to 100 yards wide, with a tabulated dredged midchannel depth of 28 feet. From here on we stay between the red and green buoys, "red right returning."

• **Fl G 2.5s "3" horn (Bl (2) 20s)** This flashing green light on the south end of the Shilshole breakwater marks the south entrance to Shilshole Marina and the north side of the Ship Canal. We watch for traffic in and out of the marina entrance. This is the only lighted green marker in the entrance channel. Seals and sea lions bark at passing vessels while lounging on rocks below the marker.

•**R N "4"** Red nun buoy on south side of the 100 yard wide Ship Canal is across from Shilshole Marina entrance.

Caution: *Inner Light "8" at bluff, dries at low tide*

• **Depths** on either side of the dredged channel shoal to one foot or less at MLLW as we continue. Vessels which yield to the temptation to shortcut this channel frequently ground here.

• **R N "6" G C "7"** These buoys mark the edge of the charted one foot shoals immediately north and south of the dredged channel. The north shore is lined now with condominiums, restaurants and businesses.

• **Fl R 4s 15 ft 3M "8" Inner Light 8** Dolphin-mounted, flashing red light on the south edge of the channel at the foot of the bluff, dries at low tide. We move far right to clear a huge outbound crabber, and we're close to homes stacked on the shore.

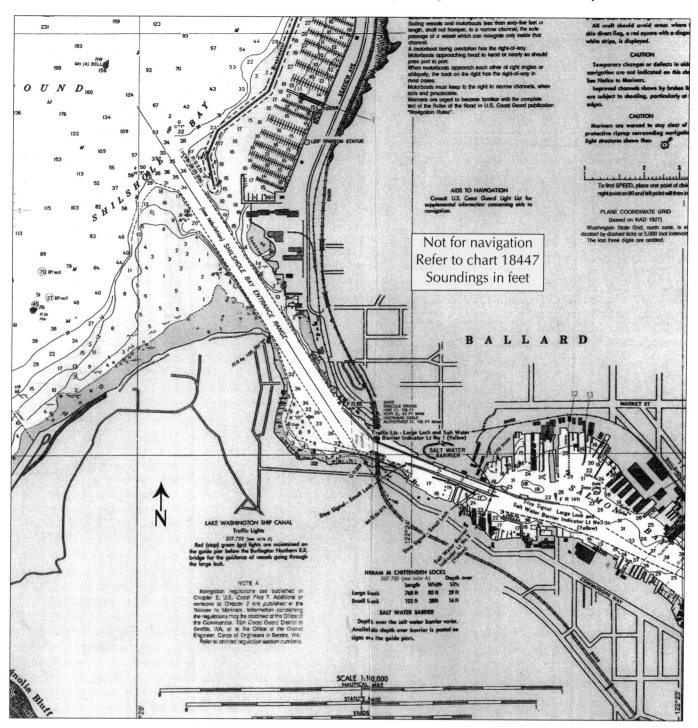

CHART A Shilshole Bay, Hiram M. Chittenden Locks, Salmon Bay

This chart includes passing under the Burlington Northern Railroad bridge. All bridge opening signals are one long and one short blast.

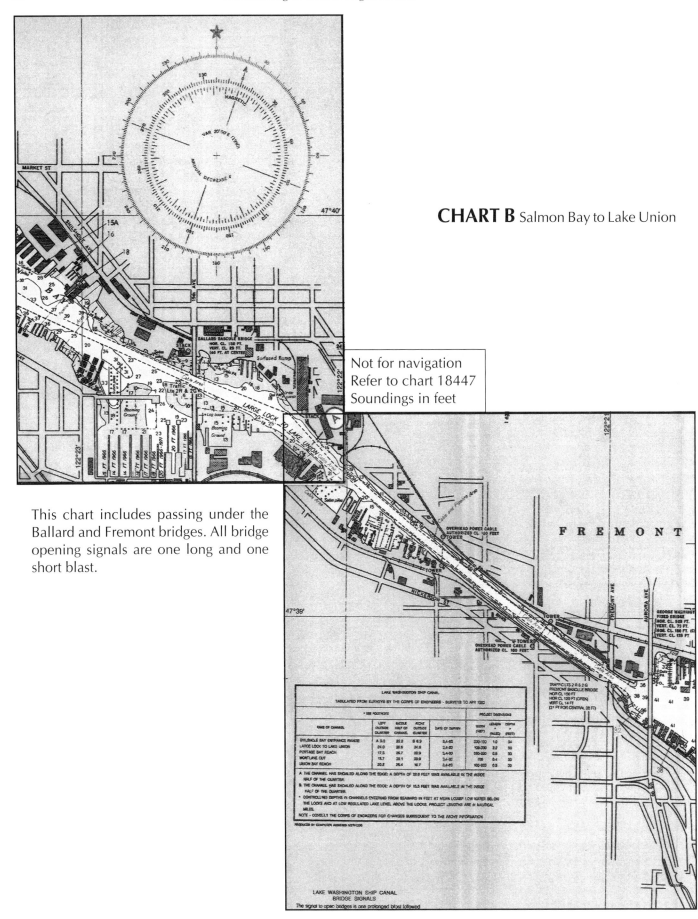

CHART B Salmon Bay to Lake Union

Not for navigation
Refer to chart 18447
Soundings in feet

This chart includes passing under the Ballard and Fremont bridges. All bridge opening signals are one long and one short blast.

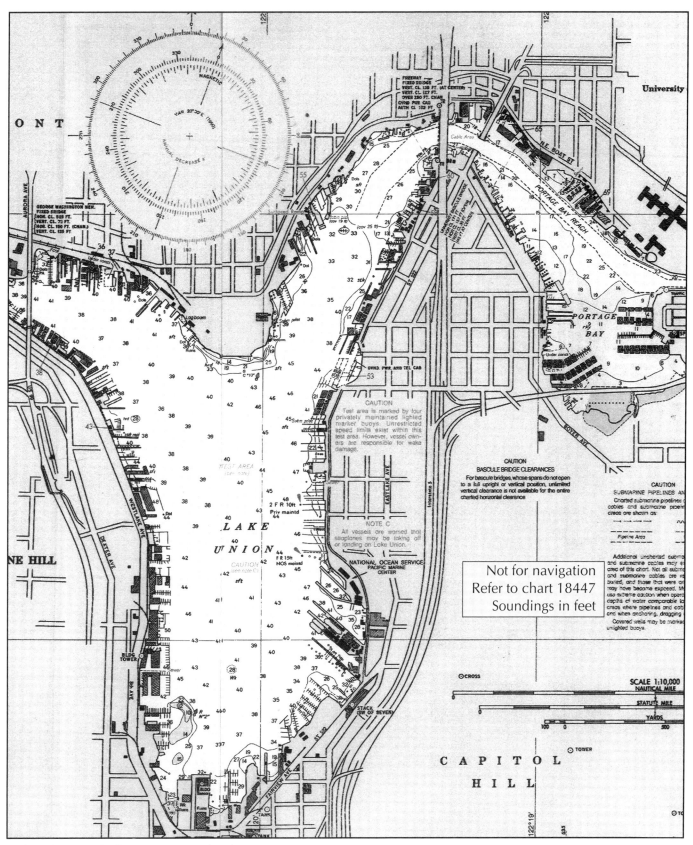

This chart includes passing under the University Bridge. All bridge opening signals are one long and one short blast.

CHART C Lake Union and Portage Bay

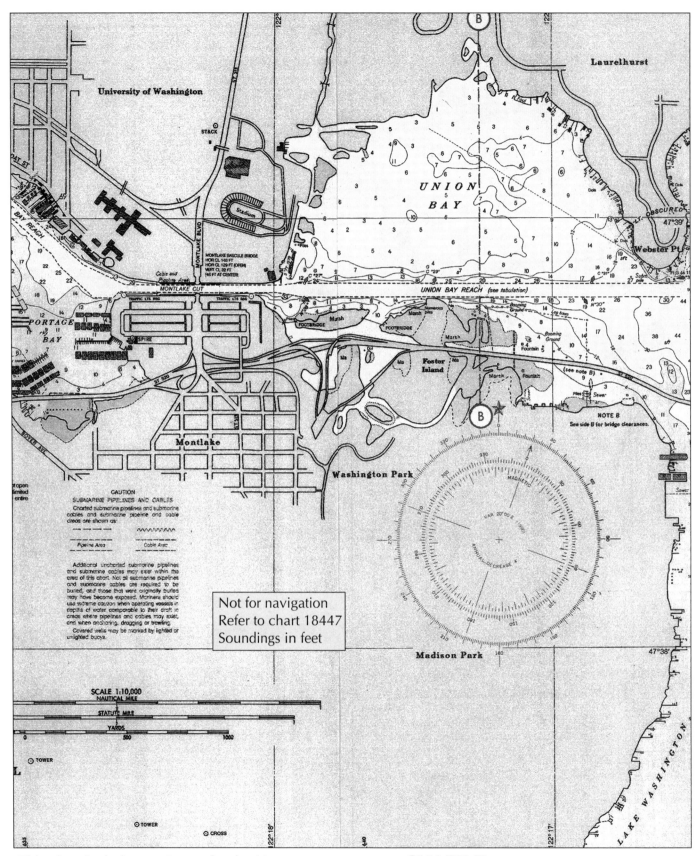

This chart includes passing under the Mont-lake Bridge. All bridge opening signals are one long and one short blast.

CHART D Portage Bay to Lake Washington

The channel widens gradually on the south side to about 175 yards as charted, and we proceed upstream.

Ballard Bait and Tackle, a deli and bait shop is on the north shore with a tie-up float. They sell bait and ice, as well as food.

• **R N "10"** Red nun buoy marks the south edge of the channel. An unnamed bay is south of the buoy where several small vessels are anchored.

We're now about 375 yards west of the railroad bridge. The entire area from here to the locks can get extremely congested with various sizes and combinations of recreational and commercial vessels, ships, tugs and tows. It's literally a "zoo" at times, especially on summer weekends and holidays, or sometimes we can be the only boat.

• **Currents** complicate maneuverability in this part of the Ship Canal. (See currents p. 35, Maneuvering, p. 36)

Locks and BNRR Bridge looking west (Photo courtesy Army Corps of Engineers)

• **F R 8 ft**. Fixed red light on the northwest end of the large lock waiting pier is on the north side of the channel west of the BNRR bridge.

• **Pipeline** area is charted west of the bridge.

• **Burlington Northern Railroad Bridge (BNRR), vertical clearance 43 ft at MHW,** is next. (See pages 39-40) Today the bridge is up and we give one long and one short blast to make sure it's going to stay up as we pass through. Occasionally the bridge tender doesn't answer, but we assume he'll keep the bridge up and we proceed with caution. Presumably he'll give us five short blasts if he's about to lower the bridge.

• **Locks, it is essential that we understand the operating procedures and requirements for the locks before we enter.** (See page 42-46)

Depending on lock traffic signals located at the entrance to each lock, the number of waiting vessels and bridge status, we may wait in the channel or tie to the small lock waiting pier on the south side of the channel east or west of the bridge.

As we approach, we see the green light for the small lock is on and we proceed into the lock

Traffic jam at the locks

as instructed by lock attendants—providing that we follow any commercial vessels—they have priority over recreational boaters. Secured to the lock wall, the gates close, turbulent water fills the lock and we find ourselves face to face with curious visitors watching the "locks show." After several minutes, the gates open and we're through the locks, into Salmon Bay, ready to continue our passage.

⚓ **Underway again,** between the locks and the Ballard Bridge is 0.68 mile. Wharves and piers along both sides of the bay include marinas, shipyards, boat repair yards, dry-docked ships, marine supply stores, sailmakers and other water-related and industrial businesses. (As we pass we note the telephone numbers of various marine businesses charted and listed on 18447 for easy reference.)

• **Seattle Coast Guard Station** is not here. Uncharted, it is noted in ***Coast Pilot***, 30th edition, "on the SW side of Salmon Bay about 0.8 mile above the entrance."

Ballard 24th Ave. public landing

Memorial at Fishermen's Terminal

• **Ballard Oil Company** is charted #12. ("Fuel docks," p. 49)

• **Rowe Machine** is charted #13, now Pacific Fishermen Shipyard.

• **The 24th Avenue Landing** is the only **public dock** in Ballard inside the locks. On the north shore, just east of the locks, it's immediately west of the large Yankee Diner Restaurant. The landing is a good stopping place inbound or outbound where you can go ashore to shop or to dine. ("Public Access," p. 51, and "Restaurants," p. 51)

• **Stimson Marina** is charted #15A; no guest moorage.

• **Covich & Williams Company,** charted #16. ("Fuel docks," p. 49)

• **Sagstad Marina** is charted #18; no guest moorage.

• **Pipeline area** is charted 0.36 mile west of the Ballard Bridge east of Sagstad Marina.

There are several other marinas along these shores, none with guest moorage.

• **Fishermen's Terminal** on the south shore, west of the Ballard Bridge, is the large commercial moorage for hundreds of seiners, trawlers, trollers, gillnetters, crabbers and factory ships that make up the large Seattle fishing fleet.

• **Public access** is available at Fishermen's Terminal which has several restaurants, a fish market, marine supplies and clothing, repair facilities, bank, barber shop, grocery and restrooms. Showers and laundromats are for commercial fishing crews only. ("Restaurants," p. 51; "Fuel docks," p. 49; "Marine Services," p. 52)

• **Cable area** crosses the channel at the Ballard Bridge.

• **Ship Canal traffic signals** are on the southwest side of the Ballard Bridge. Today it's green, indicating no major channel obstructions are obscured by the bend in the Fremont cut. ("Aids to Navigation," p. 33)

• **Ballard Bridge** with charted vertical clearance of 46 feet at the center, is next. *Guidelines for Boaters* gives the clearance as 45 feet. The bridge opens to our one long, one short blast, and we proceed east in the canal. Ballard Bridge to Fremont Bridge is about 1.3 miles. (See Bridges, pages 39-42)

• **Maritime Training Center** of Seattle Community College is east of the Ballard Bridge on the north shore. A marine engineering program is taught on board several training vessels, including the *Seattle Maritime Educator,* for hands-on experience for students enrolled in the year-long program.

• **Surfaced ramp** with parking is charted east of the college at 14th Avenue.

The south shore of the canal has piers where large warehouses, seafood processors and crabbing ships are berthed or under repair.

• **Foss Maritime Company** is huge, with its many distinctive green and white tugs, barges and cranes along the south shore. Foss Maritime Company has been on the waterfront for over 100 years. It started in 1889 in Tacoma, when Andrew and Thea Foss and their handful of rowboats grew into the Foss Tug and Launch Company. (Chapter 12)

When we're about 0.25 miles east of the Ballard Bridge, we're able to get a clear view of the canal all the way to the Fremont Bridge.

The industrial area continues east of the Ballard Bridge for about 0.5 mile when it then becomes the tree-lined Fremont Cut with office buildings on either side.

• **Fremont Cut** is about 0.55 miles long. **Wall-to-wall width** of the cut is about 100 yards.

Seafood processor fire in 1994

- **Dredged width** of the channel is tabulated as 100 feet.
- **Depth at the middle half** of the channel is tabulated as 26.6 feet in 1983.
- **Depths at the edges** of the dredged channel vary from about 18 feet to two feet; this requires attention and caution in maneuvering to clear other traffic.
- **Two overhead power cables,** clearance 160 feet, cross the canal. One is 0.55 miles west of the Fremont Bridge, the second is 0.22 miles west of the bridge.
- **Cable and pipeline crossings** are near both towers.
- **Queen Anne Hill** rises from a plateau along the south side of the canal while Phinney Ridge rises gradually along the north side of the canal.
- **Seattle Pacific University** is along the south shore and sometimes we see various games underway on the outdoor field, depending on the season.

  In spring and summer hundreds of ducks and Canada geese and their downy offspring dodge boats while begging for goodies from passing boaters.
- **Fremont Bridge**, charted vertical clearance 31 feet, but is shown 30 feet in the ***Guidelines for Boaters*** pamphlet. We signal one long and one short blast and the bridge opens. We usually wave our thanks to the bridge tender. (See p. 39-42)

  The Fremont Bridge is reputed to be the most frequently opened bridge in the country, opening an average of every 10 minutes in the busy season.

"Waiting for the Interurban" by Richard Beyer

- **Fremont Community** on the north shore—the self-proclaimed "Center of the Universe"—is a distinctive blend of old and new, funky stores, used book shops, ethnic restaurants, micro-breweries, light manufacturing, some upscale shops. The community is often looking for things new, distinctive and occasionally outrageous. It's the home of Richard Beyer's famous "Waiting for the Interurban" sculpture, the huge Volkswagen-eating troll under the Aurora Bridge, and a recently acquired statue of Lenin. Too bad there's no place to moor the boat and wander around. There are private moorages and rowing clubs on the north shore.

⚓ **Underway in Lake Union, from the Fremont Bridge to University Bridge,** the Ship Canal passage is along the north shore of Lake Union. It's 0.7 mile from Fremont Bridge to G C "13" buoy off Gasworks Park, and 0.82 miles from the buoy to the University Bridge.

Fremont's Lenin

Boat Traffic in Lake Union, includes ships, small craft, sailboats under sail, kayaks and tugs with tows. The chart notes "Caution" (see charted note C), "All vessels are warned that seaplanes may be taking off or landing on Lake Union."

- **Charted "Test Area"** is marked by four privately maintained lighted buoys. There are unrestricted speed limits in the area. Vessel owners are responsible for wake damage. The rest of Lake Union is a seven knot, no wake zone.
- **R N "16"** Red nun buoy is 35 yards off the south shore under the I-5 Bridge.

  Before passing under the University Bridge we take a closer look at Lake Union.

➡ *Caution: Kids swing out on long ropes over the canal and drop into the water, creating a hazard for boaters and themselves.*

Gasworks Park, hilly, grassy and urban, is a wonderful amalgam of old gas plant machinery. It's a favorite walking, jogging, kite-flying park with a fantastic view of the city. Kayakers seem to flit all over Lake Union often pulling their boats ashore at the park.

Gasworks Park

The old ferry Skansonia doesn't leave its moorage, and it's not a place to drop in, but interesting to note, since this vessel was once on the ferry run from Titlow Beach in Tacoma to Point Fosdick before there was a Tacoma Narrows Bridge.

Lake Union looking south

Lake Union

Is the watery heart of the city. The lakeshore is a rich mix of shipyards, yacht repair, yacht sales, moorages, restaurants, industrial sites, one large park, many tiny street-end parks, houseboats both quaint and upscale, and a couple of seaplane harbors. It's busy, noisy and endlessly fascinating, day or night, when the lights are almost as bright as day. Moorage is limited and anchoring not allowed, but this may change in the future. The "Loch Union Monster" reportedly still frequents the lake.

Queen Anne Hill crowds the lake's west shore; even larger Capitol Hill tops the east side. South are spectacular views of Seattle's towering high-rises and the city's icon— the Space Needle. Northwest is the I-5 Freeway and University bridges.

Lake Union's North Shore

East from the Fremont Bridge, under the Aurora Bridge, we see the newly-built Lake Washington Rowing Club, as well as boat moorages, haulout and repair facilities, yacht sales, including several long time marine services.
- **Vic Franck's Boat Co. Inc.** is charted #36.
- **Tillicum Marina** is charted #37.
- **Seattle Harbor Patrol** office and docks are west of Gasworks Park.
- **Gasworks Park** is a prominent bulge along the north shore.
- **G C "13"** Green can buoy is about 100 yards south of the park.
- **Surfaced ramp** is charted 0.4 mile north of the buoy at the foot of Sunnyside Avenue, easily identified by two large orange balls on the overhead power lines.
- **Seattle Marine** is charted #55.
- **Note:** Charted **"sunken ship"** just east of #55 in 32 to 33 feet, appears to be covered by 25 feet of water. A nearby submerged pile is covered by 19 feet. They have mysterious origins.
- **Puget Sound Yacht Club** is 0.25 mile northeast of Gasworks Park and has reciprocal guest moorage for about two boats.
- *Skansonia*; an old refurbished ferry, a favorite party and reception boat, is next. We might even see a wedding underway.
- **Ivar's Salmon House** is west of the I-5 Bridge, offers moorage while dining.

Southwest Shore Lake Union
- **Stewarts Engine** is charted as #32 but new location is 4600 Shilshole Ave. N.W. **Wilson Marine** is now at charted site.
- **Morrison's North Star Marine Fuel Dock** is charted #38. (Fuel docks," p. 49)
- **Con Youngquist Moorage** is charted #43, a private moorage.
- **Bellevue Yacht Club (at Lake Union)** has reciprocal moorage near China Harbor Restaurant.

Heading south along the lake's west shore, we pass marine and other businesses, yacht sales and private moorages.
- **Four restaurants with moorage while dining** are on this west shore: China Harbor, Franco's Hidden Harbor, Latitude 47, and Harborside, formerly Kayak.

- **R N "2"** marks a 10 foot shoal in this southeast corner of the lake. It seems odd this would be number "2" but it is. (Not to be confused with R N "2" in Shilshole.)
- **Kenmore Air** seaplane harbor is along this southwest shore.

South Shore of Lake Union

- **Navy and Marine Training Center** at the south end of Lake Union is used for navy training and other activities. A pre-nuclear submarine was once kept here.
- *Wawona;* the long-retired, three-masted lumber, then cod, schooner, is moored along the south shore, in a state of perpetual volunteer maintenance.
- **Center for Wooden Boats** is next with its marvelous eclectic collection of vintage wooden boats. For wooden boat lovers, visiting the center is a must—and wooden sailboats are for rent.
- **Chandler's Cove** is east of the Center for Wooden Boats at the Fairview Avenue street end, where there is a public shore park, kayaks can be launched, and where the lovely, classic, steamship *M/V Virginia V*, sometimes moors.
- **Moorage** is available on a first come, first served basis at Chandler's Cove for these restaurants: Duke's Chowder House, Cucina!Cucina! and Chandler's Cove Crab House.

East Shore Lake Union

- Private moorages and other businesses extend to the old steam power plant, charted as "stack (SW of seven)" on chart 18447, although there are really six. It now houses ZymoGenetics, Inc.
- **Kamon's Restaurant** at Lake Union Landing has 50 feet of moorage for boaters while dining, is located west of the old steam plant.
- **Chrysler Air** Seaplane Charters is north of the old plant.
- **Lake Union Drydock,** a dominant shipyard in Lake Union, is also north of the steam plant.
- **F R 15 ft**. NOS Maintd. This light is off the huge **National Ocean Service**, Pacific Marine Center docks and buildings, where some of the large, white NOAA research vessels moor.
- **2 F R 10 ft**. Priv Maintd, is charted at a houseboat moorage facility, identified as Flo Villa Lights in the *Light List*.

This eastern shoreline has boatyards and private moorages intermixed with the houseboat community.

At present, there are about 490 houseboats, according to the Floating Homes Association. Most people living in them say they wouldn't trade living in a floating home in the heart of the city for anything. The association has even published a cookbook. People who dream of buying a houseboat should expect to part with between $100,000 and $900,000.

Several public shoreline street end parks are along this shore. Kayaks are launched at these parks, but there is no anchoring offshore.

- **Azteca Mexican Restaurant** with moorage while dining is along this shore, tucked in behind some private moorages.
- **Cadranell Yacht Landing** is charted #53.
- **Lake Union Boat Repair** is charted #58, near the lake's north end.
- **American Marine Contractors** charted #60, was the former site of the Boat Yard, preceded by Blanchard Boat Company.
- **Tyee Yacht Club,** with reciprocal moorage, is at the lake's northeast end.

⎈ **Underway to Portage Bay,** we head east in the channel from Lake Union passing under two bridges.

Houseboats once numbered about 1,000 east of the Ballard Bridge, in Lake Union and Portage Bay. They were homes for fishermen, loggers, bootleggers, drunks, artists, university students, and those who loved the lifestyle. (Carl, who was born in a houseboat on Portage Bay, hasn't decided on his category.)

Today, many of the original floating houses have been transformed into modern, fashionable homes, as seen in "Sleepless in Seattle."

Dick Wagner, Director, Center for Wooden Boats

Center for Wooden Boats

Carl worked for Lake Union Drydock and lived there aboard *Winsome* for several years.

Earlier he was a cartographer for the U.S. Coast and Geodetic Survey, now a branch of NOAA.

- **R N "16"** Red nun buoy is 35 yards off the south shore under the I-5 bridge.
- **I-5 Fixed Freeway bridge,** vertical clearance is 138 feet.
- **Overhead power cables** have 182 foot vertical clearance.
- **Channel width** here is just over 75 yards wide, and narrows to 157 feet at the University Bridge.
- **Cable area** is charted west of the I-5 bridge to east of the University Bridge.
- **North and South Passage parks** are on both shores under the I-5 Bridge.
- **Between the bridges** on the south shore are rowing clubs, including the George Pocock rowing club. The shells, ranging from singles to eight person boats, skitter over Portage Bay and Lake Union, along with ever present, and increasing, kayaks.

On the north shore between the bridges, are more tug and barge out-port facilities, recreational vessel moorages, marine services and haulouts.

University Bridge has a charted vertical clearance of 45 feet, but *Guidelines for Boaters* shows 44 feet, signal one long and one short for opening. (Pages 39-42)

- **Portage Bay,** about 0.8 mile long, is 0.35 mile wide in its southern part.
- **Depths** in the bay range from seven to 25 feet.
- **University Bridge to Montlake Cut,** 0.55 mile; bridge to bridge, 0.76 mile.
- **Portage Bay Reach** is the charted dredged channel along the north shore. It is 200-350 feet wide, with a midchannel depth tabulated as 26.7 feet.

Portage Bay has its share of marinas, boat repair services, a small-boat launch ramp, small streetend parks and houseboats.

Blanchard Boat Company—where Carl worked years ago building Blanchard stock sailboats and custom boats—was once at the present site of American Marine Contractor on Lake Union.

It's a busy place, with tugs, tows, small craft and commercial vessels constantly on the move through Portage Bay Reach. Kayakers paddle in droves on their way from Lake Union to the Arboretum, east of the Montlake Bridge. Local residents swim in the waters, especially along the southwest shore, and sailboarders dart among the traffic.

Along the north shore are boatyards and yacht brokerages.

- **Wolfe's Marine,** private yard and boat sales, is charted as #65.
- Immediately east of Wolfe's is the University of Washington Police building, formerly an old sawmill.
- **Launch ramp** east of the police building at the foot of Brooklyn Avenue is poorly maintained and has no parking. It's used only for hand-carry boats. From the ramp it's just a short walk to the University district's restaurants and stores.

The sprawling University of Washington owns much of the northeast shore of Portage Bay and dominates the shoreline with Gothic and modern buildings.

Harbor Patrol officers, from left, Art Van Puymbrouck and Mary Brick, with Sgt. Duane Hoekstra—patrol office is on north shore of Lake Union

The signal to open the University Bridge has been for many years, one long and one short, the same as for the other bridges. Originally, it was one long and three shorts.

There are a couple of Canada goose nests (in wooden boxes) on wingwall pilings of the bridge. Each spring we see geese sitting on eggs here, awaiting the emergence of the little goslings.

View southeast to Portage Bay from the University Bridge
(Photo by Bernie and Elissa Rubinstein)

• **Jensen Motor-Boat Company** is charted #69. University research vessels moor at docks east of Jensen's yard where the old Showboat Theater once rested.

Portage Bay's southwest shore climbs the steep slopes of Capitol Hill with layer upon layer of homes and apartments. The shore is home to another segment of Seattle's houseboat community.

The UW campus police department is in a former old sawmill building on Portage Bay. This was once Bryant's Motor Boat Marina, then Timmerman Marine Service, with some moorage still in evidence. Although weathered over the years, the painted "Motor Boat Marina" sign still shows on the north side of the building.

Anchor Jensen

The Aquaplane Era

Carl recalls: Back in the 1930s, the limited outboard speed craze hit Portage Bay. The predecessor of today's water skier, the aquaplaner stood on a flat board—an aquaplane—while towed by an unregulated, unmuffled, speedboat.

Around and around they went in Portage Bay, those elite aquaplaning snobs. The noise and the activity were almost too much for my friend and me.

My old Evinrude and 14 foot skiff weren't up to that power and speed, which called for some original thinking. That invariably gets me in trouble.

A friend and I experimented with boards of various sizes towed behind my boat. None were quite right. They were more like sea anchors than aquaplanes.

The idea flashed through our minds that a dining room table might solve this problem: a style that had a center column with four legs that curled out onto the floor with a couple of table extension leaves clamped together securely with its reach rod—a perfect solution.

My friend had just such a table at his floating home down the bay. It was a far better style and shape and would be much easier to launch than mine, and perhaps a little safer from my point of view. Just push it out the door and into the bay, while none of our parents or family members were home.

With great care we removed the vase of flowers, doilies and lace tablecloth from the table, remembering exactly how they were arranged.

We launched the table without incident. We secured the tow line around the column next to the underside of the table.

Our first attempt was like towing a submarine—breathing was impaired.

We finally found the combination of applying power and positioning our feet and body weight, using the curling table legs as handle bars. We stood up, above the elite aquaplaners who only had rope reins to hang onto. We were up, up and away!

We circled the lake several times, the outboard motor struggling to keep us up, generating much more wake than speed, aquaplaning in slow motion. One elite aquaplaning snob was so busy pointing and laughing at us that he fell off his board, which he justly deserved.

But this entire caper would come to a terrible end if we were caught. Prudence dictated our return.

Using bath towels to dry the table, we had replaced the lace tablecloth, flowers and everything just as his mom returned. She was curious about the wet towels, which we never used because we always dripped dry.

At that point I found a compelling urge to get home to my own chores.

Later I was asked to dinner at my friend's house. We had gotten away with the caper slick as a whistle and secretly entertained thoughts of a rerun.

As we all sat eating dinner at the table, it suddenly collapsed onto our laps, dinner and all. The glue joints, weakened by the water, failed just at that moment. We looked at each other, not sure whether we'd been caught. We were as surprised as everyone else. As we cleaned up the mess I was once again compelled to return home to my own chores.

The deed that haunted us the rest of our lives was never again discussed with another soul—until now.

Anchor Jensen's well-known boatyard has been in Portage Bay since the 1920s. It was started by his dad, Marino Antonio Jensen. The yard and Anchor are among the last of the Seattle waterfront legends, which include Doc Freeman, Frank Prothero, Rupert Broom (both Frank and Rupert are deceased)Bill Garden, Vic Franck, Mark Freeman, Marty Munson, Ed Monk Sr., Norm Blanchard, his dad, N.J. Blanchard, and many others.

A large sign, "Save Portage Bay As Is," is the last vestige of a long fight to keep the UW from encroaching further on marine businesses near the school.

The UW plans to all but eliminate the taxpaying, recreational vessel moorages along the north shore.

The first graduate of the UW was Clara A. McCarty, 18, who received a Bachelor of Science degree in 1876.

Seattle Parks has restricted access to the Montlake Playfield and Community Center on Portage Bay from the water to people even in small hand-powered boats.

Asa Mercer, who at age 22 was president of the UW, and the school's only instructor, was responsible for bringing nearly 60 single women to Seattle to be brides for the large number of single men.

There are now several thousand descendants of the adventurous "Mercer Girls" in the northwest.

In summer, dozens of youngsters take sailing lessons through SYC. Their little boats scoot all over Portage Bay as the kids learn how to handle themselves in the small craft, including flipping over and righting the boats—a favorite drill on hot summer days.

*Tug **Vulcan** and log tow plugs up the Montlake Cut*

The UW was originally located in downtown Seattle in 1861, and was moved to the present site in 1891.

Rowing shells with crews from the University and various rowing clubs skim across Portage Bay, often in early morning when the waters are calmest, while their coxswain shout instructions. It's all part of the Portage Bay ambiance.

The south end of Portage Bay rises gradually into the Montlake Community. Here, two of Seattle's largest yacht clubs face each other: Queen City Yacht Club on the west shore, Seattle Yacht Club on the east. Both have guest moorage for reciprocal yacht club members.

Montlake Playfield and Community Center are between the two yacht clubs, but can't be seen from the water. Wetlands front the bay south of the 520 (Evergreen Point) causeway ascending Capitol Hill to the west.

• **Montlake Cut** wall-to-wall width scales about 150 feet. It's about 0.4 mile long with a tabulated width of 100 feet. **Midchannel tabulated depth** is 30.1 feet.

• **Traffic Lts., R & G** Red and green traffic lights as charted are at both ends of the Montlake Cut. ("Aids to Navigation," p. 33)

The bend in Portage Bay Reach blocks the view of Ship Canal obstructions and traffic until almost at the cut. Ships or tugs with tows in the cut and red traffic signals at either end of the cut are reasons to wait or use caution.

• **Montlake Bridge** has a charted vertical clearance 48 feet, but *Guidelines for Boaters* show it at 46 feet. The bridge is midway through the cut. Opening and closing schedules differ from the other bridges. (Bridges, p. 39-42)

• **Cable and pipeline areas** are charted east and west of Montlake Bridge.

➥**Caution: Montlake Cut can be a nightmare when jammed with sailboats waiting for the bridge.**

If westbound in the afternoon, the sun's in our eyes, fast boats churn up wakes, restless to reach Lake Washington where they can go **fast**; some personal watercraft (jet skis) ignore the seven knot speed limit, novice canoers and kayakers paddle naively across bows of larger boats, and we may encounter swimmers.

It's a straight shot through Union Bay Reach to Webster Point at Laurelhurst.

• **University shellhouse** is at the east end of the Montlake Cut. Small floats are here for use by university alums, as well as floats for the UW sailboat fleet near the canoe and rowboat rental, close to the crew house.

• **Union Bay,** between the Montlake Cut and Webster Point, is about 0.9 mile long and extends north about 0.5 mile. Small boats swarm all over the shallow bay.

• **Depths** throughout most of Union Bay range from about one to six feet.

• **Union Bay Reach** dredged channel is 0.9 mile long, 100-200 feet wide, and midchannel depth is 28.4 feet.

• **G C "27" "29" and "31"** green can buoys, mark north edge of dredged channel.

• **R N "28"** and **R N "30"** red nun buoys, mark the south edge of the channel.

Most of the south shore of Union Bay Reach is the beautiful marshland and woodland of the Arboretum, over 172 acres with more than 4,000 different species of vines, shrubs, trees, flowers and herbs, a wonderful wilderness in the city.

Marine traffic in the Arboretum is restricted to non-motorized craft only.

Passing close to the Arboretum's Foster Island on the south shore, we're opposite green can "29."

➡ **Caution**: In summer kids and dogs jump in the channel and swim along here—dangerously close to boats.

Next along the south shore is a log booming ground, not often used.

Sometimes in the spring, boggy floating peat islands appear–a problem for boaters in and out of the channel. Some have no vegetation and barely show above the water.

"Raisin" Schuster escapes the peat bog

• **Fl G 4s 19 ft "33" Webster Point Light**, marks the east end of the Ship Canal and **we have officially entered Lake Washington.**

• **Webster Point is the end of the seven knot speed limit except where noted.**

The information in the rest of this chapter gives details as we know them for navigating the locks and Ship Canal:

Hand powered boats are paddled across and along the channel to Foster Island and into the tiny bays of the beautiful Washington Park Arboretum on the south side. The 172.5 acre park is a beautiful woodland with boulevards, pathways and trails through the woods and gardens. The marshy islands and canals are perfect for canoeing and kayaking, bird and animal watching and, very important, relaxing.

A wonderful shiny whirligig at Webster Point marks the point and reflects the sunshine as it twists and turns. It can be seen for miles.

Important Things to Know and Have on Board Before We Go

The fewer surprises, the better and safer our cruises, lives, boats and other properties.

Run in with the trees: One otherwise uneventful, but crowded day, keeping to the right of the channel as we proceeded west to the Montlake bridge—sun in our eyes—twigs, leaves and small branches began raining on deck. Our mast had gotten into a minor skirmish with a tree.

In summer, when not cruising, Jo swims a half-mile daily from our Portage Bay home, as Carl accompanies her in the skiff for his "a-row-bic" exercise, and to run interference from window-shopping cruisers close to houseboats and shore.

In fall and spring she shortens the distance, and in winter she turns chicken and finds an indoor pool.

Federal, state, county and city regulations and procedures are enforced by the Seattle Harbor Patrol, the Coast Guard and the Army Engineers. Regulation details are covered in the Appendix.

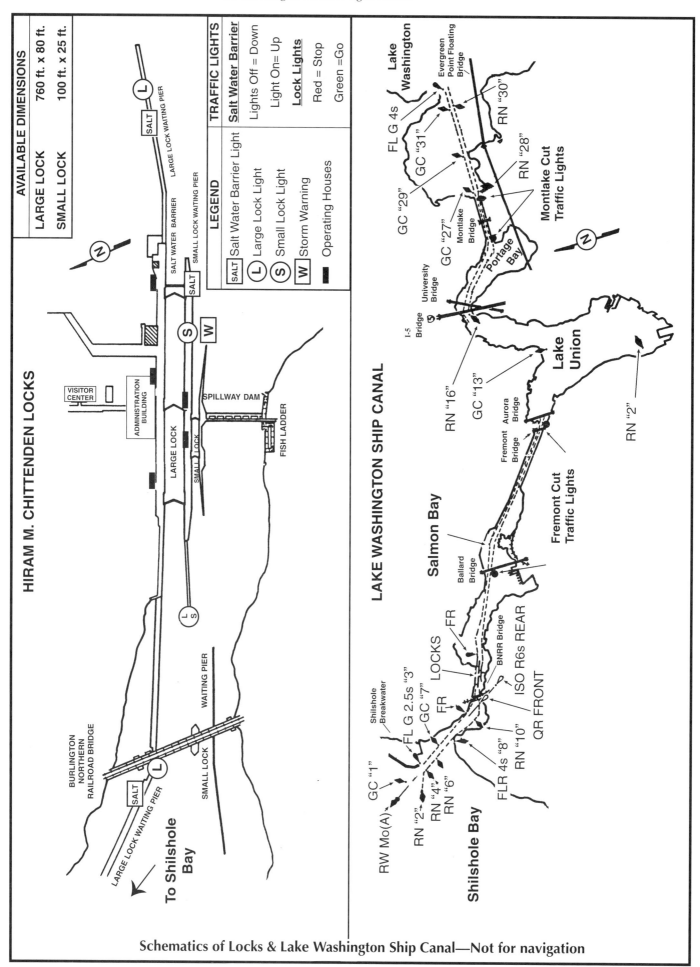

Schematics of Locks & Lake Washington Ship Canal—Not for navigation

Aids to Navigation: Lake Washington Ship Canal

The following aids are listed as charted on 18447. Information is also taken from U.S. Coast Guard *Light List* Vol. VI, 1995, and the Army Corps of Engineers, and as otherwise indicated.

The aids are from Shilshole Bay east to Webster Point Light in Lake Washington.

SHILSHOLE BAY ENTRANCE

"Approach Lighted Bell Buoy":

• R W Mo (A) [*Light List* #18110 and 16785] (Ballard Bell Buoy), red and white stripes, marked Mo A (Morse Code, dot-dash) flashing white light, is approximately 0.4 mile NNW of south entrance to Shilshole Bay Marina and about 1.4 miles north and east of West Point lighthouse.

Entrance Range Lights:

• Q R 20 ft [*Light List* #18115] "**Entrance Range Front Light**, quick flashing red light 20 feet high on dolphin with rectangular red dayboard bearing a central black stripe, visible 4° each side of rangeline."

• Iso R 6s 81 ft [*Light List* #18120] "**Entrance Range Rear Light**, isophase red, 6 second light on rectangular red dayboard bearing central black stripe, 81 feet high on skeleton tower; 250 yards, 146° from front light, visible 4° each side of rangeline."

Entrance Buoys "1" "2" "4":

• G C "1" [*Light List* #18125] "**Entrance Buoy 1** green can"
• R N "2" [*Light List* #18130] "**Entrance Buoy 2** red nun"
• R N "4" [*Light List* #18135] "**Channel Buoy 4** red nun"

Breakwater Light "3" at South End:

• Fl G 2.5s "3" Horn (Bl (2) 20s) [*Light List* #18140 and 16790] "Flashing green, 2.5 seconds, square green dayboard with green reflective border 22 feet high on white house, visible 5 miles; Horn: 2 blasts every 20 seconds (2 seconds blast-2 seconds silent, 2 seconds blasts-14 seconds silent)."

Channel Buoys "6" and "7"

mark edge of charted 1 foot shoals immediately north and south of dredged channel.
• R N "6" [*Light List* #18145] "**Channel Buoy 6** red nun"
• G C "7" [*Light List* #18150] "**Channel Buoy 7** green can"

Inner Light "8" at Bluff on South Side of Channel

• Fl R 4s 15ft 3M "8" [*Light List* #18155] "Flashing red 4 seconds, 15 feet high on triangular red dayboard with a red reflective border on dolphin, visible 3 miles."

Channel Buoy "10"

• R N "10" [*Light List* #18160] "**Channel Buoy 10** red nun"

SIGNALS & AIDS FOR LOCKS
(Maintained by the Army Corps of Engineers)

"Guide Wall Lights"

are at ends of Large Lock waiting piers on north side of channel.
• F R 8 ft as charted [*Light List* #18165] "**Lower Guide Wall Light (eastbound)** visible 11 miles, on pile structure at west end of Large Lock waiting pier"
• F R 14 ft as charted [*Light List* #18165] "**Upper Guide Wall Light**" (westbound) on pile structure at east end of Large Lock waiting pier.

Lock Traffic Signals only [*Light List* #18170]

• **F R 10 ft high** fixed red light
• **F G** fixed green
"If neither light is shown vessels bound for large lock must stop at **Stop** sign (below small lock) until directed to proceed. Red light must not be passed by vessels bound for large lock; green light indicates that they may proceed. Vessels bound for small lock may disregard lights and proceed to **Stop** sign below that lock." From *Light List* remarks (See Small Lock traffic signal.)

Eastbound:

• **Large Lock Traffic Lt.** is charted at Large Lock waiting pier on north side of channel just west of BNRR bridge.
• **Second Large Lock traffic signal** is not charted but is signed "Large Lock" at west end of middle lock- guide wall.
• **Small Lock Traffic signal** charted and signed as "Stop Signal -Small Lock" is at west end of middle lock guide wall, and is next to the Large Lock signal.

Westbound:

• **Large Lock Traffic signal** is charted roughly mid-length on the angled Large Lock waiting pier on the north side of the channel in Salmon Bay.
• **Small Lock Traffic signal** is charted as "Stop Signal - Small Lock" near the end of the small lock waiting area on the south side of the middle guide wall.

Salt Water Barrier indicator lights

are charted on 18447 but are not on the *Light List.* Information here is from *Guidelines to Boaters.*
• **Large Lock Salt Water Barrier Indicator yellow lights** are on when barrier is up, off when barrier is down, and are charted as No. 1, 2 and 3.
• **Eastbound Traffic Salt Water Barrier Indicator light No. 1** is at the Large Lock waiting pier on the north side of the channel west of the BNRR bridge.
• **Westbound Traffic Salt Water Barrier Indicator light No. 3** is about mid-length along the angled Large Lock waiting pier at the locks east entrance on the north side of the channel in Salmon Bay.
• **Westbound Salt Water Barrier Indicator light No. 2** is just east of the Large Lock gate and located on middle wing wall approximately above the saltwater barrier.
This ends the aids and signals at the Locks.

LAKE WASHINGTON SHIP CANAL
LOCKS to WEBSTER POINT

Ballard Bridge to Fremont Bridge:

• **Traffic Lts. 2 R & 2 G** as charted, west side Ballard Bridge, are not on the *Light List.*
• **Traffic Lts. 2 R & 2 G** as charted, east side Fremont Bridge, are not on the *Light List.*
• "**Vessels** of 300 gross tons and over, and all vessels with tows, shall not pass the red lights. Vessels of less than 300 gross tons without tows may disregard these signals but should travel very slowly." From *Guidelines for Boaters.* This also applies to red and green signals at Montlake Bridge.

Lake Union:

- **Fl Y 2.5s** [*Light List* #18185, 18190, 18195, 18200] "**Test Area Lighted Buoys A, C, B, D**, flashing yellow 2.5 second lights mark rectangular test area in lake; private aids"
- **G C "13"** [*Light List* #18205] "**Buoy 13**, green can," 100 yards off the south shore of Gasworks Park
- **R N "2"** [*Light List* #18210] "**Shoal Buoy 2**, red nun," marks a 10 foot shoal less than 250 yards off the southwest shore of Lake Union
- **F R 15ft NOS Maintd** [*Light List* #18215] "**National Ocean Service Dolphin Light**, fixed red, 15 feet high on dolphin"
- **2 F R 10ft Priv Maintd** [*Light List* #18220] "**Flo Villa Lights (2),** fixed red lights 10 feet high on dolphin, private aids"
- **R N "16"** [*Light List* #18225] "**Channel Buoy 16,** red nun," about 25 yards offshore under south end of I-5 bridge

Montlake Cut:

- **Traffic Lts. R & G,** as charted, 1,000 feet west and 1,000 feet east of Montlake Bridge on south side of Montlake Cut, are not on the *Light List*. (For vessel operation refer to Ballard Bridge traffic lights.)

Union Bay Channel buoys "27" through "31":

- **GC "27"** [*Light List* #18245] "**Buoy 27** green can"
- **RN "28"** [*Light List* #18250] "**Buoy 28** red nun"
- **GC "29"** [*Light List* #18255] "**Buoy 29** green can"
- **RN "30"** [*Light List* #18260] "**Buoy 30** red nun"
- **GC "31"** [*Light List* #18265] "**Buoy 31** green can"

Webster Point Light:

- **Fl G 4s 19ft "33"** [*Light List* #18270] "**Webster Point Light 33**, flashing green 4 second 19 feet high on square green dayboard with a green reflective border on a white house on pile structure, visible 6 miles. Light obscured from 121° to 199°."

Bridge Briefs
How often do they open?

There were more bridge openings in the 1970s and 1980s than in the mid-1990s. The Fremont Bridge opened between 12,000 and 13,000 times each year in the 70s and about 11,000 times each year between 1984 and 1988. In 1993 there were about 8,700 openings at Fremont.

The declining openings are attributed to more powerboats and more sailboats in saltwater moorages, and grouping boats more often so there is less disruption time opening the bridge.

Number of Openings per Month:

January	425	July	1,018
February	459	August	1,086
March	600	September	939
April	696	October	756
May	967	November	506
June	1,003	December	407

Railroad tracks to an earlier railroad bridge across the canal in the Ballard area are still charted, although the bridge was removed years ago.

The bridge crossed the ship canal and provided railroad service into Kenmore at the north end of Lake Washington. Where the tracks were torn up, the railroad bed was converted to the popular Burke-Gilman hiking-biking trail.

(Also see Bridge Details, p. 39-42)

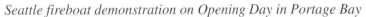

Seattle fireboat demonstration on Opening Day in Portage Bay

Shoals and Hazards

Shilshole Bay shoals are charted, marked and easily avoided, however, the area is deceptive.

- **Fishing** set nets and gillnet fishing boats (Native American) may be at Shilshole entrance and along the canal and in Lake Union in season. After dark in Shilshole there is often an attending boat which can help guide us through. The end of the nets are supposed to be lighted but are often confusing.
- **Currents** are encountered in the canal, especially in the vicinity of BNRR bridge below the locks. ("Currents" p. 35; "Bridges" p. 39-42; "Maneuvering" p. 36)
- **Locks hazards** ("Locks." p. 42)
- **Night travel** ("Canal Traffic" p. 38)
- **Fremont Cut** depths shoal abruptly to two feet as charted at several locations outside the 100 feet wide dredged channel. Caution is needed in these locations.
- **Union Bay** is shallow as charted and requires caution outside the dredged channel. Floating peat islands are occasionally encountered adrift in Union Bay and downstream in the canal.
- **Swimmers** are sometimes in the Fremont Cut, in Portage Bay, in the channel near the east end of Montlake Cut and off Foster Island. If they've fallen overboard they may be anywhere.
- **Kayaks, canoes, rowing shells and windsurfers** are just about everywhere, more in the summer, but also year round.

> ➡ **Note: Wind& or currents** can turn stopped vessels crosswise in the channel or carry them prematurely into the locks or under a closed bridge.

Currents

Our best guess is that maximum currents in the actual channels occur in the vicinities of the BNRR bridge, and in the Fremont and Montlake cuts, and can reach about at two knots during heavy seasonal flooding conditions.

- **Canal currents are fastest early in the year** when the spillway gates just south of the small lock are lowered to control flooding due to heavy rains and later snow melt.

In heavy flooding in 1996, locks administrators requested Seattle Harbor Patrol to measure the current speeds east of the spillway barrier cable.

Current was measured at three knots with about six feet of water passing over the fully lowered spillway gates. Spillway is about 235 feet long. Lock personnel felt the water might be traveling even faster than three knots at that time.

We have encountered currents of about two knots in the vicinity of the BNRR bridge and the locks during similar seasonal conditions and with a low tide.

We do not know if any or how much of that current was discharge of water from the lock chambers added to the seasonal runoff at that time.

Guide explains locks & currents to a group of school kids

These currents do complicate maneuvering, especially if westbound and unable to get a bridge opening when needed. ("Maneuvering" p. 36, "Bridges" p. 39-42)

- **Canal currents are slowest** in midsummer, continuing through November and December when little or no water runs over the spillway due to depleted snow pack and lack of serious rainfall. During this time canal currents consist only of water required to maintain the fish ladder operation and that which leaks past the lock and spillway gate seals.
- **Large and small locks literally bail** water out of the canal and Lake Washington each time lock chambers are emptied to accommodate east or westbound traffic. This volume of water only slightly increases currents upstream as lock chambers are filled. Currents downstream of the locks are later increased as water levels in lock chambers are lowered and discharged into the canal west of the locks.

Barge and Bridge Collision

When one leg of the towing bridle failed, a gravel barge veered and crashed into the protective timber structure of the middle BNRR Bridge column in October 1996.

Luckily, no one was injured and the bridge and column were not damaged, but considerable damage was done to the timber structure. Repairs lasted about a month, decreasing the space at the small lock waiting wall under the bridge.

This situation could be deadly for a vessel, caught between the barge and the bridge structure, or suddenly confronted head-on by a barge veering across the narrow channel on a divergent course caused by a failed towing bridle.

This is a classic example of the need to keep alert and be prepared to take evasive action.

Actual volume of water required to raise or lower water levels in the lock chambers varies according to the height of lake level and height of tide. The height between lake and saltwater levels may vary from six to 26 feet.

The combination of fish ladder operation, leakage of lock and spillway seals, the total of all lock operations plus evaporation, lowers the lake and canal water from the highest level in midsummer about two feet by the end of each year.

The number of lockings per day are reduced to conserve water.

Maneuvering in the Canal

Our experiences, observations and those of others, suggest maneuvering in the sometimes very crowded Ship Canal is a crap shoot.

In open water, maneuvering is less of a problem, but in the Ship Canal room is limited, channels may be as little as 100 feet wide, and must be shared with one or more other vessels of any type or size, including large ships or tugs with tows traveling the same or opposite directions.

Wind and currents generally mean boats require more speed or power to maintain control and more room is needed for maneuvering.

We're lucky to understand our own boat's maneuvering capabilities and idiosyncrasies, and can only guess at those of other vessels and the skill, experience and alertness of other vessel operators.

Twin screw vessels or vessels with bow thrusters can sometimes turn and maneuver in their own length. Single screw keel vessels can sometimes reduce their normal turning radius needed to maintain their position by alternately turning the rudder in the direction needed, then briefly accelerating power ahead and then reversing, repeated as needed.

Shallow draft vessels with little or no keel or skeg require much more power and room to turn into the wind, as they tend to slide sideways.

Tugs have more problems, and thus have right of way. Tugs towing barges or ships risk being run over by their own tows if they must stop. They lose the ability to control the direction of the tow if they must slow down, especially during windy and strong current conditions. Tugs side-tied near the stern of a barge or ship may turn crosswise in the channel if they must back down to stop, depending how the tug is tied to the barge. Tugs pushing a barge often have trouble seeing small boats ahead.

It's important we and all vessel operators stay alert and try to understand our own situations, as well as those of other vessels.

Loss of power and maneuverability in the Ship Canal becomes a real concern in the narrow channels, particularly between the locks and BNRR Bridge, and in the Fremont and Montlake Cuts.

If we are being carried toward a closed bridge by wind or current and impact is imminent and towing assistance is not immediately available, we might attempt to anchor temporarily in the channel if clear of cable and pipeline areas. Wind permitting, we might attempt to sail to a pier or out of the cut to anchor clear of the channel, and have done so in the past . . . . .

Grizzly with two "kitty litter" barges headed for Kenmore

Maneuvering in Close Quarters

Carl recalls: We were inbound from a winter cruise in the 1950s aboard my 50 foot gaff-headed yawl, *Winsome*, with a nine foot draft, and 70 feet from end of bowsprit to end of mizzen boom. Built in 1908, she was a wonderful classic of that era.

We were a half-mile west of the Fremont Bridge at 2 a.m., a very dark night, with a light southerly blowing diagonally across the cut, which is about 300 feet wall to wall. Her most reliable Chrysler Crown quit—like turning off the key. It would not restart, and there was no time to investigate.

With her deep draft, tying alongside in the shallows next to the concrete walls of the Fremont Cut was not feasible. The dredged channel was only about 100 feet wide.

To coast to windward on the south side and anchor even temporarily, the wind direction and scope would put *Winsome's* 70 feet diagonally across the middle of the channel. Uncertainty about the exact location of underwater cables in the area, on which our anchor might foul, was a concern.

She would soon be aground on the north side of the channel. No other traffic was in sight and we raised sail. *Winsome's* mizzen was well aft, and the working jib was out on the end of a long bowsprit. This combination allowed great leveraging potential for maneuvering in close quarters—we knew she ghosted very well under sail in light airs.

The mizzen hoisted and sheeted flat held her hove-to, head nearly into the wind. The jib and stays'l went up next, and then the main. We found that she would long and short tack to weather in the narrow channel quite well.

We could reach downwind, find a wide spot east of the Ballard Bridge to anchor or a place to moor, until the engine god became responsive. But, in the past I'd moored *Winsome* alongside the wood piers at the Fremont Bridge to wait out closed periods, so I decided to sail to the bridge and tie there. If we couldn't fix the problem we'd wake up the bridge tender and phone a friend for a tow. If we fixed it he'd wake up anyway.

After a couple of long and short tacks, to our surprise the Fremont Bridge whistled its long and short, and opened for a tug rapidly heading our way, towing a very large, high, empty barge.

Already we could hear the skipper on the tug cursing up a storm as he saw us, and I could imagine how he felt. No way could he stop without being run over by the barge. He knew he had to keep pulling or even the light wind would take control of the barge's direction, probably turning it crosswise in the channel.

Only an idiot would sail the cut at night, or any other time; normally we wouldn't be sailing there.

The tug had the right of way.

Either that skipper had done some sailing or his training kept him to the north side of the channel, slowing some as he approached us. *Winsome* and the tug were now head-on on our long tack, the safe distance shrinking rapidly. We came about onto our short tack, coasting and sailing to the south side of the channel. Just short of grounding we came about again, this time very slowly. We heard the tug skipper add some turns on his engine, increasing his speed.

Flattening the mizzen, we held *Winsome* in irons , allowing the tug and barge to clear us, port to port, the skipper still yelling. I yelled back our reason, apologized, and continued our long and short tacks toward the Fremont Bridge.

The Harbor Patrol happened by a few minutes later and we requested a tow to our slip at Lake Union Dry Dock. Tow line secured, we blew for the bridge which opened again, got sail off and later coasted into our slip.

Would I do it that way again? Maybe in the same boat, under a similar set of circumstances if the situation felt right. The conditions were ideal. It is not a recommended solution for any or all circumstances, but it worked for us that night.

The next day, the problem proved to be an ignition coil failure. A spare was on board, but circumstances the night before had not allowed enough time to trace the problem. Forty or so years later northbound on our Nakwakto cruise, Jo and I had an identical coil failure aboard 35 foot *Scheherazade* in a flat calm sea in Queen Charlotte Strait. One test of the ignition system prompted replacement and 20 minutes later we were underway again, demonstrating the importance of having spares on board.

Experience pays off—and we do our own engine work when possible.

***Early one morn a UW re-search vessel** went wild in Portage Bay, commanded by a lone youth. He'd fired up the engines, cast off the lines and went round the bay—out of control. He crashed ashore nearly missing houseboats and boats whose owners were aghast, bashing the bow of a moored sailboat as his wild ride ended, all in an attempt to follow in the steps of his seafaring dad.*

***Traffic signals** are located on the west side of Ballard Bridge, east side of Fremont Bridge, and at the east and west ends of Montlake Cut to indicate obstructing traffic in theses areas. ("Aids to Navigation" p. 33)*

Bridges & High Velocity Winds

In a sustained wind speed of over 35 miles per hour bridges over the Lake Washington Ship Canal are not opened all the way. The higher the wind speed, the less they can open. Figures are for the Fremont Bridge, but all bridges are approximately the same.

35 mph = 64° opening
40 mph = 44° opening
45 mph = 33° opening
50 mph = 26° opening
55 mph = 21° opening
60 mph = 18° opening
Over 60 mph = closed

"Let's hope nobody's out in that kind of weather," said Joanne McGovern, head of bridge operations.

Canal Traffic

There is a seven knot maximum speed limit and a "No Wake" restriction in the Ship Canal. In addition, there are posted areas for speed reduction. The limit when entering the locks is 2.5 knots or less.

Ship Canal traffic consists of all types of hand, sail and engine powered recreational and commercial vessels, ships of almost any size, log booms, gravel and crane barges, and an assortment of unusual floating craft. We encounter an almost infinite number and variety of pleasure and commercial vessels and ships in the Ship Canal, without knowing whether they are chartered, rented, owned, loaned or stolen. Thus there is an equally diverse level of experience, judgment, attention span and sobriety of the unknown operators. All things considered, we are amazed at how few problems there are on the water.

Night travel in the canal finds shore line lights blending with or overpowering weaker vessel navigation lights. It's not uncommon to encounter small craft, canoes and kayaks with extremely dim lights or none at all. They are not easily seen.

Between the Ballard bell buoy and Webster Point are 12 unlighted buoys which are extremely hard to see at night.

However, the night lights of the city are spectacular.

Vessel Traffic in Narrow Channels
Coast Guard Navigation Rules, "Colregs" (08-17-90) Rule 9

(a) Keep to the starboard side in the channel.
"A vessel proceeding along the course of a narrow channel or fairway shall keep as near to the outer limit of the channel or fairway which lies on her starboard side as is safe and practicable."

(b) Sailboats do not have the right of way in narrow channels.
"A vessel of less than 20 meters (about 65 feet) in length or a sailing vessel shall not impede the passage of a vessel which can safely navigate only within a narrow channel or fairway."

(c) Fishing boats should leave room for others.
"A vessel engaged in fishing shall not impede the passage of any other vessel navigating within a narrow channel or fairway."

(d) Don't cross the channel too close to other boats.
"A vessel shall not cross a narrow channel or fairway if such crossing impedes the passage of a vessel which can safely navigate only within such channel or fairway."

(e) The overtaking vessel is the burdened vessel and should sound a horn.

(i) "In a narrow channel or fairway when overtaking can take place only if the vessel to be overtaken has to take action to permit safe passing, the vessel intending to overtake shall indicate her intention by sounding the appropriate signal prescribed in Rule 34. The vessel to be overtaken shall, if in agreement, sound the appropriate signal and take steps to permit safe passing."

(ii) This rule does not relieve the overtaking vessel of her obligation under Rule 13.

(f) Be alert in areas of obscured vision and use sound signals when necessary.
"A vessel nearing a bend or an area of a narrow channel or fairway where other vessels may be obscured by an intervening obstruction shall navigate with particular alertness and caution and shall sound the appropriate signal prescribe in Rule 34."

(g) Anchor only in emergencies.
"Any vessel shall, if the circumstances of the case admit, avoid anchoring in a narrow channel."

Bridges

Lake Washington and Lake Union had railroads, trails and roads around them before the Ship Canal was completed in 1916.

After the canal cut the city, the problem was crossing it. There were settlements or villages at Ballard, Interbay, Fremont, and Ross (North Queen Anne). Heavily timbered fir and cedar forests had covered the surrounding hills, reaching to the shores.

Now seven bridges span the Lake Washington Ship Canal. Five are bascule and two are fixed spans. Large vessels and some sailboats have to open all five bridges between the Sound and Lake Washington.

Bascule bridges are built with single or double-hinged leaves which are mechanically raised and lowered. The BNRR bridge outside the locks is a single-leaf, bascule bridge. The four bascule bridges east of the locks in the Ship Canal are all double-leafed, at Ballard, Fremont, University and Montlake.

The Fremont Bridge was completed in 1917, the Ballard Bridge was built in 1918, followed by the University Bridge in 1919. The newest span over the canal, the Gothic Montlake Bridge, was completed in 1925.

When the Montlake Bridge was under construction towers were built on both sides of the cut and then the money ran out. It was several more years before the bridge was completed. North Seattle was then thoroughly secured to the rest of the city south of the Ship Canal.

I-5 Freeway Bridge, fixed, vertical clearance 127 feet, is 200 yards west of the University Bridge, and built in the 1960s.

Aurora Bridge, fixed, vertical clearance 136 feet, is at the east end of the Fremont Cut, about 200 yards east of Fremont Bridge. It connects the northeast side of Queen Anne Hill with the Fremont district on the canal's north side.

Shortly before the Aurora Bridge was completed several tall-masted sailing ships were towed out of Lake Union. Some were taken to Richmond Beach and burned. The clipper ship *Monongahela* was one of the last ships removed before the center span of the bridge was put in place. *(Photo courtesy Puget Sound Maritime Historical Society, archives at the Museum of History and Industry.)*

> ➡ **Note: Bridge regulations prohibit bridge openings for vessels under sail.**

The Aurora Bridge was formally named the George Washington Memorial Bridge because it was due to open on Washington's birthday, February 22, 1932. The bridge actually opened on February 17, 1932.

Bridge Clearance Approximations

"If it doesn't look right, don't go under it"

In the absence of bridge clearance gauges with large numbers at the water level indicating vertical bridge clearance at any time, tide or season—**like those on the Evergreen Point floating bridge**—there are a great many unnecessary bridge openings, causing delays, irritation and inconvenience to **vehicle** and **vessel** traffic.

With clearance gauges, all a mariner needs to know is mast height.

Instead, we must deal with complex variables in conventions, interpolate heights of tidal predictions, guess at seasonal variations in lake levels, all affected by floods and weather conditions; plus consequences of omissions, errors, or changed information at the time of passage.

NOAA's conventions for heights are charted on 18447, 08/15/92, latest edition:

"Vertical clearances above the locks are referenced to Mean Water Level of the lake which is 21 feet above MLLW."

"Vertical clearances for the bridge and cable of the BNRR bridge are referenced to MHW."

BNRR Ship Canal bridge is over saltwater. Clearance height conventions used by the U.S. Army Corps of Engineers, bridge tenders and NOAA seem to be the same at this bridge, but not for those over fresh water.

First let's look at BNRR clearances.

NOAA chart 18447 and Corps of Engineers *Guidelines for Boaters* pamphlet both show vertical clearance 43' feet at MHW.

At BNRR neither agency indicates an approximate least clearance during extreme high water or greatest clearance during ELW.

For 1996 we found a predicted high tide of 13.4' for 01/22/96, which indicates least clearance of approximately 40' on that date.

Curious about approximate greatest clearance, in 1996 we found a predicted low tide of -3.1' for 07/01/96, which appears to be approximately 53.6' clearance on that date.

ELW Tidal Information for Seattle is Charted on:
18440 08/05/95, latest edition, -4.5 ELW
18449 10/24/94, latest edition, -4.5 ELW
18448 10/30/93, latest edition, -5.0 ELW
18474 03/25/95, latest edition, -5.0 ELW

We wonder about different ELW charted values at the same Seattle location, and do not recall tides this low, but found a predicted -4.0 ELW on 04/13/91—so much for that.

Any clearance height based solely on a predicted time and height of tide are only approximations, as stated in tide and current tables and current charts. They are at best only predictions.

In addition, the times and heights are affected by flooding, heavy winds and barometric pressures, thus affecting clearance.

Not for the Faint Hearted . . . . . .

A friend named Raleigh, uncertain about clearance when westbound from the locks, turns the boat 180°, heading east. Idling ahead, the current carries him west, downstream backwards toward the bridge. If the mast touches, he speeds up to minimize damage to the mast. If it clears, he turns around again and continues.

Ballard, Fremont, University, Montlake bridges are east of the locks over fresh water. Here the Corps of Engineers references clearances to HWL (or least vertical clearance), while NOAA refers to MWL.

According to the Corps of Engineers and our own observations, high water usually occurs in the lake on or before July and low water on or before December. The difference is about two feet. Thus the mean lake level is one foot below HWL and one foot above LWL.

Subtracting one foot from NOAA's charted MWL should agree with Engineers HWL and give us the approximate least clearance by July.

Adding one foot to the MWL gives the approximate greatest LWL clearance in about December.

In the *Guidelines* high water clearances appear consistent with NOAA's MWL charted clearances, except at Montlake where NOAA charts the vertical clearance at 48.' It should be 47' MWL to agree with the 46' HWL clearance in *Guidelines for Boaters* and by bridge tenders.

At Montlake, NOAA appears to state clearance one foot higher than exists at MWL.

We count the planks out of the water on the BNRR north bridge pier—if enough are showing we figure we can clear the bridge. But we sometimes forget which planks we're using and how many need to be out of the water.

One bridge tender told us this method is also used by many commercial vessels.

BNRR Bridge with train, looking west to Puget Sound

Bridge Information Quick Guide

➡ Whistle signal for all bridges is one long and one short blast.

Use VHF Channel 13, low power, only for emergency or when the bridge tender does not respond to a whistle, and for one hour advance opening notice for 11 p.m. to 7 a.m. for Ballard, Fremont, University and Montlake bridges.

We do not guarantee these clearance values or equations.

SALTWATER Ship Canal BNRR Bridge		Approx. Clear	OPENINGS			CLOSED Period
			Normal Openings	Scheduled Openings		
				Hr & Half Hr	1 Hr Adv. Notice	
Ph. 206-784-2976						
Tide 13.4'	EHW*	40.1'	Bridge tender advises there are no closed or open periods			
" 10.5'	MHW	43'	Bridge is opened on request unless train is expected or on the bridge			
0.0	MLLW	53.5'				
" (-3.1')	ELW**	56.6'				

*EHW = 13.4' predicted Seattle tide in 01/22/96

MHW = 10.5' Mean High Water, Seattle 1996 is NOAA's charted bridge clearance above MHW

MLLW = 0.0 Mean Lower Low Water

**ELW = Extreme Low Water is -3.1 predicted Seattle tide 07/09/96

Equation to Determine Approximate Bridge Clearance Height at Time and Date of a Predicted High or Low Tide:

NOAA charted bridge clearance is above MHW	_____ ft.	
Plus height of MHW above MLLW datum	+ _____ ft.	
Bridge Height above MLLW datum	= _____ ft.	
Less Height of specific high or low tide prediction	_ _____ ft.	
Approximate bridge clearance at time and date of prediction	= _____ ft.	

FRESHWATER Ship Canal Bridges	Approx. Clear	OPENINGS			CLOSED Periods
		Normal Openings	Scheduled Openings		
			Hr. & Half Hr.	1 Hr. Adv. Notice	

Ballard Ph. 206-282-9525
    HWL
    MWL
    LWL
	
	45'
	46'
	47'
		
		9 am-4 pm
				
				Ph. 206-386-4251
				11 pm-7 am
					
					7-9 am
					4-6 pm

Fremont Ph. 206-386-4234
    HWL
    MWL
    LWL
	
	30'
	31'
	32'
		
		9 am-4 pm
				
				Ph. 206-386-4251
				11 pm-7 am
					
					7-9 am
					4-6 pm

University Ph. 206-684-7465
    HWL
    MWL
    LWL
	
	44'
	45'
	46'
		
		9 am-4 pm
				
				Ph. 206-386-4251
				11 pm-7 am
					
					7-9 am
					4-6 pm

Montlake Ph. 206-684-4710
    HWL
    MWL
    LWL
	
	46'
	47'
	48'
		
		9 am-12:30 pm
			
			12:30-3:30 pm
				
				Ph. 206-386-4251
				11 pm-7 am
					
					7-9 am
					3:30-6 pm

HWL = High Water Level, approximately midsummer

MWL = Mean Water Level, midway between HWL and LWL

Lake level changes approximately two feet seasonally

NOAA charted bridge clearance is to MWL

LWL = Low Water Level, approximately midwinter

Exception to Closures:

Openings may be made for a vessel of 1,000 gross tons or more, or if towing a vessel exceeding 1,000 gross tons— Federal Regs.

Closed periods are M-F except holidays or as noted in Local Notice to Mariners

Bridge Signals

One prolonged and one short blast is the whistle signal for all Lake Washington Ship Canal bridges, including the BNRR bridge west of the locks. The vessel should be close enough, about 100 yards, so the operator can hear the signal above bridge traffic noise.

Every approaching vessel needing the bridge opened is supposed to signal and receive an answer from the bridge within 30 seconds. If the bridge is open and no answer is received vessels approaching must use caution and be prepared to stop if necessary. Failure to do so has resulted in accidental closure and damage to vessels.

If the bridge cannot be opened promptly or if the bridge is being closed in response to an opening signal, the bridge operator should reply with five short blasts meaning no opening or that the bridge is being closed.

Regulations are that vessels can be held up to 10 minutes by Ship Canal bridges to allow accumulated vehicular traffic to clear or to wait for other vessel traffic. This is not always the case with the BNRR, depending on trains. Longer delays have been encountered due to train and vehicle traffic conditions.

A good whistle is worth its weight in gold, according to bridge tenders.

Hiram M. Chittenden Locks

Mariners should read this section before making a trip through the locks.

Locks Guidelines Publications:

Two brochures published by the U.S. Army Engineers are extremely helpful in understanding how the locks work and procedures for locking through;

1) *Guidelines for Boaters, Lake Washington Ship Canal and Hiram M. Chittenden Locks*— This is most important as it includes sections on equipment, the locks and canal, bridge and traffic signals, hazards, priorities and locking through. The booklet is available from lock attendants or by calling the locks at 206-783-7059. **They advise getting the pamphlet before going through the locks.**

2) *Lake Washington Ship Canal and Hiram M. Chittenden Locks, 1993*—The cover and first two pages give a graphic and written description of the operations. The booklet also gives a history of the locks and Ship Canal.

Locks "Boater Awareness" Programs

In Spring 1996, Scott Diehl began the Boater Awareness Program, on-site classes for boaters and others to learn exactly how locking-through works. The program was so successful that Diehl said they intend to do it annually, beginning each January. The program is announced through various boat dealers and boating publications.

Diehl said locks personnel also give off-site programs for boating organizations year round, using a video, with locking tips and question and answer sessions.

Phone: 206-783-7000 for more information.

From *Guidelines to Boaters:*

Equipment You Need to Lock Through

• **"Two or more** 50 foot (15.24 m) manila or other suitable mooring lines. These should be maintained in good condition (one bow and one stern) and should have an eye at least 12 inches (30.48 cm) in diameter (an eye not made with a slip knot).

• **"Fire extinguishing** equipment of the type and quantity required by the Coast Guard for your vessel.

• **"One (or more)** Coast Guard-approved Personal Flotation Device (PFD) for each person on board—required by the Coast Guard. Children and nonswimmers should wear them at all times.

• **"Fenders** for both sides of the vessel as boats may be asked to moor on either side of the lock chamber or to another vessel.

• **"Your vessel should be in good mechanical condition** to insure against the hazards of engine or reverse gear failure, fire, explosion and sinking. A fire or explosion on a vessel in the lock chamber endangers your boat's passengers, as well as passengers on other vessels and spectators on the lock wall. Escape from a vessel burning within the confines of the lock chamber could be very difficult."

• *We add: Have a sharp knife capable of cutting the lock line should it become impossible to release from the cleat.*

Ship entering large locks, as we're looking west

From *Guidelines to Boaters:*

"Hazardous conditions affecting all vessels (including kayaks)"

"Water and wind conditions can create hazardous situations when using the Locks. Water turbulence can effect your vessel in three ways.

"1.) Turbulence occurs during the filling or emptying process, when millions of gallons of water move through culverts near the base of the chamber. This water movement results in dangerous currents and undertows.

"Be alert to these dangers! They can effect rescue efforts for persons who fall overboard.

"The gates are opened when **water pressures** on either side are equal, not when **water level** is equal. Because saltwater is heavier than freshwater, it takes less saltwater to equal the same amount of pressure of the freshwater.

"2.) The interchange of salt and fresh water after the large lock gates are opened to the lake creates a second water hazard. The salt water in the lower portion of the lock chamber rushes into the lake and a corresponding surface current of fresh water rushes into the lock.

"When traveling east (toward Lake Washington), always remember to keep the bowline secure until the lock attendant advises you to release it. The in rushing current can swing the bow of your vessel around into the vessels astern if you remove the line prematurely.

"3.) Finally, whenever the spillway dam is operating, there can be water hazards. This spilling can affect navigation above or below the Small Lock. Above the locks, currents pull your vessel toward the spillway, making navigating the entrance difficult. Below, spilled water presents a strong current against your progress into the locks.

"Be alert to these potential conditions and make necessary adjustments to assure safety of your vessel.

"Windy conditions around the Locks can also influence the navigation of your vessel. Strong tail winds or side winds can make a difference in stopping speed and controlling your vessel. Always consider these elements before entering the locks.

"By paying close attention to these conditions and the lock attendant instruction (i.e. when to enter the chamber, when to hand them your line, or where to moor for the lockage), you can avoid putting your vessel in danger.

"Note to kayakers: Pay close attention to these hazards as they can create extremely hazardous conditions! Feel free to discuss them with lockwall attendants before using the locks. Also, due to hazardous currents and other hazardous conditions in using the large locks, kayakers are asked to be prepared to use the Small Lock."

We add: **Turbulence** of propeller wash from larger vessels ahead can affect your position in the lock or your ability to steer.

Damage may result to vessels from accidental engagement of forward or reverse gears coupled with propeller surges from other vessels in the locks. In 1995 several vessels were damaged and one woman injured when a large vessel was accidentally reversed while in the locks.

From *Guidelines to Boaters:*

"Who Goes First?"

"Waiting to go through the locks can be frustrating, especially on a crowded summer weekend. By understanding vessel priority, some frustrations can be eliminated. This is the established priority for vessels passing through the Chittenden Locks:

"1. Government vessels (Federal, State, City)
"2. Commercial passenger vessels on scheduled trips
"3. Freighters, fishing vessels and tow boats (with or without tows)
"4. Recreational pleasure craft
"5. Log rafts

"Larger vessels should enter first, when asked to do so. When they have been secured, smaller vessels can enter with greater safety and less possibility of being crushed.

"(Note to kayakers: Due to hazardous currents and other hazardous conditions in using the large lock, please be prepared to use the small lock. Please read section on "Hazardous Conditions" or consult the lockwall personnel if you have questions.)"

Outbound, west gate large lock open, BNRR bridge open

The Trip Through the Locks

Passing through the locks need not be a traumatic experience if we follow the motto at the locks:

BE PREPARED AND PAY ATTENTION

Whistle signals or VHF Ch. 13 radio contact are seldom used or needed for smaller vessels at the locks.

Signal to open the locks is two long blasts followed by two short blasts for all vessels other than vessels with tows. For vessels with tows the signal is two long blasts followed by three short blasts.

Speed limit when entering locks is 2.5 knots or less.

While still out in open water, we rig fenders on both sides and prepare locklines.

From *Guidelines to Boaters:*

"Be prepared! Pay attention! Are the two mottoes to live by in the Hiram M. Chittenden Locks.

"For example, be prepared to tie up on either side of the chamber or to other vessels.

"Have the correct type and amount of line and fenders to protect your vessel.

"Be prepared for the movements and adjustments of other vessels during the lockage.

"Pay attention to signals and instructions from a lock attendant, directing you where and how to moor.

"Pay close attention to your vessel during the lock process. You may need to pay out more line or bring up the slack at any time.

"Preparing to lock through: Before going through the navigation locks, always double check that you have all the equipment you need (such as lines and fenders), that your vessel's reverse gear is operating properly (this is a must!) and that you are ready for a safe passage.

"If guests are taking part in the mooring, take a few minutes before you reach the locks and review the entire lock process, including handling the lines, using the deck cleats, monitoring the vessel's security during a lockage, etc. This will prepare you and your guests for the process and help avoid a serious accident."

Locking Through:

Always follow this list of safety procedures and precautions when locking through. They will help to reduce the potential for accidents and injuries.

• "Station someone at both stern and bow to pass lines to a lock attendant and monitor the lines. (The stern line is always secured first.)

• "Arrange lines neatly to avoid hanging the vessel up on the lock wall or pulling your cleat out.

• "Place enough fenders on both sides to protect your vessel and other vessels.

• "Keep your feet away from lines. Lines can draw tight unexpectedly and you can get entangled in them and fall overboard.

• "Keep your hands away from cleats. Lines snap and cleats can fail, causing personal injury.

• "Stay behind rails or in the cockpit. On a flush deck sit down if possible.

• "Do not hang your legs over the side of your vessel. The vessel can shift and trap them against the lock wall.

• "Be prepared and pay attention!

• "Do not exceed the speed limit. You are responsible for leaving no wake which might upset other vessels."

We Add: The number of people needed on board to lock through depends on the type and size of the vessel.

If the steering station is aft one person can handle the engine controls, steering and the stern line with a second person forward handling the bow line.

With a midship steering station one person handles steering and controls, a second person aft handles the stern line and a third handles the bow.

An experienced person can sometimes rig bow and stern lines and pass through single-handed, not a recommended procedure, especially in crowded conditions.

Small Lock

Small Lock is 150 feet long, 28 feet wide.

Available dimensions are 100 feet long by 25 feet wide.

Volume is 508,000 gallons of water.

It takes about five minutes to raise or lower, depending on the tide, not including tie-up time.

Lift, depending on tide and lake level, is six to 26 feet.

From *Guidelines to Boaters:*

• **"Traffic lights** for this lock are located on the middle wall when westbound and at the waiting pier near the BNRR Bridge when proceeding east.

• "Watch these lights and listen for instructions over the public address system directing you to enter the lock. When you receive the green light, enter the lock **slowly**—at less than 2.5 knots. You are responsible for leaving no wake.

• "Watch the lock attendant for directions for mooring.

• "Pass a loop of line to the lock attendant.

• "He/she will loop the line around the button (on the floating guidewall) and pass it back to you to fasten around your cleat.

• "Use reverse gear and the stern line to stop. Keep the eye of the line on your boat cleat.

Mooring to floating guide wall in small lock, note potentially hazardous recesses in guide wall. (Photo Courtesy Army Corps of Engineers)

- **"Handle your bow line the same as the stern line.**
- "After the gates are closed, the lockage will begin. Be ready to pay out or take up lines should floating guide walls hang up.
- **"Do not secure your line with a half-hitch or under a knot. Use a figure-eight.**
- "Once the water movement has been completed, hold your lines secured to the cleats while the gates are being opened. Again, do not secure your line with a half-hitch or under a knot. Be ready for the unexpected.
- "When the lockage is complete, wait for the lock attendant's instructions before releasing the lines.
- "Move ahead SLOWLY—at less than 2.5 knots—until clear of the locks."

The above tie-up procedure is for westbound approach.

We Add:

When eastbound in the small lock the floating guidewalls with numbered mooring buttons raise and lower with water level and boats. The floating walls give vessel operators greater control over the vessel's movement and reactions to turbulent water during the locking process, and a simple method of mooring or casting off.

The attendant is high above us and the floating guidewalls, and therefore cannot put our line around the button for us. If we're unable to maneuver close enough to loop the line on the assigned mooring button, the attendant will toss a heaving line to the boat's crew. After securing it he/she will help pull the vessel within reach of the guidewall and mooring button.

On larger vessels the lock tender may instruct the operator to tie the lock line to the heaving line. Then he/she pulls the lockline to the top of the lock wall and attaches the eye to a button there. The crew can then haul or winch the vessel into position and secure it to the floating button. The line end at the wall top is turned loose by the locktender and retrieved by crew.

➡ **Warning—Floating Guide Walls in Small Lock**

At higher lake levels floating guide walls may stop rising before reaching high water level. At lower tides they stop lowering before reaching lower tidal water level.

Under some conditions they may hang up. Fixed vertical guides for floating guide walls have holes and the walls have recesses in which fenders may get caught.

Upstream gate ledge at low tide, in small lock chamber. Caution. The ledge is at the bottom of the Ship Canal.

To avoid possible damage, vessel operators must remain alert and adjust their locklines to compensate for slack or tension created by these condition. Fenders may need to be repositioned.

Large Lock

Large Lock is 825 feet long by 80 feet wide.

Available dimensions are 760 feet long by 80 feet wide .Volume is 7,700,000 gallons of water.

It takes about 15 minutes to raise or lower water in the lock, depending on the tide, not including tie-up time.

Lift, depending on tide and lake level, is six to 26 feet.

Saltwater barrier in large lock helps restrict saltwater intrusion into Salmon Bay. When raised depth over barrier is about 16 feet depending on lake level. When necessary to accommodate deep-draft vessels, the barrier is flooded and sinks to the chamber bottom.

The large lock is used primarily for ships, commercial and recreational vessels when there are large numbers of them when instructed.

In high traffic periods vessels may be rafted side-by-side, nearly wall-to-wall in the large lock.

A set of gates between east and west gates may be used when size or numbers of waiting vessels does not justify use of entire lock chamber. This reduces time required to fill or drain lock chamber, and it conserves lake water.

From *Guidelines for Boaters:*

The following applies to both **east and westbound** passages through large lock: "Traveling through the large lock is similar to the small lock, but there are several things to consider to increase your safety during lockage.

"1. **The large lock does not have floating mooring buttons to attach to**. This requires your crew to tend the lines. As the vessel moves up or down, your crew will have to pay out or take up lines smoothly and steadily with no slack. (Do not secure your lines with a half-hitch.)

"2. **A larger number of vessels can be in the lock at one time**. You must be prepared and alert and pay attention to the lock attendant's instructions.

"3. **Use caution with vessels of different sizes**.
- "You will be locking with larger or smaller-sized vessels. Larger vessels have less maneuverability than smaller ones, which is adversely affected by waves or turbulence.

- "When heading west in this lock, wait at the upstream timber guide pier, behind the traffic light. When heading east, wait at the waiting pier near the BNRR bridge. Watch the traffic lights and listen for instructions over the public address system directing you to enter the lock.
- "If you draw more than 14 feet (4.27 m), signal the lockmaster so that the saltwater barrier can be lowered. Signal with one long and two short blasts. When the flashing yellow light goes out, the saltwater barrier will be in the lowered position.
- "When you receive the green light, enter the lock SLOWLY—at less than 2.5 knots. It is your responsibility to leave no wake that might disrupt another vessel.
- "Watch the lock attendant for directions for mooring. They will instruct you where to tie either along the lockwall or alongside another vessel, stern line first.
- "Pass a loop of line to the lock attendant if you are along the lockwall. If the distance is too great, the attendant will throw you the end of a line. Use a slip knot to secure your mooring line to the attendant's line and allow the attendant to pull your line up.
- "The lock attendant will secure it to the mooring button on the lock wall.
- "The boater's end of the line should be held by a half figure-8 so that you can pay out or take up line smoothly.
- "Handle your bow line the same as the stern line.
- "As the chamber is filling or emptying, pay attention to the movement of your vessel and pay out or take up line smoothly and steadily, allowing no slack in the lines.
- "After the chamber has filled, keep your lines secured to the cleats while the gates are being opened. Do not secure your line with a half-hitch or under a knot. You may not be able to release it in the case of an emergency.
- "When the lockage is complete, wait for the lock attendant's instructions before releasing the lines. The lock attendant will release your lines from the lock wall.
- "Move ahead SLOWLY—at less than 2.5 knots—until clear of the locks. Please be cautious and leave no wake that will interfere with other vessels."

We add: After the chamber has been fully **raised or lowered**, keep your lines secured to the cleats while the gates are being opened.

A substantial current flows into the lock chamber as gates open at the lake level, or out of the lock chamber when gates are opened at the saltwater level. There is always some water passing through the gates from the freshwater to the saltwater. **Note:** There are some cavities in large lock walls which may require relocating fenders so they don't hang up.

Lock attendant heaving line to vessel

Hauling in vessel's lock line

We were aboard **Seattle Maritime Educator** *where lock lines are much larger than on* **Scheherazade**

Locks Tales: Conversation with Marvin Lund Retired Head Lockmaster

Over the years the locktenders, especially under the guidance of now retired Marvin Lund, have educated the boating public about the locks, and how to prepare for the locking process.

Be prepared and pay attention, he says emphatically. Have your lines ready.

"We get guys who have lines they bought some place, stowed them away in the chain locker and they get here and can't find them. They should be ready on deck.

"And fenders. I can't believe it. Some guy will come in the locks with a $100,000 boat and have only two small fenders. What a scramble. It's hard to understand. You've got to have enough fenders for both sides to protect your own boat and others, no matter what."

Lund cautions that it's best to have help on board when locking through. He also stresses the importance of knowing your own boat.

"Every boat responds differently. New boaters, or experienced boaters with new boats, should practice running the boat before getting into a tight situation like the locks. Some of these guys come in alone, which we try to discourage, unless they're really good and can leave the wheel to handle lines. It's not a requirement to have help, but it's sure nice if they do. If you're on the wheel and your boat's moving, you don't want to have go tend lines.

"Some people can do it easily like old **Rupert Broom**, in his *Africa, African Star* or *Wild Goose*. He was an exception, locking through for some 50 years. He knew what his boats could do and he could handle them by himself."

Lund said he's seen boaters who are in trouble because they just don't know what to do.

"So if you're in there, tied up, waiting to go through, it's sure nice if you can give the other guy a hand. Instead of getting a drink and watching this poor guy struggle while you're waiting, help him out. That's just a courtesy."

Lund has seen some stupid things in the locks.

"Some sailboaters don't think about the railroad bridge at the west end of the locks. There's 43 feet of clearance at about a 10 foot high tide. The bridge isn't always open. One guy went out in his sailboat with his girlfriend on the bow. His mast hit the bridge and she fell overboard. He had about two feet more mast than there was clearance. She was okay, but wet.

"Another time a guy coming in from the Sound went under the railroad bridge and parked at the small waiting pier on the south side because we were busy. He had a long wait. The tide was flooding and by the time he got ready to come in the locks the tide had come up so much his mast had gone in between the railroad tracks just enough so that he couldn't move. He had to sit there until the tide changed. Fortunately the mast didn't go up far enough that a train would hit it. I don't know how many hours he was there."

Marvin Lund, retired lockmaster

Lund said the current just outside the locks can be tricky.

"Somebody ran aground in a sailboat on the bar off the Magnolia side. The guy was a 'newby,' cut inside the buoy and he spent the day there. Didn't hurt his boat, but it was a little embarrassing.

"I've seen some grounds for divorce takes place in the locks. These guys get behind the wheel and they're the captain. They start giving their poor wife orders, and she's up in the bow trying to get a line over and pretty soon they're arguing."

Lund said usually several people a year fall overboard.

"It happens especially on small boats that don't have bow railings, and usually it's the woman who falls over-

board, sometimes because she doesn't have proper shoes, or perhaps she's new to the situation and the skipper hasn't adequately prepared her.

"You see a guy on a small powerboat come alongside, his wife up on the bow. He jerks the boat into reverse, stops, and she just falls overboard. It's always very embarrassing. The husband usually panics. We yell at him to shut off the engine so she doesn't get chopped up, then we get a heaving line to her. Usually she could climb out onto her own boat."

There is an emergency Jacob's ladder in the large lock, but Lund said it's pretty slimy with algae.

We asked him about the ***Coast Pilot*** referring to soaking fenders on barges when going through the locks so they don't catch fire as they drag against the lock walls.

"I've seen some fenders smoke, but I've never seen one catch on fire. That regulation was for petro barges. I don't know how many of them actually soak their fenders, but we don't have many anymore. Years ago they brought jet fuel in to Sand Point Naval Base. But since the base closed they don't bring in petro anymore."

Rupert Broom, a longtime sail-maker and legendary Puget Sound waterfront character and old friend of Carl's, died in April 1994. "We all miss you Rupe."

Years ago, *Carl saw a power boat wife in the locks bow line in one hand, beer bottle in the other, listened to her husband's impo-lite, loud hailer orders, heard in Bellingham. She finished her beer, took aim, fired the bottle into the pilothouse window, smirked, and went below.*

> **Note:** Vessels with more than an 80 foot beam cannot pass through the locks.

"The only thing wider than the locks was a floating drydock that was 81 feet wide from Marine Power and Equipment. In order to get it through they flooded one side and tipped it up and brought it through on one side. Took about four hours instead of the normal 20 minutes.

Once in a while there's an exception to the 80 ft. beam rule: the above floating drydock of Marine Power and Equipment in the locks is 81 feet wide. Yes, it does look like a ship. (Photo courtesy Army Corps of Engineers)

"The tug *Annie W.* sank in the locks in 1944. But she was raised and still running for quite a few years after I started working at the locks in '66."

Lund said he wished he'd kept a diary of what happened when he worked at the locks.

"There is always something going on. I'm not too sure if they even have the boat traffic now they had back in the early 70s. Seemed like things were really booming then. Boeing had their day and after the crunch things slowed down. For a while on any sunny weekend we'd have 2,000 boats. Now they're down to about 75,000 vessels a year, possibly because of more 'outside' moorages. A lot of people still prefer fresh water moorage. Although with saltwater moorage they don't have to hassle the locks."

Lund, whose grandfather, father and two uncles all worked for the Army Corps of Engineers, has had many unusual experiences over the years as chief of operations. (We visited with Lund in the spring of 1994.)

Conversation with Former Locks Park Manager, Dawn Wiedmeier

Dawn Wiedmeier, former park manager with the Department of Natural Resources, is a civilian with the Corps of Engineers. In 1994 she discussed some of the problems encountered over the years.

"People don't understand the possible dangers in locking, but considering the number that come through we're pretty lucky. Some problems arise when skippers can't control their vessels and they come in backwards and sideways. One boat, the *Aleutian Lady*, got jammed sideways in the large lock and needed a tug to free her. There is always a little current running and that can't be avoided."

She said there was a fatality in the locks in 1985.

"People were coming through in a boat that was quite deteriorated. The wife tied the line to the forward cleat rather than letting it slip. When the water level lowered in the large lock the pressure got so tight she couldn't release the rope. It pulled the cleat right out of the deck. The cleat hit her in the jaw and killed her.

"Around 1988 or '89 there was a barge going through. A worker on the barge put his foot through the eye of the rope. The rope went taut and his leg was severed. Lock attendants later retrieved the leg."

Dawn, and all lock employees, emphasize safety.

Heaviest floating structures to pass through the large lock were sections of the Lake Washington I-90 bridge which was built in 1940. The second span was built in 1990 and old I-90 sections were removed in 1992 and can be seen in moorages through the northwest.

A Touch of Locks History

The locks and canal were a gleam in the eye of Seattle's founders as far back as 1854 when pioneer Thomas Mercer suggested the canal be built when he named Lake Union. He said that one day Lake Washington and Lake Union would be linked with the Sound.

Between the lakes was a six foot wide log flume in what is now the Montlake Cut. In 1885, the Washington Improvement Company completed a canal 16 feet wide between Lake Washington and Lake Union. This "Portage Canal" was used mainly as a means of transporting logs to the sawmills on Lake Union.

It was 1911 before work actually started in earnest on the canal, although some preliminary digging had begun as early as 1901. During that period other routes were considered and rejected, including one from the south end of Lake Washington along the Black River to the Sound, and another across the Interbay area.

In July 1916, a dam was completed, the lock gates were closed and Salmon Bay, the present home of Seattle's large fishing fleet, was raised 21 feet above low water in Puget Sound.

In a history-making voyage on August 3, 1916, the Army Corps of Engineers vessel *Orcas* and the snag boat *Swinomish* were the first two boats to pass through the locks. Just three weeks later the cofferdam at the portage cut was removed and Lake Washington waters merged with Lake Union.

About 7,500 vessels carrying nearly 12,000 passengers used the locks during the rest of 1916. During 1917 the canal and locks saw 22,392 tugs, fishing boats and pleasure craft pass through.

Montlake Cut, circa 1889 (Photo courtesy of Army Corps of Engineers)

The Lake Washington Ship Canal and Hiram M. Chittenden Locks Project was officially dedicated on July 4, 1917, when it was about three-quarters complete. The cost by then was about $3.5 million.

Major Chittenden was responsible for the locks being built of concrete instead of wood; for constructing both a large and small lock instead of a single lock, and for eliminating a proposed lock at the eastern end of the canal. Elimination of that lock lowered the level of Lake Washington and reduced flooding.

Salmon Bay was raised 21 feet above Mean Lower Low Water of Puget Sound and Lake Washington was lowered by nearly nine feet from its original height to its present Mean Water Level when the Ship Canal and locks were completed in 1916.

Marine Fuel Docks in the Ship Canal

Salmon Bay:

Note—Ballard Oil and Covich Williams do service recreational vessels, however, boats need to be well-fendered for piling at these piers.

- **Ballard Oil Co.** (#12 on chart 18447) 5300 26th Ave. N.W., phone: 206-783-0241, on north shore east of large lock pier; diesel, gas, stove oil and marine petroleum products.
- **Covich & Williams** (#16 on chart 18447) 5219 Shilshole Ave. N.W., phone: 206-784-0171, is about 0.25 mile east of large lock pier; diesel, gas, stove oil and marine petroleum products.
- **Delta Western** fuel dock at north end of Pier 4 at Fishermen's Terminal, west of Ballard Bridge, phone: 206-282-1567; diesel only. Additional facilities at Fishermen's Terminal, public access float.

Lake Union:

- **Morrison's North Star Marine Fuel Dock**
  (#38 on chart 18447) 2732 Westlake Ave. N., is on the southwest shore as charted. Facilities include gas and diesel, oil changes, pumpout, restrooms, convenience store with groceries, ice, beer and wine. Phone: 206-284-6600. Summer hours 8 a.m. to 8 p.m. seven days a week; winter hours 9 a.m. to 5 p.m.

Moorages

Permanent moorages cover much of the Ship Canal shoreline, waiting lists are the norm.

Overnight Guest Moorage

Yacht Club reciprocal moorage may be available at Seattle or Queen City yacht clubs in Portage Bay, Bellevue Yacht Club (at Lake Union), Tyee and Puget Sound yacht clubs in Lake Union.

Lake Union:

- **Boat World,** phone: 206-284-3950, 2144 Westlake Ave. N., on west shore, has large rotating sign which can be seen from the water. Occasional moorage with electricity, water, showers, laundry, convenience store, charts, nautical supplies and clothes.
- **H.C. Henry Marine,** phone: 206-621-1142, 809 Fairview Pl. N., south shore, has occasional moorage. Contact Sam Roland for availability and facilities.
- **Chandler's Cove Marina,** phone: 206-628-0838, 901 Fairview Ave. N., south end of lake. Limited free moorage while dining at Duke's Chowder House, Cucina!Cucina! and Chandler's Cove Chowder House is on a first come, first served basis. Overnight moorage is by reservation only, fee is $1 per foot with 30-50 amp power, water, restrooms, dive shop, shopping, art gallery, hair salon.

Puget Sound Maritime Historical Society has a small display at Chandlers' Cove, but major collections and library are at the **Museum of History and Industry.** This collection may eventually be moved to a planned museum at the south end of Lake Union.

Public Access and Temporary Moorage

Public Access and temporary moorage, not overnight, are very limited for recreational mariners at this time. We understand the Seattle City Council will be rewriting regulations with an aim to open more public access areas.

Salmon Bay between Locks & Ballard Bridge:

- **Ballard Landing,** 24th Avenue, bearing about 40° true from the east end of large lock pier, is immediately west of Yankee Diner restaurant. The landing pier is about 250 feet long and 16 feet wide for vessels 40 feet or less, tied either side. No mooring from 2 a.m. to 5 a.m. Moorage fee payable to Rusty Pelican donation bird at head of pier. The landing is several blocks from two major supermarkets, laundromat, liquor store, marine supply stores and restaurants. We find this a handy last minute place to stop, shop or eat on our way in or out of the locks. Ballard Landing is maintained and was built by volunteer labor and contributions of Ballard citizens, businesses and visitors.
- **Fishermen's Terminal visitors' float** is on the south shore west of Ballard bridge between Docks 9 and 10 in front of "Chinooks At Salmon Bay" restaurant.

Float is between 100 and 140 feet long, depending on whether a vessel is in adjacent slip. For moorage confirmation call Port of Seattle VHF Ch. 19. Moorage limit is four hours for access to several restaurants, fish market, marine supplies, clothing, barber shop, bank, small grocery and restrooms. Showers and laundromats are for commercial fishing crews only.

Lake Union's Southeast and East Shore:

- **Chandlers Cove,** phone: 206-382-9963, 901 Fairview Ave. N. Dock on east side of Fairview Avenue street end at the lake's south end provides limited public moorage while dining or shopping.

Anchoring

City policy prohibits anchoring along virtually all city shoreline, including the Ship Canal. Where anchoring is allowed it requires a permit from Seattle Harbor Patrol. For information regarding anchoring call the patrol at 206-684-4071 or on VHF Channel 16.

Policy is being revised, substantially, we hope, and there may be changes in this ordinance in the future. In summer 1996, anchoring was allowed in Andrews Bay at Seward Park on Lake Washington on a trial basis.

As waterfront property owners we would enjoy having our friends visit by boat and anchor out in front.

- **In the small bay west of the BNRR Bridge,** we have anchored while waiting for traffic to clear when entering the Ship Canal.
- **Portage Bay event anchorage** for Opening Day of Yachting Season in May is limited to an area in Portage Bay south of the Montlake Cut between the Seattle and Queen City Yacht Clubs and is for participants only.
- **U. of W. event anchorage** in Union Bay is by arrangement with the U. W.
- **Emergency anchoring,** using common sense, must be out of the main channel to keep clear of large vessels and tugs with large tows frequently in the Ship Canal.

*Chandler's Cove, **Virginia V.** on right side, in back*

Public Launch Ramps

- **Salmon Bay,** north shore, foot of 14th Ave. W.
- **Lake Union,** north shore, 0.4 mile north and east of Gasworks Park on N. Northlake Way at Sunnyside Ave.

Launches for Non-Motorized Hand-Carried Boats
Lake Union:
- **Southeast shore,** Yale Street, city street end.
- **East shore,** float in front of old steam plant.
- **East shore,** four small street end parks where hand-carried boats can be launched with care:
  - **Terry Pettus Park,** just north of the NOAA ship piers at Fairview Ave. E. and E. Newton, has a tie-up float about 20' long, with about four to six feet of water. The park is landscaped, has benches and a drinking fountain.
  - **Foot of Lynn St. E.,** is a small pocket park with benches and a beach, near Pete's Market.
  - **Foot of Roanoke St.,** is a tiny park north of Azteca Restaurant with benches.
  - **Foot of Hamlin St.,** tiny park with benches, beach.
- **North end,** South Passage Park, under I-5 freeway bridge at Pocock rowing center, picnic tables, benches, beach.

Portage Bay:
- **North shore,** N.E. Boat St. at Brooklyn Ave. Ramp may be closed in the future.
- **West shore,** small park foot of Hamlin St., beach

Carl feeds Canada geese from Kamon restaurant dock, with historic steamplant in background

Restaurants with Moorage while Dining

Ballard — West of BNRR Bridge
- **Ballard Bait and Tackle**, phone: 206-784-3016, 5517 Seaview Ave. N.W. North side of ship canal. Moor at float in front.
- **Shilshole Bay Marina:** Moor four hours free at Central Pier while dining at marina restaurants.

Restaurants at Shilshole:
  - **Charlie's,** 206-783-8338
  - **Marechiaro,** 206-784-4070
  - **Little Coney Restaurant,** no phone listed

Salmon Bay — North Shore:
- **Yankee Diner,** phone: 206-783-1964, 5300 24th Ave. N.W., moor at Ballard Landing. Restaurants nearby.

Salmon Bay — South Shore:
- **Fishermen's Terminal**—Four-hour moorage at public access float between Docks 9 and 10 in front of Chinooks. For moorage confirmation call Port of Seattle VHF Ch. 17. Restaurants are:
- **Chinook's at Salmon Bay**, phone: 206-283-HOOK.
- **Bay Cafe**, phone: 206-282-3435.
- **Little Chinook's** (no phone listed)

Lake Union — Southwest Shore, North to South:
(We note that especially around Lake Union many restaurants signs are not easily visible from the water. Call first, or search them out.)
- **China Harbor Restaurant**, phone: 206-284-9539, 2040 Westlake Ave. N., no sign, large black building.
- **Franco's Hidden Harbor**, phone: 206-282-0501, 1500 Westlake Ave. N., at Marina Mart tower - straight in.
- **Latitude 47°,** phone: 206-284-1047, 1232 Westlake Ave. N., large sign in lake outside restaurant and moorage.
- **Harborside Restaurant**, formerly Kayak, phone: 206-270-8815 for reservations for guest moorage, 1200 Westlake Ave. N., in AGC building.

Lake Union — Southeast Shore:
Moor at Chandler's Cove, phone: 206-382-9963, 901 Fairview Ave. N., for the following restaurants:
  - **Duke's Chowder House**, phone: 206-382-9963
  - **Cucina! Cucina!** phone: 206-447-2782
  - **Chandler's Cove Crab House**, phone: 223-2722

Lake Union — East Shore, South to North:
- **Kamon's Restaurant** at Lake Union, phone: 206-622-4465, 1177 Fairview Ave. N., just south of old steam plant, moorage on north side of restaurant.
- **Azteca Restaurant**, phone: 206-324-4941, 2501 Fairview Ave. N., (at Roanoke) moorage along dock in front of the restaurant, inside a private moorage.

Lake Union — North Shore: .
- **Ivar's Salmon House**, phone: 206-632-0767, 501 N.E. Northlake Way, sign in front. Great fish and chips.

Activities & Special Events

Activities abound in the fresh water along the Ship Canal, and we touch on some of them here.

• **Center for Wooden Boats** Director Dick Wagner has done a great job of restoring and maintaining vintage wooden sail and rowing boats through inspiring volunteers who are regulars at the center. He's also has established a fine educational program for youngsters, and he loves what he's doing.

The Center rents boats, holds sailing classes and hosts seminars with speakers on various facets of wooden boat design and construction. They have a special festival over the Fourth of July. All in all it's a pretty terrific organization.

• **Opening Day of Yachting Season** is Seattle's splashy celebration the first Saturday each May. Decorated boats in the grand parade cruise from Portage Bay through the Montlake Cut, past the judges and hundreds of spectators in anchored boats along the way, and then out into Lake Washington in a colorful "sailpast."

Entrants in the parade rendezvous in Portage Bay between the Seattle and Queen City Yacht Clubs before the start of the parade. This is the only time anchoring is allowed in Portage Bay. During Opening Day festivities, boats moor cheek-by-jowl just east of the Montlake Cut along the north and south sides of Union Bay Reach to watch the yacht parade and crew races.

East of the cut and just north of the reach is the University of Washington football stadium. In football season hundreds of boats filled with sports fans moor just off the stadium so football devotees can troop in to watch the games.

• **Crew races** by University of Washington and other organizations are held in spring in the Montlake Cut.

• **Sailing classes** for kids and others are held from spring weekends through summer at the Seattle Yacht Club, and little boats skitter around Portage Bay and Union Bay as the youngsters learn to sail. Other sailing classes are held at some Seattle parks.

• **Weekly Duck Dodge** sail races are held on Lake Union each Tuesday during late spring and summer.

• **Fourth of July** activities in Lake Union include the festival at the Center for Wooden Boats in the south end of the lake, and a huge fireworks display from a barge. Thousands of boats, large and small, jam the lake for the annual pyrotechnics. It takes until past midnight for the boats to cruise back to their moorages in the lakes and along the canal, in a gigantic, amazing after dark "traffic jam." Red, green and white navigation lights glow like Christmas tree ornaments as the boats head for home.

• **University of Washington** fall football games attract a large number of sports fans to the stadium by both private boats and cruise ships.

• **Annual Christmas ship parades** cruise the Ship Canal and through the lakes every Yuletide season.

Emergency Assistance

• **VHF Channel 16**
• **Vessel Assist,** phone: 206-453-1176
• **Seattle Harbor Patrol,** phone: 206-684-4071
If unable to get underway or towed by another vessel, contact Vessel Assist or Seattle Harbor Patrol.

Marine Services on Ship Canal

The Ship Canal shoreline—particularly in Lake Union—its uplands and the rest of the city is filled with just about every marine service, facility and supplier imaginable. Seattle telephone yellow pages directory is probably one of the best sources of information about services since we cannot list all of them here.

Present city policy prohibits visiting mariners from anchoring and dinghying ashore at public street ends convenient to suppliers which have no waterfront access.

At this time Ballard Landing and Fishermen's Terminal are the only public accesses where boats can moor and visitors go ashore.

In Chapter 3 we completely circumnavigate beautiful Lake Washington and Mercer Island, finding moorages and unique places to visit.

Notes & Comments

Jo Testing Flotation Suit

The launching

it didn't work

oh ... it did work!

*We made it to Lake Washington! Heavy weather sailing in **Scheherazade** in Cozy Cove. Actually, it really **was** blowing, but not just then.........*
     See you in the next chapter!
*(Photo by Sally Cox Bryan from the deck of **Corsair II**)*

Headed home (patent applied)

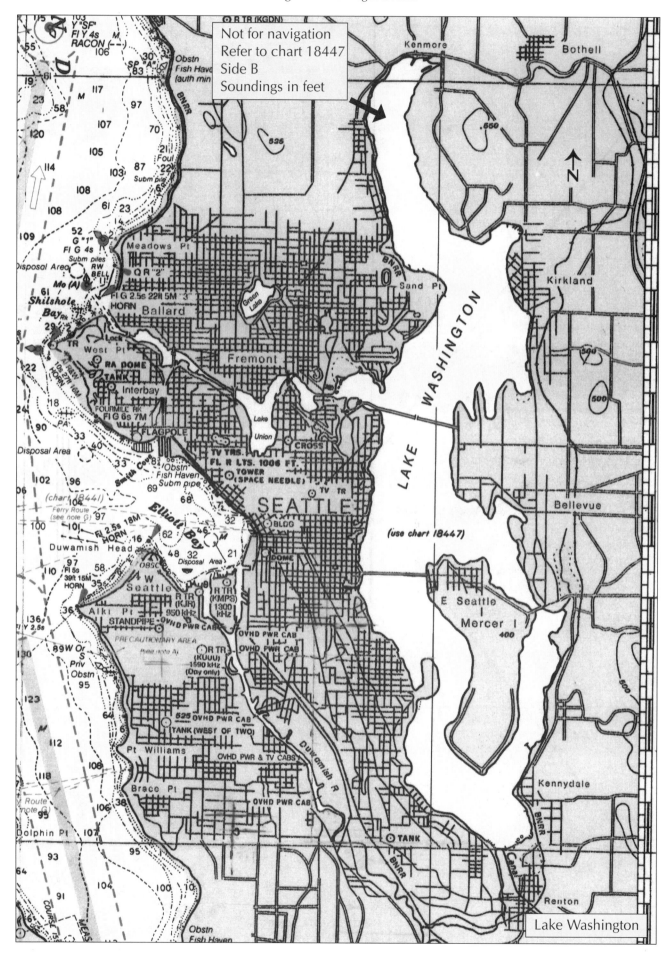

Not for navigation
Refer to chart 18447
Side B
Soundings in feet

Lake Washington

CHAPTER 3
Out and About Lake Washington

Chart	Date	Title	Scale	Soundings
Charts and publications for this chapter				
18447	08/15/92	Lake Washington, side B	1:25,000	.... Feet
		We suggest a good area road map for Seattle and		
		Lake Washington showing park locations.		

➡ *Compare chart used with the dates of the one noted above for changes and discrepancies. Review actual charts while reading book text.*

Overview of Lake Washington

The jewel of Seattle's eastern boundary is fabulous Lake Washington. Snow-capped Mount Rainier towers in mystic majesty above the southern shores of the deep, blue lake. Residents still find it an exhilarating view each time it rises out of a mist, no matter how often they see it.

Today, the beauty of the lake is unsurpassed, even though high rise buildings climb the shores on either side where once only sturdy evergreens stood. Two floating bridges, each over one mile long, and one fixed span bridge link Seattle to east side cities, communities and Mercer Island.

The lake is used year-round by boats of every size and shape: large sailboats, windsurfers, jet skis, tugboats with tows, canoes, kayaks, power boats, runabouts towing water skiers, kids paddling around in inner tubes, sightseeing boats and NOAA vessels. It can be noisy at times on the lake.

Lakeshore residents moor their boats and airplanes at private piers or floats in front of their manicured lawns. Marinas are filled with pleasure boats.

Public parks abound along much of the shoreline.

The lake is the bailiwick of the well-to-do, including Seattle's own Bill Gates, who in 1996 was the richest private businessman in the United States. His new home, which has been under construction for several years, is just south of the Evergreen Point Floating Bridge on the east side. It is huge by any standard.

Geologically, Lake Washington was apparently carved out by a glacier about 30,000 or 40,000 years ago. Evidently it was never part of the inland sea and has always been freshwater.

The lake is 17 miles long with an average width of about two and one-half miles. The widest spot is about three nautical miles from Leschi in Seattle to the east side.

The deepest spot is near Leschi Park at 214 feet, as charted on 18447.

Total shoreline of Lake Washington, excluding Union Bay and Mercer Island, is over 53 miles, with about 35 square miles of surface water area.

➡ **Note: There are five places** to buy marine fuel in the Lake Washington area. (See page 57)

Action on the lake

The Evergreen Point Bridge is really named the Albert D. Rosellini bridge, after the former governor. It was completed in 1963, and is also known as the 520 Bridge.

Commuters complain: On a summer afternoon in 1995, a tall sailboat gave notice it would need the 520 Bridge opened. The opening was granted.

However, motorists on the bridge were mighty upset when their drive across the bridge was interrupted for 20 minutes that day as the boat went through.

Traffic was stalled again several days later when it went back out. Impatient bridge commuters don't take such interruptions lightly.

Mercer Island (I-90) Floating Bridge was named for Lacey V. Murrow, a former state highway director. The original bridge was built in 1940; the second span paralleling it was built in 1990. That same year the original span flooded and sank while it was under repair. It was subsequently rebuilt.

The bridge, in theory, has a measured nautical mile painted on both its north and south sides, according to the **Coast Pilot.** *It is not charted and we don't recall seeing it.*

Submerged Forests

Three ancient submerged forests on the shores of Lake Washington are believed to be the result of landslides caused by earthquakes hundreds of years ago.

The lake level was thought to have been 10-20 feet lower than it is today. However, in time, the level apparently increased to about nine feet above its present level.

When the Hiram Chittenden Locks were completed and the ship canal opened in 1916, the lake level was lowered nine feet.

Trees which were a hazard to navigation were pulled or blasted out at that time.

Today there are still three whole groves of upright trees on submerged plateaus more than 100 feet below the lake's surface. They are identified on the chart by dotted lines.

Southeast Mercer Island submerged forest has bottom depths to 105 feet and noted clear of obstructions to navigation within 15 feet of the lake level.

West Mercer Island submerged forest bottom depths are about 130 feet, clear of obstructions to navigation within 20 feet of the lake level.

North end Manitou submerged forest bottom depths are about 139 feet and noted clear of obstructions to within about 30 feet of the lake level.

A King County harbor patrolman said a number of boaters lose their anchors when they attempt to anchor "in the forests."

His advice is to "stay clear of the sunken forests."

One fir tree that was sampled from the sunken stand was still sound on the inside after more than 1,100 years under water.

In 1995, a man was charged with "harvesting" some of the submerged trees. He scuba-dived into the forest, hooked up the logs and removed them. He was found guilty and sentenced, of what we don't know, but he was sentenced.

Lake Washington's Bridges

Two floating pontoon bridges cross Lake Washington, connecting Seattle with the east side.

Evergreen Point Floating Bridge, State Route 520, goes from the Montlake area in Seattle to Evergreen Point near Medina; **Mercer Island Floating Bridge, Interstate 90,** goes from south Seattle to Mercer Island, continues across the island and crosses East Channel to the east side.

Evergreen Point Bridge, over one mile long, has a charted vertical clearance of 44 feet at the west end in Seattle, and 57 feet at the east end at Evergreen Point.

A center drawspan opens 100 feet for large ships or sailing vessels which cannot pass under either fixed end. Two hours advance notice is required for openings between 9 p.m. and 5 a.m. Phone: 206-440-4490.

Measured courses for a nautical half-mile, a full nautical mile and 2,000 meters are marked on the north side of the bridge. The half-mile and mile courses are marked by 18 inch circles resembling an engineer's target; the half-mile markers have red and white quadrants. The 2,000 meter course is marked by one by three foot green markers with three inch white vertical stripes.

Mercer Island Floating Bridge, over one mile long with parallel pontoons, has vertical clearances of 35 feet at the Seattle end and 33 feet at the Mercer Island end.

The **East Channel Bridge** of I-90 has a vertical clearance of 71 feet.

Vessels requiring MORE than 71 feet vertical clearance no longer have access into Lake Washington south of the Mercer Island I-90 bridge because the bridge no longer has a center pontoon opening section.

Those vessels southbound in Lake Washington beyond the bridge, which need a vertical clearance between 35 and 71 feet, must use the East Channel.

Know Before You Go

➤ Speed regulations on Lake Washington: speed limit is 7 knots at bridges and within 100 yards of shore, except 5 mph. at north end of lake.

➤ It is unlawful to water-ski within 100 yards of shore.

➤ It is unlawful to swim more than 50 feet from shore or a pier, unless accompanied by a watercraft.

➤ Anchoring in Lake Washington off the City of Seattle is not allowed without a harbor patrol permit, at the present time, except for temporary anchorage in Andrews Bay.

➤ In the rest of Lake Washington outside of Seattle anchoring is permitted 100 yards offshore.

➤ Enforcement agencies on Lake Washington are Seattle Harbor Patrol, King County Harbor Patrol, Mercer Island Harbor Patrol and U.S. Coast Guard, when available.

➤ Lake cruising isn't like saltwater cruising: There's no rising tide twice a day to help get off the mud if a boat goes aground. When the wind picks up, the waves are closer together and a little steeper than on the Sound.

➤ The two best anchorages on Lake Washington are in Cozy Cove and Juanita Bay, according to the King County Harbor Patrol.

➤ The lake level is often two or more feet higher in late spring and early summer compared to late fall and early winter when lack of rain and heavy use of the government locks has drawn the lake level down.

➤ Boats and swimmers float lower in fresh water than saltwater because saltwater is heavier per cubic foot than fresh. It's a displacement thing.

Name change: Although Native Americans had used Lake Washington for hundreds and hundreds of years, the first non-Native person to view it was Col. Isaac N. Ebey in 1850.

He was so impressed with its beauty he named it "Geneva," a name that obviously didn't take hold.

Parks, Marinas, Moorages & Launch Ramps on Lake Washington

Parks abound around the lake. There is one state park, six King County parks, and large and small city parks in Seattle, Kirkland, Renton and Bellevue. We discuss the parks as we circumnavigate the lake.

There are at least eight marinas where guest moorage is available, five fuel docks and several private yacht clubs.

Marinas on Lake Washington, Guest Moorage and/or Fuel

➤ Harbour Village, Kenmore .... guest moorage
➤ Davidson's Marine, Kenmore .... gas
➤ Kirkland Marina Park .... guest moorage
➤ Carillon Point, Kirkland .... guest moorage
➤ Yarrow Bay, Kirkland .... guest moorage .... gas & diesel
➤ Mercer Marine, Bellevue .... gas
➤ Coulon Park, Renton .... guest moorage
➤ Rainier Beach, Seattle .... gas
➤ Parkshore Marina, Seattle .... guest moorage
➤ Lakewood Moorage, Seattle ...... guest moorage
➤ Leschi Yacht Basin, Seattle ...... guest moorage .... gas

On our Nakwakto, B.C., trip in 1993, we encountered a salvaged I-90 Bridge pontoon used in a marina facility in Echo Bay in British Columbia, far north of Desolation Sound. The store and other buildings were atop the large pontoon which the owners had towed to their cove.

Lake Washington
Northern Half

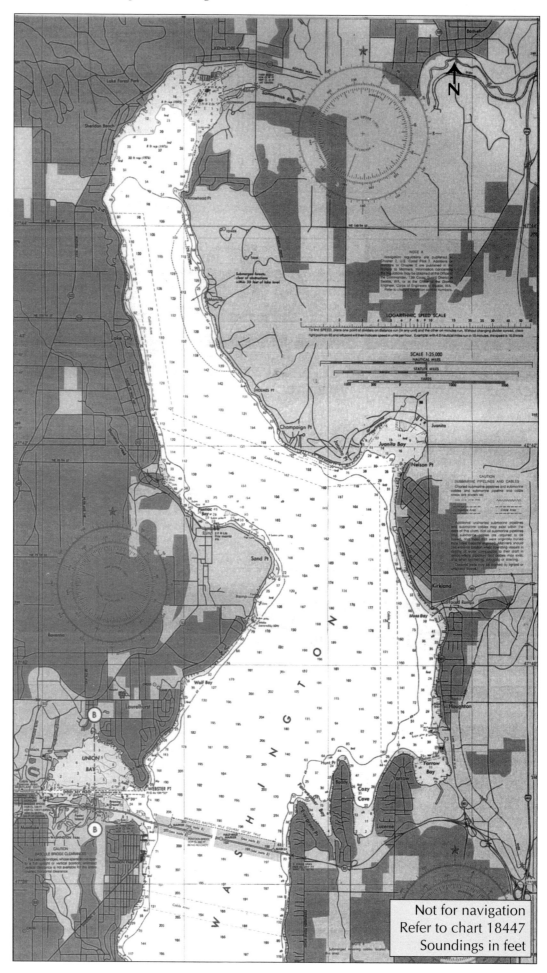

Not for navigation
Refer to chart 18447
Soundings in feet

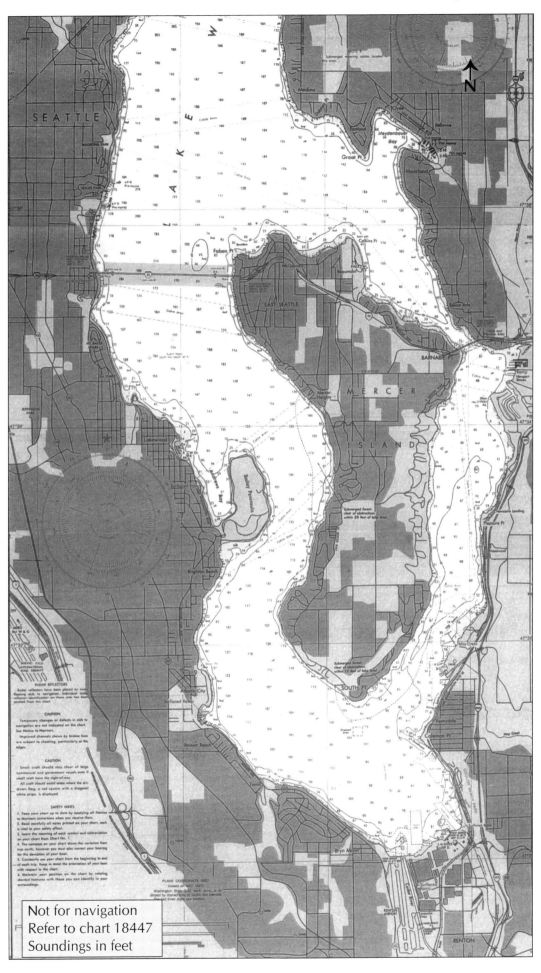

Lake Washington
Southern Half

Not for navigation
Refer to chart 18447
Soundings in feet

Public Launch Ramps

We found eight trailer launch ramps, and three car-top only ramps. There are also some street-ends designated as launch ramps around the lake, but with no parking nearby.

Public Launch Ramps on the East Side

➤ Kenmore on the Sammamish River
➤ Kirkland Marina Park
➤ S.E. 40th Street in Bellevue
➤ City Boat Launch ramp, Mercer Island, under the East Channel Bridge
➤ Gene Coulon Park in Renton

An annual pass card can be purchased at Kirkland Parks and Recreation. It is $25 for Kirkland residents and $50 for non-city residents, for boats 24 feet and less. Phone: 206-828-1217. Ramps are free from November to March 31. From April to November, a day pass is $10 plus a deposit.

Public Launch Ramps on the West Side in Seattle

➤ Atlantic City Park
➤ Stanley S. Sayres Park
➤ Warren G. Magnuson Park

The charge is $3 per day or $50 annually for frequent users at any city ramps. An option for an overnight permit is $5 per day or $75 per year, available through any rangers who might be at the ramps. Phone: 206-684-4075.

Magnuson Park at Sand Point was named for the late Warren G. Magnuson, longtime Washington State Democratic senator.

Circumnavigating Lake Washington

⚓ **Underway again,** we head north along the west shore, starting at Webster Point at the east end of the Lake Washington Ship Canal. This marks the end of the seven knot Ship Canal speed restriction.

Fl G 4s 19ft "33" Webster Point Light, flashing green 4 second light—obscured from 121° to 199°—on a square green dayboard on a pile structure, is off the point at Laurelhurst. The Evergreen Point Floating Bridge is south. We head north.

Laurelhurst is an older established community, packed with waterfront and view homes. Private piers rim the shoreline, which indents a bit at **Wolf Bay**.

Sand Point is charted as a large, rounded point along the west shore of the lake, with a small, sailboat racing watch tower and a wind chime sculpture.

Warren Magnuson Park at Sand Point is two miles north of Webster Point.
Park facilities include a mile of shoreline and 200 plus acres are dedicated to boat launching, windsurfing, swimming beaches (with lifeguards in summer), sports areas for baseball, soccer, football fields, tennis courts, picnic sites, places to relax, trails and pathways for walking, hiking and bicycling and restrooms.

Launch ramp area includes four ramps with three piers and plenty of nearby parking.

Anchoring: City park regulations do not allow anchoring off city parks at the present time.

NOAA buildings and docks, adjacent to the park, dominate Sand Point's north shore in **Pontiac Bay**. NOAA research vessels are berthed here. This is where the NOAA weather reports originate, and where we had discussions with NOAA personnel regarding charts, weather and other related matters included in this book.

Magnuson boat launch

Historic Sand Point

It's hard to believe now, but this wonderful park was once the site of Sand Point Naval Air Station. In 1926, the Navy purchased Sand Point's gently rolling forests and wetlands. It was cleared, leveled, filled and became a major naval air station and headquarters of the 13th Naval District.

The base was deactivated in 1970 following federal budget cuts, operations were transferred to Whidbey Island and Sand Point became a quiet Naval Support Center.

In 1974, Seattle voters rejected a combined airfield-park plan. In 1975 they agreed to a park as well as headquarters for NOAA (National Oceanic and Atmospheric Administration), whose buildings and property are the northern boundary of the park. Seattle will own the property eventually.

Planned uses for the site include housing, arts and cultural centers, social service agency programs, adult day care center, athletic fields and open space.

John G. Matthews homesteaded in the 1880s on the property that became Matthews Beach. By 1894 there was a sawmill on the north shore.

Matthews Beach Park is about one mile north of Sand Point and is Seattle's largest freshwater swimming beach. Lifeguards are on duty in summer and you'll see and hear kids splashing about as you cruise past this nearly 21 acre park located along the walking-bicycling Burke-Gilman Trail.

Continuing north, we pass the communities of Lake City, Sheridan Beach and Lake Forest Park, with upland and waterfront homes and private piers.

Cable areas are along much of this western shore.

Pan American World Airways office, and the dock for Pan Am's "Clipper Ships," were just south of the main bathing beach at Matthews Park.

The planes carried 70 passengers and were the first amphibious commercial air transports over the ocean.

Kenmore

It's about four miles from Sand Point to Kenmore, and the closer we get to Kenmore the more seaplane activity we find. Those little planes buzz in and out of Kenmore all day long, but don't fly after dark.

The charted, dredged waterway is an area of taxiing seaplanes heading for the air harbor, recreational vessels going into the marinas and commercial tugs with tows of sand and gravel bound for the cement plant in Kenmore.

Speed limit is 5 mph for all the waters north of an imaginary line between Logboom Park and Arrowhead Point on the east shore.

➡ **Anchoring is not permitted within this area**.

Logboom (King) County Park at the western edge of Kenmore can be recognized by the long, concrete pier, most likely covered with mallards, geese and gulls, and maybe a few folks fishing—a stopping place.

Tracy Owen Station is immediately west of the dock. This former train stop is part of Logboom Park with a sandy swimming beach (not guarded), a play area, picnic sites with outdoor cooking facilities and restrooms. Mariners enjoy it, and it's also a welcome stop for walkers and cyclists along the Burke-Gilman Trail.

Logboom Park dock is about eight feet wide and well maintained. Water depth at the end is charted at six feet, but the lake level fluctuates about two feet annually. Several 20 foot finger piers off the dock's east side are for smaller boats.

The Burke-Gilman trail, built along an old railroad bed, runs from Ballard east along the Lake Washington Ship Canal to the north end of Lake Washington and then east to Sammamish River, where it is known as the Sammamish River Trail, and on to Marymoor Park in Redmond.

The generally level trail, a favorite with cyclists, runners and walkers, is about 24 miles from Ballard to Redmond.

The park has about 1,200 feet of beach west of the dock and nearly 16 acres of upland grounds. Restrooms are onshore.

Approach the dock area with caution as it's possible to go aground here. The method recommended by one knowledgeable skipper is to stay in the dredged channel until reaching the marina, and then turn 90° to port to avoid the shallows off the end of the dock.

⚓ **Anchoring** is okay south of the Logboom Park dock in slightly deeper water. Be aware of many stub pilings sticking up off the south and west side of the dock when anchoring. They're tough on boat bottoms. In the summer the lake is high and they may be hard to see.

Logboom Park Pier, looking east

Harbour Village Marina with Logboom Park dock in the background

Dinghy to Logboom Park dock or go ashore at the beach.

Harbour Village Marina is just east of Logboom Park. This is a private moorage for about 150 boats; a "docko-minium." The marina is exposed to south winds. Permission is needed to moor overnight.

Harbormaster Caroline Gray will do her best to find a private inside slip for a visiting boat if there are any vacancies.

Entering the marina, stay in the marked channel with a dredged depth of 13.5 feet as charted. Our advice: go slow and watch the depth sounder.

Harbour Village Marina Facilities

➤ Ten undesignated spaces to tie on the outside of the fishing pier/breakwall
➤ Moor free for three hours in the daytime, which is enough time to visit the Grill House and Tap Room Pub in the marina
➤ Breakwall mooring over three hours fee $9 for boats under 30', $18 over 30'
➤ Inside guest moorage fee $10, including power, regardless of boat size
➤ Restrooms, showers and laundry for a $25 key deposit
➤ Marina monitors VHF Channel 16
➤ Phone: 206-485-7557
➤ All pier gates are locked coming and going, although the main entrance gates to the marina are open during daylight hours. There is always some one spending the night aboard to help with security.

⎈ **Boats do go aground** at this east end of the lake. Several friends have been very creative in getting off the mud in this vicinity.

Fl R 2.5 s "2" and Fl R 4s "4" Kenmore Channel Lighted red buoys 2 and 4 are to starboard entering the channel. Turn to port when past buoy "4," watching the fathometer, and then head into Harbour Village Marina breakwall for instructions.

Davidson's Marine charted as #71 is immediately east of Harbour Village. Facilities are as listed on the chart, but there is no diesel fuel. This is a marine service center with a fuel dock, no guest moorage, and has been run by the Davidson family since 1960.

Davidson's Marine

Back in the "olden days" this was a fishing resort in the wilderness of the northern end of Lake Washington. Boatloads of fishermen would come out from Leschi in Seattle and stay in the six rustic cabins. The Davidsons came from Wyoming and bought the resort because "Dad wanted to pump gas and take life easy," said son Chip. He and his brother Ed have run the marina since dad died in 1965.

Davidson's Marine Facilities

➤ Fuel dock, gas only
➤ Pumpout
➤ Travel lift
➤ Marine supplies
➤ Boat sales
➤ Engine repair
➤ Permanent moorage
➤ Dry storage
➤ Phone: 206-486-7141

Entering Davidson's, go east of Harbour Village Marina. Gas dock sign is not visible from the water. The fuel dock is between the fourth and fifth rows of covered slips. About nine feet of water is charted off the end of the fuel dock.

Sammamish River

✦ Sometimes called the **Sammamish Slough,** the river forms a delta with a small, marshy island where it empties into Lake Washington.

The south branch of the delta has two foot bridges to the mainland shore which are almost obscured by dense marsh vegetation.

The north branch has small, uncharted red and green can buoys marking the channel to the more navigable river entrance.

River adventures are for shallow draft, slower boats.

F. Bruce Stout launch ramp is about 0.3 mile upriver from Lake Washington, managed by the State Department of Game. The single-lane launch ramp is made of concrete planks, with no float or pier. Large boulders are carefully arranged along the sandy shore so that trailered boats can be launched only at the ramp. Kayaks or canoes can be carried past these rocks. This is an extremely popular launch site, judging by the large numbers of parked trucks and trailers nearby.

The launch ramp is a handy pickup point for those in kayaks, canoes or other small craft, who have enjoyed a quiet trip down the lazy river.

The slough is bordered by the Sammamish River Trail, an extension of the Burke-Gilman Trail. A highway bridge with 12 foot vertical clearance crosses the Sammamish River at the launch site.

Bothell Landing is approximately two miles upriver from the launch ramp. This city park has a float for small boat tie-up. A nice break in a trip is a visit to the nearby museum or a snack at a deli.

First settler in Bothell, Columbus Greenleaf, built his cabin on the river here in 1870. Bothell was a steamboat landing back in the days when the river was a more navigable waterway as the lake level was about nine feet higher than it is today.

➡ **Speed Limit** for the entire length of the river is 5 mph.

F. Bruce Stout launch ramp on the Sammamish River

Running the River

Marymoor Park in Redmond is at the north end of Lake Sammamish—the source of the Sammamish River.

Running downstream is a lovely, gentle ten mile trip between the fairly high banks along the river. The river passes between meadows and pastures, under freeway bridges, past lovely homes and cabins. Walkers and bikers on the Sammamish River Trail wave to paddlers as they pass.

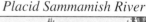

Jo kayaked down the river a few years back and thoroughly enjoyed the quiet, easy trip downstream.

When it got too warm, she just pulled into one of many small strips of sandy beach along the river, splashed in for a cooling dip, then continued on her way.

She suggests taking sandwiches and cool drinks, and to plan on a long, carefree day.

Carl recalls when he and a friend also ran the river — both ways in a flat bottomed boat in the 1930s when they were in grade school.

The water was so shallow the propeller on the outboard motor kept grinding on the river bottom, breaking off shear pins. They ran out of shear pins and had to start pulling nails out of the boat's floorboard for substitutes in order to get back home to Portage Bay.

Placid Sammamish River

Saint Edward State Park land was purchased from the Roman Catholic Archdiocese of Seattle in 1977 when seminary enrollment declined. It became part of the State Park system in 1978. The Saint Thomas Conference Center atop the hill is still owned by the Diocese and is used for retreats and other activities.

Saint Edward's shore

In 1932, Juanita Bay Park was the Juanita Golf Club nine hole course, where a round of golf cost 25 cents. On Mondays instruction and one round of golf was free for "ladies."

Before it was a golf course it was used to farm French frogs which were sold to Seattle restaurants. Then it became a truck garden. A rabbit hutch was eventually converted into a clubhouse.

Beware of Submerged Pilings

We anchored one summer evening on the lake's northeast shore near Arrowhead Point in about 15 feet of water, before we knew about the anchoring restriction.

Our friends anchored their sailboat in much less water a short distance away. We were in the shallow area near some charted submerged pilings. Although neither sailboat had any problems, we spent an eerie night.

We were relieved to leave the next morning without having been impaled atop a piling. A lesson in why there is an anchoring restriction here.

South on the East Shore

⚓ **Underway again,** we go less than one mile from the Sammamish River mouth to **Arrowhead Point**. **Saint Edward State Park** is about 1.2 miles south of the mouth of the Sammamish, between Arrowhead Point and Manitou.

It's easy to recognize the park from the north—or south—because waterfront homes suddenly cease and hiking trails are almost at the water's edge. This forested shore is at the base of a fairly high hill. There is a small state park sign along the shore. An elevated water tower and tank inland are within the park boundary and are visible from out on the lake.

There are 3,000 feet of shoreline and 316 acres of uplands with eight miles of often steep trails, some leading to the former seminary. There are soccer, tennis, handball, racquetball and softball courts, as well as birdwatching, picnicking, fishing and swimming. An indoor 25 yard swimming pool near the inland parking lot is operated by King County Parks. Grounds are open to the public for day-use only.

⚓ **Anchor** off Saint Edward Park with caution as the park is in the **Manitou submerged forest** area. It is presumably clear of obstructions within 30 feet of the lake level as noted on the chart. Just off the park is a narrow shelf about 30 to 38 feet deep with a hard bottom which drops off abruptly to about 100 feet.

Charted log storage area has not been used for some time to our knowledge.

We visited the park by land and Carl anchored here some years ago without incident, but we've not done so lately.

There is no good place to land a skiff. You can dinghy to shore, tie the boat to a bush or put out the dinghy anchor, and scramble up the low bank.

⚓ **Denny Park** at **Holmes Point** is next, about one mile south of St. Edward, it's northern boundary marked by a flagpole. It is a King County Park on a Seattle-owned site.

This again is a well used park, especially by those arriving by car. The lawns are well maintained and there are trails through 37.5 acres of uplands, picnic shelters, restrooms and a low-bank, 800 foot long beach.

There are no floats, docks or launch ramps for boaters. In fact, it would be difficult to land anything other than a small boat here as the beach is so narrow.

⚓ **Anchor** offshore, although there's a shelf which drops into deep water, similar to the one at Saint Edward Park. The chart shows this area south of the submerged forest. We have not anchored at Denny Park—but as kids we swam here.

⚓ **Underway again,** we continue on south around Champaign Point and then southeast around Juanita Point. There are many large waterfront homes here.

Juanita Bay is less than a mile from Denny Park with Juanita Beach (King) County Park along the north shore, and Juanita Bay Park (Kirkland) along the east and south shores.

Juanita Beach Park is your basic ol' swimmin' hole, updated, with 1,000 feet of shoreline. A concrete breakwater with a walkway encloses a swimming area with lifeguards during the summer. It's shallow inshore for neophyte swimmers and deeper in the outer part for the more advanced.

The 29 acres of park land include a fishing pier, tennis courts, athletic fields, concessions, picnic and outdoor cooking facilities, playground equipment and restrooms. Phone: 206-296-2964.

⚓ **Anchor** 100 yards or more away from the pier and beach a skiff west of the swimming area.

Cable areas cross from Juanita Point to Nelson Point.

☸ **Juanita Bay Park** is a passive wildlife-wetlands area, in the south end of the bay. The park has 110 acres with 3,450 feet of shoreline. There are picnic sites, restrooms and a community center. Interpretive walks along paths lead to the wetlands, where bridges extend out over the shores. A sign on the end of one walkway-dock describes 46 species of fish in Lake Washington, including four rare and 14 introduced. It advises looking for crappie, sculpins and stickleback, long-fin smelt and Kokanee salmon.

Juanita Beach ol' swimmin' hole

Cruising past this wildlife habitat, shorebirds and waterfowl are seen year round: geese, herons, ducks and loons. There's great birdwatching. You may even catch sight of a deer, beaver, eagle or hawk. This is not a place to anchor off or dinghy ashore, but is nonetheless enjoyable from the water.

Nelson Point, unnamed on the chart, is at the SW corner of the bay.

Kiwanis Park is about 0.5 mile south of the point, with 450 feet of shoreline and picnicking.

Waverly Beach Park is about 0.25 miles south of Kiwanis Park, with 490 feet of shoreline, lifeguarded swimming in the summer, fishing, picnicking, public dock (not for moorage), playground and restrooms.

⚓ **Anchor** near either park, keeping at least 100 yards offshore.

Cable areas run almost straight from Nelson Point south to Yarrow Point, both along shore and offshore. Check the chart before anchoring.

> ⚓ **Anchor** off Kirkland parks 100 yards or more.

Kirkland Area

☸ **Marina Park in Moss Bay** in downtown Kirkland is a major stop and has the only public moorage in the city.

Launch ramp is charted at the park's north end, and a long pier is at the south end. In between are gazebo-type buildings on shoreside lawns, above low stairs to the curved sandy beach. There is 695 feet of waterfront and 2.5 acres of park land.

Marina Park dock extends about 250 feet out

Kirkland Marina Park Dock

from shore, with the outer end reserved for tour boats. Space for them is clearly painted in red. Three piers extend northwesterly for guest moorages. Moss Bay is exposed to almost all winds and can be very lumpy at times.

"Puddle Jumpers"

Strolling through Marina Park we discover "Puddle Jumpers," a bronze sculpture by Glenna Goodacre, on loan from the collection of William G. Ballantine.

The expressions on the faces of these six children leaping into the air over a puddle are of sheer exhilaration. Only three of their feet barely touch the ground, the rest are in the air. No matter what angle it's viewed from it is exciting and not to be missed. We find it's worth going into Marina Park just for the joy of it.

While walking through Kirkland, you'll find more than 40 restaurants, cafes and taverns, to tempt the palate. Also find 16 art galleries, a movie theater complex, and many gift shops and boutiques to tempt the shopper.

During the summer, concerts are held in Marina Park on warm evenings. Many restaurants take part in Jazz Night on the first Wednesday of each month. The second Thursday of each month is Artwalk, and the galleries stay open for visitors.

For 50 years Kirkland was the ferry terminal for crossings from Seattle to Lake Washington's east side. Ferry service came to an end when the first floating bridge was built in 1940.

Kirkland Marina Park Facilities
➤ Guest moorage for about 65 boats, no rafting, open year round
➤ Stay up to 72 hours, no charge for brief visits
➤ Moorage fees, per day: $4 boats up to 20'/$5, 21-30'/$6, 31-34'/$8, 35-40'/$10, 41-50'/$15 over 51'
➤ Restrooms, picnic areas, playground, fishing pier
➤ Phone: 206-828-1213

Continuing south along the Kirkland waterfront, there are several city parks and marinas before reaching Yarrow Bay.

Foghorn Restaurant has a dock where boaters can moor during meals. This is the only restaurant with a dock along the shoreline between Marina Park and Carillon Point that we found. Phone: 206-827-0654

Houghton Beach Park, less than one mile south of Marina Park, has 900 feet of beach, with lifeguards in summer, picnicking, boat launch, dock, playground and restrooms.

Carillon Point Marina, a large, ultramodern waterfront development south of downtown Kirkland, was designed for luxury. **Enter** at south end of breakwater. Free moorage for 2 1/2 hours for patrons of any of several restaurants at the point. To stay longer, contact Carillon Point Marina. Moorage is approximately $1 per foot. Pumpout facility. Phone: 206-822-1110

Carillon Point Marina, looking west, entrance at south end of breakwater

Yarrow Bay Yacht Club has reciprocal moorage at Carillon Point.

Yarrow Bay is the most easterly of three bays south of downtown Kirkland. The southern shore is a large wetlands area.

Pipeline marked by several buoys crosses the bay.

Yarrow Bay Marina, charted as #73, is on the east shore of the bay, north of charted pipeline area—facilities are as listed.

Kirkland, a once bucolic east-side village, was originally home to Peter Kirk's steel mill, founded in 1890. But something wasn't quite right about ore he got from the Cascades and his plant didn't function. In spite of his dashed entrepreneurial efforts, Kirk had a city named for him.

During World War II, a large shipyard at Houghton—at the present site of Carillon Point—impacted Kirkland with the influx of shipyard workers.

Kirkland is now an upscale modern city with four miles of waterfront, many parks, light industry and much more. Each summer it hosts the Antique and Classic Society Boat Show, and a Festival of the Arts.

Yarrow Bay Marina Facilities
➤ Guest moorage is undesignated, but occasional slips are available for temporary use
➤ Moorage fee approximately $1 per foot
➤ Electricity and water included
➤ Fuel: gasoline and diesel; sign is visible beyond the covered moorage to port
➤ Marine repairs on premises
➤ Water and ice available
➤ Monitors VHF Channel 68
➤ Phone: 206-822-6066. Call ahead for available moorage

⚓ **Anchoring in Yarrow Bay** is okay in 10 to 20 feet, avoiding the charted pipeline area, offering good protection in a southerly.

☸ **Underway again**, we now head west and check out the next two bays, Cozy Cove and Fairweather Bay.

Cozy Cove, west of Yarrow Bay, is about 0.6 mile long and about 0.3 mile wide, ringed with elegant, expensive waterfront homes, many with floats and piers with yachts or seaplanes moored alongside. Manicured, emerald green lawns sweep down gentle slopes to the beach. There is no public shore access.

This is a favorite anchorage with many Seattle mariners who just want to get away for a quick overnight outing, without having to go through the locks.

Sitting in the cockpit on warm summer evenings you can watch water skiers, jet skiers, cruisers and sailboats scurrying around. Hot air balloons soar above Kirkland and the eastern coastline, carrying happy tourists on sightseeing trips. Para-sailing chutes are towed high in the air behind runabouts so daredevil passengers have a bird's eye view of Lake Washington.

By dusk all this activity quiets down.

⚓ **Anchor** in the south portion of the cove in 10 to 20 feet, soft bottom. Hard bottom is charted depths greater than 22 feet.

Ⓖ Cozy Cove is a **gunkhole,** with reservations . . . .

Para-sailing Lake Washington

Dragging in Cozy Cove

As pleasant and secure a holding ground as this seems to be, we have dragged anchor here several times. The Danforth hooks in, but then later decides it no longer likes the bottom.

This has happened twice during a rising southerly in the middle of the night. *Scheherazade's* motion changed and we awoke each time about 4 a.m. to find we had dragged nearly to the mouth of the cove, but the anchor rehooked itself securely. Both times we were rafted with one or more boats.

Another time, another southerly, we dragged and never could get the anchor to set again, try as we might in several different places in deeper parts of the cove.

We had anchored in the deeper water in Cozy Cove where the hard bottom may be covered by a thin layer of mud, and the anchor just slid across it. Or maybe we were foiled by the milfoil which was not evident when we pulled the anchor. We finally moved east to Yarrow Bay and anchored without problems, clear of the pipeline.

And yet a fourth time we slid back **into** the cove with a northerly and decided by then it was time to go back home.

On other occasions we've anchored and held in Cozy Cove just fine.

☸ **Hunt Point** is the peninsula between Cozy Cove and Fairweather Bay. Two feet of water is charted off the point, so we give it about 150 yards clearance.

Fairweather Bay is smaller and more exposed to the west than Cozy Cove.

⚓ **Anchor on the west side** of the bay because property lines for the eastern shore extend halfway out in the bay, according to a King County Harbor patrolman. Carl has anchored in Fairweather many times in the past. The head of the bay is quite protected from southerlies.

☸ **Underway again,** we continue south around **Evergreen Point** and then duck under the Evergreen Point floating bridge about 0.5 mile south of the point. Vertical clearance here is roughly 57 feet, but clearance gauges on bridge columns show the actual clearance, which does change with lake level fluctuations.

South of the bridge on the east shore is the mammoth home being built by Bill Gates of Microsoft fame—a "favorite son" who made good. His is the largest construction site around, dominating the shoreline. You can't miss it—looks like it might be a shopping center—due for completion in 1997.

Bill Gates' residence, under construction, summer 1995

The American Pacific Whaling Company's seven vessels wintered in Meydenbauer Bay for a "Scotch drydock": the lake water killed off teredo worms and barnacles.

They were there each winter from September 1918, until World War II, when the Coast Guard commandeered the ships for use as patrol vessels.

City of Bellevue

Sophisticated Bellevue is the fourth largest incorporated city in Washington. Although there is no city marina, and no moorage at city park docks, it's okay to anchor off several Bellevue waterfront parks—keeping 100 yards from all docks and floats. All Bellevue parks with swimming beaches have lifeguards on duty from mid-June until Labor Day.

We cruise south past Medina, Dabney Point and **Groat Point.**

Meydenbauer Bay, a bit over two miles south of the bridge, is lined with waterfront homes, private docks and two city parks.

Clyde Beach Park is the most northerly park on the east shore in Meydenbauer Bay. This pocket park at a street-end has a swimming beach and restrooms.

Meydenbauer Beach Park is about six blocks south. It has a swimming beach, picnic and play areas and restrooms. There are green lawns and a viewing area atop stairs onshore. The park is within walking distance of Bellevue.

Meydenbauer Bay Yacht Club is in the southeast end of the bay in Whalers Cove with guest moorage for reciprocal club members.

⚓ **Anchoring** in Meydenbauer Bay is feasible in depths of about 40 feet or so.

☸ **Underway again**, leaving Meydenbauer Bay heading south, we soon enter East Channel between the mainland shore and Mercer Island.

Cable and pipeline areas run the entire length of East Channel. Cable areas from Seattle and Bellevue enter the channel at the north end and run south to Renton, going ashore at numerous locations on Mercer Island and the eastern mainland.

Great care and attention to charted locations of cables and pipelines is needed to anchor along either shore.

Chism Beach Park is in the first little bight south of Meydenbauer Bay, about 0.6 mile from the uncharted point at Moorland, and offers a swimming beach, picnic and play areas and restrooms.

Looking SE in Meydenbauer Bay to Whaler Cove

Historic Bellevue

In 1869, **William Meydenbauer**, a prosperous Seattle baker, established the first claim here. On weekends he rowed the two miles across the lake to enjoy the natural beauty and quiet setting.

The town of Bellevue began as land was cleared and homes built. In the 1930s it was a community with truck farms, berry patches and two blocks of shops on Main Street.

Wealthy Seattle families "discovered" the east side of the lake and built elegant homes with spacious gardens. They believed the hour long commute between Seattle and Bellevue by ferries or small passenger launches, plus the trolley ride on the Seattle side, was well worth the peaceful life they could lead—much like island living in other areas.

The floating bridge changed their lives forever, although the east-side boom didn't begin in full force until after the end of World War II in 1945.

The "new" Bellevue has social and service clubs, golf courses, community theater, upscale living; including large and sophisticated shopping malls, although it still retains a strong sense of community.

Mercer Island—East Channel

The City of Mercer Island is an entity all its own.

Public access sites on the east side of the island are Luther Burbank Park, City Boat Launch Ramp at Barnabie Point, and Clark Beach. There are several small parks on the west shore including Groveland Beach and Proctor Landing.

We discuss the island now, and then go south along the mainland shore from Chism Park to Renton.

Luther Burbank (King County) Park runs from Calkins Point at the north end of Mercer Island to 0.5 mile south along the northeast shore. The park is obvious as waterfront homes stop and forested shores begin. This lovely park of 72 acres has more than 0.5 mile of shoreline.

Daytime moorage docks at Luther Burbank Park

Moorage for day-use only is at a large three-fingered pier in front of the charted "stack" at Beaumont. Short finger piers are for boats under 20 feet, while the north pier can accommodate larger boats. Overnight moorage is prohibited.

⚓ **Anchoring** is allowed. The soft bottom extends out 100 yards to the 60 foot depth curve. It becomes hard bottom farther offshore and holding ground may be questionable, so come evening it might be prudent to find another anchorage. At the park's south end is a swimming beach encircled with white floats; beyond that are fragile wetlands. A fishing pier is between moorage floats and the swimming beach, which are strung together by a small shoreside trail.

Trails crossing through the park encourage walking, jogging and cycling, and lead north to a viewpoint at Calkins Point, past the foundation of an old dairy barn. Picnic tables are scattered throughout the park, which also has tennis courts, a large playground and restrooms. Game tables near the courts and playground have chess and checker boards embedded in their surfaces.

A variety of flowers, shrubs and trees at the park are described in a self-guided tour brochure. In summer, free Sunday concerts are held in a grassy amphitheater.

Brick stack on shore near dock at Luther Burbank Park

⛵ **City Boat Launch Ramp** is at **Barnabie Point**, almost under the East Channel I-90 Bridge. This wide ramp with a float along the north side is a favorite launch for trailerable boats, jet-skis and hand carried boats. A large parking area is under the bridge. **Mercer Island** harbor patrol boat is moored here.

Clark Beach is about 2.75 miles south of the I-90 Bridge or about 0.87 miles from South Point on the east shore of the island. This nine acre park has a swimming beach, picnic area with barbecues, play area, fishing pier, restrooms and open space.

⚓ **Anchoring** here is in the **southeast Mercer Island submerged forest area**. While the chart notation shows it is clear of obstructions within 15 feet of the lake level, be cautious. The 60 foot curve is only about 100 yards offshore, and there is danger of snagging a tree in depths greater than 15 feet.

⛵ **Underway again,** we proceed around the south end of Mercer Island following the shoreline and turning to head north.

Two cable areas come ashore on Mercer Island from Brighton Beach in Seattle. We enter the south end of the **west Mercer Island submerged forest**, noted to be clear of obstructions within 20 feet of lake level. The forest runs north past charted Mercer Heights and another **cable area.**

Groveland Beach is across from Seward Park's Bailey Peninsula. This three acre park has a swimming beach, fishing pier, restrooms, picnic area and play area.

⚓ **Anchor off** this park with caution. The 60 foot curve is about 200 yards offshore. We note the 18 foot depth curve is only about 50 yards offshore.

Several street-end parks are along the west shore of the island.

Car top launch ramp is at Proctor Landing, 0.5 mile south of the I-90 Bridge.

Luther Burbank Park was named for the American naturalist, Luther Burbank.

Originally a homestead, the place was turned into a school for boys with its own orchard and farmland.

The brick stack near the piers was a coal-fired power house. The school, located in the brick building on the hill, closed down in late 1960s and King County purchased the land, turning it into a waterfront park in 1984.

The old school building houses King County Parks regional headquarters.

Mercer Island was named after Thomas Mercer, an early judge in Seattle who arrived in 1852. He brought the town's first team of horses and became the first teamster in Seattle.

On July 4, 1854, Mercer named Lake Union and suggested that one day Lake Washington and Lake Union would be joined into a single body of water and connected to Puget Sound. Sixty-two years later his dream became a reality when the Ship Canal and locks opened in 1916.

Coal was discovered on the east side of the lake in Newcastle, Renton and the Cedar River Valley in the late 1800s. They didn't even have to carry coal to Newcastle as they did in the British Isles—it was already there.

Charted railroad tracks are part of a track built for coal trains coming out of east side mines early in this century, and are still used today for log trains and for special passenger trips.

We anchored in a little bight just south of May Creek, tucked in near the booms in about 30 feet of water and 200 feet offshore. We were exposed to the south, but no winds came up.

From here we could see jumbo jets climbing into the sky beyond a ridge after they took off from distant Sea-Tac Airport. Closer in, we could see the planes at the Renton Airport on the southwest shore of the lake. It was a pleasant anchorage and remarkably quiet.

⚓ Back to the East Side

There are several Bellevue street-end public parks visible between Chism Beach Park and the East Channel I-90 bridge. Beaches in the Beaux Arts area are private.

Enetai Beach Park is immediately south of the bridge. This is another small Bellevue park with a swimming beach, dock and canoe rentals.

Mercer Slough, nestled back in the bay east of the bridge, is a 300 acre wetland and open space with trails. It has hushed, wonderland channels for kayaking or canoeing, and is an extensive wildlife habitat with deer, muskrats, herons and all manner of waterfowl and shorebirds.

Launch ramp for non-motorized boats is in the uncharted slough area.

Mercer Marine, a large marine supply center, is just north of the S.E. 40th Street launch ramp. A log breakwater is moored to pilings in front. Nip around the breakwater to get alongside the gas dock on the outer end of the middle of three floats. There is a fuel sign.

> ### Mercer Marine Facilities
> ➤ Fuel dock: gasoline, open from 8 a.m. to 8 p.m. daily all summer
> ➤ Service and repair facilities
> ➤ Rigging
> ➤ Engine repairs
> ➤ Haulouts, salvage and more
> ➤ Phone: 206-641-2090

S.E. 40th Street launch ramp is charted "ramp" next to Mercer Marine. It is 0.4 mile southeast of the I-90 Bridge—the only launch ramp in Bellevue. It's a double lane ramp with a pier on either side, limited trailer parking, and a telephone.

Newport Shores Yacht Club and community are immediately south of the ramp.

"Obstruction," reported in 1956 with no depth is charted 100 yards south of the unnamed point on the east shore 0.5 mile south of the bridge.

Newcastle Beach Park is in the bight about 0.4 mile south of the unnamed point. There is a swimming beach, a 300 foot long dock, children's play areapicnicsites, trails and restrooms.

⚓ **Anchor** here in less than 18 feet. The 18 foot depth curve is about 0.1 mile offshore and shoals abruptly.

⚓ **Newcastle Landing** is a little more than 0.5 mile farther south of the park and then we pass charted Pleasure Point and Hazelwood.

May Creek is next as the shore swings to the southwest. There are piles, piers and large log storage and an industrial lumber operation in the area.

Kennydale is about 0.3 mile south of the May Creek.

Kennydale Park is a swimming beach west of the railroad tracks. It has boomsticks fastened to pilings staking out the swimming beach and a dock. There is a terrific view of Mount Rainier.

Renton Area

➡ **Caution at Coleman Point:** Be aware that four foot shallows extend about 0.12 miles off the point with charted deadheads.

Much of Renton's waterfront is industrial, primarily Boeing, with its large office buildings, and aircraft plant. The exception is a delightful park in the southeast corner of Lake Washington.

Gene Coulon Memorial Beach Park, a 57 acre waterfront park with 1.5 miles of shoreline, is a gem. Offshore, boomsticks mark its outer limits, with chained logs extending about a mile south, paralleling the shore.

At the north end of the park is a launch area for canoes and kayaks, a float for sailing classes, walking trails and restrooms.

Coulon Park harbor

Next is Inner Lagoon, inside a breakwater. A walkway extends from an onshore gazebo out to the breakwater.

The gazebo has a large central fireplace, sinks and picnic facilities. Great place for group picnics, clean and well-maintained. The shelter may be reserved for a fee. When not reserved it's available on a first come first served basis. It's sometimes used by visiting boating groups.

Moorage is southeast of the breakwater in a boat basin with finger piers for 12 boats under 25 feet, side-tie moorage for larger boats and a six lane launch ramp.

Enter the boat basin by turning to port at the south end of the breakwater. Small boats tie at guest slips at the north side while larger boats tie to bull rails along the breakwater in front of the "picnic gallery." Paralleling the guest dock is an elevated pier with rowing shells stacked beneath.

Jo took a kayak class at Coulon Park in the late 1980s. She was amazed at how warm the water was every time she had to flip the kayak over to prove she could crawl out, right it and climb back in, without tipping over again.

Coulon Park Facilities

➤ Guest moorage for 12 boats under 25'
➤ Larger boats side-tie along by the "picnic gallery"
➤ Moorage rate $10 per night
➤ Free tie-up for four hours
➤ Restrooms with showers
➤ Ivar's restaurant
➤ During summer shells, rowboats and pedal boats may be rented
➤ Six lane launch ramp, 125 trailer parking spaces
➤ $5 to launch, parking is $2.25 daily, one-night limit
➤ Tennis and volleyball courts, children's playground
➤ Concessions
➤ Phone: 206-235-2560

Coulon Park was named for Gene Coulon, Renton parks director from 1949 to 1979.

In the south end of the park wander through well maintained, lightly treed grounds where a little bridge crosses sparkling John's Creek. You'll come out onto a sandy swimming beach (lifeguards in summer) enclosed inside a pier. Keep walking and cross a footbridge out to tiny Nature Island Conservancy where waterfowl abound.

Renton River Days festivities are held each August at the park.

⚓ **Anchor** outside Coulon Park for up to three days. Notify Renton Parks Department if you plan to stay. Phone: 206-235-2560

☸ **Underway again,** heading west from Coulon Park the chart shows dotted areas with submerged piles, shoals and foul bottom north of the wetlands and the industrial buildings.

Cedar River is just west of the large Boeing buildings, which are charted as large gray-striped areas.

Fixed bridge with four foot clearance is charted at the river's mouth. A shoal area extends about 500 yards north of the river's mouth. The chart shows it was shoaling to four feet in 1975. An apparent small island is charted in the delta area.

Cedar River launch ramp is about 0.3 mile upstream. Intrigued by the river, we checked it out by car. We found a single lane launch ramp tucked in behind large buildings in a pleasant, long, narrow park fronting the river's east side, with walking trails, landscaped grounds and grassy areas.

Nature Island Conservancy paths and bridges

The Cedar River was rerouted to its present course to accommodate the industrial development in the area.

It originally joined the Black River about a mile south of Lake Washington and together they flowed into Puget Sound by way of the Duwamish River.

The Black River, at the south end of Lake Washington, was considered a route for moving vessels built in the lake to Puget Sound.

When the lake level was lowered about nine feet after the Lake Washington Ship Canal was completed in 1916, the Black River subsequently dried up.

The Cedar River didn't have much current running that day, but it might take a bit of know-how to launch a boat here when there is current, as there is no float or pier. From here, trailered boats can head down river and out into the lake. South of the ramp is a sandbar, exposed when the river is low. Picnic areas are along the shore. This river park is a delightful, green respite in the midst of an industrial area.

Renton Airport is west of the river with its array of planes noisily taking off. There's a launch ramp at the airfield for seaplanes. A lot of small, private planes take off from this airport with great frequency.

⚓ **Underway again,** we now head north along the west side of Lake Washington.

The shore is lined with houses which seem to be stacked on top of each other; porcupined docks reach out into the lake as we go north from Renton.

Rainier Beach and the cove at **Atlantic City** are about two miles north of Renton.

Rainier Beach Moorage at the south end of the cove, is in front of the Aquamarina Apartment building. It has fuel, but no guest moorage.

Fuel dock at the outer end of moorage floats has gas, and is open Wednesday through Sunday, 9 a.m. to 5 p.m., Curt Anderson manager. Phone: 206-725-2184

Parkshore Marina is a little farther north in the cove. Marina docks A, B, C, D and E extend east into the lake. This is a condo moorage, not generally open to the public, but occasionally may have some guest moorage.

Parkshore Marina Facilities
➤ Guest moorage for four to five visiting boats
➤ Moorage is $10 per night
➤ Electricity, water included, pump-out
➤ Restrooms, showers, and laundry
➤ Call ahead. Phone: 206-725-3330

Rainier Yacht Club is at Parkshore Marina at E dock, the most southerly dock, where there are two slips for reciprocal moorage.

Atlantic City Park is adjacent to Parkshore Marina. This is a favorite spot for feeding ducks and geese paddling around in large flocks expecting handouts. The park is popular with students at Rainier Beach High School just across the street.

Four double-wide launch ramps with three piers and good parking are at the park which has over 25 acres of land, some of which includes open fields and trees with picnic shelters, a swimming beach, restrooms and benches.

⚓ **As we continue north,** the lake shore is lined with homes and private piers.

Cable areas are laid roughly northeast/southwest between Seattle and Mercer Island. They go ashore at the north and south ends of Bailey Peninsula in Seattle, in the Brighton Beach area south of the peninsula, and in Andrews Bay just north of where a surfaced ramp is charted. The cables cross to Mercer Island where they go ashore at three sites in the west Mercer Island submerged forest area.

Now we reach a favorite Seattle park . . . . . .

Seward Park is about 1.5 miles north of Atlantic City. It's a 278 acre waterfront park, with more than 2.5 miles of beach, covering all of forested **Bailey Peninsula,** jutting like a huge thumb into Lake Washington. The peninsula's upland ridge is a magnificent forest preserve.

Seward Park facilities include a sandy swimming beach, with summertime lifeguards in Andrews Bay, children's playground, tennis courts, salmon hatchery, picnic shelters, and an outdoor grassy amphitheater for up to 3,000 people.

Hand carry launch ramp with parking is on the west shore of Andrews Bay at the foot of Ferdinand Street.

There's also a Japanese Garden and Torii Gate of Welcome, and an eight ton Japanese stone lantern, given to Seattle from the city of Yokohama as thanks for American aid after the 1923 earthquake.

We've been driving our cars to city parks for years, as well as walking and bicycling to them.

While the city provides roads and parking places within the parks for automobiles—whose presence may be more hazardous than boats—the rule is that boats can't anchor off city parks.

Ⓖ **Andrews Bay** is between the peninsula and the lakeshore, open to weather from the north side of the isthmus. For years cruising mariners have anchored in the bay, even though there is a city ordinance against anchoring—an **unofficial gunkhole.** ⚓ In Spring 1996, the City Council declared Andrews Bay off-limits to boaters–no anchoring, period. Boaters formed a committee and set up a hue and cry about the lack of anchorages in the city and unfairness to boaters by Seattle officials.

In June 1996, the council enacted a temporary ordinance to allow anchoring in Andrews Bay on a trial basis. The area, marked by two "A" buoys and two shore markers, is south and west of the fishing pier on Bailey Peninsula and 300 yards north of the swimming beach. It can nominally accommodate about 80 boats. After the trial period the council will re-evaluate anchoring and decide whether or not to allow it on a more permanent basis.

⚙ **Underway again,** leaving Seward Park, we note Lake Washington Park and parkway has paths for joggers, walkers and cyclists, following the shoreline between Seward Park and the Mercer Island I-90 bridge.

Lakewood Moorage, at Ohlers Island at the north end of Andrews Bay, is on the west shore. It is charted #81, facilities exceeding those listed. A white and orange daymark indicates a rocky shoal extending from the mainland shore. Pass between the marker and the floats to enter the moorage.

This delightful, quiet marina is parklike with lawns and a gazebo. It is city-owned property run by a private concessionaire. Guest dock is on east pier, and two piers and floats are permanent moorage.

The Citizen's Anchoring Committee, in a Code of Conduct, urges boaters to maintain high standards and be considerate, responsible, smart and safe so that the council will continue to allow anchoring in Andrews Bay, and hopefully in other city areas.

Example of boats "not anchored" in Andrews Bay

Lakewood Moorage Facilities
➤ Guest moorage for three to five boats
➤ Moorage rates are 50 cents per foot per night, $10 minimum
➤ Limited electricity, water, restrooms
➤ Convenience store which includes marine hardware
➤ Locked gate
➤ Bus service on Lake Washington Boulevard to downtown
➤ Phone: 206-722-3887

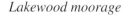
Lakewood moorage

Wildlife preserve immediately north of Ohlers Island is in a tiny lagoon. It's very shallow and filled with beaver, ducks, geese, turtles, raccoons and all kinds of waterbirds—a peaceful oasis in the city.

⚙ **Underway again,** we reach the former Wetmore Cove, now **Stanley S. Sayres Memorial Park.** It is on a small peninsula 0.7 mile northwest of Ohlers Island. Except for the Seafair hydroplane races each August, the park is open for public use. The park is charted as #81 A, services are as listed.

Turtles & water fowl in the wildlife preserve

Stan Sayres Park Facilities
➤ About eight piers, approximately 30′ long, on park's west side are used during Seafair as hydroplane pits
➤ Kayaks and canoes can be launched on west side at other times
➤ Double-wide launch ramps with piers on east side
➤ Small boats can tie to a finger pier for a short time
➤ Recreational boats cannot land here except for launching purposes
➤ Park department offers rowing and sailing programs
➤ Parking area and restrooms
➤ Swimming and diving not allowed off docks

Stan Sayres Park, canoes and kayaks

The wide Seward Park loop *trail, a 2.5-mile path around the perimeter of the peninsula, is well suited to joggers, walkers and cyclists viewing the panorama of the lake, Mount Rainier and the west shore of Mercer Island.*

It is perhaps best done with a couple of friends for safety's sake.

Our latest Lake Washington chart *is dated 10/92, 25th edition. The chart cover has a table listing some depths, services and supplies. Magenta numbers 82, 82A and 83 appear on the chart in the Leschi area. Numbers 82 and 82A are private moorages without guest slips or fuel services.*

Number 83 was formerly Lake Washington Yacht Basin and is currently Leschi Yacht Basin.

"Slo-Mo" & Gold Cup History

In 1950, Stan Sayres moved the Gold Cup hydroplane races to Seattle from Detroit. With the expertise of the well-known local boat builder Anchor Jensen, Sayres built super-fast hydros, the "Slo-Mo-Shuns." He won five consecutive Gold Cup events from his headquarters at Mount Baker Boathouse.

Gold Cup races went back to Detroit in 1955. Slo-Mo-Shun IV flipped and sank in the Detroit river in 1956. That fall, Sayres died of a heart attack. The following year the present site was dredged and converted into Sayres Memorial Park.

Seafair races with unlimited hydros still roar around the three mile course off the park each summer. During the races, spectators in boats tie to a special log boom to watch the races. They are mesmerized by the rooster tails of boats skimming over the lake's surface at nearly 200 miles per hour.

Three mysterious submerged floats—between 0.3 and 0.7 miles east of Mount Baker Park—are indicated by shaded dotted circles on charts at authorized minimum depths of 30 feet. There is no reference explaining their purpose or who owns or maintains these floats—the Loch Washington Monster perhaps?

Day Street Launch Ramp is charted as a surfaced ramp at the west end of the I-90 Bridge. This ramp was closed down during reconstruction of the bridge. Good news for kayakers and canoeists: in Spring 1996, Seattle Parks said a hand-carry launch ramp would be developed "soon" at the foot of Day Street near the bridge.

⚓ **Underway again,** we leave the southwest end of the I-90 Bridge where there is a 35 foot vertical clearance, with a 33 foot vertical clearance at the east end. Our mast is 47.5 feet off the water so we head back around Mercer Island and we'll go next to Leschi Park. Boats which don't need that much clearance will get to Leschi faster than we. En route, note charted wreck symbol at the bridge's southeast end.

Leschi Park is about 2.5 miles south of the Evergreen Point floating bridge and about 0.75 mile north of the I-90 floating bridge. It is the only marina and moorage on the Seattle side in the 3.1 miles between the two floating bridges.

Leschi Yacht Basin has no designated guest moorage, but the marina sometimes has slips available for visitors who call ahead. The yacht basin has permanent moorage slips on four floats.

A small, L-shaped floating breakwater and fuel float is located inside. Enter either end of the breakwater.

South and north Leschi moorages are charted as #82 and 82A. Facilities are more extensive than listed.

Leschi moorage with fuel float at left, floating breakwater at right, looking north

Leschi Moorage Facilities
➤ Guest moorage for one to four boats
➤ Moorage rate is $25 per night
➤ 30 amp shore power included
➤ Water
➤ Fuel: gas only
➤ Restrooms
➤ Secured moorage
➤ Restaurants, deli, video rental, supermarket, bike shop, bus to downtown Seattle
➤ Short-term moorage while dining at restaurants
➤ Phone: 206-328-6777, call ahead

Leschi Park History

Chief Leschi of the Nisqually tribe had a camp on this site in the early 1850s. He is famous for his part in the Battle of Seattle. Native Americans, upset by the 1854 Medicine Creek Treaty which gave their lands to the whites, attacked the tiny village of Seattle on January 26, 1856. Two white settlers and many Indians were killed.

Leschi was a leader who resisted sending fellow Native Americans to reservations. He and 38 men in six canoes went south to Fox Island to take John Swan, the agent in charge of the reservation, away with them.

Leschi was captured by Captain Maloney of the steamer *Beaver* from Fort Steilacoom, and sent to the reservation.

The following day Leschi left the reservation. It wasn't long before he was captured again and tried in a civilian court for a "murder" he committed during the Indian Wars.

He was hanged later, after he had been chained in public view for months until he became weak and emaciated. His executioner said he felt he was "hanging an innocent man."

Leschi's efforts to gain a more favorable treaty for his people bore fruit after his death when Governor Isaac Stevens signed a treaty giving the Native Americans better land than provided for in the Medicine Creek Treaty.

In 1889, the year Washington became a state, Leschi's campsite on the lake was turned into an amusement park at the end of the Lake Washington Cable Railway's trolley line from Pioneer Square in downtown Seattle. The park included a boathouse with canoe and rowboat rentals, a dock for sidewheel steamers, a casino, zoo animals and beautiful gardens.

The property was sold to the city in 1909, the year of the Alaska-Yukon-Pacific Exposition. Steamers quit their runs after the lake was lowered in 1916 on completion of the Lake Washington Ship Canal.

A plaque at Leschi Park cites a bit of maritime history. Steam ferries in the 1880s began carrying passengers from Leschi to Mercer Island and east side communities. The largest was the S.S. Issaquah which could carry 600 passengers. Ferry service ended when the floating bridge opened in 1940.

When the ship canal and locks lowered Lake Washington nine feet in 1916, all docks and piers became nine feet higher and the waterfront land areas increased as the shoreline shrank.

Maritime History Memorial plaque at Leschi Park

Madison Park is about 0.32 mile south of the Evergreen Point floating bridge, but boats can't land here or anchor offshore. The park has 12 acres of grassy slopes, a fishing pier and 400 feet of swimming beach.

This was the site of the most popular of all Seattle's parks in the early 1900s. Cable cars brought picnickers every two minutes from downtown so they could enjoy the boathouse, piers, promenade, floating bandstands, beer and gambling halls, athletic fields, even vaudeville acts.

⚓ **Underway again,** we return to the Ship Canal—the end of our trip around Lake Washington.

In Chapter 4 we cover downtown Seattle's urban waterfront and West Seattle.

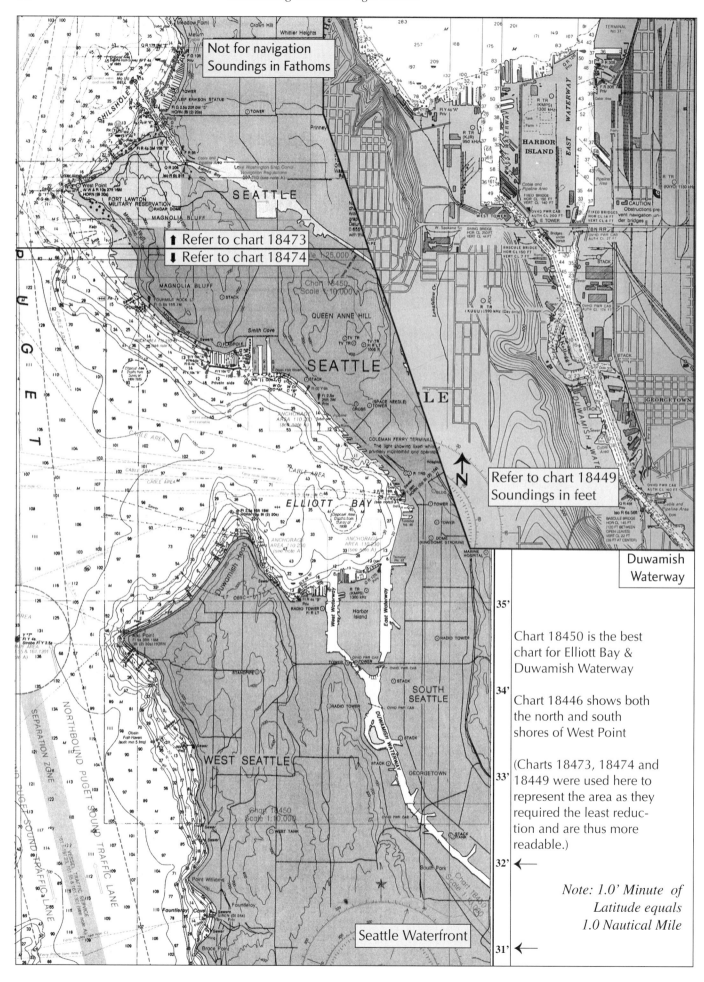

Not for navigation
Soundings in Fathoms

⬆ Refer to chart 18473
⬇ Refer to chart 18474

Refer to chart 18449
Soundings in feet

Duwamish
Waterway

35'

Chart 18450 is the best
chart for Elliott Bay &
Duwamish Waterway

34'

Chart 18446 shows both
the north and south
shores of West Point

33'

(Charts 18473, 18474 and
18449 were used here to
represent the area as they
required the least reduc-
tion and are thus more
readable.)

32' ←

*Note: 1.0' Minute of
Latitude equals
1.0 Nautical Mile*

31' ←

Seattle Waterfront

CHAPTER 4
Seattle Waterfront from Shilshole to Fauntleroy

Charts and publications for this chapter

	Chart	Date	Title	Scale	Soundings
***	**18450**	08/22/92	Seattle Harbor—Elliott Bay and Duwamish Waterway	1:10,000	Feet
**	**18449**	10/29/94	Seattle to Bremerton	1:25,000	Feet
*	**18446**	06/16/90	Apple Cove Point to Keyport	1:25,000	Feet
	18445	06/03/95	Puget Sound—Possession Sound to Olympia, Page B, Inset 4	1:40,000	Fathoms
	18474	03/25/95	Puget Sound: Shilshole Bay to Commencement Bay	1:40,000	Fathoms
	18473	08/14/93	Puget Sound—Oak Bay to Shilshole Bay	1:40,000	Fathoms
			Booklet: Puget Sound Shellfish Sites		
			Washington State Public Lands Quad Map, Seattle	1:100,000	

➡ *When using charts, compare your chart dates with ones referred to above. There may be discrepancies between different charts and different chart editions.*

Elliott Bay Overview

In this chapter we'll explore Elliott Bay, the urban Seattle waterfront and Duwamish Waterway, from Shilshole to Fauntleroy Cove in West Seattle.

Our voyage has taken us through the unique villages and fair cities of Kingston, Edmonds, Ballard, Fremont, Kenmore, Kirkland, Bothell, Bellevue, Renton and others, and circumnavigated the City of Mercer Island.

We dabbled in the Sammamish and Cedar rivers and shall return some day to explore them in more detail. Now we're off for a cruise around Elliott Bay.

✴ **Underway again,** we start outside Ballard cruising southwest, past Shilshole Marina and the entrance range leading into the locks, well offshore of the shoals along the northwest side of West Point.

Al W&R 10s 27ft 16M Horn (Bl30s) West Point Light, is an alternating white and red light 27 feet high in the octagonal tower of the lighthouse at the point.

West Point is a low sandspit for about 900 feet east of the lighthouse. It then rises to a small bump, rising again to heights over 300 feet, to become the forested areas of Discovery Park, including Fort Lawton, and residential Magnolia Bluff.

Discovery Park's more than 530 acres includes all of West Point, except for the sewage plant, and covers much of the west end of the bluffs.

Shoreline northeast of the point is dominated by the structures of the Metro Sewage Treatment Plant backed by a steep forested bluff, declining to low bank.

Depths around West Point change abruptly as charted.

North of the point the three fathom curve is surprisingly only about 100 yards offshore. Shoaling to this depth progresses to about 850 yards offshore about 1.2 miles north and east of West Point, near red nun buoy "2" at the Ship Canal entrance, the site of many groundings by careless navigators.

West Point Lighthouse looking to the north

West Point Lighthouse *is on the National Register of Historic Places. It has been here since 1881, eight years before Washington became a state in 1889.*

➡ **NOTE: Marine gas and diesel** are available at **Elliott Bay Marina** and **Harbor Island Marina.**

*Vancouver's **H.M.S. Discovery***

West and south of the point the three fathom curve extends 500 yards off-shore.

South and east of the point the three fathom shoal extends about 1,000 yards offshore for 0.85 mile, or about halfway to Four Mile Rock from West Point. This is also the site of many groundings.

G "1" Fl G 4s West Point Lighted Buoy 1, flashing green 4 second light, is about 0.3 mile southwest of the point, marking West Point Shoal.

Several charts show Magnolia Bluff as only the steep bluff along the southwest shore, but we regard the entire area from West Point to Smith Cove as Magnolia Bluff. East of Discovery Park is Magnolia Bluff residential community. Bluffs rise to about 300 feet and extend over one mile along this shoreline, then recede inland to steep contoured terrain with some residential development glued to the side of the hills. The bluffs continue southeast about 2.5 miles toward Smith Cove.

Discovery Park extends to the West Point Lighthouse from the forested area atop the bluffs. A small charted lagoon is near the point on the south shore.

Discovery Park History

Discovery Park is of one of Seattle's newest, largest and most delightful city parks. With 534 acres and 12,000 feet of shoreline, it's a wonderful spot, but we have no way of reaching the park from the water because we can't anchor off—Seattle Parks' policy.

Beaches, forests, meadows, self-guided nature trails, picnic sites, birds, raccoons, beach critters, plants and play areas, sea cliffs and sand dunes, are within this lovely spot. Creative nature programs, adventure courses, workshops and family programs are held at the park seasonally.

Shilshoh people originally inhabited the Salmon Bay beaches of West Point. Other tribes arrived during the annual lush salmon runs each fall. Daybreak Star Indian Cultural Center in the park houses a library, museum, a gallery of Indian art and an auditorium for native singers and dancers.

Discovery Park was dedicated in 1973, named after Captain Vancouver's ship the *H.M.S. Discovery*, a 96 foot long, three-masted sloop-of-war carrying 100 men. Vancouver, the first explorer to survey and chart Puget Sound in 1792, directed Peter Puget to explore South Sound.

The park was a military reservation after 1896, when it was known as Fort Lawton. Over one million troops were processed here during World War II, and it served as a prison camp for some German prisoners. Later, military and civil service employees were processed here before heading to the Far East, and lastly it was a training center for reserves.

When Seattle obtained the property, the park department declared that most of the land would continue to be nature-oriented and so it has remained. Views from the bluffs are breathtaking, and from south beach on a clear day there are fabulous views of Seattle and Mount Rainier.

Cable areas come ashore midway in the bight, roughly 0.6 mile south and east of West Point.

VTS buoy Y "SG" Fl Y 4s light flashing yellow light marks precautionary and turning area about one mile west of green buoy "1." Northbound VTS lane is about 0.3 mile west of buoy "1," which can be a bit of a squeeze if ships are leaving Elliott Bay or are in the northbound VTS traffic lane.

Fl G 6s 15 ft 7M Fourmile Rock Light, flashing green light on a square green dayboard on a tower, 60 yards offshore, is 1.65 miles south and east of West Point. Fourmile Rock is about four miles from the quick red light at the northwest corner of the East Waterway, which may be the reason for its name.

Depths of the three fathom curve at Fourmile Rock are about 300 yards off-shore and remain somewhat consistent all the way to Elliott Bay Marina.

Fouled at the Buoy

Carl recalls: "Much 'over-canvassed' aboard a friend's cutter, we were rail down in a freshening southerly and rising sea, heading toward the windward mark in the race, West Point green buoy " 1."

"We all knew we'd save some time otherwise lost to shortening sail. We'd keep the buoy to starboard, coming about just before grounding on the West Point shoal, and then flying around the buoy on our downwind leg.

"But we were knocked down immediately after coming about onto a port tack, with only a couple of feet of water under the keel. Our cleated main sheet washed over the side and trailed astern. The skipper's most able and competent wife tailed the genny sheet while struggling to keep the tiller hard to weather in order to give way to a competing boat still holding on a starboard tack. I was awash at the winch, cranking and securing the genny sheet.

"But we weren't able to give way. No one on board was able to get aft and slack our mainsheet soon enough. The competitor was forced to take evasive action and come about.

"Slacking their main sheet, their main boom swung out and the sheet looped over and instantly moored them to green buoy " 1 ."

"At the float after the race, we all remained below as skip went topside to discuss the happenings with the fouled skipper.

"My recollection is that the wind died and no one finished the race."

Elliott Bay indents the east shore of Puget Sound between West Point on the north and Alki Point five miles to the south. The bay lies east of a line between Magnolia Bluff and Duwamish Head. It is about two miles wide and extends nearly two miles southeast, as defined by the ***Coast Pilot.***

Marinas, piers, terminals, slips and berths in Elliott Bay and Duwamish Waterways are best shown on chart 18450, scale 1:10,000, soundings in feet.

Marinas are graphically shown but not otherwise identified on this chart. Four offer guest moorage and two have fuel and other services, detailed on pages 81-84.

"Terminals, piers, berths, slips," are terms used on charts, and generally apply to moorages used by large ships or commercial vessels, except as we note otherwise.

Piers are fairly consistently numbered and run along most of the downtown waterfront counterclockwise around the Elliott Bay shoreline, starting with Pier 2 west of the Duwamish West Waterway to Pier 91 in Smith Cove.

Many of the piers are remodeled warehouses from the old steamship days on the Seattle waterfront, and jut out into the bay about due west at a nearly 45 ° angle from the shore.

Elliott Bay History

The Wilkes Expedition in 1841 was the first major exploration after Vancouver in 1792, and the first by an American. We found that Lt. Charles Wilkes didn't think much of Elliott Bay. He wrote:

"The anchorage is of comparatively small extent, owing to the great depth of water as well as the extensive mud flats; these are exposed at low water. Three small streams enter the head of the bay, where good water may be obtained. I do not consider the bay a desirable anchorage: from the west it is exposed to the prevailing winds, and during their strength there is heavy sea."

*Although Wilkes named it Elliott Bay, it is not quite certain for whom it was named as there were three men in the expedition named Elliott. One was the chaplain, Jared Elliott, not a favorite; a second was the ship's boy, George Elliott, who received eight lashes for insubordination, and then there was Midshipman Samuel Elliott, a member of the **H.M.S. Porpoise** survey crew. Samuel may have been given the honor.*

About three miles of public tidelands are in this chapter.

Public tidelands unless otherwise noted are state owned. Some maybe leased for private use. We take the Washington State Public Lands Quadrangle Map when going ashore at these locations to avoid trespassing on adjacent private property.

➡ **Note: Time to change to chart** 18449 or 18450, the preferred charts for Elliott Bay.

Seattle Hills Topography

Sailing in Elliott Bay and looking up at Seattle's hills, we've found heights not what they appear. Most Seattleites might say that Queen Anne and First (Pill) Hill are highest.

Wrong. A Seattle Times article lists the high five:

Highest point *is 512 feet in West Seattle, at 35th Ave. S.W. and Myrtle St., 2 miles inland from Lowman Beach Park.*

Second *is 492 feet at N. 145th St., at Greenwood Ave., north end.*

Third *is 456 feet, Queen Anne Hill.*

Fourth *is 455 feet, at Maple Leaf north end.*

Fifth *is 443 feet, at Volunteer Park, Capitol Hill.*

The Pier 1 Imports *retail store is at Pier 70 and there is no longer a real "Pier 1."*

Terminals, berths and slips which are for large commercial vessels may or may not be numbered.

General anchorage areas in Elliott Bay for large ships and commercial vessels only, are indicated by solid magenta lines on the chart at four locations, and are referenced to section 110.230 of the ***Coast Pilot*** and Note A on the chart.

General anchorage area for large vessels west of Smith Cove starts at Fourmile Rock and continues east past Elliott Bay Marina.

Seattle skyline from Magnolia Bluff (1) to the Smith Tower (3). The tallest building in Seattle is the Columbia Center (2).

⚓ **Underway again, from West Point,** we are on our way along the north shore of Elliott Bay off Magnolia Bluff.

Elliott Bay Marina is about 0.9 mile east of Fourmile Rock. The 0.4 mile long, rock breakwater and forest of masts are impressive, with Magnolia Bluff as a backdrop. The modern new marina is second in size only to Shilshole in the greater Seattle area, with moorage for about 1,200 boats.

This is a unique location for a marina with panoramic views of the city skyline, the Cascades, Mount Rainier, the Olympics, and the ever-changing downtown waterfront with large commercial ships, tour boats and ferries.

Columbia Center *has been dubbed the "box the Space Needle came in." If the building were lying on its side it would be about the same length as the Hindenburg dirigible. It can be seen well above the horizon from many places in the Sound and from Lake Washington.*

Piers are lettered from A through N, starting with A at the west end. All 14 piers have slip sizes from 32 to 63 feet, plus pier ends which can accommodate much larger yachts. Elliott Bay Marina was built on former traditional Indian fishing grounds and each year a percentage of the income goes to the Suquamish and Muckleshoot tribes. It took 10 years for the marina to obtain all the necessary permits and three years to build it.

Enter the marina from either east or west end of the rock breakwater.

Fl Y 10s "B" and Fl Y 10s "C" mark the long straight section of the breakwater which then angles to the north at both ends.

<u>At the west entrance</u> the navigation lights are:

Fl R 2.5s "2" marks west end of rock breakwater, which angles abruptly north.

Fl Y 10s "A" is about mid-length of west vertical breakwater projecting south.

Fl G 4s "1" marks south end of west vertical breakwater.

Entering from the west we keep FL Y 10s "A" to port until Fl R 2.5s "2" is abeam, turn to starboard, keeping Fl G 4s "1" to port until it is abeam, then turn to port and proceed to the fuel dock to our assigned slip or to check in.

<u>At the east entrance</u> the navigation lights are:

Fl G 2.5s "1" marks east end of the rock breakwater which angles slightly north.

Fl Y "D" is about mid-length of east vertical breakwater projecting south.

Fl R 4s "2" marks south end of the east vertical breakwater.

Coast Pilot *states in part for general anchorage areas in Elliott Bay, "No vessel shall anchor in any general anchorage described in paragraph (a) of this section without prior permission from the captain of the port or his authorized representative."*

Entering from the east we keep FL G 2.5s "1" to port until it is abeam, adjusting our course to port until FL R 4s "2" comes into view, and we are able to enter the marina between the red and green aids and proceed to our assigned slip or check in at the fuel float.

Elliott Bay Marina, west entrance, looking SW

Elliott Bay Marina Facilities

➤ Moorage for 60 or more visiting boats *
➤ 30 amp shore power $3/day, 50 amp power $5/day
➤ Water, telephone jack, cable TV & trash facilities included
➤ Fuel: gas, diesel at end of G dock in center of marina, Phone: 206-282-8424
➤ Pump-out facilities at G dock
➤ Call ahead by radio or telephone for slip assignment
➤ Free showers and restrooms, laundry
➤ Dockhands assist with lines, gear or hazardous materials
➤ Senior and handicapped citizens can be driven to boats on electric carts
➤ Security card access system around-the-clock
➤ Marine repairs
➤ Diving services
➤ Convenience store with food, ice, bait, tackle at G dock
➤ Espresso cart in summer
➤ Palisade Restaurant, Maggie Bluff's Cafe and Sanmi Sushi
➤ Concierge assists with restaurants, rental cars, cruising plans, catered meals aboard
➤ Parklike grounds with the beginning of bike/hike path to downtown Seattle
➤ Monitors VHF Channel 78A
➤ Phone: 206-285-4817

*Moorage rates vary with season:
  Winter season (December-March) 50 cents/foot
  Buffer season (April-May, October-November) 75 cents/foot
  Summer season (June—September) $1/foot

Elliott Bay Marina person-nel say their goal is to provide unequaled customer satisfaction and state-of-the-art facilities. "We love to spoil people," said Marty Harder, marina manager.

Elliott Bay Marina, east entrance, looking NW

⚓ **Underway again, we cruise along the downtown Seattle waterfront.**

East of Elliott Bay Marina, we cruise past two of the Port of Seattle's commercial piers, 91 and 90, shown on chart 18450. The giant, paved area onshore is chock-a-block full of hundreds of brightly colored, recently arrived, imported cars.

East of Pier 89, the waterfront bends southeast and there is a 400 foot long T-shaped, concrete public fishing pier at the bend. Two private orange and white striped buoys, "A" and "B," are about 100 feet off the pier marking an artificial underwater reef. These are not mooring buoys.

Pier 89 marks the north end of Elliott Bay Park, a Port of Seattle Park which adjoins Myrtle Edwards City Park along the waterfront. The combined parks are about 1.25 miles long, extending south to Bay Street, where the large commercial piers once again line the waterfront.

Pier 86 is home to a giant grain elevator seen part way along in the parks.

From the boat we see green grass above the rock bulkhead. The parks are filled with walkers, joggers and bicyclists moving along at various speeds. This a pleasant place for city dwellers to enjoy the waterfront while stretching their legs.

Piers 90 and 91 were Navy facilities lasting through WW II. When built in 1912, the two piers were reportedly the largest piers in the world.

Space Needle, 607.88 feet high

Fl 2.5s 25ft privately maintained flashing white light, is halfway along the park.

Landmark, the impressive **Space Needle**—built as **the icon** for Seattle's 1962 World's Fair—is charted 0.5 mile inland from the 2.5 second light.

Pier 70 is the first pier at the south end of Myrtle Edwards Park. As we cruise the waterfront we see some old commercial wharves renovated for use as piers for tour boats, shopping areas, restaurants, Seattle Aquarium and Omnidome Theater.

Pier 66, Bell Street Pier and **Bell Harbor Marina,** opened in June 1996. This new, modern Port of Seattle public facility is between the Seattle Aquarium and Edgewater Hotel, and several blocks from the fabulous Pike Place Market where they sell just about every type of fresh fruits, vegetables, fish, meats, flowers, and anything else you might want, including a wide array of indigenous crafts.

Enter the marina from the south, turning to port inside the tall pylon at the entrance, and check into a slip.

Along with a recreational boat marina, the pier provides cruise ship terminal operations, fishing vessel provisioning, fish processing, restaurants, public plazas, children's play area, yacht festivities and other entertainment.

Bell Harbor Marina

Bell Harbor Marina Facilities
➤ Moorage space of 2,208' accommodates the equivalent of 96 twenty-four foot recreational vessels
➤ Maximum 3 day stay. Rates: $1/foot, May-October, 60 cents/foot November-May
➤ Moorage for four hours or less is $10
➤ 24 hour security
➤ Restrooms and showers
➤ Sewage pump-out facility and utility hookups
➤ Direct access to other Bell Street Pier facilities: Anthony's Dockside Diner, Odyssey Maritime Museum, Port Chatham Smoked Seafood, International Conference Center
➤ Direct access to downtown Seattle
➤ Phone: 206-728-3000

Princess Angeline, the eldest daughter of Chief Seattle, lived in an 8-by-10 foot cedar shack between Pike and Pine near Pier 62. She lived like a street person toward the end of her life in the late 1800s, walking the streets of the city named after her father, wearing with dignity faded skirts and clothes safety- pinned together. She was one of the city's most photographed residents.

She died at age 86 in June 1896, and was buried in Lakeview Cemetery in a canoe-shaped casket with a paddle on the stern. A handful of early pioneers accompanied the horse-drawn hearse to the burial.

Pier 63 often hosts summer outdoor concerts. Some pleasure boats drift along or cruise slowly past while listening to music wafting over the water.

Pier 59 is the site of Seattle's fascinating saltwater Aquarium.

Tug Boat Races, an annual exciting event are held in Elliott Bay, with viewing from the waterfront—or perhaps from your own boat offshore. (See p.87)

Piers 57 to 59 include a waterfront park with picnic tables, viewing towers, walkways, fountain, statue of Christopher Columbus and a public fishing pier, This is where the *Miike Maru,* a Japanese steamship, arrived Aug. 31, 1896, marking the beginning of Seattle as an international port city.

Colman Dock and Seattle's Maritime Heritage
In the days before our present large car ferries, Colman Dock, then at Pier 54, was the terminal for the Mosquito Fleet steamers. The more than 2,500 vessels carried passengers and cargo from Seattle south to Tacoma and Olympia, west to Bremerton, Bainbridge and Poulsbo, north to Kingston, Everett, Port Ludlow, Port Townsend, the San Juans, Bellingham—and just about every town and settlement in between.

Pier 53 is the present **Washington State Ferry Terminal**.

(2) F R lights 19 ft (1) F R 36 ft horn, are the fixed red lights at two heights at the ferry terminal. The lights are difficult to see at night against other city lights.

At Colman Terminal, ferries service both Bremerton and Bainbridge Island about 90 times daily, nearly around-the-clock, carrying cars and passengers. Passenger-only ferries also run to and from Bainbridge and Vashon Islands.

Pier 54 is the site of the original Ivar's Acres of Clams, probably the best-known waterfront seafood restaurant in Seattle. Ivar Haglund, a well-loved Seattle original character, was the "flounder" of the restaurant, and built an aquarium on the pier with it in 1938. By 1946, he closed the aquarium and opened more restaurants throughout the region. He was a gentle entrepreneur who loved his city and its people. His motto was "Keep Clam." He died in 1985.

Between Piers 54 and 53, it's hard to miss a couple of Seattle's well-known fireboats. Besides fighting waterfront fires, the fireboats put on spectacular displays of their abilities during some city festivals. (See photo, page 34)

Another famous landmark is **Martin Selig's Columbia Center**—now named the **Seafirst Building**—which is Seattle's tallest building at 943 feet above Fourth Avenue. The dark building is charted as "tallest building" between Columbia and Cherry Streets.

Ivar Haglund feeding gulls

This statue of Ivar in front of his waterfront restaurant, feeding four larger-than-life-size seagulls, was done by Richard Beyer, who also did "Waiting for the Interurban" in Fremont and "The Kiss" in Olympia.

Battle of Seattle

Although nothing remains of it now, the Battle of Seattle blockhouse was at First and Cherry, about two blocks east of the ferry dock. The blockhouse was one of several built by pioneers who feared Native Americans might attack. And for good reason: their lands had been taken away by treaty and they felt they were being treated unfairly by white settlers.

On Jan. 26, 1856, a skirmish began when the *USS Decatur* fired a howitzer into the forests behind the village of Seattle. The Indians answered with small arms fire and the settlers ran into the blockhouse.

The Smith Tower, for many years the tallest building west of the Mississippi at 48 stories, is named on the chart at Second Avenue and Yesler Way. Its pointed tower stands out distinctly, although now dwarfed among the high-rises.

Pier 49, public access, at the foot of Washington Street, was downtown Seattle's only public moorage for years until the Bell Street Pier was built. It is still open, but mariners are advised not to leave boats unattended as this is a high-risk area. Continuing south, the waterfront becomes heavily industrial and commercial, with large container ships quickly and efficiently loading and unloading cargo day and night.

Pier 36, U.S. Coast Guard District 13 Headquarters, includes the all-important Vessel Traffic System facilities. Pier 36 is at the north end of the East Waterway.

South End of Elliott Bay, Harbor Island and Duwamish Waterways

Elliott Bay turns sharply west at Harbor Island with its high-density cargo handlings, shipyards, ship services and wharves.

East Waterway is a dead-end commercial shipping area. Fixed bridges and obstructions prevent access to the Duwamish River, as charted on 18450.

West Waterway, west of Harbor Island and east of KJR's radio tower, is about 250 yards wide, 32-60 feet deep, 0.85 miles long and highly industrial. (Chart p. 84)

Five Duwamish Waterway Reaches angle south and east upstream. We pass under five bridges to find a mix of small craft and maritime industrial facilities.

Currents flow south during flood tide. Currents flow north in excess of 3 knots during combined extreme ebb tides, muddy river flooding—expect channel silting.

Harbor Island and **Georgetown Reach** channels are about 200' wide, dredged to about 50' for about 2.2 miles; then into **1st Ave./8th Ave.** and **South Park Reaches,** 150' wide, dredged 20-15' respectively for another 1.2 miles; ending in **14th Ave. Bridge Reach**, 150' wide, dredged to 15' for 1.2 miles. Duwamish River enters the SE end of the 14th Ave. S. Reach with charted depths of 2-3 feet.

Ferry at Colman Terminal, Smith Tower in background

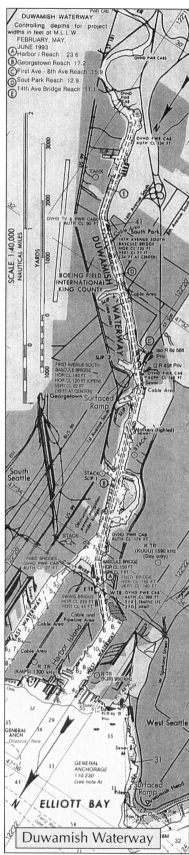

DUWAMISH WATERWAY
Controlling depths for project
widths in feet at M.L.L.W.
FEBRUARY, MAY,
JUNE 1993
(A) Harbor I Reach   23.6
(B) Georgetown Reach 17.2
(C) First Ave - 8th Ave Reach 15.9
(D) Sout Park Reach 12.9
(E) 14th Ave Bridge Reach 11.1

Not for Navigation
Refer to chart 18445,
page B, inset 4
Soundings in fathoms & feet

Upstream, the Duwamish River splits into what remains of the Black River—which flowed from the south end of Lake Washington before the Ship Canal lowered the lake nine feet when the Locks were built in 1917—and the Green River, with the source in the Cascade Range divide.

Duwamish Waterway Bridges Use whistle signals or call on VHF Ch 13			
Spokane St. Swing Bridge West Seattle			**Phone: 206-684-7443**
Closed normally, opens on request		Signal — ---	**Horiz. Clear. 250'**
At MHHW	(55.0' clr at MHW + 10.2' at MLLW - 11.1' at MHHW) =	54.1'	*(*Coast Pilot* & bridge
At MHW	**Closed vert. clear. center***	**55.0'**	tender give MHW
At MLLW	(55.0' clr at MHW + 10.2' at MLLW)	65.2'	height at 55'—
At ELW	(65.2' clr at MLLW + [-5.0'] at ELW)	70.2'	charted at 44')
West Seattle Freeway Fixed Bridge — Charted vert. clear. 140'			**Horiz. Clear. 150'**
Burlington Northern RR Bascule Bridge			**Phone: 206-935-1130**
Open most of the time (see note*)		Signal — -	**Horiz. Clear. 150'**
At MHHW	(7.0' clr at MHW + 10.2 at MLLW - 11.1' at MHHW) =	6.1'	*(Bridge tender: "Clo-
At MHW	**Closed vert. clear. as charted**	**7.0'**	sure for trains usually
At MLLW	(7.0' clr at MHW + 10.2' at MLLW)	17.2'	occur between 11 am-
At ELW	(17.2' clr at MLLW + [-5.0'] at ELW)	22.2	1 pm & 7-9 pm)
1st Ave S. (2) Bascule Bridges (West Bridge completion due in 1997/98)			**Phone: 206-767-3070**
(Both) bridges will open simultaneously by the bridge tender in a tower between the bridges on the SW side			
We understand clearances will be about the same for both bridges as currently			
Closed 6-9 a.m., 3-6 p.m. M-F		Signal: — — —	**Horiz. Clr. 145', open 120'**
At MHHW	(39' clr at MHW +10.2 at MLLW - 11.1 at MHHW)	38.1'	
At MHW	**Closed vert. clear. as charted**	**39.0'**	
At MLLW	(39' clr at MHW +10.2 at MLLW)	49.2'	
At ELW	(49.2' clr at MLLW + [-5.0'] at ELW)	54.2'	
14th Avenue S. Bascule Bridge crosses South Park Reach (King County)			**Phone: 206-767-2530**
Closed 6:30-8 a.m., 3:30-5 p.m.		Signal: — - —	**Horiz. Clear. 125'**
At MHHW	(34' clr at MHW + 10.2' at MLLW - 11.1' at MHHW)	33.1'	
At MHW	**Closed vert. clear. at center as charted**	**34.0'**	
At MLLW	(34' clr. at MHW + 10.2' at MLLW)	44.2'	
At ELW	(44.2' clr. at MLLW + [-5.0'} ELW)	49.2'	

Tide tables predict water level above or below MLLW datum, which can be greater or less than predicted, due to extreme winds, rains, river level, snow melt or barometric pressures. Predicted times may also be off for high and low tides. No values were given for extreme high tides. All values and equations should be checked for errors and against latest charts and Notice to Mariners before attempting to pass under the spans. We do not guarantee these figures.

Chart 18450, 06/29/96, was used to compile the above information. Clearance gauges at bridges would be a much safer and simpler method of communicating this information to mariners.

Harbor Island Marina is at the south end of Harbor Island where East and West Waterways meet, 0.8 mile south of West Waterway, and about 300 yards south of the railroad bridge. The marina's fuel and guest dock runs approximately east-west, and boaters are advised to check in there for guest moorage, or phone ahead. Slips are called A, B, C and D from west to east.

West Seattle Yacht Club's reciprocal moorage is at Harbor Island Marina.

Harbor Island Marina Facilities

➤ Guest moorage for at least 15 or more boats at guest dock and empty slips; maximum boat size of 65 feet
➤ Moorage fees: $9 for boats up to 20', $2 for every five feet over that
➤ 30 amp shore power at $3 per day; water
➤ Fuel dock with gas and diesel
➤ Pump-out at east end of fuel dock
➤ Restrooms with showers, no charge
➤ Basic store including snack foods, ice
➤ Deli close by, open on weekdays only
➤ Marine repairs close by
➤ Picnic area and public viewing pier
➤ Bus service to downtown Seattle
➤ Phone: 206-467-9400

There are other marinas with permanent moorage along the waterway.

Public launch ramp, free, double-wide, with parking, is on the northeast shore of the Duwamish River under the First Avenue South (Highway 99) Bridge.

South Park Marina, south of the 14th Ave. Bridge, is charted as #41 on 18445. There is no guest moorage and they no longer sell marine gas as listed on the chart.

⚓ **Underway again out of the waterway,** we continue west along Elliott Bay. Large commercial vessels are frequently at anchor here in the general anchorage area in deep water. We understand the Port of Seattle may build new facilities in this West Seattle area.

Hot Time in the Old Town

Luna Park was north of the present Don Armeni Park, at the tip of Duwamish Head. In 1907, it opened as an amusement park—of such a magnitude Seattleites were staggered. Fabulous rides included the Figure Eight Roller Coaster, the Giant Swing, Chute-the-Chutes Water Slide and the Canal of Venice. It featured the "longest bar in the bay," where teenage girls were reportedly hanging out with older, cigarette-smoking, beer-guzzling men.

For six inglorious years Luna Park was all the rage until it closed down, leaving only the Natatorium, a favorite saltwater bath house, which in turn burned to the ground in the 1930s after an arsonist set it ablaze.

West Seattle waterfront parks begin about 0.5 mile north of Pier 2 and wrap around the shoreline at Duwamish Head, almost to Alki Point for more than two miles. These are Seacrest, Don Armeni and Alki Beach Parks, with walking paths, lawns and picnic tables all along the waterfront. This is an attractive shoreline.

Seacrest Park, the southernmost park fronting this shore of Elliott Bay, has 2,200 feet of shoreline on four acres, including privately operated Seacrest Boathouse Marina. It's a good place for boating, picnicking, fishing, and scuba diving. The view of downtown Seattle across Elliott Bay is spectacular, especially at night.

Seacrest Boathouse is a replica of the old Seacrest Boathouse built in the 1920s, which was wiped out in a storm, and rebuilt about 1989. At one time the terminal for the ferry to downtown Seattle was here. The old ferry pilings are now a favorite haunt with scuba divers.

The commute back then took 8.5 minutes—a minuscule amount of time compared to today's car commute to downtown Seattle over the bridges. It may be time to consider a passenger boat scuttling across Elliott Bay from here once again.

Seacrest Boathouse Marina Facilities
- ➤ Guest moorage for an unspecified number of boats up to 60′
- ➤ Moorage fees are $10/day for boats up to 40′; $15 for boats over 40′
- ➤ No power; water, restrooms at head of pier
- ➤ Basic store with tackle, bait, deli, boutique
- ➤ Outboard repair
- ➤ Picnic tables
- ➤ Fishing pier
- ➤ Scuba diving
- ➤ Call Walt Brown at 206-932-1050

Don Armeni Park adjoins Seacrest and continues for the next 1,400 feet along the shore.

Launch ramps are at the south end of this park. The two northern lanes are posted for boat launching and the two southern lanes for boat retrieval. There's plenty of good parking, plus landscaped shoreside paths and picnic tables. This is the only trailerable launch we found in Elliott Bay.

Harbor Island was the largest man-made island in the world when it was first built. It is now the site of major industries, including the gigantic Todd Shipyard drydocks, and is filled with cranes and docks.

The Seattle Yacht Club was inside Elliott Bay in the area southeast of Duwamish Head, before the locks and Ship Canal were built in 1916.

After the canal was completed, the yacht club moved "inland" to its present home in the protected waters of Portage Bay.

Ferry Avenue runs up the hill behind the waterfront parks.

Launch ramp at Armeni Park

A public hand-carry launch ramp for non-motorized boats is between Duwamish Head and Alki Point at the foot of 56th Ave. S.W., approximately 0.5 statute mile north and east of the "Birthplace of Seattle" monument.

"Birthplace of Seattle" monument at Alki Beach Park at 63rd Avenue Southwest and Alki Avenue Southwest

***Seattle became the natural gateway to the far north** during the Alaska gold rush. Where Trident Imports now stands on Pier 56 at the foot of University Street was where the **S.S. Humboldt** departed to Alaska on June 2, 1901.*

The 320 passengers who boarded the vessel carried gear and dreams of getting rich quick in the Alaskan gold fields. Very few miners did strike it rich. It was the merchants who outfitted them and the ship owners whose vessels transported them became wealthy from the gold rush.

Fl 2.5s 15 ft 18 M Horn (Bl (2) 20s) Duwamish Head Light with an 18 mile range, 15 ft high on black and white diamond-shaped dayboard, marks Duwamish Head and offshore shallows which jut over 0.2 mile north into Elliott Bay. It is about 0.3 mile north of Armeni Park, and hills behind it rise up to more than 260 feet.

Alki Beach Park is a 154 acre park with nearly two miles of beach from Duwamish Head to within about 0.2 mile of Alki Point.

Anchoring is prohibited as this is a Seattle waterfront park. At this time small boats are unable to launch or land here.

Boats aren't the only non-allowed items in this park, where "no excessive noise, no amplified sounds, no dogs on the beach" signs are also posted. There have been problems on this once pristine, historical beach and police and local groups are working hard to make it pleasant once again. It is still a favorite park with many West Seattleites, who walk, bike, jog the paths, or swim along the sandy shores.

Elliott Bay's First Pioneer Settlement

Alki is the "Birthplace of Seattle," where the Denny Party landed on a miserable, cold, blustery rainy dawn on November 13, 1851—about 10 years after Wilkes had explored the area for the U.S. government.

In this first pioneer settlement on Elliott Bay, 10 adults and 12 children went ashore from the schooner *Exact*. The party included Dennys, Borens, Bells and Terrys, familiar names to most Seattleites. Awaiting them was a roofless log cabin.

One of the women remembered that day: " ... when the women got ashore they were crying, every one of 'em ... The last glimpse I had of them was the women standing under the trees with their wet sun bonnets all lopping down over their faces and their aprons to their eyes."

Chief Seattle was at the point when they arrived, as that was a favorite campsite for his Suquamish tribe.

The pioneers named the spot "New York-Alki"—Alki was Chinook Indian for "bye and bye" or someday. Within a year the group moved from West Seattle to the site of present downtown Seattle where the harbor was deeper.

A monument was erected, facing the water, honoring the pioneers who developed the colony into the city of Seattle. It is across the street from where that first, roofless cabin was built.

One side of the monolith is engraved, "At this place on Nov. 13, 1851, there landed from Schooner *Exact*, Captain Folger, the little colony which developed into the city of Seattle. This is the birthplace.

"Adults were: Arthur A. Denny and wife, John N. Lowe and wife, Carson D. Boren and wife, William M. Bell and wife, Louisa Boren, David T. Denny, Charles C. Terry and Lee Terry.

"Children were: Louise C. Denny, Lenora Denny, Roland H. Denny, Alonzo Lowe, Mary Lowe, John Lowe, Minerva Lowe, Gertrude Boren, Olive Bell, Laura Bell, Virginia Bell, Lavinia Bell."

We visited the monument on a cold, blustery, rainy November day, like the day the pioneers arrived. It was easy to imagine their mood.

Fl 5s 39ft 15M Horn (Bl (2) 30s) Alki Point Light, a flashing light with a 15 mile range is 39 feet high in a white octagonal tower, 1.8 miles SW of Duwamish Head.

Underway again, south of Alki Point about 0.1 mile, Alki Beach Park runs south for an additional 0.3 mile. Beyond that, there is little public beach access for boaters until about seven miles south of Alki Point where there is a small county public beach access at Three Tree Point. (Chapter 11, page 174)

Three city parks are along the way, and some public tidelands totaling about 3,000 feet.

Me-Kwa-Mooks, about one mile south of Alki, is the first park. It has 34 acres with 16 acres of tidelands and is a natural area for picnics and beach walking. The park was named for an ancestral Native American village on the flats between Alki and Duwamish Head. Me-Kwa-Mooks means "shaped like a bear's head."

Lowman Beach, about 2.6 miles south of Alki Point and a short distance north of Lincoln Park, is a "pocket park" with 300 feet of beach, popular with windsurfers and beach combers. As mentioned earlier, the highest point in Seattle is about two miles inland from the park. See if you can spot it from offshore.

Lincoln Park is on **Point Williams**, the first major point about three miles south of Alki. It's a marvelously wooded park with a mile of rocky beach in West Seattle. There are miles of walking and biking paths, 11 acres of playfields, a wonderful 50 meter outdoor saltwater heated swimming pool, picnic and play areas, restrooms, fire pits and concessions.

You can't land a small boat at Lincoln Park since it's a city park. However, the entire beach is public tidelands. A sort of oxymoron, which may change.

Fauntleroy Cove and the ferry landing are immediately south of the park. Between it and Lincoln Park is 50 feet of sandy beach at a road end, enough room to carry your kayak or canoe to the water, or to just sit on the beach and watch the car ferries come and go back and forth to Vashon Island.

And that brings us to the end of our trip along Seattle's salt waterfront.

The photo reminds us of the many working tugs we see in the area. Tugboat races are held annually in Elliott Bay and waters churn as these behemoths rev their engines, trying to reach the finish line first, in exciting displays of power and speed. Whichever throws the largest wake and gets there first is the winner.

The Stockade, a large summer resort on Alki Beach, was built from driftwood around the turn-of-the- century.

Seattleites ferried to the resort for a day of boating, hiking, clam digging and dining at Alki Beach, "the haven of the Sunday crowds." The Stockade closed down during the Depression.

In Chapter 5 we continue south from Kingston along Puget Sound's west shore, picking up the east shore again in Chapter 11.

Seattle's famous Tug Boat Race

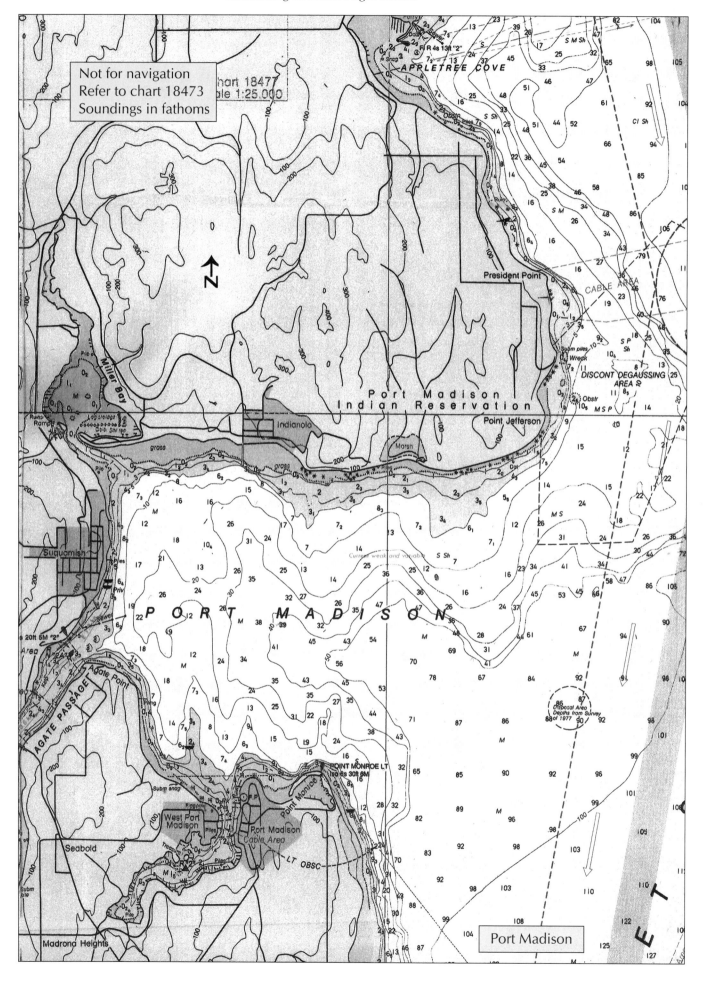

Not for navigation
Refer to chart 18473
Soundings in fathoms

Port Madison

CHAPTER 5
South from Kingston to Port Madison

Charts and publications for this chapter

	Chart	Date	Title	Scale	Soundings
***	**18446**	06/16/90	Puget Sound, Apple Cove Point to Keyport (Preferred chart for this chapter)	1:25,000 .... Feet	
**	**18473**	08/14/93	Oak Bay to Shilshole	1:40,000 .... Fathoms	
*	**18441**	02/18/95	Puget Sound, Northern Part	1:80,000 .... Fathoms	
*	**18445**	06/03/95	Puget Sound—Possession Sound to Olympia, page A	1:80,000 .... Fathoms	
	18440	08/05/95	Puget Sound	1:150,000 .... Fathoms	
			Tidal Current Charts, Puget Sound, Northern Part		
			Booklet: Puget Sound Shellfish Sites		
			Washington State Public Lands Quad Map, Seattle	1:100,000	

➡ *When using charts, compare your chart dates with ones referred to above. There may be discrepancies between different charts and different chart editions.*

South from Kingston

We started at Kingston in Chapter 1. Then we got sidetracked into Seattle in Chapters 2, 3 and 4. Now we're back on the west shore of Puget Sound, in some areas we've lived in and loved.

In this chapter we'll go south from Kingston along the west shore into the big bay of Port Madison, noting the panoramic views, concerns and communities we find along the way.

⚓ **Underway again**, leaving Appletree Cove and Kingston and heading south, we watch the depth sounder closely along this shore because at MLLW it sneakily shoals from 10 feet to two feet within 200 to 400 yards of shore.

Erratic rocks abound as the shoreline angles southeast. It's not so bad when the erratics are right along the beach, but in places they've gotten adventurous and moved farther out and underwater, where they're liable to pose a problem to mariners.

There are fairly high density residential developments and low to medium to high bluffs along the way, often with many trees, but no public tidelands on this shore. A fantastic view of the Cascades from Mount Baker to Mount Rainier emerges on a clear day.

This can also be a heavy-duty thrash to windward in adverse winds.

President Point is a little over 1.5 miles south of Kingston. Waters are shallow nearly 500 yards off the point to as low as six to 10 feet on extreme low tides.

Cable area is at President Point—important to know if anchoring off.

About midway between President Point and Point Jefferson is a white house with a red tile roof that looks amazingly like a Coast Guard or Naval station. This was the site of a Navy degaussing testing station in the 1940s, both during and after World War II.

The station has been long since abandoned, but is still charted. (Chart 18446 shows "Discontinued Degaussing Cable," and 18473 shows "Discont. Degaussing Area.") The station's dock was just offshore from the house of the former Navy quarters. It has been a private residence for many years.

➡ **NOTE:** There are **no** places to buy marine fuel and only **one protected** anchorage in this intriguing area.

Tidal Current Information

If going south from Kingston against a maximum ebb, visualize the ebb flowing from Agate Pass as it sweeps eastward along the north shore of Port Madison. This combines with the ebb current flowing north from between Bainbridge Island and West Point in Seattle as the current spills into Port Madison.

As the water level to the north recedes, a noticeable northeasterly rip spills off President Point. A favorable back eddy develops along the shore north of President Point. South of the point, we are again bucking a concentrated current, and the opposing backeddy forms along the north shore in Port Madison during flood tides.

Former degaussing station at President Point

Degaussing *is a way of making ships non-magnetic. Ships built at the Puget Sound Naval Shipyard in Bremerton, many for use in World War II, were first taken to a Deperming Range in Port Orchard channel north of Illahee. There they were rendered as nonmagnetic as possible through the use of electrically charged coils that cancel the ship's magnetic field.*

The ships had their final magnetic measurements taken at the degaussing station off President Point. The purpose was to prevent detection and destruction of ships by underwater magnetic mines.

A Suquamish tribal *canoe with Native American paddlers departed one cool, windy morning in late spring 1993 from the creek at the Port Madison Indian Reservation. The paddlers joined canoes from other tribes paddling to a rendezvous in Bella Bella, British Columbia.*

After a blessing, the paddlers sped the canoe forward through the surf and travelled north to the historic event.

About 3,500 feet of public tidelands are in this chapter.

Public tidelands, *unless otherwise noted, are state owned. Some maybe leased and posted for aquaculture or other private use. We take the Washington State Public Lands Quadrangle Map, when going ashore at these locations to avoid trespassing on adjacent private property.*

Point Jefferson is about one mile south of President Point. Called "Jeff Head" by locals, it doesn't look too much like a point, just a rounded bluff. There are more large, erratic rocks along these shores. We're comfortable at least 0.1 mile offshore.

Jefferson Beach Community private fishing pier and launch ramp are to starboard coming around the head. This is an exposed dangerous lee shore in southerly gales. The fishing pier was heavily damaged in the early 1990s when a log boom broke up in a gale and steep seas slammed logs into the dock, battering pilings.

There are 100 foot straight barren bluffs at Jeff Beach, except where a road winds steeply down to the beach, pier and ramp. Heavy rains trigger occasional slides when chunks of muddy clay slough off the bluffs and onto the beach.

The beach shoals rapidly again and we may suddenly find ourselves in 15 feet of water as far as 0.2 mile offshore along the southern face of Jeff Head.

Port Madison—the "Big Bay"

This large body of water is bounded on the north by the shore from Point Jefferson to Miller Bay, on the west by the shore between Miller Bay and Agate Passage, and on the south by all of the north shore of Bainbridge Island from Point Monroe to Agate Pass. Port Madison bay is about three miles east to west and two miles north to south. There are few navigation hazards here, although it is shallow off the north shore for as much as 500 yards.

This large bay is not to be confused with the harbor of Port Madison and the community of the same name on the north end of Bainbridge. We'll discuss the harbor in detail later in this section. Many area residents don't call this larger body of water Port Madison, unaware that is the charted name. They simply refer to it as part of "the Sound."

North Shore of Port Madison, the Jefferson Beach community extends west along this shore about 0.6 mile past the fishing pier. The bare bluffs continue above log-strewn beaches, gently tapering down to the "marsh" in the flats shown on the charts.

Port Madison Reservation of the Suquamish tribe extends along the next 0.5 mile of no-bank waterfront which includes the marsh. At high tide the marsh is filled with salt water, and at low tide a creek empties the marsh across the gravel beach. Sometimes the creek is more than waist deep—at other times we walk across without even getting our feet wet. The beach along this low area has no erratic rocks.

At the west end of the flats, just as the hills and bluffs begin again, is the Indianola Church Camp, a private camp.

⚓ Anchor in this bight in a northerly blow or in calm weather in less than three fathoms, sand bottom. All beaches are private.

✸ The land between the camp and Indianola rises to dramatic bluffs 200 feet or higher with massive numbers of rocks at the base. Silver, sea-tossed logs lie like pick-up-sticks along the beaches. For about one mile east of Indianola large rocks extend offshore from the base of the bluff for about 200 yards, some as much as 0.1 mile from the high tide line. We keep about 0.2 mile offshore.

State owned public tidelands are below the bluff, extending about 1,500 feet along the shoreline, accessible only by water.

There are homes tucked back in the trees high above the beach with panoramic views south towards Bainbridge Island, Seattle and Mount Rainier—and all the sparkling waters of Puget Sound in between.

Indianola

A waterfront community about 0.5 mile west of the bluff, the village is well known for, and identified by, its 900 foot long public fishing pier, wide sandy beaches and friendly folks.

As the tide rises over sun-warmed sand, swimmers enjoy relatively warm water.

At the end of the Indianola dock you can almost see forever, a 180° panorama of mountains, sea and sky. West past Suquamish to the looming Olympics, sunsets can be breathtaking as the sky turns dramatic shades of pink, darkening into purples over the jagged mountains. To the southeast the snows of Mount Rainier reflect the rosy glow.

Sunrises are equally spectacular from here as skies above the eastern Cascades turn glorious shades of early morning colors.

At the head of the dock the sign "community beach" means the beach is for community residents and their guests. However, the dock is public.

Indianola community dock

Indianola Country Store is one block from the head of the dock on the left corner, with the post office kitty-corner across the road. The community clubhouse is up the street. This is "downtown" Indianola, the way it's been for years. A community church less than 0.5 mile up the hill on the east side of town.

In the store, you'll find lattes, espressos, groceries, ice, beer, wine, fishing tackle, Indianola sweatshirts and T-shirts, gifts, newspapers, a copy machine, videos and much more. Sit down at one of the tables and devour the great sandwiches they make in the deli. People will say hello even if they don't know you. Please tell Rob and Tia at the store that "Jo and Carl" sent you!

They sell a charming book on Indianola history: *A Chronicle of Indianola* by Eva Pickrell Meacham. It's a delight—tells you all about remembrances of Indianola in its early days by a woman born around the turn-of-the-century who lived through all the comings and goings she writes about.

Getting to Indianola, we keep well offshore as we approach. There's less than 15 feet of water nearly 500 yards offshore at MLLW, down to less than one foot near the pier. Despite the length of the dock, it is not a deepwater pier, so we stay out past the end of it to anchor.

Quick flashing light shown on older charts at the end of Indianola dock is no longer there.

The float at the dock is for loading and unloading only, and goes aground at minus tides. The float is removed each fall because of winter storms, and goes back in late spring. It's about 25 feet long and is used by the community for swimming, fishing and landing small boats. There is no fuel or water at Indianola.

⚓ **Anchoring** at Indianola is possible, and then dinghy to the float. We consult either chart 18446 or 18473 and verify our position before we drop the hook. Know what the tides are doing, check the water depth, wind and weather. Many are the skippers who dropped anchor too near the sandy shelf and spend several hours waiting for an incoming tide. It's nearly happened to us.

We've anchored here successfully. We prefer the west side of the dock in a fair amount of water, depending on how long we're staying. Because of other boat traffic, a dependable anchor light is a must when anchoring overnight here.

We learned many years ago that even when it seems absolutely flat calm, we still roll at night from swells. They could be a precursor of winds about to arrive, from earlier winds passing through, wakes from large ship traffic, or maybe they're just built into the area. Whatever, be prepared for a rolling kind of night, or possibly having to leave for a more protected anchorage if a strong southerly comes up. The closest place for protection is two miles south to the harbor of Port Madison at the north end of Bainbridge.

A farmer's market is held on summer Saturday mornings in "downtown" Indianola at the gazebo across from the community clubhouse.

It's a great place to buy freshly cut flowers, freshly picked vegetables, many other goodies—and visit.

Indianola is NOT a gunkhole, but we love it anyway, mostly because of warm, fuzzy childhood memories . . . . . .

The Indianola dock *was formerly a Mosquito Fleet steamer landing, and later a ferry dock until the ferries quit running in 1951.*

The dock is still well loved and used, walked daily by many, and maintained by the Port of Indianola.

Indianola—Then and Now

Indianola is unlike other communities around the Sound as it was not founded by loggers, fishermen and farmers. Instead it was platted as a summer vacation community for Seattleites who loved to escape to cabins and long, sandy beaches with warm swimming.

It was about 1916 when Indianola opened as a "developer's dream." Steamers would bring city folks over to look at waterfront lots which sold for about 10 cents a front foot. A few far-sighted folks snatched them up. Their families still live in those homes built so long ago.

Jo recalls: My family started coming here in 1932 and we've been around, at least part-time, ever since. My mother did not buy property in 1916—Indianola was "too far away."

We were here when passenger-only steamships were here. The vast sandy beaches at low tide were our playgrounds. My brother, Bud, and I dug clams, caught crabs, built sand castles, played "Cut-the-Pie" tag and baseball on the hard sand with other kids. Our "summer camp" had kerosene lamps, a hand water pump and an outhouse. There was only one telephone in town—a hand-crank on the clubhouse porch.

We loved it—we had miles of beach and woods, the country store and owner Amos Pickrell, who remembered all our birthdays with a Hershey bar.

I remember watching the Indian fishermen off Indianola, standing up in their sturdy boats, facing forward as they rowed, pacing themselves at a moderate rate—so much more logical than sitting down looking back at where they had been, as most rowers do, meanwhile pulling in their catch.

Indianola Community Beach and float

Indianola was the most wonderful summer place on earth. Bud and I built rafts out of drift logs, used old sheets swiped from mom for sails. Marcia, Ruth and I built forts in the logs. Fearless Dolly picked up huge crabs in her bare hands.

The entire summer was spent on the beach—a three month picnic. We never once said we were bored. Life was perfect: peanut butter sandwiches for lunch and saltwater coursing through our systems. We swam, splashed and sailed our way through so many wonderful summers. We kids played on the beach, watched over by our moms, while our dads commuted by ferry each day to Seattle—"town" we called it then—engaged in never-ending pinochle games.

As young teenagers, we'd wait on the end of the dock for the car ferries to swing into the ferry slip. Then we'd dive in the white foaming water they churned up, never dreaming it might be dangerous.

Now in the late 20th century, the sandy beaches still stretch themselves out on either side the "fishing pier." Kids and dogs still run and play on the beaches. Every summer at Indianola Days there's a wonderful sand castle sculpture contest, usually won by a dozen or so members of an "old family" who plan all winter long for their artistic coup.

It's no longer just a summer community. There are families and retirees who fill most of the homes, once left vacant from September to June. Everyone still knows everyone else by name—and still cares for them. The depth of community is still there, even to the owners of the Indianola Country Store who know everyone. It's a community like no other.

Excerpt from *A Chronicle of Indianola* by Eva Pickrell Meacham

Amos and Eva Pickrell took over the Indianola Country Store in 1936 after the death of his dad, Cyrus Pickrell, the former Suquamish Indian agent.

Amos, long and lanky and almost always clad in overalls—Indianola's favorite folk hero. Amos was famous and unforgettable for his acting in the annual community "Stunt Night" skits each August.

Amos was appointed Postmaster on February 17, 1937, and held that post until he died April 22, 1957. At the time of his death the Bremerton Sun wrote ... "the Indianola Post Office was the center for nearly everything said and done in Indianola for over 25 years."

Eva wrote *A Chronicle of Indianola*, filled with memories of years-gone -by for her family. The booklet was printed, others read it and it became a local best seller, with a new edition printed in 1993. And although Amos, the postmaster, the storekeeper, the folk hero, is featured in the booklet, she tells other fascinating stories of Indianola's early days.

"An incident happening many moons ago, occurred during Prohibition days. One night, about midnight, our local deputy sheriff went down the dock to hang up the red lantern at the end. (A nightly ritual.) He saw a couple of men handling sacks of something or other with the wheelbarrow kept to haul freight up the dock. He bent back his coat to display has badge of authority and informed them they were under arrest. He noticed then that they were loading the filled sacks into a small boat tied to the float.

"They saw he had no arms so, offering him some of their loot, continued with their work. Bristling, he blew his police whistle. They thought it best to discontinue their activity, called to helpers on the beach and left in a boat.

"Telling loudly of his experience in the store next day, two of our adventurous young men decided to go down on the beach that night and take a look at low tide. Equipped with gunnysacks and a flashlight, they started walking east from the dock. Speck Charlesworth took his .38 automatic and Elliott Pickrell carried an old .44.

"Sure enough, they found a sack with eight bottles of whiskey in it. Speck toted it up and hid it behind a log, but he just couldn't resist sampling his find, by the time he rejoined Elliott to continue the search, he was pretty slap-happy.

"As they walked along, they found the ebbing tide disclosed a whole field of filled sacks in piles of two dozen or so. Speck was busy slitting open the sacks to see the brands when Elliott happened to look up and see a dull light glowing on the point, signaling to an anchored boat.

"Just as he looked around again, he saw behind a big stump the barrel of a gun pointing straight at them. A voice demanded that they hold up their hands and drop their guns. Speck was in a haggling mood and argued about dropping his gun on the wet sand!

"The man with the gun confiscated their arms and claimed he was a Federal man. The next day the Harbor Patrol appeared with grappling hooks and retrieved the treasure, but not before a good part of the town had slipped down and hidden away a bottle or two."

Indianola dock in the "good old days:"

As you walk the long Indianola dock imagine how it was before 1951—the year the car ferries stopped running.

The dock was wide, with both a car lane and a walking lane. There were wingwalls off the end of the dock to hold the ferries in place as they loaded and unloaded. The "transfer span," raising and lowering the ramp, was cranked by hand. A small three-sided shelter gave ferry riders a place to wait in bad weather.

The car lane on the dock was crowded with "weekenders' cars," filled with folks going back to the city each Sunday evening. Teenagers perched on the dock rails, waving good-bye to those departing.

The sandspit

In the "old" days, the sandspit at the south boundary of Miller Bay was much narrower than it is now. There wasn't a single house on it, only drift logs and scrub above the high tide line. It was a marvelous place to hike and swim off the west end in the channel leading to the bay, especially on an incoming tide when the water raced into the bay. (In fact, both Carl and Jo were doing just that in the 1940s, independently of each other, and never met.)

But in the 1950s, developers dredged, filled and widened the spit; platted and sold off the lots, and built large homes. Now it's all private. Some say it was a mistake, but it's been done. Kids no longer hike the private spit and dive into the racing currents.

⚓ **Underway again,** we pass the Miller Bay sandspit, which begins about 0.7 mile west of the Indianola dock. The 0.5 mile long spit is along the southern shore of Miller Bay. You can't miss it. The spit is filled with large homes built cheek-by-jowl on no-bank lots on the water's edge.

A close look at Miller Bay on chart 18446 shows how shallow it is. The soundings of one through seven are in **feet** at MLLW.

Inside Miller Bay, sandspit to the left, looking northwest

The only deep part of Miller Bay—originally called Squaib Bay—is at the south end along the sandspit. It was dredged so sandspit residents can moor their boats at private, front yard docks on the bayshore. The bay is seldom used as log storage anymore, even though charts show it. There is a long row of pilings off the northern shore of the sandspit.

Bay Marine, a boat sales and repair facility, and a marina, are located inside on the western shore of Miller Bay, despite the shallowness of the bay. It's used mostly by shoal draft boats since the marina floats go dry at low water. There has been a small marina here since at least the 1930s, when there was just a little cabin where fishing tackle, bait and gas were sold.

Bay Marine Facilities
➤ No guest moorage or fuel
➤ Permanent moorage and storage for small boats
➤ Engine service and repair
➤ One lane launch ramp with parking
➤ Phone: 360-598-4900.

Miller Bay is a great bay for kayaks and canoes—quiet and well-protected from weather—a safe place for small boats. You'll see herons and many different types of waterbirds in here as you paddle around. All shoreline is private. There is a fish hatchery run by the Suquamish Tribe at the very head of the bay, and although visitors are welcome, you can't kayak all the way up the stream as it gets too small. If you decide to explore Miller Bay by small boat, we advise checking tides carefully to avoid stranding.

Boat entering Miller Bay, launch ramp in foreground

Entering Miller Bay, we need at least five feet of water to get into the marina, and it's best to go in on a rising tide, they say at the marina. (They didn't say what draft vessel they meant.) Enter the channel between the west end of the sandspit and the west mainland shore. Once inside the bay, turn to port around the hook on the west shore and proceed into the marina with caution.

⚓ **Suquamish** is about one mile south of Miller Bay. Part of the town is on the Port Madison Indian Reservation of the Suquamish Tribe. The shores are covered with small erratic rocks that look like a gaggle of goslings. Homes and the business section of town are atop low bluffs.

Catch an early sunrise, or a full moon rising over the Cascades just after sunset from Suquamish—it's impressive.

A large ballfield in the center of town swells with visitors during the annual Chief Seattle Days celebration in mid-August when there are spirited Native American canoe races, salmon barbecues and handicrafts.

Suquamish village is perhaps best known historically as the site of Chief Seattle's grave. It's in the small cemetery next to St. Peter's Catholic Church, built as an Indian mission by Father Francis Blanchet about 1881. It's just a short walk up the hill from the center of town.

Today, the village may be best known locally for its two taverns, the Tide's Inn and the Tide's Out. There are several small shops, a grocery store, restaurants, hardware store, service stations, post office, in addition to the cemetery and taverns.

Charles Lawrence Memorial Boat Launch Ramp is a single-lane, fairly steep ramp on the beach below the ballfield. A 450 foot long community fishing pier with no mooring, is south of the ramp. The path to the pier has a small sign quoting Chief Seattle urging us to "love this beautiful land."

⚓ **Anchoring** is possible off Suquamish for a short period of time with care. The best area is north of the fishing pier in about 15 to 20 feet of water depending on tide and weather. It's best to anchor off when currents through Agate Pass are mild, and no strong winds are blowing. We row ashore, beaching the dinghy near the launch ramp.

State-owned tidelands run for about 1,800 feet south of the launch ramp.

Chief Seattle's gravesite at Saint Peter's Mission Cemetery is marked by uprights of a stylized longhouse with canoes on the cross-beams.

This is the grave of the legendary Indian chief for whom Seattle is named. He was head of the Suquamish Tribe and leader of the Allied Tribes in the northwest.

Seattle's baptismal name was Noah Sealth. He was probably about 81 years old when he died.

Suquamish

The village of Suquamish, as we now know it, more or less began in 1909 when Seattle real estate developer, Ole Hansen, who eventually became mayor, bought the Suquamish waterfront from its Indian owner, John Kettle. It became a successful community with steamer service and ferry service later on.

Up until 1951, when Washington State took over the ferry system, Suquamish and its sister community, Indianola, were served daily by the **Black Ball Ferry Line** from Colman Pier in Seattle.

The state built the Agate Pass Bridge in 1950, joining the north end of Bainbridge Island with the mainland just a little over one nautical mile south of Suquamish—the following year the ferry service to the two communities was stopped.

Commuters from the two communities then had to drive to Kingston and take the ferry to Edmonds, or else drive to Bainbridge Island—across the new bridge—and take the ferry from Winslow to Seattle. It was the sad end of an era for both villages. Today, dedicated "rural residents" still commute, just not as easily.

✵ **Underway again**, we cruise across Agate Passage and go east along the north shore of Bainbridge Island to complete this section on Port Madison. (We cruise through Agate Pass in Chapter 7.)

We follow along Bainbridge east of Agate Point where there are pilings from old piers along the beaches, rock bulkheads hedging against erosion, upscale houses, some with steep stairways and erratic rocks on the beach. We like to keep about 0.1 mile offshore as there are some nice, long, sandy beaches here during low tides.

From left to right, a dog, a Carl and a petroglyph

The old Agate Point Steamer Landing is shown on charts 18473 and 18446 as "piling," just about at the bulge where the land turns south. The dock is now nothing more than some old pilings.

About 100 yards northwest of this former dock is **Haleelts Rock**, a large erratic rock with petroglyphs carved on it. There are fewer than 30 known petroglyphs in the Puget Sound area and this is one of them. Haleelts means "marked face," according to Suquamish elders. The carving is thought to be 1,500 to 3,000 years old.

We had heard about the rock and decided to see it for ourselves.

Remains of steamer landing at Agate Point on Bainbridge near Haleelts Rock

The best time to photograph the Haleelts petroglyph is when the morning sun casts a shadow across the carved stone. Unfortunately, because the tide and morning sunshine didn't cooperate, we arrived in the afternoon when the sun was no longer available. As a result, we found the petroglyph to be a bit disappointing as the carvings were not deep and it was difficult to see them. If we hadn't known Haleelts was there, we might not have spotted it.

Bloedel Reserve

R "2" daymark, south of Treasure Island in Port Madison

Haleelts is at the eight foot tide level, so it can easily be seen at lower tides. The rock has several faces all looking out to sea. It's about six feet long and about five feet high and has an old brass Coast and Geodetic marker on top.

⚓ **Anchor off** and visit the rock if you feel so inclined.

There's a public road end on the island up from the old steamer pier, not too far from the rock. Local residents told us it was a difficult trail down to the beach and advised against trying to walk it.

☸ Between Agate Point and the entrance to Port Madison harbor, the 16 foot charted depth curves, and coincidentally a large mooring buoy in 16 feet of water, are 0.25 miles offshore. A subterranean ridge extends about 1.4 miles north past the buoy.

A shoulder of the ridge projects northeast from the west side of the harbor entrance where depths of four to six feet are within 200 yards of shore. Many boats have grounded here.

The uplands now taper down to no-bank waterfront. Less than 0.4 mile past the buoy is the entrance to the harbor of Port Madison.

Bloedel Reserve is about midway along this shore. From the water you can see a large white, gracious, 18th century, French country-style house in the midst of a formal lawn up on the bluff. This is the well-known Bloedel Reserve, with 160 acres of beautiful horticultural gardens, with a wildlife rehabilitation program. This treasure is the former home of Prentice Bloedel, a principal in the Canadian lumber company MacMillan Bloedel. There is no beach access to the reserve. To best appreciate it, go there by land on a self-guided walking tour. Phone: 206-842-7631 for more information.

West Port Madison Nature Preserve is immediately east of Bloedel. There's 210 feet of forested waterfront and trails in this 11.2 acre, steep-bank park. Frankly, after walking the Fairy Dell Trail near Arrow Point (Chapter 7), we opted not to do this trail as getting up the bluff is supposed to be a pretty steep hike.

⚓ **Anchor off,** go ashore, hike the trail if you want, and tell us what we missed.

Inside the Port Madison Harbor–What's Here and How We Enter

Ⓖ Port Madison is a favorite **gunkhole** for hundreds of recreational boaters and gets very crowded on summer weekends and holidays. It is an overnight anchorage for many north and southbound mariners, as well as a weekend destination.

There are no shoreside services, guest moorages or public buoys here and almost all shoreline is private residential, with very limited public access.

Many resident vessels are moored on private buoys and at private docks.

⚓ **Anchoring** is the primary reason for visiting Port Madison's protected harbor. We anchor almost anywhere harbor in charted depths of six to 21 feet, mud bottom.

Many vessels in the harbor do not display anchor lights, which complicates maneuvering after dark—radar helps a lot.

Treasure Island, a tombolo at extreme low tides, is charted off the northwest shore. The island is private with a pier on the east side.

R "2," a triangular red daymark, is on a rocky shoal approximately 150 yards south and west of Treasure Island. This is the only hazard we know of in the harbor.

Northerlies sometimes blow into the entrance but Port Madison provides a nearly landlocked harbor for anchoring within it's 0.85 mile length. The harbor zigzags west and south, ending in Hidden Cove, in the southwest end. Depth is one fathom or less, mud bottom.

Two yacht clubs are in Port Madison.

Seattle Yacht Club outstation is 0.35 mile southwest of Port Madison's private community float, which is at the harbor entrance east shore.

Port Madison Yacht Club is southwest of the Seattle Yacht Club. In its early days membership required owning a sailboat that floated at least 15 minutes.

Public access to shore is limited to several road ends and a small, newly acquired Bainbridge Island park, T'Ch-oo-Kwap Park, described below.

Road ends provide an opportunity to row ashore and walk along a road for a bit. The easiest to find is at Lafayette Avenue, just north of the Port Madison Community Club dock. From the water a short trail can be seen through the brambles. At the road end there's a plaque with a photo of the old Port Madison Mill and historical background of the harbor. The park department has put intriguing reader boards with historical information at various other viewpoints on the island.

"The giant green frog"

There are plenty of roads to walk in this beautiful area. Hike to Fay-Bainbridge State Park, or around various loop roads. Be sure and hunt for the giant green frog at an intersection on the east side.

Other accesses on the north side of the harbor are at Broom Street and Gordon Lane. You really need an island map to locate these places. Maps are available in Winslow.

T'Ch-oo-Kwap Park is the new Bainbridge Island park just east of the Seattle Yacht Club outstation and is adjacent to the corner road-end of Spargur Loop Road.

The Bainbridge Island Park Department plans to develop the 80 foot waterfront park with lawns, picnic tables, a trail and/or steps to the beach so local residents can get to the beach, kayaks can be launched, and visitors can dinghy ashore. A dinghy dock is in future park plans.

The view from atop the bank looks across the harbor and north through the entrance channel, across the big bay all the way to the Indianola bluffs.

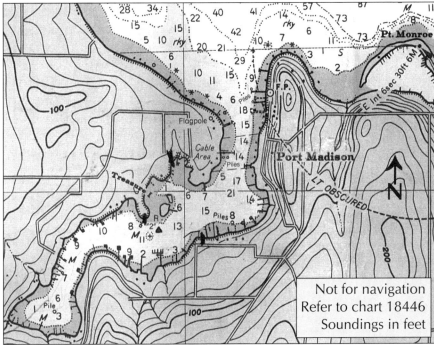

Port Madison Harbor chart

At last—there will be good public access in Port Madison. Island residents and recreational boaters very much appreciated the foresight of the park planners.

One Way to Join the Port Madison Yacht Club

Winsome—nearly 70 feet from bowsprit to mizzen boom—was usually moored to a buoy in front of Carl's family house when they lived in Port Madison.

During a Port Madison Pram race one day, Carl was sailing *Winsome* inside the little harbor and managed to come about onto a port tack exactly across and blocking the entire length of the finish line just as a gaggle of prams approached the line. Other choices were to sail *Winsome* onto the beach or crash into nearby docks and floats.

The sailor in each approaching pram, all close-hauled on starboard tacks, each looking astern at the competition, oblivious to the situation. Except in the last pram. He was looking where he was going. His large grin made everyone else suspicious. Their heads turned like a row of dominos, followed by instant panic, and they all jibed to miss *Winsome*. Everyone escaped colliding. No damage done.

All of which lead to Carl's honorary induction in the PMYC, acquisition of a Port Madison pram, family participation in subsequent races—and the layout of the finish line.

Rumor Has It ... Many years ago a collection of loud, obnoxious pleasure boaters would consistently arrive, anchor and raft up in Port Madison, with drunken partying.

At dusk one evening some local lads swam to the rafted group on the start of an ebb, pushing a good-sized log ahead of them. Reaching the rafted boats they quietly raised the anchor off the bottom, tied it to the log and swam silently to shore.

The raft was last seen in the moonlight gently drifting out of the harbor on the ebb and a south wind. None of those boats ever returned to Port Madison. There may be a message here.

Locals sailors know there is "dead air" in the stretch between Port Madison and Point Monroe for a fair distance north of the island. Sailors keep farther north to keep out of the doldrums.

> **Note: If you do go ashore,** please keep pets and kids under control and respect and keep off the private property of others.

Port Madison entrance looking north

On our first sailing date, we short-tacked **Scheherazade** *against a southerly wind into Port Madison at low tide. It can be done–it's called "local knowledge." Carl had lived in Port Madison for a number of years and knew how far we could push our luck on each tack.*

We didn't go aground, and we're still together!

Ballast rocks were offloaded from empty lumber ships and schooners arriving to load lumber from the prolific Port Madison Lumber Mill for delivery to worldwide ports between the 1850s and 1890s.

⊕ Approaching Port Madison Harbor

The chart, tide table and depth sounder are the best guides as we approach the channel in Port Madison.

From Agate Pass, the three fathom curve is about 200 yards north of the Agate Point shoreline. We roughly follow this depth curve until the top of the 900 foot nub on the northeast shore of the entrance is dead ahead, a little over one mile, following that course until we are a bit east of a line looking straight through the channel entrance. At that point we head into the channel.

From the east side of Bainbridge, the heavy shoreline development at Point Monroe is more obvious than the daymark or Point Monroe light. A depth curve of three fathoms runs 200 yards off the northeast and north shorelines of the point.

From here we proceed west, pick up the three fathom depth curve north of the rounded point on the east side of the entrance channel and follow this curve south into the entrance.

A submerged rock is about 100 yards off the rounded point and is inshore of the three fathom curve.

From the north, Point Monroe and its light will be to port as we head south toward the 140 foot nub, on the northeast side of the entrance. Although unlighted, the hill can usually be seen and identified even at night.

We stay clear of the submerged rock northwest of the rounded east entrance.

Entering Port Madison Harbor channel, the **main channel depths** of 14 to 18 feet are charted. The exact channel width at low tide at the charted depths is not known. The channel shoals appreciably toward the shore on either side of the charted depths. (Charted depths indicate depths at the precise location and time of the survey.)

Depths of six feet or less extend about 200 yards to the northwest on the west side of the entrance. We favor the east shore when entering or leaving the harbor.

Submerged ballast rocks along the channel's east shore extend to approximately the outer ends of piers, causing abrupt shoaling. Herons patrol the tide flats.

About 100 yards south of the Port Madison Community dock, the harbor opens up and we're through the channel and into the harbor.

The chart, tide table and depth sounder are the best guides into this lovely gunkhole. It's quite shallow along the west shore.

Treasure Island is sometimes a tombolo—an island joined to land at low tide. Just south of the island is (unlighted) red triangular beacon "2" to starboard marking the rock shoal.

Continue into the harbor and in about 0.2 mile into **Hidden Cove** in the southwest end of the harbor. Depth is one fathom or less, mud bottom.

⚓ **Anchor** in the center in this well protected, delightful little gunkhole, if the tide and draft permit. Homes ring the shore and all beaches are private.

> ### Keel Tracks
> Years after Carl moved back to Seattle from Bainbridge, he was returning from a New Year's cruise to Port Gamble following a long, hard thrash to weather he anchored *Zade* temporarily in Port Madison. This was before he had radar.
>
> When he later pulled the hook on that black, windy, rainy night, he decided Christmas lights on a nearby residence near the entrance would serve as a "local private" aid to navigation.
>
> *(continued on page 99)*

He ducked back under the dodger, turned off the spreader lights and, peering through rain splattered glasses and windshield, headed for the colored lights.

Later he noticed the lights were not getting closer, checked the depth sounder and discovered that *Zade* had eased her way onto the mud. Confident about the choice of Christmas lights as navigating aids, and concerned about avoiding unlighted boats at anchor, he hadn't checked the depth sounder or compass.

Turns out there were **two** houses with similar Christmas lights. *Zade* had swung about 90 and headed toward the house in the tiny bay northeast of Treasure Island—right onto the mud—instead of into the entrance channel.

The engine could not back *Zade* off. Loading anchor and chain into the skiff, trailing the anchor line, he rowed to deep water, lowered the anchor and returned to *Zade*. With the engine and anchor winch he kedged off—more or less standard operating procedure—and sailed back to Seattle.

Port Madison History

Long before the pioneers arrived there was a Native American village in Port Madison. The flat point lying opposite the old landing was called, "Where Corpses are Put." The deceased were put in boxes and placed in trees (T.T. Waterman).

In the winter of 1854-55, the Indians who lived in Port Madison helped George Meigs assemble the sawmill machinery which he moved from his earlier location in Kingston. The founding of the mill was the beginning of non-Native settlements and industry on Bainbridge Island.

An 1857 census showed 19 white men on the island; average age was 25 and occupations were all mill-related. By 1860, there were ten families and more than 100 employees in the mill or logging the island. Port Madison was the county seat of Kitsap County until 1893 when voters chose Port Orchard. The village had a general store, school, blacksmith and carpenter shops, brass and iron foundry and a machine shop. A hotel was built, but later burned.

A shipbuilding center was on the west side of the harbor and 29 ships had been built there by 1890. Largest was a four-masted schooner named *Zampa*.

A mill was established at Port Blakely at the south end of Bainbridge in 1864, and by the turn of the century the once busy Port Madison mill was shut down. A summer colony was planned in its place, mill cottages were torn down and lots sold. Wealthy Seattleites spent summers in the harbor, often sailing over in their yachts.

Over the years Port Madison has gradually changed from a summer community to year-round residences.

⎈ **Underway again,** we leave Port Madison harbor and head east toward Point Monroe.

In Chapter 6 we go south from Point Monroe along Bainbridge and then west through Rich Passage, finding towns, marinas and gunkholes on the east and south shores of Bainbridge Island.

Jo recalls: *Despite many summers at Indianola, I had never sailed into Port Madison until the summer of 1965, the year we built an El Toro—an eight-foot sailing pram. I even built the sail. I joined the first annual Bullship Race from Shilshole to Bainbridge, nearly six miles away.*

That was back in the days when the race was divided into men's and women's classes.

I sat in the hot sun on the cold, cramped bottom of that little boat, trying to catch every bit of wind possible; tossed about by large waves from nearby ships, along with the other 50 or so competitors, wondering why on earth I was submitting myself to such nonsense. Several fast chase boats whisked around the outside edges of our little fleet, making sure we were all safe and well cared for.

They tossed us cans of beer as we pressed on toward the finish line, which I couldn't even see.

However, I followed the only boat that was ahead of me, sailed by a man, and lo and behold we crossed the finish line— near that buoy outside the entrance to the harbor in Port Madison—just about together. Somehow, I was the first woman to finish! I guess I'm just as glad that back then we weren't quite equal, otherwise I'd have been in second place. This way I was first among women!

It was a great race, but once was enough. The following year I deferred to son John, who raced the same boat with the same sail and won in the junior division.

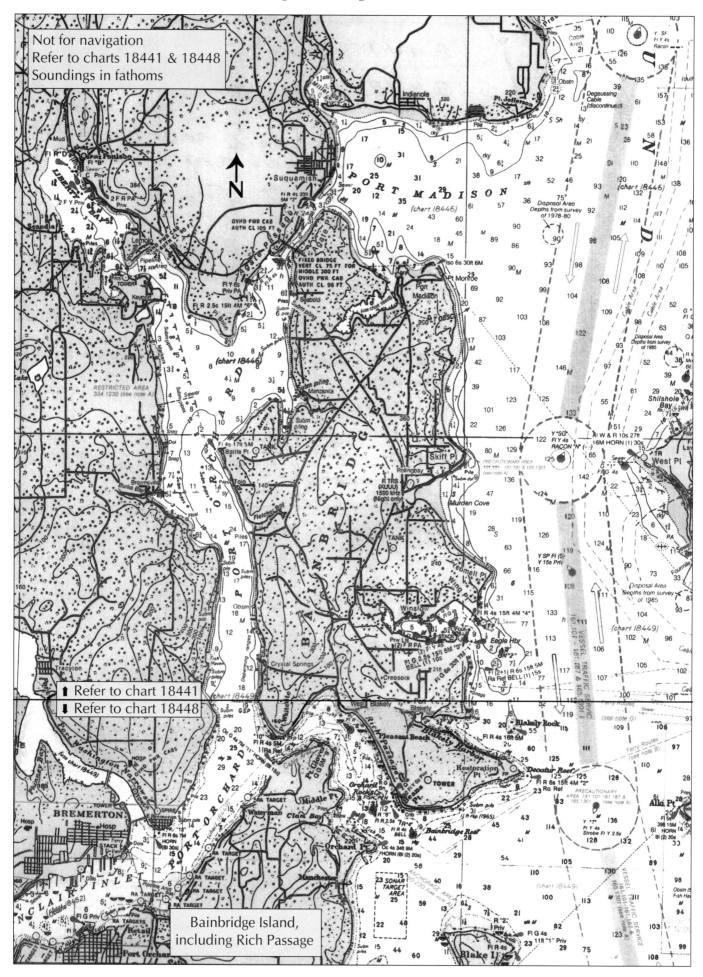

Not for navigation
Refer to charts 18441 & 18448
Soundings in fathoms

⬆ Refer to chart 18441
⬇ Refer to chart 18448

Bainbridge Island,
including Rich Passage

CHAPTER 6
Exploring Bainbridge Island, including Rich Passage

Charts and publications for this chapter

	Chart	Date	Title	Scale	Soundings
***	**18446**	06/16/90	Puget Sound, Apple Cove to Keyport, Agate Pass	1:25,000	.... Feet
***	**18449**	10/29/94	Puget Sound, Seattle to Bremerton	1:25,000	.... Feet
**	**18473**	08/14/93	Puget Sound, Oak Bay to Shilshole	1:40,000	...... Fathoms
**	**18474**	03/25/95	Puget Sound, Shilshole Bay to Commencement Bay	1:40,000	...... Fathoms
*	**18445**	06/03/95	Puget Sound—Possession Sound to Olympia, page A	1:80,000	...... Fathoms
			page B, inset 2, Agate Pass and inset 3, Eagle Harbor	1:25,000	...... Fathoms
*	**18441**	02/18/95	Puget Sound—Northern Part	1:80,000	...... Fathoms
*	**18448**	10/30/93	Puget Sound—Southern Part	1:80,000	...... Fathoms
	18440	08/05/95	Puget Sound	1:150,000	.... Fathoms
			Tidal Current Charts, Puget Sound, Northern Part		
			Booklet: Puget Sound Shellfish Site		
			Washington State Public Lands Quad map—Seattle	1:100,000	

➡ *When using charts, compare your chart dates with ones referred to above. There may be discrepancies between different charts and different chart editions.*

The City of Bainbridge Island, an Overview

Lush greenery, often hiding old cabins nestled in the woods, is slowly falling victim to the influx of development on Bainbridge—a 10 mile long island-city across the Sound from Seattle—about 2.5 miles away at the closest and six miles by ferry.

More than 17,200 residents live along the shores, in the forests and inland meadows in remodeled cabins and farmhouses, or in large new homes and condos.

While nearly half the working population commutes daily by ferry to Seattle—light years and attitudes away—the other half work in island businesses, cross the Agate Pass Bridge to jobs in Kitsap Peninsula communities, or work in at-home businesses, telecommuting with the outside world.

Each morning thousands of island and peninsula commuters board the ferries for the 30-minute trip to downtown Seattle. The vessels disgorge them back on the island in the evening, a testimony to the number of people who readily juggle the more relaxed island (or peninsula) life-style with frenetic workdays of the big city.

Bainbridge long has enjoyed the reputation of upscale island living. It has attracted well-to-do retirees and young professionals who want a less harried, less polluted life-style than can be found in the city. Even so, modern day spray-painted pictographs are emerging in public places for future archeologists to decipher.

This once rural island of small rapidly growing communities—there are more than twice as many island residents in the mid-1990s as in 1970—transformed itself into a city by a narrow vote in 1991. Islanders wanted more control over land use and growth policies which formerly had been under the control of Kitsap County.

Bainbridge has many attractions for recreational mariners, including marinas, moorages, services, supplies, protected harbors in Eagle Harbor and Port Blakely, road-end public access and sheltered anchorage in Port Madison and Manzanita Bay, and two large state parks with buoys for boaters. We'll point out several parcels of state-owned public tidelands as we cruise the east and south shorelines.

➡ **NOTE: No marine fuel** is available in the areas covered in this chapter.

Bainbridge Island Historical Museum

Carl recalls: Before developments on the Point Monroe sandspit and lagoon, Miller Bay sandspit, Port Madison, Jeff Head and other spots, these were the haunts of a rag-tag bunch of teen-aged guys with their mixed group of sailboats. (Somehow we missed Jo, who was growing up just across from us at Indianola.)

As we got older, boats got larger, girls and wives joined the group and babies appeared. Later the kids arrived with their own boats and began to show up on annual New Year's cruises to Port Ludlow, Port Gamble and elsewhere.

This started out as the Clam Bay Cruising Club, then the Pipe and Bottle Club and later became the Essex County Country Club.

We anchored in the bight just west of Monroe sand spit, and went ashore many times on beaches which are now private.

Onshore is Bloedel Reserve, where beautiful botanical gardens attract thousands annually, Bainbridge Performing Arts Center, Bainbridge Island Winery, churches, a community swimming pool and more. Winslow is filled with boutiques, bookstores, shops, restaurants, liquor store, post office, markets, hardware and other stores.

One of our favorite places is the Bainbridge Island Historical Society and Museum. The restored 1908 Island Center School in Strawberry Hill Park has photos, artifacts, videos and friendly docents who will interpret island history, folklore, archeology, cultural diversity, architecture and the natural wonders that are Bainbridge. The gift shop offers books, maps, shirts, collector's edition coffee mugs and more. Curator Jerry Elfendahl knows the island and its history intimately.

The museum is open from May to October on Saturdays and Sundays, 1 to 4 p.m., or by appointment. It's 1.5 miles west of Highway 305 at 7650 N.E. High School Road. Phone: 206-842-2773

For a time in the mid-1800s Bainbridge boasted the world's largest sawmill at Port Blakely. The lumber industry was immense, tall-masted sailing ships jammed the small bay, loading lumber for deliveries around the world.

Up until the 1940s when Japanese-Americans were interned during World War II, Japanese farmers had transformed the island economy with their extraordinary farming techniques; strawberries were the main crop. They grew vegetable delicacies in their fields and greenhouses such as lettuce, tomatoes and cucumbers, flowers, included lilies, chrysanthemums and geraniums. The island is still known today for its fabulous strawberry crops.

⚓ **Underway again,** and we start cruising at the northeast corner of Bainbridge at Point Monroe. We head south along the island's eastern shore past Fay-Bainbridge State Park, visit Eagle Harbor and Winslow, go into a favorite moorage at Port Blakely, swing around the south end of the island and go through Rich Passage. (In Chapter 5 we explored the north shore of Bainbridge and the harbor of Port Madison and we cover the western shore in Chapter 7.)

ISO 6s 30ft 6M Point Monroe Light, is an equal interval 6 second light, 30 feet high, visible for six miles, with a green and white diamond dayboard on a tower. The light is obscured from 321° to 089°. It's sometimes difficult to distinguish at night amid the lights of surrounding homes.

Point Monroe Light

The "point" actually hooks west and around back toward the island, almost surrounding a shallow lagoon. The land is crammed with cabins and beach houses which either face the Sound or into the lagoon. Many cabins have been remodeled into permanent homes on no bank waterfront lots.

Fay-Bainbridge State Park is immediately south of the homes at Point Monroe. It's easy to spot from the water: no houses, log-strewn, no-bank shoreline with two mooring buoys just offshore. If the wind pipes up or there's large wake from passing ships this can be a lumpy place to spend the night. Use caution when approaching the buoys, as one buoy is charted in about two feet of water.

⚓ **Anchoring** is possible off the park. A narrow shelf drops off sharply from about one to about eight fathoms.

Fay-Bainbridge Park land was bought in 1944 from the Temple S. Fay estate. There was a stipulation that State Parks preserve the name Fay, who taught at the University of Washington.

The park is well loved by island residents who enjoy the peace and quiet. This is the only overnight campground on Bainbridge Island. There's plenty to do at this nearly 17 acre park—including beachcombing the lovely, sandy beach and swimming in the chilly waters; no lifeguards.

Fay-Bainbridge Park Facilities
- ➤ Two mooring buoys
- ➤ 1,420 foot sandy beach
- ➤ Restrooms with showers
- ➤ 36 campsites
- ➤ Picnic tables, shelters and fireplaces
- ➤ Telephone
- ➤ Volleyball, horseshoes
- ➤ Kids' play equipment
- ➤ Trailer dump
- ➤ Phone: 206-842-3931

About 8,000 feet of public tidelands are covered in this chapter.

Public tidelands, unless otherwise noted, are state owned. Some may be leased and posted for aquaculture or other private use. We take the Washington State Public Lands Quadrangle Map, when going ashore to avoid trespassing on private property.

On warm sunny days you can sit with your back against a big drift log and let your fingers and toes sift through the warm sand, scattered with bits of shells and tiny pebbles—making for great relaxing.

Launch ramp at the north end of the beach had a warning sign in 1995 that it was unusable, covered with logs and sand. While State Parks had planned to repair the ramp, that project has been put on hold. Our latest information is that due to the slope of the beach and high rate of sand accretion, it is neither practical nor cost effective to construct and maintain a ramp here. But you can hand-carry kayaks or small boats across the logs to the beach if you don't mind a bit of a scramble.

Fay-Bainbridge "launch ramp"

⚙ **Underway again,** continuing south from the park the shore is private, except for some state-owned public tidelands. We'll point them out as we go.

Public tidelands of about 2,300 feet south is about 2,000 feet south of Fay-Bainbridge, accessible by water.

The east shores of Bainbridge are a mix of bluffs, banks and no-bank waterfront, with homes tucked among the evergreens. Across the sound to the east are fabulous scenes of Seattle and the Cascades, with Mount Rainier to the south and Mount Baker to the north—providing it's a clear day.

East across the Sound is the dense "forest" of sailboat masts at Shilshole Marina just north of the entrance to the Ship Canal and the locks.

Large ships are constantly traveling up and down the Sound, staying in their invisible marine highway in the VTS lanes.

"Port Madison Bell" in Fay-Bainbridge Park was bought by the community in the mid-1800s to be used by the town crier for important events. It was to be installed in the new school, but when Port Madison became the county seat in 1857 and had to have a court house fast, the school building was converted and the bell was put on the building. The bell was moved to the park in 1953.

Port Madison Bell

Vancouver Missed Out

Captain Vancouver and his vessels passed this way in 1792, but didn't stop until they reached the south end of Bainbridge for their rendezvous with the Chatham, Commander, Lt. William Broughton.

Vancouver did not specifically describe this area, but he wrote of the region: "To describe the beauties of this region, will, on some future occasion, be a very grateful task to the pen of a skilful (sic) panegyrist. The serenity of the climate, the innumerable pleasing landscapes, and the abundant fertility that unassisted nature puts forth, require only to be enriched by the industry of man with villages, mansions, cottages, and other buildings, to render it the most lovely country that can be imagined; whilst the labour of the inhabitants would be amply rewarded, in the bounties which nature seems ready to bestow on cultivation."

About 1.5 miles south of Point Monroe are erratic rocks off the abrupt shoreline bulge charted on 18446 and 18473, about halfway to Skiff Point. The shoreline climbs to a 200 foot high steep bank along here. We pass **Rolling Bay,** a residential area, on the way. **Skiff Point** follows, with its low yellow bluffs, and then high bank.

Depths, oddly, drop steeply at the point with the five fathom curve only 100 yards off the northeast shore of Skiff Point.

Capt. Vancouver also named many of the geographic points after his friends and shipmates, replacing the names already in use by the area's Native Americans.

The awesome panorama south and east from Bainbridge extends from Alki Point east past Duwamish Head, north past the Elliott Bay waterfront and Seattle skyline, with the tall masts of hundreds of sailboats moored at Elliott Bay Marina silhouetted below Magnolia Bluff and West Point.

Skiff Point is about 2.5 miles west of West Point; Restoration Point is about 2.5 miles west of Alki Point. With the exception of the water flowing through Rich Pass and Agate Pass, all tidal water flowing to and from South Sound passes through these constricted channels.

➠ **Time to switch charts from 18446 to 18449, and/or from 18473 to 18474.**

Native American legend is that Yeomalt Point is where North wind and South wind had a fight. North wind was chased out of the Duwamish River valley and fled to Yeomalt. The final battle took place here—that's why the big sea is here all the time.

The Native American name is "Fighter's Home." They also called Wing Point "Gradually Falling Promontory."

➠ **Strip chart 18445, has an inset of Eagle Harbor, page B, scale 1:25,000.**

East of the point a kelp-covered shoal extends about 250 yards from the shore and is apparently gradually increasing.

VTS buoy Y "SG" Fl Y 4s flashing yellow 4 second light and strobe flashing yellow 2.5 second light mark the center of the VTS lanes 1.5 miles east of Skiff Point. The **VTS southbound lane** western boundary and precautionary area are just 0.7 mile east of Skiff Point shoal.

Skiff Point—Local Knowledge

Carl recalls: Years ago I was sailing with a salt-encrusted old friend during a Port Madison Yacht Club race when the skipper sailed his 38 foot cutter aground at Skiff Point after rejecting his wife's protestations of being "too close to shore." Trying to prove his point he proved hers instead.

By the time we wiggled off the shoal and returned to the Point Monroe finish line the committee boat, *Unamae*, had retired.

Approaching Port Madison harbor a bit west of the entrance, as skip's wife and I were getting the sail down, we both warned him about shallow water—just before the boat ran aground again, proving yet another point. He started the engine, backed the boat off the shallows and headed into Port Madison. The engine coughed, spluttered and was out of gas. We hoisted sail once again and sailed into the club floats. Disasters were over for the day. Before the race started his wife had asked if they had enough gas. Sound familiar? There are days when pobody's nerfect. This was not skip's day—we all take our turn.

Public tidelands of five parcels, each about 1000 feet, are along this north shore of **Murden Cove** at **Manitou Beach.**

Rounding Skiff Point in deep water, we set a course for **Yeomalt Point,** past Murden Cove. The cove, about 3.5 miles south of Point Monroe, is shoal nearly 0.5 mile offshore and islanders term it a "terrible anchorage." A waterfront road runs along the beach and radio towers of FM station KUUU are charted above the shore.

Ahead, Seattle-to-Winslow ferries appear and disappear from behind Yeomalt Point going to and from Eagle Harbor.

We've been skirting the eastern shore of Bainbridge—as close as we dare—partly out of curiosity about this area, and it keeps us out of the southbound VTS lane 0.6 mile east of Yeomalt Point. We pass within 200 yards of the point in about 35 feet of water. The point is a low sandspit about 150 yards wide.

Tyee Shoal is a major concern after passing Yeomalt Point. It is now ahead as we proceed south. A course plotted on a line between Yeomalt and Restoration Points would put us in about four feet of water about 0.9 mile south of Yeomalt Point, which we don't want to do; it shoals rapidly in places.

However, by staying east of a straight line touching the east tips of Skiff and Yeomalt Points and projected to Tyee Shoal, we will maintain at least a two fathom depth. We use compass courses when we must—we'd rather watch the scenery.

Wing Point is next on the north shore of Eagle Harbor. The point has a narrow bluff about 30 feet high with a prominent flagpole. A shoal extends south-southeast for 0.5 mile from Wing Point. It is generally marked by kelp—and red nun buoy "2."

Eagle Harbor and Winslow

This is a destination for many recreational boaters. There are a number of private and public moorages, plus anchorages, in the harbor.

Marine traffic seldom ceases in Eagle Harbor where jumbo Washington State Ferries arrive and depart from the terminal here 24 times daily—nearly around the clock except for about three hours early in the morning. It is also the site of the large ferry maintenance shipyard.

Winslow is the hub of Bainbridge Island. It is the home of the island government and everything else that goes with a small city.

Winslow has everything within just a few blocks: restaurants, shops, supermarket, post office, banks, a hardware store carries marine items, boutiques, bookstores, a chandlery and liquor store. A laundromat is several blocks away, north on Madison Avenue. There is taxi service on the island to get you around.

The island has a plethora of activities from concerts to little theater to sports events all year round. Each spring it hosts the well-known "Chilly Hilly" bike ride around the island's hills, and there are many.

⚓ **Anchoring** in Eagle Harbor is popular in from four to six fathoms, mud bottom. There are a number of liveaboards who anchor in the harbor.

A cruise around the harbor is extremely interesting. A fair number of creatively designed floating habitations are scattered throughout the bay.

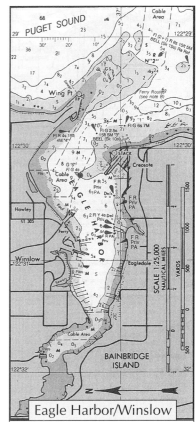

Not for navigation
Refer to chart 18445,
page B, inset 3
Soundings in fathoms

Shop Talk

We visited with Bainbridge Island Parks and Recreation director Chuck Fields and with City Police Chief John Sutton to discuss marine-related problems and water-accessible parks and road ends.

There are buoys in Eagle Harbor for the fairly large anchored liveaboard population. The city recognizes those people as living a legitimate alternative life-style—aboard some very interesting looking vessels. We think the tolerant attitude is great—and unusual.

The island police department has one marine officer who responds to calls with a 19 foot runabout. Most problems the harbor patrol division manages are usually in the summer. They include jet skiers, speeding boats, stolen dinghies, garbage complaints, boats washed up on the rocks on the south end of the island and vandalism.

The police chief said the harbor patrol program was controversial when the island first became a city. They couldn't get a grant for a patrol boat, so the marine officer did his patrolling on a jet ski. When authorities saw the officer responding to calls on the fast little machine, they gave the department a grant for a REAL boat.

In Spring 1996, the Bainbridge Island City Council passed a new speed ordinance.

"(1) Speed limit for all watercraft throughout Eagle Harbor shall be no greater than five knots per hour from buoy #5 at the east end of Eagle Harbor westward to the end of the harbor, except that during the month of May through September 15, between the hours of 7 a.m. and 7 p.m., but not before sunrise or after sunset, this speed may be exceeded by boats 16-26 feet in length, occupied by at least two persons while towing a 3rd person on one or two water skis.

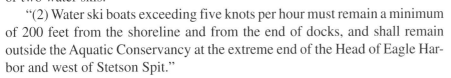

Winslow waterfront, ferry landing on right

"(2) Water ski boats exceeding five knots per hour must remain a minimum of 200 feet from the shoreline and from the end of docks, and shall remain outside the Aquatic Conservancy at the extreme end of the Head of Eagle Harbor and west of Stetson Spit."

North Shore Moorages

Eagle Harbor Waterfront Park, the first moorage on the north shore after passing the ferry terminal and the shipyards, has a 225 foot long guest float managed by the City of Bainbridge Island.

"Custom" accommodations afloat Bainbridge style

In the winter of 1996, the city installed a Linear Mooring System southwest of the waterfront park dock on a trial basis. The new system features a 200 foot taut line on each side of three "floating fence posts," interspersed with fenders and tie-up rings. The system can be easily moved and is marketed as using far less space than buoys and docks while offering increased mooring capability.

Fees are 25 cents per foot per day, the same as at the public dock.

The system, created by a local company, Ocean Spar Technologies, is based on their aquaculture net pen technology which has withstood continuous waves of 20 feet and currents of three knots during testing, they say.

Eagle Harbor Waterfront Park Facilities

➤ Room for eight to 10 boats, rafting is permitted
➤ Moorage rate 25 cents per foot per day, two day limit, pay station near the head of the float
➤ Pump-out station on outer end of float
➤ No water or power
➤ Restrooms without showers
➤ Pay phones, picnic tables and fireplaces
➤ Easy walking access to town and all amenities
➤ Single lane concrete launch ramp immediately west of float
➤ Great play area, tennis courts
➤ Phone: 206-842-2545

Eagle Harbor Waterfront Park public moorage float

The public guest float at the waterfront park has a zero tide mark painted on it so we have some idea of the tide range. Dinghies tie on the east side of the float in shallow water.

The park is an eight acre forested and grassy wonderland in the heart of the city. About 1,000 feet of waterfront are open to the public. Tennis courts, a kids' play area, and an outdoor stage are in the park, with a footpath above the beach leading to the ferry terminal. In the summer there are occasional concerts in the park.

Queen City Yacht Club outstation for members only is west of the public dock.

Winslow Wharf Marina, the next moorage with a large sign on the outside pilings, is a condominium moorage, but there is almost always room for visiting boats in open condo slips.

Winslow Wharf Marina Facilities

➤ Guest moorage space varies
➤ Moorage rates per night are by slip size: under 24', $14; 28-32', $17; 36-38', $21; boats over 38' are $26
➤ 20-30 amp power, water included
➤ Off-hours register at the outer end of B float
➤ Office is on shore at the head of the ramp between B and C floats
➤ Restrooms with showers, laundry facility, pump-out station
➤ Monitors VHF Channel 09
➤ Phone: 206-842-4202

This is a great location and the folks here have a great attitude. It helps to phone ahead for a slip. Manager is Brenda Plantz.

The Chandlery is the only marine store on the island, located at the head of the ramp of Winslow Wharf Marina.

Harbour Marina and The Harbour Public House are west of Winslow Wharf. No overnight guest moorage, but complimentary moorage if you visit the pub for food or drink. It's in a charming old house built in 1881 by Amanda and Ambrose Grow, recently remodeled, using as much original structure and wood as possible. The Grows homesteaded a great deal of land in Eagle Harbor. A periscope is built into the men's restroom. There is jazz on weekends frequently. Phone manager Jocelyn Evans, 206-842-6502, for more information.

The Eagle Harbor Yard is the site of the former Isaac and Winslow Hall brothers' famous shipyard, which moved to Eagle Harbor from Port Blakely in 1902. The Hall Brothers' ship-building company and marine railway was a repair facility for a fleet of ships that carried northwest cargoes all over the world.

During World War II hundreds of men and women built minesweepers at the shipyard. The yard closed and was demolished in 1959.

The Eagle Harbor Yard usually has one or more Washington State ferries under repair.

Creosote Plant

Chuck Fields, Bainbridge Parks director, said the old Creosote plant on the west side entering the harbor—the Wyckoff property—is undergoing EPA "superfund" cleanup. The plant originally preserved poles and logs by wrapping them in burlap and asphalt. Tankers arrived from Europe with creosote oil and steamers came in to load the processed piles.

In 1988 a plan was developed with the EPA to clean up creosote and phenols which have contaminated soil and groundwater over decades of treatment operation. The government will take over the property and dispose of it and the park department hopes there will be some public access there eventually.

South Shore Moorages

The south shore moorages are across from the ferry terminal and shipyards.

East of the drying cove at the foot of Taylor Avenue is a public road end and a boat yard, almost directly across the harbor from the ferry terminal. The schooner *Adventuress* occasionally moors at this dock. One of the conditions of the dock development was to allow public access on the docks during working hours. So you can land at the dock and go ashore here—at least in the daytime.

Eagledale Moorings, next west, is private covered moorage with no guest floats.

Eagle Harbor Marina is the last moorage. Manager Dan Hornick says he doesn't really plan for guests but seldom turns anybody down. It's a condominium marina which allows some liveaboards.

*Schooner **Adventuress** at public access dock at Taylor Avenue*

Eagle Harbor Marina Facilities

➤ Guest moorage space varies
➤ Restrooms, shswers, laundry
➤ Exercise room, sauna and a clubhouse which can be rented out
➤ Phone: 206-842-4003 for more information

Dan says many of the guests are those who have been there before and like to return. As he points out, the marina is a 3-1/2 mile walk to downtown Winslow. You can dinghy across the harbor to the waterfront park dock for supplies.

⚓ **Entering Eagle Harbor,** larger vessels, including ferries, enter the harbor from south and west of Tyee Shoal, near the center of the channel.

Fl (2+1) R 6s 15ft 5M Ra Ref Bell Tyee Shoal light, a flashing red 6 second light 15 feet high on dayboard, with horizontal bands of red and green on a dolphin is visible for five miles.

Eagle Harbor floating home

A ferry skipper tried to pass between red nun buoy "2" and Tyee Shoal, only to find that with low tide it was too shallow for his vessel. The ferry, skipper, crew and passengers spent several hours waiting for high tide while TV helicopters hovered above, broadcasting the grounding to the whole region.

R N "2" red nun buoy "2" is about 400 yards north of Tyee Shoal. It's possible for small craft to pass between Tyee Shoal dolphin and buoy "2" as 2 fathoms are charted at low tide. We gradually swing north and follow the channel between the red and green marks into Eagle Harbor.

Fl G 6s 30ft 7M "1" Creosote Light 1, **a flashing green light** on a square green dayboard on a dolphin, is kept to port.

Fl G 2.5s 15ft 5M "3" bell Light 3 flashing green 2.5 second light at 15 feet, marks where we begin making the turn to port. A flagpole is charted on the starboard shore across from "3."

Fl R 4s 15ft 4M "4" Light 4 flashing red 4 second light on a red triangular dayboard on dolphin marks the northeastern edge of the channel.

G "5" Fl G 4s, Sandspit Light Buoy 5, visible four miles, is off the tip of the sandspit west of Creosote Point.

Creosote Point, between "3" and "5" gets as shallow as two to four feet at MLLW.

We continue turning to port, watching for ferry traffic. The ferry terminal is on the north shore with a couple of docks and large parking lot beyond. Condos, the ferry shipyard, a boat repair yard and the public park and wharf are along here.

Cable areas are at the harbor entrance, crossing either side of "2."

2 Fl Y 4s lights 15ft high on piles, are Bainbridge Island Boat Yard East and West Lights.

F R Priv PA lights identify private marinas. Four lights are charted on 18445 and 2 on 18474. Several privately maintained lights are along the south shore.

✴ **Underway again,** we leave Eagle Harbor heading out the way we came in, keeping green marks to starboard. Green buoy "5" is less obvious on the way out. That's a buoy we wouldn't want to visit.

From here to Blakely Harbor, about 1.5 miles south of Eagle Harbor, we leave Tyee Shoal to port and go south along the shoreline, keeping at least 300 yards offshore to avoid shallow water, erratic rocks, kelp and snags along the beach. This is Rockaway Beach community and homes line the shore .

Fl 4s 16ft 5M Blakely Rock Light, is a flashing light on a diamond shaped board with black and white sectors on the southeast side of the rock.

Blakely Rock is about 0.6 mile east of the harbor entrance, and about the same distance north of Restoration Point. This rock heap is about 200 yards long with kelp stringing around it. We give it a fairly wide berth on the north side as it's shoal for nearly 0.2 mile where a rock is awash at low tides.

Blakely Point, unnamed on the charts, is on the northeast side of the entrance. The point is foul for about 200 hundred yards offshore east of the point.

Blakely Harbor entrance is relatively clear, once past the northeast point and we can go virtually straight into the harbor. From the south or east, pass between Blakely Rock and Restoration Point, leaving room on either side.

The harbor is a mix of old and new homes, evergreen trees and cabins.

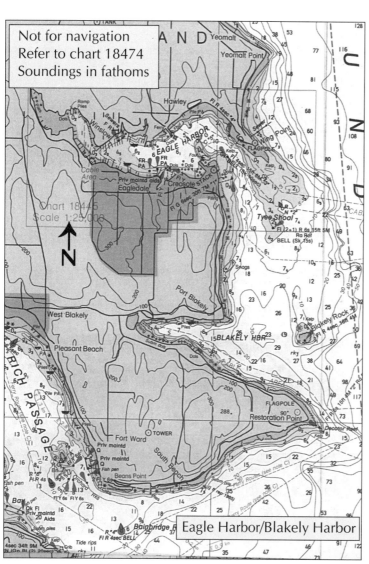

Not for navigation
Refer to chart 18474
Soundings in fathoms

Eagle Harbor/Blakely Harbor

The relics of the old Port Blakely Mill are at the head of the harbor, including an old concrete structure decorated with modern day pictographs and the remains of the dam that enclosed the holding pond, usually with tide water streaming in or out.

Ⓖ The view from here is spectacular. Looking east at night the lights of Seattle twinkle across the blackness. Here it's quiet and snug, a nearly **perfect gunkhole.** However, lest we get too carried away, the winds in Port Blakely

Blakely Rock at low tide

can be somewhat unpredictable. Not only that, Blakely Rock does not necessarily act as a breakwater from large ship wakes or waves caused by flukey winds. We have been wakened by the boat rolling in lumpy waves here several times.

Cable area in Port Blakely comes ashore at the northwest corner, far back in the harbor. The cable area sign on the beach is obscured at times by boats hauled out on the beach. The cable crossing area is used by some for limited public beach access.

The cable angles out through the center of the harbor, past the shallows on the southern shore, then follows along the shoreline as it trends southeasterly. When the cable area approaches Restoration Point it widens out, crossing the sound to Alki Point.

Looking east toward Seattle from inside Blakely Harbor

⚓ **Anchoring** is possible east of the cable area off the north shore in 25 to 50 feet, mud bottom. The south shore of the harbor bares at low tide for about 150 yards out.

We really like anchoring in Blakely Harbor. There's a contented ambiance, possibly because we can see the city without being there. Old stub pilings are along the beaches at the head of the bay, remnants of old wharves. There are a number of permanently anchored boats in here.

Port Blakely History

In 1863 the Port Blakely lumber mill started up. A 75 room hotel, houses, schools and orchards followed. A dam was built at the head of the harbor to form a log pond and dam remains are still there.

Square-rigged sailing schooners began carrying lumber to San Francisco and world ports at that time.

In 1881 the Hall Brothers built their shipyard in Port Blakely. In the next 22 years they built 77 vessels. They moved the yard to Winslow in 1902.

In 1889 the lumber mill burned and the "Great Mill" was built on the same Port Blakely site. In the next decade more than 200 houses were in the town at Port Blakely. Steam "donkeys" hauled timber, and a railroad track ran around the harbor. The mill employed over 1,000 workers from all over the world. In addition to a hotel, the town had a post office, two schools, a Masonic Temple, steamer service and a movie theater. By 1903 a Japanese community of more than 300 persons was on the south side of the harbor with a Buddhist temple, church, saloon, hotel, restaurant and bathhouses.

At extreme low tides there is a sandy shoal along the western side of Blakely Rock, complete with seals if no humans are around. At minus tides it's enjoyed by many who land small boats, dig clams or beachcomb. Blakely Rock is a favorite scuba diving spot where divers enjoy spear fishing, underwater photography and just plain watching marine critters.

"Sailing ships in Blakely Harbor, circa 1901" (Photo courtesy Bainbridge Island Historical Society)

World's largest mill: *It's almost impossible to imagine that at one time this little harbor was home to the largest sawmill in the world, and that lumber ships jammed the harbor from one side to the other—but, it's true.*

The Great Mill closed down in the 1920s and the area declined.

⚓ **Underway again,** we head south around Restoration Point to Rich Passage.

Restoration Point is the southeastern tip of Bainbridge. The point is private, a country club, with large, stately homes on shores where once the Suquamish Indians camped in meadows. The land tapers to low bank waterfront. A members' private pier is on the northwest shore.

Fl R 6s 15ft 4M "2" Ra Ref—Decatur Reef Light "2" flashing red 6 second light 15 feet high, visible 4 miles with a triangular red daybeacon and radar reflector on pile, is 200 yards offshore.

Restoration's 100 foot high bump drops to about 40 feet, steps up to about 260 feet and then to 420 feet about one mile west of the point. Here the island's south side becomes quite precipitous in the South Beach area.

Rocks are charted more than 200 yards offshore and a mile west of Restoration. **Public tidelands** extend from South Beach 3,000 feet to around Beans Point.

Group exploring old millpond dam with owners' permission

Plans by Port Blakely Mill Company *to develop the head of the bay with homes and condos, leaving 900 acres of open space and public beach access, are "on hold." The Bainbridge Park District is also interested in making a 20 acre public park at the head of the bay. One of these days there may be some access for islanders and visitors.*

Touch of History

The south shore of Bainbridge was the starting point of the exploration of South Puget Sound by Europeans. On May 20, 1792, Peter Puget and Joseph Whidbey, at the direction of Capt. George Vancouver, began their seven-day exploration in two small boats. In that one week they explored almost all of the passages, waterways and inlets in what is now recognized as South Sound.

They left from well offshore the South Beach area, west of Restoration Point. Vancouver stayed behind on Bainbridge, but left four days later in a ship's boat to survey the area and locate Puget's party.

While at Bainbridge, Vancouver visited the Suquamish tribe camped at Restoration Point. Some of the tribe were busy digging for wild onions and other roots, while others were curing clams, mussels and fish. Tribal Chief Schweabe's seven year old son, Sealth, later became one of the great chiefs of the northwest whose name will ever be remembered in the city named after him, Seattle.

(continued on next page)

> *Sealth said later that as a child he saw the great white-winged ships of Vancouver's expedition. There was an ancient legend that gods would appear in the future, and Suquamish Indians thought perhaps they had arrived in a giant canoe with white wings. Sealth often told others that Vancouver had invited his father and him aboard the Discovery. He thought that Vancouver recognized his father as a great leader and the boy as an heir to the leadership.*
>
> *Although he explored the region for 10 days, Vancouver never discovered that Bainbridge was an island. He actually named Restoration Point as Village Point because of the native camps. On his last day he renamed it in honor of England's celebration of Restoration Day.*

Replica of Peter Puget's launch

Rich Passage Overview

This sharp angular channel separates the southwest shore of Bainbridge Island from snoutlike Point Glover on the mainland shore of Kitsap Peninsula. It is the main deepwater passage connecting Puget Sound with Port Orchard channel, Bremerton, Port Orchard the city, Dyes Inlet, even Keyport and Poulsbo, and indeed to Agate Pass to the north.

Rich Passage is about three miles long, has a controlling depth of about 50 feet, and a least shore to shore width of 550 yards. It is relatively free from charted hazards, except for Bainbridge Reef in mid-channel at the eastern approach, and Orchard Rocks, on the north side just inside the east entrance.

Rich Passage Currents, from the *U.S. Coast Pilot*

Fastest extreme currents, based on **Current Charts,** may reach more than 5.4 knots during flood and 5.18 knots during ebb.

The *Coast Pilot* does an excellent job of describing Rich Passage currents, which are a major consideration in this pass, and we'll quote that book here.

"(Paragraph 352) Continuous observations in midchannel between Point Glover and Point White and at other points in the passage indicate that: Current velocities increase from east to west in Rich Passage reaching a maximum **average** velocity of 2.4 knots on the flood and 3.1 knots on the ebb at the west end off Point White. The strongest observed currents were 4 knots on the flood and 5 knots on the ebb. Ferry pilots on regular daily run between Seattle and Bremerton advised that on rare occasions they have experienced ebb currents of 'at least' 6 knots in the vicinity of light '10.'

"(353) Near the time of slack, the average period when the velocity does not exceed 0.2 knot is about 20 minutes. For strong currents these periods will be decreased; for weak currents they will be increased.

"(354) In the channel off Orchard Point, at the east end of Rich Passage, the velocity of the flood is 0.8 knot and on the ebb, 1.1 knots. Off Pleasant Beach the velocity of the flood is 1.3 knots and on the ebb, 2.8 knots.

"(355) On the flood, the lines of stream flow are nearly uniform except off the bight just northwest of Middle Point and in the large cove on the north shore opposite Point Glover. Eddies do form in those two places, but they do not extend outward to the usual vessel track. On the ebb, however, extensive eddies and counter-currents do occur, owing to the funnel-shaped configuration of the passage.

"(356) Between Middle Point and Point Glover, an extensive eddy extends from shore almost to mid-channel, and will frequently be encountered by vessels on the track between Orchard Rocks and Point Glover buoys.

"(357) An eddy fills the cove on the north shore opposite Point Glover, but does not extend outward to the vessel track.

"(358) An eddy occurs about 0.2 mile SSW of Point White and a little north of mid-channel at the west entrance to the passage. A weak counter-current occurs inshore along the southeast side of Point White.

"(359) These eddies and counter-currents on the ebb greatly diminish the effective width of the passage, and so increase the velocities in the channel.

(continued on page 114)

Rich Passage compared to Agate Passage

Agate Passage at the northwest end of Bainbridge Island is straight, about one mile long, controlling depth of about 21 feet, and has 300 yards least shore to shore width.

Its fastest extreme currents might reach 6.7 knots during flood and 6.58 knots during ebb.

Blakely Harbor *was named by Wilkes for Capt. Johnston Blakely, U.S.N., lost at sea in the War of 1812 with his ship* **Wasp**.

The earliest non-Native American settler *at Restoration Point on Bainbridge Island was Reuben Bean in 1854.*

In 1891 much of the property was sold to a group of Seattle yachtsmen who formed a private residential area called the Country Club.

The area became an exclusive summer colony for wealthy Seattleites, and large estates, tennis courts and a golf course were developed.

**TIDAL CURRENT CHARTS of
BAINBRIDGE & VICINITY**

Charts for Bainbridge Island area and points west
are for Chapters 6-8; including;
- *Rich and Agate Passages*
- *Entrance to Liberty Bay*
- *Port Washington Narrows*

Use *Tidal Current Table* predicted max flood or max
ebb speeds at Bush Point to select the factor for correcting the charted Tropic speeds.

For details and instructions on use of the factor for
correcting speeds using *Tidal Current Charts*, North
Puget Sound, see Appendix, p. 320.

These current charts are not for navigation, they are
for reference only.

Hourly charts of flood currents based on currents at Bush Point

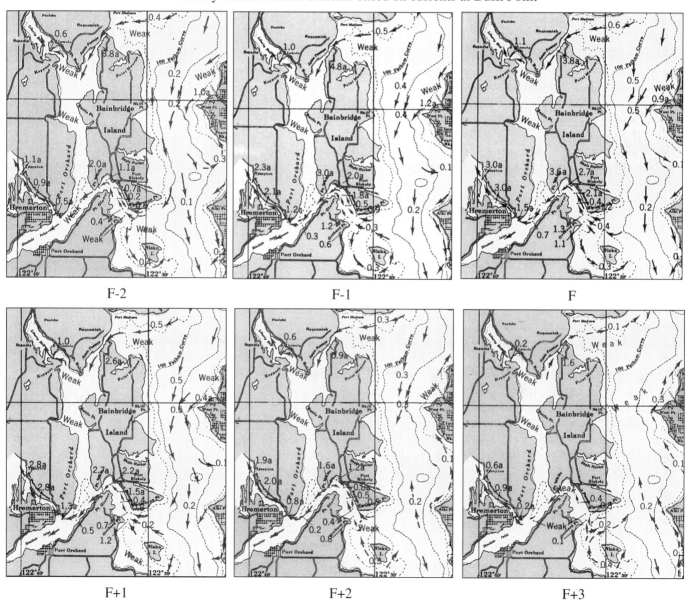

F-2   F-1   F

F+1   F+2   F+3

FLOOD FACTORS		Factors for Correcting Speeds	EBB FACTORS	

For use with speeds accompanied by solid arrows
When predicted "Maximum flood" speed (knots) off Bush Point is: / Multiply speed on chart by:

For use with speeds accompanied by dashed arrows
When predicted "Maximum ebb" speed (knots) off Bush Point is: / Multiply speed on chart by:

	Usual factor	Special Factor "a"		Factor
(*)	0.0	0.2	0.3-0.4	0.1
0.3	0.1	0.3	0.5-0.8	0.2
0.4-0.6	0.2	0.4	0.9-1.1	0.3
0.7-0.8	0.3	0.5	1.2-1.4	0.4
0.9-1.1	0.4	0.6	1.5-1.8	0.5
1.2-1.3	0.5	0.6	1.9-2.1	0.6
1.4-1.6	0.6	0.6	2.2-2.4	0.7
1.7-1.8	0.7	0.7	2.5-2.8	0.8
1.9-2.1	0.8	0.8	2.9-3.1	0.9
2.2-2.3	0.9	0.9	3.2-3.4	1.0
2.4-2.6	1.0	1.0	3.5-3.7	1.1
2.7-2.8	1.1	1.1	3.8-4.1	1.2
2.9-3.1	1.2	1.2	4.2-4.4	1.3
3.2-3.3	1.3	1.3	4.5-4.7	1.4
3.4-3.6	1.4	1.4		
3.7-3.8	1.5	1.5		

Hourly charts of ebb currents based on currents at Bush Point

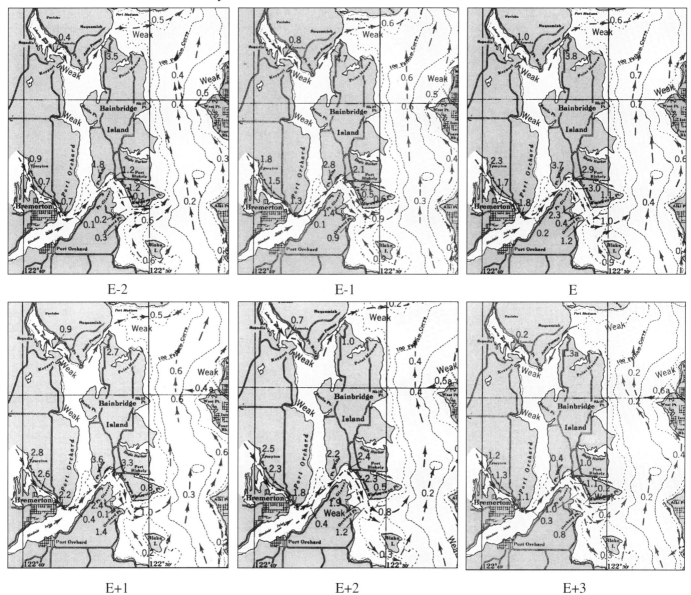

E-2   E-1   E

E+1   E+2   E+3

Toe Jam Hill Road is an almost straight road charted from Blakely Harbor to the south shore by way of a 1.3 (statute) mile-long stretch. The road reaches an elevation of almost 400 feet and then goes steeply back down again to sea level at South Beach.

The road was named for a saloon which purportedly served exceedingly poor liquor, scornfully called "Toe Jam." The saloon burned down, the name was immortalized, and the hill is low-gear steep on its southern slope.

(continued from page 111)

"(360) Strangers should not attempt to navigate Port Orchard, and particularly Rich Passage, in thick weather because of the strong tidal currents. In clear weather, however, the navigation of these waters presents no unusual difficulties.

"(361) **Caution**—Because of activities of the Puget Sound Naval Shipyard, (the) passage has a large volume of traffic. Many ferries a day each way, tugs with hawser tows, and various types of naval craft, all contribute to create a considerable collision hazard in the passage, particularly at the sharp bend off Point Glover.

"Strong tidal conditions prevail in this vicinity, and deep-draft outbound vessels making the sharp turn may be unavoidably set well over toward the east shore, necessitating a two-blast, starboard-to-starboard meeting with inbound vessels. Vessels approaching Point Glover from either direction should sound one long blast when within 0.5 mile of the point as a warning to any vessel approaching from the opposite direction."

Backeddies & Their Tide Rips as We Perceive Them

Rich Passage's convoluted bends, bumps, points and underwater contours combine with currents to create a complex challenge of backeddies and boils, in addition to the mainstream flow. Rich Passage has seven significant points or bulges and one sharp turn of 105°.

Backeddies are not always well-defined on current charts. They start to form at significant shoreline bends, bulges or points, after slack at the beginning of each current cycle, reaching their maximum current velocities near the mid-current cycle and diminishing to least velocity at next slack. Some residual inertia turbulence may be evident during the slack period before the reverse current cycle starts.

Downstream from large shoreline projections backeddies appear on the surface as tide rips which angle toward mainstream current.

Current flowing past the projection continuously drags with it water from behind that projection which lowers the water level immediately downstream of the projection.

Depending on the size and shape of the projection and velocity of the main current, a very large egg-shaped lethargic whirlpool is formed, which we term a backeddy.

Water nearest the shoreline downstream of the projection may in fact be flowing "downhill," that is, back toward the projection in the opposite direction to the mainstream current.

Viewing a tide rip from a boat—away from the shore—one side of the rip appears to be traveling in the opposite direction to the water on the other side of the rip. But, if anchored, we're most likely see the water on both sides of the rip are traveling in the same direction, but one side is traveling **faster** than the other.

However, we repeat, next-to-shore currents may be truly traveling in the opposite direction of the mainstream.

Rips and backeddy currents weaken and diminish further downstream, eventually joining and becoming part of the main currents.

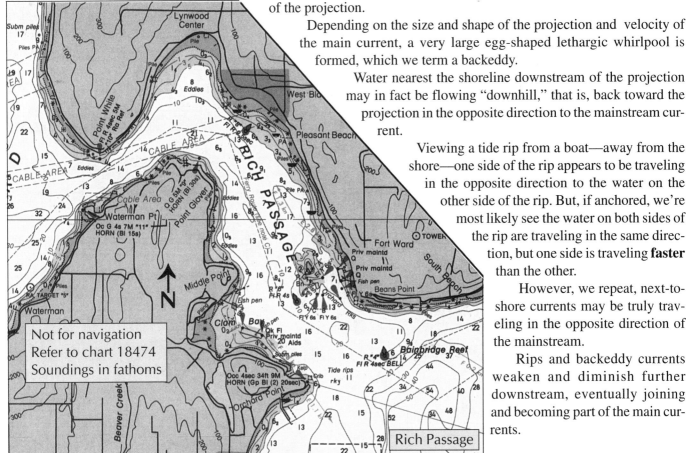

Not for navigation
Refer to chart 18474
Soundings in fathoms

For these reasons we stay in the mainstream well clear of the backeddies and rips. When traveling against the main flow we stay in backeddies as close to shore as possible.

Even without benefit of backeddies adverse currents are generally weaker nearest shore except in the long radius of a bend in the channel.

During both flood and ebb cycles, large backeddies are generated along the shore near significant shoreline projections. Thus water flows toward both sides of the bulges or points during either current cycle.

Vessel Traffic in Rich Passage

A mix of Washington State Ferries traverse the pass almost around the clock, making approximately 100 trips daily; plus tugs with tows, sometimes enormous navy ships, commercial ships of all sizes, and hundreds of recreational vessels. All suddenly appear or disappear behind Point Glover, and all need to steer courses to offset currents, avoid charted obstructions and each other.

Navigation is a major concern which increases exponentially with the size of vessel operating in this constricted channel. Throw in pea-soup fog and there are more problems. This is an exciting busy waterway, with strong currents and eddies, short chop and a lot of traffic.

Ferries in Rich Passage

Ferries have an excellent safety record, especially considering that they carry more than 20 million passengers each year.

On chart 18474, the ferry routes are shown with magenta dashed lines. But don't count on them being in exactly those routes. There is a cautionary note on the chart that ferries may deviate from the published route due to inclement weather, traffic conditions, navigational hazards or other emergencies.

Because of bends and currents it is sometimes hard to anticipate intentions of other vessels in Rich Passage. We try to stay clear of other vessels.

A brief review of Rules of the Road in constricted channels was included in Chap. 2, p. 38. We are not the authority on this matter, so please go to the source, ***U.S. Coast Guard Navigation Rules***, Rule 9, p. 20.

Thirsty anyone? It was an easy walk during early sawmill days, from Port Blakely to Pleasant Beach, on the northeast shore of Rich Passage.

As a result, many saloons prospered in the woods between the two communities.

Pleasant Beach was also the site of the first Kitsap County Fair in September 1900, and a favorite summer spot for riding bikes, swimming and bowling.

The ferry Kitsap ran aground on Point Glover in dense fog on September 18, 1996. No one was hurt, but there was over $300,000 damage to the vessel.

Ferries in Rich Passage

Rich Passage Navigation Aids

From Puget Sound, we enter Rich Passage on either side of Bainbridge Reef in mid-passage. We look first at navigation aids and then we cruise through the passage, describing what's onshore, crossing the passage several times. (Information on these navigation aids is taken from chart 18474, March 25, 1995, and ***Light List Volume VI, 1995.***)

R "4" Fl R 4s Bell, Bainbridge Reef Lighted Bell Buoy 4 (Light List #18030) flashing red 4 second red light visible 4 miles

Oc W 4s 34ft 9M Horn (Bl (2) 20s) Orchard Point Light (Light List #18035) occulting 4 second white light 34 feet high on white pyramidal concrete tower, visible 9 miles, horn which has 2 blasts every 20 seconds (2s bl-2s si-2s bl-14s si)

Fl Y 6s 4ft Clam Bay Fish Pen Lights (2) (Light List #18045) 2 flashing yellow 6 second lights charted 4 feet high, Light List height is 8 feet on pile, private aids.

R "6" Fl R 2.5s Orchard Rocks Lighted Buoy 6 (Light List #18040) flashing red buoy, 4 mile range, 0.2 mile south of Orchard Rocks, 0.3 mile west of Bainbridge.

(continued on next page)

Ferry problems: One of the few ferry collisions in more than 40 years took place in Rich Passage in dense fog on September 6, 1991, when two of the jumbo vessels crunched. While no one was injured, there was damage to both vessels. It seldom happens, but it can.

(continued from preceding page)

Fl Y 6s Rich Passage Fish Pen Lights (2) (Light List #18049) 2 flashing yellow lights on aquaculture facilities, private aids in Orchard Rocks area

Fl Y 6s Orchard Rocks Fish Pen Lights (3) (Light List #18050) 3 flashing yellow lights on aquaculture facilities, private aids in Orchard Rocks area

RG Bn Orchard Rocks Daybeacon (Light List #18055) dayboard bearing horizontal bands of red- green, red band top with red reflective border, SW side of Orchard Rocks

Fl Y 6s Beans Point Fish Pen Lights (2) (Light List #18065) 2 yellow flashing yellow lights 4 feet high on aquaculture facilities, private aids in Orchard Rocks area

R "8" Fl R 2.5s Lighted Buoy 8 (Light List #18065) red lighted buoy with 4 mile range is about 0.3 mile off West Blakely and Pleasant Beach on Bainbridge.

Q G 25ft 5M "9" Point Glover Light 9 (Light List #18070) quick green 4 second light 25 feet high mounted on square green dayboard with green reflective border visible 5 miles, with horn 1 blast every 30 seconds

Fl R 4s 5M "10" Ra Ref, Point White Light 10 (Light List #18075) flashing red 4 second light, visible 5 miles with radar reflector mounted on triangular red daybeacon on dolphin

Oc G 4s 26ft 7M "11" Horn (Bl 15s) Waterman Point Light 11 (Light List #18080) occulting green 4 second light, visible 7 miles, 26 feet high on square green dayboard on skeleton tower with horn blasts 1 blast every 15s (2s bl)

Near Point Glover there was a rock quarry in the early 1900s, called "Raven's Water" by local Native Americans.

A rock, now broken down, on the side of the bluff, looked like an "Indian dipper" or canoe bailer. This was said to have belonged to Raven in mythical times.

Orchard Rocks are a favorite spot for scuba divers who swim among pier piling and rocks. This is a good place for photography, spearfishing and just plain watching the marine wildlife swim past.

Fish pens near Orchard Rocks, looking west

Aquaculture, primarily salmon farming, is the second largest employer on Bainbridge Island.

Cruise through Rich Passage

⌖ Now that we've dealt with currents, traffic and navigation aids in Rich Passage, let's cruise through looking at what we may encounter along both shores.

Underway again, we enter the passage from Puget Sound and can pass on either side of Bainbridge Reef bell buoy "4."

Beans Point on Bainbridge and **Orchard Point** on the Kitsap Peninsula mark the east entrance to the passage.

Orchard Point is part of the oil storage area of the Puget Sound Naval Supply Center. There are some very heavy duty dolphin and offshore piling structures that are part of another portion of the Navy facility.

Clam Bay, just north around the point, is very shoal. There is no good place to anchor in the bay filled with charted fish pens.

Bainbridge Side

Beans Point on the east shore of the pass rises fairly steeply above the shore, and there is no marker. Here are remains of pilings, ruins, a shore battery, and old gun mounts, never used. Pier area with former military buildings is inshore of aquaculture.

Development becomes more dense along this coast with large white structures and riprap bulkheads belonging to the aquaculture operation.

Orchard Rocks, a 40 yard long rocky shoal, about 500 yards west of Bainbridge Island, is next. Red buoy "6" is about 300 yards south of the rocks. Vessels stay south of buoy.

It's possible to pass between Orchard Rocks and Bainbridge as there's plenty of water. We're careful to avoid shallows and keep clear of aquaculture facilities, shown in detail on charts 18474 and 18449, marked with flashing yellow 6 second lights.

Fort Ward State Park is on the southwest shore inshore and north of Orchard Rocks. This is an intriguing historical stop because of the military history involved. It would be easy to land a small boat along this shore. A launch ramp and two mooring buoys are at the park.

Buoys are preferable to anchoring because of the strong currents.

Fort Ward State Park Facilities

- ➤ About 4,300 feet of shoreline
- ➤ Two mooring buoys at opposite ends of the beach
- ➤ Single lane launch ramp near north end
- ➤ 137 acres of uplands with picnic tables, restrooms, water, hiking trail
- ➤ Historical displays
- ➤ Bird-watching blinds on shore, poison oak in the woods.
- ➤ Day-use only
- ➤ Phone: 206-842-3931

Fort Ward History

This is a rare kind of history: Fort Ward was a fortress begun in 1899 to place a submarine minefield to destroy enemy vessels which might dare to enter Bremerton. Enormous gun batteries were built on shore to protect the minefield. It was not completed for about 10 years. Guns from battery emplacements were never fired. On the beach is an old brick and metal chimney, part of Fort Ward.

Troops were stationed here in 1907. During the 1940s in World War II, Fort Ward deployed barrier nets across Rich Passage against submarine entry to Puget Sound Naval Shipyard in Bremerton. Black wooden pilings supported the heavy cables for the nets stretched across the pass. After the war ended in 1945 the government released the land and it became a park. Remains of various military sites are throughout the park, a fascinating place to visit if you're interested in military history. The fort was part of a planned group of five forts throughout Puget Sound: Fort Casey on Whidbey Island, Fort Flagler on Marrowstone Island, Fort Worden in Port Townsend and Fort Lawton in Seattle.

In 1960 much of Fort Ward was sold to private buyers with the remainder purchased by state parks.

Capt. Vancouver went through Rich Passage, but Peter Puget did not, according to our investigation.

Peninsula Side

⎈ **Manchester State Park** wraps around **Middle Point** into the unnamed angular bay. (More information on the park is in Chapter 9.)

Wautauga Beach is next, a small community with many homes on no-bank waterfront.

From here on through the pass there is a lot of wake from ferries and other marine traffic. We sometimes really roll in here with three to four foot waves building up around Point Glover.

Point Glover is next, marked by a quick green light and flashing strobe.

Rich Passage, imitation "lighthouse"

Bainbridge Side

⎈ **Pleasant Beach** is north of Fort Ward Park, and **West Blakely** area beyond is where the shoreline turns north. Erratic rocks and shoals are 200 yards offshore. Some older homes are along the shoreline, which curves into the bay at **Lynwood Center.** There is a grocery store and other services here, but it's far too shallow to anchor off easily without getting in the currents and there's no real public place to leave your skiff on the beach if you do want to go ashore.

The shoreline heads back along the west side of the bay. Dense development and no-bank waterfront gives way to rising hills, and we are nearing Point White.

The west entrance to Rich Passage is between **Point White** on Bainbridge and **Waterman Point** on Kitsap Peninsula, a nub of land jutting about 0.1 mile into the passage.

We've popped out of Rich Passage and we're in Port Orchard Channel.

➡ **In Chapter 7** we go south through Agate Pass into Port Orchard Channel on the west side of Bainbridge Island to meet Rich Passage from the north.

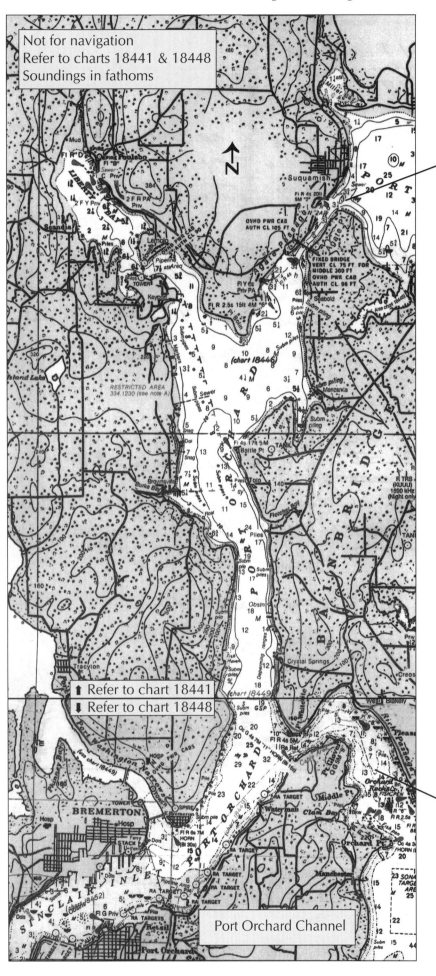

Not for navigation
Refer to charts 18441 & 18448
Soundings in fathoms

Refer to chart 18441
Refer to chart 18448

Port Orchard Channel

Agate Passage Current Details,
see Chapter 6, pages 112-113

Agate Passage Bridge clearance
details included in this chapter,
page 119

Rich Passage current details,
see Chapter 6, page 111-114

CHAPTER 7
Port Orchard Channel and Agate Passage, including Poulsbo

	Chart	Date	**Charts and publications for this chapter** Title	Scale	Soundings
***	**18446**	06/16/90	Puget Sound, Apple Cove Point to Keyport	1:25,000	.... Feet
			Agate Pass inset	1:10,000	.... Feet
***	**18449**	10/29/94	Puget Sound, Seattle to Bremerton	1:25,000	.... Feet
**	**18473**	08/14/93	Puget Sound, Oak Bay to Shilshole Bay	1:40,000	... Fathoms
**	**18474**	08/15/92	Puget Sound, Shilshole Bay to Commencement Bay	1:40,000	... Fathoms
*	**18445**	06/03/95	Puget Sound—Possession Sound to Olympia, page A,	1:80,000	... Fathoms
			Agate Pass, page B, inset 2	1:25,000	... Fathoms
*	**18441**	02/18/95	Puget Sound—Northern Part	1:80,000	... Fathoms
*	**18448**	10/30/93	Puget Sound—Southern Part	1:80,000	... Fathoms
	18440	08/05/95	Puget Sound	1:150,000	. Fathoms
			Tidal Current Charts, Puget Sound Northern Part		
			Booklet: Puget Sound Shellfish Sites		
➡			Washington State Public Lands Quad Map—Seattle	1:100,000	

When using charts, compare your chart dates with ones referred to above. There may be discrepancies between different charts and different chart editions.

Port Orchard Channel & Agate Passage Overview

Agate Passage lies between Bainbridge Island and Kitsap Peninsula shores south of the big bay of Port Madison. The narrowpassage meets the larger **Port Orchard Channel** south of the **Agate Passage Bridge**, and the channel continues more than seven miles until it joins Sinclair Inlet south and west of Bainbridge.

On the way through the channel we pass Keyport, Liberty Bay and Poulsbo, Manzanita Bay, Brownsville, and Illahee State Park, and other interesting places.

Agate Passage is about one mile long and 300 yards wide in the narrowest spot with steep forested shores, interspersed with many homes, on both sides. The bridge connecting Bainbridge to Kitsap Peninsula dominates the view through the pass. There is 75 feet vertical clearance above MHW under the bridge, and 300 feet horizontal clearance, shore to shore. Overhead power cables are 105 feet above the pass.

⚓ **Underway again** at the north entrance to the pass, we head south between **Agate Point** on Bainbridge Island and the Suquamish shore.

Fl R 4s 20ft 5M "2" Agate Pass Light 2, flashing red 4 second light, is on triangular red dayboard on dolphin 0.3 mile south of Suquamish fishing pier.

North end main channel is east of **RN buoy "2A"** marking a kelpy shoal extending nearly 0.4 mile southwest to the west shore. We passed west of the buoy, although it's necessary to be alert about kelp and depths which are between nine to 11 feet as charted at MLLW.

➡ **NOTE: Marine gas and diesel** is available at the **Port of Poulsbo** and **Port of Brownsville** in the areas covered in this chapter.

Looking south at the Agate Pass bridge

Agate Pass Bridge opened Kitsap Peninsula to development when it was completed in 1950, ending ferry runs from Seattle to Indianola and Suquamish the following year. The State Department of Transportation decided these communities didn't need their own ferry service and could drive to either Bainbridge or Kingston to take ferries to the eastern side of the Sound—whether they liked it or not.

Public tidelands unless otherwise noted are state owned. Some maybe leased and posted for aquaculture or other private use. We take the Washington State Public Lands Quadrangle Map, when going ashore at these locations to avoid trespassing on adjacent private property.

About five miles of public tidelands are in this chapter.

Fl R 4s buoy "4" Agate Pass Lighted buoy is at the south entrance to the pass, approximately 500 yards south of the bridge off the west shore. The buoy marks an extensive shoal.

Agate Pass details include:
• **Main channel** lies roughly along a line east of buoys "R2" and "R4."
• **Depths** of 18 to 20 feet are at the north entrance northeast of buoy N"2A."
• **Greatest depth** is 31 feet just south of the bridge.
• **Least width** between 20 foot depth curves is about 100 yards east of buoy N"2A."
• **Greatest width** between 20 foot depth curves is about 200 yards, near buoy "R4."

Currents in the pass can run up to six knots during spring tides. All the water is compressed into a navigable channel about 200 yards wide where the bridge crosses above the narrowest and shallowest section of Agate Passage. The flood sets southwest and the ebb sets northeast.

We usually check *Tidal Current Tables* and *Current Charts* when planning a passage. Current velocity often affect our decision whether to use Rich or Agate Passages. (See Chapter 6, "Tidal Current Chart Overview, Bainbridge Island and vicinity," pages 112-113.) This information is also useful to the many "ragbaggers" or powerboaters participating in popular "around Bainbridge Island" races.

Cable areas cross the pass at two locations. North end cable area is defined by Agate Point, buoy N"2A," and flashing red 4 second light "R2" on a dolphin south of Suquamish fishing pier.

Mid-passage cable area is about 650 yards north of the bridge.

Old Man House State Park, also known as **Chief Seattle State Park,** is on the west shore, just inshore of buoy N "2A." The site of the former huge, historic Indian longhouse, it is less than 0.5 mile south of Suquamish, or 0.7 mile north of the Agate Pass Bridge.

No trace remains today of the magnificent structure that was the largest longhouse in the region. Where it once stood is now a grassy hillside above the shore. Looking closely with binoculars from a boat, the roof of the information kiosk part way up a gently sloping hill may be seen among lovely evergreens above the beach.

The cable area sign at the north end of the park helps identify the park from the water.

Chief Seattle State Park attractions include an informational display to commemorate this extraordinary living complex, recognized as the home of Chief Seattle. No documentation has been located to substantiate the notion that the house "was razed on order of the United States Army," as stated on the plaque. The name "Old Man" is actually an anglicized version of "O-le-man," Chinook jargon for "Strong Man."

There is 210 feet of beautiful, sandy beach, a fire ring, picnic sites, water and toilet. The best way to visit the park is from a beachable boat or car.

⚓ **Anchoring** is questionable unless currents are slack. Avoid cable crossing area at the north end of the park.

Agate Passage

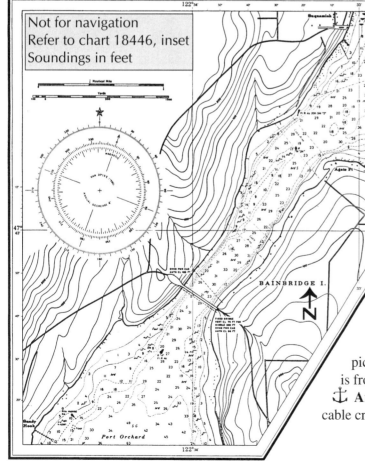

Not for navigation
Refer to chart 18446, inset
Soundings in feet

Early Agate Pass Indians

The Indian longhouse at Old Man House State Park is estimated to have been as much as 900 feet long by 60 feet wide. The shape followed the slight curve of the beach. It was about 12 feet high in front and between 8 and 9 feet in the rear.

There seem to be conflicting ideas as to when Old Man House was built. It was probably some time in the late 18th century or early 19th century after Vancouver explored in 1792, however, he does not make mention of the village in any references we found.

Chief Kitsap of the Suquamish tribe supervised the building of the structure as a place to meet and deal with the coming "Boston Men."

Our information describes the longhouse as having 40 separate apartments, each divided into rooms partitioned by mats. Each apartment had a fireplace, usually made of stone and raised a little above the ground, with an opening in the roof for smoke. Some rooms had raised bunks around the walls for beds.

The chief's apartment was very strong; the wall in front had heavy posts with several openings. On every corner post in front of the chief's and sub-chief's apartments were carved the big "Thunderbirds." (***Book I of Kitsap County History***)

Potlatches, ceremonials and dances were held in the massive house throughout the years.

Before the settlers arrived an estimate of Suquamish tribal members in 1844 included 158 men, 102 women, 113 boys, 97 girls and 64 slaves. They had five horses, 160 canoes and 63 guns.

There are variations on the demise of the huge structure. One is that when the settlers came with their usual frenzy to "civilize," they burned down the longhouse in the late 1800s to "discourage communal living," calling it an obstacle to the "civilization of the Suquamish people."

Another report is that by 1859, only the upright members of the building were still standing and eight years later most or all of the Indians were living in individual houses built with lumber from the Port Madison Mill. They were encouraged to have houses by Acting Indian Agent William Deshaw aided by Chief Seattle.

In 1870 only three upright members of the longhouse were still standing. A portion of the collapsed structure used as a shelter for a number of ship jumpers and vagabonds was burned by Deshaw. The Indians were all inoculated to prevent an outbreak of smallpox.

Old Man House Park is one of 43 Washington State Parks Heritage Sites, helping to preserve and interpret the state's human history.

Chief Seattle

Old Man House State Park– site of a former Indian longhouse

Public beach access in Agate Pass on Bainbridge is at the power line right-of-way at Reitan Road, just under the bridge. The access is mostly used by scuba divers, but some islanders use it for beach walking. We **wouldn't even suggest anchoring** a large boat here. The bottom is cobbled and it would be a tough anchorage even without currents, however, beachable boats can stop here.

This is a favorite spot with experienced divers who enjoy playing the currents, spearfishing and watching the underwater action. It was the site of a big cod fishery years ago before it was fished out.

Captain Vancouver *apparently did not find Agate Pass at the north end of Bainbridge Island, he did go through Rich Passage at the south end of the island and then into Port Orchard, which he named for H.M. Orchard, a clerk with the expedition.*

A large aeolian harp can be seen up amidst the trees about 0.25 mile south of the bridge on Bainbridge. We found it after a friend told us about it. Sometimes it's hard to see—but it's there. Thanks to Webster we learned that "an aeolian harp is a box with an opening over which are stretched strings of equal length which produce sound when wind blows over them."

Aeolus was the Greek God of Wind.

Suquamish Tribal Headquarters and Museum

This is the same Sandy Hook visited by Mosquito Fleet steamers in the 1930s that picked up guests along the way at Indianola and other steamer stops. The guests picnicked and swam in the warm outdoor saltwater pool, while salesmen tried to entice them into buying lots at the Sandy Hook development during the outings. Pilings from the old steamer dock are about 1,000 feet north of the present pier.

⚓ **Underway,** we pass several parcels of **public tidelands** accessible by water on the Kitsap Peninsula shore. About 1,800 feet are north of the bridge and about 500 feet south of the bridge; then a gap of about 500 feet and another 800 public feet.

➡ **Once through Agate Pass,** we continue on chart 18446, scale 1:25,000.

Port Orchard channel now opens up. It's the nearly eight mile long body of water between Bainbridge and the peninsula running from the south end of Agate Pass to Bremerton.

Depths range from 36 to 150 feet when past the shoals on the west shore between the bridge and Point Bolin. The shores are forested, low to medium bank with a number of waterfront homes and communities.

Currents are generally weak and variable. The channel is 0.5 mile wide at the south end and two miles wide near Point Bolin.

Fl Y 6s light marks aquaculture pens owned by the Suquamish tribe.

Suquamish Tribal Headquarters are on the waterfront in a forested setting less than 0.7 mile south of the bridge on the west shore. The large building also includes and the Suquamish Museum.

⚓ **Anchoring** is possible, then dinghy in and visit the museum, according to museum personnel. Sandy shallows with some kelp extend about 0.15 mile offshore.

Suquamish Tribal Headquarters

The Suquamish Museum is a fascinating place, giving visitors history of the Pacific Northwest from the perspective of Chief Seattle and his descendants, the Suquamish people. Set on the shores of Agate Passage, the museum tells of the world of Puget Sound's original inhabitants.

The sights and sounds of the past make the well-known exhibition, *The Eyes of Chief Seattle,* come alive. The exhibition received international acclaim in Nantes, France, as part of Seattle's Sister City Exchange.

There is an award-winning media production, *Come Forth Laughing: Voices of the Suquamish People*, which gives their firsthand account over the past 100 years.

There are displays of baskets, canoes and Indian artifacts, plus 1,000 feet of shoreline, nature trail, picnic tables and restrooms. This is an intriguing visit for all ages.

Museum guides suggest other interesting spots on the Port Madison Indian Reservation, including Chief Seattle's grave in Suquamish, Old Man House and Suquamish Fish Hatchery at the head of Miller Bay. Phone: 360-598-3311.

⚓ **Underway again, Sandy Hook** is next south, site of **Kiana Lodge,** a large log building used for weddings, receptions, company dinners and other occasions. It's private, but guests may arrive in their own boats and moor at the dock for a few hours, but not overnight. The dock is also used by charter boats transporting guests. Phone: 360-598-4311.

Fl R 2.5s 15ft 4M "6" light Point Bolin Reef Light 6, a flashing red light on a triangular day dayboard on dolphin, marks the outer edge of a shallow and kelpy area about 800 yards offshore. We keep east of this marker as we angle southwest to Point Bolin.

Point Bolin is a bluff with a vertical piling bulkhead at the base. It's also been called "Cape Horn." Onshore is a mix of evergreen and madrona trees, probably second or third growth. We understand some of the rocks may have petroglyphs—Indian rock carvings—but we haven't found them.

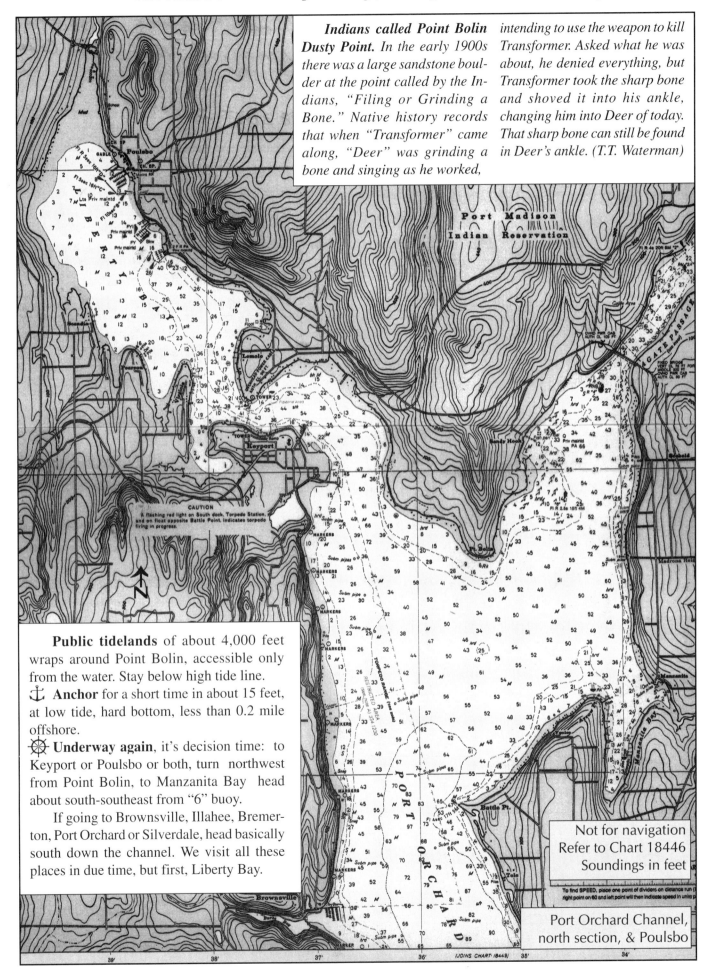

Indians called Point Bolin Dusty Point. *In the early 1900s there was a large sandstone boulder at the point called by the Indians, "Filing or Grinding a Bone." Native history records that when "Transformer" came along, "Deer" was grinding a bone and singing as he worked,* *intending to use the weapon to kill Transformer. Asked what he was about, he denied everything, but Transformer took the sharp bone and shoved it into his ankle, changing him into Deer of today. That sharp bone can still be found in Deer's ankle. (T.T. Waterman)*

Public tidelands of about 4,000 feet wraps around Point Bolin, accessible only from the water. Stay below high tide line.

⚓ **Anchor** for a short time in about 15 feet, at low tide, hard bottom, less than 0.2 mile offshore.

⚙ **Underway again**, it's decision time: to Keyport or Poulsbo or both, turn northwest from Point Bolin, to Manzanita Bay head about south-southeast from "6" buoy.

If going to Brownsville, Illahee, Bremerton, Port Orchard or Silverdale, head basically south down the channel. We visit all these places in due time, but first, Liberty Bay.

Not for navigation
Refer to Chart 18446
Soundings in feet

Port Orchard Channel,
north section, & Poulsbo

Keyport Naval installation

Keyport

After rounding Point Bolin we follow the three fathom depth curve and head northwest toward Keyport.

Public tidelands of nearly **4,000 feet** are on the NE shore across from Keyport.

Keyport Naval Facility

The large buildings of Keyport Naval facility loom along the southwest shore. This is the **Naval Underwater Warfare Engineering Station—NUWES** for short—the Navy's depot for torpedoes and mobile targets, a large employer in Kitsap County.

There's both a south pier and north pier at the naval facility and all mariners must stay 100 yards away.

Speeds are five knots passing the south pier and three knots passing the north pier where a seaplane float extends 100 feet to the northwest.

Flashing red torpedo range testing light on the end of south pier warns boaters to avoid the testing area along the west shore between Keyport and Brownsville if torpedoes are being tested. Torpedoes have been tested at Keyport since 1910.

Keyport is home to a naval undersea museum. The drawback for mariners is there is no place to moor vessels while visiting. Phone: 360-396-4148

Keyport—**"Torpedo Town, USA"**—was so named because founding fathers expected the settlement to become a **"key"** port. Keyport is west of NUWES. Two docks are in Keyport.

Keyport Marine Service is the first dock west of the naval property. It is a haulout facility with a railway and crane. They have towing in addition to other services, permanent moorage for 24 boats, and occasional spaces for guest moorage at $5 per night. Phone 360-779-4360 for information.

Port of Keyport Marina facilities—charted as #44 on 18445, with mostly permanent moorage, facilities as listed—is the second dock west of the naval facility. It occasionally has one slip for transient moorage on the west side. There is a public fishing pier here. We have no phone number for this dock.

Single lane launch ramp is at the marina.

A grocery store is about a half block from the marina; there's gas at a service station and on-street parking. Several restaurants and a gift shop are in town.

Public tidelands of about 1,000 feet are just west of the port facilities. The first bay west of Keyport, between there and Virginia Peninsula, has tidelands along much of the east, southeast and southwest shore. Public tidelands are around Pearson Peninsula also, and several areas on the north shore.

Not for navigation
Refer to chart 18446
Soundings in fathoms

Keyport, Liberty Bay and Poulsbo

Liberty Bay and Poulsbo

⚓ **Liberty Bay** runs basically north for just over two miles beyond Keyport and is about 0.7 mile wide. Homes and small communities ring most of the shores, with the charming Scandinavian city of Poulsbo on the northeast shore.

Entering Liberty Bay, at Keyport the channel narrows to about 150 navigable yards as we head west, before it opens up into Liberty Bay. Towers on either side support an overhead power cable 90 feet high across the channel to **Lemolo**.

R "2" Liberty Bay Daybeacon 2, triangular red on pile, marks navigable water off Lemolo.

Currents in Liberty Bay entrance: floods run about one knot while ebbs can be 1.5 knots. (Refer to Chapter 6, pages 112-113.)

Depths in the bay range from 44 feet to mud flats at the north end.

"No wake" signs are placed throughout Liberty Bay.

Poulsbo is on the northeast shore and the skyline is dominated by the beautiful spire on the First Lutheran Church, built by early pioneers. Rugged Olympic mountain peaks can be seen above the western shore from up in town, but not from the waterfront. Mount Rainier's snows glisten past the south end of the bay.

⚓ **Anchoring** is good and plentiful in Liberty Bay. Winds blow equally from north or south in the bay, so pick a place and set the anchor accordingly.

The bay north of Lemolo head is favored by many, although there's not much protection in a strong northerly. Anchor in about 11 to 17 feet, mud bottom.

Two small bays west of Keyport offer some protection in a southerly. Anchor in about 10 feet with a mud bottom.

In summer, many boats anchor off Poulsbo west and south of the port marina in from seven to 20 feet, mud bottom; drying mud flats are north of marina. Tie the dinghy inshore of the marina seaplane float and walkway between E and F floats at the north end of the marina. Remember the life jackets.

Poulsbo's Three Marinas

⚓ **Liberty Bay Marina**, first marina on the northeast shore, is just over one mile from the entrance channel. This is private, permanent moorage and has no guest moorage.

Poulsbo Yacht Club is next with reciprocal privileges. This is a modern new facility with room for about 10 visiting boats just a short walk from town.

Port of Poulsbo Marina is the last and northernmost marina in Poulsbo. This is a great spot, smack dab in downtown Poulsbo, with its Norwegian themes and heritage. Charted as #43A, facilities exceed those listed.

> ➡ **All of Liberty Bay is closed to shellfish gathering.**
> We wouldn't even suggest gathering shellfish in Liberty Bay without checking with the Red Tide Hotline to see if there are any closures due to PSP or other factors.
> **Phone: 1-800-562-5632**

The $10 million Naval Undersea Museum at Keyport is full of artifacts documenting undersea exploration, from Deep Submergence Vehicles to the evolution of diving gear. The Jason Project, an interactive experiment, takes scientific field studies directly into classrooms. The Museum's motto: "Explore the human experience beneath the sea ..."

Port of Poulsbo Marina Facilities
➤ Moorage for about 130 guest boats
➤ Four hour courtesy moorage
➤ Moorage rates 25 cents per foot
➤ Water
➤ Fuel float with gas, diesel
➤ Pump-out station
➤ Restrooms, showers, laundry
➤ Phone: 360-779-3505
➤ Monitors VHF Channel 16
➤ 300 boats moored permanently, including a fishing fleet
➤ Launch ramp

Port of Poulsbo Marina

Poulsbo breakwater with guard seals

Poulsbo means "Paul's Place" in Norwegian.

Entering the Port Marina

Three flashing lights mark the marina, flashing red "D" at the north end of the breakwater, and flashing "B" and "C" at the south and eastern corners.

We go northwest past the timbered breakwater and boomsticks covered with guard seals, and then angle to the right. The last two floats at the north end, E and F, are for guest moorage. Tie up at any open slip and check in at the port's handsome new floating office near the head of the E dock.

The fuel float is on the south side of E dock inshore of the office. There's even a seaplane float if you need to fly out fast.

Launch ramp is at the south end of the marina, next to the Marine Science Center. Parking for trucks and trailers is scarce.

Port Manager Gary Proutt, a good friend who lives with his wife Jan aboard their Chris Craft in the marina, will take care of you in great style. Tell him we sent you—he promises NOT to double your fees.

Port of Poulsbo Marina is at the downtown waterfront park where just about everything that's going to happen in Poulsbo does. There are picnic areas, gazebo and a giant erratic rock for kids to climb. A waterfront boardwalk meanders north along the bay and through the woods to a playground. The head of the bay was once the site of a Native American village, but now is the home of restaurants and other services.

We walk to anything we might want in town: restaurants, delis, a marine store, boutiques, clothing stores, bookstores, drug stores, bakeries, banks and a post office. It's about a one-mile walk to the major supermarkets, liquor and hardware stores. There is bus service all through town in the "cruising season."

Poulsbo's rich Scandinavian heritage is proudly retained and displayed in the unique storefronts, outside murals and annual events with participants wearing Norwegian costumes. The Sons of Norway, in their Viking hats and furs, stir up a storm of fun at community events and you may well see them during holiday festivities.

Poulsbo is warm and welcoming, with the Norwegian "Velkommen til Poulsbo" mottoes all around town. Rosemaling (painted folk art design) decorates many of the storefronts in downtown Poulsbo.

Poulsbo erratic rock, foreground, low tide in Liberty Bay in back

Poulsbo History

Kitsap Peninsula, and then Poulsbo, were settled in the 1880s by Scandinavian fishermen, loggers and farmers who felt at home in the fjord-like surroundings and the long coastline where they could fish. They logged and then farmed, once they'd chopped down most of the trees.

The Scandinavians brought their traditions and Lutheran beliefs with them when they arrived in Poulsbo. They established two major institutions in the 1900s, a home for the elderly—now modernized and still in operation—and an orphanage for 30 children, which ran successfully for many years.

As in most Puget Sound communities, early transportation was by water. Supplies and communication were through "Mosquito Fleet" steamers that plied the waters from villages and towns on the west side of the Sound to Seattle.

The Pacific Coast Codfish Company was based in Poulsbo in the early 1900s. There the codfish, caught by large schooners in the Bering Sea, was salted and preserved. Since the closing of the plant in the 1950s, Poulsbo now relies on tourism, as well as many small businesses for its economic growth.

Liberty Bay was once called "Dogfish Bay" for the small sharks in demand by early loggers and mill operators because of the smelly oil they contained. The sharks were caught and rendered down by homesteaders who sold them for greasing skid roads and mill machinery.

Port Orchard Channel—again

⎈ **Leaving** Liberty Bay, if we head southeast and cross Port Orchard we'll be in lovely Manzanita Bay on Bainbridge Island in no time. This favorite spot of ours is about 2.5 miles from Keyport. We'll go south in Port Orchard Channel after this.

Ⓖ **Manzanita Bay,** what a lovely spot—**a favorite gunkhole**—it **feels** right. We've spent many a pleasant night here, quiet, serene, secure. Lovely homes and cabins, some with private docks, line the shore, but not too close together.

It's peaceful and quiet. Add a moon rising over the trees to the east and you'll think you're in heaven.

⚓ **Anchor** in about 20 or 30 feet, mud bottom.

One of the delightful bonuses in Manzanita Bay is the public access road end in the northeast part of the bay. This gives you a chance to go ashore, stretch your legs in a brisk walk or run, take the dog and/or kids ashore, perhaps meet an island friend or go for a swim off the sandy beach in summer.

This is the old **Manzanita Landing** at the foot of short **Dock Street.** There's a sign at the landing showing it dated from 1895-1927, the years of steamer service to Manzanita..

Manzanita Landing is on chart 18446 where it shows "Manzanita." On chart 18473 it's about where it shows "subm. piles" on the little rectangular-shaped point.

From the water, the narrow beach access is at the three foot high concrete "ecology blocks" marking the street end between two waterfront homes. There are four large steps down to the beach on the north side of the blocks. A gray house with a rock bulkhead is north of the beach access. On the south side is a rock wall with a charming brown shake house.

Many islanders take their kids to the landing to picnic, sunbathe, swim, play, read and relax. All land and beaches on either side of the access are private.

Manzanita Park is nearby you want a walk through woods. This is a 120 acre park with hiking and equestrian trails. Walk north along Manzanita Road to Day Road. Take a right, walk until you see signs, turn into the forest and follow the trails.

⎈ **South along Bainbridge Island's west shore**, from Manzanita head out and around **Arrow Point** giving it a fairly wide berth, at least 200 yards off, to avoid rocks and shallows of two and three feet at low tides. There's another 100 yards or more of sandy beach exposed at low tide, and erratic rocks are along the shore.

Fairy Dell Trail is for those who want to know unusual places to anchor and go ashore. It's a charted road end near Venice, about 1/4 of the way southwest past Arrow Point on the way to Battle Point.

From the water, the shoreline has fallen trees and low clay bluffy banks. The trail can be spotted because of the ravine behind it. Fairy Dell Trail meanders through woods following the ravine of a seasonal stream. About a 1/2 dozen small wooden bridges cross the stream. Local Boy Scouts built the trail along the side of a hill. It's great for kids, but sort of steep and slippery for others, such as us.

⚓ **Anchor** in about 12 to 15 feet of water, about 0.1 mile off in mud bottom.

⎈ **Fl 4s 17ft 5M Battle Point Light,** flashing white light on a diamond shaped black and white daymark, is 1.1 miles southwest of Arrow Point. The point was called "Adolescent Girl" by Native Americans, because legend is a girl went bathing here and turned to stone.

Swimmers: A man we met in Manzanita swims across the bay almost daily in the summer.

He was once bumped by "playful" sea lions who wanted a companion. He stayed very still in the water until the large marine mammals swam away, looking for another "playmate."

Manzanita Landing public access

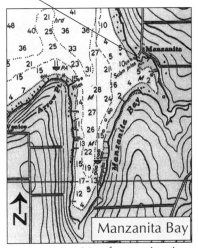

Not for navigation
Refer to chart 18446
Soundings in feet

The shore at Fairy Dell Trail was the site of the longest pier in Puget Sound about 1910.

Members of the Seattle Automobile Club would bring their cars over on a boat, unload at the pier and drive up the road. If you hike this trail, you'll wonder how they ever did it. This was their hunting lodge area and many of them had summer homes here.

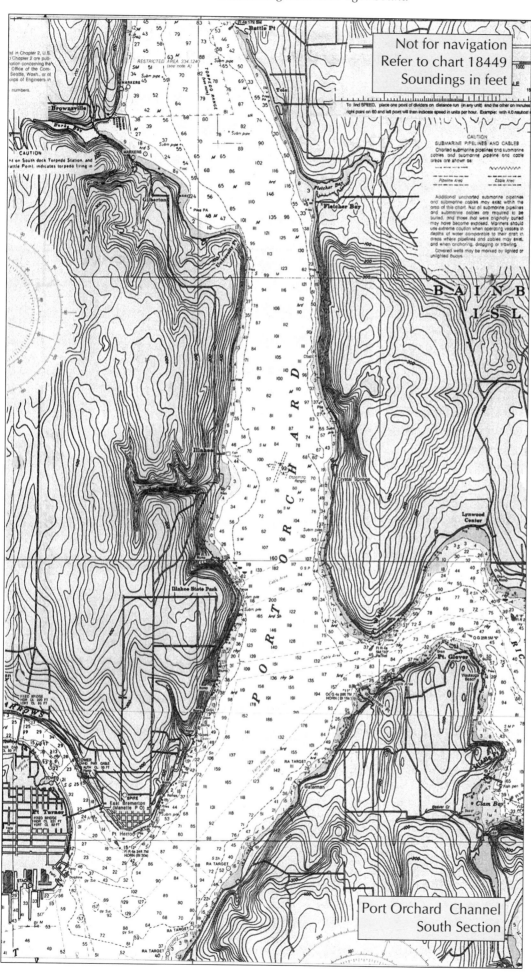

Not for navigation
Refer to chart 18449
Soundings in feet

Port Orchard Channel
South Section

Battle Point is the end of a long sandy spit that extends about 200 yards out. A short stretch of bare bluff and erratic rocks are behind the spit. Bluffs taper to low bank to no bank to the spit. It is a conservation easement to preserve as is without public access. A landlocked lagoon, except at high tides, is south of the point, site of an old Indian village.

Tolo, a small community near another drying lagoon, is about 0.6 mile south. The shore along here is fairly straight, medium-high forested bank with a number of homes, a few pilings, small erratic rocks and no real navigation problems.

Fletcher Bay is about 1.4 miles south of Battle Point. It has all the attributes of a neat gunkhole, protection from just about all wind and weather conditions, quiet, and secluded, except for two problems: one, it's all private property with no public access, and, two, you can only get in and out at high tide.

It's a pretty good anchorage inside in places, but very small and all private.

From outside looking in at low tide, there is a sandspit/bar blocking the entrance with a "No Trespassing" sign. Beyond the spit are private docks with some boats floating, some sitting in the mud.

Although the *Coast Pilot* mentions it as an anchorage, we've not gone in there to investigate, as we have peeked in at low tide and there is not much water in there.

A public road end, is south of the bay's entrance where there was once an old steamer dock, **Fletcher Landing**. Years ago this was public beach access, but the county sold off beach rights, neighbors bought them and divided them into 20 parcels. So now the beach itself is private property and we can't go ashore. There is an unlocked chain link fence on the road end above a concrete bulkhead on the beach, but since the beach is private, the road end is not accessible from the water.

The west coast of Bainbridge from here south is fairly straight with high and medium bank, homes, evergreen trees—typical scenery. We pass the communities of **Westwood, Crystal Springs** and **Gibson.**

Point White public fishing pier is south of Crystal Springs and across Port Orchard channel from Illahee State Park. There's no tie-up float or launch ramp, but you could put in a canoe or kayak here as there's 25 feet of public beach on either side of the dock. The L-shaped pier is popular with fishermen and those who like to drop crab pots. Marine critters live on and around the dock pilings.

Public tidelands of about 5,000 feet are around Point White, about 3,500 feet on the west side of Bainbridge, just about south of the public fishing pier.

⚓ **Now, back to Keyport and we're underway** south on the peninsula shore.

It's about three miles from Keyport to **Brownsville** with high forested bluffs tapering to medium bank farther south. There are some visible homes, but not high density, erratic rocks on the beaches and evergreen trees lining the shore—a pleasant shoreline, offering a good place to anchor with a muddy bottom.

This shoreline is shown as **public tidelands**, and Department of Natural Resources personnel tell us that we can **anchor** over state tidelands without a problem.

But Big Brother has a **Torpedo Range** here.

The range is charted between Keyport and Brownsville. There are seven markers along the shore between the two communities. The chart suggests reading about the testing range in the *Coast Pilot* in Section **334.1230.**

Flashing red lights on the end of the south pier at Keyport indicate when torpedo firings or noise measurement tests are in progress, or other hazardous conditions exist. If lights are flashing, mariners should not enter the test area.

Olympic Mountains from Port Orchard channel

➡ **Time to change charts, from 18473 to 18474, and from 18446 to 18449.**

The Native American name for Fletcher Bay means "Bitten Into." Legend is that a monster lived in this bay and preyed on those who crossed over at its mouth.

Fletcher's Landing steamer dock was just south of the entrance to the bay in the early 1900s. The boat went from there to Brownsville across Port Orchard channel. Not much is left of the landing except a couple of old rotted pilings.

In the 1910 era, there were resorts at Fletcher Bay that featured beaches, rental cabins, a store, dance pavilion, picnic and camping grounds.

Point White public fishing pier

Those nearby should stop engines or other equipment generating underwater noise, such as depth sounders, because some torpedoes are guided by noise and may be attracted to the boat noises. Whoops!

We called the Navy and the Army Engineers and asked both if it was okay to anchor if there were no planned tests. As of this printing, no one had been able to figure out what to tell us. We will keep after them until we get some sort of answer. You're on your own.

Port of Brownsville Marina is snugged close to the head of **Burke Bay**. There is good moorage, some services and a public fishing pier—and they tell us the squid fishing is great, especially in November and December.

Attitude is tops at the Port of Brownsville facility. Everyone is very friendly and helpful, including the port manager whose name is pretty special. He's Bill Bailey. NOT Jo's son Bill Bailey, but same name anyhow. Makes it easy to remember who's in charge.

Port of Brownsville Marina Facilities
➤ Moorage for about 60 guest boats
➤ Moorage rate 30 cents per foot per day
➤ 20-30 amp shore power, $2.75 per day
➤ Fuel float with gas, diesel and propane
➤ Pump-out station on main dock, porta-potty dump
➤ Water
➤ Restrooms, showers, laundry
➤ Launch ramp
➤ Monitors VHF Channel 16
➤ Phone: 360-692-5498

The fuel float is at the outboard (south) end of A float—the float closest to the shore. The area west of "A" dock and the fuel dock was dredged in 1994 to a depth of -6 feet at zero (0) tide level.

Port office, grocery store, deli, restrooms, showers and Brownsville Yacht Club are all in one building. The deli has groceries, large selection of Northwest wines, marine supplies, and espresso.

Brownsville guest moorage float on right

There are barbecues and picnic areas, a horseshoe pit, and a boardwalk. The large launch ramp and float have an extra large parking area.

Entering the marina, the intriguing floating "junk" breakwater that was a marina trademark for many years was replaced with a floating dock in 1994—enter from either end. Guest moorage is on the 530 foot long breakwater-float extending perpendicularly from the shore at the marina's north side. There are also small boat guest slips at A float, closest to shore on the south side. The head of Burke Bay bares at low tide and turns into mud flats.

⎈ **Underway south** from Brownsville the shoreline trends a bit southeasterly.

Public tidelands of 1,000 feet accessible by water, is 1,000 feet past the marina. There are erratic rocks along the shoreline, old pilings, lots of houses, a medium high, forested bluff. Past Gilberton, the shoreline swings into a little bay, then out again to University Point.

⚓ **Anchoring** is possible in this bight—muddy bottom, 10 to 20 feet—in calm weather or in a southerly, but we haven't done it.

The shoreline here has a moderate slope, steep enough so houses are set back a little in the trees and much of the waterfront is bulkhead.

⎈ **Illahee Community** is about 1.5 miles south of University Point, with a public fishing pier and a couple of floats for daytime tie-ups. The sign on the end of the dock announces "Illahee Foods, Coca Cola, Texaco gas, groceries, cold beer, water, ice, bait." The store is across the street from the head of the dock and the service station has gas, so portable tanks can be filled.

➡ **Time to change charts from 18446 to 18449 and from 18473 to 18474.**

Check the depth carefully as the water is pretty scant here on low tides–with a deep draft boat be wary. An artificial reef is off the pier's end—good fishing and scuba diving. Note that you need to be at least 300 yards offshore to avoid shoaling beach south of the fishing pier where it is as shallow as one foot at MLLW.

Mount Rainier unexpectedly appears to the southeast and is beautiful from here.

Illahee State Park is less than a mile south of Illahee community. This 75 acre park, built on a 300 foot high bluff which slopes steeply to the water, is a popular camping and fishing destination. A fishing pier with a 125 foot long moorage float is protected by a floating breakwater.

Five mooring buoys are strung out just south of the fishing pier. The buoys are seldom full in here, maybe because boaters don't know about them. Or perhaps they don't tie up because they know they may spend a rolly night here, as we have, from vessel wake in Rich Passage. At least you know you're on a boat.

A plus is the lovely view of Mount Rainier from the mooring buoys. You'll also be able to see the Seattle-Bremerton ferries in Rich Passage, off the south end of Bainbridge Island about one mile away.

American Navy Lt. Charles Wilkes entered Port Orchard during his voyage of exploration in 1841 and noted that, "Port Orchard is one of the many fine harbors on these inland waters, and is perfectly protected from the winds."

A replica of his chart shows that he considered Port Orchard to be the channel from Point Herron to just off Manzanita Bay.

Illahee State Park Facilities
➤ Five mooring buoys
➤ 1,785 feet of saltwater shoreline
➤ Restrooms on the beach
➤ Porta-potty dump
➤ Showers up the hill
➤ Kids' play area
➤ Hiking trails
➤ Campsites
➤ Baseball diamond
➤ Historic display
➤ Launch ramp
➤ Phone: 360-478-6460

Illahee fishing float and launch ramp

The launch ramp is sloping concrete most of the way but eventually ends in mud at extreme low tides. The ramp is tucked back in a bight just north of the fishing pier. You have to drive down a steep switchback road to reach the launch ramp and beach. Your vehicle should be able to make sharp turns and have reliable brakes. There is good boat trailer parking near the ramp.

Cable area crosses from Illahee Park to near Crystal Springs, and south toward Point Herron.

Public tidelands of several parcels are south of the park along this shore.

End of Port Orchard Channel

⚓ **We head south** and about two miles beyond the park we reach the southern end of Port Orchard channel. The shoreline along this section is like so many others, low to high bank, waterfront, homes, trees and erratic rocks.

Point Herron in East Bremerton is the end of this chapter.

Native American lore is that the word "Illahee" means "Earth" or "Country."

➡ **In Chapter 8** we explore Sinclair Inlet, including the city of Port Orchard, Bremerton, and Dyes Inlet.

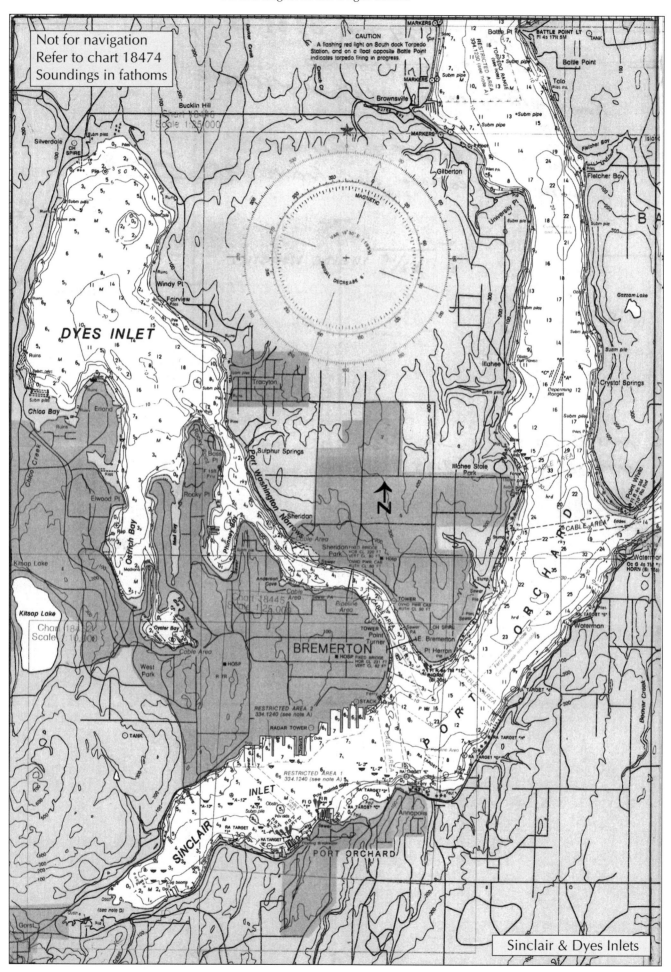

CHAPTER 8
Sinclair and Dyes Inlets, Bremerton, Port Orchard and Silverdale

	Chart	Date	Title	Scale	Soundings
***	18449	10/29/94	Puget Sound, Seattle to Bremerton	1:25,000	Feet
**	18474	03/25/95	Puget Sound, Shilshole Bay to Commencement Bay	1:40,000	Fathoms
*	18445	06/03/95	Puget Sound—Possession Sound to Olympia, page A,	1:80,000	Fathoms
			page B, Inset 5	1:25,000	Fathoms
*	18448	10/30/93	Puget Sound, Southern Part	1:80,000	Fathoms
	18440	08/05/95	Puget Sound	1:150,000	Fathoms
			Tidal Current Charts, Puget Sound, Northern Part		
			Booklet: Puget Sound Shellfish Sites		
			Washington State Public Lands Quad Map, Seattle	1:100,000	

Charts and publications for this chapter

➡ *When using charts, compare your chart dates with ones referred to above. There may be discrepancies between different charts and different chart editions.*

Sinclair & Dyes Inlets—Overview

Sinclair Inlet, about 3.5 miles long, extends in a southwesterly direction from Port Orchard channel. It's the site of the cities of Port Orchard and Bremerton and home of the Puget Sound Naval Shipyard.

Dyes Inlet is entered through three mile long Port Washington Narrows—at the northeast end of Sinclair Inlet—and extends about three miles north-northwest from the narrows. Silverdale is at the north end of the inlet.

Port Orchard, county seat of Kitsap County, is a delightful town that leans on its historic atmosphere and its forward-looking approach.

Port Orchard Marina dominates the city's waterfront. The large, modern marina is across Sinclair Inlet from the Bremerton Ferry Terminal and **Port of Bremerton Marina.**

There are passenger-only, modern-day "mosquito fleet" ferries that make runs between the two marinas about every half-hour.

Bremerton— "Navy Yard City"—is taking advantage of new waterfront developments to help create a "people-friendly" gathering place.

Bremerton's core has been the Navy ever since 1891. That's when the **Puget Sound Naval Shipyard,** the oldest permanent naval installation on the Sound, became a reality. **Lt. Ambrose B. Wyckoff** bought 190 acres of waterfront property from the **Bremer** family and others for a mere $9,500. That property has since become home to the second-largest industrial employer in the state.

The century-long naval influence is apparent. Visitors tour the decks of the historic *USS Turner Joy* at the east end of the new waterfront boardwalk.

Bremerton homeports numerous ships, including the huge aircraft carrier *USS Nimitz, CVN-68.* It is the home of the Inactive Ships Maintenance Facility which boasts the carrier *USS Ranger* and battleship *USS New Jersey.*

The pride of Bremerton, *USS Missouri,* the battleship on which the historic treaty with Japan was signed at the end of World War II, is destined to move to Pearl Harbor, Hawaii, in 1997. The carrier *USS Midway* is also to move to Hawaii.

➡ **NOTE: Marine gas and diesel** are available only at **Port Orchard Marina** in areas covered in this chapter.

More than four miles of public tidelands are in this chapter.

Public tidelands unless otherwise noted are state owned. Some maybe leased and posted for aquaculture or other private use. We take the Washington State Public Lands Quadrangle Map, when going ashore at these locations to avoid trespassing on adjacent private property.

Sinclair Inlet was named for George T. Sinclair, an acting master, with the Wilkes Expedition.

➥ The **Coast Pilot** refers to chart 18452 for Sinclair Inlet, but we find chart 18449, Puget Sound, Seattle to Bremerton, 1:25,000, which shows depths in feet, is adequate for this entire area. Strip chart 18445 has 1:25,000 scale of Sinclair Inlet, page B, inset 5.

Waterman was a steamer landing nearly 100 years ago. Bricks from a local brickyard were loaded aboard the vessels and transported to various destinations.

After the yard closed down at the turn-of-the-century, steamer service dropped off and the pier was abandoned.

We saw a large sloop come to a screeching halt, sails flapping uselessly, as the boat met the shoals east of Annapolis. After several vain attempts to get off the mud, the crew dropped the sails as the boat gently heeled over to wait out the tide.

Captain Vancouver and Port Orchard

Capt. George Vancouver sent Lt. Peter Puget and Sailing Master Joseph Whidbey south from Bainbridge Island on Sunday, May 20, 1792, to survey what is now known as South Puget Sound.

*But the captain became restless as he waited for the two men and their crews to return. In the meantime, his "gentlemen" had discovered a "very narrow passage" off the southwest coast of Bainbridge Island. He decided on May 24 to set out with a crew in the ship's yawl to "examine" it. (The quotes are from passages in Vancouver's diary from the book, **Vancouver's Discovery of Puget Sound** by Edmond S. Meany, 1935.)*

"From the west end of this narrow channel (Rich Passage) the inlet is divided into two branches, one extending to the SW (Sinclair Inlet) about five or six miles, the other to the north about the same distance (Port Orchard), constituting a most complete and excellent port, to all appearance perfectly free from danger, with regular soundings from four fathoms near the shores, to nine and ten fathoms in the middle, good holding ground," Vancouver wrote in his log.

"It occupied us the whole day to row round it ... The country that surrounds this harbor varies in its elevation; in some places the shores are low and level, in others of a moderate height, falling in steep low cliffs on the sandy beach, which in most places binds the shores. This harbor, after the gentleman who discovered it, obtained the name of Port Orchard."

In fact, Vancouver did not know that Bainbridge was an island. To the best of our information he landed at the south bay of the island and later saw and named Port Orchard, apparently assuming it was a bay not a channel.

Vancouver's estimate of about five to six miles length in Sinclair Inlet, the "southwest branch," scales out to six miles to the extreme southeast end at Gorst from Rich Passage. Port Orchard, the "branch" to the north, is about 7.5 miles to Keyport. He apparently did not investigate the full length of either pass. No mention was made of Washington Narrows and we'd guess he didn't row southwest past Point Herron or more than a few miles north in Port Orchard channel.

In any event, even with a favorable current it was a long way to row in one day, from south of Restoration Point. Not only that, neither of those "branches" were to the east, the direction he was searching for the elusive "Northwest Passage."

⚓ **Underway again,** we start at Waterman Point, a large knob that protrudes from the east shore of Sinclair Inlet (west end of Rich Passage), on our cruise around the inlet. Sinclair is about one mile wide for most of its six mile length, and depths range from 32 fathoms at the northeast end to 2.2 fathoms and then mud in the southwest.

Oc G 4s 26ft 7M Horn (Bl 15s) Waterman Point Light 11, with occulting green 4 second light "11" 26 feet high, visible seven miles, marks the end of this knob. **Waterman** is the first community along this shore, about 0.8 mile southwest of the knob. A 200 foot long public fishing pier is operated by the Waterman Port District. A float at the end of the pier blew away in the winter of 1994-95.

Public access to shore is by way of stairs from the beach on the north side of the dock. Facilities onshore are limited to a telephone and a sani-can.

⚓ **Anchoring** is possible off the fishing pier in about 15 to 20 feet, hard bottom.

Public tidelands start about 3,000 feet south of the dock and extend approximately 9,000 feet to where the shore makes a western turn.

Annapolis, a little over two miles southwest of Waterman, is a village best known for its large sprawling veterans' home, "Retsil," highly visible from the water.

A public fishing pier extends about 100 yards out to a float used by the passenger ferry which runs twice daily for commuters between the village and Bremerton. The pier is called either Annapolis Dock or Retsil Pier.

Launch ramp with parking is east of the ferry pier.

Shoals are 0.2 mile offshore in the bight just east of Annapolis and about 0.3 mile offshore between Annapolis and Port Orchard.

Ten charted radar targets are in Sinclair Inlet, appearing as "RA" targets on the chart.

⚓ **Port Orchard** is next along the south shore of the inlet, west of Annapolis. The large marina covers nearly 0.2 mile of waterfront, making it impossible to miss. A waterfront park and boardwalk, covered gazebo, nearby picnic areas, fishing pier, launch ramp, boat repair and marine supplies are also along the shore.

Port Orchard Marina, Bremerton in the background

Port Orchard Marina Facilities

➤ Moorage for approximately 100 visiting boats at 3,000' guest float, plus 44 other guest slips
➤ Moorage rates 30 cents per foot per day
➤ 30-50 amp shore power; water
➤ Rates: $2.30 for 30 amp or $2.60 for 50 amp service on east breakwater
➤ Fuel: diesel, gasoline, 2 cycle mix, oil disposal
➤ Pump-out
➤ Showers, restrooms, laundry
➤ Controlled entry requiring key card between 10 p.m. and 7 a.m.
➤ Party float for various functions
➤ About 375 permanent slips, nearly 3/4 of them covered moorage
➤ Monitors VHF Channel 16
➤ Phone: 360-876-5535

Port Orchard farmers market

Entering Port Orchard Marina, go beyond the marina and enter it from the west end. Make a hard turn to port and enter the opening between the breakwater and the farthest float west—with no number or letter. Mariners are asked to go dead slow as they pass the long north face of the breakwater float and around the curve at its west end, as the wake penetrates the marina.

Flashing green 4 second light on the breakwater **and flashing red 4 second light** on the float will help guide you in. Both the breakwater and this first float are available for guest moorage. The fuel facility is on the shore end of this float.

Six other floats are in the marina. The five in the center, A, B, C, D and E, are permanent moorage. The uncovered float at the eastern end of the marina, between the wraparound breakwater and covered moorage has about 44 guest slips. There are many places to moor in Port Orchard.

The town has parks, playgrounds, tennis courts, library, post office, liquor store and shopping. There are 70 shops at the Antique Mall in downtown Port Orchard. In fact, the town is the self-proclaimed "Antique Capitol of Kitsap Peninsula."

There are also unique community festivities at the marina, including the "In the Water Boat Show" on Mother's Day weekend, "Fathoms O' Fun" in July, "CarCruz" in August, "Mosquito Fleet Days" in September and the annual Christmas Lane parade of lighted boats.

A farmers market every Saturday from May through October at the marina park attracts boaters and others who fill up on fresh fruits and vegetables, arts and crafts, as they stroll through the large outdoor market. A block or so away are restaurants, gift shops and art galleries.

Wander along Bay Street and Sidney Avenue enjoy historic buildings. The Log Cabin Museum, three blocks up Sidney, is an authentic structure built in 1913, featuring historic memorabilia and furnishings from the life of an active family of yesteryear. Hours are Saturdays, 11 a.m. to 4 p.m., Sundays, 1 to 5 p.m., no charge.

Port Orchard, a city of about 5,600, became Kitsap County's first incorporated city more than 100 years ago. It was named the county seat in 1893, after it was moved from Port Madison. It is still the busy center of Kitsap County government.

In the 1850s, five of the world's largest sawmills were in Kitsap County.

By 1867, the county was reputed to be the richest in the U.S.

In 1884, pioneer Sidney Stevens laid out the town of Port Orchard. His teenage son suggested the town be called Sidney, but it remained Port Orchard. By 1890 Kitsap County, although the smallest geographically, was the most populous in the state.

Chris Craft rendezvous

Port Orchard Marina *is gaining a reputation as a rendezvous destination for boating groups which specialize in specific one-design models, and/or boats of special manufacturers, such as Catalinas, Chris Crafts and others. Unlike some marinas, they reserve moorage space for large gatherings, and then do their best to be friendly and accommodating to everyone. They even have a special "group" float with a barbecue. A totem welcomes visitors on the shore side of the guest moorage.*

The Gorst Aquatic Preserve *is 24 acres of tidelands that have been dedicated as a waterfowl and fish refuge by the U.S. Fish and Wildlife Service and the Port of Bremerton. Be prepared to see many seabirds.*

"Retired" sub

Stop at any local information center for a self-guided walking tour brochure of Port Orchard.

Launch ramp with two lanes and parking is west of the marina and across the street from the white concrete Port Orchard Municipal Building.

City of Port Orchard pedestrian pier, a 150 foot long dock with benches and picnic tables, is farther west.

⚓ **Anchoring** is possible on the east side of the marina. Be certain to stay out of the way of passenger ferries which run past the port's eastern float.

⚓ **Anchoring** is possible west of the marina, avoiding the charted, abandoned cable crossing,

Four golf courses are within an eight mile radius of the marina—handy for cruising golfers.

Port Orchard Yacht Club moorage and clubhouse is next west. There is moorage for reciprocal yacht club members.

Kitsap Marina, farther west, has no guest moorage.

⚓ **Underway again,** we head southwest in Sinclair Inlet. **Ross Point** is about one mile west of the Port Orchard Marina. **Public tidelands** of about 8,000 feet run from the point to the southwest into the mud flats at the head of the inlet.

Dockside Sales and Service is midway along this shore. Run by T. J. Cavanagh, this working marina has a travel lift and they do engine repair and fiberglass repair. "We can do everything by way of boat repair," T.J. said. Phone: 360-876-9016.

Gorst is a community at the southwest end of Sinclair Inlet, set far back behind tide flats, without reachable waterfront.

⚓ **Anchoring** is good in Sinclair Inlet. Depths range from 20 to 40 feet and the bottom is mud and/or sand. There are a number of navy mooring buoys in the inlet.

We ran southwest until we were where the inlet begins to shoal, and anchored in 22 feet of water, about 0.1 mile off the south shore. It was a gem of a June night; cloudless, flat calm, full moon. Nobody else was around. It was almost perfect. But we hadn't expected the noise from State Highway 16 which runs along the north and south shores of Sinclair Inlet, with a large interchange in Gorst. Even though it was a Sunday night, the loud steady hum of traffic—interspersed with an occasional siren—never let up. Live and learn. We should know by now that we have to watch out for nearby highways when we anchor.

The bottom has just about the yuckiest, smelliest mud ever, gunk like we've never seen before. But the anchor really held. It took buckets and buckets of water to clean off the anchor and deck after the hook came up. A Bremerton friend suggested the muck may be "spoils" from Drydock 6 at the Puget Sound Naval Shipyard.

⚓ **Continuing across** Sinclair Inlet to Bremerton is a somber experience cruising past the gray, silent "mothball fleet" of submarines, destroyers, aircraft carriers and other naval ships moored west of downtown, grim reminders of past wars. Navy restricted areas are charted. Keep 100 yards off naval vessels.

Port of Bremerton Marina, adjacent to the Washington State Ferry Terminal for the Seattle-Bremerton ferry run, is a major attraction for recreational boaters. It is immediately west of retired navy destroyer *USS Turner Joy,* open to the public.

Along the Bremerton waterfront and wide boardwalk is the new Waterfront Park, complete with a bronze statue of a navy yard worker and small boy admiring a ship model. The park is often the scene of arts and craft festivals, a farmers market on Sundays from May through October, and other seasonal events.

Within a short walk of the waterfront are bookstores, restaurants, antique shops, gift shops and more.

Port of Bremerton Marina Facilities

➤ Two guest floats with 45 slips:
   21 slips 32'; 24 slips 40'
➤ Moorage rates are 30 cents per
   foot per day
➤ 30 amp shore power
➤ Water
➤ Electricity $2.30 per day
➤ Fuel available across the inlet at
   Port Orchard Marina
➤ Pump-out facility
➤ Restrooms, showers, laundry
➤ Controlled entry system
➤ Ferry wake near the marina may be disturbing, but does not cause damage
➤ Monitors VHF Channel 16
➤ Phone: 360-373-1035

Port of Bremerton Marina

U.S.S. Turner Joy

Enter the marina at the east end, just past the *USS Turner Joy*. Inside the 500 foot long marina breakwater, which is also used by the Seattle passenger-only ferry, are the guest floats with slips. There is side-tie moorage on the inside of the breakwater. We found a fair amount of current runs through the marina at times.

The Navy has always had a major role in Bremerton's life, and this is shown in many ways. Take a tour boat around the Bremerton waterfront to hear the naval history. Or visit Bremerton's Naval Museum, which has a maritime collection from the early 1900s to the present, depicting the role the Navy has played in the Northwest, with interesting displays for young and old.

Port Washington Narrows, Dyes Inlet, Phinney, Oyster & Ostrich Bays

There are several other touring options in this area. It's worth a side trip to go through Port Washington Narrows into Dyes Inlet. There are three bays with good anchoring, a marina, a yacht club, Silverdale's waterfront park and several other places of interest.

Before cruising through three mile long Port Washington Narrows, we check *Tidal Current Tables* and/or *Current Charts* as currents can reach velocities exceeding four knots, according to the *Coast Pilot*. Currents will help or hinder any trip, especially in a slower boat,

Flood and ebb currents are stronger at the narrow's north end with speeds up to 4.5 knots on a flood, and 3.1 knots on an ebb.

⚓ **Underway,** we're at the south end of Port Orchard Channel and the entrance to entrance to Port Washington Narrows off Point Herron in East Bremerton.

Cable areas in this vicinity defy description. Study the chart carefully and look for signs on shore if you must anchor in the Narrows.

Public tidelands of about 25 small parcels are in the Narrows and Dyes Inlet.
⚓ **Anchoring in Port Washington Narrows** can be very "iffy." Charts indicate rocky bottom, cable area problems and currents which change direction during ebb and flood so the anchor must reset itself and may foul as the rode drags across the anchor with each current change.

Fl R 6s "12" 24ft 7M Horn (Bl 30s) Point Herron Light 12, is atop a triangular red dayboard on pile. This marks the offshore shoals at **Point Herron.**

The navigable channel narrows to 100 yards in places. Although it is shallow in spots, by carefully following the chart we find we are able to maintain about 19 or 20 feet depth. Gray whales frolicked in the channel in the spring of 1995.

➥ **Chart 18449, Seattle to Bremerton, 1:25,000,** depths in feet, is useful in this area.

Named the "Nation's Most Livable City" in 1992 by Money Magazine, Bremerton revelled in its popularity.

A by-product of that title is that a number of working artists and art-related businesses have moved to the area, expanding its population of 37,000.

Cultural offerings include a fine symphony orchestra, community theater, dance and summertime Concerts on the Dock.

Manette Bridge is the first of two narrows bridges. It has an 82 foot vertical clearance and a 231 foot horizontal clearance, crossing to East Bremerton.

Boat Shed Restaurant is almost under the bridge on the east shore. There is a float to moor a boat for an evening of dining out. Phone: 360-377-2600. Passing under the Manette Bridge we keep in mind the direction of current and our speed over the bottom.

Overhead power cables are about 600 yard west of the bridge with a 90 foot vertical clearance between towers.

Bridges over the Port Washington Narrows, Manette Bridge in foreground

Evergreen Park (Bremerton) is on the west shore north of the charted tower in a small cove. There is a single-lane, surfaced launch ramp, about 300 feet of shoreline, restrooms, picnic tables, shelters, water, fireplaces and children's play area. Not recommended for swimming, it's supposed to be good fishing here.

Cable and pipeline areas are charted between the towers and the Warren Avenue bridge, vertical clearance 80 feet.

Port Washington Marina in shallow **Anderson Cove** is on the southwest shore. Mariners are asked to watch their wake as they cruise by, because the marina has no breakwater.

Port Washington Marina Facilities
➤ Undesignated number of guest moorages
➤ Power
➤ Restrooms with showers
➤ Laundry
➤ Pump-out
➤ Launch ramp
➤ Fishing pier
➤ Restaurants and groceries available within walking distance
➤ Phone: 360-479-3037.

The Native American name for Rudy Point means "Boiling Promontory." According to legend as the current ripples around this point a spring of fine water bubbles up among the rocks off the point and at low tide one can get a drink here—if you can figure out where it is and how to get to it.

Warren Avenue bridge is next, vertical clearance 80 feet, horizontal clearance 220 feet, depths of 12 feet.

A rocky shoal is charted near the center of the narrows, west of the bridge, and shallow water is along the north shoreline, so we favor the south shore.

Lions Field (Bremerton) is on the northeast shore opposite Anderson Cove. It is a city of Bremerton and Lions Club joint effort park with 1,700 feet of shoreline.

Launch ramp with parking, fishing pier, float, jogging track, kids play area, picnic tables, restrooms and playing fields are at the park. (Beware of large cats.)

• **Cable area** is charted west of the park.
• **A rock** is charted inshore of an abrupt five foot shoal 100 yards offshore, about 0.4 mile north of Anderson Cove on the south shore.
• **"Rudy Point,"** unnamed on charts, is on the east entrance of Phinney Bay.
• **Phinney Bay,** 0.3 mile wide and 0.5 mile long, opens south from the Narrows.

Bremerton Yacht Club is charted but unnamed on the west shore of Phinney Bay. The club offers reciprocal moorage.

➡ **Caution:** A 50 foot steel hull boat sank in the southern part of the bay in the spring of 1994. The Coast Guard surveyed the area, but as yet the wreck isn't charted. It is approximately just north of the "24 foot" charted depth. Local divers say it is deteriorating rapidly. We've been told that at a minus 3.5 tide it is still in about 10 to 12 feet of water. Anchors or anchor lines may foul on the wreck. We use our depth sounder to locate the wreck and stay clear when in that part of the bay.

⚓ **Anchoring** is good in the south end of the bay in about 16 to 30 feet with mud bottom. It is nice and quiet, offering pleasant nights, and no nearby highway noise.

⚙ **Underway again,** leaving Phinney Bay, we head north.

F 15ft Priv Light is about 0.25 mile north of the yacht club.

Bass Point has abrupt ledges on the edge of the three fathom curve near shore.

Rocky Point, at the northern tip of Rocky Point peninsula, has tide rips when the current is running. The shores are lined with homes of all sizes, shapes and colors, stairways to the beaches, and refinements like manicured lawns and landscaped gardens.

Dyes Inlet now opens up to the north. There's a fetch of over three miles north to Silverdale. A blow from that direction can come in pretty heavy.

Oyster Bay or Ostrich Bay are choices for anchoring in the south end of Dyes. Oyster Bay is preferred by many cruising boaters because it offers more protection.

Tiny Mud Bay is tucked between Phinney Bay and Oyster Bay. We're told it's suitable for kayaking, canoeing, rowing, or even anchoring at high tide. We haven't tried it yet. This is a drying bay at low tides. There are some state public tidelands in the bay.

Ⓖ **Oyster Bay** is a lovely, well-protected anchorage with eight to 15 feet, muddy bottom—a tree-lined, reasonably quiet **gunkhole,** and not overrun with homes. It seems larger than it appears on charts, with a tiny island in the northeast corner where it's all shoal.

A highway is not too far from the shore so some traffic noise filters in. Water skiing is popular in this bay during the summer and can provide some entertainment, albeit at close range, sometimes too close, and goes late into the evening.

Public tidelands of about 3,000 feet are in Oyster Bay.

Entering Oyster Bay, the passage is barely 100 yards wide in places, and 0.5 mile long. The pass is lined with homes and has a least charted depth of six feet at mean lower low water.

Scheherazade draws 5.5 feet so we enter and leave on rising or high tides.

Madrona Point, at the north end of the peninsula between Ostrich and Oyster Bays, has a charted six foot shoal extending 350 yards, a bit west of north, with some rocks inshore of the four foot depth.

Entering Oyster Bay, heading south

We clear the point and cruise slowly up the inlet, waving at people in their homes—and they wave back. Some are washing windows, vacuuming, doing yard work or having coffee out on their decks. On hot summer days the pass is filled with swim rafts and ski boats.

A rather abrupt point is at the end of the passage on the east side, with a no-bank waterfront home with many trees. Pass by a point on the west side and we're inside Oyster Bay. It's a **delightful gunkhole.**

Sewer line is charted and crosses the southwest corner of the bay about 300 yards offshore.

Cable area is in the southeast corner of the bay.

A good friend in Olympia, Don Fasset, lived at Mud Bay in the 1940s or 50s. He recalls:

"I found an old log house on the West shore of Mud Bay. Moved the family there and moved the boat, a 28 foot cutter called Wunks into Mud Bay, where I kept her upright by fastening a couple of long poles from her deck to the beach. Obviously we could only go in and out at the top of the tide."

Marine Drive is charted on the small peninsula separating Mud Bay and Ostrich Bay, but early Native Americans called it the "Battling Place." Legends claim this was the scene of a great battle between myth people from Sxaqt and myth people from Port Orchard. Erratic boulders on both sides of the point are warriors who were turned to stone.

Before World War II, Japanese oysters were introduced into Oyster Bay, but when the Japanese oyster farmers were confined to internment camps, the commercial production closed down.

Duck nets were supposedly used in the south end of Mud Bay by Native Americans. As ducks in the lagoon flew through the pass, nets would be raised on poles and ducks became dinner.

⚓ **We anchor** in charted depths of about six to 16 feet in Oyster Bay, after avoiding the sewer and cable areas.

☸ **Leaving** Oyster Bay, we go out through the pass and turn left.

Ostrich Bay—we've reached the last and largest of these three bays in the south end of Dyes Inlet.

Public tideland is along the southwest shore, part of a small undeveloped marine park. It's possible to land a small boat and walk the trail to the park entrance, and from there to a market. There are picnic tables and a parking lot.

⚓ **Anchor** in the south end in charted depths of 15 to 20 feet, mud bottom, south of the deteriorating Navy dock.

Ostrich Bay was named by explorers because its shape appeared to the explorers to be like an ostrich. If you can visualize that, please advise.

We anchored near the west shore, rowed to the beach and walked the short, woodsy trail into town for ice cream.

A long row of pilings stretch from the old dock almost to **Elwood Point,** nearly 0.25 mile. It's shallow, from four to six feet between the pilings and the beach.

Bremerton Naval Hospital is near Elwood Point. This is all Navy property: housing, play areas and Jackson Park on the point. North of the point is a large drying lagoon.

Dyes Inlet beaches are permanently closed to shellfish harvesting.

☸ **Underway again, we head for Chico, Silverdale and Tracyton.**

It's nearly a mile from Elwood Point north to **Erland Point,** then out and around the point and the rounded bump north of it, staying between 0.1 and 0.2 miles off.

Chico Bay, about 0.6 mile across and about 0.5 mile long, spreads out to the south. The southern half is mud flats, especially where Chico Creek enters the bay. The rest is shoal with many pilings throughout the bay and along the western shore as well.

Chico launch ramp

Launch ramp on the west shore of Chico Bay is one block from the highway. It is surfaced, single lane with some parking. Private homes and beaches are on both sides of the ramp.

North along the west shoreline of Dyes Inlet to Silverdale are houses, houses, and more houses. There is no public beach access along the entire western shore of Dyes Inlet except for the Chico launch ramp.

Silverdale is about two miles north of Chico. **Silverdale Waterfront Park and Marina** are in Old Towne Silverdale on the northwest shore at the head of the bay. The pier, floats and launch ramps are easy to spot from the water as this is the only large moorage in the area. This is a four-acre park designed for family fun with a playground and picnic areas.

*Chico was named for a friendly local Indian chief, **William Chico** or **Chako**.*

As with most small waterfront communities, Chico had steamer service in the early days. Chico also had roads fairly early-on to serve inland settlers after they disembarked from the steamers.

Silverdale Marina & Park Facilities
➤ Moorage for approximately 40-50 boats, no power
➤ Moorage rates are $3 daily for boats under 28', $5 daily for boats 28' and over
➤ Floats are open to the public; no locked gates
➤ Restrooms
➤ Fishing pier
➤ Nearby restaurants, shops and laundry
➤ Three night maximum
➤ No rafting
➤ Double-wide launch ramp with plenty of parking
➤ Phone: 360-692-2801

Silverdale Marina

The moorage is okay in a northerly, but southerlies whistle through, although the good piers and concrete floats provide some shelter. There is about 10 feet of water at the floats at low tide.

Just cruise up to a float and tie up. Two short sets of stairs reach the beach from the park; beachcomb or swim along the 600 feet of shoreline. Youngsters enjoy the crab and starfish designs in the concrete walkways.

Kitsap County Historical Museum, in the old Silverdale State Bank building is one block from the marina, a wonderful and intriguing place to visit, especially if you love fascinating historical stuff. Restaurants and small shops are close to the marina.

The giant, sprawling Kitsap Mall with a Bon Marche, JC Penney, Sears, Lamonts, Mervyns and more than 120 specialty shops, is less than a mile away from the marina park for those who need a "mall-fix." Close by are Costco, Home Depot, Eddie Bauer and other well-known stores. This is the largest regional shopping center on the Kitsap Peninsula, and a far cry from businesses in the early days.

Silverdale hosts Whaling Days the last weekend each July, which include a parade, street fair and wine-tasting, among other events.

The northeast corner of the Dyes Inlet is shoal, with the one fathom curve nearly 0.3 mile offshore.

⚓ **Anchoring** is possible during calm weather south of this curve in charted depths of about 20 to 25 feet, mud bottom. Rocks are inshore of the four foot depth.

☸ **Underway again,** leaving Silverdale, we go south along the east shore.

Clam Island, charted but unnamed, is 800 yards west of **Barker Creek** on the 48° line. The shoal is accessible by boat and only at very low tide. It would be a great place for clam digging, except that all of Dyes Inlet was permanently closed to shellfish harvesting in 1995.

We pass east of often submerged Clam Island, using the depth sounder, dead reckoning and caution, to avoid an unwanted encounter.

J. A. and Anna Smith Children's Park, about one mile southeast of Silverdale, is south of Barker Creek. It's visible from the water with its 600 foot long, low, concrete bulkhead below a forested bank. The park is across Dyes Inlet from Silverdale Marina.

Park trails are along the hillside from beach to upper area with small, wooden bridges, a large children's garden, picnic areas, small amphitheater and restrooms.

⚓ **Anchoring** is feasible south of the shoal off Barker Creek in about 10 feet or more. Dinghy ashore at Smith Park as this is a public beach.

☸ **We continue south** along this east shore of Dyes Inlet and there's not quite as much development as on the west shore, or maybe we're getting used to it. The closer to Windy Point, the more homes there are.

Windy Point depths of 3 fathom extend about 400 yards offshore. The shoreline trends southeasterly along here toward the community of **Tracyton.**

Launch ramp, single lane, is at the end of Tracy Avenue. From the water, there's a cluster of several pilings offshore just south of the ramp. It's a four block walk to the main road where there's a deli, service station and tavern.

Public tidelands of about 2,000 feet are north of the launch ramp.

⚓ **Anchor** in about 25 to 35 feet and dinghy ashore at the ramp.

☸ **Leaving** Tracyton, we head back out through Port Washington Narrows on our way back into Puget Sound.

Murals on Silverdale Historical Museum

Silverdale was once a quiet, waterfront community in the northwest corner of Dyes Inlet that had regular steamer service to Seattle starting in the 1880s. Logging was its primary early industry, and a blacksmith shop and livery stable were the town's first businesses. Later on, farmers raised poultry and dairy cattle.

Native Americans once called the Silverdale area "Prairie" or "Open Spaces." That name no longer fits.

Dyes Inlet was named for John W.W. Dye, an assistant taxidermist with the Wilkes Expedition.

In Chapter 9, we'll be back in the main waters of Puget Sound and ready to explore Blake Island and Yukon Harbor.

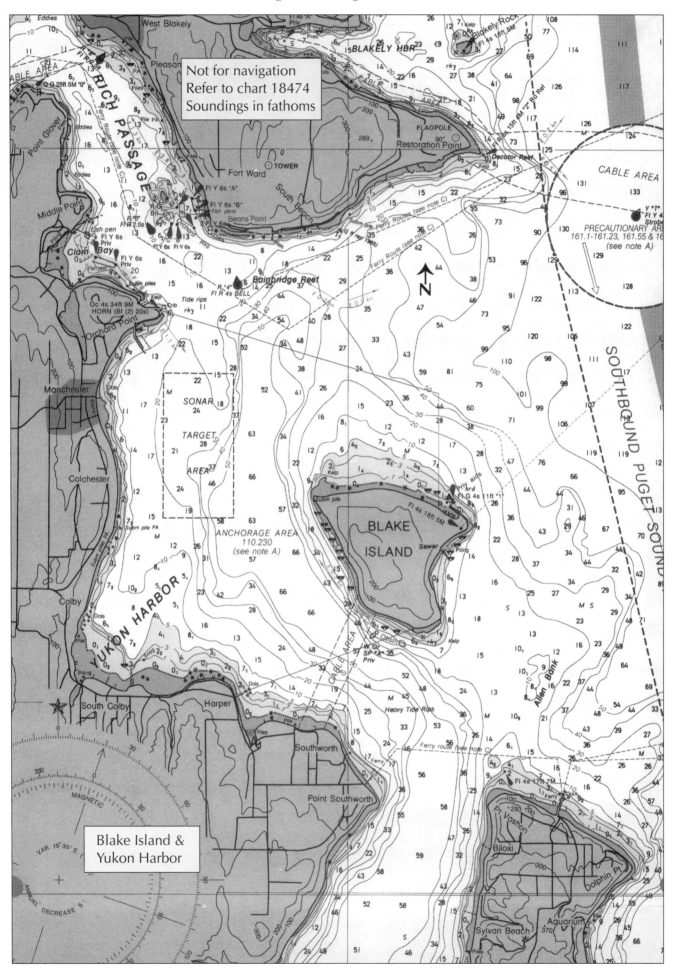

Not for navigation
Refer to chart 18474
Soundings in fathoms

Blake Island &
Yukon Harbor

CHAPTER 9
Blake Island and Yukon Harbor

Charts and publications for this chapter

Chart	Date	Title	Scale	Soundings
*** 18449	10/29/94	Puget Sound, Seattle to Bremerton (Recommended chart for this area)	1:25,000	Feet
** 18474	03/25/95	Shilshole Bay to Commencement Bay	1:40,000	Fathoms
* 18445	06/03/95	Puget Sound—Possession Sound to Olympia, page A	1:80,000	Fathoms
* 18448	10/30/93	Puget Sound, Southern Part	1:80,000	Fathoms
18440	08/05/95	Puget Sound	1:150,000	Fathoms
		Tidal Current Charts, Puget Sound, Northern Part		
		Booklet: Puget Sound Shellfish Sites		
		Washington State Public Lands Quad Map—Seattle	1:100,000	

➡ *When using charts, compare your chart dates with ones referred to above. There may be discrepancies between different charts and different chart editions.*

South from Restoration Point

Blake Island State Marine Park, just over two miles south of Bainbridge Island, is one of the most well-used state marine parks in Puget Sound. A scant six miles from downtown Seattle, the park is visited by thousands seeking the peace and quiet of a woodland refuge close to the city.

All of the thickly forested, 475 acre island is a state marine park, with magnificent views of the Olympics, Cascades, Mount Rainier, Mount Baker and the awesome Seattle skyline. It is a favorite destination for about 300,000 people arriving annually by both private and tour boats.

Replica of Puget's launch

Seattle, as viewed from the island's east shore is spectacular, especially at night—and you're not part of its hustle and bustle. Hide away from the world by anchoring or tying to a mooring buoy off the south or west shore where the view will be of forests, mountains and shorelines.

Blake is ideal for picnicking, camping, water skiing, fishing, hiking, beachcombing, swimming, scuba diving, clamming, bird watching and marine life study.

➡ **NOTE: There is no place to buy marine fuel** in the area covered in this chapter.

Puget Passes Blake

Peter Puget was the first European to pass close to Blake Island. Captain George Vancouver directed Puget:

"You are at 4 o'clock tomorrow morning to proceed with the Launch accompanied by Mr. Whidbey in the Cutter, whose directions you will follow in such points as appertain to surveying the shore ... & being provided with a week's provisions you will proceed up said Inlet, keeping Starboard or Continental Shore on board & having proceeded three days up the Inlet, should it then appear to you of that extent that you cannot finally determine its limits, and return to the Ship by Thursday next ..."

(continued on next page)

*In the fall of 1993, the longhouse on densely wooded Blake Island was the site of the annual APEC conference, attended by **President Bill Clinton** and many Asian-Pacific heads of state.*

Peter Puget's men rowed *smartly against an ebbing tide, ignoring the small island south of Bainbridge as they headed into the narrow channel, later named Colvos Passage.*

The mile wide pass was a marine corridor between splendidly forested Kitsap Peninsula and Vashon Island.

Blake Island is the "small island" Puget saw, but ignored, as they headed into the unexplored region of "South Sound."

Chief Seattle—we meet again

More than six miles of public tidelands are in this chapter.

Public tidelands *unless otewise noted are state owned. Some maybe leased and posted for aquaculture or other private use. We take the Washington State Public Lands Quadrangle Map, when going ashore at these locations to avoid trespassing on adjacent private property.*

(continued from previous page)

When Puget's two small boats departed from southwest of Restoration Point on Bainbridge Island that early morning more than 200 years ago, smoke rose from a nearby Suquamish Indian encampment. A small Indian boy had watched in awe at the arrival of Vancouver's ships the night before. His father was the tribal chief, Chief Schweabe.

Years later that boy grew up to become the beloved Indian chief, "Seattle," for whom the city is named. He remembered as a child seeing Capt. Vancouver and his ships on the waters of the "Whulge."

Chief Seattle

On the back of a large sign on Blake Island there is a picture of Chief Seattle and a narrative about him. We'll tell you about it in case you miss it.

"It is not known for sure where Chief Seattle was born. Some reports indicate he was born on Blake Island, one of the camping grounds of the Suquamish tribe. The records of Capt. George Vancouver indicate that Sealth (his Indian name) was born around 1786.

"Just who is Chief Seattle? At age 22 he successfully led a band of warriors against some hostile mountain Indians. He was then made chief of six allied tribes. Chief Seattle was baptized and given the name Noah Sealth.

"His steadfast friendship with the white settlers convinced them to honor him and name their new city after him. During the Indian wars of 1855 and 1856 he was a peacemaker between the Indians and the settlers. His tall stately appearance and tremendous sounding voice earned everyone's respect. His last years were at the Port Madison reservation. He died in 1886 and is buried at Suquamish cemetery."

It was in a speech in 1855 that Chief Seattle predicted the end of Puget Sound as it had once been; "the pleasing landscapes and abundant fertility" that Vancouver saw, were coming to an end.

Chief Seattle spoke to a gathering called by Territorial Gov. Isaac Stevens to approve the Point Elliott Treaty in which Indians ceded almost all their lands to the white men—a treaty which forever changed Puget Sound. In memborable words translated by his friend, Dr. Henry Smith, the Indian chief said:

"It matters little where we pass the remnant of our days. They will not be many. The Indian's night promises to be dark. Not a single star hovers above his horizon. Sad-voiced winds moan in the distance. Some grim fate seems to be on the Red Man's trail, and wherever he goes he will still hear the approaching footsteps of his fell destroyer and prepare stolidly to meet his doom, as does the wounded doe that hears the approaching footsteps of the hunter.

"A few more moons, a few more winters — and not one of the descendants of the mighty hosts that once moved over this broad land or lived in happy homes, protected by the Great Spirit, will remain to mourn over the graves of a people once more powerful and hopeful than yours.

"But why should I mourn at the untimely fate of my people?

"Tribe follows tribe, and nation follows nation, like the waves of the sea. It is the order of nature, and regret is useless. Your time of decay may be distant, but it will surely come, for even the White Man whose god walked and talked with him as friend with friend, cannot be exempt from the common destiny. We may be brothers after all. We shall see.

"We will ponder your proposition, and when we decide we will tell you.

"But should we accept it, I here and now, make this the first condition — that we will not be denied the privilege, without molestation, of visiting at any

(continued on next page)

time the tombs of our ancestors, friends and children.

"Every part of this soil is sacred ... Every hillside, every valley, every plane and grove has been hallowed by some sad or happy event in days long vanished. Even the rocks, which seem to lie dumb and dead as they swelter in the sun or darken in the rain along the silent seashore, thrill with the memories of stirring events connected with the lives of my people.

"And when the last Red Man shall have perished from the earth, and the memory of my tribe shall have become a myth ... these shores will swarm with the invisible dead of my tribe; and when your children's children shall think themselves alone in the fields, the store, the shop, upon the highway, or in the silence of the pathless woods, they will not be alone ...

"At night, when the streets of your cities and villages will be silent and you think them deserted, they will throng with returning hosts that once filled them and still love this beautiful land.

"The white man will never be alone. Let him be just and deal kindly with my people, for the dead are not powerless."

Blake Island's Founding Family

William Pitt Trimble, a Kentucky lawyer who became a brilliant success as a real estate promoter after he moved to Seattle in 1890, bought Blake Island in 1900—with a bit of persuasion from his wife Cannie. He developed it into a beautiful, private estate and renamed it Trimble Island.

They built a 12 room, two-story summer home, with five fireplaces on the main floor. The living room was 30 x 40 feet with 8 x 16 inch clear cedar beams. There were water and sewer systems, a 350 foot long wharf, wagon road, concrete tennis courts and other amenities.

South of the island's northeast point are ruins of an old wharf. Trimble built the original pier here. It was made with untreated timbers and pileworms ate it up in six months. He rebuilt it using creosoted pilings.

Cannie loved gardening and turned the island into a Federal Wildlife Refuge. She assembled a large Pacific Northwest History Library. She died in a freak accident when her car plunged off an Elliott Bay pier in December 1929.

Trimble was devastated. He abandoned the island and never returned. The house was vandalized and burned, until all that remained was the foundation, tennis courts and dock pilings. Trimble died in March 1943 at the age of 80.

Behind one of the park information signs are some concrete foundations. One may have been a fireplace foundation made with brick and beach rock, which looked like it was hand mixed. Rock ruins of a bulkhead with stone steps lead uphill—to what? A last remnant of the Trimble property.

⚓ Underway on a clockwise circumnavigation of Blake Island

We start a cruise around Blake Island from the marina at the northeast corner of the island, where there is room for about 25 or so recreational boats, plus tour boats. A large rock breakwater extends westward, enclosing the moorage.

Marina entrance is off the western end of the breakwater. A well-marked channel leads into the marina. It's as shallow as five feet or less outside of the channel. All navigation aids on and around Blake Island are privately maintained.

Entering the marina, Fl G 4s 11 ft "1" Blake Island Light 1 on a square green dayboard on a pile, marks the east side of the channel entrance.

Green daybeacons "3" and "5" square green dayboards on piles, are to port.

Blake Island was acquired as state park property in three parcels, the last in 1974, for a total cost of $1,588,125.

It was logged by G. A. Meigs and W.P. Sayward in the 1850s, as were many of the islands in the Sound.

It was officially named Blake in that same year. It has been known as both High Island and Smuggler Island at various times over the years.

Blake Island is an ancestral campground of the Suquamish Indian Tribe. *Chief Seattle* told Catherine Maynard (wife of Doc Maynard—one of Seattle's founders), that he was born on Blake Island in 1786.

Hundreds of tourists visit Northwest Indian Tillicum Village, a privately operated facility on Blake, to enjoy barbecued salmon and traditional Northwest Indian dancing. The festivities are held in a replica of an Indian longhouse. Striking murals on the longhouse face the water, welcoming visitors. A gift shop features native crafts and other items.

Visitors arrive by both tour and private boats. Those not on tour boats can also enjoy the festivities. Phone: 206-443-1244

Indian longhouse

Red daybeacons "2" "4" and "6," triangular red dayboards on pilings, mark the west side of the channel and are kept to starboard.

We turn to port after **green "5"** and enter the marina.

The first float inside is for tour boats; the second for state park boats; the next four floats are for guest boats. (A pump-out float parallels the breakwater.) It can be very crowded in here at times. Pick your spot, tie up and enjoy.

Blake Island Marina

Blake Island Marina Facilities

➤ Moorage for approximately 25 boats
➤ Moorage rates $8 per night for boats under 26', $11 per night boats over 26'
➤ 21 mooring buoys
➤ Buoy rate $5 per night
➤ No fuel or other marine services available
➤ Porta-potty dump station
➤ No fee pump-out station on a float (closes first fall freeze until spring)
➤ Moorage limited to three consecutive nights
➤ Restrooms with showers (at north end of island), restrooms only at west end
➤ Aluminum can recycling center
➤ Five miles of beaches
➤ Picnic tables and 56 campsites with fire ring
➤ No trash collection on Blake Island, pack it in, pack it out
➤ Moorage at the northeast end of the island is where tour boats and park boats tie up, leaving about 1,744 feet of moorage space for recreational boaters.

***In May 1841** the name Blake was given to the island by Lt. Charles Wilkes. He named it for George Blake who was in charge of the U.S. Coast Survey from 1837 to 1848.*

The island's main campground with restrooms, showers, group camp and an interpretive display are along this shore, adjacent to the marina. The longhouse is the site of Northwest Indian Tillicum Village, hosting the salmon barbecue and Indian dancing. The ranger station and remains of the old Trimble estate are also on shore. An interpretive nature trail is west of the longhouse, and other trails around and across the island fan out from here.

⊕ **Underway,** we leave the marina through the channel, head east past the breakwater, and then turn south, following the shoreline.

Fl 4s 18ft 5M light Blake Island East Light, is on a diamond shaped dayboard with black and white sectors, 18 feet high, on the northeast point of the island. Several large concrete blocks have been placed along the shoreline to help prevent erosion here. Off the east shore are six mooring buoys. From here we look east with a panoramic view of Seattle and the Cascade Mountains.

⚓ **Anchoring** is possible along this shore in three to six fathoms, sand bottom, being cautious to set the hook well because of kelp on the bottom.

Heading south from here, the island banks become steeper, as always heavily forested, and at the south end are kelpy, rock shores.

Approximately 22 mooring buoys are around Blake Island. We comment on them as we go. Buoys shown on NOAA charts may or may not agree with the actual numbers in place.

⊕ **The underwater park** for scuba divers is around this end of the island. They can dive in deep, rocky waters and enjoy spearfishing, photography and just observing sea life. As we come around the island, the diving reef buoy and two mooring buoys come into view.

The underwater reef is 800 feet south of the southern tip of Blake in about 60 to 90 feet of water offshore from the south campground. The campground has pit toilets. Trails lead around the island in several directions.

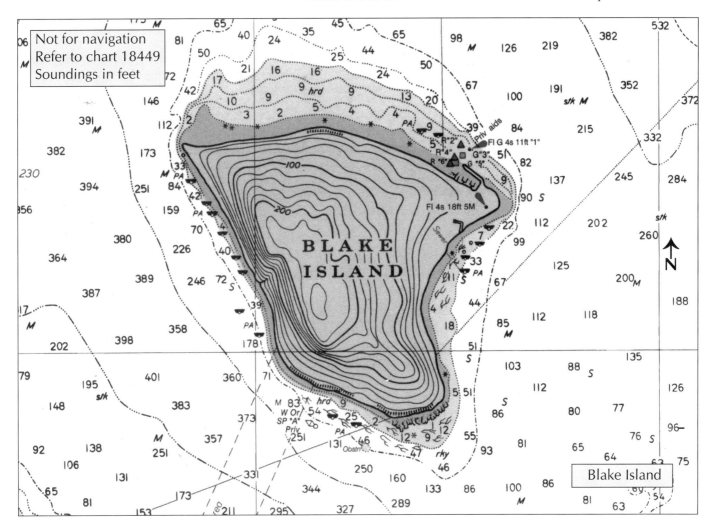

The island shore here is heavily wooded, with big erratic rocks on a beach filled with downed trees and silver driftwood.

Cable area extends from the southwest shore of Blake Island to Southworth on the Kitsap Peninsula.

We continue northwest past south end bluffs for about a 0.5 mile, then the bluffs recede and the west camping area, the "Riviera" of Blake Island, appears along the shore, extending to the point shown as North Point on island maps.

There are eight mooring buoys here, and the water is sometimes calmer than at other places around the island. This is our favorite moorage spot at Blake Island. Even though the swimming is chilly, the hiking trails are great.

⚓ **Anchoring** is feasible along this shore in about 40 feet, mud bottom, an alternative if the buoys are taken.

A sandy beach and uncharted tidal lagoon beckon those who want to swim or wade. Picnic tables, fireplaces and trails are on shore. Restrooms in the woods are not visible from the water.

From the west side of the island the views include sunsets over the Olympic Mountains.

⚙ **Underway** from the "Riviera," we complete our circumnavigation of the island as we go out around North Point and the wide sandy shoal which extends north about 500 yards, keeping well off the shallow north shore, with erratic rocks on the beach.

Six buoys are west of the marina along this shore. This can be pretty choppy with all the large ship traffic in the Sound, including ferries and other vessels going to and from Bremerton.

The highest spot on Blake Island is a 250 foot high knob on the southwest side. It was called "Bullhead" by early Native Americans.

Blake Marina & longhouse

The sea bottom is shallow and irregular for about 0.5 mile off the north shore of the island, which contributes to the chop. We found this the least comfortable of all the buoy areas around the island.

Along the entire north side of the island the three fathom depth curve extends about 500 yards off shore.

⚓ **Anchoring** is possible here, with the same lumpy water as if tied to a buoy.

We've circumnavigated the island and we've arrived back at the marina.

Tips & Trivia from the Ranger

We visited with ranger, J.P., who told us, among other things, that the little sandbar at the east end of the marina between the breakwater and the island is eroding and needs to be built up.

Moorage space: "Moorage for private boats gets pretty well packed on summer weekends. The best time to come is late Sunday afternoon because all the weekenders are heading out and only the retirees and people who have Monday and Tuesday off are coming in. On Wednesdays and Thursdays we start filling up again."

Salmon barbecue: "The Indian barbecue and dancing is a big draw. Lots of people come on the tour boats."

Garbage: "People in general are pretty good, although we still have problems with garbage. They try to burn glass and aluminum cans in the fire rings. A universal problem with boats is that garbage accumulates pretty fast and people dump it. On an average summer weekend we get 250 bags of garbage daily, even though there are no garbage facilities. We spend the next three days hauling it out." He sighed. "Hauling garbage and cleaning restrooms."

Such is the life of a park ranger.

Black Tail deer *flourish in the wooded environment of Blake Island. The herd is a source of interest and enjoyment for island visitors.*

Seasons at Blake Island

We've been at Blake Island in both summer and winter—two totally different experiences.

Summertime is crowded and noisy, the marina crammed full. You can catch a buoy if you're lucky. The trails, however, may be quiet and serene, since most folks either stay on the beaches or at the marina and Tillicum Village.

We've wandered Blake Island's trails, uphill and down, through forests, wetlands, along cliffs and beaches several different times of year. Considering the proximity to Seattle and the dozens of boats tied at the marina, we were amazed that we actually walked 45 minutes through the island's central trails on a Sunday afternoon in mid-July without seeing another human being. There were birds, chipmunks and squirrels, garter snakes and the ubiquitous slugs who love the dampness of the woods. We saw several of the nearly 75 deer who live on the island. The perimeter trails were a bit more well traveled.

In wintertime, it's pretty easy to find an empty slip at the marina. And almost all the buoys are empty. Tillicum Village is closed except for weekends.

Rules for park visitors are on a sign near the registration fee box. Outside lights come on early on the floats. The water is turned off and the place seems to be pretty well deserted. A wonderful time to visit.

(continued on next page)

On shore the trails are sloshy underfoot. Newly blown-down trees partially block some trails. Even the deer seek shelter.

We were moored in the marina just after a New Year's weekend one year. The tide was so low we couldn't see over the top of the breakwater. Then it started raining and blowing, with wind whistling through the rigging. It poured and blew. About 8 a.m., the tide was almost high. By then only three or four feet of rock breakwater was visible; the breakwater had virtually become an island. At the east end of the marina cove, which we knew to be a steep sloping sandy beach, all we could see were breaking waves flooding in, the beach a good four feet under the water. The floats, which had been very quiet during the night, were like junior grade roller-coasters.

The three sailboats bounded up and down in the slips. The saltwater was within inches of the trees on shore, within inches of a Blake Island signpost. That's about as high as the tide gets. Ramps leading to floats in the marina were almost horizontal. Grassy areas on lowlands south of the marina had turned to mud and at high tide were nearly under saltwater.

It was a typical wintry, windy day, with winds gusting 35 to 40 knots, but we were pretty well sheltered in the marina. We walked the beach, enjoying the surf and the driftwood it tossed onto the beach.

Having the island practically to ourselves, we shlumped through muddy trails inland among the variety of deciduous trees, cedars and firs. We saw blowdown trees from earlier windstorms, up-ended in the woods, as we walked the squishy trails. We walked to the island's summit, hearing our shoes sloshing with each step. It was swampy even high up. We headed back down.

As we neared the moorage we could hear surf pounding on the beach. A squall of perhaps 50 knots was coming through, bringing crashing waves.

We had a slight problem with our bow line coming undone when winds gusted that morning. *Scheherazade* broke loose and was getting ready to run away to sea without our permission. The bow swung out even as we stood on deck. Carl leaped off onto the float and we got her tied back up before she departed.

As the saying goes, "A smooth sea never made a skillful sailor."

Seas were white all across the Sound to Seattle as heavy rollers bashed the island. With the high tide we were still thrashing around a bit, the dock going up and down about a foot. We kept our headlines a lot looser than before. The swells looked at least four to six feet high outside the breakwater. A half-hour later the wind had dropped, seas were down somewhat, and it was time to leave Blake Island.

Large vessel "Anchorage" is charted in Yukon Harbor.

Note the magenta line from Orchard Point east to Blake Island and then south to Harper delineating the anchorage. Mariners are referred to Note A on the chart and section 110.230 of the **Coast Pilot**.

Blustery day and high tide at Blake Island marina

⚓ **Underway again,** we're covering the west and south peninsula shoreline of Yukon Harbor, from Point Glover in Rich Passage to Point Southworth at the entrance to Colvos Passage. (For Rich Passage current information from Point Glover to Orchard Point, see Chapter 6, pages 111-114.)

Manchester State Park, not a marine park, is west of Middle Point on Rich Passage. Offshore, it is fairly shallow with variable currents.

⚓ **Anchoring** is possible in eight to 11 feet, sand, mud or shell bottom—to let the kids run for a short while— the hook holds. We wouldn't recommend anchoring for very long; too much current and wash from passing vessels. There are better places. It does make a feasible small boat stop.

Manchester State Park Facilities
➤ 3,400 feet of shoreline
➤ 111 acres of uplands with trails
➤ Picnic tables with fireplaces, water
➤ Restrooms with showers
➤ 53 overnight campsites
➤ Historical displays
➤ Scuba diving

State Parks acquired the land for Manchester Park from the federal government in the early 1970s.

U.S. Coast Artillery Harbor Defense Structures were built at the turn-of-the-century for the protection of Bremerton and the Naval Shipyard.

It was converted to a Navy Fuel Supply Depot and Navy Fire Fighting Station during World War II, when submarine nets were stretched across Rich Passage from Manchester to Fort Ward on Bainbridge. They were opened when ferries went through the pass.

The park was named for the nearby town of Manchester.

Manchester was originally called Brooklyn. It was renamed Manchester in 1892 in expectation of an active seaport similar to Manchester in England.

The former Torpedo Warehouse is a unique turn-of-the century brick military structure with arched doorways and windows. Interpretive slide programs are given during the summer, as well as nature walks.

(2) Fl Y 6s lights Clam Bay fish pen lights, mark the pens of an aquaculture facility which pretty much fills Clam Bay, just south of Middle Point.

Orchard Point, southeast of the bay, is included in the oil storage area of the Puget Sound U.S. Naval Supply Center. Two large wharves are on either side of the point.

Oc 4s 34ft 9M Horn (Bl (2) 20s) Orchard Point light, occulting 4 second light and horn, 34 feet high, on a white concrete tower, is visible for nine miles.

Yukon Harbor
The harbor runs from Orchard Point on the north nearly 2.5 miles south to South Colby, and then east about two miles to Southworth. From Colby to Southworth the bay is shoal as much as 0.5 mile out, with low tides revealing wide tide flats.

Anchoring is possible in the harbor in up to eight fathoms along the shores. There is good protection from south and west winds in Yukon Harbor.

The communities of Manchester, Colchester, Colby, South Colby and Harper follow the shoreline from the north corner of the harbor to the Southworth ferry landing.

Manchester community is about 0.7 mile south of Orchard Point.

Public fishing pier at the village now replaces the former passenger steamer pier. There is a float where you can tie up, daytime only, with no charge. The water tends to shoal up to five feet here, so be cautious of the depths.

Launch ramp with two lanes is immediately south of the pier with a tiny park alongside.

Manchester has a grocery store that sells a bit of everything, a post office and restaurant. There's even a branch of the Kitsap Regional Library, in case you need to look up some information or check out a book— if you're a Kitsap County resident.

Housing is quite dense on the slopes around Manchester, from the waterfront to the top of the hills. Although there are some boats anchored out, we saw no private docks—a good indication of shallow water.

Fishing is supposed to be very good around here, when the season is open. In fact, there's even a Manchester Sports Fishing Club.

Early Times in Manchester
Early pioneers in Manchester included the Samuel Denniston family who arrived in 1900. There are four Denniston-built homes still on the waterfront just south of the public pier. Two of the homes are still occupied by descendants or relatives of Samuel.

The first dock was built in 1905 so steamer passengers could walk onto the shore rather than being loaded onto floats and rowed ashore. Steamer fares were from 10 to 20 cents per trip.

⚓ **Continuing on,** we pass **South Colby** is at the head of Yukon Harbor, about 1.5 miles south of Manchester, with the community of Colchester in between.

Gurley Creek is charted as emptying into the southwest corner of the harbor. Local residents tell us it's really called **Curly** Creek, but on chart 18449 it's shown as **Gurley.** The Washington State Lands Quad Map, Seattle, shows it as **Curley.**

You decide.

In southwest Yukon Harbor the three fathom depth curve projects to 700 yards or 0.35 mile offshore.

Friends advise that if you need gas for a small boat you can row ashore at high tide, climb the hillside from Curly Creek and walk to Bayside Grocery on S.E. Southworth Drive and Banner Road and buy Texaco gas. It may not be too convenient, you have to carry your own gas can, but people do it in an emergency.

⚓ **Anchor** about 0.4 mile out from shore in about 20 to 50 feet, mud bottom, with good protection from a southerly. We anchored overnight here when visiting friends ashore at Colby. It was a LONG row back to the boat at high tide.

⚓ **Harper State Park** at old Harper ferry landing, about 1.5 miles west of Point Southworth, has been turned into a fishing pier and launch ramp—the Harper State Park - Launch Ramp.

Car-top only launch ramp is at the head of the deep indent south and east of the pier. It is a sand and gravel ramp, the reason for the car-top only designation.

There's no float at the pier, which was built through the combined efforts of the Harper and Southworth Community Clubs and the state, and is managed by State Parks. There are 3.03 acres in the park with 777 feet of salt waterfront.

Local boats are anchored at least 400 yards offshore because of the tide flats here. Local boats are a good indication of possible anchorages. There are houses all along the waterfront here, and it's very civilized, no real gunkholes. Be aware of private buoys for crab and shrimp pots.

Cable area runs from Southworth to Blake Island.

Public tidelands of over one mile, in several parcels, run from South Colby almost to Point Southworth.

Point Southworth has a large terminal for the Fauntleroy-Vashon Island ferries. They keep a busy schedule. Sometimes ferries leaving Southworth turn around before heading over to Vashon, so be aware and give them ample room.

A passenger-only ferry carries commuters across Puget Sound from Vashon to downtown Seattle. Passenger only service from Southworth to Seattle is planned in the future.

Public beach access is a narrow strip of land immediately north of the ferry landing. Canoes and kayaks can be put in here. The rest of the beaches are private.

In pioneer days there was a thriving waterfront village between Manchester and South Colby. Early families came for free homesteading land, good climate and fertile soil. Soon there were stores, a post office, a hotel and school. Nothing remains of that early settlement.

The Harper fishing pier was first known as "Harmon's Landing," after George and Jennie Harmon built their home on the hillside above the beach in 1887.

The Harper Brick and Tile Company formed early on after a discovery of local clay which was suitable for making bricks. The only brick house in the Harper-Southworth area was built by the Coates family in 1925 and is still occupied by some members of the family.

Some roads near Southworth follow old cow trails around the bay.

When the Great Seattle Fire burned down much of the downtown area on June 6, 1889, it was easily seen from many waterfront viewpoints in this whole area.

Chapter 10 is a technical one on currents in Colvos, East and Dalco Passages and The Tacoma Narrows.

In Chapter 11 we continue our narrative cruising south farther into South Puget Sound.

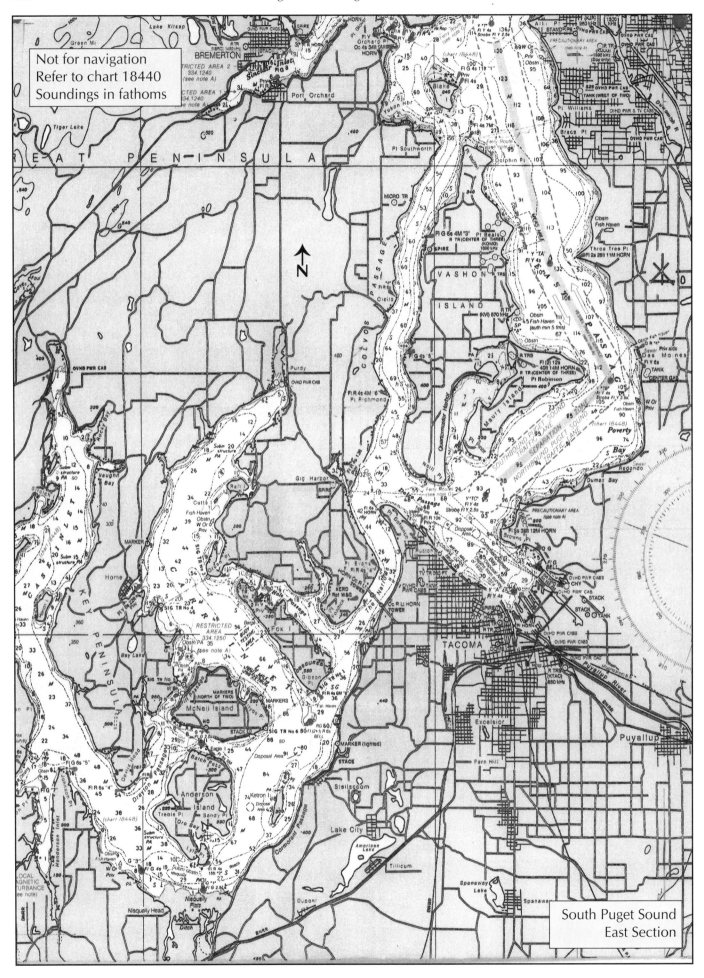

Not for navigation
Refer to chart 18440
Soundings in fathoms

South Puget Sound
East Section

CHAPTER 10
Currents: Colvos, East and Dalco Passages and Through The Narrows
A Technical Chapter on Currents

	Charts and publications for this chapter			
Chart	**Dates**	**Title**	**Scale**	**Soundings**
*** **18474**	03/25/95	Shilshole Bay to Commencement Bay	1:40,000........	Feet
** **18448**	10/03/93	Puget Sound, Southern Part	1:80,000	Fathoms
* **18445**	06/03/95	Puget Sound—Possession Sound to Olympia, pages A and C	1:80,000.........	Fathoms
18440	08/05/95	Puget Sound	1:150,000.......	Fathoms
		Tidal Current Charts, Puget Sound, Southern Part		
		Tidal Current Tables		

➡ *When using charts, compare your chart dates with ones referred to above. There may be discrepancies between different charts and different chart editions.*

Overview

We've spent the first half of *Gunkholing in South Puget Sound* cruising around what some call the **"middle"** of Puget Sound.

In this chapter it's time to get serious about heading toward **South** Puget Sound, which perhaps **really** begins at the Tacoma Narrows between South Tacoma's mainland and Gig Harbor Peninsula.

We deal with the unique nature of the currents through Colvos, East and Dalco Passages and through the 8.25 knot current potential of The Narrows.

For the first time we look at South Puget Sound current charts, which begin at Blake Island, and continue south to Olympia, west to Shelton, and all waters in between.

Anyone navigating this area will find this chapter useful, especially those in slower vessels.

The Narrows is a 0.7 mile wide, five mile-long "rapids," with a 26 fathom controlling depth. All of the waters in South Puget Sound, including river flow, must pass in or out through The Narrows twice daily. Waters in some South Sound inlets raise and lower as much as 20 feet between extreme high and low tides.

At times The Narrows surges with enormous energy and potentially dangerous currents. At other times flow is gentle, and briefly, at slack water, current is non-existent.

Time and energy afloat is precious, possibly more so to mariners in slower vessels and those opting to sail or paddle—as Native Americans have long understood—and as Peter Puget discovered on his voyage in 1792. Running ahead while going backwards is to be avoided.

Understanding, appreciating and using this awesome natural energy sooner or later confronts everyone making the decision to go through The Narrows.

We will investigate South Sound current charts, then the current dynamics and challenges of Colvos, East and Dalco Passages and approaches to The Narrows.

This is followed by a "hypothetical," non-stop cruise through Colvos and The Narrows, riding the fastest current in the year 1994. (That's the fastest current we could find.) It is hypothetical because we've not made a point of traveling The Narrows during its fastest currents.

The cruise is a mix of experiences in The Narrows, coupled with a variety of other faster rapids in U.S. and Canadian waters. The fastest rapid is Nakwakto which reaches 16 knots—the fastest salt water rapids in the world.

Tidal currents "refer to the horizontal motion of the water and not to the vertical rise and fall of the tide. The relation of current to tide is not constant, but varies from place to place, and the time of slack water does not generally coincide with the time of high or low water, nor does the time of maximum speed of the current usually coincide with the time of most rapid change in the vertical height of the tide." (From *Tidal Current Tables, Pacific Coast of North America and Asia*)

Essential current tools for mariners south of Blake Island are two NOAA publications, the *Tidal Current Tables* and the *Tidal Current Charts—Puget Sound—Southern Part*, a booklet of 12 current charts.

Mariners should purchase copies of both publications and follow their instructions for navigation purposes.

(In the Appendix, pages 328 to 335 we have printed copies of the 12 **current charts** and their instructions for reference purposes only.)

These two publications give us the ability to make simple hourly predictions of tidal currents, speeds and directions at any time, for any of the approximately 48 to 53 charted current stations south of Blake Island.

It will help in understanding the rest of this chapter to have both the Current Tables and Currents Charts nearby for reference, and charts 18474 or 18445.

Tidal Current Tables

In this instance we are using NOAA's *Tidal Current Tables for the Pacific Coast of North America and Asia.* This 200 page book contains a wealth of information. Current table books are published annually.

<u>**Table 1—"Daily Current Predictions"**</u> from **"The Narrows (north end) Puget Sound, Washington,"** lists day, date and time for:

• **Predicted "slack,"** the time at which there is no current, or the period of time at the beginning and end of each flood and ebb cycle.

• **Predicted "maximum"** flood or ebb **current speed in knots and the time** it occurs during a specific current cycle which is used to complete predictions on the hourly tidal current charts.

• **Lunar phases,** useful for fisher persons as well as for those who grow horns, fangs or undergo various romantic or other behavioral reactions during the full moon time of "lunacy."

<u>**Table 2— "Current Differences and Other Constants— on The Narrows,"**</u> lists 37 "places" or "current stations" south of Blake Island. This table includes Station Latitude, Longitude, Time Differences, Speed Rations, Average Speed and Directions of Flow for most stations, and references to "End Notes" in the Current Tables publication.

Most of the current stations listed in Table 2, "On The Narrows," appear on the Current Chart as single **tropic** speed values (explained in the Current Charts section).

Tidal Current Charts—Puget Sound— Southern Portion

This chart booklet, published in 1973, is still valid. Twelve geographically identical charts represent the direction of flow and tropic current speeds of the flood and ebb current cycles, hour by hour.

Each of six "flood" current charts refers to a specific hour: "before," "at," or "after" the time of **maximum flood.**

Each of six "ebb" current charts refers to a specific hour: "before," "at," or "after" **maximum ebb**.

The main tidal current reference station for all 12 current charts is located about one mile south of Point Defiance. It is listed in Current Table 2 as #1405, **The Narrows** (north end) mainstream current station.

The booklet has more information than we'll ever want to know. It's designed for the adult reader and gives complete instructions about current chart use and limitations. It must be used with the Tidal Current Tables.

Tropic speeds, having nothing to do with the tropics, are the greater flood and greater ebb speeds at the time of the moon's maximum declination.

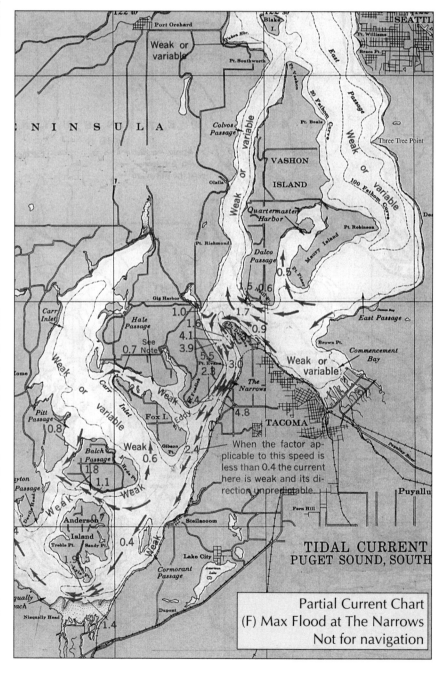

Partial Current Chart
(F) Max Flood at The Narrows
Not for navigation

Charted tropic speeds are in knots, and must be multiplied by a correction factor to produce the predicted current speeds at those locations.

Tropic speed decimal points are shown approximately on the current station sites on the Current Charts. In congested areas (on the charts) the tropic speed is located nearby with a line leading to a dot at the current station site.

Tropic speed values below 0.3 knots are charted as "weak" or "weak or variable."

We note on the Current Charts, that about nine of the 37 current stations listed as "places" in Table 2 of Current Tables appear to have between 2-5 additional unlisted tropic speed sites charted in their vicinity. (Two examples are in Colvos and Dalco Passages, see current charts.) This accounts for the rough total of 48-53 locations on the Current Charts, which indicate charted tropic speed values.

A total of about 600 tropic speeds are charted on the 12 South Sound current charts.

<u>**Factors for Correcting Tropic Speeds Range From:**</u>
- 0.1 for predicted max current at The Narrows of 0.2 to 0.5 knots
- 1.5 for predicted max currents at The Narrows of 5.8 to 6.1 knots

To predict current speed in knots at any charted tropic speed location, multiply that charted tropic speed by the correction factor for the specific flood or ebb current cycle. It is really that simple.

The answer will be the predicted current in knots, flowing in the direction shown by the charted arrows, during the specific hour of the flood or ebb current cycle, represented by the current chart, except where NOAA instructions indicate otherwise.

<u>**To Determine the Correction Factor:**</u>
1. **Refer to the *Tidal Current Tables*, Table 1.**
   - Turn to the reference station, "The Narrows (north end) Puget Sound," and the month, date and time of interest.
   - If the time of interest is other than at the time of maximum flood or ebb, refer to the "slack" time column to establish the active flood or ebb cycle.
   - Note listed date, time, maximum current speed in knots, and appropriate flood or ebb current cycle.
2. Refer to *Tidal Current Charts, South Puget Sound.*
   - Turn to the table of "Factors for Correcting (charted tropic) Speeds" on the inside front cover.
   - Match the predicted max flood or ebb current speed from the *Tidal Current Tables,* Table 1, with the "knots" column in the Table of Factors.
   - Select factor value listed in the "factor" column.
   - Multiply charted tropic speed by the correction factor.

Complicated, confusing? Well, yes, maybe at first. With some practice it gets much easier.

Be prepared: We will be referring to tropic speeds throughout the book in reference to currents in various passages and channels, which is why we've spent this time explaining about them.

(We may even spring a pop quiz at some point!)

Contemplating a Passage Through The Narrows?

Its potential 8.25 knots south flowing flood current and seven knot north flowing ebb gets our attention.

The current charts and tables help decide the best time to enter The Narrows for utilizing favorable currents to get to our destination.

We have at times struggled for hours against currents in The Narrows using every backeddy possible, succeeding only when the current was less than our hull speed, and being swept backwards when it was not.

Entering The Narrows

There are two choices for this trip: through either Colvos Passage on the west side of Vashon Island, or through East and Dalco Passages on the east and south sides of Vashon and Maury Islands. Either way intersects the Tacoma Narrows at Point Defiance.

Colvos versus East & Dalco Passages— Overview

Currents, distances and weather encountered in Colvos, East and Dalco Passages affect our decisions on the route and time to go or stay put.

We can wait out current or weather in Gig Harbor or Quartermaster Harbor if north of The Narrows.

If south of The Narrows, we can wait at Tanglewood Bay at Fox Island, or Wollochet Bay on the south end of Gig Harbor Peninsula.

Briefly, Colvos Passage is long and narrow, about one mile wide. Its north flowing currents may reach 1.9 knots, which oddly become weak or variable twice daily. Except when weak or variable, these currents are adverse to southbound vessels and beneficial to northbound vessels.

Briefly, East Passage is geographically much wider than Colvos, more than three miles in places. Currents are weak and variable all the time. However, invisible VTS boundaries and longer distances complicate its use. (See **VTS**, Appendix, pages 307-308.) East Passage south end joins Commencement Bay and Dalco Passage.

Briefly, Dalco Passage currents require close scrutiny. Its enormous backeddy during the ebb can be beneficial when westbound along the Point Defiance shore, or eastbound along the south end of Vashon.

Usually, our route is based on distance to our destination and allowances for tidal currents, although East Passage is the only way to Des Moines Marina.

Distances arbitrarily scaled from 1.2 miles north of Vashon Island to the following destinations illustrate Colvos, East and Dalco Passages mileage differences:

Distances in Nautical Miles from 1.2 miles north of Vashon To:	East Pass.	Colvos Pass.	Diff.
Gig Harbor	18.97	13.16	5.81
Narrows at Pt. Defiance	18.02	13.17	4.85
Tacoma Yacht Club	17.05	13.82	3.23
Quartermaster Harbor	15.10	14.92	0.18
Browns Point	15.22	17.02	1.80
Browns Pt. adj. for VTS	16.30	17.02	0.72

Colvos Passage

Colvos is about 12 miles long and averages about one mile in width. Least navigable width is about 0.65 mile at two places: between Point Vashon and Point Southworth, and between Command Point and near Cove, both in the northern third of Colvos.

Greatest width is 1.25 miles at two locations: between Fern Cove on Vashon and View Park, and between Spring Beach on Vashon and Sunrise Beach.

A straight edge placed on chart 18474 verifies that looking down Colvos from the south side of Blake Island we can see a tiny portion of the west shore of The Narrows, about 1.5 miles south and east of the Gig Harbor entrance, a distance of approximately 13.9 miles, bearing about 193° true from Blake Island.

Used as a course, this line-of-sight would put us aground at Point Southworth and Point Richmond on the west side of Colvos, and aground on Vashon near flashing green light "3," 0.8 mile north of Cove.

Colvos snakes from one side of the line to the other, forming numerous bulges, points and coves.

The viewing window is so narrow along this line-of-sight that from either end it's not possible to identify what we see at the other end, same as it was for Puget and Vancouver in 1792, except they had no charts.

Colvos tidal currents seem unique, confusing and a bit mysterious. Puget's voyage south may have required a lot of hard rowing in Colvos.

At first glance of NOAA navigation charts, it might appear logical for flood currents to flow south through Colvos into The Narrows. **This does not happen**.

 Colvos currents flow north during the ebb and most of the flood, at tropic speeds of 0.3 to 1.5, except during (F) and (F+1).

At the southeast end of Colvos, Dalco's west flowing flood splits and flows north into Colvos and south into The Narrows continuously, as charted on (F-2) through (F+3), with tropic speeds of 0.8 to 1.4.

Weak or variable Colvos currents are charted:
- (F-1) "weak" off Point Richmond only
- (F) (F+1) "weak or variable" full length of Colvos
- (F+2) "weak" off Points Richmond and Southworth only, oddly showing 0.3 tropic speed north of Olalla.

Colvos' unique north flowing currents have only one prolonged weak and variable period every 12 hours, twice daily. It's unlike The Narrows, Dalco, Rich, Agate and other passages that have brief slack periods and reversing currents every six hours, four times daily.

> ## "Lee-bowing"
>
> Even during the fastest tidal currents in Colvos, given enough wind, it is possible to sail *Zade* to weather against the currents—it just takes longer.
>
> We look for large backeddies downstream from prominent points and bulges. Wind direction permitting, we try to set courses to put favorable backeddy currents against our lee bow. That current then pushes us to weather, slightly increasing the apparent wind and speed along the course being sailed—an old practice called **lee-bowing.**
>
> After a number of short tacks to stay within a backeddy, with attention to depth-sounder and chart, we arrive at the point or bulge in the shoreline causing the backeddy. It's time to come about and again enter the adverse main current and work into another backeddy, or at least stay to the side of the passage with the least adverse current.

Faster vessels may disregard Colvos north flowing currents. However, fewer vessels can ignore the eight knot current potential at The Narrows. Most of us need to plan our ETA for the best use of currents to our destinations.

Southbound slower vessels may be appreciably delayed in arriving at The Narrows by Colvos' north flowing currents, especially during extreme tides and heavy rains, river run-off and snow melt.

Colvos North Flowing Currents— Fastest & Slowest—1995			
Location	Off Point Southworth North End	North of Olalla Mid Length	Off Point Richmond South End
Current Chart	(E) (E+1)	(E) (E+1)	(E+1) (E+2)
Charted Tropic (speed)	1.5	1.5	1.2
Fastest current in knots	**1.95**	**1.95**	**1.56**
Based on fastest predicted max ebb at Narrows 5.0 knots, factor 1.3, on 6/14, 12/22, 12/23			
Slowest current in knots	**0.45**	**0.45**	**0.36**
Based on slowest predicted max ebb at Narrows, 1.0 kn., factor 0.3, on 2/9, 3/10			

Estimating the Time to Travel Colvos:

Using current tables and current charts we can estimate the predicted average speed of the north-flowing current cycles during the time we plan to make the passage.

If southbound in Colvos, we **subtract** the estimated average current speed from our hull speed to obtain our estimated speed over the bottom.

If northbound in Colvos. we **add** the estimated average current speed to our hull speed to obtain our estimated speed over the bottom.

We then divide the 12 mile length of Colvos Passage by our speed over the bottom, which gives us the estimated time to travel the length of Colvos.

The equation works because Colvos currents flow only one direction—except when they're weak and variable.

When southbound we "cheat," and use backeddies, and arrive sooner—sometimes. (Hypothetical Cruise p. 159)

Northbound through The Narrows and into Colvos with the ebb, the telltale tide rips help identify backeddies so they can be avoided and the boat can run with the favorable north mainstream flow to Blake Island and beyond.

Approximate Travel Time from the North End of Colvos to The Narrows—12 miles
No allowances for current speed

Speed in knots:	Hours to Travel thru Colvos:
2	6.0
3	4.0
4	3.0
6	2.0
8	1.5
12	1.0
24	0.5

East Passage

East Passage, from the north end of Vashon Island to Commencement Bay is approximately 13.5 miles long. At the narrowest places it is about 1.75 miles across between Point Robinson, Des Moines and Piner Point and Dash Point. It is 3.7 miles wide between Tramp Harbor and the bight south of Three Tree Point near Normandy Park.

Currents in East Passage are shown as weak or variable in all 12 tidal charts, but on calm days there are faint indicators of back eddies at prominent points.

VTS Considerations

All mariners need to know the explicit rules when navigating in or near VTS. They supersede standard "rules of the road." (See Appendix, pages 307-308)

VTS lanes begin in Commencement Bay, continue north through East Passage and Puget Sound into the Strait of Juan de Fuca, west to the Pacific Ocean, and north, east and west of the San Juan Islands.

The lanes are 1.25 miles wide, constricting a large central area of East Passage.

Before VTS went into effect in 1972, whether under power or sail, we laid direct courses to our destination.

Sailing to weather in East Passage we'd arrive at our destination after a few long tacks, sometimes with shortened sail, plunging against normal seas which are minimally angered by weak or variable tidal currents.

Since VTS, we can still power or sail north or south along the mainland or Vashon-Maury shores, but we need to stay clear of traffic lanes, except as noted.

VTS lanes on the Vashon-Maury side are shown on chart 18474 (03/25/95), touching shore at Robinson Point.

Southbound, we can briefly merge with the southbound VTS lane at Robinson Point or cross the lanes at 90° and continue on our way.

Northbound along the Vashon-Maury shore, we are not supposed to sneak around Robinson Point by going north in the VTS southbound lane. Technically we should be south and stay clear of the VTS, proceeding in the same direction and parallel with its northbound lane.

Rounding the VTS "TB" buoy, we continue parallel with the VTS northbound lane. After Robinson Point is abaft our port beam, we can cross VTS at 90 degrees and then follow the island's shoreline, keeping clear of the southbound VTS lane.

The mainland side of VTS in East Passage can be traveled north or southbound without crossing or merging with VTS between Browns Point in Commencement Bay to Edmonds and beyond.

Sailing to weather in East Passage on either side of the VTS, keeping off the beach and out of the invisible VTS lanes, is a challenge and will take a lot of short tacks. There will be some tight squeezes along the way and it will require close attention to position and depths, but it can be done. Under power or downwind under sail, with caution, it's a piece of cake.

Critical Distances —VTS lanes to 10 fathom curve— Scaled from Chart 18474
Distances off Vashon-Maury Shores at:

Dolphin Point	0.4 miles
Point Beals	0.2 miles
Robinson Point	0.0 miles
Piner Point	0.1 miles

Greatest width on the west side of the VTS is 1.5 miles at Tramp Harbor.

Distances off Mainland Shores at:

Dash Point	0.25 miles
Zenith	0.30 miles
Three Tree Point	0.15 miles
Brace Point	0.50 miles
Point Williams	0.60 miles

Greatest width on east side is 1.75 miles at Poverty Bay.

Dalco Passage

Dalco, between Point Defiance and the south end of **Vashon Island,** connects the south end of Colvos Passage and The Narrows to East Passage and Commencement Bay, making Quartermaster and Gig Harbors accessible. Dalco is about 1 to 1.25 miles wide between Point Defiance and Vashon, and three miles long, east to west.

East flowing current potential at the south end of Vashon can exceed 3.5 knots during extreme ebbs.

West flowing mid-channel current potential can exceed 2.55 knots during extreme floods.

Dalco does have brief periods of slack

Understanding Dalco's currents helps us save time, fuel and energy. This is important to paddlers and in minor skirmishes between rag-baggers. It's a great area to utilize lee-bowing if sailing to weather against wind and currents.

Those areas having the fastest currents will have the most severe chop during strong winds, and it does get nasty.

The "Dalco Table" is our own (Carl's) creation, out of curiosity, using information off the NOAA current charts.

Predicting current speeds in knots in Dalco Passage for any specific hour in any flood or ebb tidal current cycle we use the basic current chart procedure:

• Determine the correction factor.

• Multiply the charted tropic value on the hourly current chart by the correction factor.

West Flowing Currents in Dalco Passage

Currents along the north shore of Point Defiance flow west most of the time during the flood and ebb.

Flood currents flow west the full width of Dalco, as charted on (F-2) through (F+3), reaching a mid-stream tropic speed of 1.7 at (F).

West flowing currents continue along the north shore of Point Defiance during the ebb, from (E-2) through (E+3), although charted as "weak" from (E-1) through (E+2).

Currents along the south shore of Vashon Island flow west during the flood.

During the ebb, Dalco currents form an elongated clockwise eddy between the north shore of Point Defiance and Vashon Island.

East Flowing Currents in Dalco Passage

Current directions reverse from west to east off the south end of Vashon between (F+3) and (E-2).

East flowing currents continue at the south end of Vashon from (E-2) through (E+3), reaching brisk 2.7 charted tropic speeds at (E+1).

Current directions then reverse from east to west between (E+3) and (F-2), as charted. The full passage width flood current then splits, flowing north into Colvos and south into The Narrows.

Dalco Passage Table of Fastest and Slowest Currents									
WEST FLOWING CURRENTS					**EAST FLOWING CURRENTS**				
		Speed in Knots				Speed in Knots			
1	2	3	4	5	6	7	8	9	10
Chart #	Tropic	Fastest Speed	Specific Speed	Slowest Speed	Tropic	Fastest Speed	Specific Speed	Slowest Speed	Chart #
F-2	1.4	2.10		0.39	WF	WF	WF	WF	F-2
F-1	1.6	2.40		0.48	WF	WF	WF	WF	F-1
F	1.7	2.55		0.51	WF	WF	WF	WF	F
F+1	1.4	2.10		0.42	WF	WF	WF	WF	F+1
F+2	1.0	1.50		0.30	WF	WF	WF	WF	F+2
F+3	0.5	0.52		1.50	WF	WF	WF	WF	F+3
*E-2	0.4	0.52		0.08	1.0	1.30		2.20	*E-2
E-1	Weak	Weak		Weak	1.8	2.34		0.36	E-1
E	Weak	Weak		Weak	2.4	3.12		0.48	E
E+1	Weak	Weak		Weak	2.7	3.51		0.50	E+1
E+2	Weak	Weak		Weak	2.4	3.12		0.48	E+2
*E+3	0.8	1.41		0.16	1.3	1.69		0.26	*E+3
F-2	1.4	2.10		0.39	WF	WF	WF	WF	F-2

West Flowing Current favors Pt. Defiance shore during ebb　　　*East Flowing Current favors south Vashon shore during ebb*

*Note: Tropic speeds shown are for both west and east flowing currents.
WF equals West Flowing current only.

Currents at Point Defiance—Dalco, The Narrows Shore & Gig Harbor

Currents: Flow in knots is based on 1.5 speed correction for extreme tides.

Point Defiance: Along Dalco and The Narrows shoreline currents flow NW most of the time as charted.

Dalco side is weak on (E-1) thru (E+2). Fastest tropic is 1.6 on (F-1) or about 2.4 knots.

The Narrows side is weak on (F-2) only. Fastest tropic is 4.6 on (E) or about 6.9 knots.

Gig Harbor entrance is weak on (F+3) and (E+3). Fastest NW tropic flow is 1.2 on (F-1) or about 1.8 knots; fastest SE tropic flow 1.6 on (E) or about 2.4 knots.

Hypothetical Non-stop Cruise South Through Colvos & Beyond The Narrows

This hypothetical cruise gives us a glimpse (after dark, unfortunately), of progressive changes of currents along Colvos, past Dalco then through The Narrows and beyond.

Join us onboard the weekend of December 3 and 4, 1994, at the north entrance to Colvos. We're headed south through The Narrows to Longbranch on Key Peninsula or to Oro Bay on Anderson Island. Both are about 25.5 miles from the north end of Colvos Passage.

We plan to enter the north end of Colvos Passage about 2300 on Dec. 3, about 2.5 hours after the 5.1 knot maximum ebb predicted for The Narrows.

If things go well, we hope to arrive about 4:30 or 5 Sunday morning, Dec. 4, before the end of favorable currents of the 5.9 knot predicted max flood at The Narrows.

This hypothetical cruise is simply one way we deal with the dynamics of currents and weather in Colvos Passage and in The Narrows into South Puget Sound.

We don't recommend making this particular passage at night or to anyone without local knowledge, with a capable vessel and a compelling reason.

Current dynamics on Dec. 3 and 4 are the fastest predicted flood and ebb for The Narrows in recent years.

Correction factors used with the current charts for:
- 5.1 knot predicted max ebb is 1.3
- 5.9 knot predicted max flood is 1.5

Referring to the current charts, we find the greatest tropic speed value for the ebb on any of the six ebb charts is charted at 4.6, east of Point Evans and at Point Defiance on (E).

The fastest ebb in The Narrows on Dec. 3 was 1.3 (factor) x 4.6 (tropic) which equals 5.98 knots.

The greatest tropic speed value on any of the six flood charts is charted at. 5.5, east of Point Evans on (F).

The fastest flood in The Narrows on Dec. 4 is 1.5 (factor) x 5.5 (tropic) which equals 8.25 knots.

Before we cast off, let's review a scenario likely to occur in The Narrows. This can be a **worst case** scenario

depending on how you feel about night travel, tide rips, currents and winds which can change abruptly—our apologies for not mentioning this before you signed on.

Let's say our average speed through the water on this cruise will be four knots because it's dark, there is no moon, and there's high potential hazard of drift and deadheads which have floated off the beaches from previous high tides or down rivers. Sooner or later even high-speed boats, if still afloat, get humble in these conditions or in heavy weather.

Steering gets very difficult as the boat enters the severe shearing action of water on one side of violent tide rips racing past water on the other side of the rip. It is important we learn to anticipate and quickly correct the boat's heading when crossing tide rips, whirlpools or upwelling boils caused by abrupt changes in depth. It is necessary to maintain as steady a course as possible, particularly under sail, to avoid collisions or other problems.

Under sail it's best not to be over-canvassed, beyond self-tending working sails, to make recovery of control easier after accidental jibes, or being forced about and held aback, with subsequent loss of steerage-way and control. If there is serious wind—and it doesn't take much—the chop can be very high and steep with short wave lengths complicating steering and control, making work on deck dangerous.

Boats under power or sail in severe chop may span more than one wave at a time with water coming aboard the fore and aft decks and over the lee rail—if sailing—all at the same time. Not the environment for open boats without self-bailing cockpits.

There is danger of being knocked overboard, with the added problem of recovery by a now short handed crew in an over-canvassed, out-of-control vessel. It's too late to practice recovery drill if we haven't already done it. Darkness makes it much worse, maybe impossible.

Extreme care with equipment including floating strobe lights, life jackets, ladders and life sling are vital to help avoid injury or death during recovery on a vessel caught in current and wallowing in severe chop. Boats have sunk and people have died in The Narrows.

Caution: Don't get sucked into the maw of The Narrows to run with strong currents, wind and chop conditions, with which we have no ability to cope or retreat. If in doubt, don't enter.

Among other things, the times and currents we actually encounter can be appreciably affected by heavy rains, snow melt, barometric pressures and storms.

Well, after all of that it turns out the weather for our cruise is calm, except for heavy tide rips.

Had the weather turned bad we would have probably put in at Gig Harbor.

See summary of this cruise, for much less dynamic conditions and passages, on page 160.

Follow this cruise on charts 18474 or 18448, and the ***Tidal Currents Charts*** for South Puget Sound. Time references of the current charts are before, at or after maximum ebb and flood at The Narrows.

⎈ We're finally underway and entering Colvos:

At 2300 we are abeam of Point Vashon, bucking adverse currents of about 1.56 knots..

(E+3) — Three Hours After Maximum Ebb — 2330 —Sat., Dec. 3

The north Colvos current station indicates 1.43 knot adverse current. To escape it, we moved east into the Fern Cove backeddies, next to the Vashon shore.

(F-2)—Two Hours Before Max Flood—0030— Sun., Dec. 4

The mid-Colvos current station indicates about 0.75 knots in the mainstream. We're past flashing green light "3" and Cove.

We are very close to Vashon's shore, bucking the declining north-flowing current, but out of the mainstream, and soon we'll be in what's left of the major favorable backeddy north of Point Sandford.

(F-1)— One Hour Before Max Flood— 0130

We have angled across Colvos and are now past Point Richmond.

The adverse northerly current is weak, 0.5 knot or less.

Keeping to the peninsula shore we escape the remainder of the adverse flood which flows north from Dalco Passage into Colvos.

We are now entering the favorable flow into The Narrows.

(F)—Max Flood at The Narrows—0230

We are past the entrance to Gig Harbor and Point Defiance and are being sucked rapidly into the maw of The Narrows.

We stay west and well out of the adverse backeddy south of Point Defiance. Half-way to Point Evans current computes at 6.15 knots, or 10.15 knots over the bottom.

Under the overhead power lines the favorable current computes at 8.25 knots. We move toward mid-channel to stay in the main stream.

With our 4 knot speed through the water, plus the 8.25 knots current, our speed is now 12.25 knots over the bottom!

If headed north against the current, we'd be going south, backwards, at 4.25 knots. It's important to plan ahead to avoid head-on, broadside, or rear-end collisions with The Narrows bridge piers as we may be set toward them. There should be plenty of maneuvering room (horizontal clearance between bridge piers is 2,565 feet), as long as we're awake and alert.

We move east of mid-channel to stay in the mainstream flow and out of the heavy boiling adverse back eddies that are south of Point Evans and near Hale Passage, Fox Island and the entrance to Carr Inlet.

East of Fox Island the flood is slowing to maybe 3.5 to 3.9 knots, according to charts (F) or (F+1) when the corrected current speed is added to our speed through the water, speed over the bottom is maybe 7.5 to 7.9 knots.

We need to stay clear of the buoys off Toliva Shoal.

(F+1)—One Hour After Max Flood—0330

We are past Fox Island, possibly even to McNeil, if we have been careful about the back eddies and stayed in the main flow of favorable currents.

Now riding the waning flood south east of McNeil Island, we must decide whether to head into Balch Passage and proceed to Longbranch or head south along Anderson Island to Oro Bay.

(F+2)—Two Hours After Max Flood—0430

If we're not already at Longbranch or Oro Bay, we're near Eagle Island in Balch Passage, a half-hour or two miles from Longbranch, or we're east along Anderson Island about the same distance from Oro Bay. We carry on to either destination on the last of the favorable currents.

0430 to 0500. We have arrived to anchor or moor and go ashore and wake up our friends.

(F+3)—Three Hours After Max Flood

We note adverse currents have already started at this end of the cruise.

Summary

In heavy weather Colvos, and particularly The Narrows, will be much less turbulent if traveled:
- During or near slack
- Wind and current are traveling the same direction
- During predicted periods with lowest max flood or ebb speed values.

Let's take a quick look at a few other current options in any year:

The fastest 1994 corrected flood current on the hypothetical cruise was 8.25 knots in The Narrows.

In 1994 there were about 62 predicted max flood speeds of under two knots.

The slowest predicted max flood was 1.3 knots, correction factor is 0.3. So the slowest corrected max flood current in The Narrows was 1.65 knots.

Tidal Current Tables **notes on The Narrows:**

"On the west side the current floods most of the time (flowing south) while on the east side it ebbs most of the time" (flowing north).

Note: Average current speeds charted with directional arrows on 18445 and 18474 can be misleading.

What is really important are the real current speeds, not just the average speeds.

Tropic current speeds, possibly a creation of NOAH, may explain construction of the Ark and its final resting place high on Mount Arafat, and after which, as a frugal man, using only a single letter, changed his name to NOAA and published a book called ***Tidal Current Tables*** at which he dined until he died.

In Chapter 11 we continue exploration of historic and present Colvos, East and Dalco Passages, circumnavigating Vashon-Maury Islands and cruising the east shore of the mainland.

*Dall porpoise and Jo's **Sea Witch** running with a mild tide rip—note arrows indicate direction of currents and rotation of swirls*

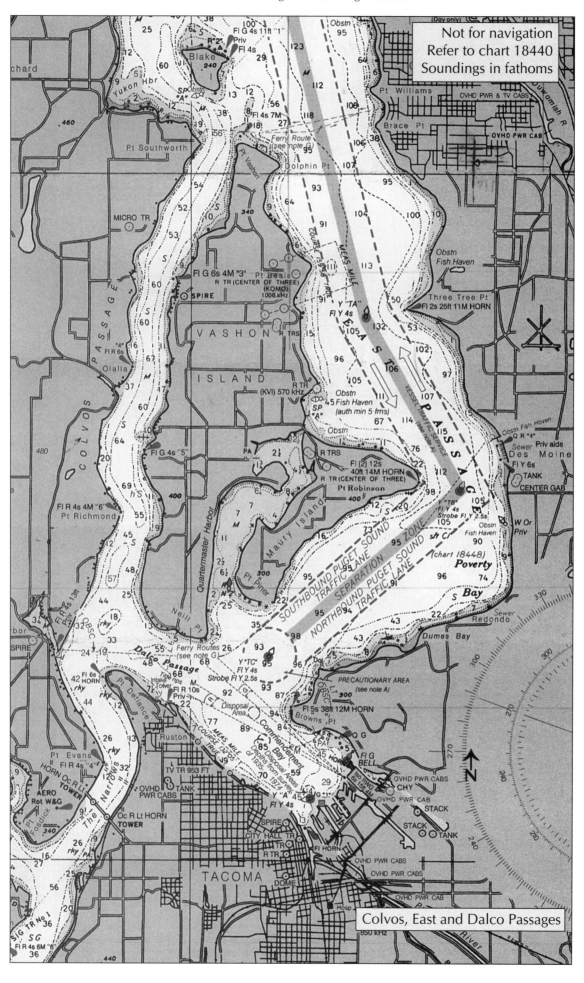

Colvos, East and Dalco Passages

CHAPTER 11
Colvos, East and Dalco Passages; Vashon-Maury Islands

	Chart	Date	Title	Scale	Soundings
***	**18474**	03/25/95	Shilshole Bay to Commencement Bay	1:40,000	Feet
**	**18445**	06/03/95	Puget Sound—Possession Sound to Olympia, pages A and C	1:80,000	Fathoms
**	**18448**	10/30/93	Puget Sound, Southern Part	1:80,000	Fathoms
	18440	08/05/95	Puget Sound	1:150,000	Fathoms
			Tidal Current Charts, Puget Sound, Southern Part		
			Booklet: Puget Sound Shellfish Sites		
			Washington Public Lands Quad Map—Tacoma	1:100,000	

Charts and publications for this chapter

➡️ *When using charts, compare your chart dates with ones referred to above. There may be discrepancies between different charts and different chart editions.*

Overview

Colvos Passage off Vashon Island's western shore isolates the island from Kitsap Peninsula. The beautiful, narrow, nearly straight, 11 mile long pass is lined with forests on both sides, with hills reaching 350 feet and higher in places, just as in Peter Puget's time, but no longer as pristine.

Tidal currents in Colvos are most unusual in that they **almost** constantly flow north, except twice daily for brief periods of time when they are "weak or variable." (See Chapter 10 "Currents")

Several communities on both shores of Colvos, county parks, ruins of old steamer docks, a youth camp and Olalla help make the trip through the pass scenic.

Navigation lights, with daymarkers, on both sides of Colvos are especially valuable to mariners at night.

Several launch ramps are charted on 18445 along Colvos. A check with Pierce County Parks Department staff informed us the only public ramp along Colvos is at Olalla on the mainland shore of the pass.

"Downtown" Vashon is inland, about one-third of the way south from the north end's Vashon Landing to Burton and then to Tahlequah at the south end. Vashon is connected at its southeast shore to smaller **Maury Island** by a narrow isthmus.

There are about 9,000 residents on the island, including a fair number of retirees who enjoy island living.

New technologies thrive on the semi-rural island, from manufacturing high-tech skis to growing orchids and making tofu. Computers link the island to the rest of the world for many who work at home or in cottage industries on Vashon. We understand about 20% of the island's residents commute off-island by ferry.

A passenger-only ferry runs to downtown Seattle from Vashon Landing. Car ferries run between Vashon and Southworth on the Kitsap Peninsula, and then to Fauntleroy in West Seattle. At the south end, a car ferry travels between Tahlequah and Tacoma.

Residents have discouraged the idea of a bridge from Vashon to the peninsula, possibly to avoid becoming a "bedroom community" as sometimes happens when progress strikes.

➡️ **NOTE: Marine gas and diesel** are available at **Des Moines Marina** in the area covered in this chapter.

Public tidelands parcels of about 8.5 miles are on Kitsap Peninsula, Vashon Island and King County shores.

Unless otherwise noted, they are state-owned; some may be leased for private purposes. We take the Quad map with us when we go ashore to avoid trespassing on adjacent private property.

Flight training for Carl

Replica of Puget's launch

Point Southworth was named for Edward Southworth, quartermaster with the Wilkes' expedition.

*The waters off Point Southworth were the scene of two ships destroyed in the 1859 Indian wars: schooner **Ellen Maria** was destroyed just north of the point by Indians; schooner **Blue Wing** was plundered and sank just south of Southworth.*

Quartermaster Harbor is at the south end between Vashon and Maury Islands. Since pioneer days it has been a favorite protected moorage and anchorage. The harbor, which includes Dockton and Burton, is entered from Dalco Pass.

East Passage separates Vashon and Maury Islands from the mainland. Des Moines, Tacoma and city suburbs fill the mainland shore.

Even with the dense population on the mainland there are several state and county waterfront parks, a couple of launch ramps and even a memorial to Capt. Vancouver. He sailed south in East Passage in May 1792, hoping that Commencement Bay might lead to the elusive Northwest Passage.

Currents in East Passage are unusual because they are weak or variable at all times, in dramatic contrast to Colvos' almost constantly north-flowing currents.

VTS lanes in East Passage may hamper cruising, especially if sailing to weather.

Puget & Colvos

More than 200 years ago Peter Puget and his men encountered Colvos Passage. Puget, Joseph Whidbey and their men were the first recorded non-native explorers to enter Colvos Passage on May 20, 1792, when they began their memorable voyage of exploration of South Sound.

Puget wrote: "Early in the Morning we left (from about one mile southwest of Restoration Point on Bainbridge where Vancouver's **Discovery** was anchored in 38 fathoms) with the two boats well armed ... provided with a weeks provision we began the examination of the Inlet."

On either side of the approximately mile-wide pass deep green forests marched from hilltops to shoreline, still dark in the early morning. Two small boats with 4 officers and 12 crewmen were the first white men to enter these waters. Indians, of course, knew them well as they used them as their highways and fishing grounds.

Puget went south and returned by way of Colvos Pass during his seven day expedition to South Sound. Capt. Vancouver returned via Colvos after he also made a voyage into South Sound.

North Entrance of Colvos

Let's start cruising through Colvos. We check out both sides of the passage as we tack back and forth, identifying the shoreline on each side as we go. (If coming from the south, we suggest you read from the other end of this section.)

We may encounter tide rips approaching Colvos off the southern end of Blake Island. We'll cross the ferry lane between Point Southworth on the Kitsap Peninsula and Vashon as we head south.

Point Southworth is at the northwest entrance to Colvos. It's easily identified by the large ferry dock and huge parking area upland.

Point Vashon, at the island's northern tip, is the northeast entrance of Colvos.

The Vashon ferry landing is on the island's north shore at Vashon Heights, east of the point.

Launch for hand-carried craft only is immediately east of the ferry landing.

An underwater recreation area near the ferry terminal is for scuba divers who enjoy the underwater landscape. Diving is not allowed within 100 feet of any state ferry terminal because of the danger from ferry propellers.

Fl 4s 17ft 7M Point Vashon Light, flashing white, is on a black and white diamond shaped daymark on a dolphin 300 yards north of Point Vashon. The water is between four and seven fathoms for nearly 0.2 mile north of the point.

Vashon ferry landing, hand-carry boat launch

At extreme low tides this is a great beachcombing and clam digging beach. Low bank homes are along the point and then the land rises to steep and wooded bluffs about 300 feet high.

Heading south, **View Park** is on the peninsula shore with forested bluffs nearly 400 feet high. A microwave tower and a 1,000 foot high TV tower are on the heights.

Public tidelands of about 3,000 feet are north of View Park.

Biloxi and **Sylvan Beach** are communities along the Vashon shore, now medium to low bank waterfront, well developed with many homes.

Fern Cove, about two miles south of Point Vashon, is a right-angled shallow cove, an excellent place to get out of currents and into back eddies off **Peter Point.** As along many of these shores, there are beach cabins mixed in with new, larger homes, and some boats are moored offshore seasonally.

Fl G 6s 4M "3" Light 3, 15 feet high on a square green daymark on a pile, is on an unnamed point 1.2 miles south of Peter Point. An old pier on a small spit is just north of the marker.

Public tidelands about 760 feet are about 500 feet north of Light "3." Some private mooring buoys are along the shore.

Cable crossing goes from a cove south of the light to Fragaria north of **Command Point** on the peninsula.

Fragaria is a community at the foot of a steep road; a cluster of beach homes, many built out over the water on pilings. Bluffs are more than 400 feet high near Fragaria. A stream empties into Colvos south of the homes on pilings.

Public tidelands of about 1,000 feet are south of Fragaria, while another 2,500 feet wrap around Command Point.

Cove is the next community across Colvos on Vashon**,** where the charted **"spire"** of a white country church is visible on the side of the forested hill.

Two public tidelands parcels totaling nearly 4,000 feet are south of Cove.

Sunset Beach community on Vashon is across from **Anderson Point** on the peninsula**,** just north of some erratic rocks and old pilings. High forested hills are above the beach. Sunset Beach isn't on all charts.

Fl R 6s 5M "4" Light 4, 15 feet high on a triangular red daymark on a tower, is between Anderson Point and Olalla on an unnamed point on the peninsula.

Public tidelands of about 4,000 feet begin about 1,000 feet south of Light "4."

Olalla Bay and community are in a bight just a little over halfway through Colvos. The red-roofed, white-painted market at water's edge is easy to see. A bridge crosses the lagoon, Olalla Bay, south of the store. A handsome, older, large white home south of the bridge is a bed and breakfast.

Olalla Bay was the first stop of Peter Puget on his voyage south, the famed "breakfast place." The community celebrates the anniversary of his arrival each May 20 with a reenactment of his first visit.

The Native American name for Command Point meant "Small Sized Mat." Grass, which was woven into mats, grew and was gathered here, according to anthropologist T.T. Waterman.

"Olalla" means "strawberry." When L. P. Larson, the first white settler, arrived in 1881 a local Indian approached him and said, "Mamook olallie," which roughly translated, meant "Have you picked berries?" Larson assumed this was the name of the place where he had beached his boat after a long row from Tacoma.

In the early 1900s the strawberries in these parts ripened three weeks earlier than those in Seattle and they were in great demand. They were taken by Mosquito fleet steamer to Seattle and sold at Pike Place Market.

Olalla—Puget's first stop

Fragaria is an Indian word meaning "native strawberry."

Puget and Olalla

About halfway through the pass Puget's men grew tired and hungry. They had been up since well before daybreak and had been working hard at their oars. Puget wrote:

"We found it trended nearly South for about 4 leagues & and in that distance preserving the Breadth of One Mile, we were induced to stop to Breakfast in hopes of enticing two Indians, who had deserted their Canoe & fled to the Woods to come to us. It was hauled up close to the Trees & before we went away some Beads Medal & Trinkets were put among their other Articles in the Canoe as a Proof that our Intentions were friendly.

(continued on page 166)

Among those steamers on the early-day Colvos run was our still-running favorite, the *Virginia V.* The trim 110 foot long vessel was built in Olalla in 1922 and was wrecked in Olalla in 1934 when she ran aground on a rock and just sort of fell over.

She was salvaged, and is the last of the real "Mosquito Fleet" vessels.

Now registered as a National Historic Landmark, she is still actively plying Puget Sound as a tour boat—an authentic survivor.

(continued from preceding page)

"At the Back of this Place is a Small Lagoon & as the Tide was out the Water was perfectly fresh in it. The Entrance is sufficiently broad to admit the Chatham to go in at high Water as the Tide had by the High Water Mark then fallen fourteen feet. The Land here is in general Low & rizing gradually a little Distance from the Beach to Hills of a Moderate Height & is everywhere covered with wood consisting chiefly of tall Straight Pine Trees."

They breakfasted at Olalla and rested while waiting for the tide to change before they resumed their watery trek through the unknown forested passages.

Puget noted in his journal that they left the "breakfast place" about 9 a.m. with a fine fair wind and tide as they continued south.

"We proceeded on a further investigation of the Inlet which still continued its Breadth & Direction. Soundings were frequently tried for but no Bottom could be reached with 40 fathoms of line."

Launch ramp (Pierce County Parks Department) is just inside the bridge on the little bay, where there's also a picnic area and parking.

Rock bares at half tide about 400 yards north of the old Olalla wharf, now just a few pilings. We find Olalla a delightful stop—by beachable boat (and car).

Al's Grocery and Old-Fashioned Butcher Shop is the full service store owned by John Robbecke. Hot foods, salads, sandwiches are served, in addition to being a well-stocked neighborhood grocery store, serving many area residents for many years. Great historical photographs cover the walls and Johnny can tell you all about them. One even shows the *Virginia V* aground on a rock at Olalla.

⚓ **Anchor** briefly offshore or stand off and row ashore for supplies.

Cable crossing goes from Olalla to Lisabeula.

Public tidelands of about 2,000 feet on Vashon are about 1,600 feet north of **Lisabeula**. The northern end of the beach begins at a small bight.

Olalla had a hotel, garage, bakery, warehouse, blacksmith shop, lumber mill and shingle mill in the early 1900s. Bridges were built across the lagoon in 1910.

Nowadays the community has an enormously popular "polar bear swim" every New Year's Day. Thousands of participants from all over come to the event, many leaping from the bridge into the icy waters—their way of starting the New Year.

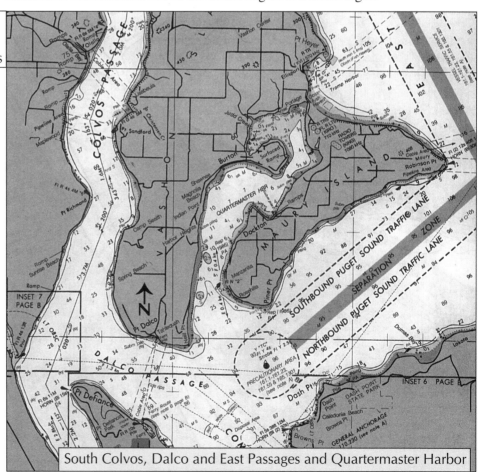

Not for navigation
Refer to chart 18445
Soundings in fathoms

South Colvos, Dalco and East Passages and Quartermaster Harbor

⚓ **Lisabeula (Vashon Island) Park** has about 300 feet of waterfront, 5.5 acres of upland, **launch for hand-carried boats**, picnic area and parking lot. The park is at a road end with old stub pilings nearby. It's easy to identify from the water by a bright orange cable crossing sign, a green sani-can and cars in the parking lot. It's part of the Washington Water Trails system campsites for kayakers.

Fl G 4s 5M "5" Light 5 at Point Sandford, is on a square green dayboard on a building 17 feet high, less than one mile south of Lisabeula. A shipwreck symbol offshore is charted between Lisabeula and the point. We didn't see any signs of the wreck.

Paradise Cove on Vashon is a large crescent-shaped bay unnamed on charts, south of Point Sandford.

Camp Sealth, the Campfire camp, shares the cove with numerous waterfront homes. Old, low, gray-green buildings are at the camp's north end near the pier. A couple of hundred yards south are more modern main buildings with flags and an open grassy area.

Lisabeula Park

Spring Beach (Vashon Island) Park is about 1.3 miles south of Sealth, accessible only by boat. The undeveloped park has nearly 46 acres of uplands and 1,400 feet of gravel public beach near charted ruins. While it is public, lack of facilities makes it not much more than a short stopping place for kayakers as they head through Colvos Passage. At high tide only a smidgen of beach remains. Some homes are built up in the ravine at Spring Beach community.

Pipeline crosses from Point Sandford to the peninsula, bearing 285° true.

Maplewood, on the peninsula shore just south of the pipeline, has a long private dock, a flagpole with a U.S. flag and a low rambling red house above a sandy beach.

Fl R 4s 4M "6" Light 6 at Point Richmond, is on a triangular red dayboard on a pile structure 15 feet-high, on the peninsula side of Colvos across from Camp Sealth. The light is obscured from 022° to 153°.

Private residences line the no-bank beach, with a lot of American flags flying. The housing density has built up considerably in recent years.

Public tidelands of 2,500 feet in five parcels are between Point Richmond and Sunrise Beach.

Sunrise Beach (Pierce County) Park on the peninsula is about midway between Point Richmond and Gig Harbor on the southwest end of Colvos. The lovely park, with about 500 feet of waterfront, has picnic tables and a sloping green lawn, which helps identify it from the water. A nice stop for beachable boats.

Point Dalco is a rounded bluff at Vashon's south end entrance to Colvos.

Mount Rainier looms larger than ever to the east, with smoggy Tacoma at its base, past the southern tip of Vashon Island.

Puget & Dalco

When Puget reached this spot he wrote: *"About 4 Miles from the Breakfast Place the Eastern Shore which had hitherto been compact branched off to the Eastward & afforded us a view of an excessively high Snowy Mountain, which though frequently seen before I have omitted noting it.*

"The Snow was yet, notwithstanding the Heat, more than 2/3 down & its Summit perfectly white appeared to reach the Clouds. From the Foot of the Mountain, we were of Opinion that the Inlet (East Passage) branched off to the North or NW, in which Case, it may communicate with the SE Branch that was seen from the

(continued on page 168)

Sandford Point was named for Thomas Sandford, quartermaster with Wilkes.

➡ **If using strip chart 18445, it's time to switch from page A to page C.**

Camp Sealth: Time was when hundreds of young Bluebirds and Campfire girls, including Jo, played games, sang songs around campfires, made handicrafts, swam the chilly waters, and learned to sail in this popular camp.

You'll see just as many boys as girls enjoying the beaches and uplands each summer. Campfire Girls became Campfire for both boys and girls a few years back. The campers are transported to and from Sealth aboard tour boats instead of on old Mosquito Fleet boats.

The camp is going strong, building skills and memories for generations of youngsters.

Colvos Passage *was named by Wilkes for George Musalas Colvocoresses, a Greek refugee from a Turkish massacre in 1822. Wilkes was renowned for his poor spelling and this name tested it.*

Luckily for the rest of us it he shortened the name to Colvos. (Colvocoresses wrote a bestselling book, **Four Years in a Government Exploration Expedition in 1852,** *and he spelled Wilkes' name accurately throughout the book.)*

(continued from preceding page)

Ship on our Departure, admitting that Supposition we must now be in the Main Inlet & the Eastern Shore of the Arm we have this Morning examined, will be an Island.

"Passing the Eastern Branch we continued our Progress along the Starb Continental Shore, which still was in a Southern Direction & of the same Breadth."

Mount Rainier looms above the Tacoma smog

Vashon Island *was named by Capt. Vancouver in honor of Capt. James Vashon who had commanded the flagship* **Europa** *when both Vancouver and Puget served under him.*

⎈ We continue east and enter **Dalco Pass,** the sometimes turbulent, sometimes calm waters between the south end of Vashon Island and Point Defiance. It gets choppy in here when the wind is blowing and the current is running. (More on Dalco in Chapter 10 "Currents")

Tahlequah, east of Point Dalco, is Vashon's southern terminal for the ferry crossing to Tacoma. There was once a big pier just northwest of the ferry dock with berths, gasoline, water and ice, but no more. It's a residential community now and all that remains of the pier and facilities are some run down piers and pilings.

Scuba divers like this underwater recreation area with its smooth but rocky bottom for spear fishing.

Tahlequah ferry landing

A small ferry, usually the *Rhododendron,* scuttles back and forth between Tahlequah and the landing at Point Defiance Park**,** a stone's throw west of the Tacoma Yacht Club and other moorages. (See Chapter 12)

Quartermaster Harbor, a popular harbor which opens up about 0.8 miles east of Tahlequah, is a nearly five-mile-long indentation between the southern portion of Vashon and Maury Islands.

The whole of the harbor is 10 fathoms or less. There are many places to anchor.

Quartermaster Harbor is entered between Neill Point on Vashon and Piner Point on Maury Island. Neill Point has a two fathom shoal about 0.2 mile offshore.

R N "2" Quartermaster Harbor Shoal Buoy 2 marks a shoal off **Manzanita** on Maury Island.

The rock off Manzanita was known to early Indians as "Killer Whale's Mother." Killer whales supposedly play around this rock even today.

Forested bluffs on the straight western shore are south of the communities of Harbor Heights, Indian Point, Magnolia Beach and Shawnee. Several two fathom shoals are less than 0.2 mile off this shore. The shoreline curves east just beyond Shawnee with its wide tideflats and creates the peninsula at **Burton.**

Public tidelands of 12 parcels totaling about 12,000 feet are off the shores of Quartermaster Harbor.

Dockton is around the east point about two miles into the harbor. There are some old buildings and net sheds on the low bank point. Once inside the bay a dozen or more sail and power boats ride at private buoys.

⚓ **Anchoring** is possible in many places in Dockton harbor in 3 to 5 fathoms, mud bottom.

Ⓖ Another **gunkhole,** but not too private.

Dockton (King County) Marine Park is in the southeast corner of the harbor, a fine park. This is the site of an old drydock and shipyard.

Dockton Harbor

The park has 23 acres of uplands, a great swimming beach enclosed with small white buoys, hiking trails, pay phone and a bus stop is close by. A nearby grocery store has closed its doors, but the post office remains open.

There are concrete floats with good heavy cleats, and the pilings are well-braced overhead and are usually occupied by at least one seagull per brace; fire hoses are on the docks. There is no potable water on the floats.

Enter the moorage at the northeast side of the park behind the breakwater float, heading toward the shore. Make a hard starboard turn between the end of the pier and a piling 30 feet or so inshore from the float. This piling has a depth gauge which shows the water depth at all tides. It's a great help.

Thirty-foot slips are inside the breakwater float and 25 foot slips are in the first tier out from the shore.

Boats can tie outside on the breakwater float also, but if it's breezy out of the north it will likely be lumpy. Better protection is inside the breakwater.

Dockton Marine Park Facilities
➤ Moorage for 58 boats
➤ Moorage fee $8 per night boats under 26'; $11 boats 26' and over
➤ Three night limit
➤ No fee — Oct. 1 to April 30
➤ No buoys
➤ No electrical or water hookups
➤ Pump-out station
➤ Restrooms on dock open 24 hours
➤ Onshore restrooms have hot showers, open 8 a.m. to dusk
➤ Fishing pier
➤ Playground
➤ Picnic areas
➤ Launch ramp with parking
➤ Phone: 206-463-2947

Dockton Marina

Burton Peninsula is the site of an old Native American village which was the scene of the famous War with the Snakes.

Warriors came here to avenge the death of a snake in the Duwamish Valley. The only house they spared was one in which the folk were singing "crying songs" for the dead snake. (T.T. Waterman)

Dockton

In 1891, a 325 foot drydock was towed to Maury Island and set up at Dockton. The huge drydock installation, 100 feet wide and 12 feet deep, was a major employer, with more than 400 workers who built and refurbished ships. Many workers commuted from Tacoma by company steamers.

Vashon was considered extraordinarily convenient because it was midway between Seattle and Tacoma, with protected Quartermaster Harbor at the south end. This was back in the days before highways, when all transportation was by water and communities were linked by steamers and even rowboats. Vashon was right on the main watery thoroughfare.

It wasn't until the early 1900s that Dockton began to lose its monopoly on the boat building business. Railroads and highways became the transportation of the day around Puget Sound. Steamboats were on the way out. Vashon, the center during the boat building era, became an isolated island, passed over by what was then considered new technology.

⚓ **Continuing north** around Burton Peninsula and into the community of Burton, we pass between the end of the peninsula and Maury Island. Depths from here on are under five fathoms, with no charted obstructions.

Raab's Lagoon is in the north end of the bight east of Vashon's Burton Peninsula. The lagoon, bight and peninsula are unnamed on charts, but named on island maps.

⚓ **Anchor** in three to four fathoms at the mouth of the bight. The lagoon and much of the bight dry at low water. All shoreline is private.

⚓ There are mostly low, treed banks on the eastern shore of the harbor north of Raab's Lagoon with only a few homes, until directly opposite Burton Peninsula. Waterfront homes and cabins line the north shore.

The charted high radio towers of KIRO and KING are excellent landmarks. There are several long, substantial private docks and floats in Burton harbor.

Burton Acres (Vashon Island) Park is on the eastern knoll of Burton Peninsula. Attractions include **Jensen Beach launch ramp**, swimming beach, a mile of hiking trails, picnic tables and restrooms at this 68 acre day use park.

⚓ **Anchoring** is possible in one or two fathoms.

⚓ **Inner Harbor,** unnamed on the charts, is north of the Burton Peninsula.

Burton village has a general store, an espresso stand with great pastries, post office, restaurant and some marine supplies and a bus stop. Island buses take you around Vashon. The Back Bay Inn, a bed and breakfast, serves dinners Wednesday to Saturday with Sunday brunches. Phone: 206-463-5355

Quartermaster Marina in Burton is at the southwest corner of the Inner Harbor in Burton, shows as #60 on chart 18445, facilities are as listed.

"Gospel Spit" was the name settlers gave to the southeastern tip of Burton Peninsula in the early 1900s.

Old-fashioned revival camp meetings were held on the spit. Hallelujah!

The lowlands between Vashon and Maury Islands are where Native Americans "portaged" their canoes across the isthmus, now named Portage.

Quartermaster Marina Facilities
➤ Moorage for about four boats
➤ 20 amp electricity, water
➤ Fees: $10; $15 with hookup
➤ 20 ton haulout
➤ Hull and engine repair
➤ Open 6 days week, 9 a.m. to 5 p.m.
➤ Charter boats
➤ Small boat rentals
➤ Lodgings
➤ Groceries, ice, hardware, bait, tackle
➤ Phone George Correll: 206-463-3624

Enter the Quartermaster Marina through a channel marked by uncharted red and green buoys, and check in for moorage at the office.

Quartermaster Yacht Club, north of the marina, has some facilities available to members of reciprocal yacht clubs.

⚓ **Anchoring** is possible in this harbor in charted depths of 10 to 15 feet, along with permanently anchored boats. We can dinghy to the dock by the marina haulout for shore access during daylight.

Heading South in East Passage

⚓ **Leaving beautiful Quartermaster Harbor,** we return (a quick trip) to the northeast shore of Vashon Island and make our way south in East Passage along both Vashon and mainland shores. Again, for those coming from the south, start at the other end of this section.

Dolphin Point at the northeast end of Vashon is a low rounded nub with beach homes restrained by rock bulkheads.

Southbound VTS lanes are only about 0.4 mile from the point and large ships and commercial vessels heading to or from Tacoma and Olympia may be traveling nearby. They generate some pretty large wakes.

Vashon shore angles southwest into a crescent-shaped bay, unnamed on charts. **Northeast Vashon Park** is in this bay about 0.5 mile south of Dolphin Point. The park is also known as **Wingehaven,** unname on the chart. It's near **Aquarium**.

We recognize the park from offshore because of two old pilings standing knee deep in the bay, and also because of the unusual bulkhead. An elaborate, old-fashioned concrete balustrade runs along the top of the bulkhead; a stairway leads to the beach at the north end. At the south side of the park an old dock and pilings stand slightly tilted in front of scattered beach houses.

Wingehaven Park has 400 feet of gravel shoreline with 12 acres of heavily treed uplands, part of Washington Water Trails for kayakers and other human powered boaters who are allowed to camp onshore.

There are two picnic tables, a sani-can, and a nice beach with gentle slope where you might even find a few clams.

Remnants of the old estate include a fireplace overgrown with greenery where the house once stood, and a fountain on the bulkhead. Wingehaven is named for the former owners.

The park's winding road leads to 200 foot high hills above, and takes you from a brilliant, sunshiny beach into the deep green shade of a forest, trees lacing overhead, and a pervasive feeling of abandoned dankness. Since you can actually go into the uplands this is a good place to rest or an interesting hike.

⚓ **Anchoring** is possible in two to nine fathoms and dinghy ashore.

⚓ **Point Beals** is about two miles south of the park. **A measured nautical mile** is off Point Beals with the first set of range markers north of the point. They are steel towers with round orange targets. Line them up and start the clock for speed, knotmeter and rpms, all of which may be affected by wind and sea conditions. The course is 159° 58' true.

Southbound VTS lanes are only about 0.25 mile off the point. Be aware of ship traffic if doing the measured mile.

Cable crossing runs northeast from Point Beals to Brace Point on the east shore. Radio towers of station KOMO are visible between the point and Dilworth.

Quartermaster Marina

Quartermaster Harbor *was named by Wilkes whimsically as a haven for petty officers' spirits.*

Wingehaven Park

There were early Native American settlements in the general area of Tramp Harbor.

The Indian name for Point Heyer meant "Hidden Spring." The legend is that a young girl was to marry a certain man, although she was unwilling. She was hidden by friends, and an old woman carried water to her in a basket. The water basket was transformed into a spring. The girl was in such a secret place the spring is still hard to find.

Native Americans used the portage from Tramp Harbor into Quartermaster Harbor as a site for netting ducks.

As birds flew from Quartermaster Harbor to open water over the isthmus, the Indians would quickly raise nets, as much as 360 feet long, on tall poles and snare the birds.

Robinson Point was named for John Robinson, captain of the fo'csle in the Wilkes Expedition.

We're now less than a mile from the inland village of Vashon.

Public tidelands of about 1,500 feet are approximately 0.5 mile south of Point Beals. With luck you might find rock crab and sea cucumbers if beachcombing.

Cruising south along the Vashon shore there are views to the east of the suburban shoreline between Seattle and Tacoma, the Cascade range and Mount Rainier to the southeast.

VTS buoy Y "TA" Fl Y 4s light, near the center of the channel south and east of Point Beals directs shipping traffic to angle more southeasterly.

Erratic rocks and pilings are along the forested Vashon shore.

Public tidelands in two parcels are located less than a mile north of Point Heyer. One is about 1,500 feet long, the other about 2,000 feet.

Point Heyer is next at the north end of crescent-shaped Tramp Harbor. A bluff rises steeply behind it, a sandspit with a shoreside lagoon extends about 0.2 mile southeast from the point. The radio towers at Point Heyer are those of KVI.

"KVI Beach" is the local name for this lovely, sandy beach at Ellisport. It is open for public use, courtesy of KVI. Island maps show it as Chautauqua Beach.

Tramp Harbor runs from this point southeast past the isthmus which connects Vashon and Maury Islands, then along the northern shore of Maury Island. The harbor is shoal with a long, sandy beach at low tide, and is home to many different kinds of waterfowl and shore birds, several aquaculture sites, a fishing pier and some radio transmission towers. The beach is enjoyed by many for beachcombing, exercising dogs and running the kids, in whatever order.

Cable area runs from the harbor to Three Tree Point on the mainland.

⚓ **Anchoring** is possible, but check depths and weather.

A 300 foot long fishing pier is a revamped old steamer dock that King County Parks rejuvenated. No boat mooring is allowed. A barbecue, picnic table and portable toilet are on the shore.

⚙ **An artificial fishing reef** is about 600 yards east of Portage, marked by four buoys, "A," "B," "C" and "D." It's a Department of Fish and Wildlife reef, visited by fish, fishermen, scuba divers and other wildlife.

Public tidelands of about 2,000 feet start a mile east of Portage at the south end of Tramp Harbor along the shore of Maury Island, a fascinating shoreline for dedicated beachcombers. Submerged piles, charted as inshore of the 10 fathom curve halfway between the radio towers and Robinson Point, help position the east end of the public shore.

The towers of radio stations KIRO and KING are highly visible on Maury Island, especially at night; their blinking red lights aid mariners in locating the area.

Robinson Point on the eastern tip of Maury Island juts far out into East Passage. It is the turning point for large ships.

Southbound VTS lane for commercial traffic passes just off the point. The chart shows the southbound edge of the lane almost coming ashore on the point.

Cable area from the north side of Robinson Point crosses to Des Moines.

Fl (2) 12s 40ft 14M Robinson Point Light, is mounted on a white octagonal tower atop the lighthouse. A fog signal is at the station, and storm warnings are hoisted here. The picturesque lighthouse was first activated in 1887 and is an old Coast Guard facility.

Robinson Point Lighthouse

Robinson Point County Park, 10 acres with about 1,600 feet of trails and picnic tables, is owned jointly by King County and the Coast Guard. A low spit extends 140 yards from the wooded shores and there are several hundred feet of shoreline for beachcombing. Views of the Sound are spectacular from the point.

East Passage is slightly less than two miles wide between here and the mainland at **Zenith** where a huge retirement center, charted, can be seen across the water. From Robinson Point , Vashon Island trends southwesterly for about four miles.

The charted shipwreck is about 0.4 southwest of the point—we didn't find it.

Pipeline area crosses from the point to the mainland.

Lost in the Fog

A couple cruising East Passage in their 35 foot boat in the fall of 1995 became lost in fog, and reportedly anchored until the fog lifted.

Suddenly they felt the impact and heard the shattering of their boat and they rushed up on deck. Their boat had been hit by a freighter. It was ripped apart and sank beneath them, but they were rescued.

The Coast Guard advises the incident occurred in reportedly 700 feet of water in a VTS lane. Seems like a long anchor line for a cruising boat—or perhaps the anchor never set.

Good reason for using GPS and/or radar, knowing where you are, what you're doing, and advising VTS on VHF Channel 14 of your location when disabled in or near the VTS lanes.

Maury Island (Vashon Island) Marine Park, a recent 300 acre acquisition on the southeast shore of Maury Island, is around the point from the lighthouse. The island's newest park includes 1.3 miles of shoreline, with planned improvements.

This **Gravel Coast** shoreline has 300 foot high bluffs, several enormous gravel pits and two barge-loading docks. Two other docks are no longer usable and others are only stub pilings. The gravel pits are prominent, easily seen from East Passage. Much of Maury Island has been shipped away.

Gold Beach, next on this southwest shore, has homes built on terraced remains of earlier mining.

Piner Point is a bulge at the southwest end of Maury Island.

Public tidelands in two parcels are here, each about 1,000 feet long.

We curve gently around the point, keeping about 0.25 of a mile offshore to avoid erratic rocks and shoal waters, passing the communities of Rosehilla and Manzanita.

R N "2" Quartermaster Harbor buoy 2, about 400 yards offshore from Manzanita, marks the eastern entrance into Quartermaster Harbor. Been there, done that.

Gravel Coast

The Native American name for Robinson Point translated to "Hollering Across."

On January 28, 1995, an earthquake of 5.0 magnitude was centered about 10 miles beneath the point and was named Point Robinson Quake. Geologists feared that calling it the Maury Island quake would lower property values.

"Where Snakes Landed" is the translation for the Indian name at a gully about one mile southwest of Robinson Point along the Gravel Coast. According to legend, a war party of Snake people came from the mainland to take revenge on the Indians in Quartermaster Harbor for a killing. They landed on the beach here and created the gully at the pit as they crawled up the cliff.

South on East Passage—Mainland Shore

Now, another quick trip and we're back across Puget Sound where we'll cruise the mainland shore of East Passage south of **Fauntleroy Cove.** We're picking up where we left off 'way back in Chapter 4 at Fauntleroy Cove and the ferry terminal.

Brace Point is next, less than 3.6 miles south of Alki. **Cable crossing** runs from Brace Point to Point Beals on Vashon Island.

Public tidelands of about 1,200 feet in two parcels are south of the point.

➡ **If using strip chart 18445 it's time to turn to page A.**

Capt. George Vancouver

Vancouver in East Passage

Although Peter Puget never investigated East Passage, his captain, Vancouver, did. He had directed Puget and Whidbey to make their explorations along the starboard or western shore when they departed May 20, 1792, from south of Bainbridge, which took them south in Colvos Passage.

By May 26, when they hadn't returned, Vancouver decided to take off in the Discovery's yawl, along with James Johnstone in the Chatham's cutter, and explore East Passage.

"We directed our route along the western shore of the main inlet, which is about a league in width; and as we proceeded the smoke of several fires were seen on its eastern shore. When about four leagues on a southwardly direction from the ships, we found the course of the inlet take a south-westerly inclination, which we pursued about six miles with some little increase in width."

Three Tree Point is referred to as Point Pully on South Puget Sound Tidal Current Charts and on older navigation charts.

➥ **If using chart 18445, it's time to turn to page C.**

Ed Munro Seahurst (King County) Park is tucked into the cove about seven miles south of Alki Point and about two miles north of Three Tree Point.

Park attractions, while not a marine park, there is nearly one mile of sandy, seaweedy beach. A long concrete seawall divides the upper picnic area from a walkway alongside a gabion bulkhead. Both bulkheads curve along the shoreline above the tidal area. This would be a good place to haul up a kayak or other beachable boat.

Onshore are nature trails, restrooms with outside showers, picnic tables, shelters and a playground. Beachcombing, swimming, fishing, hiking and diving can be enjoyed here.

There is also a Marine Technology Center, part of Highline Community College, where students study marine life. Viewing windows shaped like portholes are along the outside of the building giving visual access to sea life.

⚓ **Anchoring** is possible offshore but protection from a southerly is better a little farther south in this rather wide bay.

⛆ **A sunken artificial fishing reef** is charted as a designated state underwater recreation area, so keep a watchful eye out for scuba diver flags.

Fl 2s 11M Horn Three Tree Point Light is 25 feet high**,** visible 11 miles, is about 7.5 miles south of Alki Point. It is a low point projecting about 300 yards west from the base of a 30 foot sloping ridge.

King County public beach access is at Three Tree Point on both the north and south sides of the point, although the land is private in between.

Launching hand-carried boats is possible at either the south access at the site of an old deteriorated, unusable charted ramp, or at the north access, a single lane gravel road. The two county sites are usable from sunrise to sunset.

⚓ **Anchoring** is possible in calm weather—dinghy ashore. Both sides of the point are subject to prevailing winds, and it's shallow for a good 100 yards off the beach. There are no services; even the Three Tree Point Store is closed down.

Cable area along the point's south shore crosses to Tramp Harbor on Vashon.

VTS buoy Y "TA" Fl Y 4s light is 0.8 miles offshore from the point.

⛆ **Des Moines** is 3.5 miles south of Three Tree Point and two miles across East Passage from Robinson Point. The city's large modern, marina is the only protected moorage on either side of East Passage between Seattle and Tacoma.

This might be the closest place to take shelter in a storm or limp into if help is needed. Or maybe it's time for a night in a protected marina and dinner out. There's guest moorage and two restaurants in the marina. The downtown Des Moines district with shops, post office, liquor store, restaurants and other supplies and services is an easy walk from the marina.

Enter the marina between the concrete fishing pier and the north end of the 2,200 foot long rock breakwater. We stay clear of the fishing pier to avoid snagging gear of those fishing.

Des Moines fishing pier

Q R Light "4" 13 feet high, visible four miles, is on a triangular red daybeacon on the rock breakwater. **F G 35ft Light 1A** is at outer end of the pier. **Fl Y 35ft Lights B and C** are also on the pier.

We head in toward the fuel dock, which is to port. The guest moorage check-in is north of "N" dock (the most northerly moorage dock), south of a timber breakwater.

Des Moines Marina entrance

Port of Des Moines Marina Facilities

➤ Moorage for 50-60 guest boats
➤ Moorage rates 25 cents per foot per day for seven days, 40 cents per foot per day over seven days
➤ 20-30 amp shore power, $3 per day
➤ Water
➤ Free pump-out, porta-potty dump, garbage disposal
➤ Restrooms, showers, laundry
➤ Fuel dock: gas, diesel, bulk propane
➤ Slings for launching trailerable boats
➤ Full service private boat yard offers complete repair services, 37 ton travel lift
➤ Two restaurants in the marina, the Breakers and Anthony's Home Port
➤ Small store that carries ice, tackle, and some marine supplies among other items
➤ Phone: 206-824-5700
➤ Monitor VHF Channel 16

Des Moines Yacht Club reciprocal moorage is at the south end of the marina, past "A" dock.

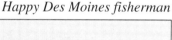

Happy Des Moines fisherman

Fl Y 6s 5M Breakwater Obstruction Light, is on a diamond shaped yellow dayboard at south end of breakwater. There is no entry to the marina from the south.

A few blocks inland from the north end of the marina on Marine Drive (immediately north of the QFC Market) is a tiny town park with a rather infamous statue of a very happy fisherman holding a giant salmon. You need to see it to believe it, but we've included a photo just in case you miss it.

Des Moines Beach Park is immediately north of the marina with 19 acres of upland and beach. There are picnic tables and restrooms.

⚓ **Underway again**, and we continue south from Des Moines. Midway between Des Moines Marina and Saltwater State Park is the huge retirement home at **Zenith**, highly visible from the water, and charted.

Saltwater State Park is about two miles south of Des Moines. The park, with nearly 88 acres of uplands, has been in the state system since 1929. We recognize it from the water by the familiar state park mooring buoys and the buoy marking the fish haven. The sandy beach is a particular favorite with youngsters.

⚓ **Anchoring** off is possible in about two to five fathoms, mud bottom, and dinghy in to the beach.

Saltwater Park beach

Three Surveys for Commencement Bay

In the mid-1800s, three survey expeditions, two U.S. and one British, explored and charted the Commencement Bay area.

In 1877, USN Lt. Cutts led a second survey expedition and it was this chart where the name Point Brown and Dash Point appeared.

The name Dash Point is still unclear as to its derivation. Perhaps named after the men or ships from either the 1846 British Expedition or the 1877 U.S. Expedition.

(From the 1993-1995 Biennium Area Reports of the Washington State Parks and Recreation Commission.)

Dash Point State Park beach

Before Dash Point became part of the state park system the beach was a haven for local recreationalists, beach combers and fisherman. The beach was variously known as Olson Landing, Fairview Beach and Woodstock Beach.

Saltwater State Park Facilities
➤ Three mooring buoys
➤ 1,445 feet of shoreline
➤ State underwater park with a sunken barge and tire reef for scuba divers
➤ Scuba rinse station
➤ Restrooms
➤ Picnic tables and shelters
➤ Group camp
➤ 52 tent campsites
➤ Two miles of hiking trails
➤ Swimming beach, no lifeguards.

Poverty Bay is at an elbow about three miles south of Des Moines, or 4.3 miles northeast of Browns Point. The 10 fathom curve runs 200 to 300 yards offshore.

Redondo Beach (King County) Park, less than two miles from Saltwater Park, is in the bight of **Poverty Bay,** where the shoreline begins to curve west. The park has three acres of uplands, lighted T-shape fishing pier, swimming beach, **two lane launch ramp**, parking lot, restrooms, no moorage.

Anchoring off the park is possible in about three to five fathoms.

Continuing south, two more King County Parks are along the coast; neither has any boat facilities, although there is shore access.

Lakota County Park is about 1.5 miles west of Redondo Park along Poverty Bay. Not easily identified from the water, the 0.25 mile beach at Lakota is north of where the shoreline dips into Dumas Bay.

Dumas Bay is about two miles from either Poverty Bay or Dash Point. Depths are very shoal; the 10 fathom curve is 800 yards offshore with 1/2 fathom charted at 500 yards offshore.

Dumas Bay Park Wildlife Sanctuary in the northwest curve of Dumas Bay, is protected and quiet, good for birdwatching and beachwalking. A lagoon marsh in 450 feet of shoreline hosts a variety of small animals, land and sea birds. No place to land a boat because of long, shallow tideflats, and the critters are better left alone. We didn't find the wreck charted west of Dumas.

Dash Point State Park is a non-marine state park with 3,301 feet of saltwater shoreline. Because of its gently sloping, sandy beach that extends more than 1,500 feet at minus tides, it's not a very good anchorage for larger boats. There are no buoys, but is identified by the gully through which Thames Creek runs.

Should you get ashore at Dash Point, you will find the beach, 398 acres of uplands, 110 campsites, five comfort stations, picnic tables and shelters. You can hike more than seven miles of trails, beachcomb or swim in saltwater warmed by sun as the tide slowly rises over the sandy beaches.

Dash Point (Pierce County) Park is south of the state park, almost at Dash Point. This day-use park has a 200 foot long public fishing pier. There are no facilities for docking or launching, but shallow-draft boats can land here. Onshore are picnic areas, children's play area and sandy beach about a block long.

Browns Point is next, about one mile south and west of Dash Point.

Fl 5s 38ft 12M Browns Point Light, flashing white, horn, is on a square white light house. The light is obscured from 002° to 217°.

Browns Point Park is a 4.2 acre Tacoma Metropolitan Park. The park wraps around the point at the northwest corner of Commencement Bay.

This is where Capt. George Vancouver landed for lunch on May 26, 1792, certain that the elusive Northwest Passage would be just southeast around the corner. We were delighted to find the small plaque commemorating his landing here. The plaque is on the ground amidst well-tended flowers at the foot of a flagpole in front of the former lighthouse keeper's home.

Vancouver & Browns Point

Vancouver's small boats sailed and rowed south along the east shore of Vashon Island and then cut across the Sound, presumably to Browns Point for lunch. They hoped to find an inlet to the east at what is now the Tacoma Harbor.

Vancouver wrote in his journal: Towards noon we landed on a point on the eastern shore whose latitude I observed to be 47°21', round which we flattered ourselves we should find the inlet take an extensive eastwardly course.

He was disappointed to find the inlet terminated in a bay.

"Here we dined, and although our repast was soon concluded, the delay was irksome as we were excessively anxious to ascertain the truth, of which we were not long held in suspense. For having passed round the point, we found the inlet to terminate in an extensive circular compact bay, whose water washed the base of Mount Rainier."

They had entered Commencement Bay.

*(The above quote was taken from **Vancouver's Discovery of Puget Sound** by Edmond S. Meany, in which Vancouver established a latitude at Browns Point of 47° 1.')*

On chart 18474, the latitude of Browns Point is 47°18.36.' This is a difference of 2.64' of latitude or miles from Vancouver's latitude which puts him at 0.4 mile north of Piner Point on Maury Island.

This may have been an error in recording or transcribing the records. Those studying Vancouver's exploration claim much greater accuracy on his part most of the time.

***"This tablet in memory of May 26, 1792, when Captain George Vancouver** and his associates dined at this point. This site recognized by the Browns Point Garden Club in 1934, rededicated by the Browns Point Improvement Club in 1988."*

Browns Point Park attractions include two mooring buoys on the north shore, picnic tables, restrooms and lawns. There used to be four buoys, but storms carried two of them off.

Residents of the area say the park is a well-kept secret. But for those who know about it, Browns Point Park is a favorite fishing site, whether from the beach or offshore. They go to the park for kite-flying, to run their dogs, walk the beach, enjoy peace and quiet, or picnic and play on a gently sloping lawn.

The park is used as a site for weddings, family get-togethers, picnics and many other events, including a bi-annual salmon barbecue.

Private launch ramp is on the west shore.

Browns Point Park Memorial

In Chapter 12, we visit Tacoma and Gig Harbor, and then head south through The Narrows into the "real" South Sound.

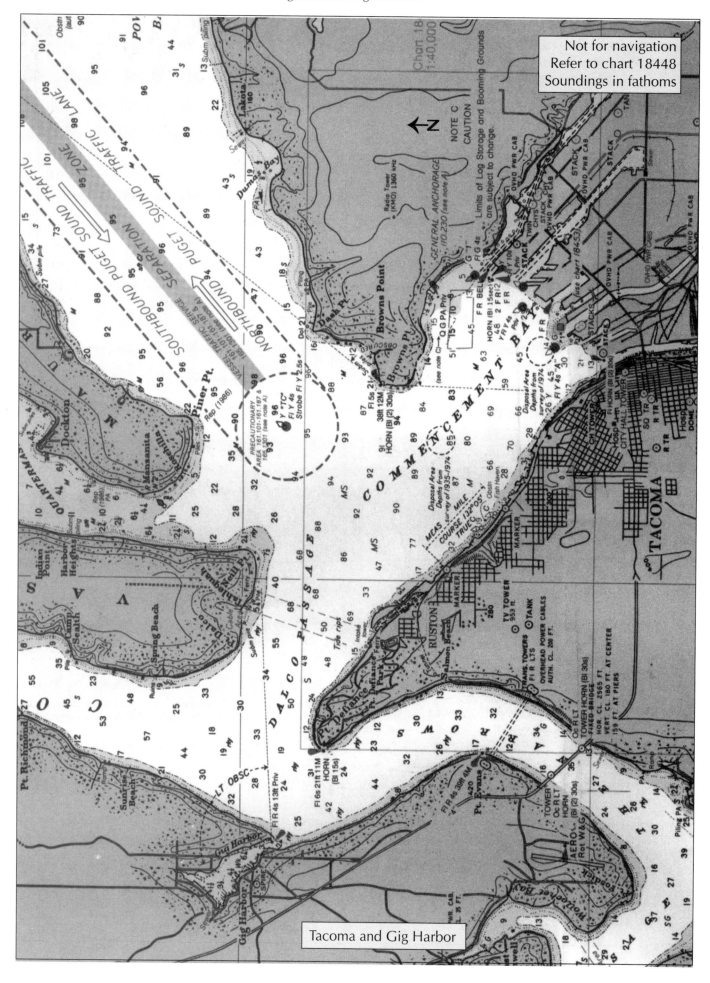

Not for navigation
Refer to chart 18448
Soundings in fathoms

Tacoma and Gig Harbor

CHAPTER 12
Tacoma and Gig Harbor

	Chart	Date	Title	Scale	Soundings
***	**18453**	08/05/95	Tacoma Harbor	1:15,000	Feet
**	**18474**	03/25/95	Shilshole Bay to Commencement Bay	1:40,000	Fathoms
**	**18445**	06/03/95	Puget Sound—Possession Sound to Olympia, page C;	1:80,000	Fathoms
			page B, Inset 6	1:40,000	Fathoms
			Page B, Inset 7	1:20,000	Fathoms
*	**18448**	10/30/93	Puget Sound, Southern Part	1:80,000	Fathoms
	18440	08/05/95	Puget Sound	1:150,000	Fathoms
			Tidal Current Charts, Puget Sound, Southern Part		
			Puget Sound Public Shellfish Sites		
			Washington State Public Lands Quad Map, Tacoma	1:100,000	

Charts and publications for this chapter

➥ *When using charts, compare your chart dates with ones referred to above. There may be discrepancies between different charts and different chart editions.*

Overview of Today's Commencement Bay

Tacoma, the city on the shores of Commencement Bay and the Tacoma Narrows, is booming. Now a thriving metropolis of 184,500, it was a secondary seaport for years. It is now a major port on Puget Sound, rivaling and sometimes topping Seattle in worldwide shipping. Competition is stiff between the two cities.

The beautiful bay at the mouth of the Puyallup River, was embraced with great enthusiasm by early settlers and visitors. The Settlement of Old Town was built early in 1865 by Job Carr, the first settler in the town. He also served as postmaster out of his home.

The bay has been turned into eight dredged waterways between commercial flatlands, and the highly industrialized Port of Tacoma.

Formerly forested hills surrounding the bay have been transformed into homes and businesses.

Cargo loading cranes, containers, warehouses and huge ships dominate the landscape, permeated by industrial smoggy haze. There are days when Mount Rainier still shows its gleaming flanks.

Today this seaport city has made a great effort to transform some of its waterfront into people-friendly parks. Much of the southwest shoreline of the bay, north from Thea Foss Waterway to Point Defiance, is parkland.

From Browns Point, at the northeast edge of Commencement Bay, follow the shoreline under steep bluffs which rise to 200 feet, and check out marine facilities along the way. We venture into Hylebos Waterway, then southwest past the industrial waterways and the Puyallup River. Next we investigate Thea Foss Waterway, and finally continue along Commencement Bay parks to Point Defiance.

➥ **NOTE: Marine fuel is available at three places** in the areas in this chapter:
- **Breakwater Marina** near Point Defiance—gas and diesel
- **Boathouse** at Point Defiance Park—gas only
- **Stutz Fuel Oil** in Gig Harbor—gas and diesel

When Captain Vancouver ventured into Commencement Bay in May 1792 after lunching at Browns Point, he had hoped to find an inlet heading east to the elusive Northwest Passage. Instead he found an "extensive circular compact bay, whose waters washed the base of Mount Rainier, though its elevated summit was yet at a very considerable distance from the shore ... "

Historic Commencement Bay

Nicholas Delin, a Swedish born cabinetmaker and carpenter from California, built a sawmill on Commencement Bay in 1852 at the confluence of two small streams. Logs for the mill were sent down a gully, called Shu-bahl-up, the "sheltered place," by the Indians.

The following year more than 150 persons had settled in or near this tiny but growing town, called "Old Town." Included in these newcomers was an English couple; William Sales was a millhand for Delin, his wife Eliza was a cook. Their son James, born on October 23, 1853, was the first white child born in what later became Tacoma. So began the "City of Destiny."

Tacoma was first known as Commencement City, then became Tacoma, named after Tahoma, the Native American name for Mount Rainier.

Historic fireboat, now retired, at Ruston Way Park (see p. 186, Fireboat Station)

Winthrop, a Romantic Traveler

When **Theodore Winthrop** traveled Puget Sound by canoe before the Civil War in 1853, he refused to call the Sound by anything except the native term, **"Whulge."** He was absolutely awestruck by Mount Rainier and all the surrounding beauty. He praised it lavishly when he wrote:

"We had rounded a point, and opened Puyallop (sic) Bay, a breadth of sheltered calmness, when I ... was suddenly aware of a vast shadow in the water ... No cloud, but a cloud compeller. It was a giant mountain dome of snow, swelling and seeming to fill the aerial spheres as its image displaced the blue deeps on tranquil water ... Only its splendid snows were visible, high in the unearthly regions of clear blue noonday sky ... Kingly and alone stood this majesty ... of the peaks this one was royalist. 'Mount Regnier' ... it has been dubbed, in ... nomenclature perpetuating the name of somebody or nobody. More melodiously, the siwashes call it Tahoma ... under its ermine, a crushed volcanic dome."

In 1855, the Indian War swept through what is now the Kent-Auburn Valley, killing men, women and children and burning farms; followed by the "White River Massacre" leaving Tacoma a ghost town. Settlers fled by any means they could to the town of Steilacoom for safety until tempers subsided.

In 1869, Tacoma got a post office, the first steamer called, a wedding was held, and a Tacoma school district started. It was the first railroad destination on Puget Sound, beating out Seattle. Tacoma was thriving. In the 1880s, the city was promoted as, "Tacoma! A new city, carved out of the primeval forest, dipping its feet into the waters of Puget Sound!"

Now we're into the 1990s and Port of Tacoma has eight industrial waterways from northeast to southwest are former tideflats. They are Hylebos (mouth of Hylebos Creek), Blair, Sitcum, Milwaukee, Puyallup (mouth of Puyallup River), St. Paul, Middle and Thea Foss, previously called City Waterway. Only Hylebos and Thea Foss waterways have facilities for recreational vessels. As we pass the port's industrial area we identify the aids to navigation.

After visiting Tacoma, we'll cruise northwest through Dalco Passage, cross The Narrows and explore delightful Gig Harbor in a protected harbor. Our main interest is cruising, finding interesting places to visit, moor and anchor and locating public access, but other information is important and include it as we find it.

Public tideland parcels of about four miles belong to the Tacoma Metropolitan Park District.

Unless otherwise noted public tidelands are state owned; some may be leased for private use. We take the Washington State Public Lands Quadrangle Map, when going ashore at these locations to avoid trespassing on adjacent private property.

Marinas with facilities listed on chart 18445 (6/1/95) were found to be inaccurate or incomplete. Businesses come and go from year to year and those facilities we list will also change over time. Information on Tacoma facilities listed in this book are by name; by the 18445 charted number, if any; by location, followed by comments and approaches.

Phone numbers and VHF channels, when known, are indicated so that continued existence of the facility can be verified before traveling long distances only to find that needed fuel and facilities don't exist.

⎈ Underway, from Browns Point we head southeast toward Hylebos Waterway.

"General Anchorage" for commercial vessels, barge storage and booming grounds, is charted along the north shore of Commencement Bay.

Floating breakwater, charted, 700 yards long in two sections, is made up of barges, pontoons and old ship hulls. It's about one mile south and east of Browns Point, protecting two marinas and a boatyard.

Q G, quick green private light at east end of the 500 yard long section marks the entrance into the marinas and yard. The smaller breakwater section continues southeast about 200 yards more.

Enter immediately south of the green light, between the two sections.

Tyee Marina is charted #61 on 18445. Facilities are not as listed. We understand this is the home of the **Corinthian Yacht Club of Tacoma**, with reciprocal moorage for perhaps two boats. There is permanent moorage for 700 boats, but no guest moorage. Phone: 206-383-5321

Also at or near charted #61 are:
- **Puget Sound Sailing Institute**, no listed phone
- **Seaward Canvas**, sailmakers and sail repair — Phone: 206-272-7542
- **Crow's Nest Marina,** see below

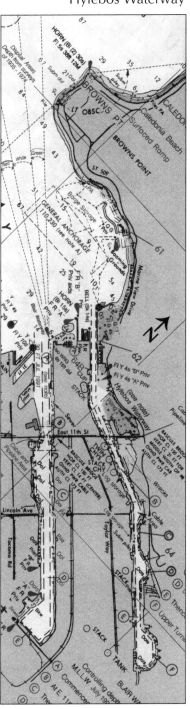

Browns Point to
Hylebos Waterway

Crow's Nest Marina Facilities
➤ Guest moorage on request
➤ Rates: $10 boats under 32'/ $15 boats over 32' — electricity, water included
➤ Pump-out
➤ Restrooms, showers, laundry
➤ Restaurants and stores within two mile radius
➤ Phone: 206-272-2827, Vic Hepperlen

Sunnfjord Boats, Inc., is a full service yard owned by Floyd Miller since 1980. The yard has two marine railways, 40 ton and 70 ton. They do repairs, including engines, hulls, electronics, boat maintenance, bottom painting, woodworking and new boat construction. Phone: 206-627-1742

⎈ **Underway,** heading southeast to **Hylebos Waterway.** This is a commercial waterway. Two marinas have guest moorage and several boatyards are along the east shore. One bascule bridge at East 11th Street crosses the waterway. There are commercial wharves, log storage, wrecks, tanks, scrap metal yards and constant activity of tugs with tows in the waterway.

Length of Hylebos Waterway is a little more than 2.5 miles.

Depths at MLLW range 27 feet at Commencement Bay entrance to 24 feet at the lower turning basin and 28.6 feet at the upper turning basin.

Widths range from 200 to 300 feet and wider in turning basins for large ships.

Fl G 4s "1" Hylebos Waterway Lighted Buoy "1," a flashing green 4 second light visible six miles, is at the northeast entrance to the waterway. It marks a shoal between the waterway and the shore.

F R PA, a private fixed red light seven feet high on the end of Pier 25, marks the southwest entrance to Hylebos. A fog signal bell which strikes every 14 seconds is in a tower on the dock.

Ole and Charlie's Marina, charted as #62 on 18445, is about 500 yards southeast of buoy "1." It is the first marina inside Hylebos Waterway. Facilities are not as listed on the chart; there is no dry dock, no chart sales and no fuel as shown. They do, however, have some guest moorage.

➡ Anchoring is not permitted in Tacoma waterways.

Not for navigation
Refer to chart 18445, page C
Soundings in fathoms

Ole and Charlie's Marina Facilities
- ➤ Guest moorage for about five boats
- ➤ Fees $7 per night up to 26'/ $10 per night over 26'
- ➤ Electricity and water included
- ➤ Groceries, water, ice, hardware
- ➤ Frozen herring
- ➤ Boat storage and moorage
- ➤ Service yard, boats to 26 feet
- ➤ Two sling hoists
- ➤ Phone: 206-272-1173

Chinook Landing Marina is on the northeast shore about 0.6 mile inside the entrance to Hylebos Waterway. Chart 18445, Ed. 26., shows #64B on the west side of the waterway as "Chinook Landing" **in error.**

Two Fl Y 4s two flashing yellow 4 second lights, "A" and "B," private, are charted at the location of the marina. There are more facilities than listed.

Chinook Landing Marina Facilities
- ➤ Moorage for 25-30 guest boats at 430 foot guest float and slips
- ➤ Guest moorage rate approximately 50 cents per foot
- ➤ 30 amp shore power at open slips only, not on guest dock
- ➤ Shore power $5 per day
- ➤ Water
- ➤ Pump-out facility
- ➤ Restrooms, showers, laundry
- ➤ Chandlery
- ➤ Basic convenience store
- ➤ Security with gate card access
- ➤ Oil recovery station, trash disposal
- ➤ Phone: 206-627-7676
- ➤ Monitors VHF Channel 79

Chinook Landing Marina in Hylebos Waterway looking northwest from 11th Street Bridge

Chinook's is a state-of-the-art marina run by members of the Puyallup Indian Tribe. It was designed and built without dredging or filling to preserve local marine life and the adjacent wildlife conservancy area and was completed in March 1993.

Enter the marina at the northwest end. Guests may tie up at the guest float at the end of A dock and check in, or call ahead for moorage.

Cable and pipeline area are north and south of the East 11th Street Bridge.

East 11th Street Bridge, a bascule bridge, is about 1.95 miles southeast of the entrance to Hylebos Waterway. Vertical clearance of the bridge is 21 feet for middle width of 98 feet, so most sailboats and many powerboats, tugs and workboats need the bridge raised. Horizontal clearance is 150 feet at water level. Bridge tenders monitor VHF Channel 16 and work on Channel 15, call sign KZN-574.

Tide clearance gauges on bridges would be a much safer way of communicating actual clearance to mariners, especially in tidal areas. In our opinion, they should be required on all federal waterways.

Overhead power cables have authorized vertical clearance of 173 feet.

East 11th Street Bascule Bridge—Hylebos Waterway

Horizontal clearance 150', closed vertical clearance 21' for middle width of 98'

At MHHW	(21.0' clr at MHW + 10.9' at MLLW - 11.8' at MHHW)	=	20.1'
At MHW	**Vertical Clearance as Charted**	**=**	**21.0'**
At MLLW	(21.0' clr at MHW + 10.9' at MLLW)	=	31.9'
At ELW	(31.9' clr at MLLW + [-4.5'] ELW)	=	36.4'

The tide table indicates a predicted height above or below MLLW datum. These heights can be considerably greater or less than predicted due to extreme winds, rain, snow melt or barometric pressures. Times predicted may also be off for high and low tides.

Values shown should be checked against the charted Tidal Information Table. The formula should be checked for errors before attempting to pass under the span. In other words, don't just take our word for it. We do not guarantee these figures.

Chart 18448, 10/30/95, was used for the above tabulation. We note no values were given for extreme high tides.

Hylebos Boat Haven, charted #64 on 18445 at 0.9 mile south of the 11th Street bascule bridge, is no longer in business.

Hylebos Marina, Inc., repair yard, is about 1.5 miles southeast of the 11th Street bridge, on the northeast side of the waterway. There is no guest moorage, but there is permanent moorage, travel lift, and boat repairs up to 50 feet. Phone: 206-272-6623

Nordlund Boat Co. Inc., boat builder and repair yard, is about 1.6 miles south of Hylebos Marina. Phone: 206-627-0605

And that about completes our trip through this basically industrial waterway.

⚓ **Underway,** we leave Hylebos, again passing the fixed red light at the southwest entrance to the waterway.

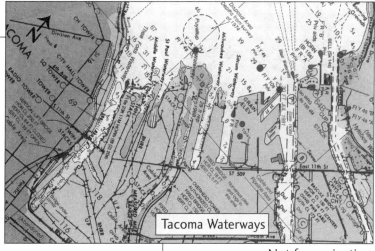

Tacoma Waterways

Not for navigation
Refer to chart 18445,
page B, inset 6
Soundings in fathoms

Aids to navigation crossing about two miles to Thea Foss Waterway, passing entrances of the 6 waterways at industrial Port of Tacoma, include:

(2) F R PA, fixed red lights "A" and "B" are 7 feet high at the end of Pier 23, the National Guard pier west of the entrance to Hylebos. A fog horn on "A" blasts every 15 seconds, mounted on house on dock.

Iso WRG 6s 15ft 4M Commencement Bay Directional Light, is at the northeast side of **Blair Waterway.** This three sector white-red-green 6 second light is on a centerline bearing 124°. White light is visible 3.25° each side of centerline; red is visible from 116.5° to 120.75°; green is visible from 127.25° to 131.5°.

Fl Y 10s Blair Waterway Lighted Buoy, is flashing yellow, private aid, southwest side of waterway.

Fl Y 4s Tacoma Outfall Lighted Buoy, is 400 yards northwest of Pier 5.

F R, a fixed red light on a pile structure, is the **Sitcum Waterway Light** at the northeast entrance to the waterway.

No lights are charted at Milwaukee Waterway entrance.

G "1" daybeacon, square green daybeacon on a dolphin, is **Puyallup Waterway Jetty Daybeacon 1,** and marks shoals off the **Puyallup Waterway** which extend nearly 500 yards north and west of Pier 2.

Fl Y 4s "A" is Commencement Bay Shoal Lighted buoy A, northwest of Puyallup Waterway.

A charted disposal area is north of the buoy.

No charted lights are at the entrance to **St. Paul** or **Middle waterways**

Fl 6s 23ft 11M Horn (Bl (2) 20s), **Thea Foss Waterway Light,** marks the northeast entrance to Thea Foss Waterway with facilities for recreational craft.

Tacoma Dome with its blue-gray roof rises at the south end of Thea Foss Waterway.

A 15 block long walkway lines much of the west shore, going up and down stairs, even along a boardwalk. A pocket park with benches and an overlook is at the south end of the walkway and Northwest Point Park is at the north end. Views from the walkway are of the nearly constant metamorphosis along the waterway as old buildings are torn down and new ones sprout up.

Thea Foss Waterway (formerly City Waterway) is mostly an industrial waterway, but there are a couple of places to moor here and a restaurant with moorage.

Length of the waterway is about 1.2 miles.

Depths charted, range from 30 feet at entrance to one foot at southern end.

Widths are nearly 200 yards at entrance to less than 100 yards at the south end where a bridge is charted as under construction.

South 11th Street vertical lift bridge is just under 0.5 mile south of entrance. Vertical clearance is 64 feet at MHW closed (down) and 139 feet when open (up).

South 11th Street Vertical Lift Bridge—Thea Foss Waterway

Horizontal clearance 200,' Vertical clearance closed 64' at MHW		**Closed**	**Open**
At MHHW	(64.0' clr at MHW + 10.9' at MLLW - 11.8' MHHW) =	**63.1'**	**+ 75' = 138.1'**
At MHW	vertical clearance as charted =	**64.0'**	**+ 75' = 139.0'**
At MLLW	(64.0' clr at MHW + 10.9' at MLLW) =	**74.9'**	**+ 75' = 149.9'**
At ELW	(74.9' clr at MLLW + [-4.5'] at ELW) =	**79.4'**	**+ 75' = 154.4'**

Values shown should be checked against charted Tidal Information Table. The formula should be checked for errors before attempting to pass under the span. In other words, don't just take our word for it. We do not guarantee these figures.

Chart 18448, 10/30/95, was used for the above tabulation. We note no values were given for extreme high tides.

Thea Foss

Thea Foss Waterway was named for the woman, who with her husband Arthur, founded the enormous Foss Tug and Launch Company.

In 1889 while Arthur, an immigrant carpenter, was away from their Tacoma houseboat building a shed, his blonde Norwegian wife bought a rowboat for $5 from a discouraged fisherman rowing past. She sold it for $15 and bought two more, renting them out at 10 cents an hour and 50 cents per day.

When Arthur returned with $32 and realized his wife had earned $41, he was so impressed with her entrepreneurial activities he decided to build rugged clinker-built rowboats—about 200—which they rented for a while.

Tug ***Arthur Foss***

From these inauspicious beginnings they moved to a naphtha launch, *Hope*, which they used to transfer people and supplies throughout the harbor, to and from ships and shore. Later they bought shallow draft launches. Arthur then designed and built snub-nosed tugs with rounded sterns—the design still seen on working tugs around the Sound.

The familiar green and white tugs—small yarders to large ocean-going craft—are prime movers of all types of tows on Puget Sound; the trademark, "Always Ready," on the vessels' stacks.

⎈ **Underway again along the west shore of Thea Foss Waterway.** Enter the waterway keeping Thea Foss Waterway Light to port.

First stop for recreational mariners after entering the waterway is the large marina about 0.3 mile in the waterway which extends north and south of the South 11th Street Bridge.

Totem Marina, charted #69 on 18445, does not have all the listed facilities. They no longer sell diesel or gas. There are 20 piers at this marina; for moorage check-in at the former fuel float on the end of Pier 4. Piers are numbered from north to south, starting with Pier 1.

Totem Yacht Club guest and reciprocal moorage is on Piers 4 and 5. Phone: 206-572-3120

Totem Marina Facilities
➤ Guest moorage for about 20 boats
➤ Moorage rates 50 cents per foot
➤ 20-30 amp power, $2 - $5 per day
➤ Water, pump-out, garbage
➤ Restrooms, showers, laundry
➤ Haulout for boats 10,000 - 20,000 pounds
➤ Basic store with marine supplies, fishing gear
➤ Security on all docks
➤ Walking distance to public services and shopping
➤ Engine repairs nearby
➤ Deli/restaurant, gift shop nearby
➤ Phone: 206-272-4404

*Totem Marina and south 11th St.
Bridge, closed, looking north*

⚓ **Continuing south** in Thea Foss Waterway, next is **City View Marina,** with no guest moorage. Owned by the city of Tacoma, there are plans to develop the marina. Presently there is permanent moorage for about 53 boats. Phone: 206-572-3120

15th Street Public Dock is about 0.25 mile south of South 11th Street Bridge. A 240 foot long float extends from behind Johnny's Seafood Market and is managed by City of Tacoma Fire Department. The dock is within easy walking distance of downtown, but is in an industrial area and security is an issue.

15th Street Dock Facilities
➤ Guest moorage for eight to 10 boats
➤ No charge
➤ No amenities
➤ 24 hour limit
➤ Boats over 30 feet call harbormaster
➤ Official policy is that boats over 30 feet must have approval of the harbormaster
➤ Phone: 206-591-5740

Not for navigation
Refer to chart 18445,
page B, inset 6
Soundings in fathoms

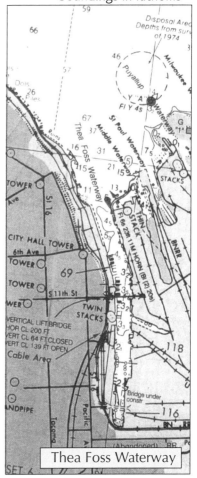

Thea Foss Waterway

⚓ **Thea Foss Waterway's** east shore includes **Martinac Shipbuilding** across from Totem Marina, south of the South 11th Street Bridge. It is near a charted, unnamed small, shoal waterway. They build and repair commercial vessels, including ferries. They also built *Corsair II* in 1926, the beautiful, custom cruiser owned by Bob Bryan and his wife, our editor and angel/exorcist, Sally.

City Marina, charted #118 on 18445, is 0.35 mile south of the South 11th Street Bridge, next to Johnny's Dock. There is no guest moorage as listed, only permanent moorage.

Johnny's Dock Restaurant is about 0.5 mile south of the South 11th Street Bridge. Facilities include guest float paralleling the shoreline with room for two to four boats free of charge while dining, first-come, first-served. Lunch and dinner daily and Sunday brunch. Phone: 206-627-3186

Pick's Cove, charted #116 on 18445, has no fuel facility as listed on the chart. It is about 0.45 mile south of South 11th Street Bridge and south of Johnny's Dock. Facilities include permanent moorage, but no guest moorage, full service repair yard, haulout facility with a 35 ton travel lift and retail store with marine hardware. Phone: 206-572-3625

Ruston Way Park looking SE

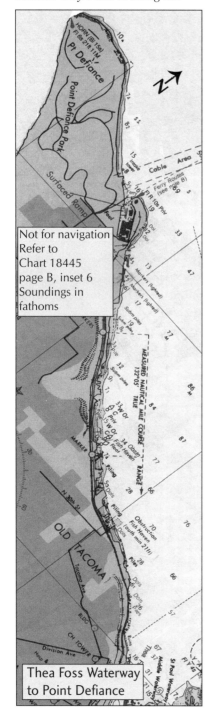

Not for navigation
Refer to
Chart 18445
page B, inset 6
Soundings in
fathoms

Thea Foss Waterway
to Point Defiance

Ruston Way Waterfront Parks (Tacoma Metropolitan Parks) start about 1.5 miles from the north end of Thea Foss Waterway and continues more than two miles along Commencement Bay.

Included are parks, fishing piers, 44 mooring buoys, erratic rocks, restaurants, concessions stands, latte stands, office buildings, ruins of old piers, benches, restrooms, telephones, lawns, picnic tables, waterfowl, fitness course, and pocket beaches with plenty of people room—all part of Tacoma's urban renewal program.

The level walk amidst lawns is a popular place for running, jogging, walking, cycling, and roller-blading. Mariners can tie to a mooring buoy or anchor, row ashore anywhere and run the kids, dogs or themselves. Kids can build sand castles and wade or paddle about while the folks sit on the sandy beach, backs against a drift log, contemplating the sun, sky and sea.

⚓ **Underway again,** we start at the south end of the waterfront park and work our way northwest to Point Defiance.

Commencement Park's unique ring sundial marks the south boundary of the waterfront parks. Made of structural steel, the sundial is 2 semicircles welded together and tipped at an angle, set inside a concrete embankment about 25 feet across. (We stopped here to set our chronometer, but it was a cloudy day and couldn't get any setting without shadows.)

The terraced park has benches with views of Commencement Bay and Mount Rainier near the display explaining history and geology of this region.

Old Town Dock fishing pier, built in 1973, just down the hill from historic Old Town Tacoma, abuts the west end of Commencement Park. Two large floats with eight slips are at this L-shaped dock with two mooring buoys offshore.

Artificial fishing reef charted as "Obstruction Fish Haven (auth min 21ft)" is just east of the Town Dock.

Hamilton Park with one picnic table, benches and an exercise station is two blocks west of Old Town Dock.

Dickman Millsite is west of Hamilton Park. Dickman Lumber Co., closed in 1977, was the last of the early sawmills operating along this once busy waterfront.

Measured nautical mile is charted on a course of 132°05' true along the shore halfway between Ruston and Old Town. Charted markers are on the shore.

Puget Park is a small park southeast of the fireboat moorage.

Fireboat station #5, dedicated in 1981, has fast 70 foot hovercraft fireboats moored at the pier. Onshore is a large, decommissioned fireboat that nearly everyone stops and checks it out. (See photo p. 180) The fire station is close to the end of North 38th St. An Italian restaurant is next door.

2 W Or C Priv buoys, white-orange can buoys, are charted about 0.25 mile apart on either side of Les Davis Pier.

Obstn Fish Haven is charted between the buoys.

Les Davis Pier, a popular 300 foot long T-shaped pier, is next, with fish cleaning stations and fishing rod holders. Bait and tackle concessions and restrooms are onshore.

Ruston Way sculpture, west of Davis Pier, is a gift from Kitakyushu, Japan, celebrating Tacoma's Sister City/Sister Port relationship.

Marine Park is the westernmost of Ruston Way parks with small, sandy beaches nestled between large rocks. Mooring buoys are offshore. There is a many-station fitness course for health addicts on the grassy strip; planters filled with bright flowers add welcome color.

The lovely waterfront parks end about Ferdinand Street and North 49th Street, and we continue northwest and to the wonderful park area of Point Defiance.

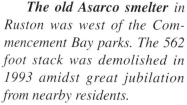

The old Asarco smelter in Ruston was west of the Commencement Bay parks. The 562 foot stack was demolished in 1993 amidst great jubilation from nearby residents.

No longer does the reminder of heavy pollution stand in their backyards. The stack is still charted on 18474, June 1991, but not on others.

Point Defiance—Breakwater Peninsula

About 0.8 mile past the parks and the defunct smelter we reach the west end of a man-made breakwater peninsula. The Tacoma Yacht Club and Breakwater Marina are in the 0.35 mile long boat basin inside the peninsula. Entry is from the northwest.

Fl R 10s Priv appears to be charted on a dolphin on the north side of the entrance to the breakwater boat basin on charts 18453 and 18445. We did not find a flashing red light or dolphin as charted. It is identified on the 1995 *Light List* as the "Point Defiance Ferry Dolphin Light." People at the yacht club said they weren't aware of a navigation light on the peninsula. However, there appears to be a light on a ferry dolphin on the south side of the entrance.

The octagonal Tacoma Yacht Club building with its lighted burgee dominates the end of the peninsula.

Point Defiance ferry landing is on the southwest mainland shore of the boat basin entrance. The ferry runs to Tahlequah on Vashon Island.

Inside the boat basin are the Breakwater Marina, the Tacoma Yacht Club and public access moorage floats and launch ramps.

Tacoma Yacht Club moorage is to port along the inside of the northeast shore; register for reciprocal moorage at the third float nearest the walkway to shore.

Breakwater Marina is along the south shore beyond the pile breakwater. For marina moorage or fuel, proceed down the channel to the fuel float where guest slips are assigned. Moorage is on the starboard side.

Point Defiance ferry landing, with Tacoma Yacht Club in background, photo taken looking east from Boathouse Marina

---

Breakwater Marina Facilities
➤ Guest moorage for 10 to 15 boats
➤ Moorage rate approximately 50 cents per foot
➤ 20-30 amp shore power is $2 per day, water
➤ Fuel dock: gas, diesel, kerosene and propane, open daily
➤ Pump-out on nearby city float
➤ Restrooms, showers
➤ Tidal grid for boats up to 50 feet
➤ Full service boat and engine repairs
➤ Basic store that carries marine supplies
➤ Phone: 206-752-6663

Breakwater Marina in background with public moorage in foreground, looking SE

Enter the basin for either the yacht club or marina by skirting the west end of the peninsula and heading southeasterly. The ferry landing, moorage floats, launch ramp and a piling breakwater wall are to starboard.

Public access to Point Defiance area (Tacoma Metropolitan Parks), offers: **Two public moorage floats** immediately east of the ferry dock. The shore-ends of the 150 foot long floats can be high and dry at low tide, with deeper water in the outer 50 feet. The floats are removed in winter months.

Overnight moorage fee $6, boats under 19'; $8, boats 20' to 29', and $10, boats over 30', 72 hour limit. Pumpout is on the west float; no power or water on floats.

Public moorage floats SE of Point Defiance ferry landing looking towards Breakwater Peninsula

When there aren't any boats at the Point Defiance moorage floats, a heron or two may dance about on stilt-like legs on the floats.

Within easy walking *of the moorage and launch ramp is fabulous Point Defiance Zoo and Aquarium, specializing in northwest critters, with some of the best naturalistic exhibits in the country. Great for the whole family. Phone: 206-591-5337*

The Boathouse Grill *has been at Point Defiance since 1890. Its popularity began when street cars took passengers to the park on the Point Defiance railway. Pleasure seekers strolled along the waterfront and admired the scenery. No Sunday outing was complete without a picnic on the beach.*

An arson fire at the old facility in 1984 ruined most everything. The new quarters were occupied in 1988.

Three surfaced launch ramps are immediately east of the moorage floats. Parking is available.

Point Defiance Park, next west, is a major Tacoma Metropolitan Park, the second largest metropolitan park in the country. The park has mooring buoys, 698 beautiful, wooded acres covering the Point Defiance peninsula, chock full of miles of hiking and biking trails, and history with the restored Fort Nisqually trading post, the Camp 6 Logging Museum and Never Never Land. The park includes a complex west of the ferry terminal with a large boathouse building, moorage, restaurant, marina and fuel dock.

Boathouse Marine Facilities
➤ Courtesy moorage
➤ Eight to 10 free moorage buoys along shore between Owens Beach & boathouse
➤ Fuel dock: pre-mix gas and regular
➤ Sewage pump-out
➤ Fishing pier
➤ Store with fishing gear, selected grocery items, snacks and souvenirs
➤ Hourly or daily boat rentals
➤ Lift-out hoist for rental boats
➤ Dry storage for 320 boats up to 17 feet
➤ Phone: 206-591-5325

Boathouse Tackle Shop has fishing gear, T-shirts, sweatshirts and Northwest novelty items. Friendly workers in the tackle shop will help rig fishing gear.

Boathouse Grill has dining with spectacular views, phone 206-756-7336.

Cable area is charted from the ferry pier to west of Boathouse Marina, crossing to Tahlequah on Vashon.

⎈ **Owens Beach** in Point Defiance Park, about 0.5 mile west of Boathouse Marina, is accessible by land or sea. Mooring buoys are offshore. This is a great beach to swim and play, but most shoreside sea treasures have already been picked over. It still provides a good place to just do nothing, which sounds like a great idea.

⚓ **Anchor** off in three fathoms or so, if you can't get a mooring buoy. Bottom here is sand, gravel and shell and does not hold as well as mud. Be aware of currents which can be strong. See chart below for further explanations.

Current Speeds in Knots at Point Defiance & Gig Harbor Entrance—
Based on extreme tides using a current correction factor of 1.5.
(Refer to Chapter 10 and/or Appendix Current Charts, pages 328-335.)
Point Defiance currents near Dalco and The Narrows shorelines flow northwest most of the time as charted, with classic backeddy characteristics.
 • **Dalco shoreline current** is weak from (E-1) thru (E+2). Current increases to about 2.4 knots at (F-1). (Note: Charted 1.6 tropic speed)
 • **The Narrows shoreline current** is charted weak at (F-2). Current increases to about 6.9 knots at (E). (Note: Charted 4.6 tropic speed)
Gig Harbor entrance currents are weak during the ends of the flood and the ebb, (F+3) and (E+3). They flow northwest into the harbor on the flood at about 1.8 knots at (F-1). (Note: Charted 1.2 tropic speed) They flow southeast out of the harbor on the ebb, and can reach about 2.4 knots at (E). (Note: Charted 1.6 tropic speed)

⎈ **Underway again,** knowing about the currents, we continue northwest in sometimes lumpy Dalco Passage, passing Point Defiance and all those sport fishermen—trying not to get tangled in their lines—crossing the often turbulent north end of The Narrows as we approach Gig Harbor.

Gig Harbor, a charming, historic small city, is a favorite destination for boaters on weekend trips from the greater Seattle area.

Entrance to Gig Harbor is between the developed west shore and the sandspit marked by a lighthouse on the east side. **Fl R 4s 13ft 3M Gig Harbor Light**, a flashing red light, is on the sandspit lighthouse at the northern side of the harbor entrance. A private aid, it is on an octagonal wood building and is obscured from 162° to 273°.

Width of the navigable channel between the sandspit and the western shore at extreme low water may be well under 100 feet.

Charted depths may be 10 feet or less in the channel center at extreme low tide. On extreme high tide the channel will be wider and maybe 24 feet deep.

We usually head for the west shore about 300 yards south of the light. When we start raising about two fathoms on the depth sounder we swing north and follow that depth along the west shore.

On extreme low tides, we may move west into seven or eight feet to be sure we get inside the 1 fathom 4 foot shoal extending about 120 yards south and west of the point (which then might be 6 feet or less) —staying clear of the pier and piles on the west shore. For *Scheherazade's* 5 1/2 foot draft, that could leave 6 inches under the keel.

Just before we are abeam of the hook on the sandspit we move east to pass close to the hook to avoid the shoal to the west. The entrance can be dicey on busy summer weekends when all manner of large and small craft enter and leave at the same time. We go slow and try to be ready to take evasive action, realizing some others may have different opinions about the channel.

And here we are . . . . . .

Ⓖ **Well-protected Gig Harbor** is about one mile long and 0.5 mile wide, with a fabulous view of Mount Rainier. Gig Harbor is known for its relaxed atmosphere, friendly people, services and shops within easy walking distance of the marinas—**a pleasant gunkhole.**

The southwest harbor shore is lined with marinas for the large local commercial fishing fleet and for pleasure boats; boatyards, marine repair facilities, several restaurants and condos. The sidewalk along the shoreline is a favorite for strollers and "serious" walkers alike. There are supermarkets, a hardware store, post office, banks, boutiques and bookstores near the waterfront. The northeast shore is mostly homes, many with private docks, floats and buoys. Transient moorage is located along the southwest, west shore and at the head of the harbor.

Piles, submerged piles and dolphins are charted around the harbor perimeter.

Tides Tavern and Restaurant on the south shore of the harbor, just inside the entrance, has the first guest float, with a sign painted on the building. The Tides is a favorite watering hole for racing sailboat crews, and cruising boaters and local residents, who enjoy the pizza, beer and entertainment.

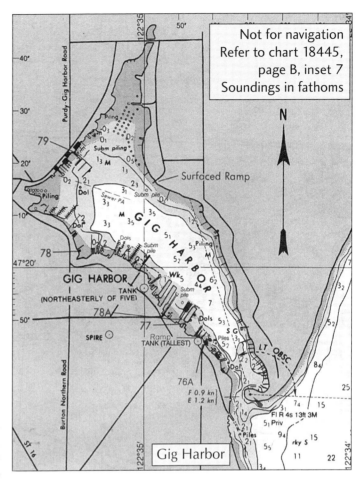

Not for navigation
Refer to chart 18445,
page B, inset 7
Soundings in fathoms

Gig Harbor

*Gig Harbor entrance,
looking east*

Gig Harbor lighthouse, *built in 1989 by a community association, is on a public beach, so it's okay to row over to the end of the spit and sunbathe or swim in the chilly (from personal experience) water.*

Gig Harbor was first explored by the Charles Wilkes expedition in 1841. He sent men in one of the ship's boats—a *gig*—to investigate. Midshipman Joseph Sanford called it a "pretty little bay that is concealed from the Sound."

Once soundings were taken, we understand Wilkes followed into the harbor in his 88 foot Porpoise. Pretty impressive sailing. He decided it was necessary to explore the harbor and this part of the Sound because, "... I deem it highly important as vessels are likely to be detained here in consequence of the difficulty of getting through the Narrows ... "

Jerisich Park public float

> **City of Gig Harbor** marine patrol enforces the 4 miles per hour (not knots) limit for all vessels.

Tides Tavern Facilities
➤ Complimentary moorage for restaurant patrons, 10-20 boats
➤ Rafting is mandatory if requested
➤ Float goes partially dry on extreme low tides
➤ 24 hour limit
➤ No water, electricity or restrooms
➤ Phone: 206-858-3982

Stutz Shell Service is charted as #76A on 18445. They carry diesel, gas, kerosene, lube oils, no propane. Hours are 8 a.m. to 5:30 p.m. daily, 8:30 a.m. to 2:30 p.m. on Saturdays, and closed on Sundays. Phone: 206-858-9131

Surfaced ramp, charted on 18445 between Stutz and Gig Harbor Marine, is gone.

Gig Harbor Marine, charted #77 on 18445, is west of Stutz. The yard has a marine railway for boats to 65 feet, a 25 ton travel lift, hull repairs, and permanent moorage for 120 boats. Phone: 206-851-7157

Jerisich Park city float and fishing pier, 500 feet long, is perpendicular to the shore. It's farther in the harbor, past several long piers, floats and boatyards, and is easily identified from the water because of the huge American flag onshore at the picnic area. This is a popular moorage for many visiting boaters on a first come, first served basis. Built in 1989, it's practically in the center of town.

Jerisich Park Facilities
➤ Guest moorage for 15-20 boats
➤ Moorage rate 25 cents per foot
➤ Restrooms
➤ Picnic tables onshore
➤ Loading float at outer end
➤ Rafting is not permitted
➤ The area up to 100 feet from shore is too shallow for sailboats at most tides
➤ Phone: 206-852-8145

Early Harbor Settlers
Samuel Jerisich, originally from Yugoslavia, arrived in Gig Harbor in 1867 with two fishing partners. They took shelter in the harbor after rowing there in a flat-bottomed skiff from Canada. When they arrived a band of Puyallup Indians was living in a longhouse by a small creek at the bay head.

Sam and his Canadian Indian wife lived in a one-room cabin with their family of ten. His wife hunted, fished, farmed, spun and wove, while he fished, rendered dogfish oil and smoked fish. He rowed his products to Olympia and Steilacoom as he felt they were better markets than Tacoma.

Pleasurecraft Marina has 54 permanent slips but no guest moorage, charted as #78A on 18445. They have not carried marine fuels since Labor Day weekend, 1995. Phone: 206-858-2350

Arabella's Landing is next west along the waterfront, the newest marina in the harbor. The owner said he built the marina because he couldn't find a place to moor his sailboat *Arabella* when he visited Gig Harbor a few years back. The guest float is the first float visible directly out from shore while permanent moorage slips are on A and C floats. The marina is within walking distance to many amenities in town, and service is first class. Just stop at the 250 foot long guest float perpendicular to shore for tie-up, and enjoy yourselves and Gig Harbor.

Arabella's Landing Facilities
➤ Guest moorage for 10 to 30 boats
➤ Moorage rates approximately 50 cents per foot, $15 minimum
➤ 30-50 amp shore power, water included
➤ Pump-out station at shore end of guest float
➤ Restrooms, showers, laundry
➤ Dock-hand assistance in tying up
➤ Furnished lounge where guests can relax
➤ Coffee on weekend mornings
➤ Beautifully landscaped uplands
➤ Meeting rooms available for groups
➤ Phone: 206-851-1793
➤ Monitors VHF channel 68

Northwest Boat Yard, formerly Northwest Yachts charted #78 on 18445, has no guest moorage. It is a full service yard for yachts including woodwork, fiberglass, paint, electrical, plumbing, engine installation but not repair, and has two marine ways for boats up to 40,000 pounds. It is located between Arabella's and Murphy's, owner Harold Palmer. Phone: 206-858-7700

Many of the early inhabitants of Gig Harbor were from Croatia and Scandinavia. Fishing and boat building were major industries in the harbor. While boat building is no longer a major industry, commercial fishing and boat repair are occupations of many harbor residents.

Murphy's Landing Facilities
➤ At the head of the harbor on the west shore, this is a modern condominium moorage 0.5 mile from downtown Gig Harbor.
➤ Guest moorage for two to three boats
➤ Moorage rates approximately 30 cents per foot
➤ 30 amp shore power and water included in moorage
➤ Restrooms, showers, laundry, pump-out
➤ Phone: 206-851-3539

Neville's Shoreline Restaurant has complimentary moorage for guests at the head of the harbor on the northwest shore. The guest docks go partially dry at low tide. There is some electricity and water. Phone 206-851-9822

Peninsula Yacht Basin is immediately north of the Shoreline charted as #79 on 18445. There is permanent moorage and open slips are rented to over-nighters.

*Genius—fish boat
in Gig Harbor*

Peninsula Yacht Basin Facilities
➤ Guest moorage for approximately 10 boats
➤ Moorage rate approximately 40 cents per foot
➤ 30 amp shore power, $1 per day, water
➤ Restrooms, showers
➤ Phone: 206-858-2250

⚓ **Anchoring,** we stay clear of the sewer charted in the northwest end of the harbor, otherwise anchoring is good most anywhere in the harbor in four to six fathoms. It gets shallow in the upper end. Set the hook well to be sure it's not fouled in seaweed, which may cause it to drag, in the middle of the night, of course. There are a fair number of permanently anchored local boats. We often anchor out, row to the city float and tie the skiff in the dinghy section.

Surfaced ramp is on the north shore of the harbor as charted. The bay becomes shoal tideflats and old pilings appear at low tide. Be aware of tides when launching here. Parking is nearby.

Gig Harbor is a great anchorage we really enjoy. We leave delightful Gig Harbor and head south for The Narrows.

As in most early communities around the Sound, Gig Harbor's "highway" was the Sound and steamers were the main form of transportation.

The first ferry, the side-wheeler City of Tacoma, arrived in 1917. Soon the larger Gig Harbor replaced it, followed by other ferries, including Defiance, Skansonia and Elk.

In Chapter 13, we take a scenic trip south through The Narrows, into Hale Passage and circumnavigate fascinating Fox Island.

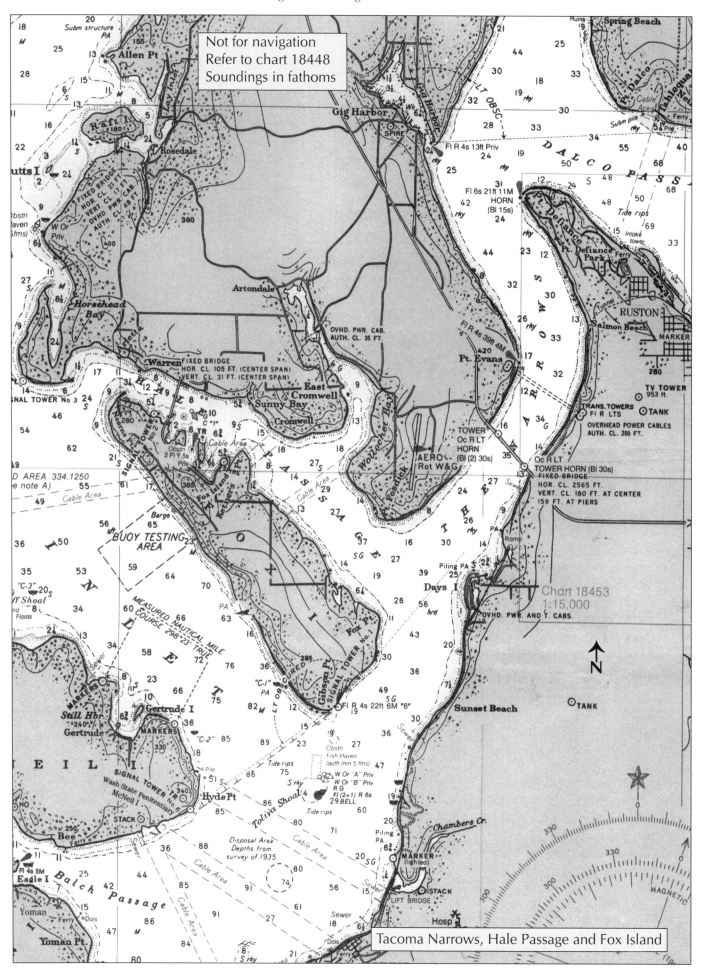

Not for navigation
Refer to chart 18448
Soundings in fathoms

Tacoma Narrows, Hale Passage and Fox Island

CHAPTER 13
The Tacoma Narrows, Hale Passage and Fox Island

Charts and publications for this chapter

Chart	Date	Title	Scale	Soundings
**18445	06/03/95	Puget Sound—Possession Sound to Olympia, page C	1:80,000	Fathoms
**18448	10/30/93	Puget Sound Southern Part	1:80,000	Fathoms
18440	08/05/95	Puget Sound	1:150,000	Fathoms
		Tidal Current Charts, Puget Sound, Southern Part		
		Booklet: Puget Sound Shellfish Sites		
		Washington State Public Lands Quad map, Tacoma	1:100,000	

➡ *When using charts, compare your chart dates with ones referred to above. There may be discrepancies between different charts and different chart editions.*

The Narrows — Overview

The vast waters of Puget Sound's many inlets south of Point Defiance and Gig Harbor rush in and out through this spectacular channel twice daily. It can be a wild millrace, churning millions of gallons of water into turbulent seas and rips between periods of extreme high and low tides, or it can be a millpond when the tidal difference is relatively minor or at slack.

Steep bluffs of 200 to 300 feet are on both sides of the Narrows, with water from 12 to 44 fathoms deep. There are no shoals or hazards offshore—except for currents and bridge piers.

The Tacoma Narrows separates the mainland from **Kitsap Peninsula**. This 4.5 mile long body of water runs from Point Defiance past Days Island on its east shore; on the west shore it runs from Gig Harbor to Point Fosdick.

Some mariners don't venture south of the Tacoma-Gig Harbor area, or north past Fox Island, because they've heard The Narrows can be frightening. Others have gone unprepared and had bad experiences. Some have even drowned in The Narrows.

We cruise The Narrows using the following information we consider essential:
- **First**, *Tidal Current Tables* and *Tidal Current Charts, Southern Puget Sound*
- **Second**, a good nautical chart of the area
- **Third**, knowledge of our boat, its speed and how it handles

In addition to the above, we add information from other boaters who can share experiences of going through The Narrows—local knowledge.

- **Chapter 10** in this book, "Currents," is a technical explanation of South Sound currents we consider essential, especially to mariners about to go through The Narrows for the first time.

Underway in The Narrows—Eastern Shore

⚓ **We enter The Narrows** as we round Point Defiance and head south.

Fl 6s 11M Horn (Bl 15s) Point Defiance Light, flashing white is on a green and white diamond on a dolphin 21 feet high just off the beach at the point. The Narrows trends southerly from here, and waters are deep off the point.

➡ **NOTE: Marine gas and diesel** are sold at **Narrows Marine Tackle and Marine** at Days Island.

The 200-foot high-bluffs at Point Defiance led Wilkes to give it that name in 1841. He said the point would, "if strongly fortified ... bid defiance to any attack and guard its entrance against any force."

Looking south to Point Defiance

*Salmon Beach homes,
train & tunnel*

More than 12 miles of public tidelands are noted in this chapter.

Public tidelands *unless otherwise noted are state owned; some may be leased for private use. We take the Washington State Public Lands Quad Map when going ashore at these locations to avoid trespassing on adjacent private property.*

Only for experienced scuba divers, *the rock ledges, wreckage of the old Tacoma Narrows bridge and turbulent currents can be a fascinating experience in this underwater recreation area, opportunities for photography, historical artifacts and sea life. This area is only for the very experienced because of strong currents.*

Looking north to Point Evans

➡ **"On the west side of The Narrows** the current floods most of the time ... on the east side it ebbs most of the time." (Tidal Current Tables)

Salmon fishing is usually excellent around Point Defiance, where it is often a traffic jam of kicker boats, fishing lines streaming out in all directions, often tangling in the propellers of the uninitiated.

The five fathom curve is sometimes less than 50 yards offshore at the west side of the point.

The Narrows Bridge is approximately three miles south of Point Defiance, and looms huge down the passage.

Salmon Beach, along the water on the east shore, is a cluster of older, brightly painted homes built out on pilings, just a bit over a mile south of Point Defiance. The unusual, picturesque community, visible from the water or the west shore, is reached by private trails down a steep hill. The most northerly cottage has an old sign declaring it "Daffodil Committee Boat," a souvenir, no doubt, from an old Tacoma Daffodil Festival Boat Parade.

Two of the homes slid into the water during the heavy rains and mudslides of February 1996. The slides also damaged several other homes along The Narrows.

Burlington Northern Railroad tracks hug the east shoreline and trains rumble past frequently, disappearing into or emerging from a tunnel at the south end of Salmon Beach. The tunnel curves under Point Defiance and then trains burst out near the Tacoma waterfront at the community of Ruston.

Public tidelands start about 3,500 feet south of the train tunnel entrance at Salmon Beach and run south for over 7,000 feet, almost to The Narrows Bridge.

Timbered bluffs above The Narrows on both shores have been replaced by ever-burgeoning million dollar homes, whose owners have million dollar panoramic views.

The Narrows—Western Shore

Fl R 4s 39ft 4M "4" Point Evans Light 4 flashing red on a triangular red daymark on a pile, is less than one mile north of The Narrows Bridge.

Bluffs in this area reach 420 feet high, and most homes on this shore are atop them with fabulous panoramic views; only a few are on the beach far below.

Power cables cross the channel at a height of 200 feet from Point Evans to the mainland. Their transmission towers are marked with flashing red lights.

Public tidelands are at the base of the bluffs along much of this western shore south of Gig Harbor almost to the bridge. Two parcels are south of the bridge. They are 2,300 feet and 900 feet long respectively, sandy, gravel beaches with rock crab and clams on them—if they haven't been all dug out.

These western beaches are accessible by water and could be very useful as a stop for canoeists and kayakers especially if currents are not favorable. Several are accessible by land—except at high tides—from one place, a steep brushy path at the west end of The Narrows Bridge. We see many beach walkers and surf fishing people using the beaches as we cruise past. All uplands are private.

Following the starboard or western shore through the Narrows, as did Puget, if we are in close enough to shore the houses at the bluff tops are not visible. What we see is almost what he saw: the pristine beauty of the bluffs.

The Narrows Currents

The Narrows currents are predicted daily in the ***Tidal Current Tables*** book, with predictions for midstream. ***Tidal Current Charts*** give details of the complicated currents which can be encountered. Currents in all the inlets and passages in South Sound are figured on these predictions. (See **Chapter 10** "Currents")

The Narrows — and the Bridges

The Narrows Bridge is nearly one mile long, with a span between piers of 2,565 feet, nearly one-half mile. Vertical clearance is 180 feet at the center.

Oc R Lts occulting red lights, are atop both bridge towers. West pier fog signal is a horn, low-tone, with two blasts every 30 seconds. East pier fog signal is a horn, high-tone, one blast every 30 seconds.

The First Bridge—Galloping Gertie

When the first Narrows Bridge, "Galloping Gertie," fell into The Narrows' turbulent waters a short four months after completion, it was a shocking blow to the whole region—especially to the insurance agent who had pocketed the premiums.

"Galloping Gertie"
Photo courtesy Seattle Post-Intelligencer Collection, Museum of History & Industry, Seattle

The bridge collapsed on November 7, 1940, when southerly winds blew steadily at 42 miles an hour. A little after 9 a.m., the bridge—already nicknamed "Galloping Gertie" because of its oscillating movements—began a sickening corkscrew, twisting motion. The north railing rose above the south in some sections and the south railing twisted above the north in others. Engineers wisely closed the bridge high above breaking waves and swirling tidal currents.

A *Tacoma News Tribune* editor, Leonard Coatsworth, abandoned his car between the towers and crawled to the Tacoma side of the bridge and safety. His dog, Tubby, refused to leave the car and bit him.

Just for thrills, a college student walked across the bridge. It was more frightening than thrilling.

University of Washington civil engineering professor F. Bert Farquarson drove from Seattle to film the bridge in its death throes. Commissioned to study untoward movements of the young bridge, it was gone before his studies had hardly begun.

Blocks of concrete broke loose and bashed and crashed across the two-lane roadbed, finally smashing through guard rails and dropping to the churning waters below. Lamp posts swayed and broke.

Tacomans on the shore—who had called the bridge a "dream come true"— watched in horror as a 100 foot section of roadbed broke loose and crashed to the sea's bottom. Most of the roadbed between the two towers dropped out of sight within minutes. Miraculously, Tubby, the dog was the only fatality.

The mile-long bridge was begun in 1937 after years of lobbying by Tacomans, who watched its construction with parental pride. The federal Public Works Administration granted half the money to build the bridge, estimated at more than $6 million. Dedicated on July 1, 1940, it was the third largest suspension bridge in the world at that time, linking Kitsap Peninsula to Tacoma over the narrowest channel in Puget Sound.

With Gertie's collapse, the Peninsula was again isolated from the east side of the Sound—except for ferries or driving around through Olympia and Shelton.

Hard hat time for mariners sailing under The Narrows bridge—note loose strut

"Sturdy Gertie"

Puget's expedition *was the first recorded group of non-Native Americans, to run The Narrows during maximum flood.*

On May 20, 1792, Peter Puget's two-boat flotilla had an easy run south through Colvos Passage from their "breakfast place " at Olalla, passing the south end of Vashon, looking east through Dalco Passage to view "an excessive high Snowy Mountain." From there "our Progress was along the Starb or Continental Shore, which still was in a Southerly Direction.

*"The previously friendly flood tide became a millrace as the surging waters of the inland sea were suddenly constricted in a channel less than a mile wide. Amid whirlpools and eddies the oarsmen had all they could do to keep the boats under control." (**Peter Puget** by Robert Wing and Gordon Newell)*

Puget wrote: "A Most Rapid Tide from the northward hurried us so fast past the Shore that we could scarce land ... "

Botanist Archibald Menzies noted: "We pursued our southerly direction with a strong flood tide in our favor ... "

Vancouver entered The Narrows several days after Puget, writing, " ... the western shore of the main inlet, into which ran a very strong tide ... With the assistance of the strong tide we rapidly passed through a fair navigable channel, near half a league wide, with soundings from 24 to 30 fathoms, free from any appearance of shoals, rock or ... interruptions."

The dream vanished. The "Gateway to the Peninsula" was no longer. It was 10 years—with World War II in between—before the new bridge was completed.

The concrete piers remained; the towers and cables were salvaged for scrap metal used in the war.

The Second Bridge— "Sturdy Gertie"

The second bridge opened October 14, 1950, a modern four-lane bridge across the Sound. Three men died building the bridge.

That spectacular piece of structural engineering is a little more than 180 feet high at the center of the span. It sometimes feels awfully close to mast top as we pass under. Through the grated bridge deck the underside of cars can be seen driving overhead on the four lanes, and we hear the traffic's roar.

It is an awesome bridge, especially from down under. When we pass under we remember "Galloping Gertie." Could that disaster happen again—especially while our boat is here? Not likely. "Sturdy Gertie" has proven to be substantial for more than 40 years. Although motorists often see high wind warning signs as they drive over it, the bridge has held in place well.

The biggest challenge now is with tremendous growth on the peninsula there is talk of adding another bridge across The Narrows.

The Narrows—South of the Bridge

Titlow Beach is on The Narrows' east shore just over one mile south of the bridge in a crescent bay, a wonderful 49 acre Tacoma Metropolitan Park. We recognize it by the forest of old pilings offshore, once supports for the old ferry dock.

Public mooring buoys off the beach seem to vary in number. We have counted from three to five at different times. Boaters heading north who can't make it through The Narrows because of adverse currents might consider tying to a buoy until the current slacks off. This is not a good place to anchor because of the strong currents.

Titlow Beach Park attractions include the buoys, of course, a drawing card for boaters. There's also 2,800 feet of beach, and the uplands have walking and hiking trails inshore of the railroad tracks. In addition, there are playfields, tennis and volleyball courts, a playground, outdoor swimming pool, fitness course and community center with restrooms. There is no public launch ramp. Phone: 206-591-5297

Private launch ramp north of Titlow belongs to Tacoma Outboard Association.

Public tidelands of about 4,500 feet run almost all the way along the eastern shores of The Narrows from the bridge to Titlow. They are suitable for beachcombing at low tides.

Days Island is a private, almost completely residential island immediately south of Titlow Beach. The south end has been filled in, making a small peninsula with a tiny bay between it and the mainland. A bridge over the railroad tracks and the peninsula is the only access to the island.

Several marine business are located in the vicinity of Days Island, including Marrows Marina Tackle and Marine, Narrows Marina, Day Island Marina and Day Island Yacht Harbor.

Narrows Marina Tackle and Marine and **Narrows Marina** are on the mainland in a bight at the northeast shore. They are charted as #81 on 18445, but are two separate entities. Narrows Marina Tackle and Marine runs the fuel float and tackle shop. Narrows Marina runs the moorage, storage and launch ramp. Facilities are not as listed on the chart.

Narrows Marina Tackle and Marine Facilities
➤ Fuel: gas and diesel
➤ No guest moorage
➤ Restrooms
➤ Fishing tackle, marine supplies, including charts
➤ Fish pens stocked with live herring; also sell frozen herring
➤ Snacks and ice
➤ Phone: 206-564-4222

Day Island Yacht Club,
looking north from
Note: Drying mid-channel shoal

To reach the fuel dock, stay close to the mainland shore, noting the two fathom four foot shoal north of the entrance. Tie up along the nearly 100 foot long fuel dock.

Narrows Marina facilities include permanent covered moorage, garage storage and warehouse for 200 boats, a vertical boat lift for boats in dry storage and large parking area.
Phone: 206-851-7394

Launch ramp is self service; fees are $10 on weekends, $6 weekdays.

Day Island Marina, charted as #82 on 18445, is across the road from Narrows Marina. It has private moorage, boat sales and service. Chart lists shows guest moorage, hull and motor repairs and gas sales; those facilities are not available.

Day Island Yacht Harbor, a full service boatyard that's been in business since the mid-1960s, is across the channel entrance on the island side. They also help bring in boats with problems. They do maintenance, annual service, engine and fiberglass repairs; 15 ton or 46 foot haulout capacity, but shallow harbor discourages sailboats. Permanent moorage only. Phone: 206-565-4814

Day Island Yacht Club is at the south end of the tiny bay between the mainland and the island. Use extreme caution, enter on rising tide, three or four feet above zero. Yacht club members say to skim close to boathouses on west side to miss midchannel shoal. There is guest moorage for reciprocal yacht club members only.

⚓ **Sunset Beach** is a little less than 1.5 miles south of Days Island, with undeveloped bluffs along the way. Views across the water are to Hale Pass and Fox Island.

Public tidelands of about 1,000 feet are at Sunset Beach. Beach cottages and untamed shore take up the next 0.5 mile.

Then we come upon the enormous remains of the largest sand and gravel mine on Puget Sound—one of the five largest in the nation—Pioneer and Glacier Gravel Pits. The sand and gravel bluffs are almost dug out, leaving gigantic valleys reaching nearly one mile inland, with sandy beaches along the shore. There are loading docks at the gravel mine where barges are still loaded with sand and gravel.

⚓ **Anchoring;** friends from Steilacoom tell us of a lovely sandy beach where they occasionally anchor off the gravel pit. In addition, some Stellar sea lions hang around near the gravel pit. It's one of a very few places we didn't try.

➡ **This is as far south as we're going in this chapter. Now we're going to chase Peter Puget into Hale Passage and Carr Inlet.**

South Sound

⚓ **Underway again, we're through The Narrows** and in a different world. Spaces open up; inlets are wider, more trees along the shores. It's quieter somehow. The huge Washington State ferries no longer ply the waters, replaced by tugs and tows, pleasure craft, fishing boats and a very occasional cargo ship on its way to Olympia.

Skies are bluer, clouds whiter, sun brighter. Gone are urban high-rises and smoggy cities. Suburban homes fitted tightly into waterfront lots eventually give way to more modest shoreline development the farther south and west we cruise.

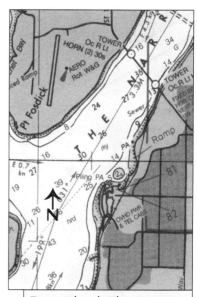

Days Island, The Narrows

Not for navigation
Refer to chart 18445
Soundings in fathoms

The chart shows "Days" Island, but most people drop the "s" and call it Day Island. Days Island was named for Stephen W. Days, a hospital steward with the Wilkes Expedition.

➡ **Time to change charts, as 18474 just ran out. From now on (until we get near Olympia and Shelton) we'll be using either 18448 or strip chart 18445, both with a scale of 1:80,000.**

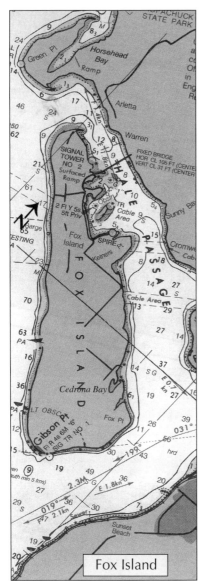

Not for navigation
Refer to chart 18445
Soundings in fathoms

Point Fosdick was named for Stephen Fosdick, a gunner's mate with the Wilkes Expedition.

We're in South Sound where there are no large cities, in fact, there are only three waterfront cities in this whole area: Steilacoom, Olympia, Shelton. Now we find small communities, small marinas, shoreline parks, pristine public lands, and some neat **gunkholes.** We check out these wonderful new cruising areas that have opened up.

Hale Passage, five miles south of Point Defiance, is about four miles long from the southeast end between Point Fosdick and Fox Island, to where it meets Carr Inlet off the northern tip of Fox Island and the sandspit east of Green Point.

Depths in Hale Passage range from eight fathoms near the Fox Island Bridge near the northwest end to 37 fathoms at the southeast entrance.

Navigable widths in Hale Passage are from 0.8 mile at the southeastern end of the pass to about 300 yards at green buoy "C1.

Currents in Hale Pass, based on predictions at The Narrows, are sometimes more than three knots, with ebb stronger than flood. Currents are best described for the time of travel based on *Tidal Current Charts* referenced to the *Tidal Current Tables*.

Fox Island fixed span bridge is three miles northwest of Point Fosdick and 1.1 miles from west end of Hale Passage. **Horizontal clearance** is 105 feet, center span.

Vertical Clearance at the Center Span of Fox Island Bridge:		
At MHHW: (31.0' clr at MHW + 12.6 at MLLW-13.5' at MHHW) =	**30.1'**	
At MHW vertical clearance as charted	=	**31.0'**
At MLLW (31.0' at MHW + 12.6' at MLLW)	=	**43.6'**
At ELW (43.6' at MLLW +[-5.0'] at ELW)	=	**48.6'**

Tide tables indicate a predicted height above or below MLLW datum. These heights can be considerably greater or less than predicted due to extreme winds, rain, snow melt or barometric pressures.

Values shown should be checked against the charted Tidal Information Table. The formula should be checked for errors before attempting to pass under the span.

Chart 18448, 10/30/95, was used for the above tabulation. Note, no values were given for extreme high tides.

Fox Island Bridge

"Heights above Mean High Water" were omitted from chart 18448, instead "Heights in feet" were used. Tide clearance gauges on bridges would be a much safer and more accurate way of communicating the actual clearances to the mariner.

G C "1" Fox Island Rock buoy 1, green can buoy about 450 yards east of the bridge, is roughly in the middle between Fox Island and the mainland peninsula shore. It marks the south side of the navigable channel in this area.

Boulder-strewn shoal charted about 350 yards east of Fox Island Bridge, west of the green buoy, bares at low tide.

Hale Passage

Peter Puget arrived here on the first afternoon of the exploration, May 20, 1792. His men had struggled with the currents as they came through The Narrows. When they reached Point Fosdick they found themselves in a surging backeddy, against them. We believe it was a clockwise backeddy, resulting from the flood current.

Puget wrote: "At the Distance of about Six Leagues from the Breakfast Place (Olalla on Colvos Passage) the Continent took a Sudden turn to the Westward (Hale Passage) & from this Direction the current came so Strong that all our Efforts could not make way against it, we therefore landed to dine on the Point," which they named Dinner Point.

(continued on next page)

(If one league equals 3 nautical miles that would have placed them through all of Hale Passage near Green Point. Possibly he was calculating his distance through the water using a chip log with no correction for adverse currents in Colvos Passage. The scaled distance on the chart appears to be about 3.6 leagues rather than 6.)

Menzies wrote of their first encounter with tidal "back eddies" in his journal: "About two in the afternoon we came to another arm leading off to the westward (Hale Passage) which we entered and found a very strong tide against us. At this time we were at a loss to account for this as it evidently appeared to be the flood tide by rising on shore, though we afterward found that it was occasioned by a number of islands 'round which the tide had reverted and as it was very strong against us we disembarked on the point to dine till it should slacken a little."

Later, taking advantage of the current, they followed the land around Point Fosdick and into Hale Passage, making a brief trip into Wollochet Bay where they encountered Indians in a village near the head of the bay.

Puget described the land as flat for about a quarter of a mile rising to hills, "which everywhere is thickly covered with large Pines, & difficult of being penetrated through a quantity of Gooseberry Raspberry and Currant Bushes now highly in Blossom which intermixed with Roses exhibited a Strange variegation of Flowers but by no Means unpleasant to the Eye."

Underway along the North shore of Hale Passage from Point Fosdick

The currents still eddy around the east end of Hale Passage as they've always done. No longer is Point Fosdick "thickly covered with large pines." It is thickly covered with large homes on nearly clear-cut slopes.

This isn't the first time this area has been denuded. Around the turn of the century many settlers were interested in developing the land for farming and so the forests were cleared. The story is that at one time you could stand on Point Fosdick and see the entire length of Wollochet Bay.

State underwater recreation area is offshore of the rounded point, with wrecks and sunken hulks plus shellfish—great for underwater photography.

Across the top of the land above the point is the Tacoma Industrial Airport which is charted with **Aero Rot W&G**, rotating white and green light. It can't be seen from the water but is the reason there are many airplanes in the area.

Public tidelands of about 1,000 feet are at the southern tip of Point Fosdick.

(G) **Wollochet Bay** opens up west of Point Fosdick, a well-protected anchorage when it's blowing briskly—**a good gunkhole**. The elongated bay trends north for the first mile off Hale Pass, where it is about 0.5 mile wide and depths range from 18 to four fathoms. In the second mile it narrows and bends northwest, giving the best protection from south winds.

Anchoring is possible in about two to four fathoms, gravel bottom. The bay shoals and narrows in the north portion, with mud flats in the last 0.5 mile.

Wollochet is ringed with homes, cabins and private docks and is often busy with small boat traffic. The bay is full of activity, especially in summer months, when small sail and power boats, kayakers and swimmers enjoy warm water and sunshine.

Launch ramp at the bay's east entrance is south of the remains of the old dock that once served steamers. Parking is limited at the no-fee ramp

Cable crossing from Fox Island comes ashore on the east side near the ramp.

Charted rock resides at **East Cromwell** about 150 yards off the west shore.

Public tidelands of about 3,000 feet are on either side of the second small bight on the east shore. The tidelands start about 900 yards north of the launch ramp.

Public tidelands of about 800 feet are near the west entrance of Wollochet at the rounded bulge.

Picnic Point on Wollochet's east shore, about 0.5 mile from the north end of the bay, is the site of an abandoned Indian village. The point was used by early settlers for gala picnics and festivities.

Point Fosdick's moment of glory was in the 1940s when President Franklin Delano Roosevelt rode up and down the streets of the community on his way to Bremerton and the Puget Sound Naval Shipyard.

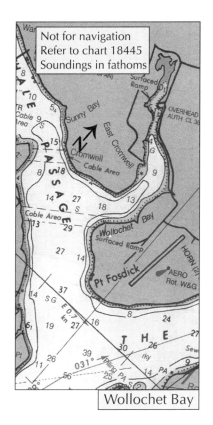

Not for navigation
Refer to chart 18445
Soundings in fathoms

Wollochet Bay

The old steamer dock at Point Fosdick was used by the ferry that crossed The Narrows to Titlow Beach in Tacoma before the bridge was built, and rebuilt, in the 1940s. About all that's left of the dock are seagull dominated pilings.

Wollochet is a Native American term for "Squirting Clams," which were plentiful on the beach when the Indians lived here. "Civilization" has decimated the clam population.

The bay was called Vander Ford's Harbor by the Wilkes Expedition before it reverted to Wollochet.

*A **purple horse** is in a field in this area, although it's NOT visible by boat. It was great fun to find, especially if you've never seen a purple horse. Someone has a wonderful sense of humor. Makes us remember the old poem about a purple cow . . .*

⚓ **Anchoring** is possible throughout the bay, but is most protected in the northern portion, past East Cromwell. There are glorious views of Mount Rainier from inside Wollochet.

Charted overhead power cable with 35 foot vertical clearance near Picnic Point was removed about 1992.

Public tidelands in two small parcels under 1,000 feet each are near the head of the bay on the east shore.

Artondale community at the head of the bay has no facilities for boaters.

Wollochet History—An Indian longhouse was on the beach along the eastern shore in Wollochet Bay. Even after settlers arrived about 500 Native Americans lived on a reservation north of Point Fosdick. Indian families fished and traded their fish, goods, beautiful hand-woven baskets and other items with the settlers. Smelt sold for 25 cents a bucket.

By late 1800s a large population of different tribal backgrounds, including Squally, Puyallup, Yakima and Cowlitz, lived on the government military reservation in the area.

Wollochet Bay is one of the older settlements on the Gig Harbor Peninsula, begun when Miles B. Hunt homesteaded in 1876. It was a boating community from the beginning.

The first grocer, a Mr. Uhlman, used a launch to sell meats and vegetables to residents along the shore. In 1879 Hunt's son Emmet started delivering mail from Steilacoom in a 16 foot rowboat. He also taught the first term at the original log Artondale School at the head of the bay. He and his brother Arthur built steamboats for their delivery business. By 1885, they bought the *Susie,* which they used to tow scow loads of bricks from the Fox Island brickyard, log booms, and hauled freight and passengers.

This area was settled in the 1880s and the pioneers logged, fished, trapped, and farmed. In 1887, local children went to school in a rough board shack on the beach near an old Indian campground between Warren and Arletta. Children walking to and from school by way of the beach found beads and agate arrowheads, which they carried home in their lard-bucket lunch boxes.

The Wollochet Bay Store near Picnic Point was the center of activity for many years after it was opened in 1914. It is now a craft shop.

Inner Wollochet Bay

Peter Puget found Shaw's Cove an attractive place to spend his first night out. His men hauled their boats ashore about 8 o'clock, tired after more than 16 hours of hard rowing. Botanist Menzies noted there were small trees of American and Mountain Ash which he'd never before seen on this side of the continent. Puget was also impressed with the "gentle northern wilderness." It was the end of their first day exploring this vast new territory.

⊕ **Underway,** leaving Wollochet Bay, we head west in Hale Passage along the mainland shore. We found places we'd never been aware of along this part of the pass: **Cromwell** and **Sunny Bay.** They are pleasant shoreside communities but have no facilities for boats.

Cable area runs from Cromwell to Fox Island.

Public tidelands of about 1,500 feet are in Cromwell east of the cable crossing. Two smaller parcels of about 500 feet are between Cromwell and Sunny Bay. The road runs just above the beach in places. Then there are small private docks and a few erratic rocks. Two more parcels of about 800 feet are east of the bridge along the north shore, while about 1,000 feet more are 2,000 feet west of the bridge.

Shaw's Cove, unnamed on the charts, is at the northwest end of Hale Passage on the mainland, inside a sandspit where a wreck is charted, about 0.5 mile east of Green Point.

⚓ **Anchoring** is possible in 1.5 fathoms, but it is exposed to southeast winds.

⚓ **Public tidelands** of about 4,000 feet are in four parcels along the southern shore of **Green Point**; three are on the point and the fourth is on the outside of the sandspit, with several hundred feet between each parcel.

It's difficult to imagine how exciting it must have been to see all this wonderful new country for the first time, as Puget did, yet we sometimes sense the zest of discovery ourselves when we sail these waters.

Fox Island

This most northerly of South Puget Sound islands is our next destination. Roughly five miles long and just a little over one mile wide, we find it to be a delightful place.

Public tidelands totaling nearly 30,000 feet, or more than five miles, in at least 22 parcels, surround the island. These tidelands are available to the public, taking care not to trespass on nearby private lands.

Up until 1954 when the Fox Island Bridge was built, Hale Pass between the island and mainland gave boaters a clear shot into upper waters of Carr Inlet and Henderson Bay from The Narrows.

Those islanders who commuted to work by ferry from Fox Island to Point Fosdick were delighted with the bridge. Those who lived on the island because they wanted the isolation of island living were less than thrilled. The bridge opened up the wooded island to developers, almost turning it into yet another suburb of Tacoma. In addition to formerly self-sufficient pioneer types, content with ferry service and semi-isolation, there are now suburban, city commuters who also love island living. Meanwhile, the old island ferry landing has fallen into disrepair.

Fox Island has a wonderful historical museum inland, but you pretty much need a car to get there.

⚓ **Underway—North end of Fox Island at Hale Passage,** we explore the intriguing island shoreline, ignoring the bridge height for the time being.

Several small coves are tucked away along this shore. Rumrunners and sailors jumping ship often sought refuge in these coves in the "good old days." The navigation charts do not name coves along this part of the shore, but we'll share what we gleaned from friendly islanders.

⚓ **Small anchorage** is inside a sandspit at Nearns Point at the northwest tip of Fox Island. It's less than one mile west of the bridge with some protection from southerlies. The beach is private and some boats are moored here.

Fox Island Historical Museum

⚓ **Towhead Island**, unnamed on charts, is at the south end of Fox Island bridge. The tiny island joins Fox by a long sandspit and the bridge.

Public launch ramp on the west shore of Towhead is built of concrete planks giving good traction with some parking, but no facilities.

Scuba diving is **supposed** to be good in here among bridge pilings and shallows to the east.

⚓ **Anchoring** is possible in the small bay on east side of Towhead Island between Towhead and the unnamed peninsula east of it. Use caution in the vicinity of the shoal and green buoy "C1." The bay shore has a number of homes and docks, and some boats anchored off, but there is occasionally room to anchor with care.

⚓ **Public tidelands** in three parcels are around this small peninsula.

Salmon fishing is rumored to be good in Hale Pass.

Echo Bay, with tiny **Tanglewood Island** in the center (unnamed on the charts), looks small, but nevertheless there are delightful anchorages on the Fox Island shore.

Off the west side of the small island is an aquaculture facility, charted as "obstruction."

Hale Passage was named for Horatio Hale, a language expert with the Wilkes expedition who catalogued a precise dictionary of Chinook jargon.

Not only that, Hale's mother wrote the children's poem, "Mary Had a Little Lamb."

Former Washington State Governor Dixy Lee Ray, who died in 1994, is Fox Island's best known citizen.

United Church of Christ

Tanglewood Island "tower"

The fish farm looks pretty substantial, with big round buoys about 3.5 feet in diameter, and small red anchor buoys marking the perimeter, with two flashing yellow, five second lights. In behind the fish farm is a small bay with anchored boats.

Note the charted rock in the bay near the aquaculture.

⚓ **Anchor** on the west side of Tanglewood Island, clear of the aquaculture buoys and their anchors.

⊕ There's enough water for us to go behind Tanglewood Island, about 15 to 20 feet or more, depending on the tide. It is a beautiful little island with only a few homes along its shores.

Cable area is charted south of the island.

On the shore east of Tanglewood Island is white-spired United Church of Christ, tucked among evergreens, with few changes made since it was built about 1900. The "spire" is charted, but blocked from view until you're almost in the bay.

⚓ **Anchoring** here is pleasant, one of the quietest spots we found. We anchor in about 30 feet and enjoy the peace.

Ⓖ There is protection in here from almost everything, a **charming gunkhole.**

Village of Fox Island is inshore from this cove, with a grocery store, gas station and several other amenities. The beach is private here so no one can go ashore.

⊕ **Public tidelands** of about 1,500 feet wrap around the first point heading east from Tanglewood, barely a nudge and unnamed on the chart.

Ketners Point is the main point on this Fox Island shore, named for an early pioneer.

Public tidelands of less than 1,000 feet are along the eastern shore.

Cable area from Cromwell goes ashore at the point.

Bee Bay, also known as **Baker's Cove**, is the first cove east of Ketners Point.

⚓ **Anchoring** is possible in here in just under two fathoms.

⊕ **Public tidelands** of under 1,000 feet are here.

There are usually several boats permanently moored in the bay. New homes have sprung up along the shoreline, but in 1906 there were only two logging camps on this shore.

Cable area is west of the abandoned, dilapidated ferry dock.

The dock is in sad shape with practically no planking remaining on the deck. It's been closed down for ages and it is fenced off with "no trespassing" signs posted. It is located where charted roads angle west and south at the shoreline.

Public beach access is by way of old concrete stairs east of the old dock.

Public tidelands in four parcels of about 1,000 feet each are along this shore.

Still heading southeast, we reach the nearly obscured entrance to a small, charted cove, about 1.2 miles east of the old ferry landing.

Cedrona Bay, unnamed on the charts, looks formidable on the chart which shows all green, shoal water inside the bay, a big rock at the west side of the entrance and a sandspit at the east side. Who would want to enter such a jumble . . . . . .

Fox Island Yacht Club is in this lovely bay.

Entering Cedrona Bay, Fox Island Yacht club members say not to try and enter unless there is at least a four foot rising tide. Caution is necessary entering the cove without "local knowledge." Deep draft sailboats may want to avoid the shoal bay.

Once inside the bay with green waters reflecting evergreens lining the shores, we can understand why the yacht club chose this spot. Their handsome new building on the west shore of the bay was dedicated in October 1992.

Fox Island Yacht Club has about 150 families for a membership of about 400. They're friendly folks and have reciprocal moorage with other yacht clubs.

Tanglewood Island was first called Tahatowa by the Indians and was used as a burial ground. It was bought in 1897 by a Mr. Hoska, who named it Tanglewood, and planted orchards.

The charted "tower" is at Tanglewood Lodge—which resembles a small lighthouse—on the north end of the island.

In the l940s the island was bought by a Dr. Schultz who built a boys' camp which he ran there for many years. In addition to the lodge there are docks and floats.

The lodge is now a multi-purpose facility used for educational or church retreats, summer youth camps, or by yacht clubs and other organizations. Call Bill Simpson at 360-549-2302.

The club has a good long dock with about four feet of water at the outer end at low tide. There are also about a half-dozen mooring buoys for use by their guests.

The yacht club bought the sandspit at the entrance and about 600 feet of waterfront along the eastern shore in 1995 and intend to leave it just the way it is. The extensive grounds include an outdoor kitchen, a deck and their own launch ramp. The yacht club is renowned for its annual August luau.

⚓ They tell us it's not necessary to be a yacht club member to anchor in Cedrona Bay, but it might be a good idea to discuss it with them. Phone: 360-549-2603

Ⓖ This is a **good gunkhole,** especially at high tide.

Launch ramp on the bay's eastern shore provides public access. It is undeveloped, a small gravel ramp with no facilities.

⚙ **Underway again,** leaving Cedrona and on the "outside" once more, we see lots of erratic rocks, diving birds, comfortable homes, forested bluffs along the shore.

Smuggler's Cove is next, about 600 yards east of Cedrona. The shore along here is called **Hope,** unnamed on charts. The cove is tiny and shoal, and only those who own property in here use it as a moorage. There's scarcely enough room to turn around and it's all private. But it was a place where small, shoal draft rumrunners hid from revenuers during Prohibition.

Public tidelands of about 3,000 feet are along the shoreline east of the cove.

Fox Point is at the northeast tip of the island. We go out around it, and we're back in The Narrows. This is low bank with waterfront homes, and then forested bluffs take over and homes climb the heights.

Toy Point is an unnamed bump along the eastern shore between Fox Point and Gibson Point, formerly marked by the landmark Concrete Dock.

In summer 1995, the state built a public fishing pier at this site.

Public tidelands of about 10,000 feet wrap around Fox Island from Toy Point to Gibson Point and continue along the western shore. This would be a difficult anchorage because of tide rips and steep shores.

Fl R 4s 6M "6" Gibson Point Light 6, flashing red 4 second light on a triangular red dayboard on a dolphin, marks the point and high bluffs at the island's south end. Note the light is visible from 055° to 222°.

Sig Tr No 1 is still charted, but no longer stands. (See page 204)

Tide rips are charted south of Gibson Point. Significant clockwise backeddies form in the Point Fosdick area and south of Fox Island during the flood. Counterclockwise backeddies form just north of Fox Island's east end near Fox Point during the ebb.

Fl (2+1) R 6s Toliva Shoal Lighted Bell Buoy, is flashing red light on a red and green banded buoy about 0.9 mile south of Gibson Point. This well-known buoy is a challenging sailboat race rounding mark, used in the annual Toliva Shoals race from Olympia.

Tide rips are strong near the buoy.

Depths at Toliva Shoal are 1-3/4 fathoms as indicated by the ***Coast Pilot*** and chart 18445. Chart 18448 shows four fathoms over the shoal.

State artificial reef is about 1,300 feet northwest of Toliva. Divers and fishermen alike enjoy the reef, marked by two white and orange buoys, "A" and "B."

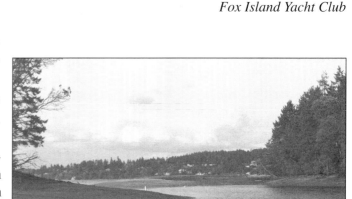

Fox Island Yacht Club

Inside Cedrona Bay,
looking out

There was once a variety of industries on Fox Island—logging and the brick and clay works businesses, which started in 1888. At one time there were five kilns for brickmaking. Additionally, there were vineyards, a huge prune dryer, dogfish processing, bulb and flower farms, plus farming and fishing.

*At the old Brick and Clay Works Company the "Railroad tracks and cars on roadbeds surrounded the sides of the hill (along the western shore). Clay was poured down a big chute. A tall smokestack stood in the center of the grounds and boats landed at a wharf to load the bricks for market. In 1910, the company ceased operation because the clay deposits had been exhausted." (From **Along the Waterfront**)*

Mike Bass, head of a testing program for both the Navy and private firms, said there are no restrictions in the testing area at Fox Island as there are at Bangor on Hood Canal.

"If we're testing, we're interested in the safety of boaters and we'll personally go out and advise them"

He said the testing does not include torpedoes or explosive devices. He does ask that mariners keep clear of the charted test area.

Bass said there will be revisions in the 1997 edition of the Coast Pilot noting changes.

Fox Island was originally called Batil Merman by the Indians. Early British explorers called the island Rosario.

It was named Fox not for the little four-legged critters, but for J.L. Fox, an assistant surgeon in the Wilkes expedition.

Washington pioneer Ezra Meeker and brother Oliver paddled north in The Narrows in 1853. Ezra wrote:

"As the sun shone nice and warm and the tide was taking us rapidly in the direction we wanted to go, why not ... ?

"We had by this time drifted into the tide rips in the Narrows, pulled for dear life for the shore, and found shelter in an eddy. A ... bluff rose from the high water mark, leaving no place for a camp fire or bed. The tide seemed to roll in waves, with contending forces of currents and counter currents, yet all moving in a general direction.

(continued in sidebar, p. 205)

Heading northwest into Carr Inlet around Fox Island where several erratic rocks are charted around Gibson Point and along the shore.

"C1" mooring buoy, charted about 0.65 mile from Gibson Point, has been removed according to the Coast Guard. We slide along below steep bluffs, some nearly 200 feet high, for about 2.5 miles to the buoy testing area. We didn't see the charted wreck shown at about 1.5 miles along the shore.

The south shores of island bluffs are primarily clay, which is important to island history, and not just because of brickmaking.

Public tidelands in two parcels are along this shore, both about 2,000 feet.

The legend of Batil Merman happened along these southern bluffs.

The Legend of Batil Merman or The Legend of the Mud Babies

A young Indian maiden on Fox Island, daughter of Batil, used to play in the sand many, many years ago. She shaped the mud into various forms, such as birds, fishes or animals. After she tired of her play she would wash her hands in the creek, making the water muddy. The place came to be known by the name Tcekwila'go, or Muddy Water.

As she grew to womanhood she rejected many young suitors who courted her from near and far. Then one evening while walking along the beach to her usual playground, an unusual young brave suddenly appeared. For four nights he visited her and departed mysteriously the following mornings. The maiden decided to follow him home the fourth morning. She saw him reach shore, walk into the water and disappear.

She told her parents of her suitor. They feared he might be the son of the "Old Man of the Sea," who had power to dry up the island's springs if their daughter did not marry his son.

Sure enough, water in the springs disappeared as if by magic, grass became brown and crops died. When that happened, they agreed to let their daughter go to her lover.

The springs once again gave forth their normal amount of water.

When the brave came and claimed his wife, they held hands and stepped into the water, disappearing beneath the surface. Three times she returned to visit her parents. On the fourth visit, there was kelp growing on her face and she was becoming a sea creature. Her parents told her it was better if she didn't return. She then stayed with her husband under the water.

Now, when the princess becomes lonesome she goes to her old beach playground on Fox Island and makes pebbles shaped like birds, fish or animals.

But she always returns to her "Son of the Old Man of the Sea," and their underwater home, now marked by the Toliva Shoal buoy, a spot midway between Fox Island and Steilacoom. (Legend courtesy of *On the Waterfront*)

Signal Towers

Six "signal towers" are charted on Fox Island, Green Point, Penrose Point and McNeil Island. For years their lights were activated when the Navy was buoy testing off the southwest shore of Fox Island as charted.

The towers have been removed, except at Green Point, although they are still shown on 1995 charts, and discussed in the *Coast Pilot*. There seems to be discrepancies between information on charts, in the *Coast Pilot,* and with what we see and have been told by test site personnel.

Information that we have obtained indicates vessels are advised to stay south and west of the middle of Carr Inlet to avoid obstructions that may be in the "buoy testing area." If the Navy plans to test, mariners are notified in advance through the weekly *Notice to Mariners* publication.

Vessels are advised to stay in the middle of Carr Inlet to avoid obstructions that may be in the buoy testing area.

Monitor VHF Channels 14 and 16 for information, or phone: 360-549-2301.

Navy "buoy testing range" as charted is about two miles from Point Gibson along the southwestern shore. It extends about one mile offshore and is 0.6 mile long, marked by buoys. The *Coast Pilot* advises that, "No vessel shall, at any time, anchor or tow a drag of any kind within 1,000 yards of the buoy testing area." The rest of the area is open to navigation at all times except when the range is in use or when hydrophones are being calibrated.

Northwest of the range is the area of the long defunct Brick and Clay Works Company, close to the sandspit near the north end of the island.

Public tidelands of about 3,000 feet are on the northwestern side of the island.

Nearns Point, at the northwest end of Fox Island, the last point and the end of our circumnavigation of Fox Island, is named on chart 18448, but not on chart 18445.

Fox Island History—Indian Wars

After the 1854 **Medicine Creek Treaty** was signed, the Indians realized they had actually signed over their lands to the white men—forever.

They then engaged in several uprisings. Chief Leschi and his half brother Quiemuth of the Nisquallys protested the takeover of their lands. Leschi debunked the treaty and the proposed reservation land as totally unsatisfactory, saying the land was both too small an amount and too poor for farming. Some Indians were ordered to go to a temporary reservation on Fox Island or be treated as "hostiles."

In the fall of 1855, the Indian War began. By 1856, the Indian Wars in the west were essentially over and Chief Leschi was charged with murdering Volunteer Colonel A. Benton Moses during the war.

Leschi was betrayed to the authorities by a nephew, Sluggia, who was later murdered by another Indian, Yelm Jim. Leschi was tried as a civilian, not as a soldier, in a civil court. Army officers who had fought against him in the Indian Wars protested the procedure.

Leschi was found guilty of murder and hanged from a tree near the land of his youth. Charles Grainger, his executioner, said, "I felt I was hanging an innocent man." (For a detailed account of the Indian Wars in the area and much more, see Murray Morgan's fine book, *Puget's Sound*.)

In August 1856, the first Territorial Governor, Isaac Ingalls Stevens, met on Fox Island with the peaceful Nisquallys and Puyallups. He agreed to grant much larger reservations on both the Puyallup and Nisqually Rivers, a result of efforts by Chief Leschi for a more favorable treaty. Some Fox Island roads are named for Leschi.

In Chapter 14 we'll investigate some most unusual places in Carr Inlet.

(continued from p. 204)

"It was our first introduction to a real genuine, live tide rip, that seemd to harry the waters as if boiling in a veritable caldron, swelling up here and there into a foam, and, where light breeze prevailed, into spray.

"Then it would seem waters in solid volume would leap up in conical, or pointed small waves broken into short sections that would make it difficult for a flat bottom boat like ours to float very long.

"We congratulated ourselves upon escape, while belittling our careless imitation of the natives.

"Just then some Indian canoes passed along moving with the tide. We expected to see them swamped as they encountered the troubled waters, but to our astonishment they passed right through without taking a drop of water. Here came two well-manned canoes creeping along shore, against the tide. I have said well-manned, but, in fact, half the paddles were wielded by women, and the post of honor, or that where most dexterity was required, was occupied by a woman. In shore, short eddies would favor the party, to be ended by a severe tug against the stiff current.

"'Mi-si-ka-kwass kopa s'kookum chuck,' said the maiden in the bow of the first canoe, as it drew alongside our boat ... we understood her to ask if we were afraid of the waters.

"We replied, part in English and part in Chinook, that we were, and it was impossible for us to proceed against the strong current.

"'Ne-si-ka mit-lite,' that is to say ... they were going to camp with us and wait for the turn of the tide, and accordingly landed nearby."

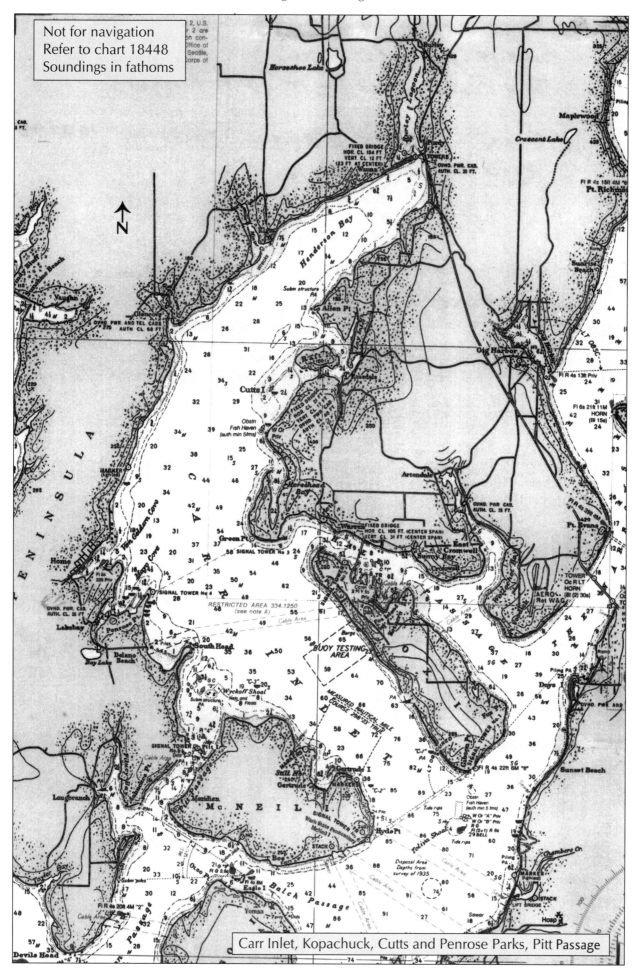

Not for navigation
Refer to chart 18448
Soundings in fathoms

Carr Inlet, Kopachuck, Cutts and Penrose Parks, Pitt Passage

CHAPTER 14
Carr Inlet, including Kopachuck, Cutts and Penrose Parks, Pitt Passage

Charts and publications for this chapter

Chart	Date	Title	Scale	Soundings
** 18445	06/03/95	Puget Sound, Possession Sound to Olympia, page C, page D, inset 8	1:80,000 .... 1:20,000	Fathoms Fathoms
* 18448	10/30/93	Puget Sound, Southern Part	1:80,000	Fathoms
18440	08/05/95	Puget Sound	1:150,000	Fathoms
		Tidal Current Charts, Puget Sound, Southern Part		
		Booklet: Puget Sound Shellfish Sites		
		Washington State Public Lands Quad Map—Tacoma	1:100,000	

➥ *When using charts, compare your chart dates with ones referred to above. There may be discrepancies between different charts and different chart editions.*

Carr Inlet Overview

Carr Inlet runs northwest between Fox and McNeil Islands for about six miles to Green Point. From there it trends north and then northeasterly for about seven miles, terminating in the mud flats of Henderson Bay at Purdy and Burley Lagoon.

Three state marine parks, one Department of Natural Resources Park, public tidelands, a fish hatchery, an historic hotel and several communities are on Carr Inlet shores.

The eastern shore of Carr Inlet is **Gig Harbor Peninsula,** unnamed on charts, and the western shore is **Key Peninsula**.

This is a beautiful cruising area, and when the wind pipes up there can be great sailing and windsurfing.

Widths in the inlet vary from less than 1.5 miles wide at the southeast entrance between Fox and McNeil, to about 2.5 miles wide in several places.

Depths in Carr Inlet are over 50 fathoms in some places, with no charted hazards except as shown near the shores.

Our cruise in the inlet takes us north to Green Point and along the entire eastern shore into Henderson Bay, then down the western shore, passing Wyckoff Shoal and south through Pitt Passage, roughly following in Puget's wake.

McNeil Island is state prison property and mariners must keep 100 yards offshore at all times. Although it's off limits to people, the island is a state Fish and Wildlife Preserve and seals, seabirds, deer and other animals abound on and around the island.

For mariners in a jam, with the boat dead in the water and drifting toward McNeil, we suggest calling "McNeil Island" on VHF Channel 16 and tell prison officials of the predicament. If it's after hours, call "McNeil Island tugboat" or "McNeil Island passenger boat." After all this, if grounded on the island, we understand the procedure is to wait there with your boat until found by the prison staff.

Underway in Carr Inlet

⊕ We skirt 100 yards off McNeil Island's northern shore as required and posted by the state Department of Corrections. The state prison is on the south shore.

➥ **Note: Marine gas** is available only at **Lakebay Marina** in Mayo Cove, although hand-carry gas cans can be filled at **Island View Market** in Rosedale.

About 14 miles of public tidelands are in this chapter.

Public tidelands unless otherwise noted are state owned; some may be leased for private use. We take the Washington State Public Lands Quadrangle Map, when going ashore at these locations to avoid trespassing on adjacent private property.

Chart 18445 has more names of small coves than 18448.

Both charts have scales of 1:80,000; 18445 has a Pitt Pass inset on page D, scale 1:20,000.

Chart 18448 shows topographic contours better than 18445.

We note charted discrepancies in Pitt Pass which we discuss fully on pages 218-219.

Still Harbor

A measured nautical mile is about one mile northwest of **Hyde Point** on the north shore of McNeil Island, course 298°23' true. Two diamond-shaped, red and white markers are amidst trees at the shoreline east of Still Harbor, the southeast marks. The second markers are one mile northwest on the west side of Still Harbor. May as well check out the knotmeter since we can't go into, anchor or go ashore in this beautiful harbor. (Well, we did the mile today in a little over 11.005421 minutes. We're still trying to figure out how fast we were going.)

Still Harbor with lovely wooded shores was once home to many early McNeil Island settlers. Now it is seldom visited, because it is environmentally sensitive—and off limits. On the harbor's south shore is a large dock, sometimes with moored vessels belonging to the Department of Corrections or Department of Fisheries.

Gertrude Island in the east half of the cove is one of the few harbor seal rookeries left in Puget Sound. There are about 500 seals who are protected and feel free to breed, bask in sunny weather and play whenever they want to, without worrying about any humans bothering them—a true wildlife sanctuary.

Two large mooring buoys are charted at the east and west ends of McNeil Island, "C2" and "C3" although we didn't see numbers on them. Buoy C2 at the east end is often used by commercial vessels, such as tugs with log booms, that need to wait for favorable currents at The Narrows. Buoy C3 is frequently used by the Navy while doing underwater research and development tests, often for acoustical data as explained in Chapter 13.

It's just a little over 1.5 miles from Still Harbor to sandy shoals off McNeil's northwest tip. These shallows extend to **Wyckoff Shoal,** just north of Pitt Passage, which we visit at the end of this chapter.

Now, north toward **Green Point,** a nub about three miles north of the west end of McNeil Island on Gig Harbor Peninsula. Green Point signal tower "No. 3" is the only tower still working. (See Chapter 13)

Public tidelands of about 6,000 feet in several parcels are along the shore north of Green Point, extending around the point at Horsehead Bay, and for about 3,000 feet more into the bay.

Ⓖ **Horsehead Bay** entrance is about one mile north of Green Point. The one mile long bay is an excellent shelter in most weather, a jewel of protected water circled by private homes, **another gunkhole.**

Widths in Horsehead go from 0.3 mile in the north end, tapering to about 0.1 mile wide in the south.

Depths range from about eight fathoms in the north to two fathoms in the south before becoming tide flats which extend about 0.1 mile from the head of the bay.

The protected waters might be a place to practice dinghy sailing, kayak paddling, or perhaps meet friends at the launch ramp.

Launch ramp in the southeast portion is less than 0.5 mile from the head of Horsehead Bay, a single lane ramp with little nearby parking. It's less than a mile to the grocery store at Arletta, if you decide you need a walk, or forgot to buy milk or marshmallows.

Public tidelands of about 2,000 feet are on the southeast shore.

⚓ **Anchoring** is possible in two fathoms, mud bottom, in the south end of the bay.

Not for navigation
Refer to chart 18445
Soundings in fathoms

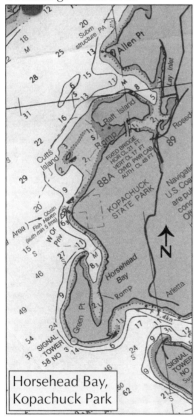

Horsehead Bay,
Kopachuck Park

The land at Horsehead *received its name originally because of its shape, and the cove was called the "little bay back of horsehead." Eventually the bay took on the name.*

Entering Horsehead Bay, we give the spit off the northern entrance plenty of room and go down the middle of the bay.

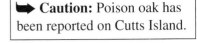

Caution: Poison oak has been reported on Cutts Island.

Kopachuck State Park is on the north side of the point less than 0.5 mile north of Horsehead Bay. It's charted as 88A on 18445, with more facilities than listed.

Two state park mooring buoys and a bulk-head shoreline with stairways to the beach make it easy to recognize this prime, unspoiled waterfront.

Kopachuck State Park beach

White and orange buoys mark a charted five fathom fish haven offshore at the point. Scuba divers find an opportunity here for underwater photos, spear fishing, observation of marine wildlife and shellfish collecting.

Exploring Kopachuck uplands on well maintained, sometimes hilly, hiking trails which take you through towering second-growth stands of Douglas fir and often dense undergrowth. Deer, bears, foxes, raccoons, squirrels, many varieties of birds and harbor seals are at home in Kopachuck. The park is a favorite destination for youngsters on school field trips, so watch for excited kids traipsing in the woods.

To the west, Carr Inlet and the Olympics beyond are spectacular, especially at sunset when varied hues outline jagged mountain peaks.

Anchoring is possible north of the mooring buoys in two to nine fathoms.

Kopachuck State Park Facilities
- ➤ Two mooring buoys by our count—three according to the state
- ➤ 109 acres of uplands
- ➤ 5,600 feet of delightful shoreline to explore
- ➤ Beachcombing, clamming, wading, swimming on a sandy beach
- ➤ State underwater park for scuba divers with sunken artificial reef
- ➤ Campsites, picnic sites, kitchen shelters, telephones
- ➤ Restrooms with hot showers
- ➤ Outdoor showers for scuba divers and swimmers
- ➤ Cascadia Water Trail campsite planned
- ➤ Phone: 206-265-3606

Kopachuck Park's musical name originated from Chinook jargon, which was the trade language of the Pacific Coastal Indians. Kopachuck is two words: "kopa" means "with" or "by," and "chuck" means "water," according to Theodore Winthrop, the adventurer who spent three months in the area in 1853. In a remarkably short time he mastered the vocabulary of the Chinook jargon.

Cutts Island Marine State Park is 0.5 mile offshore, north of Kopachuck and about 0.5 mile southwest of **Raft Island**.

Cutts is a 5-1/2 acre island with 2,100 feet of shoreline, a veritable treasure, a satellite of the mainland park. This is the kind of place we love: a tiny island, easily accessible by small boats, yet isolated from the world. A peaceful place.

Seven mooring buoys are off the east shore of Cutts facing Kopachuck. Hard to imagine, but even in the middle of summer they are often empty.

Some boats pass between Cutts and shoals off Raft Island, staying close to Raft to clear the sandspit projecting from Cutts' north end. It's charted one fathom, one foot at MLLW between the islands. We went through the pass ourselves—in a kayak.

At the southern end of Cutts, a 50 to 60 foot high barren bluff rises up to fir trees on top; large erratic boulders are scattered on the beach below.

Cutts Island was also known as Deadman's Island as it had been an Indian burial ground. The dead were placed in canoes in the forks of trees.

Cutts Island Marine Park, looking west

Cutts' Cave

Cutts Island Park attractions, include seven buoys by our count, although State Parks claims 10 buoys. The island is pristine and undeveloped, a pit toilet its only sign of "civilization." No overnight camping allowed, no fires. Minimal trails cross the forested island. It's wonderful.

A shallow cave on the west side of the island makes for wonderfully imaginative exploring by youngsters—pirates, hidden treasures and all.

The whole island can be walked around in a short time. It's a good beachcombing, picnicking, relaxing kind of place. Sunrises can be dramatic from a buoy at Cutts.

⚓ **Raft Island,** all private, is immediately northeast of Cutts. The island is about 0.7 mile east to west and 0.4 miles north to south.

Depths along the south shore of the island are charted at less than one fathom, with several charted rocks.

Raft Island is joined to the mainland of Gig Harbor Peninsula by a fixed span bridge from its south shore which has a 17 foot vertical clearance at MHW, and 21 foot horizontal clearance. The bridge and shallows may prohibit many boats from going all the way around the island but small boats slide under easily. At lower tides there would, of course, be more vertical clearance, but the water would be shallower.

Lay Inlet, between Raft Island and Gig Harbor Peninsula, is about 0.7 mile long and about 0.3 mile wide at best. A shoal cove less than 100 yards wide trends north at the eastern end. The inlet tucks southeast towards the community of Rosedale, where there are two small drying bays, and then heads south around Raft Island.

Depths in the inlet range from about 11 fathoms in the west portion to one fathom one foot in the southeast portion.

Public tidelands are on either side of Raft Island bridge on the mainland shores. The parcel west of the bridge is about 1,000 feet and the parcel east of the bridge is about 750 feet. Four small parcels of public tidelands totaling about 1,800 feet are along east shores of Lay Inlet.

Ⓖ Docks and permanently moored boats are fairly thick in the inlet. We would call this an okay anchorage, if there's room to drop the hook—a **gunkhole** in a developed area. Trees and homes are clustered around the bay; some on bluffs with stairways down to bulkheaded beaches, others on low bank.

⚓ **Anchoring** in Lay Inlet is possible in most weather in about two fathoms, mud bottom. We were here one time during a heavy southerly blow and it was so protected, there were scarcely any ripples on the water's surface.

Island View Market at Rosedale, charted as #89 on 18445, is accessible by shore boat, which can tie to a float below the store. The market is in a tan building on a bank on the southeast shore next to a small bridge over a stream, not the Raft Island Bridge. All kinds of items are in this store, with especially friendly service. They carry basic groceries, beer, snacks, canned food, as listed on chart 18445, and have a pay telephone. The owners have been here over a quarter-century and know just about everybody in Rosedale and environs.

Peter Puget was the first recorded non-Native to visit Cutts Island. He and his men breakfasted their second morning on the island. Puget named it Crow Island, after the cook made crow stew.

"The tide prevented our making any considerable Progress before Breakfast to which we Stopped on a Small Island about six Miles from Last Nights Sleeping Place (which was Shaw's Cove at the western end of Hale Passage). This Island was named after its only Inhabitants, an astonishing Quantity of Crows between it & and the Mainland (at the north end), it was almost too Shoal for the Boats."

Raft Island bridge

Gas pumps are on shore in front of the store, not on the float, and gas is available to those who carry their gas cans up stairs to pumps for fill-ups.

Allen Point is on the mainland at the north entrance to Lay Inlet, about 0.7 mile north of Raft Island. The point is a bump of vegetation on the end of a spit.

Early Rosedale

Early settlers in Rosedale depended on rowboats for their principal means of transportation before there were roads. Whether they were selling or trading goods, or sending youngsters to school—rowboats were the way to go. Some early homesteaders lived in small log cabins built by the Hudson's Bay Company in the mid-1800s.

By 1883, there was a post office in Rosedale village and a school was planned. Victor Tomlinson and another boy were to transport a load of bricks for the school chimney from Arletta to Rosedale in their rowboat. They loaded the bricks and began the trip. All went well until about halfway along when the load shifted—boys and bricks were dumped overboard.

A second load was ordered, transported safely, and the schoolhouse was finished in 1884. The boys survived both the trip and the school.

That was the same year steamer service took goods and mail to Rosedale on the *Sophia*. Later the sternwheeler *Tyconda* was on the run, and the trip from Tacoma to Rosedale included stops at Cromwell, Sylvan, Warren, Arletta, Home, Lakebay, Glen Cove, Minter and Vaughn. (From *Along the Waterfront*)

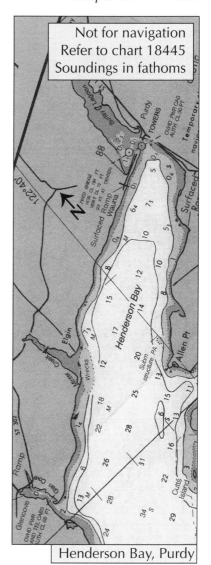

Henderson Bay, Purdy

Leaving Lay Inlet we pass charted rocks at Allen Point and head northeast for about three miles into Henderson Bay and the town of Purdy.

Public tidelands of about 5,000 feet in three parcels are on the east shore north of Allen Point, including a shallow bight about 0.8 mile northeast of the point.

Henderson Bay maintains a depth of five to 10 fathoms until about 200 to 300 yards from shore.

Launch ramp (charted on 18445) on the east shore a little over one mile southwest of Purdy eluded us.

Purdy is at the east end of a 3,500 foot sandspit and bridge at the northeast corner of Henderson Bay. There are a number of services including a shopping center with a market, bank, barbershop, pub and grill, and motel, but no public dock or float. A women's state correctional institution is in the Purdy area.

Purdy fixed span bridge has a charted center vertical clearance of 23 feet at MHW declining to 12 feet at either end, with horizontal clearance of 184 feet. State Highway 302 crosses this bridge.

Burley Lagoon north of the bridge has drying mudflats and private oyster beds. The lagoon is about 0.4 mile wide, ending at Burley community about 1.7 miles north. There are several scattered areas in the southern portion of the lagoon where depths may reach 13 feet.

Burley lagoon tidelands are private commercial oyster beds and should be respected as such. Not recommended as a gunkhole.

Overhead power cables cross near the bridge, charted clearance at 30 feet.

Charted on 18445 in the southwest corner of Burley Lagoon near Wauna is a #88. However, #88 is missing from tabulations on the strip chart and we're not sure what it's supposed to be.

Wauna, a small community, is at the west end of the two-lane Purdy Bridge.

Launch ramp, single lane, is at the west end of the spit. Parking space and sani-can are on the south side of the shoulder along the highway east of the ramp.

The ramp is alongside a vacant, gray building, once **the store** in Wauna.

The south shore of the sandspit is public and in summer is heavily used by clam diggers, swimmers and most especially sailboarders. This is a favorite spot with sailboarders, who thrive on sailing at high speeds on relatively calm, reasonably warm water.

Anchoring is possible in five to 10 fathoms at the head of Henderson Bay.

In 1898, Burley was home to 16 people who wanted to "secure control of the politics and start the cooperative commonwealth."

Socialists were encouraged to move to Washington after a large Populist vote in the state in the 1896 election. The colonists built a schoolhouse which they rented out to the local school district, and the income helped pay the teacher. They also used the building for cooperative meetings and hoped they could make "Burley the social and intellectual center of a considerable district."

It worked for a while, but the movement died out in 1924.

Old store at Wauna

This wooden building, once the home of the historic W.E. White Flour, Feed & Grocery Store, was built in 1906, the year Wauna was named.

Originally platted in 1889 as Springfield, the area of Wauna was asked by the government to change its name because there were so many Springfields in the country, including at least 14 in Washington state.

Postmaster Mary Frances White chose the Native American name "Wauna," which means "mighty waters."

Wauna was a hub for nearby communities for years, with a hotel and a long wharf with deep water moorage, which are no longer there.

In April 1995 a 35 foot juvenile gray whale swam into Henderson Bay. Marine researchers said the youngster may have been with a group going from Mexico's Baja Coast to breeding grounds in the Bering Sea. They feared the whale was desperately searching for food and might die as do one out of three grays after they enter South Puget Sound. The teen-aged mammal was in the area several weeks before making its way back out to the Pacific.

Purdy: Legend & Lore

Purdy was named for Joseph Purdy, a Tacoma grocer, who donated lumber to build the first school—with the proviso that the area be named for him.

Previous to that was an Indian legend:

"The area was a beautiful green Eden lying beside a quiet bay. The envious eyes of the animal world on the shore led to a gathering of all the beasts of the forest. An appeal was made to a great builder, the beaver, and a dam was constructed. The dam began at Wauna and ended at Purdy where the present bridge joins the shore.

*"For many moons it was the cross trails of Peninsula territory. The salmon and all the fishes of the outside bay were very angry so they appealed to the sea lions to dig a channel through the inner waters. This led to a savage war between the seals and beavers which threatened to exterminate all concerned. A great storm came up during the height of the conflict and when it subsided, the huge dam was broken at the Purdy end." (From **Along the Waterfront**)*

Puget at Henderson Bay

When Peter Puget first sighted the tideflats at the head of Henderson Bay with his "glass" he realized he had come to another dead end inlet. He saw a small Indian village among the trees along the western shore. He called the inhabitants "surly Gentlemen."

Shortly before noon on May 21, 1792, as Puget and his men were exploring the head of Carr Inlet, a canoe approached them. Puget wrote, "They lay about Twenty Yards from us & kept continually pointing to the Eastward, expressive of a wish that our Departure would be more agreeable than our Visit."

To show they were friendly, the British made some gift offerings: "Some Copper Medals, Looking Glasses & other Articles were tied on a Piece of Wood & left floating on the water, then pulling away to a Small Distance (we saw) the Indians immediately Picked them up."

Puget and his men then headed south along the west shore of Carr Inlet to Von Geldern Cove. Several Indian canoes, led by "One-Eye," followed the two boats.

⚓ **Underway again**, we cruise south and west from Henderson Bay, now following along the shoreline of Key Peninsula.

Public tidelands of two 2,500 foot parcels, two 1,000 foot parcels and one smaller parcel—places to dig clams or beachcomb—are between Wauna and Minter Creek, a distance of about 2.5 miles.

Elgin is the community at Minter Creek. The creek flows down from surrounding hills into drying mudflats and then it's shoal for 0.25 mile offshore. We never found the charted wrecks along the outside shores of the sandspit. But we did learn how they got there. (See page 214)

Minter Creek, formerly a favorite Indian fishing ground, is the home of a large salmon hatchery where about 10 million Coho are raised each year. About 1.5 million of the tiny fish are released into Carr Inlet. The rest are released from other areas. Chinook, chum and pink fingerlings are also raised. The hatchery is open to the public.

⚓ **Anchoring** is possible outside Minter Creek cove in two to four fathoms on a calm day; dinghy in for a hatchery visit. Pretty interesting, for kids of all ages.

⚓ **Glen Cove** is about two miles southwest of Elgin. The bank is relatively high along here, covered with trees and homes, of course.

The winding channel into the cove is charted, but we chickened out taking *Zade* in. Jo had seen the cove at low tide from the shore. She saw low, muddy lumps with practically no water in between them. If you go in, tell us how it works out. Someday maybe we'll go back and give it a try ourselves—at high tide.

Launch ramp charted on 18445 at the head of the bay is no longer operational. The other charted ramp is private, part of YMCA Camp Seymour.

Glen Cove is used by canoeists and kayakers, many of them boys and girls from the camp on the east shore of the cove.

Overhead power cables with a clearance of 68 feet are charted near the entrance to Glen Cove.

Thompson Spit, unnamed on charts, is off the southwest entrance to Glen Cove.

Two parcels of public tidelands totaling over 3,000 feet are south of the spit.

Lighted marker on pilings is charted about 2.3 miles south of Glen Cove on the beach below forested bluffs.

Public tidelands of about 1,500 feet are about 2,000 feet north of Maple Hollow.

Maple Hollow Picnic Area, a DNR park, unnamed on charts, can be identified by the lighted marker offshore which is just about at the park's center. A mooring symbol is also charted. It's a good stopping off place and there is one mooring buoy.

Maple Hollow Picnic Area Facilities

➤ 1,420 feet of saltwater shoreline
➤ One mooring buoy
➤ Littleneck clams, horse clams, mussels and sand dollars
➤ Includes 20 acres of hilly forested upland with hiking trails
➤ Picnic tables tucked away in little glens, interpretive signs
➤ Water
➤ Pit toilets
➤ Hike, beachcomb, dig clams, swim

⚓ **Anchoring** is possible along the park in two to eight fathoms, sand bottom.

⚓ **Cruising south** along the shore, we approach **Von Geldern Cove** and the charming community of Home. Shoals and erratic rocks extend about 0.3 mile offshore, off the cove's north entrance.

Von Geldern is about 0.8 mile long; the southwest half terminates in **Joe's Bay,** unnamed on charts. Pilings of the long steamer dock remain in the inner bay that served Home area residents in the days before roads were built.

Depths in a dog-leg channel shoal from five fathoms at the entrance to the cove to three feet and less in Joe's Bay.

Fl 8s 22 ft Von Geldern Cove Light, a flashing yellow light on a steel pile, privately maintained, is on the south point approaching Joe's Bay and across from the ramp.

Launch ramp, single lane with some parking (charted on 18445), is on the west shore. It's possible to dinghy ashore at the ramp and walk along the shoreside road to the head of the bay near the newly rebuilt bridge.

On a high tide, the old steamers used to go into the dock near the entrance to Glen Cove. Later a store, post office and barbershop were built at the same location.

There was a marina at the head of the bay until it burned down in 1976.

Glen Cove looking southeast

Glen Cove Hotel is the gem in Glen Cove. It's a wonderful handsome historic and restored hotel, built in 1897 by Nick Petersen. He and his family originally lived in a floathouse on the bay and sometimes provided lodging and meals for loggers.

Ship Wrecks in Carr Inlet

A junk dealer bought some surplused World War I wooden transport ships for scrap and took them into Lake Washington. Later the ships were taken to Minter sandspit where they were burned for scrap iron.

Heavy cables secured to the hulks eventually rusted away. Some of the remains broke loose while some stayed on the spit, only to be buried in sand.

One of the loose wrecks was seen drifting past Green Point in the 1920s. A resident hailed a passing tug and requested they beach the hulk on the sandspit east of the point to help prevent the tides from eroding the spit any further. That hulk is now nearly gone, too, almost 70 years after it was beached.

Puget & "Alarm Cove"

Peter Puget named Von Geldern "Alarm Cove," because it was the only place in his South Sound explorations where there was a confrontation with hostile Indians. All other meetings with them were generally friendly.

Puget's two boats with 16 men stopped on the eastern shore near the streams at the head of Von Geldern Cove for lunch. The weather was hot and sultry and the men were tired and hungry.

Very shortly they found themselves confronted by about 24 Indians warriors led by One-Eye, who had silently and swiftly arrived in the bay by canoe. Rather than attack, one of Puget's men shot a crow flying in the air, and then fired another volley of shot which impressed the Indians.

The natives then turned to trading with the British and the confrontation turned into a friendly barter session.

The community of Home has a store, service station, fire station, laundromat, Lakebay Post Office and Homeport Restaurant and Lounge at the head of Von Geldern Cove. An old barn on pilings inshore of the highway bridge is a popular subject of artists and photographers.

Residences along the waterfront and those along the hillside above the cove seem comfortable and less ostentatious than in some other communities. Folks who live in Home say they really are "at Home."

Public tidelands in Von Geldern Cove include one parcel of about 1,000 feet near the launch ramp, and two parcels totaling about 2,000 feet on the south shore. ⚓ **Anchoring** is possible in about one fathoms four feet, but check the weather first. The bay is exposed to the north.

Home History

Home was founded when Joe Faulkner claimed land in the 1870s. Joe's Bay was a secluded area with only a few residents.

In 1897, three men arrived at the bay, disenchanted with an experimental socialist colony near Tacoma. They wanted a rural community where the only requirement was that men respect the rights of others to do and think as they pleased.

They organized the Compact of the Mutual Home Association and divided their 26 acres into equal lots of two acres per person. The "rule of tolerance" was their guideline. Their lifestyle included a newspaper, **Discontent—Mother of Progress**, which gave **"yes"** answers to, "Is sin forgivable?" and "Do women have the same rights as men in sexual relations?" They found a fairly widespread audience and more colonists arrived. By 1900, there were about 75 residents. A county dock was built.

Home was a haven for free thinkers, most noted for its attitudes on free love and nude bathing. Anarchist Jay Fox wrote in an early Home newspaper: "Home is a community of free spirits, who came out in the woods to escape the polluted atmosphere of a priest-ridden society. One of the liberties enjoyed by Homeites was the privilege to bathe in evening dress or with merely the clothes nature gave them, just as they chose. No one went rubbernecking to see which suit a person wore who sought the purifying waters of the bay. Surely it was nobody's business. All were sufficiently pure-minded to see no vulgarity, no suggestion of anything vile or indecent in the thought of nature's masterpiece uncovered."

However, the intellectual Fox was convicted of criminal libel for advocating that residents shun their neighbors who complained about nude bathing. He was eventually granted full pardon. Later reports say that only the children swam nude; most men and women wore something because to expose very much of the body was shocking at that time.

Home lost its post office in 1902 because of supposed anarchy, and residents had to go to Lakebay for their mail. A post office was finally reinstated at Home in the 1950s, but even today it is still called the Lakebay Post Office.

Home filled with enterprising persons who established businesses and orchards, farms and fishing in a cooperative effort, which still exists today. And few pay attention to what people wear—or don't wear—while swimming.

⚙ **Underway again** from Von Geldern, after telling you more than you may ever want to know about Home, we head south and round the bluffy bump of land separating Von Geldern and Mayo coves. We keep about 400 yards offshore and stay in about three fathoms. In a matter of minutes we are at the north side of Mayo Cove. The cove is exposed to the north and northeast.

Signal tower "No. 4," charted and once located at Penrose Point, has been removed. (See "Signal Towers" Chap. 13, page 204)

Mayo Cove is about one mile long and roughly 0.4 mile wide at the mouth, and is exposed to the north and northeast.

The cove is the site of Penrose Point State Park, Lakebay Community and Lakebay Marina.

Depths in this area are interesting and entering here requires prudent judgment and attention to tides as well. Depths of six fathoms are found about halfway into the cove, and charted depths of two fathoms are near the head of the cove. When approaching Mayo Cove, depths near Penrose Point are deceptive. Check the charts.

Entering Mayo Cove, preferably on a low and rising tide, we follow the charted dogleg. The channel goes towards the south, then trends west to avoid charted shoals off both the north and south shores, then again goes southwest into the tiny inner harbor at the west head of Mayo Cove.

Penrose Point State Park covers the southeast shoreline of Mayo Cove into the inner harbor where a park float is in the southeast corner behind a sandspit. Park shoreline then wraps around Penrose Point, which has an extensive erratic rock garden, and continues along the shores on the south side of the point into Delano Bay.

Lakebay Marina is on the west shore in the inner harbor of Mayo Cove, across from the small park float. This small inner harbor offers some protection from northerlies in about two fathoms.

When approaching Mayo Cove, depths near Penrose Point are deceptive. A close look at the chart reveals a sandspit that dries at low tide paralleling the whole east shore of the cove. It is defined more clearly on chart 18448 than on 18445. Three state park mooring buoys are as charted off the west shore of this sandspit.

We look first at Lakebay Marina and then explore Penrose Park.

Lakebay Marina, is charted as #90 on 18445. Facilities are as listed on 18445, except no lodging or camping were available in 1996. Tabulations show an approach depth of six feet and the alongside depth of 12 feet.

Fishpens are off Lakebay Marina's north end float.

Mayo Cove, Home
& Penrose Park

Lakebay Marina Facilities
➤ Guest moorage for 6-10 boats at end of dock
➤ Fees approximately 30 cents per foot per night
➤ 15 amp shore power included, water
➤ Restrooms
➤ Fuel dock: gas only
➤ Boat launch ramp
➤ Store on dock has limited groceries, ice, fishing bait and tackle
➤ Phone: 206-884-3350

Mayo Cove looking north-northeast at the channel (arrow) into Lakebay at low tide

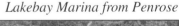
Lakebay Marina from Penrose

Marina owner Dewey Hostetler was remodeling the store in 1995. He has photos of a 25 foot long shark caught in Carr Inlet and beached in Mayo Cove in 1991. That's larger than some cruising boats.

A planked dock leads from the marina to the beach where there are a number of small cabins from a former resort in various stages of disuse.

Launch ramp inshore of the marina is usable, but may be covered with sand. Fees are $5 for a round-trip launch, $3 for a cartop launch.

Lakebay was settled in 1871 with William and Sarah Creviston as the first permanent residents. Their son Bill was the first white child born on the Key Peninsula. His mother was the first schoolteacher on the Peninsula.

Penrose Park sandspit

Carl Lorenz started one of the first businesses at Lakebay— a sawmill. There was also a brickyard. Then came steamer service, when a long dock was built into the bay. This was followed by a hotel, store, barber shop, pool hall, roller skating rink, and a community hall. A woman and her date were asked way-back-then to leave the hall because they were smoking, as few people smoked in the hall in those days.

A petroglyph—Indian rock carving—has been reported somewhere on Sandy Beach at Penrose. Jo spent some time hunting for it, but it's covered by sand and she couldn't find it. If you find it let us know. The ranger assures us it's there— somewhere.

Public tidelands of a little over 1,000 feet in two parcels are along the northwest shore of the cove.

Ⓖ **Penrose Point State Park,** a well loved and much used marine park, has over 150 acres of wooded uplands and about two miles of saltwater shoreline to beachcomb, dig clams, swim or whatever. The park covers the whole southeast shore of Mayo Cove and wraps around Penrose Point, and we're willing to call it a pretty **nice gunkhole**. The sandspit that parallels the shoreline in Mayo Cove is a great clamming ground. At high tide the three mooring buoys look almost in the center of the cove. At minus tides they seem almost on the sandspit. We picked up a buoy at a (-) minus three foot tide and were in just six feet. *Scheherazade* draws 5-1/2 feet.

Onshore is a lovely grassy picnic and day use area. Many people launch kayaks or other hand-carried boats from here and paddle out to Wyckoff Shoal at low tide. This beach was once a swamp, which we now call wetlands. Nearby the "Touch of Nature Interpretive Trail" winds through the forest. The walk takes about 20 minutes, and is a delightful self-guided nature trail through silent woods. The basic amenities of the park are on the Mayo Cove side of Penrose Point.

Penrose Park float is charted as 90A on 18445. Facilities at Penrose exceed those listed. The float has room for perhaps a dozen boats in the small protected yacht basin just inside a park spit called Sandy Beach. Alongside depth is charted at 2-1/2 feet. However, we have seen the inshore portion of the float go dry at minus tides and have seen boats aground alongside the float. At an extreme low tide of (-) minus five feet, the entire float would be high and dry.

Penrose Park was named for Dr. Stephen Penrose, president of Whitman College in Walla Walla from 1884 to 1934. Dr. Penrose and his family spent their summers on what is now park property. A firm believer in outdoor recreation for his children, he was a prominent educator and church leader. The community played an important part in developing Penrose Park.

Penrose Point State Park Facilities
➤ Three mooring buoys on Mayo Cove side of the park
➤ Five mooring buoys on Delano Bay side of the park
➤ Mooring buoys $5 per night
➤ *135 foot guest float inside Sandy Beach spit, room for 9-12 boats
➤ Moorage at float: $8 per night boats under 26', $11 per night, boats over 26'
➤ No moorage fees from September 30 to May 1
➤ Four restrooms, two with hot showers
➤ 11,751 feet of saltwater beach to explore
➤ 152 acres of wooded uplands laced with 2.5 miles of trails
➤ 83 camp sites, group campsite, 90 picnic sites
➤ Water on shore
➤ Pay phones
➤ Porta-potty dump station onshore
➤ Easy place to hand launch kayaks
➤ Access to Wyckoff Shoal
➤ Phone: 206-884-2514

Ⓖ **Five mooring buoys** off the park's east shore in Delano Bay allow a fabulous view of Mount Rainier (see book cover). Dinghy ashore to the undeveloped beach where several park trails go through the brush to the beach. This is a beautiful, quiet moorage— a nice **gunkhole.**

⚓ **Underway again, we head for Wyckoff Shoal and then Pitt Passage,** first checking out Delano Beach. This crescent shaped beach is between Penrose Point and South Head, a long peninsula jutting northeast for about 0.5 mile. Large erratic rocks are around both points, and a large rock and several pilings are near the head of the bay. It's about one mile across from Penrose Point to South Head.

Penrose float at low tide

Public tidelands in Delano Bay include one parcel of about 2,500 feet south of the state park and another parcel of about 5,500 feet from the southeast corner out and around South Head. We stay 0.5 mile or more offshore in the bay.

Leaving Delano Beach area we go out past **South Head** and head south towards Wyckoff Shoal, about 0.7 mile away.

We've arrived at Wyckoff Shoal wonderland. The shoal, all DNR public tidelands, extends 0.8 mile northwest of McNeil Island. It's about 0.3 mile east of Key Peninsula and 0.6 mile north of Pitt Island at the north end of Pitt Passage. The shoal is marked by two green can buoys at the western edge of its three fathom curve. It is partially used by private aquaculture as charted.

Wyckoff Shoal Buoy "1" marks the NW corner of three fathom curve.

Wyckoff Shoal Buoy "3" marks the SW corner of the shoal and is charted on the west end of Wyckoff's one fathom depth curve.

At extreme low tides of minus (-) five feet, this jumble of rocky tidelands is exposed for about 800 yards east of buoy "3" and about 400 yards north and south, roughly within Wyckoff's one fathom curve. Public access is by boat only.

Wyckoff Shoal disappears below the surface when the tide rises two feet or more above the MLLW level. The broad expanse of open water between McNeil and Key Peninsula is deceptive and hazardous to the unwary mariner, marked only by the two green buoys.

At a minus tide beachcombers can land their beachable boats on the shoal and marvel as treasures unfold: butter clams, geoducks, sea cucumbers, red rock crabs and whatever else might be the "catch of the day" on the shoal.

We have friends who anchor more than 100 yards off McNeil in this shallow area and dinghy over so they can explore. Others go to the shoal in shore boats after tying their cruising boats to buoys on the Delano Beach side of Penrose Park, about 1.5 miles from the shoal. Kayakers put in at Penrose to paddle to this unique reef. Small runabouts also often land on the shoal.

Shallow, unmarked channel is between Wyckoff Shoal and McNeil Island. It is about 150 yards wide, between the one fathom depth curves of both the shoal and island.

Depths in the channel are charted as about one fathom, three feet. Controlling depth in this shallow eastern channel at extreme low tide, minus (-) five feet, is reduced to four feet. At MHHW of 13.5 feet it may be as deep as 22.5 feet.

This channel is difficult to locate visually except at lower tides and requires good local knowledge, but may be useful to shoal draft boats and kayakers.

Captain and Mrs. Delano built an impressive hotel at Delano Beach in 1889, with landscaped gardens, tennis courts, cottages and a dance pavilion. This was a popular vacation spot, famous for grandiose dinner parties featuring geoduck chowder. Yachting parties were organized and guests stayed on for days.

As with many of these pioneer structures, the hotel burned down long ago.

Wyckoff Shoal

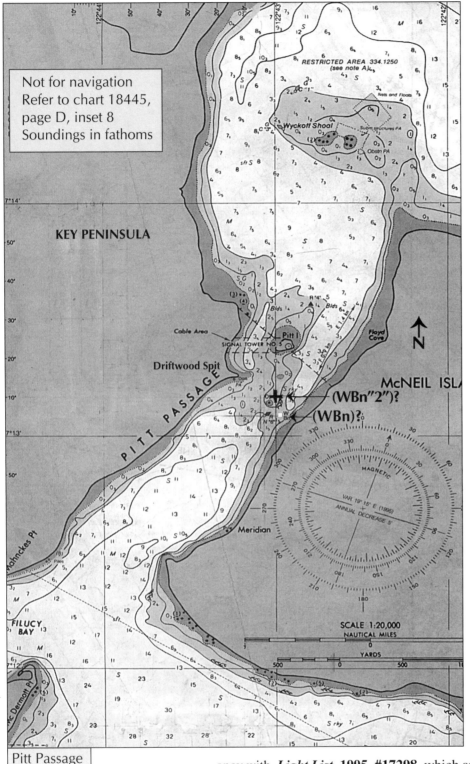

Not for navigation
Refer to chart 18445,
page D, inset 8
Soundings in fathoms

KEY PENINSULA

Driftwood Spit

Pitt Passage

For Pitt Passage Currents, see page 220.

Pitt Passage is a small craft channel two miles long between McNeil Island and Key Peninsula.

Chart 18445, 26th Ed. (06/03/95), page D, inset 8, scale 1:20,000, was the latest available and is used to illustrate our concerns.

Pitt Passage marked channel lies W of Wyckoff Shoal buoys GC "1" and "3," then S and E to Pitt Island North Shoal red daybeacon R "4," then between tiny Pitt Island and McNeil, and finally past buoy RN "6" to Balch Passage.

Controlling charted depth in the marked channel is 1 fathom, 5 feet at MLLW, near Pitt Rocks.

Pitt Island in the middle of Pitt Passage, is Department of Wildlife property.

The McNeil Island prison security restricted area extends 100 yards offshore from both McNeil and Pitt islands—in other words, no visiting— and don't pick up any swimmers.

South of Pitt Island for about 0.25 mile, it's a veritable stew of jumbled rocks, which emerge at low tides, sometimes marked with kelp.

Pitt Passage Rocks, charted about 275 yards offshore from McNeil Island and 450 yards south of Pitt Island, is within the SW end of the one fathom curve from Pitt Island.

We have used Pitt Passage from the 1970s into 1995, but not since the charted changes on Ed. 26.

We became concerned about charted changes on 18845, 26th Ed., when we saw a newly charted **(WBn)** Daybeacon, and noticed the absence of **(WBn "2,")** Pitt Passage Rocks Daybeacon. We also noted a discrepancy with *Light List,* **1995, #17298,** which appeared to relocate Pitt Passage Rocks Daybeacon to WBn Daybeacon site. So that's when we contacted the very patient and helpful Seattle Coast Guard about these three concerns, which we detail below.

(WBn "2"), Pitt Passage Rocks Daybeacon, has for several years been charted about 60 yards northeast of the rocks, and was **not** charted on Ed. 26. Its approximate position was Lat. 47°13'10.0", Long 122°43'1.0".

Coast Guard advised us that the daybeacon, discontinued in February 1993, was temporarily replaced by a white buoy with orange stripes marked "Danger Shoal." The buoy is to be replaced by a permanent pile-mounted dayboard worded "Danger Shoal" in Spring 1997. Approximate Coast Guard position for the new daybeacon is Lat. 47°13' 9.643", Long. 122°43'1.293", closer to Pitt Rocks than the original position.

WBn, a square white daybeacon, was charted on Ed. 26. about 140 yards SE of Pitt Rocks, about 140 yards from McNeil's shoreline and about 140 yards east of R N "6." The approximate position was Lat. 47°13'5.5", Long. 122°42'59", as scaled from the chart.

Coast Guard advised WBn was destroyed on March 5, 1996, by a vessel which cut it too close and it will not be re-established at this location.

Light List Concerns:

As mariners, we all depend on the Light Listed Name and Location columns, and/or the latitude and longitude—to the nearest tenth of a minute—in the Position column, to clearly identify specific charted aids or *Light List* numbers.

"Pitt Passage Rocks Daybeacon," is a non-lateral white dayboard, "NW on pile worded **Danger Shoal**. It had been located about 60 yards NE of Pitt Rocks at least since 1984, charted as WBn "2," and assigned *Light List* **#17285**, prior to Ed. 26 of chart 18445. Its Light Listed position should be Lat. **47°13.2.**'

However, the identical daybeacon description in the 1995 Light List was assigned to #17298 and its Light Listed position was Lat. **47°13.1'**, about 0.1 NM from WBn "2," 140 yards SE of Pitt Rocks on the opposite side of the channel from Pitt Rocks. (We note here that 0.1 minute of latitude equals 0.1 NM.) In other words, #17298 identifies the Pitt Rocks Daybeacon site where WBn was, instead of at WBn "2," the real site of Pitt Rocks Daybeacon.

It is very important that mariners using Ed. 26 understand the above details and not try to pass on the west side of the <u>real</u> WBn "2," Pitt Rocks Daybeacon, and know that WBn no longer exists.

Pitt Island & Pitt Pass markers

This 1992 photo was taken from Jo's kayak near Pitt Passage Rock, looking approximately 20° east of true north. It shows the original (WBn "2") Pitt Passage Rocks daybeacon in the foreground, with a white diamond-shaped dayboard worded "Danger Shoal."

R "4" daybeacon is north and east of Pitt Island.

The marked channel is east of these daybeacons.

Note absence of signal tower on Pitt Island. (See Chap. 13)

The above explanation is necessary if using Ed. 26, which was the latest chart available at the time of publication.

We expect new chart editions of **18445, 18448 and 18440**, *Notice to Mariners* and *Light List* will reflect the above changes—readers should check these out.

The important thing to note is that there is no longer a WBn off McNeil's shore and that by Spring 1997 there will probably be a new Pitt Passage Rocks Daybeacon, WBn "2."

⚓ **Underway again,** now after all this discussion, let's go south through Pitt Passage from Carr Inlet.

Entering Pitt Passage we keep west of Wyckoff Shoal green buoys "1" and "3," and then head south and east toward **Floyd Cove** on McNeil. Keeping north of Pitt Passage North Shoal Daybeacon R "4," (off Pitt Island), we may need to offset our course to compensate for currents. It's about 0.75 mile from green buoy "3" to daybeacon R "4."

Distance between R "4" and charted RN "6" buoy is about 0.5 mile. Passing R "4" we head south and (slightly) west between Pitt and McNeil Islands, favoring the McNeil shore, aware of the charted 1 fathom, 5 ft depth at MLLW in the channel east of Pitt Rocks.

An unmarked channel off the west side of Pitt Island requires offsetting the course to port and then to starboard between Pitt Island and Driftood Spit, to avoid grounding in the shallows. We've seen other traffic in this channel but we've never used it.

Controlling depth in the unmarked channel is charted at 2 fathoms, 2 feet at MLLW, just west of buoy RN "6."

Going through Pitt Passage can actually be easy and interesting.

Public tidelands of about 1,000 feet are on the Key Peninsula side, with about 1,000 feet north of Driftwood Spit and over 5,000 feet south of the spit.

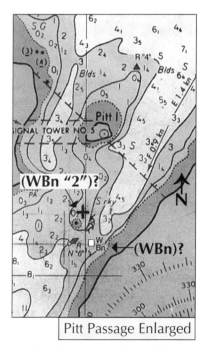

Pitt Passage Enlarged

Not for navigation Refer to chart 18445 Soundings in fathoms

Driftwood Spit

Jo: I beached my kayak on the sandspit at extreme low tide and trudged up the steep slope through sand and gravel to the top of the spit. It was a soft summer morning, not another soul in sight.

A small totem stood tilting slightly to one side. Surely it was too modern to have been carved back before the "invasion" by settlers, although this was a spot where the Indians camped during their trips around South Sound in their wonderful cedar canoes. They were the first real "discoverers" of the Sound.

I was where Puget's expedition had spent their second night. I looked around and saw much of what Puget must have seen: forested Pitt and McNeil Islands, except then it was virgin forest, not second or third growth.

I saw where they may have dug clams, built a fire and made camp.

I saw the rocky shoal south of Pitt Island, visible only at low tide, the Pitt Rock daybeacon and McNeil just a short distance beyond. I mused about how Puget and his men had cruised all through this area, charting and sounding as they went, gathering food and water under way, with none of the amenities we take for granted. They were pretty remarkable voyagers.

I thought about Driftwood Annie and her humanitarian outlook on the McNeil escapees. The Indians, Puget and Annie are gone from Pitt Pass, but in the solitude of the spit there is a presence, possibly of the earlier voyagers and the kindhearted woman, or maybe it's because I just wanted to feel something special.

There are forested bluffs and long sandy beaches south of the spit where it's okay to dig clams or walk the public beaches at low tides. There is no upland access along the shore. Kayakers enjoy the area, as do deer and other wildlife.

⚓ We find anchoring off the public beaches should be restricted to periods when currents are minimal.

Be aware that currents can be challenging in the pass, as Native Americans knew and Peter Puget discovered. During part of the flood they flow northeast, and during part of the ebb they flow southwest.

Currents in Pitt Pass			
Currents flow NE during (F+3) thru (E+2), and SW from (E+3) thru (F+1).			
Refer to current charts and current tables for The Narrows. (See Chapter 10)			
	Current Chart	**Charted Tropic**	**Knots at Extreme Tides**
NE flow starts during	F+3	0.8	1.20
Fastest NE current	E-2 thru E-1	1.8	2.70
NE flow ends after	E+2	0.3	0.45
NE flow becomes weak, reversing to SW flow between (E+2) and (E+3)			
SW flow starts during	E+3	0.4	0.60
Fastest SW current	F-1	1.2	1.80
SW flow ends after	F+1	0.4	0.60
SW flow becomes weak, reversing to NE flow during (F+2)			
Correction factor for extreme tides is 1.5 multiplied by charted tropic speed			

Driftwood Annie and the Sandspit

"Driftwood Annie"—Anna Halvorson Peyser—was a remarkable woman with a love for all living things. The widow of Max Peyser, she lived above the sandspit on the mainland shore. From her house she could see down to the spit and across Pitt Passage to Pitt and McNeil Islands. Her home was also the closest haven across the narrow pass from McNeil Island—and the penitentiary.

Annie lived in her driftwood-filled house for about 80 years before her death in the mid-1980s. Her guests included not only lost pets and injured wildlife, but also cold and wet escaped felons from their enforced lodgings on McNeil. She didn't remember how many fleeing convicts came to her door seeking dry clothes and hot food, but by her own loose count she probably cared for well over 20 men who swam across the chilly pass in front of her house. She didn't remember the dates they arrived, or bother with their names or what their crimes were. Nor did she care. All she knew was that they were fellow human beings in need of comfort. Usually the men slipped off into the woods after her ministrations.

Law officers weren't exactly pleased with Annie's caring ways with fleeing prisoners. It annoyed her that they lectured her rather than thanking her for helping out hypothermic and sometimes nearly dead fugitives. They didn't quite charge her with aiding and abetting escapees. When she was in her 90s, she complained that every time a prisoner escaped from the island prison officials sent someone to her home to keep an eye out for the missing man. She was not intimidated by law enforcement officers and she was not afraid of the felons they sought. She said no prisoner ever laid a hand on her. She simply wanted to help those in need.

Annie felt prisoners should learn how to live productive lives during their incarceration, rather than depending on others. She thought they really didn't want to do bad things. She also felt that people should help each other. That's why people were always welcome on her beach. She was a hard worker, and she vowed never to leave her beautiful, isolated home.

She had fun, too. When there was a local dance, she had the reputation of "dancing the legs off" the young men.

Annie's gone now, but before she left she deeded her land over to a church which is now subdividing it. She always felt the Lord was watching over her.

Peter Puget and Pitt Passage

Puget and his men camped on the low sandspit on Pitt Passage on their second night out, May 21, 1792. The spit overlooks tiny Pitt Island—which they dubbed "Mosquitoe Island"—and McNeil Island, called "Pidgeon" by them. In his journal Puget told of a great flock of pigeons that nested in holes on the steep banks of a "small island" he named for them.

They took refuge on the spit as a southeasterly squall hit them, bringing a "perfect deluge of rain." They pitched their tents in the downpour in an early dusk, ate their hot dinners in front of roaring beachfires and went to bed early. In spite of the rainstorm they had recorded a high of 90° earlier in the day. Even the weather has changed little since they were here.

The men broke camp by four the next morning, launched their boats in the early dawn and were practically stopped dead in the water. They had just discovered that, as in many channels between islands in South Sound, the waters running through narrow or dead-end channels often follow their own patterns and don't conform to normal ebbs and flows. Just when they thought they'd have an easy time of it, they were fighting what Puget called "a most rapid stream in this narrow channel" with such a strong current they only "got through with great difficulty." Had they waited a few hours, they would have had the current with them.

Once through the pass, they headed east in what is now Balch Passage between McNeil and Anderson Islands, bypassing Filucy Bay to starboard. A chart drawn by Puget indicates they were aware of the bay, but apparently didn't explore it.

Driftwood Spit totem

Kayakers in Pitt Pass

In Chapter 15 we go into delightful Filucy Bay and visit Longbranch, then through Balch and Drayton Passages, circumnavigating Eagle and Anderson Islands.

Cruising through Pitt Pass, we can see how close we are to McNeil Island. On extreme low tides some "guests" of McNeil Island prison have managed to escape across Pitt Passage, a practice frowned upon by prison officials.

The prison has several patrol boats whose crews are alert for boaters getting too close to the island—they don't want any inmates leaving by private boat.

Daredevils

If you think going through Pitt Pass by boat is a tight squeeze, consider the young pilots in World War II who flew through the pass at about 20 feet above the water, taking out the telephone line to McNeil Island as they went, much to the consternation of islanders.

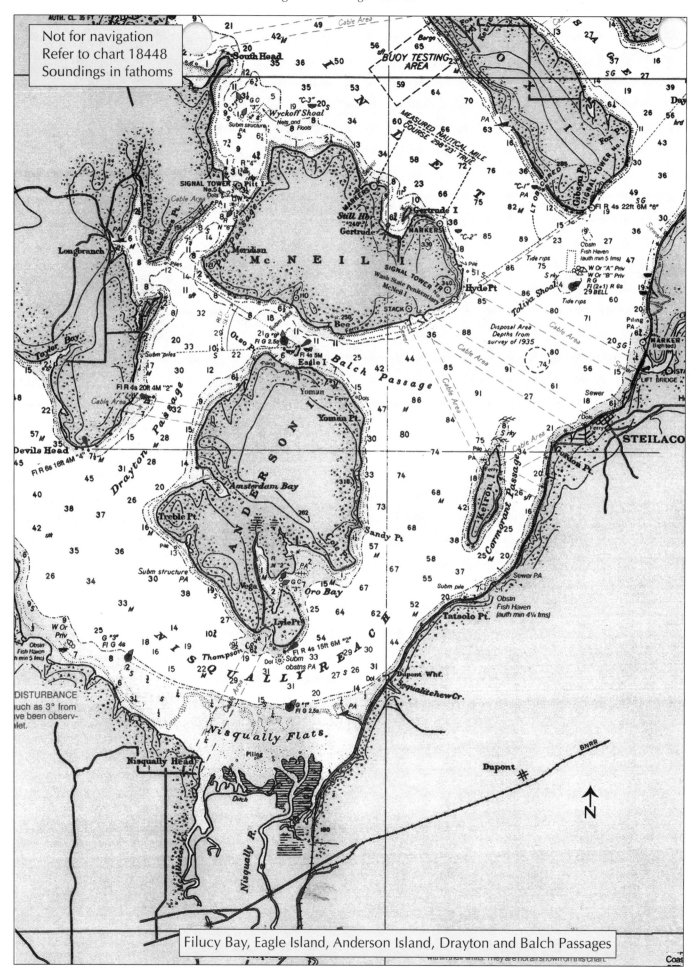

Not for navigation
Refer to chart 18448
Soundings in fathoms

CHAPTER 15
Filucy Bay & Longbranch, Eagle & Anderson Islands, Balch & Drayton Passages

Charts and publications for this chapter

	Chart#	Date	Title	Scale	Soundings
**	18445	06/03/95	SC Possession Sound to Olympia, page C	1:80,000	Fathoms
			inset page D	1:20,000	Fathoms
**	18448	10/30/93	Puget Sound, Southern Part	1:80,000	Fathoms
	18440	08/05/95	Puget Sound	1:150,000	Fathoms
			Tidal Current Charts, Puget Sound, Southern Part		
			Puget Sound Shellfish Sites		
			Washington State Public Lands Quad Map—Tacoma	1:100,000	

➥ *When using charts, compare your chart dates with ones referred to above. There may be discrepancies between different charts and different chart editions.*

Overview

Filucy Bay is on the east shore of **Key Peninsula** at the junction of **Pitt, Balch** and **Drayton Passages.** It is one of the joys of cruising South Puget Sound. There are good places to anchor—a gunkholing treasure— with all the attendant beauty of the area, including spectacular views of Mount Rainier.

Anderson Island is a delightful, rural island whose north shores, including **Eagle Island,** are across Balch Passage from McNeil Island; east shores face the mainland across from Steilacoom; south shores look to Nisqually Flats, and the west shores border on Drayton Passage, across from Key Peninsula. **Drayton Passage** is two miles long, between Key Peninsula and Anderson Island.

There are a couple of good anchorages in this area; one state marine park at Eagle Island, and one waterfront village at Longbranch.

⎈ **Filucy Bay and Longbranch** have long been destinations for boaters, including the Nisqually Indians. For hundreds of years, they arrived in dugout canoes to harvest clams in the bay. Clam middens from these early diggings can still be seen along the shores. Now recreational boaters arrive, not quite in droves, but in small numbers to enjoy the peace and quiet beauty.

The gentle bay is tree-lined, with mostly low-bank shores dotted with summer cabins and a few posh homes; beaches are private. The feeling is rural, although larger homes are being built as land is subdivided.

Ⓖ This is a **favorite gunkhole** for many, including us.

Longbranch community is the center of this part of Key Peninsula. The Longbranch Marina and Longbranch Mercantile are on the west shore, straight ahead in the bay.

The north arm of Filucy Bay is about two fathoms deep for about 0.3 mile long and just over 100 yards wide. On shore is a substantial barn-like structure, the old Sipple Boat House.

➥ **NOTE: No marine fuel** is available in the areas covered in this chapter.

➥ **Chart 18445** has more names of small coves than **chart 18448.** Both charts have a scale of 1:80,000. Chart 18445 has several inset charts with 1:20,000 scale.

Longbranch Marina, Mount Rainier in background

There are about eight miles of public lands in the area covered in this chapter.

Public tidelands surround much of Anderson Island; several parcels are south of Filucy Bay. We take the Washington State Public Lands Quadrangle Map, Tacoma, with us when we go ashore to avoid trespassing on adjacent private property. Unless otherwise noted, the public tidelands we mention are state-owned; some of them may be leased for aquaculture.

William Sipple, master craftsman, built pleasure boats, fish boats, tugs and just about everything else around the turn-of-the-century.

Inside McDermott Point sandspit is the southeast arm of Filucy Bay, which carries about two fathoms for about 250 yards and is about 100 yards across.

"Far-A-Way," a large, white, turn-of-the-century former home, is south of the point. It's used for weddings, receptions and other festivities. Be aware of a small spit that extends out from the resort beach, with the Far-A-Way dock south of it.

There are also a number of private docks, floats and moored boats in this small southeast arm of Filucy Bay. South of about two fathoms it begins to shoals terminating in tideflats. There may not be much swinging room among permanently anchored boats.

Entering Filucy Bay, the entrance is between the spit at **McDermott Point** on the south and the green house on the north shore just inside **Mahnckes Point**. From there, go north or south into either arm or straight ahead to Longbranch.

Boaters are asked to slow engines and leave no wake upon reaching the entrance. It takes just five minutes for wake to reach Longbranch Marina. Dockmaster

Dockmaestro Glen Miller, left

Miller says "It feels like we've been hit by a tsunami when that happens."

⚓ **Anchor** in either arm of Filucy Bay or near Longbranch Marina in two to six fathoms. The bay is basically protected and there's good holding ground with a mud bottom. It's okay to dinghy to the marina and walk to the store and restaurant.

Longbranch Marina has newly remodeled floats and room for transients at reasonable rates—stay two hours for free. Dockmaster Glen Miller (no, he isn't a dance band leader) makes docking at the marina a treat. He's handled lines for Robert Ripley on his boat *Believe it or Not,* and for media moguls Jack Anderson and Tom Brokaw, all about as authentically rich and famous personalities as he. He'll tell you everything you want to know about his community with unabashed enthusiasm. A "one man chamber of commerce," Miller is happily back on the docks again after an absence.

"This is the place to be if you want a beautiful and quiet marina. There are no discos or bars," Miller says. "Quiet hours are from 10 p.m. to 7 a.m., and you can just relax on your boat. A lot of yacht clubs have discovered Longbranch and plan annual visits."

There's an assortment of paperback books by the dock office if you want to trade some of your tired, already read books, or just buy some. Each transaction has a 25 cent fee, and the money goes to a vocational scholarship fund for Peninsula High School students.

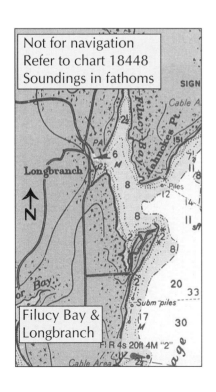

Not for navigation
Refer to chart 18448
Soundings in fathoms

Filucy Bay & Longbranch

Longbranch Marina Facilities
➤ Guest moorage for about 30 boats; rates about 35 cents per foot
➤ 30 amp shore power, $3 per day
➤ Water
➤ Porta-potty facilities
➤ Paperback book exchange
➤ 20' x 50' covered social and potluck area
➤ Monitors VHF Channel 16
➤ E-mail address: KBFD97A@PRODIGY.COM
➤ Phone: 206-884-5137 FAX: 206-884-9854
➤ Peace and quiet

Longbranch Mercantile has a diversity of merchandise, and it's a lot more fun than shopping at any mall we know of. If they don't have what you need, they'll figure out a substitute.

They claim to have the lowest meat prices and freshest produce on Key Peninsula. They carry fishing gear, hardware, nuts and bolts, kitchen utensils, general food, toys, health and beauty aids, life jackets and marine supplies, beer and wine, ice, T-shirts, propane bottles, kerosene, candles, videos and video machine rentals, a few magazines and local newspapers.

Not only that, they have the "prettiest views" ever of Mount Rainier, claiming the mountain is "just awesome" at 6 a.m. and 6 p.m., spring through fall. Phone: 206-884-3721

Longbranch Mercantile

The Chowder House Restaurant, next to the mercantile, is a longtime tradition in Longbranch now under new ownership. Alan and Susan Collins served soups and salads in 1995. By the summer of 1996, they were in full swing with Susan's own chowder recipe and "real boating food:" burgers and fries and the like. They also have a gift shop.

The restaurant, a favorite with boaters and local residents, had been closed down for several years. Many cruisers are delighted to stop in once again.

Yeazell's Longbranch

Longbranch was named in 1889 after Long Branch, N.J., a well-known resort at the time. That year Edward and Katherine Yeazell bought 13,500 feet of Longbranch waterfront, worth about 7 1/2 cents per front foot, for $1,009 in gold coin.

The Longbranch sandspit was a sliver, a hook—with most of the spit under water at high tide—and it included a lagoon. Yeazell created a warm water swimming pool in the lagoon by adding a gate to impound the water. He also built a bath house and dance pavilion.

The New Jersey resort featured gambling casinos, burlesque theaters, horse racing, entertainment clubs and luxury hotels, which is what Yeazell planned to do with his new purchase in South Sound. Nicknamed the "Summer Capitol of Presidents," famous guests included presidents Grant, Hayes, Garfield, Arthur, Harrison, McKinley and Wilson, as well as visitors from the world of finance, fashion, theater and high society.

Yeazell's stationary read, "The Popular Summer Resort of Puget Sound, Fine Saltwater Bathing, A Good Restaurant, Shady Groves, Beautiful Views, Excellent Drinking Water." He added a covenant: "No wine, spirituous or malt liquors shall ever be sold on said premises, that covenant shall annex to and run with the land."

In 1895, Yeazell sent invitations to hundreds: "Yourself and friends are most cordially invited to partake of a genuine Rhode Island Clam Bake at Long Branch, Wednesday, July the 24th, 1895. There will be a sale of lots on that day, ranging in price from Ten Dollars upwards. A Naphtha Launch will be at the services of visitors during the day. The steamboat *Monte Cristo* will leave the N.P. Wharf at 8:30 a.m. sharp and the *City of Aberdeen* from Commercial Dock (Tacoma) at 10 a.m. Round trip fifty cents."

Longbranch Mercantile Company is the only remaining Key Peninsula store which grew out of the "grocery boat" era of sternwheelers and sidewheelers of Puget Sound's "Mosquito Fleet." Longbranch was a regular stop for many years, starting in the late 1880s.

The store was built by Bill Otto in 1934 as the Maple Leaf Tavern. He and his wife Mae turned it into a grocery store several years later. In 1942, it became the Longbranch Mercantile.

The two-story Wyatt Hotel was built in the late 1890s for traveling salesmen, early schoolteachers and overnight visitors. The roof was later lowered and became the home of Bill Otto, and later the Chowder House.

Far-A-Way

(continued on next page)

We spoke with a state parks planner who said that "hopefully" the state will be able to purchase McDermott Point for a new state marine park.

Good news for mariners who love South Sound and Filucy Bay!

The Longbranch Community has always had 4th of July celebrations. In the book, **Along the Waterfront,** the story is told of how in early days the community always sent someone to Steilacoom to get a keg of beer for the party. One year the rower got drunk and didn't get back to Longbranch until   July 5.

Residents had their celebration one day late.

When Wilkes was here in 1841 he called Filucy Bay "Titusi Bay." It's not known if that was the actual name or a mistake made when copying the name Filucy.

(continued from previous page)

Some 200 people arrived and partook of free sarsaparilla, cigars—and the modest dispersal of liquid spirits. The Yeazell estate was decorated with garlands and wreaths of wild flowers. Tables were laden with a variety of entrees, delicacies, desserts, baked and steamed clams and bowls of nectar. Yeazell hired farmers to plow up clams with teams of horses while local and Indian women and kids gathered clams in such quantities that not all could be baked Indian-style in the rocks and seaweeds on the beach, nor could all be eaten.

Fun at Filucy Bay

Jo recalls: Back in the 1960s and 70s when we lived in Olympia we cruised to Filucy Bay with family and friends. We'd anchor just inside the sandspit and pile into the dinghy to go ashore. That was before "No Trespassing" signs. There was a tumble- down, no longer operating lighthouse on the point for kids to explore. We'd swim and play on the beach and sail the dinghy around Filucy Bay. One friend always carried a volleyball and net on his boat, so he'd set it up in the meadow on the sandspit for a game for everyone on the beach.

We'd row over to the marina and get ice cream at Longbranch Mercantile. We'd plan to be at Longbranch for at least one of three summer holidays— Memorial Day, Fourth of July or Labor Day—to take advantage of the fireworks displays at Far-A-Way and wonderful dances at the Longbranch Improvement Club building.

All that remains of the lighthouse on McDermott Point is a concrete base. The lighthouse itself was burned down by vandals in 1971, although the point is still called Lighthouse Point. The meadow is private property, so no more volleyball games. We can walk the beach below the high tide line, but that's about all.

The Longbranch Improvement Club still holds dances in its impressive building, about one-half mile up the road from the marina. The building has been on the National Historical Register since 1987. It was built by the WPA in the 1930s, and has enormous log rafters, stone walls and a chalet-style metal roof. For those who don't want to walk, shuttle service is provided. It's sure to be a good time.

Filucy Bay's Early Settlers

Joe Shettleroe arrived in 1859 and operated a one-yoke oxen logging camp. He had a man called "French" helping him; "Soldier Sally," an Indian, was Joe's housekeeper. Nearby lived Pierre Legard, whom Indians called "Old Clearwater," a French trapper and interpreter for Hudson's Bay Company at the Nisqually Trading Post in 1833—the first real encroachment of "civilization" in Puget Sound.

William Sipple arrived on board the sternwheeler *Messenger*, the vessel with a double-noted whistle pitched at different harmonic tones. There was no float or dock in Filucy Bay, so they just shoved her nose into a sand spit and Sipple jumped off in 1887, a year after Henry Mahncke homesteaded in Filucy Bay. The sternwheeler wiggled loose and continued on her way, delivering supplies to logging camps along forested shores.

Sipple wrote, "after gathering up my tools and about a week's supply of groceries, I set out at once for the little log cabin squatting on the beach just beyond reach of high tide to which I had acquired title by virtue of buying the land on which it stood. This cabin had only one room with a floor area of about 16-by-20 and an opening looking out over the bay. In the opposite end there was a fireplace built with cobble stones laid in mortar. The door with its rawhide hinges had fallen to the ground where it lay in the last stages of decay.

(continued on next page)

The roof was covered with shakes about an inch in thickness, but on the weather side these had been beaten to shreds with the storms of perhaps half a century and I often wondered how long it had stood there. 'Gig Harbor Joe,' a Puyallup Indian and my almost constant companion during summer months, said it had been there many, many years."

Sipple opened his carpentry and shipbuilding shop and waited for his prune orchard to mature. He was Justice of the Peace for 40 years, built the light-house on McDermott Point, and built and repaired boats and houses. Sipple described the outline of Filucy Bay as a monster human ear, looking through the ear's orifice off towards Steilacoom and Mount Rainier.

Sipple's boathouse was a meeting place for locals, because, in addition to the boats he built, he made a bowling alley in the boathouse. What better product to make from his plum orchard than plum wine? Combine plum wine, a bowling alley and a gathering of Longbranch gents and it's a good time of a Sunday afternoon.

Sipple said "Filucy" was a Haida Indian Princess brought by trapper Pierre Legard, who built a cabin in the 1830s where the boathouse now stands. Supposedly there's an Indian grave on the property.

Sipple Boathouse

Drayton Passage—Key Peninsula Shore

⚓ **Underway again**; leaving Filucy Bay, we head south in Drayton Passage between Key Peninsula and Anderson Island. The pass is about two miles long—from its juncture with Balch Passage at the north until it meets Nisqually Reach at **Devils Head**. It's 0.7 mile wide at the narrowest spot to about 1.2 miles wide at the widest. We usually keep almost 0.2 mile offshore to be comfortable.

Public tidelands of about 2,000 feet are about 1,500 feet north of the launch ramp—on the outside of the sandspit which terminates in McDermott Point.

Launch ramp about 0.5 mile south of McDermott Point is well used by Key Peninsula residents. The ramp leads to the water between medium high banks. Beaches are signed private on both sides of the ramp, with parking nearby.

Fl R 4s 20ft 4M "2" Drayton Passage Light 2 is flashing red on a triangular red dayboard on a dolphin. It's about one mile south of McDermott Point and marks a sandspit that extends nearly 0.5 mile into the pass.

A long dock is south of the spit, part of a youth camp, and in summer you can watch kids leap from the dock into chilly waters as you cruise past.

Cable area runs from here to Anderson Island.

Halfway between the spit and Devils Head is a private launch ramp. Onshore is a mix of homes, beach cabins, trees and bluffs along this shore of Key Peninsula.

Currents, based on predictions at The Narrows, can run one to two knots in the south portion of Drayton Pass. Check *Tidal Current Tables* and *Tidal Current Charts*.

Fl R 6s 4M "4" Devils Head Light 4 flashing red light is on a red triangular dayboard on a dolphin offshore of 280 foot high, heavily-wooded, Devils Head bluff at the southwest entrance to Drayton Pass. We stay well outside this marker as there are many erratic rocks on the beach. This marks the southern end of Key Peninsula.

Key Peninsula was called the Great Indian Peninsula by Lt. Charles Wilkes when he cruised through here in 1841.

Devils Head was named by Capt. Vancouver who claimed if he turned the chart upside down the area at the south end of Key Peninsula looked like Satan's head.

⚓ **We're underway again** and heading back to Balch Passage. The passage, between McNeil and Anderson Islands, is approximately two miles long. It can be entered from the east off The Narrows, west from the Longbranch area, north from Pitt Pass and from Drayton Passage to the south.

Width of the pass is about 0.5 mile, but as there is only about 100 yards between 10 fathom curves in Balch, and deep draft vessels need to stay in the center. Going west we stay offshore enough to avoid the erratic rocks along the McNeil coast.

Depths are up to 11 fathoms in midchannel. Eagle Island extends about halfway across the pass.

Currents in Balch Pass can swirl through at a fairly strong rate. Max ebb in the pass is 40 minutes before max ebb at The Narrows, and can run as high as 3.6 knots. Max flood is 1 hour 7 minutes after max flood at The Narrows, and can reach 2.2 knots. Currents are based on predictions at The Narrows. We check the ***Tidal Current Tables*** and ***Tidal Current Charts,*** but usually manage to make way when we want, even against the current.

The grim Washington State Corrections Center penitentiary, which occupies about 100 acres of the island along Balch Passage shoreline, comes into view as we round Hyde Point from the east.

The harshness of this severe, fort-like facility descends and we vow never to do anything that could put us here, as lovely as the setting may be. And we wonder, couldn't they have built a prison in a less beautiful place? There's been a prison on the island since the 1870s.

The buildings are stark, a sort of cream-color, but feel gray—it all feels gray here. Guards in towers keep watchful eyes on everything. This is a medium-security prison with about 1,100 men. Inland is a minimum security prison with about 200 inmates.

The prison has its own dock and vessels transporting employees, prisoners, visitors and other personnel to and from Steilacoom. All other boats must keep 100 yards off all shores of McNeil Island at all times.

McNeil Prison

West of the penitentiary are several quite attractive staff residences, white, with red roofs—a vivid contrast to penitentiary buildings.

Bee, the island's ferry landing, is one mile west of the institution. Tugs bring in landing barge-type vessels which accommodate a fair number of vehicles. The cars belong to island residents who are state employees.

After we pass the ferry landing at Bee, we're well into Balch Passage.

Between what we've said about 4,400 acre McNeil Island in this chapter and the last, Chapter 14, we've actually gone all the way around the island. And since we can't go ashore anyway, that's it.

Ezra Meeker, Pioneer

We understand the first settler to stake a claim on McNeil was well-known pioneer Ezra Meeker in 1853, although it was never recorded. Ezra and his brother Oliver built their log cabin near where the penitentiary later had a shipyard. Ezra and his wife moved to the mainland after a short time on the island.

Meeker wrote in his book, ***Pioneer Reminiscences of Puget Sound***, "My cabin stood on the south side of the bight or lagoon within stone throw of where the U.S. penitentiary now stands, and only a few feet above high tide level. The lagoon widens and deepens from the entrance and curves to the south with gentle

(continued on next page)

slope on either side, the whole forming a miniature of sheltered valley of light, timbered, fertile land ... In the front a long flat or sandy beach extended far out from the high tide line where the clams spouted in countless numbers, and crows played their antics of breaking the shells by dropping to the stony beach the helpless bivalve they had stealthily clutched and taken to flight with them."

His cabin was about 18 by 18 feet with seven foot high walls. The fireplace was of round stones and had a "cat-and-clay chimney" nine feet high. The floor was of rough lumber, and bookshelves covered the walls.

Other settlers arrived and the island was settled just as in all the other Puget Sound communities. In 1870, the government bought 27 acres from James Smith near the east end of the island and set up a territorial prison. More land was purchased in 1904. The prison expanded.

In 1936, the federal government took possession of the entire island and everyone in the large, cohesive community was forced to leave. It remained a federal prison until 1979 when the Feds closed it down and surplused it out. In the mid-1980s they deeded the island to the state which decided to continue to use the buildings as a correctional institution, however, 3,100 acres are managed by the state Department of Wildlife.

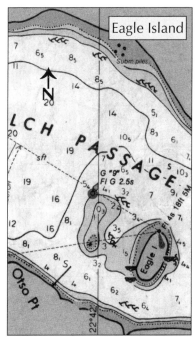

Not for navigation
Refer to chart 18445,
page D, inset 8
Soundings in fathoms

Eagle Island

⚓ **Eagle Island** in Balch Passage between McNeil and Anderson Islands is a treasure and the entire 10 acres has been set aside as a State Marine Park.

Accessible only by water, the island has been left natural, with the only additions being three mooring buoys and a few overgrown trails crisscrossing the island.

Bask in the luxury of surrounding evergreens and water. Study the large number of madrona trees, their twisted trunks of light colored, shedding, paper-thin bark are a constant amazement. Walk the 2,600 feet around the island's gravel beaches at low tide, swim, wade, or just sit and enjoy.

Overnight camping is not allowed as this is a day use only park. When summers are dry, there is fire danger on the island.

Mooring buoys, if you choose to stay at Eagle Island, there are two mooring buoys off the southwest shore and a third buoy is off the east shore. Some sailing friends said the west buoys lack adequate depth and swinging room for larger boats, although a ranger said he received no complaints.

⚓ **Anchoring** is possible in three to six fathoms, sandy bottom.

Currents, especially if there are very high and low tides, may run fairly strong around the island. The ebb can reach as much as 4.5 knots and the flood can be up to 2.7 knots.

Good clam beds once surrounded the island, but have been pretty well dug out.

Seals and California sea lions thrive off the west side of the island. They romp and play, diving and cavorting enthusiastically in the water off the island's shores, sunning themselves on Eagle Reef 300 yards west of the island at low tides.

⚓ **Approaching Eagle Island** from east or west it is possible for a boat to stay fairly close to Anderson and run between Eagle and Anderson in six to eight fathoms. From the north, we go around either side of Eagle.

Eagle Reef, 300 yards west of Eagle Island, bares at its south end on a one foot tide. It has a depth of three feet on zero tide at the north end.

Fl G 2.5 "9" Eagle Island Reef Lighted Buoy 9 marks the northwest end of the reef.

Detail on Wilkes's original 1841 charts show two islands between McNeil and Anderson that he dubbed The Peppercorns, Tom and Ned. Tom is Eagle and Ned is the shoal—he must have been there at extreme low tide.

➡ **Caution:** Poison oak flourishes on Eagle Island.

Shores of Eagle Island

A fog bell was installed on Eagle Island in 1963. Up until about the mid-1900s, the echo of steamer whistles resounded in the small island's dense forest. But a fire ravaged the island and the trees fell. The sparse remaining forest lets the sound of whistles penetrate freely—the echoing-back no longer works.

Eagle Island was at one time an Indian burial ground with burial canoes placed in the trees, as were many other small islands around the Sound.

Anderson Island was settled by loggers, farmers, fishermen, as were most other Puget Sound early settlements. These pioneers built and worked on the many boats in the Sound.

One of the first settlers on the island was Michael Luark, an early logger. He kept a 25 volume diary (now at the University of Washington), in which he describes logging on the island in 1854 and complains about the rain. He tells of paddling from Steilacoom in a storm, in a canoe taken from an Indian graveyard from a small nearby island—possibly Eagle.

The 54 foot steam tug, Magnet, was built on Anderson Island in 1907. It was the only tug that operated on both Upper and Lower Puget Sound that was built on the island.

Fl 4s 18ft 5 M Eagle Island Sector Light is a flashing 4 second white light with a red sector from 081° to 121°. It's mounted 18 feet high, on a black and white diamond shaped dayboard on a skeleton tower off Eagle Islands's north end.

The light is to insure safety for vessels coming from the "Upper Sound," which is west or southwest towards Olympia, through Drayton Pass. When a vessel approaches from that angle to where the white sector is visible, it can change course to an easterly direction, which will put it in mid-Balch Passage, avoiding Eagle Reef.

Eagle Island Light—& the Johnsons

With the arrival of settlers and steamers, Eagle Island became important to navigation through Balch Passage. On December 13, 1887, Bengt Johnson of Anderson Island was appointed "Keeper of Eagle Island Post Light" by the U.S. Lighthouse Department. The Post Light was located at the island's north end.

In 1889, the light was ordered moved to the south end for the convenience of the keeper and his family—who all pitched in with the twice-daily chores.

The kerosene lantern was tended by Johnson for more than 30 years. In 1917, son Ben became keeper. By 1919, an eight day blinker light was installed at the island's north end.

The Johnsons served as keepers of the light for 48 years total.

The light was lit each evening and put out each morning. The lamp was in a heavy brass frame with a chimney of thick, ridged glass. The fuel container had to be filled every 24 hours; filling and cleaning were done each evening.

"The boys (brothers Gunnard and John) took pride in tending the light. We all learned at an early age to perform this twice-daily chore. Not only did we become familiar with the seven-day-a-week responsibility, we also learned how to deal with the ebbing and flowing tides which swirl about Eagle Island," wrote Betsey Johnson Cammon in her charming book, ***Island Memoirs***.

"We grew up with the island seemingly in our front yard; consequently a touch of sentiment crept into our hearts over the years. We affectionately called it the 'little island'," she wrote.

Anderson Island

☸ **Underway again,** we circumnavigate Anderson island counterclockwise starting from the northwest shore about 100 yards south of Eagle Island.

The island has approximately 14 miles of mostly forested shoreline, indented by two harbors and several smaller bays. No navigational hazards are charted off Anderson's shores as rocks and shallows are close to the island.

Public tidelands of about 20 parcels surround the island. We point out general locations as we reach them. Beaches are accessible only by water and uplands are private.

Settlements and developments scattered around the island with the grocery store inland, serving as the chatting-gathering place on the island. This is a friendly, close community, brought together by the circumstance of isolation from urban areas.

Along Anderson's gently sloping northern shores are farms, fields, cabins, and a few new large homes.

East of **Otso Point,** at the northwest corner of the island, are remains of **Johnson's Landing,** for many years the island's main steamer stop until ferry service to Steilacoom started and the ferry landing was moved north of Yoman Point.

Drayton Pass opens up after rounding Otso Point.

Higgins Cove is the first bay along the northwest shore, **West Bay** is the second, both charted but unnamed. They're too shallow for anchoring and dry at low tide.

Public tidelands of about 2,500 feet are between the two bays.

Cable area to Key Peninsula is south of West Bay.

Public tidelands extend from south of West Bay for about 1.1 miles. to across the entrance of Amsterdam Bay, a little less than two miles south of Otso Point.

Amsterdam Bay has a sandspit across the entrance, and is nearly 0.5 mile long with homes along its forested shores. Islanders anchor small boats in the bay and run in and out frequently. We would go in only a rising tide, but we haven't done it yet. Local knowledge is necessary to enter the inner bay because of extensive sandbars. ⚓ **Anchoring** is possible in an outer bay in calm weather, especially to dinghy ashore and explore the public tidelands. The outer bay is one fathom at low tide and can offer some protection from a strong southerly, but there's better protection in Longbranch across Drayton Pass, out of the weather. A charted large rock is off the northern tip of the bay.

☸ **Treble Point** is the most westerly point of Anderson Island, with a high bluff.

Public tidelands of about one mile wrap around the point. As we continue around the point, we're now in the waters of **Nisqually Reach.**

Carlson Bay, tiny, drying and not suitable as an anchorage, is about 0.5 mile south and east of the point. In the bay is a beautiful beach, **Andy's Marina Park**, a great place for kids to play, with a nature trail, but no overnight camping. ⚓ **Anchoring** is possible outside the little bay if it's calm, then dinghy in and enjoy this delightful little park. Washington Water Trails may establish a campsite here for hand-powered boats.

☸ **Continuing** along this southwest shore of Anderson depths range from 13 to 27 fathoms about 0.1 mile offshore.

Public tidelands are along the shore from Carlson Bay, past Thompson Cove on the southwest edge of the island, all the way to Lyle Point, more than two miles.

Thompson Cove shoals to just one fathom. During an unusually low tide (minus) -three feet, we saw the cove was dry. Outside the cove, depths are between six and nine fathoms.Erratic rocks are along the east shore.

Cable area comes ashore in Thompson Cove from Nisqually Head.

Fl R 4s 6M "2" Lyle Point Light 2, flashing red, is on a triangular red daybeacon on a dolphin at the southern tip of the island. Charted submerged obstructions are at unknown depths offshore. Tide rips and chop may make the water turbulent off the point.

Onshore there's a gradually sloping bank which rises back from the shore at a fairly even rate.

After we pass Lyle Point, we can continue northerly around the island or head into East Oro Bay and then into the western arm where there's good anchorage.

East Oro Bay, between Lyle Point and Cole Point, is about 0.7 mile across and about 0.5 mile long. There's a charted rock along the south shore, a charted wreck along the northwest shore and shallow water in a north cove.

A small channel opens to the west leading to Vega, charted, and to what we think of as West Oro Bay, but is called Vega Bay on island maps.

West Oro Bay has three docks with floats in the south end, Anderson Island's Oro Bay Yacht Club and outstations for both Tacoma and Bremerton yacht clubs. Mostly the shores are tree-lined and fairly low bank. ⚓ **Anchor** in Oro Bay in one to two fathoms (at low tide), mud bottom.

It's peaceful and quiet in here—we're in a **lovely gunkhole.**
Ⓖ **Public tidelands** cover much of inner Oro Bay, especially north of the entrance. There's also about 2,000 feet

Christian and Helda Christensen, who lived in a little log cabin at the outer limits of New Amsterdam Bay in February of 1872, were the first settlers on Anderson Island.

➡ **Currents in Nisqually Reach** south of Lyle Point may flow west at 2.85 knots at (F) thru (F+1), and may flow east at 1.6 knots at (E) thru (E+1) during extreme tides.

State Parks had hoped to acquire some land in the north part of Oro/Vega Bay for use as a State Marine Park, but were stopped during the 1995 legislative session.

Too bad, it would have been a wonderful spot for a park.

Private moorages in West Oro Bay south of entrance channel

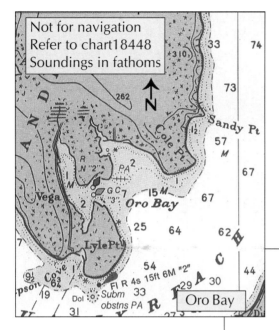

Not for navigation
Refer to chart18448
Soundings in fathoms

around the south side of the channel entrance to the bay, around the north side of the channel entrance into East Oro Bay and along the bay head.

Entering West Oro (Vega) Bay, we swing wide around a shoal on the Lyle Point side of Oro Bay until we can see straight into the inner bay. We stay slightly to the north of midchannel. Lighted buoys marking the channel keep us from straying onto the shoals.

R N "2" Oro Bay Lighted buoy 2, a red nun buoy off the north shore entrance, has a flashing red 2 second light.

G C "3" Oro Bay Lighted buoy 3, a green can buoy off the south shore entrance, has a flashing green 2 second light.

We enter the bay on a rising tide if possible. We go slow and watch the depth sounder. Channel depths are as charted.

Puget, a Storm and Oro Bay

Peter Puget and his drenched band of explorers camped their third night out after a squally, rainy afternoon thunder storm thwarted progress. They found shelter in a small bay on the southeast shore of Anderson Island.

Puget's group may have been the first non-Native Americans to camp on Anderson Island.

On Tuesday, May 22, 1792, as Puget and his men headed south after exploring Pitt Pass and Ketron Island, they were hit with thunder, lightning and drenching rain about 3 p.m. That's when they found Oro Bay.

Archibald Menzies wrote in his journal: "Here three canoes with some men in them came to us from the eastern shore ... they had a quantity of the young shoots of raspberries & of the Triglochin maritimum which they gave us to understand was good to eat & freely offered us all they had which were accepted of & though we made no use of them yet we did not leave their generosity unpaid making a small present to each which was infinitely more valuable to them. We requested them to get us some fish & they went over immediately & brought us some Salmon & if we understood them right they told us there were plenty up a river on the eastern shore where they came from ... They paddled off again in the dusk of the evening so that we remain quiet & unmolested all night."

We left West Oro Bay one time on a falling tide, dropping to minus 2.5 feet, and our depth got a little scant and the water was too murky to see bottom. However, we went slowly and made it out just fine—after a few tense moments. No keel tracks this time.

An old ferry, Ocean City, is moored partially on the beach in Oro Bay while being restored

A Walk on Anderson Island

We anchored in West Oro Bay near the old pier and store building at Vega, rowed ashore and went for an island walk. When the owner of the Vega store tired of running it, he shut it down and it's been sitting vacant ever since, we were told. A weathered, old painted "Shell" sign on the building faces the water, a remnant of days when there was a fuel dock here.

We walked to Island General Store about 2.5 miles north of Vega on Eckenstam-Johnson Road. A good walk, and we caught some island flavor. Everyone waves driving by, it's rural and quiet. We passed a charming bed and breakfast, one of four on the island.

On our way we found "Wide Awake Hollow," the old, one-room Anderson Island School—no longer a school, but now on the National Register of Historic Buildings—and then passed the island cemetery.

At the shopping center is a market and deli owned by Jeff and his wife, the post office, a beauty shop and real estate offices. Jeff, wife and kids have been living on the island for years and he says they can't imagine living anywhere else. The store has everything you could possibly need, plus the deli has great yogurt cones, home made cinnamon rolls and all manner of luscious foods.

(continued on next page)

We talked with Jeff for quite a while. He was the "Knight in a Shining Van" who drove us back to Vega after we were caught in a heavy downpour while visiting his market. About a mile north of the shopping center is Johnson Farm, the island's historical museum and gift shop. Jo is about ready to move to Anderson Island, she's so enchanted by it, and having lived in the San Juans, she understands "island living."

We were, however, somewhat taken aback by sounds of firing practice from Fort Lewis Military Reservation south and east on the mainland, sounds which intruded into the peace and quiet of Anderson.

Old Vega store

⚓ **Underway again**, we head out of Oro Bay—carefully. **Cole Point** has some houses, and a fairly high, sandstone bare bluff.

Public tidelands of about 2,500 feet are along the south shores of the point. We saw deer grazing along the beach as we cruised past on several different occasions.

Less than 0.1 mile east of Cole Point, the water is over 60 fathoms.

Sandy Point, sheer and steep, north of a shallow cove, one fathom deep.

Riviera Country Club Marina is north of Sandy Point, a landscaped, parklike private facility with a pier, two mooring buoys, gazebo and launch ramp. This is part of a private residential development.

Public tidelands run from north of this development to Yoman Point, over 1.5 miles of sand and gravel beaches. Above are evergreens atop bluffs with no beach access, the only access is by water.

Yoman Point is a forested bluff about 0.3 mile south of Anderson ferry landing. The island has had ferry service since 1922. From the ferry landing, it's about a mile along the shore.

We're back to Eagle Island, ending our circumnavigation.

"Deerus Aquaticus"

Naming Anderson Island

Anderson Island was named by Commander Wilkes when he arrived in 1841 for Alexander Caulfield Anderson, who was in charge of Fort Nisqually. Anderson had done many "kindnesses" for Wilkes, who also named McNeil Island for Captain Henry McNeil of the Hudson's Bay Company steamer, the Beaver.

The Inskip Chart of 1846 showed the British frigate **Fisgard** *was stationed in the area from 1844 to 1847. Unaware that Anderson had been named, Inskip called it Fisgard. He also called McNeil Island Duntze for Capt. John A. Duntze of the frigate.*

In the mid-1870s Anderson was called Wallace Island, possibly either for a murdered young Pierce county man, Leander C. Wallace, or for William H. Wallace, appointed governor of Idaho Territory. Neither seems very plausible. It once again became Anderson when Washington Territory became a state in 1889.

The ferry Steilacoom makes a number of trips daily from Anderson Island to Steilacoom.

There are working commuters who prefer the ambiance of island living and enjoy the daily ferry ride. Anderson high school youngsters also commute by ferry to a mainland high school.

In Chapter 16 we visit the mainland shores from north of Steilacoom through Nisqually and Johnson Point to Henderson Inlet, an area which includes the incredibly beautiful Nisqually National Wildlife Refuge.

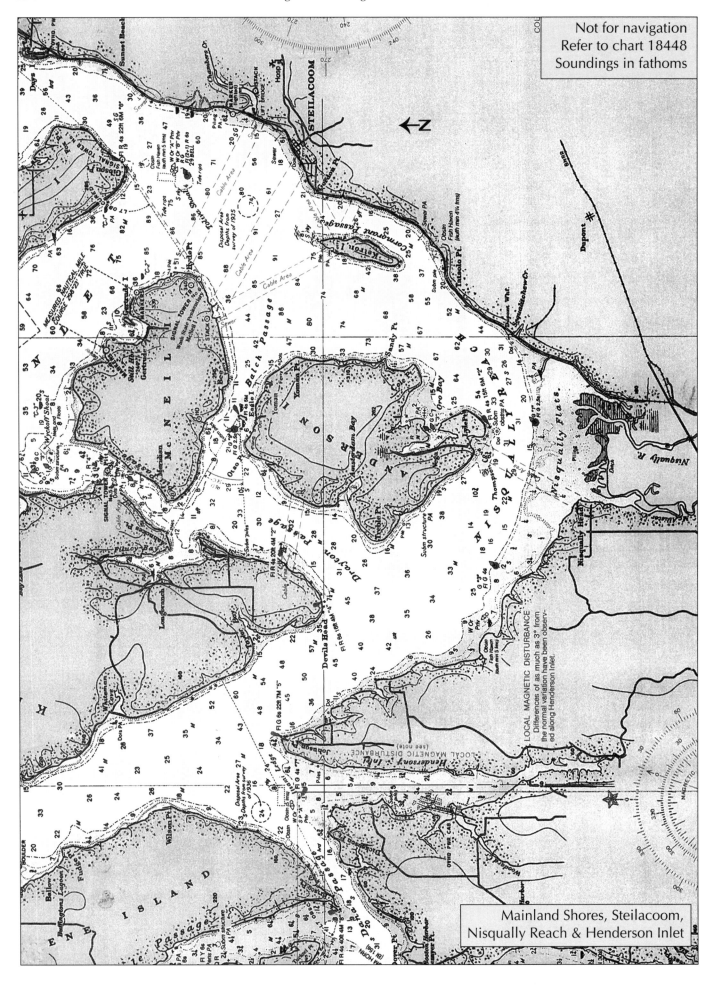

Not for navigation
Refer to chart 18448
Soundings in fathoms

Mainland Shores, Steilacoom,
Nisqually Reach & Henderson Inlet

CHAPTER 16
Mainland Shores: Steilacoom, Nisqually Reach & Henderson Inlet

Chart	Date	Title	Scale	Soundings
** **18445**	06/03/95	Puget Sound—Possession Sound to Olympia, page C	1:80,000	Fathoms
** **18448**	10/30/93	Puget Sound Southern Part	1:80,000	Fathoms
18440	08/05/95	Puget Sound	1:150,000	Fathoms
		Tidal Current Charts, Puget Sound, Southern Part		
		Booklet: Puget Sound Shellfish Sites		
		Washington State Public Lands Quad Map—Tacoma	1:100,000	

Charts and publications for this chapter

➡ *When using charts, compare your chart dates with ones referred to above. There may be discrepancies between different charts and different chart editions.*

Mainland Shore

Let's go back now to Toliva Shoal and the confluence of the south end of The Narrows, Carr Inlet and waters to the south. We left off at the gravel pit on the eastern mainland shore back in Chapter 13 after following Peter Puget into Hale Passage.

In this chapter, after cruising past Toliva Shoal once again, we head south, looking into Chambers Creek, Steilacoom, Ketron Island and Nisqually Flats. Then we go west to Tolmie State Park, north to Johnson Point, and south into Henderson Inlet, a distance of about 18 to 20 miles.

This whole area is charged with historical events that affected the entire Northwest. We'll touch on history, now and then, and continue cruising, blending past with present.

Trains rumbling along the shore are almost constant companions from Salmon Beach north of The Narrows Bridge to Nisqually Reach where they turn inland.

The reverberation of Fort Lewis firing practice detracts from the usual peace and tranquillity of Nisqually Reach.

Underway again

⚓ We start heading south along the east mainland shore, east of Toliva Shoal.

Fl (2+1) R Toliva Shoal Lighted Bell Buoy, with a flashing red light, is on a red and green banded bell buoy. The well-known navigational marker is about one mile south of Gibson Point on Fox Island, 1.7 miles east of Hyde Point on McNeil Island and about 1.3 miles northwest of Chambers Creek on the mainland.

The Pioneer and Glacier Gravel pits are about one mile east of Toliva Shoal on the mainland shore. The pits are charted as two ravines on 18448 with two buoys offshore. On 18445 only the buoys are charted. The gravel pits extend south almost to Chambers Creek—they're enormous and hard to miss.

Lighted marker is charted with no other description about 0.6 mile south of the gravel pit buoys. There is no charted reason, color, light or ownership of the marker that we could see.

Stack is charted on the southeast side of Chambers lagoon, about 0.5 mile southeast of the lighted marker.

➡ **NOTE: Marine fuel** is available in the areas covered in this chapter at **Puget Marina,** gas only, and **Zittel's Marina,** gas and diesel.

Toliva, Steilacoom, Ketron Is.

Not for navigation
Refer to chart 18448
Soundings in fathoms

Public tidelands of about six parcels cover about 4.5 miles of shorelines in this area.

We take the State Quadrangle Map, Tacoma, with us when we go ashore to avoid trespassing on adjacent private property. Unless otherwise noted, the public tidelands we mention are state-owned; some of them may be leased for aqua-culture.

In addition, there are federal public lands in the Nisqually National Wildlife Refuge.

When pioneer Ezra Meeker visited Steilacoom in 1853, he was impressed with "an air of business bustle that made one feel here was a center of trade ... we had not proceeded far before we came in sight of a fleet of seven vessels lying at anchor in a large bay of several miles ... We had never before seen so many ships at one place as were quietly lying at anchor in front of the embryo city."

Each July 4th a fireworks barge is taken from McNeil Island prison to Sunnyside Beach Park and anchors off the beach. One year the anchor dragged, creating a moving fireworks display.

Steilacoom

Lighted marker is charted on the west shore of Carr Inlet about 5.3 miles northwest with no other description and is exactly in line with the stack and lighted marker on the eastern mainland shore described above. We have no other information on these markers. We also do not know if the markers on this southern mainland shore are really in place at this time.

Chambers Creek is 0.2 mile south of the charted marker and less than one mile north of Steilacoom. It empties into a natural preserve at Chambers Lagoon at the south side of the gravel pit. The creek's canyon, to the east and north, is the habitat for spawning salmon runs. The steeply forested banks are home to small mammals, deer, bobcats, birds, and all types of other small critters.

Depths of zero (0) fathoms, one foot, on chart 18445, and 1/4 fathom on 18448 are near the entrance to Chambers Creek. We have no information about a dredged channel or depths in the lagoon.

Railroad lift bridge with uncharted vertical clearances or opening signals cross the entrance.

Chambers Creek Boat Owners Association has private, covered moorage for approximately 50 powerboats. Some boats moored here need the bridge raised to transit the low, shallow, narrow entrance under the railroad tracks, and must call the bridge tender. At low tide some of the boats sit in the mud. A storage facility for 100 trailerable boats is located just east of the moorage in the creek.

Launch ramp is inside Chambers Creek on the south shore.

Cable area immediately south of Chambers Creek crosses to McNeil Island.

Sunnyside Beach Park, about 0.5 mile south of Chambers Creek and about the same distance north of downtown Steilacoom, is a popular spot in summer.

⚓ **Anchoring** is possible in less than six fathoms. This is about the only place to land a skiff safely on the beach because of large rocks along the shore.

Sunnyside Beach Park attractions include a good swimming beach and fishing. Scuba diving is great at nearby Toliva Shoal, 1.5 miles north-northwest. There are restrooms, a play area and a picnic area.

⚙ **The historical city of Steilacoom is our next stop,** and for the historically-minded Steilacoom is a treasure. In 1854, Steilacoom became the first incorporated town in Washington territory.

Large sailing ships no longer lie at anchor in the bay, as they did in the late 1800s. Instead, Steilacoom is the terminus for the ferries to Anderson, Ketron and McNeil Islands, and launches which run to the prison on McNeil.

Arriving at Steilacoom by boat, the city is easily identified by the ferry terminal and adjacent docks. While there is no guest moorage for recreational boaters in downtown Steilacoom, there is a small float on the northeast side of the ferry dock for loading and unloading boats under 26 feet.

Clyde B. Davidson Fishing Pier, public and popular, is southwest of the ferry dock. There is private moorage.

Launch ramp goes under waterfront railroad tracks just north of the ferry dock. There is parking for boat trailers on the land side of the tracks. A short distance beyond the parking area is Steilacoom Marine Service which carries supplies for small boats and does motor repairs.

⚓ **Anchoring** is possible in calm weather for a short time to row to the beach near the launch ramp. Holding ground is poor; the bottom is rock ballast dumped from sailing ships which anchored here 100 years earlier.

Depths from the beach slope steeply to more than 10 fathoms 150 yards offshore.

The ***Coast Pilot*** warns, " ... off Steilacoom there are tide rips which, with a wind opposing the current, are dangerous to small boats."

Cable area is on either side of the ferry terminal crossing, to McNeil Island.

Boaters who do get ashore have discovered that within three blocks of the ferry dock there are two small grocery stores with delis.

Steilacoom launch ramp

The Steilacoom Historical Museum in the Town Hall basement has an excellent display of pioneer artifacts. There are some 27 historic home sites in the town, several listed on the National Register of Historic Sites, plus monuments honoring historical occasions.

Walking tours conducted by docents from the Steilacoom Historical Association may be arranged. Phone: 206-584-4133

The Steilacoom Tribal Cultural Center and Museum occupies an historic building, the old Oberlin Congregational Church. There is a collections repository, a gift shop featuring traditional, handmade gifts, books on Indian culture, contemporary artwork, Indian artifacts and a snack bar features traditional Native American foods.

Delightful Bair Drug and Hardware, built in 1895, is a combination living museum and restaurant. The store housed the town post office for a time. You can eat great food while browsing amidst relics of years past in a friendly, Victorian setting. It's quite unique—and just a couple of blocks up the hill from the town dock.

⚓ **Underway again, we pass Gordon Point,** about one mile south of the Steilacooom ferry dock.

Steilacoom Marina, charted as #84 on 18445, is just south of Gordon Point. Facilities are as listed, except gas is no longer available.

The marina is adjacent to **Saltar Point Beach Park**, a Steilacoom recreation area. The day-use park has both picnic and play areas.

The only land access to the marina or the park is by way of a foot bridge over the railroad tracks.

Fort Steilacoom was built near Gordon Point, but the present city of Steilacoom is the amalgamation of two rival towns built one mile apart on this large bay in 1851.

Captain Layfayette Balch established Port Steilacoom on January 23, 1851. About a mile west Steilacoom City was built on a land claim by John B. Chapman on August 23, 1851. The two men eventually got together and in 1854 Steilacoom became the first incorporated town in Washington territory.

Other territory "firsts" for Steilacoom include the first Protestant church in 1853, the first public library in 1858, and the first jail in 1858.

Steilacoom Marina Facilities

➤ Moorage for 5-10 guest boats in the unoccupied spaces at the north and south ends of the marina
➤ Moorage rates 40 cents per foot per day
➤ 20 amp shore power at $2 per day, water
➤ Restrooms, showers, laundry
➤ The marina is exposed to most winds, weather is a caution
➤ Covered, elevated, dry storage building in the center of the marina
➤ Small-boat sling for haulouts
➤ Marine repairs
➤ Basic store, tackle, bait
➤ Rental boat facility
➤ Phone: 206-582-2600

Cable area runs from Gordon Point to Ketron Island.

⚓ **Ketron Island**, wooded and private, is a little more than one mile southwest of Steilacoom by ferry across Cormorant Passage. The island is about 1.25 miles long and 0.3 mile wide, with a fair number of homes rimming the island's bluff shores.

Steilacoom Marina

Ketron Island was named by Wilkes during his 1841 expedition for William Kittson who supervised construction of Fort Nisqually for the Hudson Bay Co. Cartographers misspelled his name, and it's been Ketron Island ever since.

A train derailed during heavy rain in February 1996. The engine and a freight car slid into Puget Sound after hitting a mudslide south of Steilacoom.

➡ **Currents in Cormorant Passage** may flow north at 1.35 knots at (E+1) thru (E+2), and may flow south at 0.6 knots at (F+1) thru (F+2) during extreme tides.

Cormorant Passage was named in 1846 by R.M. Inskip of the Royal Navy, for the **S.S. Cormorant,** the first steam naval ship to visit this region.

The marina near the Ketron ferry landing on the northeast shore is now abandoned. It did feel lonesome there, with no one around, just empty floats where there had apparently once been a fuel float and moorage. There were old pilings, a couple of fuel tanks on the shore, a high bank with houses above it, a cable area with a "do not anchor" sign, and a private launch ramp with some trailered boats parked nearby.

We understand several different yacht clubs have shown an interest in the marina to turn it into an outstation, but to our knowledge it hasn't happened yet. They're nervous it might blow away in a bad storm.

The ferry landing is definitely not abandoned, it is the lifeline for those who live in the relative isolation and privacy of Ketron.

Vancouver, Puget & Ketron Island

Both Capt. Vancouver and Peter Puget and their parties ended up on Ketron Island in 1792, just a couple of days apart.

On May 22 Puget's men landed on Ketron (he called it Long Island) for a short time "as Mr. Whidbey wishd to take up his former angular bearings."

Four days later, on May 26, Vancouver and his men camped on the island for the night. Vancouver wrote of it ... "Whilst employed in arranging our matters for the night, we discovered, coming out of the southernmost opening (between Anderson Island and the mainland), two small vessels, which, at first, were taken for Indian canoes, but, on using our glasses, they were considered to be our two boats. (Those rowed and sailed by Puget and Whidbey and their men.) The evening was cloudy; and closing in very soon, prevented a positive decision. The original idea was, however, somewhat confirmed on firing two muskets, which were not answered."

Menzies, the botanist traveling with Puget, entered in his journal on the same date. . . " In the dusk of the evening as we were passing the Island on which we dind on the 22d near the Eastern shore of the Main Arm we saw a fire kindled upon it which we could not suppose then to be any one else but the Natives, till we afterwards understood that it was Capt. Vancouver and his party putting up for the evening, they likewise observed our Boats & Sails, but as we were at some distance they took us for Canoes & so they went on surveying & examining the very ground that we had gone over."

Cormorant Pass between Ketron and the mainland is about 0.5 mile wide with no charted navigational hazards.

Public tidelands in two parcels are about 500 yards south of Gordon Point in Cormorant Pass, one with about 1,500 feet of shoreline and the other over 2,000 feet, separated by about 800 feet of private beach.

Cable area runs from Ketron to about 0.6 mile south of Gordon Point.

Public tidelands of two parcels totaling about 3,000 feet are along the mainland shore of Cormorant Pass, and about 2,000 feet of tidelands are around the southwest shore of Ketron, below barren bluffs.

Fort Lewis Military Reservation begins less than one mile south of Gordon Point, covering hundreds of acres inland and more than 3.5 miles of shoreline along forested banks. While cruising in this area we may occasionally hear the blasts of shelling practice. Fort Lewis Military Reservation is south of Steilacoom and east of Nisqually Flats. Its boundaries are defined on the quadrangle map.

Fish haven is charted at four fathoms depth about 0.5 mile northeast of Tatsolo Point.

Launch ramp is charted on 18445. It appears to be on the military reservation.

Sequalitchew Creek is about 1.25 miles south of **Tatsolo Point,** the site of the 340 foot long **Dupont Wharf** at the mouth of the creek. The abandoned, old barge near the wharf has been there for years.

The shoreline is still fairly untouched with a sandy beach near the wharf. Crabbing is supposed to be good here, at least that is what those who catch them tell us.

The railroad tracks along the shore, which have been with us since south of Point Defiance, now turn inland and sounds from the passing trains diminish into the distance. The sounds now are the cry of the gulls and the wind in our rigging.

The village of Dupont, inland, is the new home of Intel computer chips.

Depths south of the Dupont Wharf marked by green buoys "1" and "3" (to the west) shoal abruptly from as much as 20 fathoms to zero (0) fathoms with drying mudflats at MLLW. The wide expanse of open water is deceptive.

We are at the eastern end of Nisqually Reach.

This broad sweep of water runs south and west between the mainland and Anderson Island for about four miles, with two green buoys marking the shoals off Nisqually Flats. West of buoy "3," the reach trends northwest another four miles to Case Inlet.

G "1" Nisqually Flats Lighted Buoy 1 with flashing green 2.5 second light, is nearly 1.5 miles west of Dupont Wharf and 0.7 mile north of the Nisqually delta.

G "3" Nisqually Flats Lighted Buoy 3 with flashing green four second light, is almost 2.5 miles west and only slightly north of the first buoy. The two green buoys mark the northern edge of the flats.

The shallows off the flats extend over one mile north from shore and bare at low water. They are soft mud and the edge drops abruptly to 10 fathoms and more.

Fishing is good in the Nisqually Reach area, and we know a number of people who set their crab pots here during the season and catch beautiful Dungeness crabs.

> ➡ **Currents in Nisqually Reach** are described briefly in Chapter 15, page 231. For more detail, see Appendix, pages 328-335.

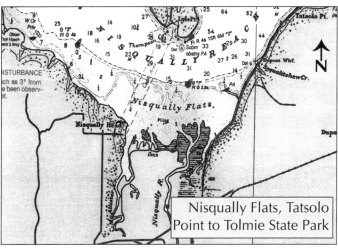

Nisqually Flats, Tatsolo Point to Tolmie State Park

Not for navigation
Refer to chart 18448
Soundings in fathoms

A Touch of Nisqually History

Nearby Indians appreciated the bounty of the delta, intimately familiar with all the creatures that lived there, reaping only that which they needed in the grasslands and marshes. They established a village on the bluff east of the delta.

The delta is the site of the original Hudson Bay Company trading post, built in 1833, about 0.25 mile inland.

The Nisqually Hudson Bay Company Post was built in 1836, a mile farther east and convenient to Sequalitchew Creek.

The Wilkes Expedition arrived at Fort Nisqually on May 11, 1841, and were greeted by Captain McNeil and Mr. Anderson of H.B.C. They spent some time at Nisqually while Wilkes was surveying and charting much of Puget Sound and related areas. He measured the altitude of Mount Rainier and wrote in his diary that he concluded it was 14,850 feet high, an error of only 440 feet from the 14,410 feet actual height. They left May 19 for Astoria, returning on June 23, when they once again directed officers in charting and surveying, and enjoyed a 4th of July celebration. (See page 242)

In 1854, the post was described by George Gibbs: "It is situated at some distance from the water, on a high, undulating prairie, and is a cluster of small buildings, of no great value, within a stockade."

The historic **Medicine Creek Treaty of 1854**, in which the Indians gave up just about everything and were moved off their native lands to reservations, was signed at Medicine Creek, two miles inland, near the present, heavily traveled Interstate-5 Freeway.

Nisqually name

The Native American name 'Squally' originated from the beautiful wild flowers and herbs which grew in abundance.

In Indian jargon 'squally' means beauty and peace. Our big Webster's says it means gusty and stormy.

The Squally Indians who lived in what is now Pierce County, were peace-loving people who got along well with the Hudson Bay Company men, the first non-Natives in the area.

Another version of the name is that Nisqually originated from the French explorers, who called the Indians "nez quarre," meaning "square nose."

They say the word was altered by the Indians' inability to pronounce the letter "r."

Nisqually National Wildlife Refuge

Capt. George Vancouver *visited the flats on Sunday, May 27, 1792. He said: "... The inlet here terminated in an expansive though shallow bay, across which a flat of land extended upwards of a mile from its shores; on which was lying an immense quantity of drift wood, consisting chiefly of very large trees. The country behind, for some distance, was low, then rose gradually to a moderate height; and, like the eastern shores of the inlet, was covered with wood, and diversified with pleasant inequalities of hill and dale, though not enriched with those imaginary parks and pleasure grounds we had been accustomed to behold nearer to the sea coast; the whole presenting one uninterrupted wilderness."*

Nisqually National Wildlife Refuge

The refuge was established in 1974 to protect the delta and its rich diversity of fish and wildlife habitats. Nisqually is a stop for migratory birds with more than 15,000 ducks, geese and shorebirds flying in during fall and winter months. Later in the winter other birds arrive, while in spring there are goldfinches, warblers and tree swallows. Bald eagles frequent the flats in winter.

Salmon and steelhead pass through the estuary as they head upriver to spawn. Small mammals, songbirds, woodpeckers and hawks live in the dense woodlands and grasslands of the refuge. A detailed list of the 176 species birds observed at the wildlife refuge, and 36 other birds species, is available at the information center at the refuge. The list also contains mammals, reptiles, amphibians and fish that live in or on the delta. There are also pamphlets giving a much more detailed history of the delta than we can provide here. The Nisqually River winds through the whole refuge. With 3,780 acres, it is one of the largest remaining undisturbed estuaries in Washington.

You can visit the Wildlife Refuge by land and hike the easy trails that are 0.5 mile, one mile and 5.5 miles long. Visit the Twin Barns Education Center. From the trails you'll see wildlife habitats and enjoy the birds, the wildlife, the beauty and peace of the delta.

Boating is permitted in waters outside the Brown Farm Dike. This is a fabulous place to explore the wildlife refuge of saltmarsh and creeks, inland meadows and forests. The view of Mount Rainier and the Nisqually delta from here is absolutely spectacular. Canoeists, kayakers and small boaters should beware of hazardous tides, shallow waters, wind and weather conditions around the Nisqually Delta. No boat landings are allowed on refuge lands. The nearest public boat ramp is at Luhr Beach.

Fishing is allowed from boats in the Nisqually River or McAllister Creek, or from designated areas along the river banks which can be reached by foot or by boat.

Tideflats are open to fishing and shellfishing. Access is by boat or by foot from Luhr Beach. Access to the tideflats is not permitted from the Brown Farm Dike. All state fishing regulations are in effect.

Mt. Rainer from Luhr Beach

Nisqually Delta is truly a national treasure.

Beginning about where the Nisqually Flats start, Nisqually National Wildlife Refuge boundaries are best defined on the quadrangle map. The Burlington Northern railroad tracks near Red Salmon Creek, unnamed on the charts, mark the eastern boundary of the refuge; the western boundary is along McAllister Creek, the southern boundary skims bustling noisy Interstate-5 Freeway.

For more information, contact the Refuge Manager, Nisqually NWR, 100 Brown Farm Road, Olympia, WA., 98506.
Phone: 360-753-9467

Luhr Beach boat ramp (unmarked on charts but marked on the quad map) is at the eastern shore of **Nisqually Head.** The ramp is accessible at mid-to-high tides.

Nisqually Reach Nature Center is just south of Luhr Beach launch ramp. Not affiliated with the Nisqually Wildlife Refuge, there are environmental displays and a mounted bird collection in the building.

Public fishing pier, partially covered, is at the Center.

⚓ **Underway again**, we head west and north from Nisqually Head to Tolmie Park. There are four very small, drying bays along the way. The water is shoal from Nisqually Head to buoy "G3."

A small, "midden point" sticks out into Hogum Bay, unnamed on the charts (between the first and second tiny bays); white oyster shells are on the beach near the Hogum Bay Oyster Company.

Next is the community of Beachcrest with its waterfront homes and tiny lagoon. Trees are along the shore, and so are plenty of waterfront homes.

Then we see the old Atlas Powder dock. We understand there are plans to build an industrial port here, and we wonder how this can happen so close to the National Wildlife Refuge. How dreadful for the environment and the beauty of the delta.

We pass buoy "G3" which has a couple of resident sea lions who check us out as thoroughly as we check them out as we sail past.

There's a channel south from the buoy to the old Atlas dock. Nearby is a large boat which looks like an old, shipwrecked tug, as shown on the charts.

Now, more homes on the banks and "Butterball Cove"—just a tiny tidal lagoon (unnamed on the charts). Ⓖ We've reached **Tolmie State Park,** about 2.4 miles north and west of Nisqually Head, an absolute jewel along this shoreline, well worth visiting. The park is a lovely place to spend a day or two, a **gunkhole**.

Tolmie is one mile west of green buoy "3." It's easy to spot not only because of the state mooring buoys, but also because it's the only place along the shore without homes. Mooring buoys, "fish haven" buoys, and a scuba diving area are charted at the park.

Let the kids play, hike in the woods on more than three miles of well marked trails, scuba dive, swim, dig clams and beachcomb. It has just about everything, and you can land your skiff anywhere along the park beach.

Even Peter Puget, our intrepid explorer, found that "The water had shoaled quite across to four and five feet. That stopped our further progress toward the shore as it was falling tide and I was fearful of ... " being grounded.

Buoy G "3" at Nisqually Flats and wreck at Lat. N122° 46.4" Long. W47°05.5"

Tolmie State Park Facilities
➤ Five mooring buoys
➤ 1,800 feet of shoreline
➤ 106 acre day-use park
➤ Outside shower for divers and swimmers next to lower restroom
➤ Artificial reef for scuba divers, fishermen, marked by two white can buoys with orange stripes, not suitable for mooring
➤ 42 picnic tables and two kitchen shelters
➤ Phone: 360-753-1519

White and orange buoys mark three barges sunk below the low water mark to form the artificial reef which attracts fish and other sea life. It provides recreational scuba diving in an area relatively free of currents.

Big Slough is a large salt marsh in the park between a long sandspit and the uplands, with a bridge across the marsh. Throughout the park are five interpretive sites describing the hydraulics of the sand flats, the estuary fauna and flora, and explaining the view from the high ground of the park, with a brief history of sea-shore life in the area. This is a peaceful, lovely park to enjoy nature.

Sandy Point, unnamed on the charts, is immediately northwest of Tolmie Park.

Dogfish Bight, unnamed on the charts, is a long shallow bay, just beyond Sandy Point. There are many homes along the waterfront.

Puget Marina is next, about 1.75 miles northwest of Tolmie Park, and about two miles southeast of Johnson Point. It's easy to locate because of the long float leading into the water below the repair yard. Both NOAA charts show a road access to the shoreline which is visible from offshore.

Puget Marina Facilities
➤ Launch ramp with float, fee $5
➤ Fuel: gas only
➤ Parking for trucks and trailers
➤ Operates Memorial Day to Labor Day
➤ Boat and engine sales and service
➤ Phone: 360-491-7388

A windmill is between Puget Marina and Mill Bight.

Mill Bight, unnamed on charts, is the next bay northwest of Puget Marina.

Depths charted at one fathom at the mouth of the cove, it goes dry at low tides inside the bay. Shores are private.

Baird Cove, unnamed on the charts, is about one mile northwest of Mill Bight or about 0.8 mile southeast of Johnson Point.

Zittel's Marina is on the west side of the entrance. Depths in this cove are not charted, and we believe it to be shallow at best. Friends have anchored here in high tides when tidal change is not significant. We haven't tried it. Surrounding shores are private.

Zittel's Marina is at the entrance of Baird Cove. Zittel's is a favorite spot with South Sound fishing persons. The fuel dock is on the northeast end of the guest float, which is also the moorage check-in. There is a log boom breakwater to the east of the dock. In between the two sets of permanent moorage floats, near the store and snack bar, is a launch ramp.

Zittel's Marina

Zittel's Marina Facilities

➤ Guest moorage for 10 to 15 boats along outside float, exposed to north wind
➤ Moorage rates approximately 35 cents per foot per night
➤ Some shore power
➤ Water
➤ Fuel: gas and diesel
➤ Restrooms
➤ Launch ramp
➤ Haulout lift for boats up to 50 feet or 50,000 pounds
➤ Marine repairs done on premises
➤ Boat storage
➤ Rentals, boat and motor sales
➤ Marine supplies, fishing supplies
➤ Store with groceries, snack bar
➤ Phone: 360-459-1950

We attempted to ease *Scheherazade* into Zittel's on a minus (-) 3.4 tide. Heading for the guest float from the north, her 5.5 foot draft grounded gently on soft mud about 25 feet from the dock. We backed off with no problems, and we left our trademark keel tracks.

Zittel's later said had we approached from farther east we would have been in the channel leading directly into the fuel dock and would have had enough water. New "local knowledge" learned by the touch system.

⚓ **Johnson Point** is at the northwest end of Nisqually Reach and about two miles northwest of Devils Head on the southern tip of Key Peninsula.

Fl G 6s 22ft 7M "5" Johnson Point Light 5 flashing green light on a square green dayboard on pile is just off the end of the point.

The bluff behind Johnson Point rises to 90 feet above the many residences that wrap around the point.

Not for navigation
Refer to chart 18448
Soundings in fathoms

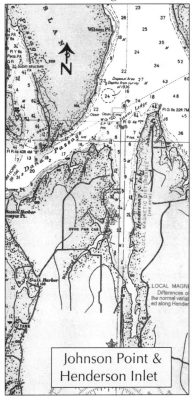

Johnson Point &
Henderson Inlet

Johnson Point & a Clam Bake

Johnson Point was originally named Moody Point by Wilkes, but the name was changed later when the point became the home of J. R. Johnson, M.D.

Pioneer Ezra Meeker, his brother and their wives visited Johnson during the summer of 1853. They had spent the previous night camping in Henderson Inlet, and they found Johnson the next morning in his cabin on the point.

"He had the pretentious name of 'Johnson's Hospital,' opened, as he said, for the benefit of the sick, but which, from what I saw in my later trips, think his greatest business was in disposing of cheap whisky of which he contributed his share of the patronage," Meeker wrote.

At a large Indian encampment nearby, the Meeker party was introduced to a "regular, old-fashioned clam bake," which Meeker raved about later.

(continued on next page)

(continued from preceding page)

"And so the kitchen of the camp was surrendered to the native matron ... who began tearing down our camp fire. She quietly covered the hot pebbles and sand where the fire had been with a light layer of pebbles, upon which the clams were deposited and some fine twigs placed on top, upon which earth was deposited.

" ... If you never have participated in a clam bake then go straightway, before you die, to the end that you may ever after have the memory of the first clam bake."

The pioneers soon realized they need never go hungry, that twice a day when the tide was out there would be food ready for the taking.

The Indians lived remarkably peacefully with the English and traded with them at various posts after the Europeans arrived in "Whulge" country. Whulge was the Indian name for the inland sea or saltwater, and occasionally there are movements to rename Puget Sound to its original name. Why not?

Fl G 4s "4" Itsami Ledge Light 7 flashing green light on a square green dayboard 20 feet high on a dolphin, marks Itsami Ledge. The light is about one mile west and south of Johnson Point, roughly in the center of Henderson Inlet entrance.

This has long been considered a good fishing area.

There is good scuba diving on a reef near Itsami Ledge, about 1,100 feet northwest of the light, in 50 to 70 feet.

Henderson Inlet, called **South Bay** locally, is just west of Johnson Point.

Dickenson Point marks the western entrance to the inlet, which extends about 4.5 miles in a southerly direction from Itsami Ledge.

Depths of five to nine fathoms are charted in Henderson Inlet. The three fathom curve extends about 2.1 mile into the inlet from Itsami Ledge, shoaling to about one fathom in the next 0.6 mile. The southern 1.7 miles of extensive mud flats dry at MLLW.

Widths of Henderson shore-to-shore are about 0.7 mile near the entrance, tapering irregularly to about 0.5 mile at the charted one fathom depth toward the south end. The width shrinks to about 300 yards wide for the last 1.5 miles of mud flats.

Possibly the most interesting things about shallow, narrow Henderson Inlet are the magnetic disturbances and the enormous number of seals.

"Beach cruising"
Henderson Inlet

Magnetic Disturbance

A local magnetic disturbance is noted on the charts of Henderson Inlet. Difference of as much as 3° from the normal variation have been observed along the inlet, and it is also noted in the **Coast Pilot**. Frankly, we're lucky if we can steer within plus or minus 3° on any course on a calm day, so we haven't found the magnetic disturbance to be any problem.

According to the **Coast Pilot,** the definition of local magnetic disturbances is:

"If measured value of magnetic variation differ from the charted values by several degrees, a magnetic disturbance note will be printed on the chart. The note will indicate the location and magnitude of the disturbance, but the indicated magnitude should not be considered as the largest possible value that may be encountered. Large disturbances are more frequently detected in the shallow waters near land masses than on the deep sea. Generally, the effect of a local magnetic disturbance diminishes rapidly with distance, but in some locations there are multiple sources of disturbances and the effects may be distributed for many miles."

About midway along the west shore of Henderson Inlet, are many old pilings and some log booms, some of them covered with seals. There are signs on the pilings warning boaters to keep 100 yards away from the sunbathing mammals. Some looked up nonchalantly as we cruise past, others quietly slide into the water and keep a wary eye on us.

In places along the inlet, especially along the northern portion of the west shore, there is heavy residential development with many small boats anchored offshore.

Henderson Inlet
log booms & sunning seals

North of the charted pilings is a little nub of a point, Cliff Point, unnamed on the charts. While it is quite shallow north of this point, we noted several anchored boats tucked back in the small bight which were well out of a strong southerly. This could be a good place to seek temporary refuge in a south wind.

Woodard Bay Natural Resources Conservation Area is on the western shore of Henderson Inlet. It includes the Woodard Creek area on the southwest and the bay extending to the northwest, locally known as Chapman Bay. The boundaries are defined on the quad map.

The area is tucked back in behind the log booms. These inlets and the surrounding lands are managed by DNR as a wildlife conservation area, and they prefer people stayed out. However, it's okay to take a kayak, canoe or rowboat into Woodard Bay, but it will be muddy if you want to walk and there are no shore facilities.

The state Department of Natural Resources and Thurston County plan a series of hiking and biking trails to reach all over the county from the Woodard Bay Natural Resources Conservation area on the west shore of Henderson Inlet. Thurston County Parks Operation Manager Chuck Groth said the trail system could be in place by 1997. He said there would be public access from the water to the shore to reach the start of the trail.

Public tidelands of nearly 10,000 feet extend throughout the conservation area. The southern third of Henderson Inlet is mud flats and oyster beds.

Public tidelands starting about 2,500 feet north of the head of the inlet, extend north 4,000 feet along both shores in these tideflats.

⚓ **Anchoring is possible** in Henderson Inlet in two to five fathoms along the shores of the bay. The eastern shore has few indentations. Anchoring there would give little protection from northerlies and marginal protection from southerlies due to the fetch at the south end.

> **In Chapter 17** we explore Case Inlet—a fascinating place—one of our favorites, with some excellent places to cruise, anchor and moor.

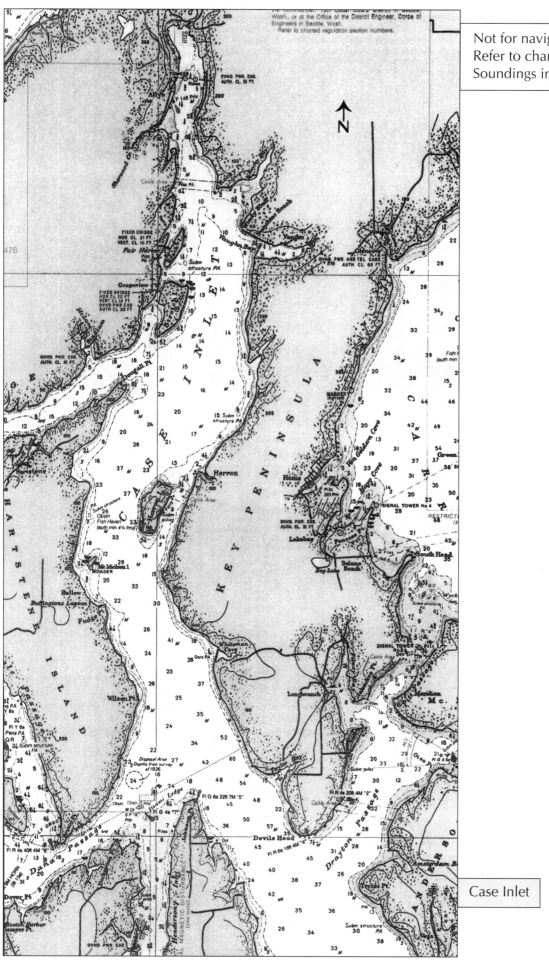

Not for navigation
Refer to chart 18448
Soundings in fathoms

Case Inlet

CHAPTER 17
Case Inlet

Charts and publications for this chapter

Chart	Date	Title	Scale	Soundings
**18445	06/03/95	Puget Sound—Possession Sound to Olympia, Page C	1:80,000	Fathoms
**18448	10/30/93	Puget Sound, Southern Part	1:80,000	Fathoms
18440	08/05/95	Puget Sound	1:150,000	Fathoms
		Tidal Current Charts, Puget Sound, Southern Part		
		Booklet: Puget Sound Shellfish Sites		
		Washington State Public Lands Quadrangle Map—Tacoma	1:100,000	

➡ *When using charts, compare your chart dates with ones referred to above. There may be discrepancies between different charts and different chart editions.*

Case Inlet Overview

This chapter covers 14 mile long Case Inlet between Hartstene Island and the mainland to the west and Key Peninsula to the east. The inlet runs from Devils Head and Johnson Point at the south, to muddy tide flats at Coulter Creek north of Allyn.

We feel the cruising just gets better and better the farther into South Sound we go, which is something of an oxymoron since at the moment we're actually going north up Case Inlet.

In this chapter we visit four state parks: Joemma Beach, McMicken Island, Hartstene Island and Stretch Point, the Port of Allyn, Fair Harbor Marina, and at least a couple of wonderful gunkholes in Case Inlet.

Currents north of Dana Passage in Case Inlet are shown as weak and variable in the *Tidal Current Tables* and *Tidal Current Charts*. The current station for Case Inlet is southeast of McMicken Island.

No navigational obstructions are charted in the inlet.

Although there are homes along the shores, the feeling is definitely not suburbia. It's basically bluffs, forests, beaches and small communities, and it feels quiet and comfortable, almost rural and pristine.

⚓ **Underway again,** starting from Devils Head at the southern end of Key Peninsula, we look up at the 280 foot high, heavily-wooded bluff, with its share of erratic rocks on the beach. Watch for eagles soaring the air currents above the bluff.

Fl R 6s 4M "4" Devils Head Light 4 is on a triangular red dayboard 22 feet high on a dolphin, just offshore of the southern end of Devils Head.

Currents between Devils Head and Johnson Point can be important to ragbaggers deciding to sail or power this area in light airs.

More than once we've had to shorten down and thrash to weather against heavy, southerly, squalls from Nisqually Reach. We've dived into steep, ebb chop sending spray over the entire vessel. At times solid water comes over our weather bow, soaking us and sending unsecured items below astray. The sea would be less troubled during weak or slack currents, and maybe a little less exciting.

So as we perceive the currents in this area from our own experience, and from the *Current Charts* and *Current Tables,* we have the following information:

➡ **NOTE: Marine gas** is available only in **Fair Harbor** in the areas covered in this chapter.

➡ **"The Current Thing"** regarding current information west of Case Inlet, is a four page special section on currents in this area of South Sound, found at the end of this chapter, pages 260-263.

Devils Head light

Approximately 12 miles of public tidelands are in this chapter.

Public tidelands unless otherwise noted are state owned. Some maybe leased and posted for aquaculture or other private use. We take the Washington State Public Lands Quadrangle Map, when going ashore at these locations to avoid trespassing on adjacent private property.

Devils Head was named by Capt. George Vancouver who claimed if you turned the chart upside down the area at the south end of Key Peninsula looked like Satan's head. We-l-l-l-l, possibly, with a bit of imagination.

Charles Taylor settled as the first permanent white pioneer on the Key Peninsula. A Scotsman, he had jumped ship from a British boat, married an Indian girl he called Bridget, and built his home and furniture entirely from driftwood they collected from the beach.

There was ferry service from Taylor Bay to Johnson Point from 1937 until 1942.

Maximum current speeds are based on the extreme max flood and ebb currents predicted in 1994 for the Tacoma Narrows. The northwest and southeast currents are mainstream currents. There will be backeddies forming downstream from projecting shoreline points and bumps.

To understand progressive changing current speeds and direction, we must study the hourly current charts in the order given below. (See Current Charts in the Appendix, pages 328-335.)

Currents between Devils Head & Johnson Point:
Flow roughly NW during the flood, as shown on charts (F-1) through (F+2)
　Maximum NW flood currents can exceed 0.75 knots during extreme flood ranges
　Maximum NW flood occurs at the same time as max flood at The Narrows, as shown on chart (F)
Flow roughly SE as shown on charts (F+3) and (E-1) through (E+3)
　Maximum SE current can exceed 1.17 knots during the extreme ebb ranges.
　Maximum SE ebb occurs about + 20 minutes after max ebb at The Narrows, as shown on charts on (E) and (E+1)
Weak currents and slack water occur **briefly** about 2 hours before max flood at The Narrows, that is, between charts (E+3) and (F-2). They occur again for a **longer period** of about one hour between two and three hours after max ebb at The Narrows as shown on charts (F+2) through (F+3).

Just after rounding Devils Head there are two tiny drying lagoons behind little hooks of land that are charted about 300 yards apart.

Public tidelands of about 1,500 feet are between the hooks; a sand and gravel beach. As with most DNR beaches, there is boat access only. This is a lovely beach and there are clams, sea cucumbers and red rock crabs.

"Johnson's South Sound Wildlife Refuge" is on a sign at the north lagoon.
⚓ **Anchoring** is possible for a short time, in calm weather, at low tide to be able to explore the beach. It is against the law to disturb the wildlife.

☸ **Taylor Bay** is next along the way north, a little over one mile from Devils Head. It's a rather picturesque bay with old pilings at the entrance and overhanging trees at the head. It's not a gunkhole, it goes dry at low tide. There are often shrimp and crab pot buoys just off the entrance during the seasons.

Public tidelands of more than 3,000 feet are immediately south of Taylor Bay, and another 1,500 foot long parcel is north of the bay. About 500 feet of private shore is next north, and then there is another 3,000 foot parcel of public tidelands. These public beaches have high forested private bluffs behind them, but no houses are on the shores.

⚓ **Anchoring** is possible in calm weather and at low tide. Kayakers find these beaches good stopping places to stretch their legs and beachcomb at low tides.

☸ **Underway again,** much of the shoreline along here has not been developed. It is still pristine because there are few roads in this part of Key Peninsula. Charted rocks are along the shoreline.

Public tidelands of about 4,000 feet are midway between Taylor Bay and Whiteman Cove, which is about 2.5 miles north of Taylor.

Whiteman Cove is no longer a "cove," but a landlocked lagoon behind a silted-over entrance, with another 1,000 feet of public land outside the lagoon.

Joemma Beach State Park is just north of Whiteman Cove, shown on chart 18445 as #91B, beside a "surfaced ramp." Park facilities exceed those listed. It is identified on the chart tabulation as Robert F. Kennedy Department of Natural Resources Education and Recreation Area.

The area has been called Joemma Beach almost as long as anyone can remember. DNR obtained it in 1966, when it was named in memory of RFK. In 1994, it was transferred to State Parks and renamed Joemma Beach.

There are no charted hazards approaching Joemma Park. The park is easy to locate because of the long, sturdily-built fishing pier—the only one along this shore.

The exposed high bluff immediately north of the pier is glacial till, partly covered with vegetation. We've seen deer, eagles and ospreys.

The park is in a nice little bight, but is exposed to southerly winds, which are the prevailing storm winds in winter, sweeping up Case Inlet.

This is a popular fishing spot for both locals and others who have "discovered" it. It's a great place to beachcomb, hike, camp, dig clams and swim.

Joemma Beach, pier and floats

Moorage floats at the end of the fishing pier are removed each winter and replaced each spring. Five park mooring buoys are north of the pier.

Launch ramp of concrete planks on a fairly steep grade is immediately north of the pier. There is a large parking area.

The long beach is wonderful, flooding with warm water for summertime swimming as the tide creeps in over the sun-warmed sand.

Joemma State Marine Park Facilities
➤ Five mooring buoys
➤ Guest moorage for approximately 20 boats at the dock
➤ Moorage rates: $5 for buoys, $8 for boats under 26', $11 for boats over 26'
➤ 22 acre park
➤ 1,100 feet of shoreline
➤ Campground and picnic area
➤ Telephones
➤ Launch ramp
➤ Toilets
➤ Phone: 206-884-2514

Joe Smith and Joemma Beach

Born about 1875 and raised in Eastern Washington, Joe Smith was a "kind-of" old time cowboy. He lived in the last place on the frontier where there were "old style" cattle ranches. Then he became the first war correspondent for the *Seattle P-I* in the war in the Philippines in 1898.

When he came back from the war, he became involved in Seattle politics in the early 1900s. He left it all and got title to the uplands behind what is now the Joemma Beach Park area. He began raising flower bulbs and published the *Joemma Bulletin*. In it he wrote meandering articles on politics and growing bulbs—it was an eclectic newsletter that charmed all who read it. His wife was named Emma, of course.

A note from a *Joemma Bulletin* in 1925: "Joemma is on North Bay, on the west side of Puget Sound, three miles west of Longbranch, 28 miles south of Port Orchard and about 24 miles from Tacoma. It is most conveniently reached from the outside world via Tacoma and Steilacoom and the ferry *City of Steilacoom* to Longbranch. A personally conducted Bi-Monthly Periodical, Part Flower Magazine, Part Catalog and Part Report of the Activities of the Joemma Experiment in Living Simply and Endeavoring to Pass the Good Things Around."

Joemma beach at high tide

Ferry at Herron Island

Dutcher Cove was originally the small settlement of Little Sweden. Most of the men were loggers while the women looked after the family cows, chickens and children. (The original CCC—Civilian Conservation Corps—of the 1930s. Hardly.)

Herron Island was not named for the graceful big water birds (one "r") but for Lewis Herron, a petty officer with Wilkes.

Peter Puget and his crew camped their fourth night on Herron Island, calling it Wednesday Island because that was the day they were there. In fact, Puget and his group had run north around Devils Head and were going north in Case Inlet until early on that Wednesday afternoon, May 23, 1792. They were hit with a brutal squall and made camp for the night under miserable conditions on the island.

Archibald Menzies wrote, "On account of the heavy rain, thunder and lightning which set in soon after, we were obliged to pitch our tents and remain on the island all night . . . The rain fell in perfect torrents."

Hartstene Island was named for Lt. Henry J. Hartstene, a member of the Wilkes expedition.

⚓ **Continuing north** of Whiteman Cove about 0.7 mile we see a sandy private beach fronting a small lagoon, dry at low water. There are pilings on the beach—the remains of an old dock—small houses on the shore. Bluffs along this shore reach up to 220 and 240 feet high.

A rounded, westerly unnamed "point," with still another sandspit and lagoon, are less than a mile north of Whiteman. There are a fair number of summer cottages, beach houses, two teepee frames and private buoys along here; other than that there's not much development.

Herron Island, 2.5 miles north of Whiteman Cove, is private. It's served by a small, open car ferry, the *Charlie Wells* of Lakebay, which runs from the **Herron** community dock on Key Peninsula to a landing on the northeast side of the island.

The island's south end has a 140 foot high barren bluff. Houses perched atop the bluff have fabulous bird's-eye views to south, east and west.

Public tidelands of about 1,500 feet are on the mainland shore opposite the south end of Herron Island.

Charted three fathom, three foot shoal is off the northeastern tip of Herron Island. A charted two fathom, one foot shoal projects west of Herron community. This is a good place to watch the depth sounder. We jog a bit west at the north end of the island to avoid both island and mainland shoals.

Public tidelands of about 5,500 feet in six parcels are scattered along the shore from south of Herron community to Dutcher Cove, a distance of just over three miles. All beaches are private property between these parcels. Modest homes and cabins are tucked into the low forested shores along this section of the inlet.

Dutcher Cove, unnamed on chart 18448, is two miles north of Herron. It dries at low tide, so it wouldn't make much of an anchorage.

Public tidelands totaling about 5,000 feet are in five parcels along the two mile shoreline between Dutcher Cove and Vaughn Bay.

We now cross Case Inlet to Wilson Point on Harstine Island and go north along the shore of the island to Dougall Point.

Harstine Island Overview

Harstine is a rural gem in South Sound. Individual homes and several fairly large residential developments are spread across its 19 square miles. It is joined to the mainland at Graham by a fixed bridge from the island's western shore across Pickering Pass.

How do you spell "Hartstene?"

Hartstene is spelled a variety of ways: Harstine, Hartstein, Hartstine, Harstene and Hartstene. NOAA charts show the latter spelling as preferred. Even Wilkes spelled it one way in his journal, another way on his chart.

Islanders spell it Harstine—and we understand the state may soon make this the official spelling—so some of the time we'll also spell it **Harstine.**

The island has more than 26 miles of shoreline, is about eight miles long, and 2.5 miles wide in places. It's densely covered with second and third growth evergreens, madronas, salal, huckleberries, ferns and other northwest trees and shrubs.

The majority of islanders live on the periphery of Harstine Island near the beaches, but some roads turn inland to homes deep in the woods. Originally, there were three island schools until the bridge was completed in 1969, when the schools consolidated with Pioneer Schools of Shelton. Now all the kids go off island to elementary school and then on to Shelton High.

Artists and writers, retirees, commuters and those who have small "cottage industries" are important island residents. We'll visit the island in both this chapter and the next.

⚓ **Underway again,** we cruise about 1.5 miles across Case Inlet from Joemma Beach Park to Harstine Island.

From Wilson Point we head north along the eastern shore. At low tide, a sandy bar extends from the point about 0.2 mile into the inlet. At MLLW a drying, off-shore shoal is very evident.

Public tidelands start about 3,000 feet north of Wilson Point and run for about 6,500 feet. Cruising north past these tidelands, we see beautiful evergreen-forested island shores with few houses interspersed for about 1.7 miles where we reach:

Fudge Point—the **REAL** Fudge Point. We're not fudging about Fudge Point. An interesting dilemma developed when a state publication of *Puget Sound Public Shellfish Sites*, the state quad map, and several other maps and publications, showed Fudge Point at the unnamed point 1.5 miles **north** of McMicken Island State Park.

Fudge Point is shown on the NOAA navigational charts as **south** of McMicken Island. Neither NOAA nor the state could explain the reason for the mix-up, but both agencies said to stick with the NOAA version, and so we are.

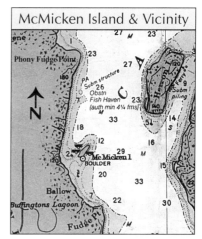

Not for navigation
Refer to chart 18448
Soundings in fathoms

Buffingtons Lagoon & Ballow

Both are north of Fudge Point. The drying lagoon was named for a colorful, early-island character, John Buffington, who lived on the lagoon at Ballow, had horses, coon dogs and a colony of beehives filled with fierce bees. Stories are told of his ventures, including farming, logging, and even bootlegging—he's a legendary island pioneer character.

By the 1920s, Ballow was a community of more than a dozen families, including that of Moses Sutton, a man of many talents and trades, including publishing the Ballow Breeze, filled with local news. His son Mel hewed a wooden bathtub out of a six-foot cedar log which in summer was filled with water and warmed in the sun.

---

*You'll find more wonderful stories in **The Island Remembers a History of Harstine Island and Its People**, by Beulah Hitchcock and Helen Wingert.*

It's now only 0.7 mile north to one of our favorite stopping places.

Ⓖ **McMicken Island State Marine Park**—we've arrived. This is the kind of place we'd like to keep secret and have all to ourselves—but it's way too late. Just about all South Sound boaters **do** know about McMicken—a great **gunkhole.** Jo was anchoring here long before it became a state park in 1974.

It is a pristine 11.45 acres of isolated island where bald eagles soar, blue herons stalk shallows for snacks, deer feed in the fields and seals cavort nearby.

McMicken is joined to Harstine at low tide by a sandy bar or "**tombolo**," about 30 feet wide. The first 100 yards west of the park are state park property. The rest of the bar is private and Harstine islanders are displeased with traffic from boaters visiting the park. "No Trespassing" signs are on Harstine, posted by oyster growers.

At high tide the tombolo is deceptive. It could probably be crossed carefully by boat at high water, but we didn't do it. This is a great example of a tombolo: "a sand or gravel bar connecting an island with the mainland (or another island)," usually covered by water at high tide.

Along the tombolo's ridge are very fine white shell deposits on the north side. On the south side there are few shell deposits, so the beach is darker and more or less mixed gravel.

One time we saw three large island dogs romping across the bar, barking and chasing seagulls, each other and having a marvelous run.

Wilson Point *was named for Thomas Wilson, sailmaker's mate with Wilkes.*

Tombolo at McMicken

➡ **Caution**: There is poison ivy on McMicken Island.

McMicken Island's water is unusually clear and you can often see bottom in 12-15 feet, which doesn't ordinarily happen in this part of the Sound. In the mid-1970s during a South Sound Sailing Society cruise, one friend dived down to pick up a "loose" anchor he could see lying on the bottom. Turns out the anchor was attached to the anchor line on the Sea Witch—Jo's former 29' sloop.

He surfaced, chagrined—and she kept her anchor.

"Boulder" at McMicken, Sea Witch in background, low tide

McMicken's name: A Swedish sailor who jumped ship settled on McMicken Island originally, naming it Lundquist for himself. However, when he attempted a legal claim of the island with the government, they said there was no record of its existence. A surveyor was sent to establish the island on U.S. maps and he named it for himself, McMicken. The name stuck, and it's been McMicken ever since. Poor Mr. Lundquist.

Another story is that the Swedish sailor who claimed McMicken Island could not get the government to record the claim until he proposed to claim the island for the King of Sweden.

Some of McMicken's beaches are almost completely white from broken shells right up to the grasslands, which makes us think this may be an old Indian midden.

Waves against the island's shores leave little ledges of sand and gravel that are quite pronounced and unusual. On the rocky south beach are remains of old, reddish bricks with holes in them.

> ### McMicken Island State Park Facilities
> ➤ Five mooring buoys; two off the south shore and three off the north shore
> ➤ 1,661 feet of saltwater shoreline
> ➤ 11.45 acres
> ➤ Peace and quiet
> ➤ Hiking, clamming, fishing, swimming

The south shore of McMicken boasts—see the charts—a **boulder.** And it **is** a boulder—huge and covered by water at high tide. It's another of those erratic rocks that are so common, but this is larger than most. In fact there are so many erratic rocks along the shores of McMicken, they look like pimples on a 14 year old.

Ashore there are no facilities. State Parks plans a camp site on the island for Cascadia Water Trail kayakers after a new composting toilet is installed, which will be built when funding is available. But for those whose boats have legal heads, shore facilities aren't necessary.

We enjoy walking the beach all around the island to see the sights at low tide, although it's not the easiest walking because of large rocks on the beach.

We like to hike across the island on the several trails wandering through the woods. The trails are narrow and twisting with tree roots in the paths making the walk a challenge. Even on a bright and sunny day it's dark on the forest trails with only occasional views through thick underbrush. On a rainy day it's fairly dry and protected because there are so many branches and leaves overhead.

⚓ **Anchoring** is good on either side of the island if all the buoys are taken, depending on which way the wind is blowing. In the "off-season" you might be the only boat here—as we have been several times.

A triangular area on McMicken's southeast shore (near the charted boulder) is fenced off and privately owned. A small house with a steep roof and several out-buildings are inside the fence with a "No trespassing" sign by the gate. A one-lane vehicle track is barely discernible in tall grass near the gate.

The fence crosses the meadow, which is rough and covered with clumpy grass with a lot of snaky ruts and channels underfoot. We thought the channels might be mole holes that had washed out as the surface is caved-in in several places.

We met a couple who have been coming to McMicken even longer than Jo, and wondered aloud about those ruts. The woman said she'd been curious a few years back and pulled up a board lying over a rut. Underneath the board was a whole bunch of writhing, squealing, smelly, beady-eyed rats. She beat a hasty retreat. We don't pick up boards on McMicken.

Her husband said in days past the owners drove motorcycles or tractors across the tombolo at low tide. That's how materials got there and how people got back and forth to the house—and accounts for the faint vehicle track across the meadow.

⚙ **Underway again, Hartstene Island State Park** lands begin less than 0.25 mile north of the McMicken Island tombolo. The southern boundary is marked by a small state park sign on two posts.

Hartstene Island State Park attractions include 315 acres of uplands, as well as 1,600 feet of saltwater shoreline. A beautiful beach and trails through the forests and ravines are the joys in this park, with parking for seven vehicles at the trailhead for those who arrive by land.

A large oyster bed at the south end of the park beach has over one million oysters available for the picking.

The park ranger asked us to mention that clam and oyster pickers must have proper state shellfish licenses and know the limits. Oysters must be shucked on the beach, leaving the shells where you find them, as they are usually covered with "spat"—baby oysters.

Shoreline at the entrance to the uplands of Hartstene Island State Park

State Parks purchased the park property from DNR in 1990, but DNR manages the shoreline.

⚓ **Anchoring** is possible all along the park's shoreline in about two fathoms at low tide. It's easy to dinghy ashore and stroll beaches and hike trails, which include three small footbridges. A trail starts on the beach at a ravine between 100 foot high forested bluffs, about 0.7 mile north of McMicken Island. (Chart 18448 shows topographic features best.)

Fish havens and a submerged structure are off the park's north end as charted.

Public tidelands extend north from McMicken Island for about 8,000 feet, including tidelands at Hartstene State Park.

⚙ **Underway again**, about 1.4 miles north of McMicken island is the unnamed point—on charts, shown as Fudge Point on some state maps and books. (We already discussed the **real** Fudge Point charted **south** of McMicken Island.) Forested banks just south of this point are up to 180 feet high.

***Zade** at McMicken*

Spencer Cove, unnamed on charts, is tucked in north of the phony Fudge Point.

Depths of the three fathom curve are charted about 400 yards offshore in the southwest part of the cove and 300 yards offshore in the west and northwest areas.

Land rises to 140 feet high on shore behind the cove, and there are houses on the point. This is a pleasant cove with little traffic.

⚓ **Anchoring** is possible a little north and west of the point, dropping the hook in a sandy bottom to wait out a southerly blow. The beaches are all private.

Public tidelands start approximately 3,000 feet south of Dougall Point and extend south another 3,000 feet.

Dougall Point is at the northeastern tip of Harstine Island. A charted shoal extends about 0.25 mile off the long sandspit at the point. Two charted "surfaced ramps" are part of the private "Hartstene Pointe" development on the island. But before we round Dougall Point and go down Pickering Pass, we have other plans.

⚙ **Underway again,** we go across Case Inlet to Vaughn Bay on Key Peninsula.

Ⓖ **Vaughn Bay** is a nifty spot—**a great gunkhole**—12 miles north of Devils Head.

Public tidelands of nearly 2,000 feet are along the sandspit at Vaughn Bay. It is accessible only by boat—but there's a bay to anchor in while exploring the spit.

The spit, with silvered driftwood carelessly flung across the top by wind-driven

***Vaughn Bay** and the surrounding areas were first settled by William J. Vaughn in 1852. He filed a homestead and began clearing the ground and logging the timber on his claim. In fact, his was the first log boom shipped to San Francisco to be used in gold rush construction. (From **Along the Waterfront**)*

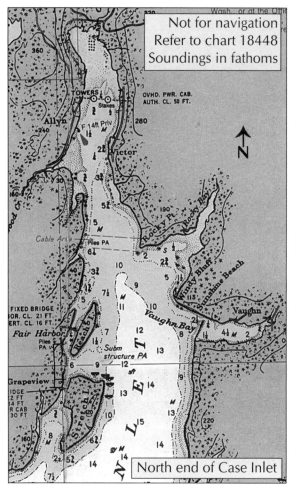

Not for navigation
Refer to chart 18448
Soundings in fathoms

North end of Case Inlet

Early settlers in the Vaughn Bay area logged, farmed, picked oysters and huckleberries. There were stores, a dock, post office, community center, schoolhouse, library and a literary society. Eventually all this burned down,

Vaughn Bay entrance channel at high tide— bay is to the right

waves, is great for beachcombing and clam digging: littlenecks, butters, horse clams. Red rock crabs are here, too.

The old dock on the spit is long gone, only old stub piles and rusted out old cables remain. The outside (Case Inlet side) of the spit slopes gradually to the water, with fine, pea-gravel along the beach. In fact, when some friends anchored their 40 foot sailboat along this shore, the tide went out, the boat grounded and laid over on its side. Embarrassed, but always prepared, the skipper went below and brought out scrapers. Barnacles were removed from most of the bottom before the tide came back in.

The Vaughn Bay side is quite steep, especially near the entrance. There are no facilities on the beach—just a wonderful place to bask in the sun and let the kids run.

Public tidelands also extend east about 2,000 feet from the southwest corner of the bay.

Launch ramp is charted on 18445 on the north shore of Vaughn Bay about 0.5 mile from the entrance. At low tides it is unusable; there is limited parking.

Several boats are permanently moored boats in Vaughn Bay.

Depths at MLLW approaching the entrance are charted as two fathoms three feet outside, shoaling to zero (0) fathoms one foot, just inside. Depths increase to one fathom three feet behind the spit. Mid-length of the bay depths increase to about four fathoms.

Currents in the channel during both flood and ebb tides may exceed skiff rowing speeds and are not shown in the ***Tidal Current Tables*** or in the ***Current Charts***.

Entering Vaughn Bay, considering the zero fathom, one foot depth inside the entrance, we enter only after we are sure there is enough water to clear our 5.5 foot draft, plus a couple of feet, preferably on the last stages of the flood. Favoring the spit side of the entrance we proceed at dead slow with the current, heading south immediately inside the spit to avoid the shoal projecting from the north shore. Then we turn east into more comfortable depths. Prudent judgment suggests leaving the bay on the flood also.

⚓ **Anchoring** is possible inside the spit toward the south and east corner of Vaughn Bay, in two to four fathoms, mud bottom.

We've found it fun to run the channel in the skiff with the current, though we may have to walk back along the shore towing the skiff against the current.

This a protected, favorite anchorage with many South Sound boaters, especially because of the wonderful spit tidelands to explore on the Case Inlet side. Except for the noted public tidelands, the rest of the Vaughn Bay shoreline is private.

Vaughn Bay community is a pleasant mix of summer residences and permanent homes. At the bay head, near the bridge, is the Key Peninsula Community Center.

✹ **Underway again**, we leave Vaughn Bay, passing Sunshine Beach on the north shore.

Windy Bluff is the point just around the corner to the west and north of Sunshine Beach and Vaughn Bay.

Depths off the bluff are shoal—the three fathom curve runs about 350 yards offshore.

Immediately around the point at Windy Bluff on its northwest shore is a sandspit with a charted rock at its northeast end and a charted depth of one fathom three feet. Shores are private.

It seems a bit too small for us and exposed to the west and north, though shoal draft boats might investigate and find it interesting.

Rocky Bay is about 0.6 mile wide at its entrance between Windy Bluff and Rocky Point to the northwest. About 1.4 miles northeast to its head the bay mostly dries at MLLW.

Looking south from the north end of Vaughn Bay Spit, with the bay to the left

The bay is open to the south and west and there are better anchorages for overnight. We dinghied around the shallows in Rocky Bay and it **is** rocky, with many large erratics.

Depths at the three fathom curve extend 0.2 mile northeast of the bay entrance.

Public tidelands of about 2,000 feet are in the drying lagoon in the narrower section of Rocky Bay.

⚓ **Anchoring** might be possible in the bay in about two fathoms for some protection from a northerly, but it would be wide open to a southerly.

Cable area crosses Case Inlet from Rocky Point west.

☸ **Underway again,** still heading north, depths north of Rocky Point shoal from 10 to under three fathoms as the navigable midchannel virtually ends at **Victor,** a residential community on the east shore 1.4 miles north of Rocky Point.

Depths along the west shore of Case Inlet shoal to one foot or less as we near Victor, and shrink to 1/4 fathom from Victor north to the towers between the overhead power cables.

Overhead power cables cross the head of Case Inlet about 0.6 mile north of Victor with a charted clearance of 50 feet above MHW.

There are numerous oyster stakes in these parts, with about 4,000 feet of private oyster reserves on the east shore north of Victor.

North Bay is the local name for the head of Case Inlet.

Coulter Creek Salmon Hatchery is at the head of the bay.

Captain Vancouver turned up in Case Inlet also. He had left Restoration Point about five days after Puget had and was concerned about what had happened to his lieutenant. In fact, nothing had happened except that Puget had discovered it took TIME to really explore South Sound. Especially when they had only sails and oars to power their small vessels.

So when Vancouver got to Case Inlet on May 28, after failing to meet Puget along the way, he was trying to find a short cut back to his ship off the south tip of Bainbridge Island. But Vancouver found, as had Puget, that the inlet "terminated like all the other canals in a shallow flat before a low swamp bog. Here we dined."

After that they headed south and camped near Whiteman Cove and enjoyed fresh venison killed near Dougall Point on Hartstene by Mr. LeMesurier.

Canal to Hood Canal?

On the chart, it's only two short miles from North Bay at the head of the inlet across the land to Lynch Cove at the head of Hood Canal. The hills rise over 350 feet in places between the two bodies of water, which is probably why no one has ever built a canal linking them.

As far back as 1889, a canal was urged by enterprising settlers to connect the two bodies of water. Over 100 plus years later there is still no canal. It is an interesting idea. It does make you wonder how such a canal would affect tides and currents in Hood Canal and South Sound.

During a survey expedition in 1841 led by Lieutenant Case of the Wilkes Expedition for whom the inlet was named, one group opened a trail and portaged their boats across the hills separating Case Inlet and Hood Canal.

Allyn is the northernmost community on Case Inlet's western shore, and although it's not often a cruising destination, we found it a neat place to go. It's about 0.4 miles northwest of Victor.

Port of Allyn has a public fishing pier nearly 600 feet long with a T-shaped end where there are floats for transient and overnight moorage.

Fl 14 ft Allyn Dock Light, flashing white, privately maintained, on the float at the end of the dock, marks the outer end of the Allyn pier.

Approaching Allyn, once we're certain we're north and east of the zero fathom, one foot shoal, we proceed north from two fathoms, four feet at Victor until the Allyn pier lines up with St. Hugh's white church. We head west toward the dock.

> ➡ **Caution:** Depths shoal to about one fathom, three feet as charted. From Victor we approach the Allyn float with caution.
> **"Danger Low Water Hazard"** signs are posted on the Allyn floats and dock. Draft and tide range are definite factors in mooring at Allyn.

Allyn can be a good stopover with reasonable tides. We were here above midtide range and had enough water. The dock is open to southerly winds.

Permanent moorage from October 1 through May 1 is available at $1.13 per foot per month and $1.50 per foot per month May 1 through October 1. Summer monthly rates by arrangement. Contact the Port of Allyn: P.O. Box 686, Belfair, WA. 98528.

Port of Allyn public dock

Port of Allyn Facilities
- ➤ Guest moorage for six to eight boats
- ➤ Guest moorage rates 25 cents per foot, May through October
- ➤ Restrooms
- ➤ Water and telephone at head of pier
- ➤ Waterfront park with kids' play area
- ➤ Launch ramp
- ➤ Phone: 360-275-2346

Allyn, named for Tacoma jurist, Judge Allyn, was platted and settled in 1853.

The town's first real business started a year later with a sawmill founded by Joe Sherwood, the so-called "Hercules of Allyn," at the mouth of Sherwood Creek just south of Allyn.

Reach Island was locally known as Oak Island because of an unusual stand of oak trees on the 86 acre island. The first resident was Joseph Pickard, who homesteaded and built a log cabin on the island in 1885.

He left after five years and no one lived there until 1905 when Alfred W. Zizz bought the island for $1,000. At some point the island's name was changed to Reach, because someone thought it a humorous complement to neighboring Stretch Island. Zizz lived there until 1952, when developers bought it.

The Mosquito fleet served the Grapeview area for years around the turn of the century because of pick-ups and deliveries at Stretch Island with its abundant fruit orchards and wineries.

It's just a short walk from the public dock and waterfront park, past picturesque St. Hugh's Episcopal Church—built in 1909—to grocery stores, ice cream cones, or pizza and beer at the Allyn Tavern. Allyn has a full hardware store, fast food restaurants, espresso stands and other services, including a liquor store.

The waterfront park has a pavilion and picnic tables, telephone and a launch ramp north of the pier with nearby parking. There is no clam digging south of the dock without permission.

Allyn could be a good place to launch kayaks or rendezvous with friends.

We took our own advice and visited the pizza parlor in Allyn. It was great. They had encouraging words about the public moorage. They told us that although **their** waterfront was on mud flats the port dock is always available for boats, except on minus tides. They have a lovely view out over Case Inlet, and the owners put in an outdoor beer garden for their customers to enjoy. But they said the inlet does get pretty dry in the north end. Boaters should be aware of the oyster stakes that can be seen and stay outside of them.

⚙ **Underway again,** let's leave before we hit the "low swamp bogs." We head back south along the western shores of upper Case Inlet. From Allyn, in 2.2 miles we come to Reach Island.

Reach Island is the northernmost of two small islands on the western shore of Case Inlet. Both Reach and neighboring Stretch Island are joined by bridges to the mainland. Reach is the name shown on charts, but it's been renamed Treasure by developers. It is private and covered with homes ranging from cabins to imposing.

Public tidelands of about 2,500 feet are along Reach Island's eastern shore.

There's nothing on Reach for the recreational boater, except to know the bridge to the mainland has a vertical clearance of 16 feet at MHW. There are many rocks in the narrow, shallow channel. We went through the channel—slowly—in a small boat, and can attest to that.

Fair Harbor Marina on the mainland is 0.25 mile south of the Reach Island bridge. The marina is charted as #99 on 18445 with more facilities than listed, however, there is no longer a 10 ton lift, lodging or camping.

Fair Harbor Marina

Fair Harbor Marina Facilities
- ➤ Guest floats for 40 to 45 boats
- ➤ Moorage rate is 35 cents per foot
- ➤ 30 amp shore power, $2.50 per day
- ➤ Fuel float: gas only
- ➤ Restrooms, showers
- ➤ Convenience store carries foods including gourmet goodies, beer and wine; gift shop, fishing gear, ice, marine supplies, espresso bar
- ➤ Two mechanics
- ➤ Book exchange
- ➤ Telephones
- ➤ Picnic and play area
- ➤ Permanent moorage for 58 boats
- ➤ Phone: 360-426-4028.

The attractive buildings and shoreside park tucked off in this corner of the world are unexpected to newcomers. The marina has been there for about 30 years, but was rebuilt in its present form in 1991.

Marina owners Susan and Vern Nelson help moorage guests in many ways: they'll arrange tee times and transportation to nearby Lakeland Village Golf Course in Allyn for golfing boaters; they plan wine-tasting for visiting yacht clubs, and see to it their guests visit Bill Somers' fascinating Maritime Museum on Stretch Island.

Entering the marina, the entrance is between Reach and Stretch Islands. We turn west after reaching the south end of Reach Island, keeping nearly 0.3 mile offshore to avoid the charted one fathom, three foot shoal, and the submerged offshore structure if coming from the north. If coming from the south, we turn west at the north end of Stretch Island, past Stretch Point State Park on the northeast corner of the island.

We head toward the mainland community of Grapeview, midchannel between Stretch and Reach, and turn north in the channel between Reach and the mainland. Fair Harbor, with it's blue covered moorages, is on the mainland about 300 yards north of the turn. The gas float, store and office are at the north end of the marina.

Depths between Reach and Stretch Islands are charted at six fathoms at the south end of Reach. Just south of the Reach Island Bridge depths on chart 18448 show 1/4 fathom and zero fathom, one foot on 18445.

A rock is charted about 300 yards south of the bridge, roughly 100 yards west of Reach Island across from Fair Harbor Marina.

We have about 18 to 20 feet or more whenever we enter, usually about midtide.

Launch ramp immediately north of the marina is owned by the Port of Grapeview. Parking is nearby.

The marina store is open year round. At Christmas, the store becomes a Christmas shop; the community does a lighted boat parade out of the marina. Santa Claus arrives by boat and there is a bonfire, carols, cookies and cocoa.

Grapeview has a water festival the last weekend each July with an adult fishing derby and a derby for kids fishing off Fair Harbor Marina floats; a community salmon bake, serving about 250 people, and an old fashioned picnic with croquet, horseshoes, and volleyball. The marina has become an unofficial community center.

Fair Harbor Marina started out in the 1950s as a fuel barge.

When Vern and Susan Nelson cruised in their 42 foot Grand Banks they would make notes on what they liked about marinas and why, and bought Fair Harbor Marina several years ago.

After they took possession they were hit by a major northerly windstorm that devastated the place.

"After the storm, it all just needed to be repaired so badly that there was nothing to save, so we decided to tear it out and rebuild, store and all, and turn it into the kind of place **we** liked to visit. We got the permits, put in 40 new piling. We get so much positive response from the community, first of all for cleaning the marina up, that now they think of it as 'their' marina. I let the kids come down and fish and have some pretty strict rules about fish guts on the dock and stuff like that. But they're pretty good about it," Susan said.

Bill Somers

Stretch Island Maritime Museum

Stretch has a most impressive Maritime Museum inland, operated by Bill Somers. For maritime history buffs, the museum is a treasure. It's in the oldest winery on Stretch Island.

Bill showed us wonderful memorabilia, including photos of the old Colman dock in Seattle, a sign from Percival Dock in Olympia and many other photos. He rang a deep-toned, ship's bell. We ran our fingers over a worn wooden block from an old battleship, saw rum puncheon (barrels) from back in the days when barrels were $10 each.

We saw photos of part of a crew that ran a boat between Seattle and Vashon; of the old Hyak, which ran between Seattle and Poulsbo in 1910. We saw a model of the Flyer, that ran between Seattle and Tacoma, logging more than 2,000,000 miles, and a photo of people waiting for the Flyer in 1900, round trip 75 cents. The list goes on—it's great if you love maritime history.

Visit the museum and talk to Bill to really experience it.

One way to see the museum is to arrange a visit through Susan Nelson at Fair Harbor Marina, as you can't get there from Stretch Point State Park because of the private property surrounding the park.

Grapeview—Then & Now

Grapeview was originally called **Detroit** by early settlers, hoping to build a city that would rival Detroit, Michigan. The Malaney brothers, Tom, Albert and John, arrived in 1885 with grandiose plans.

The land was platted, 300 settlers began farming and logging the area, a hotel and two saloons were built. But the developers saw it differently ...

In the May 23, 1890, issue of the **Shelton Journal,** it was written, "It is most refreshing even in these days when veracity is at a premium to reward the efforts of the cheerful liar as exemplified in the following extract from an exchange. We have nothing whatever against this embryo city, and desire to see it grow with us, but this conjuring up a full-fledged city from among the stumps by the facile writer's pen is amusing: 'The City of Detroit is only three months old, yet it has seven miles of graded streets, three sawmills, one sash and door factory, one newspaper office, three merchandise stores, one hardware store, one $15,000 hotel, three restaurants, one law office, five real estate offices, one shingle mill, one planing mill, one brick and tile factory. Water mains and electric lights are being put in. This example illustrates the rapid growth of our coast cities'."

The investors quickly left and within a year lawsuits and counter-suits were filed. A couple of years later a notice in the same newspaper noted the "report that John and Albert Malaney have been arrested for smuggling is not verified." The hotel was mentioned again in 1910, but there seems to be no more news of it after that.

In 1950 Charles Bill (Bill) Somers bought 10 acres of the original Detroit and developed it into a lot with a common beach access. The sign at the entrance reads "Detroit Townsite."

⚓ **Underway again**, leaving Fair Harbor Marina we now look at Stretch Island and its neat little State Marine Park.

Stretch Island is shaped a bit like a pixie boot with the toes turned up, if you "stretch" your imagination. The island is in Case Inlet; the waters of Pickering Passage lap its southern shores.

Stretch Point State Marine Park is at the northeast point of the island. It extends around both sides of the point. It is easy to spot the mooring buoys on either side of the point. The buoys look close to shore, but they're in about 40 feet of water. The beach is fairly steep and gravelly.

The park, accessible by water only, is undeveloped and adjacent to private property on either side. It is a satellite of Jarrell Cove State Park on Hartstene Island.

Stretch Point Park looking west

Stretch Point Park Facilities
➤ Five mooring buoys, three east of the sandy point, two in the north shore bight
➤ 4.2 acres of land with 610 feet of shoreline
➤ No picnic, water or toilet facilities

The park is a favorite spot for water skiers. There's also swimming, beach-combing, clamming, fishing and picnicking, on either side of the point. By sunset the water-skiers usually quit and it's a quiet, peaceful anchorage.

(G) The little bight inside the northeast corner of the island is **a nifty gunkhole,** a choice spot. It's lovely.

We tie to a mooring buoy and enjoy a delightful, peaceful evening at Stretch Island Park after a quick dinghy trip ashore and a swim. The sun sets slowly over the trees and all's right with the world.

⚓ **Anchoring** in the bight is possible if the buoys are all taken. It's protected from all but a northerly in here.

Wooded bluffs are along the eastern shore of Stretch, large boulders on the beach. Although there are a fair number of homes on Stretch Island, it somehow seems not quite as urbanized as other places in this area.

❋ **Public tidelands** stretch around much of Stretch Island. There are about 2,000 feet of tidelands along the northwest corner and nearly 7,000 feet in two parcels along the eastern shore.

Most of the public beaches are below barren bluffs, which along the eastern shore can reach 120 feet in height, with homes along the bluff tops.

⚓ **Anchoring** is possible along the eastern side in calm weather to row ashore, beachcomb the area and maybe dig a few clams along the public tidelands, unless otherwise posted.

An unnamed bay curves in between the southwestern shore of Stretch to the mainland south of the Stretch Island bridge to Grapeview. The bridge has a vertical clearance of 14 feet at MHW, but at low tides it is mudflats in parts of the channel between the island the mainland. The bay is enjoyed by water skiers, jet skiers and small boats of all types. Depths of about eight fathoms, mud bottom, continue into the bay.

Public tidelands of about 800 feet are on the eastern shore of this bay.

Before we go on to the next chapter, let's take a look at the four page special section following this, from pages 260-263. We call it, The "Current Thing" West of Case Inlet.

➡ **In Chapter 18** we head south into Pickering Passage, go west into Hammersley Inlet to Shelton, south into Totten and Little Skookum inlets, and through Squaxin Passage, stopping at the new Hope Island State Marine Park and the little pass between Hope and Squaxin.

Years back, Stretch was called Grape Island because of the grapes grown for Washington wines, and for the winery on the island, which closed down in 1965, but the grapes are still used for jam and juice.

Stretch Island was named for Gunner's Mate Samuel Stretch with the Wilkes Expedition.

Mason County has a legal age limit of 16 to operate a motor boat with more than a 10 horsepower motor unless accompanied by someone over 18.

Spruce Beer
Several times during Puget's exploring expedition in 1792 we read about the men making "spruce beer."

*Robert Wing, who co-authored the book, **Peter Puget**, explained spruce beer.*

"Many of the conifer trees in the northwest were loosely termed 'spruce' trees. The drink was made from the tender spring tips of the trees which are lemony-tasting. They boiled the tips, added molasses yeast and then drank it before it had time to ferment. The drink was high in vitamin C and beneficial in preventing scurvy. They also boiled early spring green nettles which made a 'half-tasteless' spinach," Wing said.

The "Current Thing" West of Case Inlet

Refer to Tidal Current Charts — Puget Sound — Southern Part (Not for Navigation)

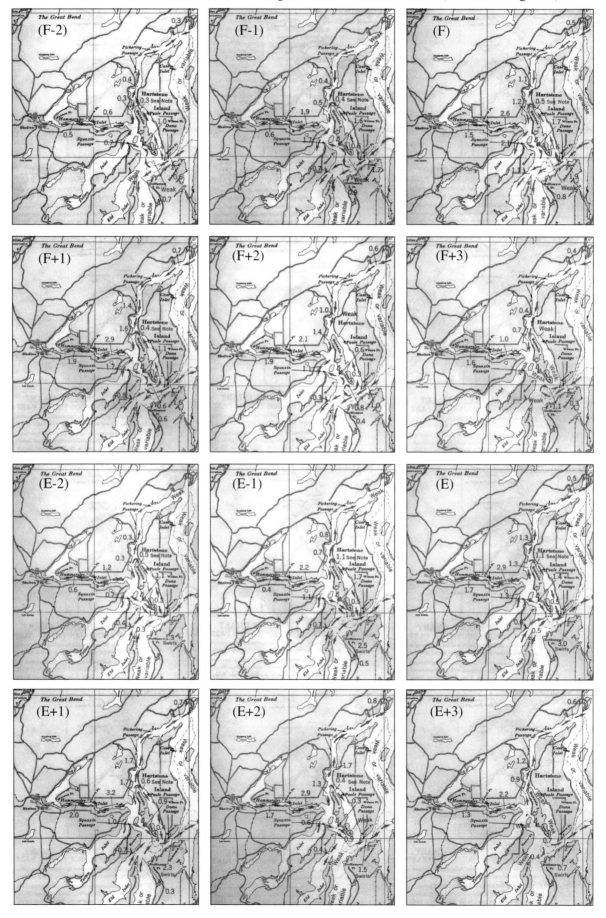

The "Current Thing" West of Case Inlet

A quick overview of currents is important for paddle, sail and slower power vessels, fishermen and scuba divers, and faster vessels interested in fuel economy.

We're tired of thumbing through 12 pages of Current Charts, the Current Tables and its "Table 2, Current Differences and Other Constants," to determine what we need to know; trying to recall what we've found from hour to hour and place to place about direction, speed and when the current flows or is slack. All of that, plus taking advantage of backeddies from shoreline bulges and points, watching the depth sounder and nautical charts, drove us (Carl) to develop the "Current Thing" West of Case Inlet.

We use it as a quick reference and planning tool when making a passage or a casual sail in this area. We use it in deciding when to sail or power for best use of time, energy and fuel, or as a quick reference of where we'll end up if there's no wind and the engine won't work.

"Current Thing" West of Case Inlet is easily understood after becoming familiar with the navigation, tidal current tables and current charts in this area.

The 16 current stations listed are located on the **Current Charts**. For more details refer to:

• **Tidal Current Charts, Puget Sound, Southern Part,** in our Appendix, pages 328-335

• **Tidal Current Tables**

• Chapter 10

"Current Thing" West of Case Inlet lists an estimate of fastest currents which might be encountered during each hour of extreme flood and ebb current cycles in Column K.

A simple formula is provided.for predicting the current speed and directions at any hour during any specific flood or ebb cycle.

Schooner Alcyone,
Port Townsend

The "Current Thing" West of Case Inlet
FLOOD CURRENTS

COLUMN	1			2			3			4			5			6		
CURRENT CHART	F - 2			F - 1			F			F + 1			F + 2			F + 3		
ROW STATIONS	T	D	K	T	D	K	T	D	K	T	D	K	T	D	K	T	D	K
1 DANA	0.6	✎	0.90	1.7	✓	2.55	1.9	✓	2.85	1.6	✓	2.40	1.0	✓	1.50	0.3	✎	0.45
2 BUDD ENT.	0.7	✓	1.05	0.9	✓	1.35	0.8	✓	1.20	0.6	✓	0.90	0.4	✎	0.60	W	W	W
3 ELD ENT.	W	W	W	0.7	✎	1.05	1.1	✓	1.65	0.8	✓	1.20	0.3	✎	0.45	W	W	W
4 SQUAX.	1.0	↖	1.50	1.6	↖	2.40	1.7	↖	2.55	1.1	↖	1.65	0.6	↖	0.90	W	W	W
5 PEALE S.	0.4	↑	0.60	0.6	↑	0.90	0.6	↑	0.90	0.5	↑	0.75	0.3	↑	0.45	W	W	W
6 TUCKSEL PT.	W	W	W	W	W	W	W	W	W	0.6	⤵	0.90	0.8	⤵	1.20	1.1	⤵	1.65
7 ↑N SCHEMATICS Values Indicated are Tropic Speeds	TUCK. SQUAX 1.0 / PEALE S. •0.4 / W / W•ELD •0.6 DANA / 0.7 BUDD			TUCK. SQUAX 1.6 / PEALE S. •0.6 / 0.7•ELD W 1.7 DANA / 0.9 BUDD			TUCK. SQUAX 1.7 / PEALE S. •0.6 / 1.1•ELD W 1.9 DANA / 0.8 BUDD			TUCK. SQUAX 1.1 / PEALE S. •0.5 / 0.8•ELD 0.6 •1.6 DANA / 0.6 BUDD			TUCK. SQUAX 0.6 / PEALE S. •0.3 / 0.3•ELD 0.8 •1.0 DANA / 0.4 BUDD			TUCK. SQUAX W / PEALE S. •W / W•ELD 1.1 •0.3 DANA / W BUDD		
8 TOTTEN ENT.	0.7	↓	1.05	1.7	✓	2.55	2.1	✓	3.15	1.7	✓	2.55	1.1	✎	1.65	W	W	W
9 HAMM. E.	0.6	→	0.90	1.9	←	2.85	2.6	←	3.90	2.9	←	4.35	2.1	←	3.15	1.0	←	1.50
10 HAMM. W.	0.5	→	0.75	0.6	←	0.90	1.5	←	2.25	1.9	←	2.85	1.9	←	2.85	1.6	←	2.40
11 PICK. S. ENT.	0.3	↑	0.45	0.5	↓	0.75	1.2	↓	1.80	1.6	↓	2.40	1.4	↓	2.10	0.7	↓	1.05
12 * PEALE N.	0.3	↖	*	0.4	✎	*	0.5	⌃	*	0.4	✎	*	W	W	W	W	W	W
13 PICK.PEALE N.	PK	↗↖	PN	PK	↙↗	PN	PK	↙⌃	PN	PK	↙✎	PN	PK	↙w	PN	PK	✎w	PN
14 PICK.GRAH.	0.4	✎	0.60	0.4	✎	0.60	1.1	✓	1.65	1.4	✓	2.1	1.0	✓	1.50	0.4	✎	0.60
15 PICK.N. ENT.	0.3	✎	0.45	W	W	W	0.5	✎	0.75	0.7	✓	1.05	0.6	✓	0.90	0.4	✎	0.60

Note: Tucksel Point on navigation charts is "Unsal Point" on current charts.

* See Note on Current Charts— Apply no correction factor

KEY DEFINITIONS

F = Time of predicted **max flood** at The Narrows

E = Time of predicted **max ebb** at The Narrows

-/+ = **Hours before(-) or after(+)** max flood or ebb

T = **Tropic Speed** charted at current station on current chart. (Tropic Speeds are the greater flood & greater ebb speeds at time of moons max. declination)

D = **Current direction** arrows, (example ↑ = North) Bold arrows indicate change of direction

S = **Swirls** as charted at Dana Passage on all six ebb charts

W = **Weak current** as charted at current stations

K = **Knots** during extreme current cycles, approx. the fastest current speeds, based on a speed correction factor of 1.5 x the charted tropic speed

COLUMNS: 1 through 12 reference *Current Charts*

ROWS:

1 - 15 = Current info. for 2 hours before max flood thru 3 hours after max flood

16 - 30 = Current info. for 2 hours before max ebb thru 3 hours after max ebb

7 & 22 = Composites diagrams of the tropic currents flowing around Tucksel Point area charted from hour to hour on *Current Charts*

13 & 28 = Provide the hourly behavior of currents at the junction of North Peale and Pickering Passages

The "Current Thing" West of Case Inlet
EBB CURRENTS

COLUMN	7			8			9			10			11			12		
CURRENT CHART	E − 2			E − 1			E			E + 1			E + 2			E + 3		
ROW STATIONS	T	D	K	T	D	K	T	D	K	T	D	K	T	D	K	T	D	K
16 DANA	1.3	↗	1.95	2.5	↗	3.75	3.0	↗s	4.50	2.3	↗s	3.45	1.5	↗s	2.25	0.7	↗s	1.05
17 BUDD ENT.	0.3	↑	0.45	0.5	↑	0.75	0.5	↑	0.75	0.3	↑	0.45	W	W	W	0.4	↘	0.60
18 ELD ENT.	0.4	↑	0.60	0.7	↑	1.05	0.8	↑	1.20	0.7	↑	1.05	0.4	↑	0.60	W	W	W
19 SQUAX.	1.1	↘	1.65	1.7	↘	2.55	1.4	↘	2.1	0.9	↘	1.35	0.3	↘	0.45	W	W	W
20 PEALE S.	0.3	↓	0.45	0.5	↓	0.75	0.5	↓	0.75	0.4	↓	0.60	W	W	W	W	W	W
21 TUCKSEL PT.	1.6	↘	2.40	1.6	↘	2.40	1.5	↘	2.25	1.4	↘	2.10	0.9	↘	1.35	0.7	↘	1.05
22 SCHEMATICS — Values Indicated are Tropic Speeds (with N/A compass)	*see schematic values below*																	
23 TOTTEN ENT.	0.7	↗	1.05	1.1	↗	1.65	1.3	↗	1.95	1.0	↗	1.50	0.6	↗	0.50	W	W	W
24 HAMM. E.	1.2	→	1.80	2.2	→	3.30	2.9	→	4.35	3.2	→	4.80	2.9	→	4.35	2.2	→	3.30
25 HAMM. W.	0.6	←	0.90	0.4	→	0.60	1.7	→	2.55	2.0	→	3.00	1.7	→	2.55	1.3	→	1.95
26 PICK. S. ENT.	0.3	↑	0.45	0.7	↑	1.05	1.3	↑	1.95	1.7	↑	2.55	1.3	↑	1.95	0.9	↑	1.35
27 * PEALE N.	0.5	↖	*	1.1	↖	*	1.1	↖	*	0.6	↖	*	0.4	↖	*	W	W	W
28 PICK.PEALE N.	PK	↗	PN	PK	↗	PN	PK	↗	PN	PK	↗	PN	PK	↗	PN	PK	↗w	PN
29 PICK.GRAH.	0.3	↗	0.45	0.8	↙	1.20	1.3	↙	1.95	1.7	↗	2.55	1.7	↗	2.55	1.2	↗	1.80
30 PICK.N. ENT.	W	W	W	W	W	W	0.5	↗	0.75	0.7	↗	1.05	0.8	↗	1.20	0.6	↗	0.90

Row 22 schematic values (Tropic Speeds):
- Column 7: TUCK.; SQUAX 1.1; PEALE S. 0.3; ELD 0.4; 1.6; S 1.3; DANA; 0.3 BUDD
- Column 8: TUCK.; SQUAX 1.7; PEALE S. 0.5; ELD 0.7; 1.6; S 2.5; DANA; 0.5 BUDD
- Column 9: TUCK.; SQUAX 1.4; PEALE S. 0.5; ELD 0.8; 1.5; S 3.0; DANA; 0.5 BUDD
- Column 10: TUCK.; SQUAX 0.9; PEALE S. 0.4; ELD 0.7; 1.4; S 2.3; DANA; 0.3 BUDD
- Column 11: TUCK.; SQUAX 0.3; PEALE S. W; ELD 0.4; 0.9; S 1.5; DANA; W BUDD
- Column 12: TUCK.; SQUAX W; PEALE S. W; ELD W; 0.7; S 0.7; DANA; 0.4 BUDD

Note: Tuksel Point on navigation charts is "Unsal Point" on current charts.

* See Note on Current Charts— Apply no correction factor

How to Use "Current Thing" Information West of Case Inlet	Factors for Correcting Speeds

How to Use "Current Thing" Information West of Case Inlet

To predict current speed in knots for any hour during any flood or ebb current cycle for any day or year for the listed locations:

1.) From **Tidal Current Tables** look up and note for The Narrows for the day and time of choice:
   — Times of maximum flood and speed in knots
   — Times of maximum ebb and speed in knots

2.) Compare these speeds with the **"Knots"** column in the **"Factors for Correcting Speeds"** table to determine the correct factor for the specific flood cycle and specific ebb cycle.

3.) Using the appropriate **"Factor"** for the flood and/or ebb, multiply the tropic speed listed in the **COLUMN " T"** for the location.

The result indicates the predicted current direction and speed during each hour in the specific tidal cycle.

Factors for Correcting Speeds

When predicted speed in The Narrows (north end) is: — Multiply speed on chart by —

Knots:	Factor
0.2–0.5	0.1
0.6–0.9	0.2
1.0–1.3	0.3
1.4–1.7	0.4
1.8–2.1	0.5
2.2–2.5	0.6
2.6–2.9	0.7
3.0–3.3	0.8
3.4–3.7	0.9
3.8–4.1	1.0
4.2–4.5	1.1
4.6–4.9	1.2
5.0–5.3	1.3
5.4–5.7	1.4
5.8–6.1	1.5

All the details and tabulations are taken from the NOAA Current Charts and are subject to the same irregularities as described therein, plus any omissions, errors or oversights that we have made.

We find "Current Thing" West of Case Inlet useful, but others using it do so at their own risk and peril.

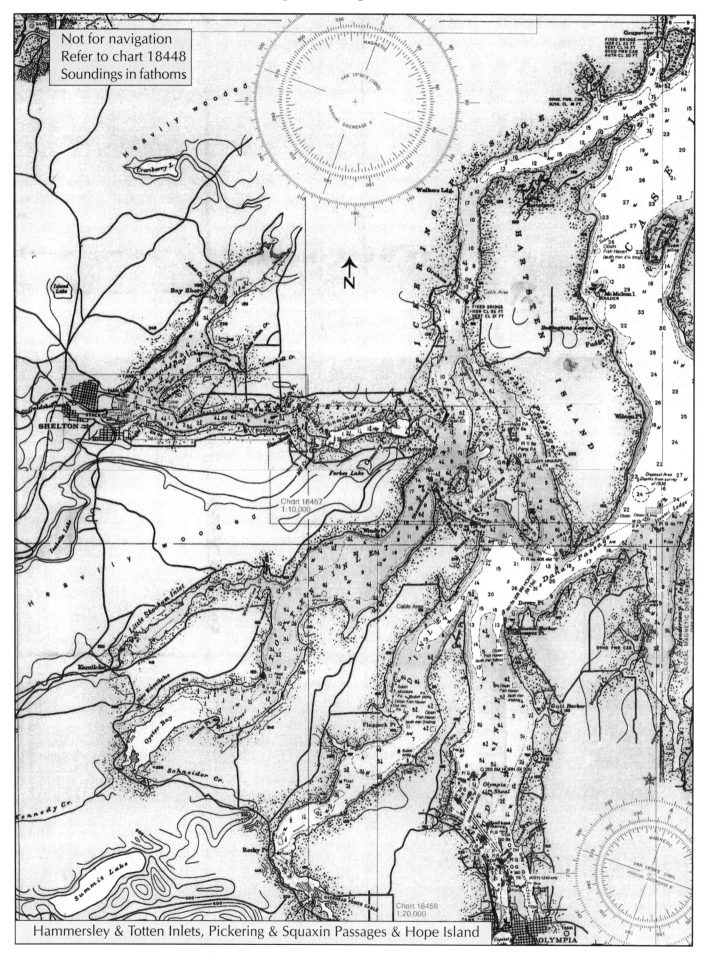

Not for navigation
Refer to chart 18448
Soundings in fathoms

Hammersley & Totten Inlets, Pickering & Squaxin Passages & Hope Island

CHAPTER 18
Hammersley and Totten Inlets, Pickering and Squaxin Passages and Hope Island

<table>
<tr><th colspan="6" align="center">Charts and publications for this chapter</th></tr>
<tr><th>Chart</th><th>Date</th><th>Title</th><th></th><th>Scale</th><th>Soundings</th></tr>
<tr><td>*   18445</td><td>06/03/95</td><td colspan="4">Puget Sound, Possession Sound to Olympia,</td></tr>
<tr><td></td><td></td><td>page C</td><td></td><td>1:80,000</td><td>..................... Fathoms</td></tr>
<tr><td></td><td></td><td>page D, inset 10, Shelton</td><td></td><td>1:10,000</td><td>..................... Fathoms</td></tr>
<tr><td>*   18448</td><td>10/30/93</td><td>Puget Sound Southern Part</td><td></td><td>1:80,000</td><td>..................... Fathoms</td></tr>
<tr><td>***18457</td><td>09/02/89</td><td>Puget Sound—Hammersley Inlet to Shelton</td><td></td><td>1:10,000</td><td>........................... Feet</td></tr>
<tr><td>18440</td><td>08/05/95</td><td>Puget Sound</td><td></td><td>1:150,000</td><td>................... Fathoms</td></tr>
<tr><td></td><td></td><td colspan="4">South Puget Sound Tidal Current Charts</td></tr>
<tr><td></td><td></td><td colspan="4">Puget Sound Shellfish Sites</td></tr>
<tr><td></td><td></td><td>Washington State Public Lands Quad Map, Tacoma</td><td></td><td>1:100,000</td><td></td></tr>
<tr><td></td><td></td><td>Washington State Public Lands Quad Map, Shelton</td><td></td><td>1:100,000</td><td></td></tr>
</table>

➡ *When using charts, compare your chart dates with ones referred to above. There may be discrepancies between different charts and different chart editions.*

Overview

In this chapter we explore Pickering Passage, including McLane Cove, Jarrell Cove State Park and Jarrell's Cove Marina. We go south under the fixed Hartstene Island bridge, pass by the north entrance of Peale Passage, proceeding to the south end of Pickering at Hungerford Point. Here we turn west into Hammersley Inlet leading to Shelton and Oakland Bay. After that we once again head south and explore Totten and Little Skookum inlets, then go east through Squaxin Passage and visit Hope Island State Park and the surrounding waters.

The next and last chapter explores Dana and Peale passages and their currents, Eld and Budd inlets and finally Olympia.

Currents for Pickering and Squaxin passages, Hammersley and Totten inlets and around Hope Island are in the "Current" section, pages 260-263.

Now, let's rediscover Pickering Passage as we follow the same course as Peter Puget did, but, unlike Peter, we use charts and navigation aids.

Pickering Passage, its size, shape and obstructions:

Length is roughly nine miles long, the north entrance is at Dougall Point at the northeast end of Hartstene Island across from Stretch Island. The pass trends southwest for about three miles and then bends south for the rest of the passage.

At Hungerford Point, near the southern end of Pickering, the pass joins the confluence of four other inlets and passages; Hammersley and Totten Inlets, Squaxin Passage, and the small unnamed pass between Hope and Squaxin Islands.

Width of Pickering is about 0.6 mile wide at the north, widens briefly then narrows at the bend where is shrinks to 0.3 mile. About two miles farther south it again narrows to 0.2 mile at Graham Point at the fixed bridge to Hartstene, with a vertical clearance of 31 feet at MHW. (See Bridge Clearance details on page 269.)

South of the bridge the passage width is 0.3 mile. At Salmon Point on the north end of Squaxin Island the width is about 0.5 mile, where Peale Passage joins Pickering Passage.

➡ **NOTE: Marine gas and diesel** are available only at **Jarrell's Cove Marina** in the areas covered in this chapter.

Peter Puget and his hearty band of explorers rowed and sailed from the head of Case Inlet through Pickering Pass on Thursday, May 24, 1792.

Puget's boats passed by McLane Cove as they went south in Pickering Pass, but as far we know they didn't stop.

Public tidelands of more than 13 miles are in the areas covered in this chapter.

Public tidelands, are state-owned unless otherwise noted; some of them may be leased for private purposes. When we go ashore on public tidelands we take the Washington State Public Lands Quadrangle Map with us to avoid trespassing on adjacent private property.

Hartstene Pointe at Dougall Point, a 231 acre private development, includes three miles of beaches and a private marina.

Not for navigation
Refer to chart 18445, page C
Soundings in fathoms

McLane Cove

Abandoned prune drier

Pickering continues south between Squaxin Island and the mainland; widths vary from 0.2 to 0.4 mile for the next 1.3 miles to Hungerford Point.

Depths in Pickering range from 18 fathoms at the north end of the pass to five and six fathoms at the south end. The only charted hazards are shoals off the entrance to Hammersley Inlet.

Underway again, starting at the northeast entrance off Harstine Island, we follow Puget's wake through Pickering Passage, except we use charts and he had only the touch system. He also didn't make all the stops that we will.

Charted shoal of two fathoms, three feet extends about 0.25 mile off the east pointing sandspit at Dougall Point.

Indian Cove, unnamed on charts, is a small bay 0.6 mile southwest of Dougall Point. Hartstene Pointe private marina is in the cove.

Public tidelands of about 9,000 feet in two parcels run along the island's north shoreline, starting about 2,000 feet west of Dougall Point.

From Indian Cove let's cross to the north shore of Pickering Passage, west of Stretch Island and travel along the shore to McLane Cove.

Public tidelands of about 3,000 feet are in two parcels between the bay west of Stretch Island and McLane Cove. About 1,000 feet are directly off McLane Cove's east entrance; another 3,000 feet are west of the cove. It's easy to dinghy to these beaches at low tides.

Deep green forests cover uplands of these shores, with an occasional home peeking through; silvered drift logs line the beaches. Banks on these mainland shores rise about 40 or 50 feet above.

G **McLane Cove** opens up and we find a quiet bay with sandstone bluffs pocked with large holes at the east entrance. There are no charted hazards except a rock off the east point. The cove, near Stadium, is about 0.1 mile wide by about 0.2 mile long— a **delightful gunkhole.**

Depths in the cove are 12 to 20 feet. A red house on a bluff is at the west entrance. Several houses are scattered around the bay. An abandoned prune dryer left over from early farming days is hidden in trees on the east shore.

Anchoring, we find the cove has good protection except from a southerly. We anchor west center in mud bottom, 12-20 feet.

Beaches inside the cove are all private. We can glimpse Grapeview Road bridge farther up at the western head of the cove. It's quiet and inviting here.

Underway again, we leave McLane Cove continuing southwest along the mainland shore about one mile near a drying cove where there is public beach.

Public tidelands of about 2,500 feet in three parcels are here.

Anchor in about two fathoms off the cove to dinghy ashore and explore.

Three other small drying coves are west along this mainland shore.

Now, we cross Pickering Passage to Harstine Island again. It's about 1.7 miles from Dougall Point west to Jarrell Cove. Forested banks are as much as 120 feet high and slowly being covered with homes.

Jarrell Cove is home to Jarrell Cove State Park and Jarrell's Cove Marina. Immediately east of the cove's entrance on Pickering Pass are several large homes on the bank, and just off the beach are old dock pilings and fallen trees. We turn south into the cove past the pilings to reach the park and marina.

Jarrell Cove is about 0.6 mile long and about 200 yards wide, with a drying arm about 0.3 miles long off the east side.

Depths in the cove are from five fathoms at the entrance to drying tidelands in the south and east coves.

Public tidelands surround all shores of the cove, totaling about 8,000 feet.

Jarrell Cove State Park is charted as #98A on 18445. Facilities are as listed, except there is no electricity on the floats.

Two park floats with mooring space are in the cove, and both have trails leading to the park's uplands with campgrounds, restrooms and other facilities.

The first park float is roughly 300 yards inside the cove and has a pump-out. The second float is 500 yards farther into the cove, also on the east shore.

Uncharted drying sandspit north of the second float extends west from a small barren bluff on the southeast shore. We've seen boats run aground on this spit when entering, particularly at low tide, so we give it plenty of room.

At the inner float we will settle in mud on low tide so we move out in the cove to a buoy or to anchor off.

> ### Jarrell Cove State Park Facilities
> ➤ 14 mooring buoys—at our last count
> ➤ 682 feet of total moorage space at two floats
> ➤ Year round moorage fees: $5 per buoy; floats: $8 for boats
>   under 26', $11 for boats over 26'
> ➤ Restrooms, showers
> ➤ More than 3,506 feet of shoreline
> ➤ 42.6 acres of uplands
> ➤ Pump-out station on north float
> ➤ 20 campsites, including #20, a Cascadia Water Trail site
> ➤ Day-use area, water, kitchen shelter near inner float
> ➤ Play area for loosely organized games
> ➤ Phone: 360-426-9226

McLane Cove was the site of a lively community in the early part of the century. Residents of Stadium lived on both sides of the cove, had their own post office and a newspaper column. But to get together they had to have boats. A bridge was built in 1923 and Stadium folks had direct access to the school and their neighbors at Grapeview.

The bridge was 840 feet long, 30 feet high, with a graceful curve at one end. After 10 years of ever-increasing car traffic it was unsafe and demolished. Other wooden bridges were built, but it wasn't until 1953 that a permanent 60 foot steel bridge was built at the head of the cove.

Jarrell Cove State Park float

ⓖ Exploring Jarrell Cove shoreline by skiff at high tide is best as the beaches are muddy at low tide and yucky to walk on. The main cove continues about 0.25 mile farther south where private homes line the shore. The small secluded arm east of the park's inner float, complete with deep green overhanging trees, is a beautiful spot to drift quietly at high tide in a small boat, a **popular gunkhole**.

⚓ **Anchoring** is often the only way to find a spot on crowded weekends. On the other hand, we've been there in the winter—and even in the summer—when there have been very few boats.

Much of the park has been left natural and is a delight for the family. A one mile foot trail winds through the meadows and trees in the park for those who want to stretch their legs. Or leave the park on Wingert Road and walk Harstine's roads.

Deer Crossing, whether walking, bicycling or driving, watch for the many deer going in and out of the woods—who knows which way they may turn.

An old dock at the head of cove is all that remains of the Jarrell homestead.

✯ **Jarrell's Cove Marina,** charted as #98 on 18445, is on the cove's west shore across from the park. Facilities at the marina are as listed.

The marina has both guest and permanent moorage. It is a hub of the island community and has the only store and gas station on the island. Open year round, they get visitors winter and summer by land and sea.

Many who stay at the state park find the store ideal for extra supplies, or to refuel.

Gary and Lorna Hink bought the resort in 1980 because they wanted a "great place" to raise their twin sons. The sons are grown and they say it **has** been great.

Robert and Philura Jarrell were the first non-Native American settlers on Harstine Island, arriving about 1872. She was the only white woman during their first 15 years. On Philura's 75th birthday in 1905, a reporter wrote that 75 persons attending the party had, "Perhaps the most pleasant and most lively time Harstine Island had ever known." She ran the post office until her death March 23, 1913.

The Jarrells logged, farmed, sailed, and were friends of the Indians. A neighbor said that "quite often Indians would come single file in their canoes to visit the Jarrells. The string of canoes reached from one end of the cove to the other, and they would probably have a clambake."

*For those who want to know more about this lovely island we recommend the delightful book, **The Island Remembers, a History of Harstine Island and Its People**, by Beulah Hitchcock and Helen Wingert. Published by the Harstine Women's Club in 1979, the book tells of the pioneers, their joys and their sorrows, in a very personal way. We thoroughly enjoyed it. It's sold at the Jarrell's Cove Marina store.*

Jarrell's Cove Marina Facilities
➤ Guest moorage for approximately five to seven boats on shore side of G float
➤ Moorage rates about 50 cents per foot
➤ 30 amp shore power at $3 per day; water
➤ Restrooms, showers, laundry
➤ Fuel: gas, diesel and propane at both fuel float and on land
➤ Free pump-out, porta-potty dump, garbage
➤ Check in at fuel float or call ahead by telephone.
➤ RV and tent campsites at the resort
➤ Store carries groceries, beer, wine, ice, some marine hardware, books, magazines, fishing supplies
➤ Fishing is good, they say, even off the dock
➤ Phone: 360-426-8823

Public tidelands of about 3,500 feet are along Pickering Passage adjacent to their property. The Hinks granted an easement to DNR so visitors may reach the beach through the marina.

Jarrell's Cove Marina

⚓ **Underway again,** west and south in Pickering Passage, we head out from Jarrell Cove, cruising towards the unnamed northwestern point of Harstine Island.

Public tidelands of about 4,000 feet wrap around the point. Homes and beach cabins, bluffs and forests are on both shores of this stretch of Pickering Pass.

Walker's Landing is on the mainland shore as Pickering turns south.

Depths are two fathoms off the landing. A few boats are sometimes anchored here, but all beaches are private. A charted drying lagoon is north of the landing.

Harstine Island bridge, joining the island to the mainland, now comes in view.

Public tidelands of over 5,500 feet in four parcels are on Harstine's western shore between the northwestern point and the bridge. These tidelands are accessible by boat only; surrounding beaches are private.

Latimer's Landing public launch ramp on the mainland shore, charted as "surfaced ramp" on 18445, is just north of the bridge. It's a single lane concrete ramp with adjacent float and parking for a dozen or so trucks and trailers. Latrines and garbage cans are on site.

Public tidelands of about 500 feet are about 3,000 feet north of the ramp.

Cable area is just north of the bridge.

Public tidelands of about 4,000 feet run south from Latimer's Landing around the two tiny spits at Graham Point and into the two, small, drying bights.

Harstine Island Bridge at Graham Point has a charted vertical clearance of 31 feet at MHW, 95 feet horizontal clearance.

Tide clearance gauges on the bridge would be a much safer way of communicating the actual clearance to the mariner. In our opinion, they should be required on all federal waterways.

Public tidelands extend south from the bridge along Harstine Island to the entrance to Peale Passage in two separate parcels totaling 6,000 feet.

The bridge was dedicated on June 22, 1969. It replaced the last shallow draft ferry, old **Harstine II,** which ran from the island to Graham Point.

Salmon Point at the north tip of Squaxin Island separates Pickering Passage and Peale Passage.

Lorna Hink of Jarrell's Cove Marina talks about island life: "It's still pretty isolated on Harstine. No one delivers milk and bread here, we go to Shelton for that. We have potlucks and a little theater group which gives a free show at Christmas time. We all have Shelton addresses, not Harstine Island. There used to be a post office on the island, but no more. The only 'government' we have is the fire department and the community club."

There is a good emergency system on the island, with a paramedic on duty all the time. There are two fire stations, one at Hartstene Pointe and one at the south end of the island; two engines and a tanker.

Vertical Clearance at Center Span of the Harstine Island Bridge:

At MHHW:	31.0' clr at MHW + 13.2' at MLLW - 14.2' at MHHW	=	**30.0'**
At MHW	Vertical Clearance as Charted	=	**31.0'**
At MLLW	31.0' at MHW + 13.2' at MLLW	=	**44.5'**
At ELW	44.5' at MLLW + [-5.0' at ELW]	=	**49.5'**

The tide table indicates predicted heights above or below MLLW datum. These heights can be greater or less than predicted due to extreme winds, rain, snow melt or barometric pressures. Times predicted may also be off for high and low tides.

Values shown should be checked against the *Tide Table*. The formula should be checked for errors before attempting to pass under the span. In other words, don't just take our word for it. We do **not** guarantee these figures.

Chart 18448, 10/30/95, was used for the above tabulation. We note no values were given for extreme high tides.

Venerable Harstine Islander John Erickson—an old salt with many years of sailing & island living—said if he could see mussels on bridge piers it was safe to go under in his Bristol Bay boat with a 32 ft. mast.

Sailing friends from Olympia whose mast was too tall to go under the bridge would put the whole family on one side of their sailboat and heel it far enough over so they could squeak under.

⚓ **Underway again**, back to the west mainland shore south of the Harstine Bridge, where there are two small unnamed coves on Pickering Passage just south of the bridge. Homes and cabins are on the shores of both coves, and both have private buoys and floats.

"Graham Cove" is our name for the north cove.

"Tr," tower is charted in the cove, but it's one of those "stealth towers" which NOAA charted but we couldn't see, as its removal apparently was not charted.

Harstine Island Bridge

Depth of one fathom one foot is charted about 250 yards offshore and three to four fathoms in a radius of about 350 yards here.

A tiny unnamed island is about 0.7 mile south of Harstine bridge near the south end of "Graham Cove." A bridge connects this tiny island to the mainland. Olympia Yacht Club's delightful outstation facility is on the island. The yacht club's private moorage floats are on the north side of the bridge to the island.

Public tidelands of less than 1,000 feet are on the mainland shore west of the yacht club.

Olympia Yacht Club outstation looking south

"Rectangle Bight" is our name for the second cove on the mainland.

Development is moderate along the western shore of the cove, including a painted "guard eagle" at a private dock; the rest of the shoreline is private and forested.

⚓ **Anchoring** in "Graham Cove" and "Rectangle Bight" appears questionable without local knowledge, giving attention to depths, shoaling, charted rocks, currents and bottom characteristics.

Current potential at extreme mainstream flood and ebb may reach 2.1 to 2.5 knots in this general area. Changes in direction of flow can cause anchors to break out and hopefully reset in the direction of the current change.

Bottom symbols in this area are charted sand and gravel, which usually do not hold an anchor as well as mud.

South of "Rectangle Bight," where pilings are charted, is a lovely, sandy beach. Along this same beach is a sign we love on an upland building: *Port Schoumburg Wharfing*.

Hungerford Point at the entrance to Hammersley Inlet is about 0.7 mile south of Rectangle Bight.

Peter Puget's men rowed south through Pickering Passage along the shores of Hartstene Island on Thursday, May 24, 1792. They camped that night on the west shore of the pass, and we wouldn't be at all surprised if it was in one of the two small coves. Either one is the kind of place they usually picked.

Hammersley Inlet, Shelton and Oakland Bay Overview

Hammersley Inlet is an intriguing, nearly six mile long inlet through a narrow, shallow, river-like channel leading west to Shelton and Oakland Bay.

It keeps us alert as we cruise past the entrance at Hungerford Point, then encounter Cape Horn and Cape Cod in a few minutes' time. We pass bends and points: Church, Libby, Cannery, Skookum, peering into bays and coves. It's a trip like none other in South Sound, and we made our first trip through after careful study of the chart and current tables.

Width, shore to shore Hammersley Inlet is 0.4 mile wide at the east entrance, narrowing abruptly to 0.125 miles at Capes Cod and Horn and later at Libby Point.

Navigable channel width of 75 yards is between the charted six foot depth curve just east of Cannery Point, with controlling depth of about seven feet at MLLW.

Controlling depth in Hammersley Inlet is "about eight feet," according to the *Coast Pilot.*

Between Cannery and Libby points, along the south shore, the six foot depth curve projects about halfway across the channel. A drying shoal is along this shore. The deepest water in Hammersley is along the southwest side east of Skookum Point and along the north shore between Skookum and Church points. Between Church and Miller points we stay more or less midchannel where depths are greatest.

Currents may reach max speeds of about five knots during extreme tidal ranges. Because of current and shoals, it's best to travel Hammersley on a rising tide.

When running with the current, the speed of a vessel, plus the speed of the current, determines the impact in event of grounding. Backing off a shoal against a current is difficult and sometimes not possible. Grounding is less likely to occur, or at least with less impact, near the end of the flood when currents are diminished. And if grounded, it's easier to back off in slower currents.

The *Coast Pilot* is cautious regarding Hammersley and suggests "entering on the flood, usually after half tide, and leaving on the ebb, usually before maximum strength." It warns that "vessels with sharp rise of bilge should avoid the inlet as there is danger of capsizing in the strong current in case of grounding." It also suggests the inlet "is considered dangerous to strangers"— those without local knowledge, because of currents and shallows. (1995, page 380, paragraphs 565 and 566)

Vessels without tows must give way to tugs with tows, which cannot maneuver easily in this constricted waterway.

Shelton, at the west end of Hammersley Inlet —the carrot at the end of the stick—is a city of about 7,500 friendly folks, nestled in the bend of Oakland Bay. It's the only incorporated city in Mason County, and is also the county seat. Shelton's nickname is "Christmastown, U.S.A.," for the millions of deep green, fragrant Christmas trees it produces and ships annually up and down the coast.

The Simpson Timber Company's mill operations dominate the downtown waterfront south of the Port of Shelton small craft moorage. Other industries, also dependent on nearby woods and water, include lumber, shellfish farming, the Christmas tree industry and ITT Rayonier's research division. A large employer in the Shelton area is the state at the close-by Washington Corrections Center.

Pickering Passage was named for Charles Pickering, a naturalist with the Wilkes' expedition in 1841.

An alternate channel, about 100 yards wide, is west of Cape Horn with controlling depth of eight to nine feet along the north shore between Cape Horn and Cannery Point.

Similar to Nakwakto?

At times we likened the trip through Hammersley Inlet to four mile long Schooner Channel leading to Nakwakto Rapids, just a bit south and east of Cape Caution in B.C. Except at Schooner Channel there wasn't a single home or habitation—totally primeval wilderness. And at the north end were the rapids which can run as much as 16 knots on an ebb. This makes Hammersley fairly tame, but nonetheless an exciting and special passage.

**Charts Used in Getting to Hammersley Area,
Without Suitable Details for Navigating the Inlet:**

- **18448**, **10/30/93**, **scale 1:80,000**, fathoms, *Puget Sound Southern Portion*
- **18445**, **6/3/95**, **Page C, scale 1:80,000**, fathoms, *Puget Sound, Possession Point to Olympia.*
- **18445**, **6/3/95 Page D, inset 10, scale 1:10,000**, fathoms, from Miller Point to Shelton north to Lat. 47°13'10.2" in Oakland Bay. Inset is a duplication of the 1:10,000 scale of the area on chart 18457, soundings in feet; also indicates ramps, facilities and services.

(continued on page 272)

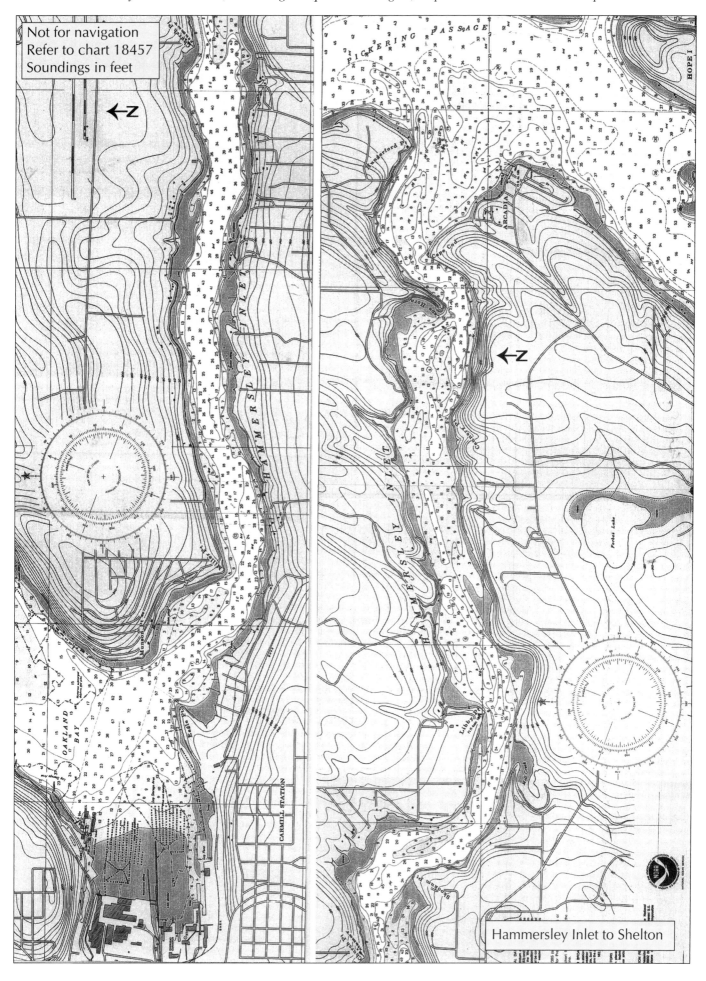

Not for navigation
Refer to chart 18457
Soundings in feet

Hammersley Inlet to Shelton

It hasn't happened for quite a while, but in August 1920, a 55 foot humpback whale supposedly made a side trip into Oakland Bay instead of staying on the prescribed coastal migration route. Unfortunately he was killed. We heard of another who decided to run down Hammersley in the 1970s, but apparently made it back out intact.

Entrance to Hammersley at Hungerford Point, looking west

Logs and barges are towed in and out of Hammersley. Simpson Timber Company tows logs to its Shelton operations. Manke Lumber Company tows logs out of Shelton to its mills in Tacoma. Barges full of wood chips are sometimes towed to Tacoma. In the future, gravel barges may be towed through the inlet.

Most tugs plan to leave at high water before the current is running too fast. We understand when there are extreme high and low tides they may not leave at all. We've been told some tows are over 800 feet long and 200 feet wide. Most difficult spots for tugs and tows are the same for all boats: Capes Horn and Cod, Libby, Skookum and Church points. Indolent sea lions and seals often hitch rides on the log rafts, basking in the sun when it shines and enjoying the free trip.

(Continued from page 270)

Chart used approaching and in Hammersley Inlet to Oakland Bay, Shelton:
- **18457, 9/2/89, scale 1:10,000, soundings in feet, Puget Sound—Hammersley Inlet to Shelton,** is terrific. We clung to it in rain, fog, thick and thin.
- **Area covered** is north from Hunter Point in Squaxin Passage and about 0.8 mile south of Steamboat Island in Totten Inlet to about 0.4 mile north of Hungerford Point in Pickering Passage; west from Squaxin Island, including Hope Island, through Hammersley Inlet into Oakland Bay and Shelton. In Oakland Bay it extends for about 0.4 mile north of Shelton to Lat. 47°13'10.2." Oakland Bay details north of this latitude are available on the 1:80,000 scale on charts 18445 and 18448.
- **Discrepancies exist between these three charts, dating from 9/2/89 to 6/3/95, and clarifications are needed.**

Aids to Navigation, Entrance to Hammersley Inlet:
- **Fl R 4s "2" PA Hungerford Point Light 2** flashing red on triangular red dayboard on pile structure, "Position Approximate"
- **Black square** symbol for structure only and no light or beacon is charted at **Hungerford Point** on 18457. The black symbol is not on 18445 or 18448.
- **Depths** across most of the entrance to Hammersley do shoal in some places to drying flats at MLLW and lower, between the **Hungerford Point channel** and a shallow channel off **Arcadia.**
  - **Two fathom** curve extends east nearly halfway across Pickering Passage
  - **Green buoy "C 1"** previously charted about 225 yards south of Hungerford Point has been permanently removed, but is charted on 18457, 9/2/89, and on 18445, 6/1/91. (It is not charted on 18445, 6/3/95, or 18448, 10/30/93.)
  - **Obstr ED or Obstn ED** (submerged obstruction, **E**xistence **D**oubtful) is charted on 18448 about 150 yards south of Hungerford Point. No depth is given. A channel between the submerged obstruction and the charted rocks at Hungerford Point shoreline does not look feasible on this chart, but does on 18445 and 18457.
- **Chart 18445**, 6/3/95, or its previous edition, 6/1/91, does not indicate a submerged obstruction in the above location. The shaded edge of the 18 foot or three fathom curve on 18445 shows a narrow 3-5 fathom channel entering Hammersley from east of Hungerford Point.
- **Chart 18457**, 9/2/89, soundings in feet, shows the submerged obstruction "ED" about 200 yards south of Hungerford Point. It appears well clear of charted shoreline rocks. The absence of the obstruction on later charts might indicate the obstruction is non-existent, but we don't count on it.

Hungerford Point channel: A shaded two fathom curve and dotted three fathom curve (depths of 14 to 42 feet) is well-defined along the north and west shore from Hungerford Point to **Cape Horn** and south and west almost to **Cannery Point.**
- **Red buoy "2"** charted about 125 yards west of Cape Horn on 18457, has been permanently removed. It is not charted on 18445 or 18448. U.S. Coast Guard advised it was discontinued due to its being snagged and towed off station by log rafts.
- **A buoy off station can be worse than no buoy at all.**

Now, back to the entrance at Arcadia Point:
- **Fl G 4s light** charted on 18457 at Arcadia Point, has been permanently removed. This light is not charted on 18445 or 18448.
- **Arcadia channel**: Depths are charted on 18457 as 8-14 feet roughly 50 yards off shoreline points and bulges from Arcadia Point to Cape Cod. This is shallower and narrower than Hungerford Channel along the north shore. We have seen several boats use this approach to Hammersley, but have not done so ourselves.
- **Charts 18445 and 18448**, 1:80,000, soundings in fathoms, do not define depths well enough to indicate this south channel.

Entering Hammersley Inlet

We start our trip into Hammersley at Hungerford Point, following the charted channel along the north shore, making an arc which brings us past Cape Cod on the south, with trees overhanging rocky shores.

At Cape Horn, we see caves in barren bluffs on the east side and aim for the channel off the south shore.

A six foot depth curve begins about 150 yards west of Cape Horn and extends about 525 yards west toward Cannery Point. A small area of a shoal, about 300 yards west of Cape Horn, dries at MLLW. Depths of three and four feet are common elsewhere on this shoal. The west end of the shoal is roughly 100 yards north and east of Cannery Point.

Two channels north and south around the shoal are indicated on the chart. We've not used the north channel, but it might be a retreat to escape a tug and tow.

Controlling depths of nine feet are charted in the channel north of the shoal.

Controlling depths of seven feet are charted in the channel at the Cannery Point end of the shoal, along the south shore. This begins to feel a bit shallow.

West of Cannery Point and east of the "bulge" about 0.5 mile east of Libby Point, we keep well north of a line-of-sight between Cannery Point and Cape Horn. At the north shore bulge we head southwest to the south shore big bump.

Public tidelands of about 5,000 feet in four parcels are along the inlet's north shore between Cape Horn and Libby Point area.

Fl R 4s 18ft 4M "4" Libby Point Light 4 flashing red, is next on the north shore, 1.2 mile west of Cannery Point. From here we stay about midchannel.

Mill Creek is on the south shore, west of Libby Point. It's a shallow creek leading back into a quiet bay where there was once a sawmill in the last century.

Homes abound along the inlet in some places, and in others the inlet is lined with trees, bluffs and beaches, like it was before "civilization" arrived.

Approaching Skookum Point, we favor the south and west shore and find deeper water, up to 72 feet (charted), continuing northwest across the inlet to the Church Point channel along the north shores.

Fl R 6s 20ft 4M "6" Church Point Light 6 is on a triangular red dayboard on a white structure. There's a channel from 14 to 42 feet deep 100 yards offshore. Directly south of Church Point, extending west of Skookum Point, is a long shoal with charted shallows of one-nine feet, shown in both green and blue on chart 18457.

We continue more or less midchannel for the next two miles towards Miller Point. Tide flats extend off both north and south shores, but navigable depths range from 13-58 feet once west of Church Point, with widths about 150-200 yards.

A private navigation light is charted on 18457 and 18448, but not on 18445, 6/3/95, or in the *Light List.* Location is about 0.7 mile west of Church Point on the bulkhead at a private home on the south shore.

Public tidelands of about 6,000 feet in five parcels are along the north shore between Church Point and Miller Point.

Cable area crosses Hammersley Inlet 0.25 mile east of Miller Point, not charted on 18448.

Walker (Mason) County Park is on the south shore across from Miller Point. The park has about 1,650 feet of gravel beach, picnic tables, restrooms and water.

Charted "surfaced ramp" is abandoned.

Anchoring about 100 yards offshore to avoid shallows will put a boat in the current and possibly in the way of tugs with tows. We don't recommend this.

Jacoby Shorecrest (Mason) County Park is on the north shore, in the bay between Miller and Munson Points**.**

Cape Horn caves

Hammersley Inlet was named for George W. Hammersley, a midshipman with the Wilkes Expedition.

Peter Puget either missed the Hammersley Inlet entrance as he went past it about dawn on the morning of Friday, May 25, 1792, or decided it wasn't worth bothering with. Instead they rowed and sailed to the head of Totten Inlet.
It was Wilkes who first noticed and explored the inlet in 1841.

Private navigation light

Jo recalls: Hammersley Inlet always held a mystique for me. During the 18 years I lived in Olympia I never cruised the inlet. Carl and I did it on a cold, rainy day, which enhanced my apprehension. Once past Church Point I realized we were through the shallows, and suddenly found it had been a special trip and I was pleased we had done it.

We understand a proposed gravel loading dock may be constructed north of the Shelton Port docks.

Gravel would be brought by conveyor belt to this dock where it would be loaded aboard barges. This of course, will increase barge traffic in Hammersley Inlet.

Park facilities include 320 feet of shoreline, picnic, play areas and a sani-can.

Charted "surfaced ramp" is at the park.

A muddy shoal with depths of one fathom to zero (0) fathoms two feet, parallels the shoreline extending southeast from Munson Point.

⚓ **Anchor** off Jacoby Park between the shore and the charted shoal, keeping out of the current, mud bottom, 10 to 17 feet.

Cable area from Munson Point to Shelton marina area is charted on all charts.

☸ **As we head across** Oakland Bay, northwest toward the boathouses, we can see that most of the bay to the south and west is a maze of log storage, piles and dolphins and the constant activity associated with a working waterfront.

Shelton Marina on the west shore is a small craft moorage owned by the port and managed by **Shelton Yacht Club** whose members are most helpful.

Enter the marina by going between two floats lined with boats and boathouses where the inner float is signed, "Welcome to the Port of Shelton." There the 65 foot long guest float with moorage on either side awaits the visitors. What the moorage may lack in amenities is more than made up for by the friendly people in the port and in Shelton itself.

Shelton waterfront, marina to the right

Port of Shelton Marina is charted as #96A on 18445. Listed facilities show showers, diesel and gas; **none** are presently at the port.

There were no marine fuel facilities in Shelton in 1996, but we were told they hope to have them again "in the future." The nearest gas station is on a highway in town where fuel can be purchased for portable tanks. It's at least a 0.5 mile walk from the port dock.

Port of Shelton Facilities
➤ Guest moorage for about eight boats at guest dock
➤ Moorage fee 25 cents per foot
➤ 30 amp shore power for $2 daily; water
➤ Sani-can
➤ Pump-out on float
➤ Shelton Yacht Club offers guest moorage for members of reciprocal yacht clubs free for first 48 hours, not including power
➤ Phone: 360-426-6435

In the mid-1800s, the restless, westward-moving settlers saw the low shores, covered with beautiful timber, and decided to move to Hammersley Inlet.

David Shelton moved to the area with his family in 1853 and filed a 640 acre claim in 1855. The area's first sawmill was built at the entrance to Mill Creek on the southern shore of Hammersley Inlet.

The old Shelton mill town had a company store, a railroad that ran down the main street, and a railroad roundhouse in the center of town. For many years a pulp mill shared the waterfront with the Simpson lumber mills.

It wasn't until 1888 that "Sheltonville" won the election for county seat of Mason County.

⚓ **Anchoring** is possible if there's no space at the float, or if that's your choice, between the cable crossing and log storage area, two to four fathoms, mud bottom. Be aware of charted and uncharted submerged dolphins and pilings.

Launch ramp, usable at high tide only, is on the northwest shore, behind the marina.

It's about a mile or so walk into downtown Shelton from the marina. There you will find restaurants, stores, post office and other services. The hardware store is about 0.75 mile, the liquor store is about 1.5 miles, and marine supplies and fishing gear are about two miles.

When we stayed at the Port of Shelton, the whistle of a nearby logging train surprised us, until we realized they still bring logs in by train from Dayton to the Simpson Mill.

Simpson claimed in 1996 to be the largest lumber mill in the country, producing about one million board feet daily.

To learn more about historical Shelton, visit the Chamber of Commerce office in a restored railroad caboose behind the old Shay locomotive downtown. They'll head you on a historical walking tour through downtown.

You can get even more information about the town at the Mason County Historical Society Museum at Fifth and Railroad. Built in 1914, it is Shelton's combined library and city hall.

The town has an enormous statue of its favorite hero, that legendary logger, Paul Bunyan.

Shelton guest dock looking east

⚓ **Oakland Bay** is about four miles long and 0.6 miles wide and we admit to not having cruised the bay, mainly because it has so many submerged piles, dolphins, snags, ruins, and we've not yet explored it by skiff. We'll do that later.

Public tidelands of about 4,500 feet in three parcels are on the north and south shores of shoaling Chapman Cove off the east side of Oakland Bay. Without checking it out we can't recommend anchoring.

Depths in the north portion are mostly 1-1/4 fathoms with a couple of three and four fathom depths, and one five fathom hole in a large drying north end lagoon. The entire north half of the bay is shown as "oyster reserves" on the state quad map.

Underway again

⚓ We've been through Hammersley into Shelton, made our way safely back out of the inlet, and now we're off Arcadia Point, again.

"Arcadia Point public launch ramp, Squaxin Island Tribe," is on the east side of the point on Pickering Pass. Formerly owned by the Port of Shelton, the ramp was sold to the Squaxin Tribe about 1984 for access to their tribal-owned Squaxin Island. Private property is on either side of the charted surfaced ramp with parking about a block away.

From the center of the ramp magnificent Mount Rainier towers over the whole scene. Views of Squaxin and Hope islands are to the east, Squaxin Passage and Steamboat Island to the southeast. Totten Inlet, our next destination, is slightly to the southwest.

Overview of Totten Inlet

The inlet trends southwest for about nine miles from the entrance, between the west end of Squaxin Passage and Arcadia Point. Although there are a fair number of homes along its shores, Totten is not as crowded as Eld and Budd Inlets.

Widths in Totten Inlet vary from about 0.25 miles at the northern entrance to nearly 1.5 miles at unnamed Gallagher Cove on the east shore.

Depth at the entrance is about 16 fathoms. A charted 3.5 fathom shoal is mid-channel west of the point at Carlyon Beach. Depths of nine fathoms are east of the shoal and 16 fathoms on the west side.

South and west from Windy Point depths shoal from 19 fathoms to drying flats at Burns Cove and those massive flats of Oyster Bay west of steep, 100 foot high Burns Point.

Oyster Bay, at the head of the inlet, has private oyster beds, as we might suspect.

The ***Coast Pilot*** states in paragraph 564, "Oyster Bay, south of Burns Point (it's really west), is an extensive mudflat; oysters are grown in this area and there are log booms.

Shelton's Historic Shay locomotive is gear-driven, powered by three cylinders tied to a line shaft geared to all right side wheels. It could traverse steep grades and twist around short radius curves that rod-driven locomotives could not.

This Shay was built in Lima, Ohio in 1924, went to Simpson Timber Co., where it was used in the high woods, then in Shelton until 1955, and finally McCleary, until retired in 1958.

It was named "Tollie" in honor of Mrs. Sol Simpson when it was donated to Shelton by the Simpson Timber Company in 1959.

➡ **Chart 18457,** scale 1:10,000, is best for Totten entrance, but in less than one mile the chart ends. Switch to chart 18448 or 18445, page C. Both have a scale of 1:80,000.

Totten Inlet has the greatest tidal range in all of Puget Sound, followed closely by Eld and Budd.

Burns Point has a maximum high tide of 17.82 feet with a maximum low tide of minus (-) 3.18 feet, which can produce a tidal range of 21 feet or more.

(Tidal predictions are based on Seattle tides with a ratio of 1.33 on the highs and 1.06 on the lows for Burns Point.)

"South of the entrance to Little Skookum Inlet, along the shores of Totten Inlet, are rock or concrete walls enclosing the oyster beds," according to the ***Coast Pilot.***

"The walls are a danger to navigation, and the oyster industry discourages boatmen from entering these waters. Oyster-processing wharves are on the north side of the inlet. Local knowledge is required to get to them. Good anchorage may be had anywhere inside the entrance of Little Skookum Inlet."

Enough of this, let's get back to chasing Peter Puget into Totten Inlet.

Underway Again

⎈ **We enter Totten Inlet** running south from Arcadia along the western shore toward Windy Point.

G "1" Totten Inlet Daybeacon 1 is a square green daybeacon on a pile on a charted sandspit which extends about 100 yards west of Steamboat Island. We keep it to port, and continue along the west shore. This is the narrowest part of Totten where currents will be the strongest.

About two miles farther south we reach **Windy Point,** a 70 foot high bluff, two miles from Arcadia.

Staying along this west shore, running in about two to three fathoms as far as 0.5 mile offshore, we reach the entrance to Little Skookum Inlet.

Barron Point, unnamed on charts, on the north shore of the entrance, rises abruptly to 180 feet.

Kamilche Point, also unnamed, on the south shore of the entrance, rises more gradually to the same elevation. A private community moorage with private launch ramp is just inside Kamilche Point.

South end of Totten Inlet

Ⓖ **Wildcat Cove** on the south and **Deer Harbor** on the north, are the two small bays inside the entrance to Little Skookum, **potential gunkholes,** if there is room.

⚓ **Anchoring** is possible in about 1 3/4 fathoms in either arm. Both bays provide shelter, although room may be limited as there are a number of local boats already anchored here

⎈ **Little Skookum Inlet,** is possibly the last natural inlet in the Sound—a tranquil, shallow, winding, narrow estuary about three miles long.

Width at the inlet entrance is about 300 yards; west of Wildcat Cove and Deer Harbor it squeezes to about 100 yards. It widens irregularly to about 0.3 mile for nearly 2.25 miles to the west and the south, ending in a saltmarsh.

Depths in the inlet range from the charted zero (0) fathom, one foot depth about one mile west of the entrance, at the narrowest part of the channel, to its southwest end, where it goes more or less dry at MLLW.

Current predictions or reference stations are not given for the narrow passage of Little Skookum.

Traveling the inlet by small boat, kayak or canoe is a delight. Around each bend is a step back in time to glorious solitude, as kayakers quietly explore the protected waters of the inlet.

Little Skookum Inlet

Common sense suggests the inlet's shellfish beds not be contaminated by motorized boats. These oysters may end up on our own dinner table. Not only that, but because of the shallows and the concrete ledges in the inlet, outboards sometimes get hung up and boaters are stranded until the next high tide.

There are no places to go ashore in the inlet. All beaches are privately managed, most with commercial oyster beds.

Kamilche, site of Squaxin Tribal facilities and tribal trade center, is just past the head of the inlet.

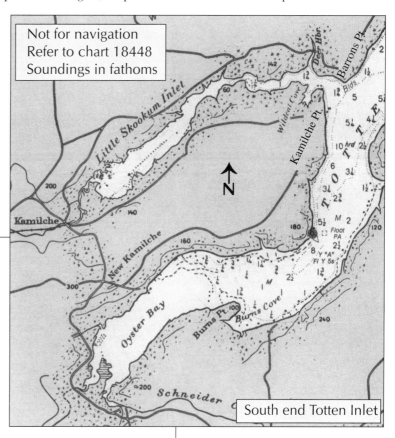

Not for navigation
Refer to chart 18448
Soundings in fathoms

South end Totten Inlet

Whales in Skookum

For a moment, we thought we had finally caught up with Peter Puget, but as we got closer it turned out to be long time inlet residents Steven and Ann Ness, well up on local history, who told us others have discovered Little Skookum. In spring of 1994, Steve saw a small gray whale had swam up the inlet.

"It wasn't very spectacular. It came, blew, and went out. But in the early 1980s, a really big gray whale came up the inlet—maybe 30 to 35 feet long. It surfaced, rolled, and came out of the water. We could see all the barnacles on it. It was incredible. We were caught totally off guard. We ran out to the shore and the whale turned around in this wide spot out in front and then went back out. I guess it was just curious. We called the Whale Society and they thought it was looking for food," said Ness, whose wife Ann is the daughter of Shelton residents Lee and Pearl Calloway, Carl's friends of nearly 60 years. (The men first met in Mats Mats Bay in the 1930s when Carl powered and sailed his 24' schooner Condor from Seattle to the small bay nearly every other weekend with the currents for years, but that's yet another story.)

Steve said we might possibly go up the inlet as far as their place at high tide in our sailboat and then turn around and head right back out—just like the whale. We'll pass on that, and stick to kayaks and skiffs in the inlet.

Oysters & Other Shellfish

There's more to Little Skookum than misplaced whales and muddy tideflats. Several South Sound inlets are nationally known for growing oysters and clams. Of those, Little Skookum is one of the highest mollusk-producing inlets for its size. Taylor United, Brenner, Kamilche, Little Skookum, Olympia and other oyster companies farm Little Skookum, Totten, and other inlets.

Taylor United, with headquarters in Shelton, has hatcheries and farms up and down Puget Sound and in Hood Canal. Justin Taylor, former president of the old family business, said they are presently growing more clams than oysters, and starting to harvest mussels as well. The Taylor family has grown shellfish for over 100 years, but the company is only about 25 years old.

At one time, they started building dikes to replicate tidal pools for the Olympia oysters, and there are still remnants of the log or cement dikes in some inlets which can be seen at extreme low tides.

(continued on next page)

Carl suggests: Consider for a moment, 2.25 miles long Skookum Inlet has an entrance less than 100 yards wide.

The average width is about 0.2 mile, which equals about 0.5 square mile of water in the inlet.

The highest of tides is about 17.82 feet. All of that water must run in and out of this channel in periods of about six hours. Currents can be "pretty strong," according to residents.

The logical approach is to ride in and out with the current in a small boat.

Historian Steve Ness, left, Pearl and Lee Calloway

Commercial shellfish gatherers

Peter Puget reached the head of Totten Inlet about noon Friday, May 25, 1792, but couldn't get closer than two miles because of minus tide and extensive shoals. Menzies noted, "we found an abundance of small oysters."

"We had ... been successful in procuring a good Quantity of Clams which with Nettle tops, Fat Hen and Gooseberry Tops greatly assisted the customary allowance of Provisions," Puget wrote.

They turned, headed northeast; Puget noted "in this branch were many beautiful spots ... low surrounding country thickly covered with wood had a very pleasant appearance, now in the height of spring."

(continued from previous page)

Introduction of the Shelton pulp mill in the 1900s devastated the industry.

"Each time they had new methods of increased production, it worsened the effluent, which affected the shellfish," Taylor said.

Times have changed, with the Department of Ecology monitoring just about everything, production of shellfish has improved once again.

When he was a youngster Taylor said oyster growers usually lived in floathouses which were anchored near the oysters they harvested in Totten, Little Skookum, and other southern bays. He said they worked from their own places, picking oysters, washing them, culling them and putting the market oysters in another float ready to sack up. A boat picked them up and took them to Olympia where they were sold. The first oysters shipped from Oyster Bay left Kamilche in 1878, the start of the thriving industry.

Taylor said shellfish growing and harvesting is a unique business and people from all the over the world visit their facilities.

"It's something the average person doesn't know a whole lot about. Little Skookum is an easy place to get to (by car). It's easy for kids to walk out and see the clams, crabs, oysters and barnacles on the beach."

There aren't oysters for the taking on these beaches—they're all private. But there are public tidelands where the public can pick oysters and dig clams, or buy them from various producers in the area.

Little Skookum Inlet History

At the turn of the century, the town of **Rollway** was on the south side of Little Skookum about one mile west of Wildcat Cove, according to Steve Ness. It was a lumber town run by Port Blakely Mill that started about 1885. There were houses, commercial buildings, a school, and a turnaround for trains.

A steamer from Olympia serviced the area. Passengers got off the boat in Rollway and took the train to the head of the inlet to Kamilche.

More important than Shelton early on, it was called Rollway because it was the terminal for all early logging trains which dumped logs in the water on both sides of the inlet. The roundtable at Rollway turned the trains around and they went back toward Kamilche. Little Skookum Inlet was full of boomed logs.

All Rollway's buildings are now gone—everything was pushed into the water. Stub pilings from the old pier are all that remains. Bottle collectors have discovered treasures in Rollway. The land is still owned by Port Blakely Mill.

Remnants of Rollway

Totten Inlet was named for George M. Totten, a midshipman in the Wilkes Expedition.

Underway Again

⎈ Out of Little Skookum and still going south in Totten Inlet, it's less than two miles south of Kamilche Point to 180 foot high **Deepwater Point,** unnamed on charts.

Fl Y 5s Y "A" Kamilche Sea Farm Lighted Buoy A is a flashing yellow light off Deepwater Point. Depth is eight fathoms about 100 yards offshore.

Shallow **Oyster Bay** south and west has many oyster barges; aquaculture buoys and oyster stakes are all along shores which shoal to Burns Point and Burns Cove.

Public tidelands, leased and privately managed, surround the entire bay head.

Now it's about time to call it quits in the south end of Totten, and head back north along the east shore.

Hudson Cove, unnamed on chart 18448, about two miles north of Burns Point and south of Cougar Point, the unnamed "bulge" on the east shore of the inlet. The cove, tucked back in with about 1-1/2 fathoms, is opposite the entrance to Little Skookum, might offer protection in a northerly, but be aware of pilings and oyster stakes along the shore.

Typical Totten Inlet aquaculture buoys

Cougar Point rises about 120 feet and homes are mushrooming atop the bank; stairways lead to the beach. Oyster reserves are along the shores of the point.

Gallagher Cove, unnamed, on the north side of Cougar Point, has aquaculture, ever-present oyster stakes, and some permanently anchored boats and floats. It's difficult to get very far into the cove because of drying tideflats about 0.6 mile offshore. This might be a good place to duck into in a southerly, although the wind whistles through a ravine between Hudson and Gallagher Coves.

This eastern shore from here to Steamboat Island has clusters of homes amidst banks of evergreens; a few erratic rocks along the beach. Anchoring is possible along these shores in good weather, beaches are private.

We've reached the northeast side of the Totten Inlet entrance at Steamboat Island, keeping at least 200 yards offshore. We round green daybeacon "1," marking "Steamboat Spit" west of the island, and then pass the north end of Steamboat Island. We're now heading south and have just entered Squaxin Passage.

Squaxin Passage Overview—Navigation Concerns

Squaxin Passage is a major connection linking Totten Inlet, Hammersley Inlet and Pickering Passage to Eld Inlet, Budd Inlet, Peale Passage and Dana Passage. It runs in a northwesterly-southeasterly direction for about 1.3 miles between the mainland and Hope and Squaxin Islands.

Puget and his men landed for dinner along the east shore of Totten Inlet on May 25, 1792, then proceeded to Squaxin Passage for the night.

Hope Island splits the northwest end of Squaxin Passage into two channels. The named and charted west passage is between the mainland and Hope Island. A smaller unnamed passage is between Hope and Squaxin islands.

Width shore to shore of Squaxin Passage west and south of Hope Island is roughly 500 yards.

Depths in Squaxin Passage are charted six to seven fathoms in midchannel.

A small pinnacle shoal is charted 150 yards off Hope Island's west shore across from the north end of Steamboat Island, at 19 feet, MLLW. It's more of a curiosity than concern to most mariners.

A shoal of seven to 12 feet at MLLW is charted about 175 yards east of Steamboat Island causeway, northwest of the private marina.

Steamboat Island, north end

Navigation Aids in Squaxin Passage:
- **Q Fl 15 ft Carlyon Beach Light** white flashing light privately maintained, is charted at the southeast pier of the private marina for Carlyon Beach residents.
- **R N "2" Reef Buoy 2** red nun buoy, marks an unnamed drying shoal about 650 yards northwest of Hunter Point and 650 yards southwest of Belspeox Point on Squaxin Island. A two fathom depth curve surrounds the buoy, extending about 200 yards north. The shoal is an obligatory stop for ragbaggers and stinkpotters who insist on cutting it too close at low tide—then spend hours in an enforced "layover."
- **Main passage** between red nun buoy "2" and mainland shore is about 400 yards.

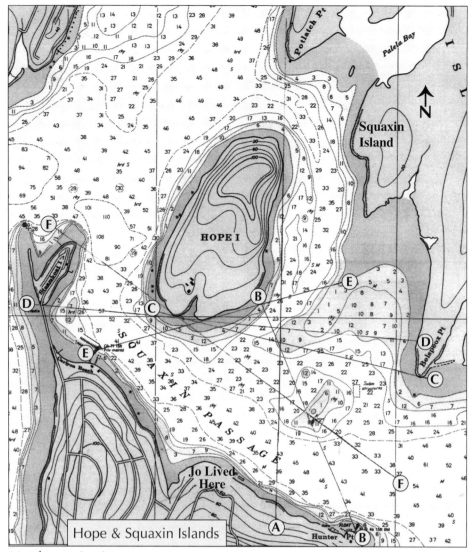

Hope & Squaxin Islands

Not for navigation
Refer to chart 18448
Soundings in fathoms

Squaxin Island is private land of the Squaxin Tribe. Landing on the island or anchoring in island coves is not permitted by the Squaxin Tribe.

(continued from previous page)
- •**"Submerged structures"** are charted, but not marked, about 300 yards northeast of the red buoy toward Belspeox Point.
- • **Fl G 4s 15ft 7M "1" Hunter Point Light 1** flashing green on a square, green dayboard on a tower, is on Hunter Point on the mainland at the southeast entrance to Squaxin Passage.

Currents of 2.5 knots may be encountered in Squaxin Passage during extreme tidal ranges, with the usual backeddies downstream of points and bulges and upwelling boils from shoals.

Squaxin's unmarked north passage between Hope and Squaxin islands is about one mile long between red buoy "2" and the north entrance between **Potlatch Point** and Hope Island.

Width shore to shore of the passage and east to the unnamed Squaxin bluff is about 0.2 mile.

Width shore to shore between **Belspeox Point** and eastern bluffs off Hope Island is about 0.5 mile, 0.3 of which shoals from 12 feet to drying flats at MLLW off Squaxin's west shores.

Depth curves of 12 feet between Hope and Squaxin at this location are about 125 yards apart, and about 100 yards off Hope Island's shore. The shoal west of Belspeox Point is massive and deceptive.

Controlling depth of 20 feet for this north passage is east of the bluff on Hope Island. A nine foot "pimple" is about 100 yards south of Hope's charted 12 foot depth curve "finger" pointing south.

Across on Squaxin, **Palela Bay** is beautiful—remote, pristine and peaceful, with a tiny island in the entrance. The bay dries almost entirely at MLLW. Cruising past we saw hundreds of diving birds, while firs, cedars and madronas overhang beaches.

The channel angles roughly NNE toward Squaxin's western unnamed bluff.

At the northeast side off Hope Island the distance between the 12 foot curves between the islands increases to about 200 yards and the channel swings west. The 12 foot curves are about 100 yards off Potlatch and Hope Island shores.

Currents in Squaxin's north passage are not given in either the *Tidal Current Tables* or in the *Current Charts*, so local knowledge takes over. Our guess is that the currents here will be less than those encountered in the main Squaxin Passage.

Carl's Line-of-Site Ranges
Line-of-site ranges between charted objects and natural terrain are important to us when sailing or powering channels near the massive shoals and flats west of Belspeox Point, especially during low tides. **Refer to chart on this page for range lines.**

(continued on next page)

(continued from previous page)

They best verify our ongoing position, regardless of the effects of wind and currents on compass courses on our real direction and distance traveled over the bottom. They are approximate positions, variations can occur.

Line-of-site ranges are the ultimate back up, with a lead line, when electronic depth sounders, GPS and radar fail. No matter what, knowing the depth is vital, so keep an eye on the depth sounder or use a lead line to verify depths.

<u>Line-of-Sight Ranges Refer to the High-Water Shoreline:</u>

• **(A) Range:** Bluffs west side of Potlatch Point **in line with** east shore of Hope Island. This line is tangent to the west edge of Belspeox Point's 12 foot depth curve, and is almost true north-south.

• **(B) Range:** From Hunter Point green light **in line with** red nun buoy "2" provided it's on station where charted on 18457. This line is tangent to the west edge of Belspeox Point's 12 foot depth curve.

• **(C) Line drawn** between shoreline at Belspeox Point and shoreline at south end of Hope Island. The line crosses the 12 foot depth curve at a charted depth of about 10 feet.

• **(D) Range:** Line from shoreline at south end of Steamboat Island **in line with** shore line at south end of Hope Island.

• **(E) Range:** Line from Carlyon Beach marina **in line with** SE shoreline of Hope Island.

• **(F) Range:** Line from high-water shoreline at north end of Steamboat Island **in line with** high-water shoreline of south end of Hope Island, bearing to drying shoal.

<u>If northbound,</u> we keep south of Line C unless we are maintaining a northbound course on Range A or west of Range A.

• Heading north on Range A or west of Range A we cross Line C.

• Looking west to Range D, the south end of Steamboat Island disappears behind Hope Island in a few minutes. We then alter course to suit our fancy toward our northbound destination.

<u>If southbound,</u> when we cross Range E Carlyon Beach marina comes into view from behind Hope Island. We then swing west to establish a southbound course on Range A or B before crossing Range D. When looking west, Steamboat Island comes in sight and appears to be moving south of Hope Island.

• When we've crossed Line C we proceed to our destination to the south, east or west, staying clear of the shoal at red nun buoy "2" and "submerged structures" which show no authorized depth. Charted blue color makes us think depth is 12 feet or less.

• If our southbound destination is west around the end of Hope Island, we would follow the 12 foot depth curve around the island.

⎈ **Underway again** in Squaxin Passage we go west to east, following the southern or mainland shore first, then work our way back to Hope and Squaxin islands.

Steamboat Island, about 100 by 400 yards in size, is surrounded by shoals on all sides and is chock-a-block filled with cabins, houses and trees sitting atop its bluffs, which are especially steep at the north end. The island is joined to the mainland by a one-lane causeway on pilings.

Experienced scuba divers like diving the steep ledges in the swirling tidal currents off the island's northern shores—not a place for novices.

Carlyon Beach development is immediately east of the Steamboat Island causeway. Obviously built on clear-cut land, the houses seem almost stacked one on top of the other. After the lovely forested bays and inlets we've seen in South Sound, finding this urbanized community 15 miles from the nearest city is a shock.

There are no visitor facilities at the private Carlyon Beach marina.

*Sailing around Hope Island reminds Carl of sailing **Winsome** with her 9 foot draft in and out of similar situations using only a lead line.*

Steamboat Island Causeway looking east

About 700 yards southeast of the marina is a shoal bight where Jo lived in an A-frame cabin on the eastern shore in the late 1970s, before the area was built up.

Puget's group camped for their sixth night on the south shore of Squaxin Passage on May 25, 1792, "in a very pleasant situation." They had spent the day exploring Totten Inlet, and planned to explore Eld Inlet the next morning.

Sea Witch Grounding

Jo anchored her sloop *Sea Witch* about 75 yards offshore in front of her cabin on the bight at Carlyon Beach on Squaxin Pass.

"On a dark and stormy winter night I looked out from the cabin to see the *Witch* had laid all the way over on her starboard side at an extreme low tide—in the middle of the nasty night.

"I had never seen her over like that before. All I could think was, 'Will she fill before she floats?'

"I sat in my dark little house watching the ghostly white shape of the boat on her side; agonizing if I should drag my skiff far out on the sandy beach to 'rescue' her. Although what I thought I could do to help escapes me. Finally, as the water lapped up the *Witch's* sides, she slowly righted and then floated in the wee hours before dawn.

"Don and Willa Fassett helped me re-anchor her farther out the next day. No damage."

Public tidelands of about 3,000 feet run from just east of the bight to Hunter Point along the south shore.

Now let's cross Squaxin Passage to Hope Island. This is an enchanting spot, and is the newest of the state's marine park acquisitions—another treasure. The day use park is great for hiking, picnicking, clamming and fishing.

The one lone mooring buoy off the island's south cove is vulnerable to currents. We are reluctant to anchor off the cove during strong tidal currents. The island's caretaker lives in a small, red cabin in the cove. It was once a favorite place for high school students who held numerous beach parties there over the years.

We've circumnavigated Hope Island staying about 150 yards offshore, in depths of nine to 50 feet.

Charted erratic rocks are mostly along the western shore.

Jo: "I had the feeling over the years that the 'very pleasant situation' where Puget camped might have been right on the cove in Squaxin Pass where I lived. Who knows for sure? It felt right. It was the type of spot that Puget usually found—a sheltered cove and a sandy beach where they pulled their boats ashore."

Hope Island Marine State Park Facilities
➤ One mooring buoy
➤ 106 acre island with hiking trails
➤ 8,541 feet of saltwater shoreline to beachcomb
➤ No drinking water
➤ No facilities

➡ Caution: Watch for poison oak and poison ivy whenever it's shrubby off Hope Island trails.

⚓ **Anchoring** is possible off the eastern shore of Hope in about 12 to 20 feet where currents aren't too strong. It's easy to dinghy ashore at any of several delightful little beaches sprinkled around Hope.

Ⓖ This eastern shoreline qualifies as a **gunkhole**, but be aware of currents.

The 106 acre forested island, covered with mix of evergreen and deciduous trees, has several miles of trails weaving around and through small hills and dales, tall trees and underbrush.

The main trail begins up behind the caretaker's house and winds amidst the trees gently upward to 120 feet at the north end of the island, then dips back down at the southeast end to relatively low land. It's a peaceful, wonderful, not always well-defined trail. Although the caretaker told us we might get lost, we only strayed off the trail a couple of times and never felt "lost."

Caretaker's home on Hope

Hope Island—Present, Past and Future

In the summer of 1995 we met Hope Island caretaker, Barry Wallis, a *volunteer* steward. While he's **presently** earning a masters degree in environmental studies at The Evergreen State College, he's caring for Hope Island. Barry paddles his kayak back and forth to the mainland in most weather. He swims in the chilly salt water most of the year. He's restoring the old windmill at the old well. He's friends with the island's deer, watches the eagles, herons, the seals swimming by.

Barry told us some of the island's fascinating **past.**

Hope was purchased by the state from the Munn Estate in 1990 for more than $3 million. It was originally owned by the Schmidt family of Olympia Brewing Company fame, who bought it in 1896 and used it as a family retreat and home for one of their sons. The Schmidt family took out large Douglas firs, planted orchards, a vineyard, and the island became self-sufficient. They built a charming home on the island, including a dock for their 36 foot launch.

Barry was enthusiastic about the island's heritage fruit and nut orchard, the oldest in Mason-Thurston counties. The vineyard, now abandoned, still has some renegade grape vines over 80 feet high, tangled and clinging in the tall firs.

Future state plans are to add about four more mooring buoys off the northwest shore, not off the south cove, where there is the one buoy currently.

They also expect to develop a small four to eight site campground, a small group camp and a composting toilet as part of the Washington Water Trail system for hand-powered boats. This would be either the beginning or the end of the trail, depending on where kayakers put in. Since funds for these improvements were cut, they may not happen until 1998. No camping will be allowed on the island until a composting toilet is built.

Several Olympia area boaters said they hope the state will leave the island natural, allowing only limited camping. They also say they always look for anthills every time they go to the island. There are a couple of big anthills with little red ants, but we didn't find them.

The island may also be renamed due to the Hope Island near Whidbey Island, but we haven't heard what the new name might be. We like it as it is—it offers **Hope**.

Barry Wallis, volunteer steward on Hope

Puget went past Hope Island *in 1792, Wilkes cruised past in 1841, but it wasn't charted until 1853.*

From much of Hope Island the views are lovely— Mount Rainier down Squaxin Passage to the east on a clear day, the friendly old evergreen forests to north and northeast, Arcadia Point at the entrance to Hammersley, and sparkling waters surrounding the island— while to the southwest the view is across Squaxin Passage— to hundreds of houses.

Public access from the mainland closest to Hope Island is the launch ramp at Arcadia.

From Hope Island, we continue southeast, cruising past Hunter Point with its flashing green light. We are now near the confluence of Squaxin, Peale and Dana Passages, with Eld and Budd Inlets to our south.

Forested interior of Hope

In Chapter 19—the final chapter— we pick up Dana and Peale Passages, then follow Puget into Eld Inlet, and end up in Budd Inlet and the capitol city of Olympia, Puget's last stop before heading back north.

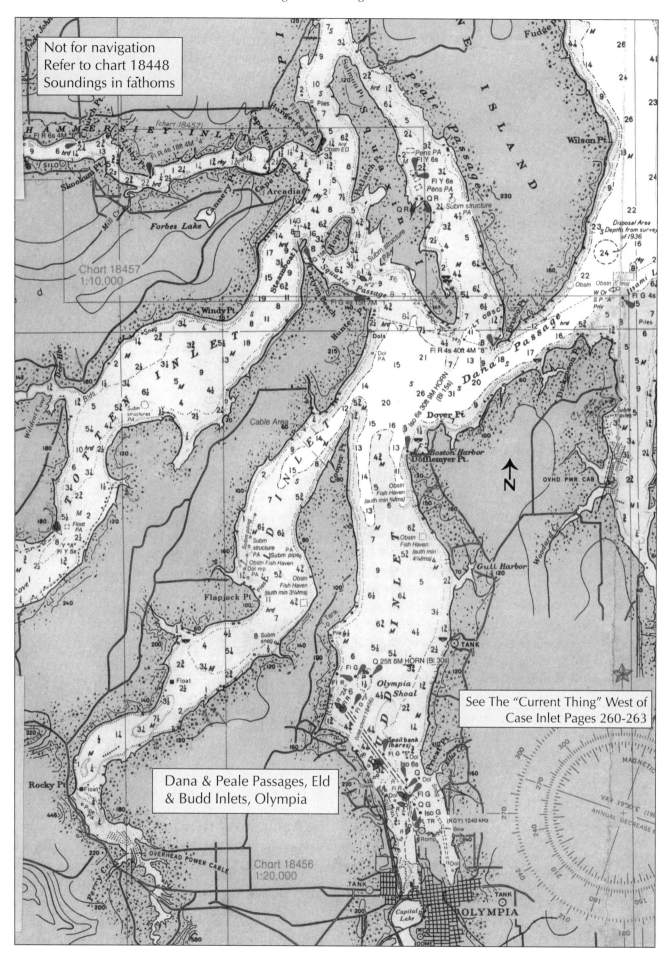

Not for navigation
Refer to chart 18448
Soundings in fathoms

Chart 18457
1:10,000

Dana & Peale Passages, Eld
& Budd Inlets, Olympia

Chart 18456
1:20,000

See The "Current Thing" West of
Case Inlet Pages 260-263

CHAPTER 19
Dana & Peale Passages, Eld & Budd Inlets, Olympia

Charts and publications for this chapter

	Chart	Date	Title	Scale	Soundings
***	18456	05/20/95	Olympia Harbor and Budd Inlet	1:20,000	Feet
**	18445	06/03/95	Puget Sound—Possession Sound to Olympia, page C	1:80,000	Fathoms
			Olympia, page F	1:20,000	Fathoms
*	18448	10/30/93	Puget Sound Southern part	1:80,000	Fathoms
	18440	08/05/95	Puget Sound	1:150,000	Fathoms
			Tidal Current Charts, Puget Sound, Southern Part		
			Booklet: Puget Sound Shellfish Site		
			Washington State Public Lands Quad Map, Tacoma	1:100,000	
			Washington State Public Lands Quad Map, Shelton	1:100,000	

➡ *When using charts, compare your chart dates with ones referred to above. There may be discrepancies between different charts and different chart editions.*

Overview

It's time to cover the places we by-passed in our preoccupation with following Peter Puget . . . . . .

In Chapter 17, we followed Puget to the head of Case Inlet. In Chapter 18, we pursued him south in Pickering Passage, and we ducked into Hammersley Inlet which he missed.

Then we nearly caught up with him in Totten Inlet, but he got away, so we headed southeast through Squaxin Passage as far as Hunter Point, while he spent the night in a tiny cove on the pass (at Jo's place).

So in this last chapter, we return to Wilson Point on Harstine Island and Itsami Ledge in Dana Passage to cruise southwest through Dana, north into Peale Passage and then follow Puget into Eld and Budd inlets. We find a couple of shoreside county parks and gunkholes along the way, and end our cruise in Olympia.

Dana Passage

Dana Pass is about two miles long and is the main route from The Narrows to Olympia and Budd, Eld, Totten and Hammersley inlets, and the south end of Peale and Pickering Passages. Dana runs northeast/southwest between the mainland and Harstine Island.

Fl G 4s "7" Itsami Ledge Light 7 flashing green light on square, green dayboard on a 20 foot high dolphin, marks eastern end of Dana Passage and entrance to Henderson Inlet (Chapter 16).

"Obstruction" charted at five fathoms is 300 yards north of Itsami. We don't recall seeing white and orange buoys charted at this site on 18448 (1993), and they were not on the 1995 light list.

Disposal area with depths of 24 fathoms from a 1936 survey is charted about 0.3 mile off the southeast shore of Harstine, about 1.5 miles south of Wilson Point.

Depths in Dana Passage are 12 to 24 fathoms.

➡ **NOTE: Marine gas and diesel** are sold at **both Boston Harbor Marina** at the entrance to Budd Inlet, and at **West Bay Marina** in Olympia.

➡ **The chart** we use for most of Dana Pass, north part of Eld Inlet, and all of Budd Inlet is **18456**, scale of 1:20,000, soundings in feet. It's excellent.

There are about seven miles of public tidelands in the areas covered in this chapter.

Public tidelands, unless otherwise noted, are state-owned. Some may be leased for private use. When we go ashore we take the Washington State Public Lands Quad Map, to avoid trespassing on adjacent private property.

Dana Passage was named by Wilkes for James Dwight Dana, a mineralogist on the expedition.

*He was also the brother of Richard Henry Dana, author of the classic sea story, **Two Years Before the Mast.***

Width in Dana Passage narrows to about 0.5 mile off the southern tip of Harstine Island at **Brisco Point.**

Currents in Dana are discussed in the "Current Thing" Chapter 17, pages 260-263. Currents may reach 4.5 knots under extreme conditions. (Note: "Swirls" are indicated on all Ebb current charts.)

Six Fl Y 6s Priv. Hartstene Island Fish Pen Lights, mark aquaculture floats 1.8 miles southwest of Wilson Point, approximately 300 yards offshore.

⛵ **Underway again,** along the south shore of Dana Passage, we pass **Dickenson Point** at the mouth of Henderson Inlet, about 1,500 yards southwest of Itsami. Charted erratic rocks, drying shoal and sandspit are 0.1 to 0.2 mile off Dickenson and the rounded point at the northwest entrance to Henderson. Private mooring buoys are on either side of the point. Banks above the beach here reach 100 feet high, with numerous homes along the bluffs.

Big Fishtrap is about 0.7 mile southwest of Dickenson Point. Much of the outer cove dries at MLLW, and drying arms reach south and east. A charted mooring buoy symbol indicates private buoys. Beaches are all private.

Big Fishtrap, outer cove

"Big Fishtail" is the name an Olympia friend has given to Big Fishtrap. He claims the charted two inner arms are shaped like a fishtail.

⚓ **Anchoring,** there is enough depth—14 feet at MLLW—to duck into the outer cove and anchor temporarily in a southerly blow.

⛵ **Leaving Big Fishtrap** we continue southwest.

Little Fishtrap, about 0.5 mile west of Big Fishtrap, is a drying lagoon that is not an anchorage, but a former fishing area. It is charted as a 0.2 mile long notch between bluffs.

Zangle Cove is on the south shore 0.8 mile west of Little Fishtrap, south and east of Dover Point. This area is all private, heavily settled and chances are on a nice day we'll see lots of local home owners out strolling the beaches, or, heaven forbid, working on their homes or yards. Much of the cove dries at low tides as charted. A few local boats may be anchored off.

Southwest past **Dover Point** bluffs, staying at least 100 yards offshore, we clear **Jeal Point** at the entrance to Boston Harbor. Dana Pass ends as Budd Inlet begins.

We're saving Budd Inlet, Boston Harbor and Olympia until the end of this chapter. Now we go back to Wilson Point on Harstine Island and cruise south and west along the island's south shore, using chart 18445 or 18448 for a bit.

Jo recalls: When the kids were young in the mid-1960s, we'd cruise to Zangle Cove to visit friends, anchor, swim, water-ski and barbecue in the summers—and shiver through a polar bear dip each New Year's Day.

⛵ **Wilson Point,** with shoals about 300 yards offshore, is our starting point.

Public tidelands in Dana Pass in four parcels of about 6,000 feet are along the southeast shore of Harstine, starting about 2,500 feet south of Wilson Point.

Forested bluffs of about 100 feet rise above the shores, with some houses and cabins back in the trees along this part of Harstine.

The farther south and west we go toward Brisco Point, the more homes we find, many with intriguing and creative stairways from the beach climbing up the 160-200 foot high bluffs along this coast.

Large erratic rocks are on the shore, most of them visible by midtide. In summer, small boats are moored off or hauled onto the beach.

Two tiny drying coves are charted, but there are no places to take shelter along this shore.

Brisco Point, at the very southwest tip of Harstine, is a little over three miles from Wilson Point. Brisco is a long, skinny, rocky point with a bluff over 40 feet high that rises abruptly from low beach on all sides.

Fl R 4s 4M "8" Brisco Point Light 8, obscured from 105° to 242°, is a flashing red light on a triangular red dayboard at 40 feet.

Sometimes called

Brisco Point, looking northerly up Peale Passage, Tucksel Point at far left

"Raggedy Ass Point" by fishermen and others because of the jagged rocks, kelp and turbulence at its outer end, Brisco has a rocky ledge that extends over 200 yards off the point. This clutter can be seen at low tides. It's a killer for an outboard boat—or any other—that gets in too close. We keep at least 300 yards off as we round the point and head north up Peale Passage.

Current chop and fetch of southwesterlies from Budd and Eld inlets gets downright nasty in the whole area between Hunter Point and Dana Passage.

Tucksel Point at the south tip of Squaxin is at the SW entrance of Peale Pass.

Current chart reference station 0.3 mile south of Tucksel Point provides a useful study of currents in this area. (See "Current Thing", Chapter 17, pages 260-263)

Peale Passage

The southern end of Peale Passage connects with Dana and Squaxin Passages and Budd and Eld inlets. Verifications, clarifications and possibly even corrections are needed here.

Length of the pass is about four miles, extending northwest between Harstine and Squaxin islands where it connects with Pickering Passage at its north end.

Widths in Peale Pass are a little over 0.5 mile at the south end narrowing to 300 yards at the north end, maybe 100 yards or less navigable width, depending on the boat's draft.

Depths in Peale are charted at 60 feet at the south end and 16 feet in the narrow channel at the north end on chart 18445 6/3/95 and on 18448 10/30/93. It has a controlling depth of 10 feet according to the *Coast Pilot.*

The "10 foot depth" indicated in the *Coast Pilot* appears to be charted along the Hartstene shore, east of the three fathom curve which extends nearly into the narrows. We are uncertain whether the controlling depth here is really 16 feet as indicated on the charts or 10 feet as indicated in the *Coast Pilot.*

Charted depths of 1 fathom, 4 feet, on 18445, and the equivalent of 1 3/4 fathoms on 18448, are about 10 feet and are near the Hartstene shore but do not appear to extend into the charted channel.

Currents in Peale Passage: *Coast Pilot* (Paragraph 534, 1995) cautions rather strongly, "Strangers should not attempt [Peale Passage]. The current at times attains a velocity of 2.0 knots in the narrow part of the passage, and sets north on the flood."

Currents at the north end of Peale Passage: "Apply no correction factors to speed given for ... the north end of Peale Passage." (See "note" on Current Charts)

We note the fastest charted **tropic flood** speed of 0.5 occurs on (F) and it **does flow north**. But the **faster charted tropic ebb** speed of 1.1 flowing south,occurs on charts (E-1) and (E) according to current charts.

> ➡**Navigation charts refer** to the southeast point on Squaxin Island as "Tucksel Point."
>
> **Current charts refer** to the same point as "Unsal Point."

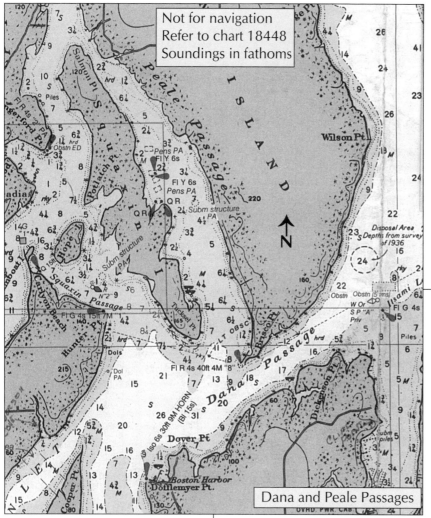

Not for navigation
Refer to chart 18448
Soundings in fathoms

Dana and Peale Passages

If we apply the highest speed correction factor of 1.5 on the table to the 1.1 tropic ebb, corrected speed in Peale would be 1.65 knots if a predicted current at The Tacoma Narrows maxes out at 5.8 to 6.1 knots.

This suggests fastest current of 1.65 knots occurs during the south-flowing ebb.

The *Coast Pilot* states "the current at times attains a velocity of 2.0 knots in the narrow part of Peale Passage and it sets north on the flood."

Our best guess is that during severe rain and snow melt and barometric or other conditions, the current might reach **2.0 knots and set south on the ebb.**

Squaxin Island State Marine Park

This park in the cove 0.5 mile north of Tucksel Point was closed in 1993, although it is still charted as #85A on 18445. None of the listed park facilities are available as they have all been removed.

Squaxin Island and its bays and coves are off limits to anchoring or going ashore, according to Squaxin Tribal policies at this time.

This was a delightful 31.4 acre park in a protected southeast cove on the island, was closed when State Parks and the Squaxin Tribe were unable to agree on an annual lease payment to the tribe for tidelands use.

State Parks acquired the land in two parcels in 1961 and 1965, at a cost of $41,310, but apparently did not include tidelands use or access, according to the "1993-95 Biennium Area Reports" of Washington State Parks.

The park, with 2,673 feet of shoreline, was a favorite with recreational boaters. It was an easy weekend destination for years in South Sound. Many have wonderful memories of days or weekends at Squaxin Island: barbecues, softball games, hikes, swims. It was a wonderful place. Total park attendance dropped from 23,000 in 1988 to 7,900 in 1992.

A large erratic boulder with a carved Indian petroglyph was on the Harstine shore for many years. The big rock was moved to the state museum in Olympia some time ago.

"Squaxin Navy," we understand, is a 100 foot former navy patrol boat. It was anchored off Squaxin, blew ashore in a winter storm, and when last seen in 1995 was spruced up and looking good, according to a friend.

⚓ **Underway again,** along Peale Passage, the view is of all sizes and shapes homes among the trees along Harstine. Some are cabins remodeled from the turn of the century buildings or before, as the island has been settled for well over a century.

A private park and campground with launch ramp is obvious about midway through the pass.

"Submerged structure" is charted in about seven fathoms, two miles north of Brisco Point, and about 0.2 mile off Harstine's west shore.

Aquaculture pens of the Squaxin Tribe are across from this on Squaxin in a cove north of an unnamed rounded point.

2 Q R Peale Passage Fish Pen Lights, two quick flashing red lights, mark the southern pens.

Fl Y "A" and Fl Y "B" Squaxin Island Fish Pen Lights A and B 2 flashing yellow lights, mark more pens about 0.5 mile north of the Peale Pass pens.

Squaxin Island

The island was named "Jack's Island" by Commander Charles Wilkes when he surveyed Puget Sound in 1841. The name didn't catch on and the Indian word, *duskwak-sin*—Squaxin—meaning "alone," became official.

In 1864, Indian agent A.R. Elder said of the Squaxin Indian reservation, "The island is surrounded by logging camps which are occupied by men of very loose and immoral habits, who are continually taking the Indian women and furnishing the men with whiskey."

Peale Passage was named by Wilkes for Titian R. Peale, a naturalist and artist.

⚓ **Anchoring** is possible off Harstine's shore in three fathoms or less. As we cruise through Peale Pass, we can see that there are places we could stop, although there is no public tideland or places to go ashore until north of the oyster plant.

☸ We see a fairly large oyster operation, complete with conveyer belt and piles of oyster shells, is near the north end of Peale Passage on Harstine.

We keep west of center here to avoid oyster beds, many marked by slender oyster stakes, making it easier to miss them.

Public tidelands of less than 1,000 feet are at the north end of Peale, past the oyster operation.

As the navigable channel narrows and shoals to 10 or possibly 16 feet at the north end of the pass, we keep an eye on the depth sounder and note the currents.

Oyster processing plant

Once through Peale Pass, we have the choice of continuing north around Harstene Island, being aware of the Harstine Island Bridge and its 31 foot vertical clearance at MHW (clearance details on p. 269) or head south through Pickering Pass.

Since we've already been both places, let's now head back to take a good look at Eld Inlet and then head south in Budd Inlet to Olympia. Once again, we're chasing Puget's keel tracks.

Eld Inlet Overview

Cooper Point is at the north end of the turkey-headed mainland peninsula which separates Budd and Eld Inlets.

Eld Inlet, nearly eight miles long, trends more or less southwesterly, ending in Mud Bay. The last two miles angle to the southeast and are mostly drying mudflats at MLLW.

Widths of Eld Inlet range from 0.2 mile at the northern entrance to one mile wide from the cove north of Flapjack Point to the east shore, ultimately narrowing and then disappearing to the southeast in muddy tideflats under overhead power cables and highway bridges.

Depths in Eld Inlet are 10 to 15 fathoms in the first 1.5 miles. The three fathom curve ends in the next 2.5 miles, except for an apparent cartographic oversight at Latitude 47°5' where three to seven fathom depths are charted, but not defined by a three fathom curve.

There are no charted hazards in Eld Inlet except some erratic rocks near the shores. Some places go dry at low tide more than 0.1 mile offshore.

Currents in Eld entrance might exceed 1.65 knots during extreme tidal ranges, and are discussed in The "Current Thing" in Chapter 17, pages 260-263.

➡ **Chart 18456** is good in Eld Inlet to about 0.8 mile south of Flapjack Point, and then we must switch to either 18445 or 18448.

Eld Inlet is home to The Evergreen State College, delightful Frye Cove County Park, a fine wooden boat builder, launch ramp, but very little public tideland, except at the park and tideflats in the south end—and a couple of gunkholes.

The shores of the inlet have many residences, from elegant homes to beach cabins, especially on the east side. The inlet has long been suburban Olympia. Second growth evergreens remain and the view is green and forested.

Kayakers paddle Eld Inlet, water-skiers and jet skiers kick up their wakes, small sailboats tack back and forth, but the inlet is not really used much as a cruising destination, mainly because of the lack of public access and anchorages.

⎈ **Underway again,** at Cooper Point we enter Eld Inlet and cruise south past the long slender finger of sand, which trails into the sea. It's shoal about 300 yards to the north and east of this unmarked sandspit.

Sanderson Cove, unnamed, is a skinny, private, drying cove nearly 0.4 mile long, indenting the northwest shore due west of Cooper Point. Erratic rocks are charted along the shore north of the cove.

Cable area south of Sanderson crosses to and straddles a drying lagoon south of Cooper Point.

Public tidelands of about 500 feet are about 4,000 feet south of Sanderson Cove.

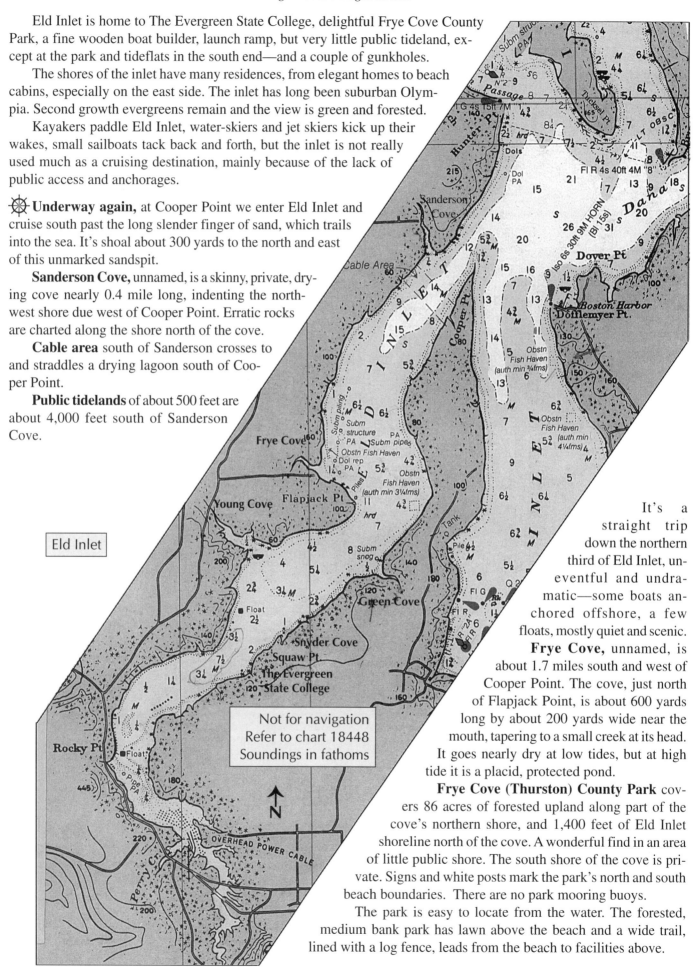

Not for navigation
Refer to chart 18448
Soundings in fathoms

It's a straight trip down the northern third of Eld Inlet, uneventful and undramatic—some boats anchored offshore, a few floats, mostly quiet and scenic.

Frye Cove, unnamed, is about 1.7 miles south and west of Cooper Point. The cove, just north of Flapjack Point, is about 600 yards long by about 200 yards wide near the mouth, tapering to a small creek at its head. It goes nearly dry at low tides, but at high tide it is a placid, protected pond.

Frye Cove (Thurston) County Park covers 86 acres of forested upland along part of the cove's northern shore, and 1,400 feet of Eld Inlet shoreline north of the cove. A wonderful find in an area of little public shore. The south shore of the cove is private. Signs and white posts mark the park's north and south beach boundaries. There are no park mooring buoys.

The park is easy to locate from the water. The forested, medium bank park has lawn above the beach and a wide trail, lined with a log fence, leads from the beach to facilities above.

Large rocks are along the bottom of the bank just above the sandy shore.

Three miles of trails wind through trees along the cove and a northern loop trail, thanks to hard-working area Boy Scouts who help maintain it. Restrooms proclaim the "most modern in recycling toilets." Picnic shelters and lawn on the uplands are at the site of an original homestead near the old apple orchard. A fabulous view from the park is east across Eld Inlet and beyond to Mount Rainier.

Frye Cove park shore

Thurston County Parks has done a fine job of cleaning out the underbrush while preserving the orchard and forests in the park. The park beach is sand and good steamer clams can be dug there. Oysters and clams are planted annually by the State Fisheries Department for public digging.

Ⓖ The cove is a quiet, **peaceful gunkhole**, unless there's a strong northerly blow.

➡ On chart 18456, 5/20/95, we noted 15 **"Submerged pilings"** charted in a row paralleling the shore—pilings from early logging activity north of the park. Thirteen of them are spaced along a 1,450 yard long straight line, about 300 yards offshore at each end, starting 150 yards north of the north corner of Frye Cove. One piling at each end is charted 75 yards east of the row in depths of 25 to 35 feet.

Thurston County Parks operations manager Chuck Groth said that to the best of his knowledge the charted, submerged, old pilings appear to be gone. Groth said park staff had been through the area with sonar fish finders.

"The bottom is real clear and we found no pilings," Groth said.

Groth also said water skiers run a slalom course in the area in the summer and had not encountered any sign of the submerged pilings. Nonetheless, we use caution in the area.

"Submerged structure PA" is charted between the 4th and 5th piling north, in a depth of 34 feet and is shaded.

"Obstn. Fish Haven" is charted inshore at the south end of the row of piling. This artificial reef made up of several thousand tires, was put in during 1978, according to Groth. There are no buoys marking the reef, used by many divers and fishermen.

"Dolphin PA" charted about 200 yards off the south shore entrance to Frye Cove, appears to be in line with and 300 yards south of the charted row of submerged piles.

Frye Cove park is a great place to dinghy ashore for some beach walking, picnicking, shellfish digging and swimming.

⚓ **Anchoring** is good about 400 yards off the park in this delightful gunkhole in about 30 feet, mud bottom. It is protected from south, west and northwest winds, but is exposed to north, east and southeast.

☸ **Underway again,** leaving Frye Cove, we head around **Flapjack Point**, the 100 foot high rounded knob which juts out from Eld Inlet's western shore, keeping outside the three fathom curve.

➡ **Switch to charts 18445 or 18448 for the southern portion of Eld Inlet.**

Young Cove, unnamed on the charts, is tucked back in the southwest side of Flapjack Point. It was called Friendly Cove by Peter Puget. It is charted as a drying cove almost 1,000 yards long and 200 yards wide, with about 1/2 fathom of water near the entrance. Erratic rocks are scattered along the shores.

View east across Eld Inlet from Frye Cove

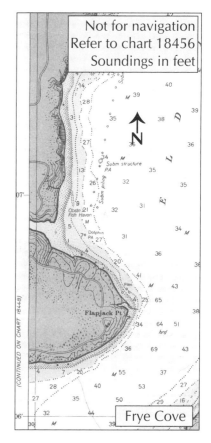

Not for navigation
Refer to chart 18456
Soundings in feet

Frye Cove

*Flapjack Point viewed from
Frye Cove beach*

*Native Americans used to
camp in the Frye Cove park area
when they dug clams. The cove
itself was an easy place to land
canoes. The area fell prey, as did
others, to logging in later years.*

*Young Cove is where Peter
Puget's group visited the "friendly
Indians." His band of sailors entered Eld Inlet on the morning of
Saturday, May 26, 1792. By the
time they'd rowed an hour they
found two Indian villages facing
each other across the inlet. Puget
wrote that "... we landed for a
short time and were received by
the inhabitants with all the friendship and hospitality we could
have expected ... from the 60 or
more persons in the village." He
named the quiet bay "Friendly
Cove."*

*He wrote that the Indian
women were curing clams and
fish and making neatly woven
baskets when he visited the village. The men apparently fished,
built canoes and did the "labori-
ous work" of the village. And although the Indians were the
"friendliest, most gentle and
agreeable" he had met, they also
ornamented their faces with red
and black ochre which conveyed
"a sense of savageness."*

We found the cove still friendly and quiet when we visited boat builder Sam Devlin in his shop here.

Devlin says during midsummer's extra low tides we could almost walk across the entrance to Young Cove—and it's mud into the head of the forested cove.

Ⓖ It's another **gunkhole**, especially in west and northerly breezes— if that's the case, we should be sailing. Just outside the cove he says there is almost always about 12 feet of water at the entrance. Some private mooring buoys are shown by a charted mooring buoy symbol.

⚓ **Anchoring** is okay here, Devlin said.

Launch ramp with floats along the northwest shore of Young Cove is owned by Doug Keyes. From the water the ramp is easily visible, and so is the big bell in front of his house east of the ramp.

Conversations with Custom Boat Builder Sam Devlin

A superb craftsman, Devlin designs and builds beautiful, custom wood boats in his shop on the north shore of Young Cove's entrance. He moved to the cove in 1982 and opened his boat yard. He's never deviated in his construction medium—wood—specializing in stitch-and-glue construction. He said this gives him great flexibility to vary his designs, and each boat is "built to order."

Devlin used to include boat repair and a marine railway in his operation. Even though he had the "first ecologically clean operation" on the west coast, he decided to quit running the railway, mainly because of liability reasons. The unused marine railway and some floats are on the west side of a launch ramp. Devlin's shop is on shore behind the ramp.

Sam Devlin enjoys the story of Puget's visit to Friendly Cove in 1792:

"He (Puget) had poked around Flapjack Point, rowed in here and found the Indian village in the cove. Back in this cove is one of the few spots on Puget Sound that Indians didn't haul their canoes up out of water. If you think about the process, lugging these big dugout canoes out of the water is a high caloric expense. You couldn't do it without a lot of effort, and that took energy which had to be replaced by food sources. In this cove the Indians never ever hauled their canoes out. They could leave them sitting in mud; no winter storms beat up into the cove; ice never formed enough to hurt anything. That alone, plus ready access to fish and shellfish and everything else made their lives so much easier that they had no inclination to be warlike or unfriendly."

Devlin said another spot where Native Americans left their canoes in the water year round was farther north near Bremerton, probably at Mud Bay in

Dyes Inlet. Few Indians had that privilege along the coast, and they had to yard canoes out of water, using logs for rollers.

Not many geographic locations on Eld Inlet shores are named on charts. Devlin told us some names, some are on the quad map, and we added some to the chart on page 290.

⚓ **Leaving Young Cove**, we cross Eld Inlet and find **Green Cove,** unnamed, at Lat. 45°5.9,' on the eastern shore.

Extending south from Green Cove for 3,300 feet is Geoduck Beach, the waterfront property of The Evergreen State College campus, a school with a reputation for innovative, independent programs. There is also a mandate to not develop their beautiful sand and gravel shoreline. Forests of firs and madronas overhang the beach, a favorite place for sunning and beachcombing.

The school has a campus of more than 1,000 acres of uplands.

Squaw Point, unnamed at Lat. 45°05.2,' the tiny hook charted on the southeast shore, is the location of the college's Marine Ecology Studies Center in Geoduck House.

Snyder Cove, the drying, minuscule bay inside the hook, is the moorage for the school's small boats.

We're now nearing the southern third of Eld Inlet and can see why its nickname of **Mud Bay** is well deserved.

About 1.5 miles south of Young Cove, south and west of the 140 foot high unnamed point on the west shore, we begin to run out of water with one fathom depths. From here on it is shallow and muddy with sandbars, eelgrass and oyster beds. Forget cruising any farther south, although it might be interesting to explore the tidal areas which trend east, then south, by canoe, kayak or dinghy.

Public tidelands of about three miles are here in the head of Eld Inlet on both shores.

As we turn around and head back north we encounter another artificial reef**, "Obstn. Fish haven"** 200 yards off the east shore of the inlet directly across from Flapjack Point.

➦ **We shift back to chart 18456,** 1:20,000 scale, soundings in feet, from charts 18445 or 18448. We will continue to use this chart with its good detail for the rest of the chapter.

⚓ **Leaving Eld Inlet,** we again allow about 400 yards to round Cooper Point and we find ourselves at the entrance to Budd Inlet.

Now let's cross the 0.8 mile of the inlet from Cooper Point to Boston Harbor. This crossing can be a millpond at times, but prevailing northwesterly winds can hit with little warning, except for darker water as winds approach. Sudden gusts can cause knockdowns and chop can be suddenly steep.

Boston Harbor

This crescent-shaped bay is between Dofflemeyer and Jeal points at the northeast entrance to Budd Inlet. Attractive, beach front homes line the low bank shore, with side-by-side residential development. Private floats and docks extend from the shore and permanently anchored boats are spread about the bay.

The harbor is somewhat protected from southerlies, but is exposed to northerlies and westerlies.

Early settlers named the bay and community after Boston, Massachusetts, hoping that it would be as successful in attracting commerce as its namesake. The idea never took hold and Olympia with its more protected harbor became the major city. Smugglers did dart in and out of the harbor around the turn of the century.

Boston Harbor Marina is on the south shore of the harbor, charted as #95 on 18445. Facilities at the marina are as listed.

The marina has guest and permanent moorage. Check-in at the store at the head of the dock on pilings, where a big sign announces "Marina."

Gary Jessen and Pam Vladeff took over the friendly community marina in 1995.

"Nude Beach:" Some local residents of Eld Inlet call one area of The Evergreen State College shoreline "nude beach," for the "summer passion of full body sun worship" practiced by many of the Evergreen students.

Eld Inlet was named during the Wilkes Expedition for Henry Eld, a passed midshipman. Cooper Point was named for John Cooper, an armorer aboard one of the ships in the Wilkes Expedition.

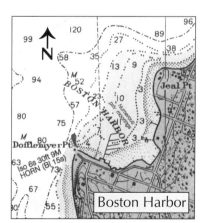

Not for navigation
Refer to chart 18456
Soundings in feet

Boston Harbor Marina, looking NE, with forested Jeal Point in background

Gary makes two important points about the marina:

1) Currents sometimes run through the marina and he urges mariners to be aware of this when docking.

2) The fuel float is on the east side of marina, at the outer end of the second float from shore. Coded card holders may pump their own fuel. Others need to call the attendant.

There's a picnic table on the deck outside the store to sit, visit and enjoy the view. This is a friendly, neighborhood place. The owners also sell fresh salmon, clams and oysters in season, which they buy from local Indians.

Boston Harbor area was platted and put up for sale in small lots in 1907, as a promoter thought it would be the metropolis of the west. Steamer loads of citizens came to view the potential property. The unscrupulous developer eventually ended up behind bars.

Boston Harbor Marina Facilities
➤ Guest moorage for about 15 boats
➤ Moorage rate about 30 cents per foot, $6 minimum
➤ 20 amp shore power at $2 per day; water
➤ Restrooms
➤ Fuel: diesel, gas; propane in containers
➤ Basic store carries ice, fishing gear, limited marine supplies, groceries, deli, beer, wine, ice cream, snacks
➤ Book exchange
➤ Call ahead for reservations
➤ Phone: 360-357-5670

A district fire department boat is moored alongside the main float. An unusual looking craft made of flotation tanks is used for beach-landing bulldozers and other equipment in areas that can be reached only by water. Several local dive boats are moored at the marina.

Surfaced launch ramp is charted on 18445 and operated by Thurston County. It is immediately west of the marina with parking across the street. Parking for boat trailers is limited to three days.

Telephone, restrooms and information about bus service into downtown Olympia is in the parking lot.

The only public beach access in Boston Harbor is at the launch ramp.

⚓ **Anchor** in the harbor, in about nine to 13 feet, if there's room in among permanently anchored boats, of which there are a fairly large number.

☸ **Dofflemeyer Point Lighthouse** is at the northwest point of Boston Harbor. The

Dofflemeyer Point Lighthouse from Marina floats

lighthouse, and its comforting horn, is a welcome sight and sound entering or leaving Budd Inlet, especially in the fog. All beaches are private, so it is not possible to walk to the lighthouse.

Iso 6s 30ft 9M Horn (Bl 15) Dofflemeyer Point Light, is an isophase white light at Dofflemeyer Lighthouse. Older charts show it as an equal interval six second light. Both terms mean the light's on and off time is of equal duration.

Budd Inlet Overview

This is the southernmost of all South Sound inlets, locally called Main Bay.

The capitol city of Olympia surrounds the head of the bay, with the striking Capitol Dome visible during much of the cruise up the inlet. Homes of all sizes and shapes, from cabins to mansions, line almost all of both sides of Budd Inlet, but there are still some forested shores.

Olympia is a port of entry with customs clearance.

Three marinas with guest moorage are in Olympia. **Percival Landing** is in downtown Olympia, **East Bay Marina** is a short 0.5 mile from town and **West Bay Marina** is about one mile away.

Two public waterfront parks are in Budd Inlet, both on the east shore:

Burfoot County Park is about 0.5 mile south of Boston Harbor and boats can anchor offshore.

Priest Point Park is in Olympia on both sides of Ellis Creek; nearby anchorage is not easily available because of muddy tideflats which extend several hundred yards off its shores.

Budd Inlet/Main Bay is a great sailing area. There is often a steady "afternoon westerly," especially in the summer. No charted navigational hazards are in the northern half of Budd Inlet. It's generally protected sailing, except during storms, of course, and most Olympians on or near the bay take advantage of it's delightful shores and water—which is often warm enough for enjoyable swimming.

Entrance to the nearly six mile long inlet is between Dofflemeyer Point at Boston Harbor on the east shore and Cooper Point on the west shore.

Width shore-to-shore at the entrance of Budd Inlet is about 0.8 mile; it widens to about 1.5 miles at Tykle Cove, and shrinks to about 0.7 mile near Priest Point. South of that it divides into two arms, East and West Bays, with narrow, navigable dredged channels through the shallows.

Depths at the entrance of Budd are charted 28 feet at midchannel, 42 to 88 feet east of midchannel and 111 feet west of midchannel. The 30 foot depth curve tapers south and west of Olympia Shoal, connecting with the dredged Outer Channel.

East shore 18 foot depth curve runs south and west from **Gull Harbor** for about two miles until about midchannel. The curve then progresses south and east to the "spoil bank."

Spoil bank bares at low tide, revealing sandbars and submerged pilings, and extends as much as 800 yards off Budd Inlet's eastern shore.

It is important for us to stay west of the 18 foot curve until it intersects with the dredged **Outer Channel** (chart 18456) or **"500 foot"** wide channel (chart 18445), due west of north range light, "Iso 6s 23 feet."

West shore 18 foot depth curve rarely extends 200 yards offshore from Cooper Point to about 400 yards south of flashing red nun buoy "4," where the curve turns east and intersects the dredged **Outer Channel.**

Depths south of here are less than 18 feet except in dredged channels.

Budd Inlet is free of charted navigational hazards for the northern three miles until we encounter the well-marked Olympia Shoal.

South of Olympia shoal are charted shallows and shoals along the east side of the inlet and on either side of the dredged and buoyed channels leading to the Port of Olympia's East and West Bay facilities and services.

⚓ **Anchoring** with caution, judgment and good weather is possible almost anywhere along Budd Inlet's shores in mud bottom and modest depth.

Partial Budd Inlet chart south of Tykle Cove showing dredged channels and aids to navigation from Olympia Shoal south are on pages 304-305.

Peter Puget went through Dana Passage after he surveyed Eld and Budd inlets, although as far as we can tell he never did go through Peale Passage.

His exploration of these southernmost inlets marked the end of his survey of South Sound, and he headed back to the *H.M.S. Discovery,* still anchored off Bainbridge Island. Imagine doing all this without charts and in one week's time.

Budd Inlet was named for Midshipman Thomas A. Budd by Lt. Charles Wilkes during his exploratory expedition in 1841. Budd had been acting master of the *Peacock* and then transferred at Fiji to the *Vincennes.*

Lush trails at Burfoot Park

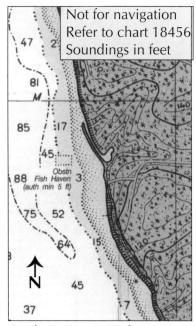

Burfoot County Park

South in Budd Inlet

⊕Underway again, we head along the eastern shore, past forested bluffs and homes for about 0.5 mile, until we reach a lovely park beach.

Burfoot (Thurston) County Park is identified on the chart by a ravine, a north-pointing sandspit, a drying lagoon and a "fish haven" 150 yards offshore.

Low to moderate partially forested bluffs rise to about 50 feet with small caves and holes along the bank immediately north of the cove and ravine. Silvered drift logs are scattered along the shore at the top of the gravel beach.

The 200 yard long sandspit has eroded since it was charted, and only a tiny drying cove remains at the base of the ravine between the uplands which rise to about 130 feet to the north and about 120 feet to the south.

"During heavy rains of the 1995 winter, the charted sandspit on the north end was breached and washed out," according to Chuck Groth, Thurston County Parks operation manager. "Everything changed, it's not as it was 40-50 years ago," he said. Wind and rain storms over the last couple of years have taken a toll, according to neighbors.

There are no mooring buoys to help identify this park from the water, but the sudden lack of homes and many madronas and evergreens along more than 1,100 feet of shoreline are good indicators of the park. A dark red caretaker's house above a rock bulkhead is about midway through the park, north of the ravine. White sign posts and markers identify the north and south boundaries of the park. South of the park boundary homes again climb the bluffs.

Attractions in this beautiful park include a good place to anchor off, paddle ashore and enjoy some shore time. Trails in the ravine lead from the beach across bridges over skunk cabbage wetlands, through forests to plank and gravel stairs to uplands where picnic tables and shelters, restrooms, three miles of trails (built with the help of local Scouts), interpretive trails and a new children's play area are within the park's 60 acres.

The beach, like most of those in the

Caretaker's house at
Burfoot Park

Archie and Mildred Burfoot *bought 20 acres here in 1936, built their home and lived here until they sold it to Thurston County for a park in 1968. The county later added 40 more acres.*

George Burfoot said, "My folks liked people to use the place and they wanted it preserved as a park for the community. People were always coming here for picnics, swimming or whatever. My folks encouraged it."

north part of Budd Inlet, is sand and gravel, great for children of any age. There's plenty of beachcombing, picnicking, swimming and fun here.

"Obstn fish haven" (auth. min. five feet) is charted across the 18 foot depth curve about 200 yards offshore of the drying cove, not marked by buoys.

Two fish havens or reefs are actually at the park, made up of several thousand old rubber tires tied together and anchored on site, but only one is charted. The reef north of the caretaker's house runs east and west and is visible at low water. We understand some of this reef has been damaged but still remains. It's shallow enough for snorkelers to dive around. The second reef is south of the house and at an "L" angle to the first. Both reefs were put down in 1978. "There is lot of interesting sea life to see around here. The sun stars are close to 14-15 inches across," Groth said.

⚓ **Anchoring** is possible providing the weather is calm enough to anchor and leave the boat comfortably. We drop the hook in about 45 feet, or less, mud bottom. Depth sounder may be useful to locate the fish haven before anchoring. Here we'd stay well north or south of the fish haven in at least 45 feet at MLLW depths. Groth said anchoring is feasible south of the caretaker's house or between the reefs in front of the house in about 60 feet at MLLW. The important thing is to not snag the anchor on any tires or structures.

⚓ **Underway again**, we leave Burfoot Park and cruise south along the shoreline. The shores here are steep bluffs, partially treed, up to 120 feet high. About 0.5 mile south of the park is a **"Obstn fish haven** (auth. min. 26 feet)" 200 yards offshore.

Gull Harbor is the next indentation south, on the east shore, 1.8 miles south of Dofflemeyer Point. It's private and shallow, drying at low tide. We have friends in Gull Harbor who have their 32' sailboat moored inside in a "puddle" at low tide.

Anchor off Gull Harbor in 10 feet or so, about 250 yards offshore.

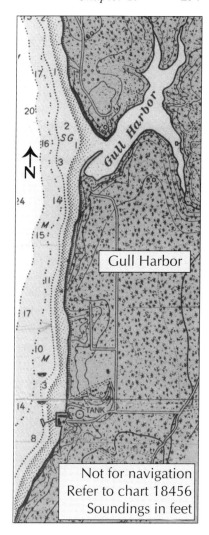

Gull Harbor

Not for navigation
Refer to chart 18456
Soundings in feet

Liberty Ships

Following World War II a huge number of retired, rusting vessels—mostly Liberty and Victory ships—were anchored in the east half of Budd Inlet north of Priest Point Park. By 1960 there were 185 ships chained together in dismal gray rows, to the dismay of many of boaters and waterfront home owners.

The ships clogged the cruising area and interrupted views; they were ugly; rats were rampant on them when grain was stored in them. Teenagers dared each other to clamber up anchor chains and board the ships so they could jump into the water—a definite "no-no"—but they did it anyway. Boaters were warned to stay 100 yards away.

Eventually, the ships were all towed away to meet their destinies, sold and/ or junked out. Nobody in Olympia shed a tear. The bay was opened to cruising and attractive views once again.

⚓ **Underway again,** we cruise past **Indian Road County Park,** about halfway between Gull Harbor and the Department of Natural Resources Center with its large dock, 0.7 mile farther south. The park property is in two long narrow charted gullies, one large, one small. No public land shows on the quad map at the park's location.

There is 330 feet of shoreline, a good, sandy beach and five acres of uplands in the steep ravines above. There is no parking or other facilities.

Although Thurston County has owned the park since 1940, no improvements have been made and none are planned because of the inaccessibility of beach lands. The park is identified from the water by gullies, trees and lack of homes.

⚓ **Anchoring** is possible about 200 yards of in 15 to 20 feet, mud bottom. Go ashore on this sandy, pleasant beach, but there are no park boundary stakes.

⚓ **Underway, Department of Natural Resources Research and Development Center** is next south along the shore. A large pier, two mooring buoy symbols and a "tank" are charted at the site. A mobile home park is visible above the DNR facility.

Priest Point Park, an Olympia city park, is about 1.4 miles south of the DNR facility. A large, lovely waterfront park, it is not conveniently accessible by boat, due to drying mudflats as much as 500 yards offshore. (See pages 304-305) We discuss the park and possible approaches after we enter East Bay.

Now we return to Cooper Point and work our way south along the west shore.

South from Cooper Point, the west side of Budd Inlet from Cooper Point south to Tykle Cove is about 2.9 miles. Homes cover the hills, which rise to over 100 feet in places, above beaches.

Tykle Cove is the first major indentation on the west shore, north of Olympia Shoal, all private shoreline.

"Pile PA" is charted on a radius of about 350 yards offshore in about 27 feet.

⚓ **Anchoring** is possible inside the 30 foot curve of Tykle cove, mud bottom. There is protection from westerlies and southwesterlies.

⚓ **Underway,** we look at **Butler Cove** on the west shore, 0.7 mile southwest of Olympia Shoal, or about 1.2 miles south of Tykle Cove. It's almost a right angle bight with a drying flat pursuing a steep ravine to the southwest between the 120 and 130 foot uplands.

A friend told of powering his 30 foot sloop slowly through the narrow entrance into Gull Harbor with the last of the flood.

"Current in the narrow entrance was still strong. It carried me in at a most alarming rate. About 30 feet past the sand spits at each side of the entrance we grounded on a gravel bar. The current swung the stern around so that we were beam-to on the bar with the current heeling us against it. No way to power off.

"After some time the harbor filled and current eased, I rowed upstream with an anchor and kedged the bow around to where we could power out. Flood tide can hurt, but help, too."

➥ **If using strip chart 18445,** turn to page F where there is a chart from Olympia Shoal south to the harbor in a scale of 1:20,000, otherwise continue with chart 18456.

Along with residential development in the cove is the Olympia Golf and Country Club on the hills above. All docks and shoreline are private, with one exception.

Public tidelands of about 500 feet are along the south shore of Butler Cove.

⚓ **Anchoring** is possible in Butler Cove about 200 to 500 yards offshore in 12-25 feet, mud bottom. Protection is good in a westerly or southwesterly.

☸ **Underway again,** we head towards Olympia Shoal and south to Olympia.

Olympia Shoal is about three miles south of Dofflemeyer Point and 0.4 mile off the west shore.

Looking at charted depths, small craft can easily pass either side of Olympia Shoal.

Mandatory pilots or skippers of larger ships may feel more comfortable using the dredged channel west of the shoal because of slightly deeper controlling depths.

Depths from 1/2 foot to four feet are charted within the six foot depth curve on the shoal. In addition, the 12 foot, 18 foot and 30 foot depth curves help define the shoal. This rock pile bares at low water.

➥ **Note: Budd Inlet south of Gull Harbor is closed to shellfish digging.**

The head of Budd Inlet was an immense expanse of muddy tide flats and decaying trees blocking access to a river (DesChutes) twisting through the shifting sands when viewed by the first early European explorers.

Peter Puget and Joseph Whidbey, their two boats and crews entered Budd from Eld Inlet on Saturday, May 26, 1792. They stopped a short distance south of Cooper Point for a late breakfast, and continued on until the boats nudged the mudflats that ended their journey south. Whidbey took a noon sun sight which fixed the latitude as 47°03'. Charts today show the head of Budd Inlet at Percival Landing at 47°03.'41." Darn close, we'd say.

Puget's small boats turned and headed back north, the only direction they could go.

"Memoir" of Olympia Shoal

Jo recalls: In the 1960s, during a summer Lakefair Festival, we looked out our dining room window and saw one of several invited Navy ships hard aground on Olympia Shoal. The vessel's crew spent several hours in utter embarrassment waiting for a tide to lift the ship off. We had the feeling that chart-reading lessons would be the order of the day aboard that vessel.

"In 1967, our family had both the 29 foot sloop *Sea Witch* and the 19 foot sloop *Winsome* (not to be confused with Carl's 50 foot yawl *Winsome*). I left Olympia in the dark of night on the *Winsome* with the three teenage daughters, to meet their dad and our two sons aboard the *Sea Witch,* 'somewhere near Seattle.' This was before cell phones, we had no radio on the little *Winsome* and we were heading out into a large area. How crazy we were sometimes.

"At that time I wasn't familiar with the navigation lights and aids on the buoys, piles and dolphins in Olympia Harbor and I freaked out trying to figure what was what. Megan, Robin and Debi took over and got us past all those confusing, blinking lights, and into the dark waters north of Olympia Shoal. Underway all night, we stopped in the morning at Days Island in The Narrows for gas. We finally met up with the *Sea Witch* later in the day, somewhere in Colvos Pass. Did she ever look good. That's when I learned about navigation aids and lights. I'm sometimes amazed we all survived our early years of sailing, given how little we knew, and how much more we have yet to learn."

When Jo lived in Olympia she spent about three hours aground on the south side of Olympia shoal in a women's race. She says she was not the skipper and was overruled when she wanted to go to starboard and the woman skipper wanted to go to port—and did—and onto the shoal as well. However, the women took advantage of the enforced layover, relaxed, sipped a bit of wine and sailed off the shoal when the tide came in. Needless to say, They didn't finish the race.

She was also in another race, on another boat, at another time, and ran aground on the east side of the shoal, but that time they got off quickly. She claims she wasn't steering that time either.

We now cruise into Olympia and discuss what we find there.

➠Before we get underway, let's take a close look at **Olympia Harbor Chart 18456,** on page 304, from Tykle Cove south, past Olympia's shoals and into the harbor. Aids to navigation are listed on pages 304-305.

Touch of Olympia History

In spring 1845, a group of settlers reached the Olympia area and started farming. Leaders were Kentucky-born Michael T. Simmons and George Bush, a black man from the French Colony of Louisiana. Simmons built a gristmill and a sawmill at the Des Chutes River falls, now called Tumwater Falls.

Edmund Sylvester, a former Maine fisherman, and his associate, Levi Smith, each settled on a half section of land, 320 acres each, in 1846. When Smith fell from a canoe and drowned a few months later, Sylvester inherited Smith's land on the waterfront of what later became a landfill at the foot of Capitol Way.

Olympia was named in 1850, the first American port in Washington territory. The Brig *Orbit* was the first ship to call in the new port, and she loaded pilings for San Francisco, beginning a very productive trade. The fledgling town had the first post office on Puget Sound; soon there were general stores, saloons, newspapers, a livery stable, churches, and public school—which collapsed under heavy snow.

The Steamship era began in the 1850s, when the side-wheeler steamer *Fairy* tied at high tide to the dock built by Samuel Percival, a sea captain from California. Steamers were the best source of news of the outside world to tiny waterfront settlements. The busy little ships stopped wherever there was a store or post office, the most important vessels ever on the Sound. Landings became community centers where townsfolk met to gossip and pick up mail.

By 1851, Olympia had a Customs House. All ships had to register in Olympia whenever they plied the Sound, regardless of their destination. Three years later it was moved to more convenient Port Townsend, but by then Olympia had a solid reputation as a port. Customs services were later re-established.

In 1853, Olympia had 250 settlers and was the largest village on Puget Sound. It became territorial capitol, in spite of objections from other cities. It was again named capitol when Washington reached statehood in 1889.

In 1871, the Puget Sound Steam Navigation Company was incorporated in Olympia. Business was good, with lumber the mainstay of the young port.

Holidays found steamers filled with folks on excursions.

In the 1890s, the channel into Olympia Harbor was first dredged and landfills built up on Cheetwood peninsula and elsewhere, creating industrial sites.

The Deschutes River was dammed in 1951, creating Capitol Lake and establishing the head of the harbor at the 4th Avenue bridge.

Today, little more than 200 years after Puget first saw the area, the elegant 187 foot high domed capitol building dominates the energetic city of Olympia at the tip of the Sound.

Olympia was the terminus of Puget Sound steamer runs. Later it was a huge log-shipping facility, which has declined somewhat in recent years. It is now, more than ever, a destination for recreational vessels.

"Cheetwoot," meaning "bear," was the Indian name for the peninsula between East and West Bays. It was a favorite shellfish gathering spot for the Nisqually, Duwamish and Squaxin Indians.

Great Blue Heron

Jo recalls: For 15 years our family lived in a wonderful big house on the water on East Bay, slightly north of the marina— long before it was built. We watched the tide slide in and out daily over the muddy flats, much preferring high tide The kids built boats, forts and rafts; swam to their heart's content, sailed and rowed about in various and sundry rafts and boats, often followed by harbor seals. It was an idyllic time.

⚓ **We have arrived in Olympia . . . . . . !**

We've actually made it to our last destination—Olympia. We'll take a look at the three marinas and some of the other facilities in this wonderful capitol city.

West Bay Marina, is charted as # 97A on 18445; facilities exceed those listed.

To reach the marina, we turn west at red buoy "6" at the jog in the entrance channel and go straight over to the entrance between the two floats paralleling the shore, B, north, and C, south. The fuel dock and check-in are visible straight ahead, tucked inside, between F and G docks.

Depths here range from nine to 19 feet. Note: 12 foot depth curve between the main channel and the marina extends about 150 yards north of buoy "6."

West Bay Marina Facilities
➤ Guest moorage as available for 5-10 boats
➤ Moorage rate $10 per night up to 30', $15 per night 30' and over
➤ 20-30 amp power, rate included in moorage; water
➤ Fuel: gas, diesel
➤ Restrooms, showers, laundry
➤ Pump-out
➤ Restaurant
➤ Permanent moorage for 400 boats
➤ Full service boat yard with boat repair, haulout, and marine supplies
➤ Phone: 360-943-2022, call ahead for reservations

It's a quiet marina, with a small park and pet area overlooking the water, about 1.5 miles from downtown Olympia. After a devastating fire a couple of years back, the office and restaurant area were rebuilt in the summer of 1995.

West Bay Yacht Club has reciprocal moorage on C dock.

⚓ **Continuing on,** we might opt to follow the small craft, dredged channel into East Bay by turning to the southeast from the Outer Channel at the Junction Light, and end up in Olympia's newest marina.

East Bay was mostly mud flats and log booms until dredged for the marina in the 1980s.

East Bay Marina is on the east side of the peninsula separating East and West bays. Entering from the Outer Channel we angle southeast at the flashing green junction marker, strangely enough keeping the green junction light to starboard. (We must remember to keep the junction light to port when leaving.) We continue into the 100 foot wide dredged channel, noting locations of navigation aids "1" through "4," until reaching the marina breakwater, a distance of about 0.6 mile.

East Bay Marina breakwater and launch ramp are to starboard. Boats may side-tie to the guest moorage at the breakwater, or to Float A, the first float beyond the ramp.

➥ **Note:** The dredged channel into East Bay Marina had a depth of 13 feet, with a depth of eight feet or less outside the channel on both sides, in 1991.

East Bay Marina, looking NW

East Bay Marina is owned and operated by the Port of Olympia. It's about 0.75 mile from downtown (a level walk, no hills). The marina is modern, quiet and secure, the staff is friendly, the waterfront park and picnic areas are pleasant.

East Bay Marina Facilities

➤ Guest moorage for more than 85 visiting boats
➤ Moorage fees $7.50 per day for boats up to 20', after 20' add .30 per foot
➤ 30-50 amp shore power included in moorage fee; water
➤ Restrooms, showers, laundry facilities
➤ Double lane launch ramp
➤ Security gates
➤ Pump-out on end of guest float
➤ Picnic and play area
➤ Nearby boat yard
➤ Monitors VHF Channel 65 and CB Channel 9
➤ Phone: 360-786-1400

Port of Olympia's future plans for East Bay include marina expansion, the Swantown Boat Works with a haulout facility and travel lifts; a chandlery, boat sales and sailmaker.

There is plenty of parking for trucks and trailers, boat owners and visitors at East Bay Marina.

Priest Point Park, as we came south from Boston Harbor we mentioned this park on the east shore and promised to tell more about it. The 265 acre landmark city park has about a mile of saltwater shoreline, with Ellis Creek tucked away inside. Olympia acquired the property in 1906.

Heavily forested, the park has picnic tables and shelters, a children's wading pool, play equipment, an extensive interpretive trail system and saltmarshes and beaches to explore.

However, the park is not conveniently accessible by boat and is easier reached by land than by sea. A quick glance at the chart shows drying mudflats extending over 500 yards off Ellis Creek, over 100 yards off the north part of the park and 300 yards off the south.

Even if mooring at East Bay Marina and taking a shore boat to the park we suggest going on an incoming tide and leaving before it ebbs to prevent getting mired in the yucky mud. This is a good place to use retrievable, dinghy anchor-gear. Wear boots or shoes as there's a lot of unknown "cutting edge" materials under the mud's surface.

Not for navigation
Refer to chart 18456
Soundings in feet

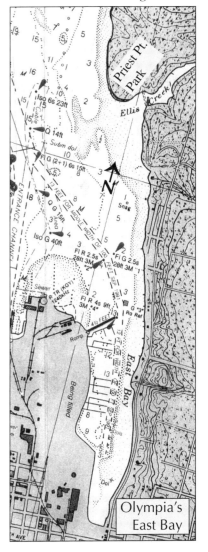

Olympia's East Bay

Priest Point Park History

Catholic missionary priests started St. Joseph Mission at Priest Point Park in 1848. The quiet, forested shores were used by Squaxin Indians as a gathering place and site of early potlatches.

Missionaries of Oblates of Mary Immaculate arrived to minister to nearby Indian tribes. Father Pascal Ricard and three other priests cleared land, planted a garden, built a chapel, operated a school for Indian boys, and claimed the 324 acres as St. Joseph's of New Market.

The Squaxin, Nisqually, Puyallup and Snoqualmie tribes used the mission as a trading center. Pascal left the mission in 1857 and it closed in 1860.

Approaching downtown Olympia marina facilities in West Bay from the Outer Channel, we enter the 300 foot wide Entrance Channel between the flashing green junction light and R "6" buoy, continuing south past the Turning Basin.

We stay in the marked channel until reaching the beginning of the small craft facilities, about 1.0 mile from the junction light, otherwise we may find ourselves planted in mud for a few hours.

Depths on either side of the channel are charted at 11 feet or less. Channel depths south of the Turning Basin are charted between nine to 15 feet.

Channel width south of the basin is charted about 150 yards.

Percival Landing

Percival Landing *was named for pioneer entrepreneur Samuel Percival.*

We found Percival Landing to be a delightful moorage—especially when we discovered the harbormaster had been one of Jo's fourth grade students when she taught school in Olympia.

Olympia Harbor & Capitol building

"The golden age of steamboating *with the lovely smell of steam and hot paint and salt water," was from 1872 to 1920. (From* **So Fair a Dwelling Place** *by Gordon Newell)*

⚓ **Anchoring** is possible south of the turning basin in about 13 feet at MLLW, and we see boats anchored here at various times. Be aware that south and west of red buoy N "18" there are old pilings, and depths are charted as shallow as one foot.

⎈ Several small private moorages are on the east shore south of the basin.

Fiddlehead Marina is charted as #97 on 18445. Guest moorage has not been available here since the early 1980s.

Olympia Yacht Club floats and boathouses are at the head of the bay west of Percival Landing. They have reciprocal guest moorage for four to six boats.

Percival Landing, a public moorage at the head of the bay, is as far south in Budd Inlet as a boat can go. It's a great spot and is the centerpiece of Olympia's downtown waterfront.

As we enter Percival Landing we pass:
- **"E" float** with pumpout station on the east side.
- **"B" 90 foot float,** immediately south with guest moorage; no power.
- **Observation lookout** is next. After you get moored this is a great place to get a bird's eye view of the marina and Olympia.
- **"A" 600 foot float** is next, paralleling the east side, guest moorage with power.
- **"B" 250 foot float,** guest moorage, no power, south end on the west side.

And here we are, at Percival Landing in downtown Olympia.

Percival Landing Facilities

➤ Guest moorage for 45 to 60 boats in 940 ft. of dock space
➤ Moorage rates are $6 boats under 29'/$7, 30-39'/ $8, 40-49'/ $9, over 50'
➤ Moorage with 30 amp shore power is an additional $3 daily
➤ Water is available to fill tanks but not to hook up
➤ Restrooms, showers
➤ Pump-out and porta-potty dump
➤ Moorage is limited to seven days in a 30 day period, self-register
➤ Walking distance of just about everything in Olympia
➤ Phone: 360-753-8382

Managed by the City of Olympia, Percival Landing opened in 1978 and was completed in 1988. It has nearly one mile of boardwalk along the south and eastern shoreline of West Bay with open space areas, picnic spots, benches and viewing sites, restaurants and other shops.

The observation tower allows panoramic 360 degree views of the city and the capitol, Budd Inlet, the nearby hills and the distant Olympics. There are many cities that could benefit by such a boat and people friendly facility as Percival Landing.

Olympia

The city has just about everything: marine hardware, fishing tackle and bait, groceries, restaurants, liquor store, post office, retail stores, boutiques, art galleries, museums, medical facilities, performing arts center and movie theaters.

Tour the beautifully manicured Capitol Grounds and buildings. They are lovely in spring when pink Japanese cherry blossoms are rampant. (Phone: 360-586-INFO)

Farmers' Market is open May through October on the Port of Olympia property, north of Percival Landing and west of East Bay Marina, with baked goods, flowers, fresh produce, seafood, crafts and other wonders every Thursday through Sunday.

Walk or take a bus to Olympia Brewery (in Tumwater) for a tour; walk four miles around Capitol Lake for exercise. The swimming beach is closed, but there are picnic tables, fishing piers, boat rentals, an interpretive center and rest rooms.

South of Capitol Lake are Tumwater Historical Park and Tumwater Falls Park. The parks encompass the original abandoned brewery, closed down when Prohibition was the law, hiking trails, restrooms, historic sights, picnic areas, fish ladder and other sights viewed from above Tumwater Falls. The falls are about 1.7 miles from Percival Landing as the crow flies.

Something is always going on in the capitol city, whether the Legislature is in session or not. There's a Wooden Boat Festival in May, Capitol Lakefair in July, Olympia Harbor Days and the Tug Boat Festival on Labor Day weekend in September, among other community festivals.

During pioneer days the East Bay area was called "Swantown."

We understand that in the late 1800s, young boys would skinny-dip. The tideflats were bare mud at low tides, and on hot summer days impetuous boys would peel off their clothes and roll about in the muck until the rising tide rinsed them clean, a mother's fondest wish.

Olympia later passed regulations which prohibited swimming within the city limits without a suit.

In early days when Olympia first became a shipping terminal, the harbor was usable only at high tides as it emptied almost to Priest Point Park on extreme low tides.

"The Kiss," a delightful sculpture by Richard Beyer, captivates many who see it. It's at the very head of Olympia harbor on the boardwalk and was dedicated July 7, 1990, by the Patrons of South Sound Cultural Arts. If you enjoy Beyer's "Waiting for the Interurban," in Seattle's Fremont District, and "Ivar and the Seagulls," you'll understand our enthusiasm and appreciation for "The Kiss."

Finis

⚓ It's hard to believe, but somehow we've just finished our great gunkholing cruise of Puget Sound from Kingston/Edmonds south to Olympia. Now we're in Olympia, and the cruise has gone by so quickly, although it took us over three years to compile it.

All we can say is thanks for coming along with us through a cruising area we've lived in for so long and dearly love.

We hope you've had as good a time as we have, for that's what this is all about.

➡ Other Gunkholing books, co-authored by Jo Bailey, on the *San Juans, Gulf Islands and Desolation Sound,* will be available in expanded, revised versions, plus a new *Gunkholing in North Puget Sound* book in 1997-98.

Check with your local nautical bookseller.

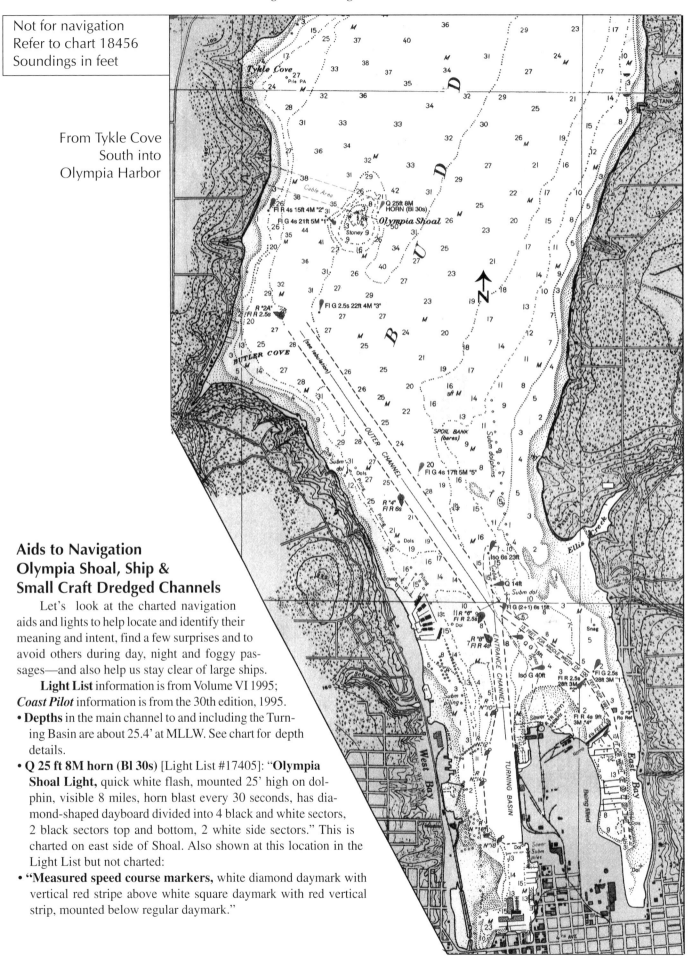

Not for navigation
Refer to chart 18456
Soundings in feet

From Tykle Cove
South into
Olympia Harbor

Aids to Navigation
Olympia Shoal, Ship &
Small Craft Dredged Channels

Let's look at the charted navigation
aids and lights to help locate and identify their
meaning and intent, find a few surprises and to
avoid others during day, night and foggy passages—and also help us stay clear of large ships.

Light List information is from Volume VI 1995;
Coast Pilot information is from the 30th edition, 1995.

• **Depths** in the main channel to and including the Turning Basin are about 25.4' at MLLW. See chart for depth
details.

• **Q 25 ft 8M horn (Bl 30s)** [Light List #17405]: "**Olympia
Shoal Light,** quick white flash, mounted 25' high on dolphin, visible 8 miles, horn blast every 30 seconds, has diamond-shaped dayboard divided into 4 black and white sectors,
2 black sectors top and bottom, 2 white side sectors." This is
charted on east side of Shoal. Also shown at this location in the
Light List but not charted:

• "**Measured speed course markers,** white diamond daymark with
vertical red stripe above white square daymark with red vertical
strip, mounted below regular daymark."

Curious about the term, "measured course," rather than "measured nautical mile," and it's being uncharted, we found the measured course to be about 125' longer than a nautical mile. Then we plotted the distance between the markers at about 6,300' which is about 224' longer than a nautical mile, or 99' longer than the Coast Pilot's distance. All of which may explain its not being charted—if the marks are still in place.

Keep in mind Aids to Navigation are subject to change.
Cable area crosses to Olympia Shoal from the west shore.

- **Fl G 4s 21ft 5M "1"** [Light list #17410]**: "West Olympia Shoal Light 1.** Flashing green 4 second light mounted 21' high on dolphin with **square green dayboard,** visible 5 miles," marks the east side of the main ship channel.

- **Fl R 4s 15ft 4M "2"** [Light list #17415]: **"Budd Inlet Light 2.** Flashing red 4 second light, mounted 15' on dolphin, has a red triangle dayboard, visible 4 miles;" charted about 100 yards off the west shore, marks west side of main ship channel.

- **FL R 2.5s R "2A"** [Light List #17425]: **"Olympia Entrance Lighted buoy 2A,** flashing red 2.5 second lighted buoy, visible 3 miles," marks west side of dredged 500 ft wide Outer Channel. Light is about 400 yards off west shore, north of Butler Cove.

- **Fl G 2.5s 22ft 4M "3"** [Light list #17420]: **"Olympia Entrance Light 3**. Flashing green 2.5 second light, 22' on white platform on dolphin, has square green dayboard, visible 4 miles," charted on east side near north end of dredged 500 ft wide Outer Channel.

Outer Channel Range Lights Mark Center of 500' wide Channel:

- **Q G 15ft** [Light List #17430]: **"Range Front Light,** quick flashing green light visible all around, with **rectangular red dayboard** bearing central (vertical) **black stripe,** mounted 15' on dolphin; higher intensity on rangeline." Front range light is 1.4 nautical miles south of Outer Channel entrance.

- **Iso G 40 ft** [Light list # 17435]: **"Range Rear Light,** isophase green light visible 4° each side of rangeline. Rectangular red dayboard bearing central (vertical) **black stripe** mounted 40' high on skeleton tower. Light is 325 yards, 144.6° from range front light."

500 ft dredged Outer Channel aids:

- **Fl R 6s R "4"** [Light List #17445]: **"Olympia Channel Lighted Buoy 4,** flashing red 6 second light visible 3 miles on red buoy." Buoy is about 400 yards off west shore and 0.9 miles south of R "2A," marks west side of dredged Outer Channel.

- **Fl G 4s 17 ft 5M "5"** [Light List #17440]: **"Olympia Channel Light 5,** flashing green 4 second light, 17' high on pile structure with square green dayboard, visible 5 miles." Light is on east side of ship channel about 600 yards off west shore and 0.75 miles SE of "3."

Note: This is also the south end of measured course marker.
Fl R 2.5s R "6" [Light List #17450]: **"Olympia Channel Lighted Buoy 6,** flashing red 2.5 second light on red buoy, visible 3 miles." Buoy is at SE end of 500' wide Outer Channel; marks west side of channel and is about 550 yards off west shore and 0.55 mile SE of R "4."

Cable crossing runs between junction light and range lights in vicinity of junction area.

- **FL G (2+1) 6s 15 ft** [Light List #17455] **"Junction Light,** flashing green (2+1), repeats 2 flashes then 1 flash every 6 seconds, mounted 15' high on pile, has dayboard bearing horizontal bands of green and red, green band topmost with green reflective border, visible 3 miles, 40' outside channel limit."

Olympia Inner Range Lights for 300 ft wide Entrance Channel:

- **Q 14ft** [Light list # 17480]: **"Olympia Inner Range Front Light,** quick flashing white light 14' high on dolphin with rectangular red dayboard bearing central black stripe, visible 6 miles." South light is located about 225 yards north and slightly west of **Junction Light.**

- **Iso 6s 23 ft** [Light list # 17485]: **"Olympia Inner Range Rear Light,** isophase 6 seconds, 23' high on dolphin with rectangular red dayboard bearing central black stripe, 235 yards, 354° from front (north) light."

300 ft wide "Entrance Channel" Buoys:

- **Fl R 4s R "8"** [Light List #17490]: **"Olympia Channel Lighted Buoy 8,** flashing red 4 second light on red buoy, visible 3 miles." Buoy is 550 yards off west shore and about 200 yards south of buoy R "6." Buoy marks west side of 300' wide Entrance Channel.

- **R N "10"** [Light List # 17495]: **"Olympia Channel Buoy 10,** red nun," approximately 570 yards south of "8," marks south end of **Entrance Channel** and north end of **Turning Basin.**

- **Buoys RN 12, RN 14, RN 16 and RN 18** define **Turning Basin** on its west side and south end. Basin is 300-800' wide and 0.5 mile long. East side of basin is bordered by commercial piers.

Small Craft 100 ft wide Dredged Channel into East Bay:
starts at **Junction Light Fl G (2+1) 6s** 15', 40' outside channel limit.

- **Charted depths** are 12 to 13' for middle width of channel, Sept. 1991.

- **Fl G 2.5s 28ft 3M "1"** [Light List #17460]: **"Light 1,** flashing green 2.5 second light, 28' high on square green dayboard on pile, visible 3 miles, 40 ft outside channel limit," about 850 yards SE of Junction Light and 200 yards off east shore. Light marks NE side of smallcraft channel where it angles southeast.

- **Fl R 2.5s 28ft 3M "2"** [Light List #17465]: **"Light 2,** flashing red 2.5 second light 28' high with triangular red dayboard on piling, visible 3 miles, 40' outside channel limit," approximately 180' southwest of "1."

- **G "3" Ra Ref** [Light List #17470]: **"Daybeacon 3,** square green daybeacon with radar reflector on pile, 40' outside channel limit, about 125 yards off east shore, 350 yards southeast of "1."

- **Fl R 4s 9ft 3M "4"** [Light List # 17475]: **"Light 4,** flashing red 4 second light, 9' high on platform with triangular red dayboard," at northeast end of East Bay Marina breakwater.

That friends, takes us past the Olympia Shoal and through the Ship Channels into the capitol city.

Appendix

Coast Guard Group Seattle

Coast Guard Group Seattle handles many different areas of boating. Their basic mission is safe boating for all.

Group Seattle is responsible for search and rescue operations, promoting water safety and education through Coast Guard Auxiliary classes and public speaking programs. They have a law enforcement mission, and units conduct boardings to make sure boats are in compliance with federal regulations.

The Coast Guard assists immediately if there is any danger to boaters. However, their search and rescue policy is to not interfere with commercial assistance. In a call that a vessel is broken down but in no immediate danger the Coast Guard operator will advise that all persons on board put on life jackets, and the operator helps the boater get appropriate assistance.

(Vessel Assist is one of several private groups which comes to the aid of stranded boaters—much like AAA. For more information contact 206-453-1176.)

We recommend those new to boating or who want to learn more about seamanship, navigation and other facets of boating, take Coast Guard Auxiliary or Power Squadron classes. They are generally free, except for supplies, and are given by both groups throughout the northwest.

The Coast Guard Boating Education Branch published a 49 page pamphlet in 1992 titled *Federal Requirements and Safety Tips for Recreational Boats,* available at most marine stores or directly from the Coast Guard, 1-800-368-5647.

The Coast Guard has established minimum safety standards for vessels and associated equipment. Briefly, this means each vessel must have:

- Proper registration/numbering/documentation
- Personal flotation devices (PFDs) in appropriate sizes
- Visual distress signals
- Know FCC regulations
- Adequate ventilation
- Sound producing devices
- Marine sanitation devices
- Navigation lights and shapes
- Fire extinguishers
- Backfire flame control
- Know pollution regulations

The booklet includes sections on:

Additional Recommended Equipment

- Aids to navigation
- Anchoring
- Boaters check list
- Boating while intoxicated
- CME additional requirements
- Cold water survival
- Display of Numbers
- Equipment Requirements
- Float plan
- Fueling management
- Fueling precautions
- Law Enforcement
- Loading your vessel
- Marine rated parts
- Nautical charts
- Navigation rules
- Negligent operation
- Operating Procedures
- Rendering assistance
- Reporting boating accidents
- Safety and Survival Tips
- Small boats and water activities
- Staying afloat
- Stern anchoring
- Termination of use
- Vessel conditions
- Weather

Coast Guard Lt. Ben White on Law Enforcement: Boardings and the Law

Many boaters are rankled by Coast Guard boardings and inspections, feeling their right to be secure "against unreasonable searches and seizures" is being violated.

We discussed these boardings with the officer in charge, Lt. Ben White. He said that "basically boardings are to check for compliance with federal regulations. People see it as being a borderline encroachment on 4th amendment rights, and that's what gets them upset," he said.

"We're trained to come on board and say 'I'm here to just check for compliance.' If the boater has all the required equipment nothing thrills us more than to give the gold sheet that says 'you got it all, you look good.' Those in compliance aren't the ones we're talking about. Those without required equipment are the ones we need to check. We want to get that across to people.

"How do we decide who to board? We basically pick at random: fishermen, power boaters, sailors. Sometimes it comes down to the experience of the boarding team and officer. If we see faulty equipment or an unhealthy-looking situation, then we're likely to board. When a boat is being boarded, we ask for an INTEL check so the team knows what they're walking into."

A vessel underway, when hailed by a Coast Guard vessel is required to "heave to," or maneuver in such a manner that permits a boarding officer to come aboard.

The Coast Guard may impose a civil penalty up to $1,000 for failure to comply with equipment requirements, report a boating accident, or comply with other federal regulations.

A Coast Guard boarding officer who observes a boat being operated in an unsafe condition, specifically defined by law or regulation, and who determines that an especially hazardous condition exists, may direct the operator to take immediate steps to correct the condition, including returning to port.

An operator who refuses to terminate the unsafe use of a vessel can be cited for failure to comply with the directions of a Coast Guard boarding officer, as well as for specific violations which were the basis for the termination order. Violators may be fined not over $1,000 or imprisoned not over one year or both.

Patrolling Coast Guard cutters are always underway or on call year round. There are no more boats patrolling in the summer than in winter, but they are much busier in the summer with many more recreational boaters out on the water.

The Coast Guard does check to make certain that heads are in compliance. Which means that vessels under 65 feet may use Type I, II or III Marine Sanitation Devices which must be Coast Guard certified.

Generally, the Coast Guard will give a warning citation if all their requirements are not met and the citation will be forwarded to a hearing officer who will then decide on appropriate action.

There are not many instances of drug smuggling in the Puget Sound area that the Coast Guard responds to, although U.S. Customs may have a different story, White said.

Boating While Intoxicated

Boating while intoxicated can now be prosecuted under civil tests, and Coast Guard vessels carry breathalyzer equipment on board.

"We do enforce the boating while intoxicated law. It's dangerously unacceptable to abuse alcohol and operate a boat. We want to get the drunks off the water.

"Boating accidents are even worse in Puget Sound because of the effects of 40°- 50° water," he said.

Yacht clubs are encouraging their members to abstain from drinking while running their boats.

Operating a vessel while intoxicated (blood alcohol content

of 0.10 or higher) became a Federal offense on Jan. 13, 1988. Negligent or grossly negligent operation of a vessel which endangers lives and/or property is prohibited by law.

"Common Sense" Boating

- **Never cut between a tug and a tow:**
  The cable/lines connecting the tow lie low in the water and are difficult to see and could rip your boat in half. The distance between the tugboat and the tow or barge may be as great as 1,000 feet.
- **Never pass closely behind a tugboat:**
  Towed barges can also unexpectedly yaw from side to side. Log tows are deceptively dangerous with their "bundles," which may be difficult to see.
  Don't try to "out race" vessels with the intent of crossing ahead of them.
- **Other vessels, especially from afar, never appear to be as fast as they are actually traveling:**
- **Always maintain a sharp lookout.**
  Dead heads (logs drifting upright), large vessels masked by background lighting from shore and fog banks—and other surprises—can make for unpleasant experiences.
- **A sailboat not under sail and under power:**
  This is considered under the RULES OF THE ROAD to be a power driven vessel.
- **Carrying people in an unsafe manner:**
  While it may be fun to dangle hands and feet in the water, it's easy to be crunched by another boat at a dock, or to fall off the boat and go into the propeller. There must be a sufficient railing for bow, gunwale or transom riding to be safe.

For more information on boating safety and boating courses, contact your State Boating Agency, Coast Guard District or the Boating Safety Hotline, or call 1-800-336-2628.

Vessel Traffic Service

General Information about VTS

There are close to 273,000 ship movements annually in all of Puget Sound, the San Juan Islands and the Strait of Juan de Fuca. That means approximately 750 plus ships transit some part of the area daily. This includes freighters, tankers, tugs and tows, Naval and Coast Guard vessels, including submarines and surface vessels. This figure includes the more than 212,000 ferry movements annually, or about 580 daily. It does not include the tens of thousands of recreational boats on the waters.

This kind of boat traffic almost makes you wonder if there's room enough for all of us, and helps us understand why the waterway traffic needs to be monitored and/or controlled.

The mission of the Puget Sound Vessel Traffic Service is to enhance safety on the waterways, particularly by preventing collisions, groundings and environmental damage, and to protect the beauty of the local waters. Certain laws apply to all vessels that ply the waters.

The more recreational boaters understand about the rationale behind the VTS, the safer the waterways will be for both commercial and recreational vessels.

What VTS Is

The Puget Sound Vessel Traffic Service (PSVTS) managed by 13th Coast Guard District is similar to air traffic control in monitoring vessel traffic, but 99% of the time it is advisory.

VTS was commissioned in 1972 as a voluntary system for vessel traffic; at that time about 140 boats transited the area daily. U.S. and Canada signed an international agreement in 1979 establishing the Cooperative Vessel Traffic Service; the Canadians monitor shipping in Haro Strait and west of Cape Flattery.

Full participation in VTS is required of those vessels over 132 feet (40 meters) in length to comply with VTS reporting requirements. "Passive participation" is required of vessels between 66 and 132 feet (20 and 40 meters) in length which must monitor designated VTS frequencies and comply with general VTS operating rules.

How it Works

The Traffic Separation Schemes (TSS) are shown on NOAA navigational charts in purple dashes. TSS is a two-lane water highway with each lane 1,000 yards wide. The lanes are separated by a 500 yard "median" or separation zone—pretty much like the freeway. Large vessels use the traffic lanes.

Lt. Dan Precourt gave us a tour of the Vessel Traffic Center in Building 1 at Pier 36, the C.G. Support Center in Seattle, for a complete briefing on how the system works.

Vessels in the TSS are monitored by round-the-clock crews in the Vessel Traffic Center. In a large, dimly-lit room three highly trained operators and one watch supervisor manage the 12 radar screens tracking the movements of all vessels in the TSS lanes. All personnel have instant recall of all the prominent geographic points in the entire VTS area. The same number of operators and supervisors are on duty during each of three daily watches in a highly labor intensive operation. Soon, with new state-of-the-equipment many functions will be automated and the center will be even more efficient.

The center receives radar surveillance information from 12 strategically located radar sites in the area: Point Defiance, Point Robinson, Elliott Bay (at Pier 36), West Point, Point No Point, Point Wilson, Smith Island, Shannon Point (Guemes Channel), Village Point, Port Angeles, Clallam Bay and Cape Flattery.

"We have the authority to direct the movement of the vessels. In one percent of the time we will recommend or **urge**—such as telling them to pass port-to-port to avoid a collision. They can tell just by the tone of voice we use. First we **advise**, then **recommend**, then **tell** them what to do. We reserve that right as sometimes situations develop very fast with large vessels," Precourt said.

Colregs (Collision Regulations) Rule 10 details conduct within the TSS, which includes crossing the lanes at as close to right angles as possible.

Colregs Rule 10:

Any vessel in the TSS is bound by the TSS rules. The following is a summary of Rule 10. Actual copies of COLREGS Rule 10 are available in Rules of the Road books found in nautical bookstores.

1. A vessel shall, if possible, avoid crossing traffic lanes but, if obliged to do so, shall cross on a heading as nearly as practical at right angles to the general direction of traffic flow.

Crossing at right angles makes you much more easily detectable, both visually and by radar, by providing a beam view of your vessel. It also reduces the amount of exposure time to large vessels operating in the traffic lanes.

2. A vessel other than a crossing vessel or vessel joining or leaving a lane shall not normally enter a separation zone.

Separation Zones provide areas where a vessel can "bail out" in the event of an emergency. Fishing vessels, particularly in the Strait of Juan de Fuca, tend to fish in these "medians."

3. A vessel not using a TSS shall avoid it by as wide a margin as possible.

Recreational boaters are more maneuverable than a large vessel or a tug and tow. These vessels rely on the predictability of the traffic flow when following the traffic lanes. Recreational boaters that congest the TSS tend to reduce the predictability and therefore safety of vessel traffic.

4. Vessels, when leaving or joining traffic lanes, shall do so at as small an angle to the general direction of traffic flow as practicable.

This allows vessels to safely "merge" with existing traffic in the lanes and minimizes disruptions to existing traffic flow. Merging in this manner is similar to using a highway on/off ramp.

5. A vessel of less than 20 meters (66 feet) or a sailing vessel shall not impede the safe passage of a power-driven vessel following a traffic lane. A vessel engaged in fishing shall not impede the passage of any vessel following a traffic lane.

"Shall not impede" means a vessel MUST NOT navigate in such a way as to risk the development of a collision with another vessel (i.e., when a vessel following a TSS is forced to make an unusual or dangerous maneuver in order to avoid one of the vessels listed above, then the vessel following the TSS has been impeded).

The larger the vessel the more room and time it takes for that ship to maneuver or stop. Large vessels must maintain speed to steer. A 900 foot container ship or a tug with a cumbersome tow can't turn or stop on a dime. Stay well clear. The master or pilot must anticipate rudder commands or speed changes miles in advance. Remember, the master of a large vessel or tug and tow doesn't always know what YOU are going to do!

6. All vessels are required to keep the center of the precautionary area to port. A precautionary area is usually marked by a yellow lighted buoy and is clearly marked on all nautical charts.

This is an area where vessels following the TSS are negotiating course changes and where other vessels join or depart the TSS; therefore, all mariners must exercise caution in these areas. If you are in the TSS and encounter a large vessel, or a tug and tow in a precautionary area, BEWARE, for the vessel is most likely changing course and may be less able to avoid you.

Failure to comply with these regulations could create an unsafe navigational situation and may result in a civil penalty of up to $5,000.

Radio Contact with Vessel Traffic Services

VHF-FM channel 14 is the primary working frequency south of a line from Marrowstone Point to Lagoon Point, and across Possession Sound from Possession Point due east. North of these lines the primary frequency is VHF-FM channel 5A.

If unsure of your situation or another vessel's intentions you are urged to contact the vessel or PSVTS. The call sign is "Seattle Traffic" or simply "Traffic." Recreational boaters are asked to monitor the primary channel in their area—5A or 14—to get a feel for how congested the waterways are, offer radio assistance to disoriented mariners, relay distress calls to the appropriate Coast Guard rescue unit, and broadcast hazards to navigation—such as broken log booms, problems with the locks and other developing situations. Mariners are asked to report navigation

aids they think may be missing or malfunctioning.

If you need to call VTS you should provide:
- Vessel name (not the call sign)
- Vessel type (sail/power)
- Vessel position (relative to a point of land or buoy)
- Nature of the distress or inquiry
- Keep your call short.

Miscellaneous Information

Heavy Traffic: The busiest times for heavy marine traffic are summer afternoons and weekends because of the increase in recreational boating traffic. There will often be 30 to 50 vessel movements in any shift, depending on weather, fishery openings, search and rescue operations and recreational boats. Sailboat races are also a busy time. As an example, Precourt said the annual "Round Vashon Race" attracts about 150 sailboats.

"They go around Allen Bank (at the north end of Vashon), south through East Passage and past Tacoma—which is a busier commercial port than Seattle. Take 150 sailboats, several deep draft vessels leaving or going into Tacoma, add commercial and pleasure boat traffic in Colvos Passage, ferry crossings at both the north and south end of Vashon, and there's a lot more to a race than just a race. Particularly if the sector operator has 50 other vessels to keep track of and it's foggy and there's a search and rescue going on!"

Unpredictable Peculiarities: During the winter of 1995, the very important Sierra Charlie buoy in Admiralty Inlet went underwater during an ebb current. Rains, swollen rivers, and quickly dropping tides caused the predicted four knot ebb current to run at closer to six knots. The buoy was pulled under water so far that someone reported it missing. When the current subsided the buoy surfaced, but the light was knocked out and had to be replaced.

Whoops!

A large container ship was steaming south in Puget Sound within the recommended vessel traffic lanes. At about the same time the vessel's captain spotted a sailboat ahead of him the sailboat skipper called the ship on VHF radio.

"Captain, are you aware I'm a sailboat and have the right of way?" queried the sailboat's owner.

"I am," said the captain. "And are you aware I'm backing down full power and am going to run over you if you don't get out of the way?"

The sailboat beat a hasty retreat.

Note: Sailboats do not have the right of way when following the traffic separation schemes—the Rules of the Road apply to everyone, not just those big vessels.

For more information about the Vessel Traffic System, call 206-217-6040 and ask for a free PSVTS Users Manual. Or arrange for a tour any day of the week from 8 a.m. to 6 p.m. Boaters are encouraged to visit and view Vessel Traffic Center in operation. Vessel Traffic Services also provides speakers for boating organizations and yacht clubs.

Seattle Harbor Patrol

Seattle Harbor Patrol, a division of the Seattle Police Department, is responsible for water patrol, crime prevention, boardings, search and rescue, boating safety, waterborne fire fighting assistance and the general safeguarding of life and property.

Headquarters for the Harbor Patrol and its marine facilities are located on the north shore of Lake Union about 0.4 miles east of the Aurora Bridge, just west of Gasworks Park. The park is unmarked on the chart, except for green buoy C "13" off Gasworks Park Point.

To Contact the Seattle Harbor Patrol:

Headquarters phone 206-684-4071, or 911, VHF Channel 16, or CB Channel 9 React. Address: 1717 N. Northlake Place, Seattle, WA. Zip 98103.

Seattle Harbor Patrol fleet of 7 boats is based in Lake Union:
- (2) Patrol boats No. 1 and No. 3, 38 feet long
- (1) Patrol boat No. 2, 34 feet long
- (1) 20 foot trailerable jet boat
- (1) 17 foot Boston whaler
- (2) Rigid hull inflatables
- The unit plans to get an additional boat with fire-fighting capabilities by Spring 1997

Jurisdiction and patrol area for the Harbor Patrol unit includes city, county, state and federal waters within the Seattle city limits from North 145th Street to South 106th Street. It extends east to the middle of Lake Washington and between Seattle and the shores of Mercer Island; the entire length of the Lake Washington Ship Canal, Shilshole Bay and the harbor limits from North 145th Street to West Point.

Jurisdiction and patrol area from West Point south including Elliott Bay, Duwamish River and south to the city limits, is by the U.S. Coast Guard and Seattle Fire Department, unless there is a police investigation.

Enforcement Duties:

The Harbor Patrol is mandated to provide a waterborne patrol to insure compliance with city, county, state and federal laws within their jurisdiction. In addition to normal police duties it is required to enforce compliance with all U.S. Coast Guard regulations pertaining to registration, required equipment and operation of vessels within its jurisdiction. (See U.S. Coast Guard, Group Seattle for requirements.)

Conversation with Sergeant Hoekstra:

Sgt. Duane M. Hoekstra of the Harbor Patrol told us of the patrol's operations and concerns;

The Harbor Patrol advises boaters that the most important thing they watch for is safety, especially life jackets, carrying proper equipment and following the Rules of the Road. They also watch for current registration decals on vessels.

He said they give more warnings than citations. If they do give citations the average fine is $50.

The most common problems include: inexperienced, brand new boat operators; speeding, drunken boat operators, people falling overboard, carrying passengers in an unsafe manner—and the list goes on.

A major problem with inexperienced boaters is a lack of boating education. Boats are often sold and bought buy those who don't know what equipment is legally required on the boat, he said. Operating a boat is more than turning on the engine and blasting off. There ARE rules and regulations.

Driving a Boat While Intoxicated:

While there are more drunken boaters due to increased boating, the overall percentage is going down because being drunk is no longer "in" for an increasing number of people, according to Hoekstra. It is legal to drink on boats, but it is not legal to operate a boat while drunk. Standards for intoxication are much the same as those used for drivers of motor vehicles.

Anchoring

In Seattle, anchoring is limited to anchoring on private property but only with permission of the property owner, according to city ordinances. There are anchorages for loading and unloading ships with cargo, but you can't just drop your anchor off city parks or street ends, or go ashore in these locations.

There are three exceptions.

(1) Portage Bay: Boaters are allowed to anchor during preparations for the annual Opening Day of Yachting Season the first Saturday in May.

(2) Union Bay: Anchoring is allowed during UW football games east of the stadium along the north and south sides of the canal. In fall the water level is low and peat islands may pop up in Union Bay.

(3) Andrews Bay in Seward Park: In June 1996 the city of Seattle installed 10 mooring buoys in Andrews Bay for use by recreational boaters. The buoys are on a first come, first served basis. No other anchoring is allowed.
Phone: 206-684-4071.

Small Boat Access

There are several launch ramps within the city where small boats can land, but not at city parks or street ends parks.

Jet Skis: If the operators wear wet suits and follow proper rules of operation, then they're part of the boating scene.

Problems: There may be problems in downtown Seattle for those who tie to a public piers; drunks or druggies have been known to climb aboard and sleep on boats tied to the pier at the foot of Washington Street —even when the owners are on board.

Be Aware: Some scofflaws "outfit" their boats in the spring by swiping gear off other people's boats ...

Seattle Vessel Speed Limits

This applies to speed limits within the city of Seattle.
- **Shilshole Marina and approaches to the locks:** Speed limit 4 knots.
- **Locks:** Speed limit 2.5 knots.
- **Lake Washington Ship Canal**, including **Salmon Bay, Lake Union, Portage Bay** and **Union Bay**: Speed limit 7 knots, except as otherwise noted.
- **Lake Union** speed test course marked by four buoys: **No** posted speed limit, see "vessel operators" below.
- **Lake Washington:** Speed limit 2.5 knots within 100 yards of shore, docks, bridges, or other fixed objects, unless otherwise posted.
- **Andrews Bay in Lake Washington:** Speed limit 3 knots.
- **Elliott Bay** and **Duwamish River:** Speed limit 7 knots within 200 yards of shore or any shore installation.
- **Negligent Wake:** Wake, by definition, includes waves made by the vessel's operation.

All vessel operators, including those of jet skis, runabouts and larger vessels, are responsible for damages caused by their wake regardless of the posted speed.

Coast Guard, Seattle Police or other law enforcement agency personnel can stop any vessel even if it isn't going over the speed limit if it's creating a wake likely to cause damage to life or property, or if they get a complaint that a wake has damaged a houseboat or a delicate rowing shell or any other such problem.

Ferry Information

There are about 212,000 ferry crossings in all Puget Sound and the San Juan Islands annually, carrying more than 23 million people—more than pass through SEATAC Airport.

Consequently, all recreational boaters need to know what to expect in ferry crossing situations while cruising in Puget Sound.

We talked with personnel at both Washington State Ferries and the Coast Guard to gather the best information we could on what we need to know about ferry crossing situations.

Ferry skippers are extremely diligent and are as anxious to avoid confrontations or collisions as we are, and they need help from all of us.

Whether you are new to boating or an old hand, we hope you'll find this information useful.

Ferry Rules of the Road

1. **In narrow channels, small boats shall not impede deep-draft vessels**—such as ferries—in docking maneuvers or in channels. In open seas, however, sailboats do have the right of way over most other vessels.
2. **Five or more short rapid blasts** from the vessel's whistle means extreme alert—a collision is imminent—or a confusion over the other vessel's whistle signals.
3. **One short rapid blast** means vessel is altering its course to the right (starboard).
4. **Two short rapid blasts** means vessel is altering its course to the left (port).
5. **Three short rapid blasts** means vessel is reversing engines.
6. **Approaching another vessel head on, pass port to port.**

We were cautioned, always keep a sharp lookout. Be aware of where your boat is and where other boats are.

For more information on commercial vessels, see the section on the Vessel Traffic System.

"Local Knowledge"

Local knowledge is best learned from experienced mariners cruise area in which they live. We make a point of meeting and talking with local mariners and others about their areas and experiences to glean as much local knowledge as we can.

We have cruised to, anchored in or moored at virtually every place of which we write. We've also visited these areas by car, when possible. We visited every marine park, checked out shorelines for public access, and visited almost all marinas, public and private.

We have cruised our way around Puget Sound separately or together for a combination of 80-90 years.

We have contacted the Coast Guard, Harbor Patrol, NOAA, Washington State Parks, Department of Natural Resources (DNR), Department of Fisheries, Washington State Ferries, locks and bridge tenders, park rangers, various state and local park departments, marina owners and managers, local boaters, residents and others, for information.

None of this information is intended to replace official U.S. navigational charts, current charts, tide tables, tidal current tables, current charts and other publications by NOAA and other services.

It is up to each boater to learn and use good seamanship and judgement. We encourage novice boaters to take Coast Guard Auxiliary and/or Power Squadron classes to help gain necessary skills for safe boating before casting off.

When afloat you're entirely on your own.

"Warning: The prudent mariner will not rely solely on any single aid to navigation, particularly on floating aids. See U.S. Coast Guard Light List and U.S. Coast Pilot for details." (From NOAA charts.)

Puget Sound Wildlife

Whale watching is one of the exciting highlights of cruising this region. You're happily slipping through the water and suddenly spot a whale surfacing nearby. It's always a thrill. Orcas, grays and minkes swim in the area, although the orcas are more commonly found in the San Juans.

Dall's porpoises are also common throughout the Sound, and we often find them diving across our bow as we make our way around the Sound.

Harbor seals seem to be everywhere, poking a curious head above the surface and sinking back under leaving scarcely a ripple. Report seal strandings to the Whale Hotline, 1-800-562-8832.

Sea lions don't breed in the Sound, but they do hunt and feed here.

The Federal Marine Protection Act passed in 1972, makes it illegal to kill, capture or harass marine mammals.

If you encounter orcas or other whales while cruising, keep at least 100 yards away. At a speed no faster than the slowest

whale, approach slowly from the side. Turn off your engine and drift—if under sail, head into the wind to slow down without excessive maneuvering.

The 100 yards distance applies to other marine mammals and sea birds, especially those nesting or caring for their young. Never separate a mother from its baby.

Grab your camera or video recorder and enjoy!

Whale harassment incidents may be reported to the National Marine Fisheries Service, 206-526-6133. Include the name of the vessel and its identification number.

While out on the water or beaches, you can feast on the sight of dozens of different waterfowl. If you're a "birder" you're bound to have plenty to keep you happy for ages. Avoid discharging any fuel, oil or petroleum products into the waters as even small amounts of oil have devastating impacts on marine life.

Puget Sound State Marine Parks

Nineteen state marine parks are in the area covered in *Gunkholing in South Puget Sound*.

These parks, accumulated by the state over a period of as much as 50 years, give boaters an exceptional opportunity to enjoy many different aspects of Puget Sound—from the pristine peace of undeveloped islands in South Sound, to the Indian dances and salmon bakes on Blake Island.

Some of the parks are accessible only by water, others may be reached by land as well. There are underwater parks for divers; some launch ramps, docks, floats and mooring buoys; some have buoys only, some have neither. Many have overnight camping areas, others are day use only. Where overnight camping is allowed there are picnic areas and sanitary facilities.

Fees are charged year round at Blake Island and Jarrell Cove, others charge from May 1 thru September 30. Fees at floats and docks are $8 per night or $50 per year for boats under 26 feet, and $11 per night and $80 per year for boats over 26 feet. Moorage buoys are $5 per night.

Rafting is encouraged at mooring buoys in crowded moorages. The number of recommended boats that may tie to a buoy varies depending on boat length, location, currents and sea bottom. This information is printed on each buoy.

Annual moorage permits, valid for a year, can be used at all fee marine parks. The permits are economical if you moor at floats and docks or tie to buoys more than six nights a year. They are available at most State Park Offices or contact Washington State Parks and Recreations Commission, PO Box 42664, Olympia WA 98504-2664, phone 360-753-5771.

Public Tidelands—State Owned

A large number of parcels of state-owned tidelands are located throughout Puget Sound and the Department of Natural Resources (DNR) wants the public to know about them. As they point out, we pay for them, we should use them.

The state tideland ownership shown on the DNR Washington State Public Lands Quadrangle Maps includes public-use beaches, which are leased to private parties, environmentally sensitive beaches and beaches otherwise not suitable for public use.

To help locate these tidelands the quad maps with a scale of 1:100,000 show where the beaches are, along with other items of interest. We have relied on three of these maps, the Seattle, Tacoma and Shelton regional maps, for information about state tidelands in the areas in this book.

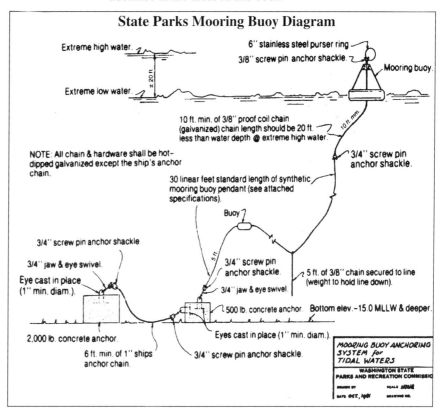

State Parks Mooring Buoy Diagram

State Parks South of Kingston - Edmonds
Accessible by Water & Visited in This Book

Fay-Bainbridge	15446 Sunrise Dr. N.E., Bainbridge Is., 98110	206-842-3931	Buoys
Satellite Parks with same address and phone as Fay Bainbridge:			
Fort Ward		206-842-3931	Buoys
Old Man House (Chief Seattle)		206-842-3931	No buoys/floats
Illahee	3540 Bahia Vista, Bremerton, 98310	360-478-6460	Buoys/ floats
Blake Island	P.O. Box 287, Manchester, 98353	360-447-1313	Buoys/ floats
Manchester	P.O. Box 36, Manchester, 98353	360-871-4065	No buoys/floats
Harper (Satellite)	P.O. Box 36, Manchester, 98353	360-871-4065	No buoys/floats
Saltwater	25205 8th Pl. S., Des Moines, 98198	206-764-4128	Buoys
Dash Point	5700 SW Dash Point Rd., Federal Way, 98033	206-593-2206	No buoys/floats
Kopachuck/Cutts Island	11101 56th St. N.W., Gig Harbor, 98335	206-265-3606	Buoys
Penrose Point	P.O. Box 73, Lakebay, 98439	206-884-2514	Buoys/float
Joemma Beach State Park	321 158th KPS, Lakebay, 98429	206-884-2514	Buoys and floats
Tolmie	6227 Johnson Point Rd. N.E., Olympia 98506	360-753-1519	Buoys
Jarrell Cove	Route 4, Box 162, Shelton, 98584	360-426-9226	Buoys/ floats
Satellite parks with same address and phone as Jarrell Cove:			
McMicken Island		360-426-9226	Buoys
Hartstene Island State Park		360-426-9226	No buoys/floats
Eagle Island		360-426-9226	Buoys
Hope Island		360-426-9226	Buoy
Stretch Point		360-426-9226	Buoys

The state has made every effort to verify beach locations and property boundaries on these maps; however, the agency is not responsible for errors. Usually "boat-only access" beaches are publicly owned to the mean high tide line. Beach users should first verify property boundaries—the absence of posted signs does not automatically identify public tidelands. Shellfish may not be taken from private tidelands without the owners permission.

Some state tidelands are bounded on the water side by private oyster beds. Oyster Reserve Tidelands are managed by the State Department of Fisheries.

We urge all our readers to buy the maps in order to locate the state tidelands with accuracy and to take them ashore to avoid getting in trouble with private property landowners. Using dividers and a chart to complement the map, it's possible to scale off the locations of the public beaches.

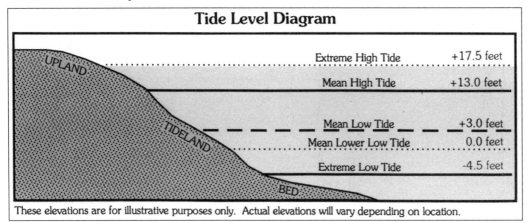

Tide Level Diagram

Extreme High Tide	+17.5 feet
Mean High Tide	+13.0 feet
Mean Low Tide	+3.0 feet
Mean Lower Low Tide	0.0 feet
Extreme Low Tide	-4.5 feet

These elevations are for illustrative purposes only. Actual elevations will vary depending on location.

(The above diagram from Wash. State Public Land Quad map.)

DNR staff also said it's possible to anchor anywhere over saltwater bottom that is continuously wet as long as the boat is on a transient basis of a couple of nights, and not in a restricted area. Don't anchor off the restricted areas of Keyport, the Bremerton Navy Yard or Bangor in Hood Canal, etc.

The maps are $5 each and they indicate public lands in each area. Contact DNR Photo and Map Sales, 1065 S. Capitol Way, M.S. AW-11, Olympia, WA. 98504, or call 1-800-527-3505; DNR, P.O. Box 68, Enumclaw, WA. 98022-0068.

Puget Sound Public Shellfish Sites is a booklet published by the State Game Department which gives information about locations of public areas for shellfish collecting and species at these various sites.

Fish Haven/Artificial Reefs

Six major artificial reefs, plus many smaller ones, are in the areas covered in this book:
- The Trees, 2.1 miles S. of Point Wells
- West Seattle, 2 miles S.E. of Alki Point
- Blake Island, 800 ft S. of south tip of island
- Point Heyer, 1,000 ft S.E. of KVI radio tower on Point Heyer, Vashon Island
- Toliva Shoal, 1,300 ft N.W. of Toliva Shoal navigational buoy
- Itsami Ledge, 1,100 ft N.W. of Itsami Ledge navigational light

Artificial fishing reefs are made by placing scrap concrete, quarry rocks or even tires at depths of 45 to 100 feet for access to lingcod, rockfish, cabezon, greenling, surfperch and other species. Some are marked by orange and white striped buoys. Scuba divers also enjoy these reefs.

Tying to the buoys is not permitted. Anchoring near the reefs is allowed.

Anchoring tip (suggested by the Department of Fisheries which develops and maintains them): to avoid snagged anchors, pass a biodegradable hemp line through the opening in a concrete building block; keep both ends of the line in the boat. Slide the block down the looped line until it snags the reef. Attach the line to the boat. If the block cannot be retrieved, simply release one end of the line and pull it through the block. You will have made a contribution to the reef and still recovered your line.

Consult the Washington State Department of Fisheries for the current sport fishing pamphlet and latest regulations and changes. Address: 1111 Washington St. S.E., P.O. Box 43144, Olympia, WA. 98504-3144, or pick one up from your local fishing license dealer.

State underwater recreation parks: Established by Washington State Parks, these are used by SCUBA divers in addition to many numerous wrecks and several artificial reefs. Parks are:
- Orchard Rocks, Fort Ward, Bainbridge Island
- Blake Island
- Saltwater State Park
- Tolmie Beach State Park
- Kopachuck State Park

Sunken barges are at Kopachuck and Saltwater state parks and at Seahurst County Park.

For more information on the numerous underwater recreation sites contact Washington Council of Skin Diving Clubs, Washington State Parks or the Department of Natural Resources.

Shellfish—PSP

As early Puget Sound settlers learned, when the tide is out the table is set. There are many public places where shellfish can be harvested in Puget Sound. It's fun and delicious.

Shellfish are filter feeders which take in large volumes of water during feeding, contaminates and all. When boats anchor near shellfish beds and discharge sewage, shellfish may take up some of the disease-causing bacteria present in sewage. Eating contaminated shellfish can cause gastrointestinal disorders, nausea, diarrhea, infectious hepatitis or other diseases.

Mariners are asked to not anchor where there are known shellfish beds and to not discharge *any* sewage in shellfish areas. Don't harvest shellfish near marinas, popular anchorages, sewer outfalls or heavy industrial areas. When harvesting shellfish, watch for posted signs warning of possible contamination.

Paralytic Shellfish Poisoning (PSP), commonly known as "red tide," occurs when clams, oysters, scallops and mussels consume a microscopic algae that contains a strong toxin. Eating infected shellfish can cause PSP which causes respiratory problems and even death.

Infected shellfish do not look, smell or taste any different than those not infected. The only way to be certain the shellfish are safe is if they have been tested.

Rubbing them on your lips to see if your lips tingle is not a valid test of PSP.

Cooking will not kill the bacteria.

The state regularly tests shellfish and if there is any chance of PSP, the areas are posted. You can also call the PSP Hotline at 1-800-562-5632 for current information.

Puget Sound Pollution

Sound Information: A Boaters Guide, a booklet published by Puget Soundkeeper Alliance, an organization dedicated to protecting Puget Sound, is recommended reading for all boaters concerned about preserving our unique water environment.

With their permission, we reprint some of their information. The Puget 10 Step: The Boaters Solution to Pollution.

1. Minimize use of toxic chemicals. Most marine stores carry a full line of non-toxic products for the bilge, holding tank and boat cleaning.
2. Buy only what is needed if you have to use a toxic chemical.
3. Be a good neighbor and see of others can use leftover chemical or paints rather than dispose of them.
4. Keep your dock box safe by lining bottom with tarps to contain spills. Store all chemicals in labeled closed containers.
5. Spills aren't slick. Recycle used oil, filters, paint and batteries. For the nearest locations call 1-800-RECYCLE.
6. Know where it goes. Puget Sound recreational boaters can dispose of hazardous wastes from routine maintenance at any household hazardous waste site.
   - Hazardous Waste Hotline 1-800-633-7585
   - King Co. Household Hazardous Waste 206-296-4692
   - Pierce Co. Household Hazardous Waste 206-591-5543
   - Snohomish Co. Household Hazardous Waste 206-388-3425
   - Thurston Co. Household Hazardous Waste 360-786-4663
7. Don't throw it away—recycle aluminum, plastic and paper.
8. Keep it out of the water. Use tarps or paper to keep paint, debris, cleaners out of water when doing slip-side maintenance.
9. Get involved in a group working to protect and enhance the Sound. Call 206-286-1309 or 1-800-42-Puget.
10. Don't keep it to yourself. Spread your knowledge of environmentally safe products and processes with others: "Pier" pressure really works.

Sewage Disposal—Do's & Don'ts

1. Don't discharge even treated sewage at the moorage. The same breakwaters that protect your boat also limit the flow of water through most moorages.
2. If you don't want to pump your holding tank, several commercial pumpout companies will come to you. Check your phone book.
3. If there's no room for a holding tank aboard use a portable toilet.

Pumpout Locations in Central and South Puget Sound:

Port of Edmonds	206-774-0549
Port of Kingston	360-297-3545
Seattle:	
Ballard Mill Marina	206-789-4777
Berg's Marina	206-285-2250
Chandler's Cove	206-628-0838
Elliott Bay Marina	206-285-4827
Fisherman's Terminal	206-728-3395
Harbor Island Marina	206-467-9400
H.C. Henry Pier	206-625-1580
Marina Mart Moorings	206-281-8260
Morrison's North Star	206-284-6600
Parkshore Marina	206-725-3330
Shilshole Bay Marina	206-728-3006
South Lake Union Moorage	206-682-0159
Kenmore:	
Davidson's Marina, Inc.	206-486-7141
Kirkland:	
Carillon Point	206-822-1700
Bainbridge Island:	
Eagle Harbor Marina	206-842-4003
Harbour Marina	206-842-6502
Winslow Wharf Marina	206-842-4202
Blake Island State Park	360-731-0770
Port of Poulsbo	360-779-3505
Port of Brownsville	360-692-5498
Bremerton:	
Illahee State Park	360-478-6460
Bremerton Marina	360-373-1035
Port Washington Marina	360-479-3037
Port Orchard Marina	360-876-5535
Des Moines Marina	206-824-5700
Vashon:	
Dockton Park	206-463-2947
Tacoma:	
Chinook Landing Marina	206-627-7676
Pick's Cove Marina	206-572-3625
Pt. Defiance Marina	206-591-5325
Totem Marina	206-272-4404
Tyee Marina	206-383-5321
Gig Harbor:	
Arabella's Landing	206-851-1793
Murphy's Landing	206-851-3093
Olympia:	
East Bay Marina	360-786-1400
Percival Landing	360-753-8380
West Bay Marina	360-943-2080
Shelton:	
Jarrell's Cove Marina	360-426-8823
Jarrell Cove State Park	360-426-9226

There's much more information in the booklet and we suggest you pick one up.

Important Services & Agencies for Mariners in Puget Sound at-a-glance

Department of Ecology:
- Northwest Region 206-649-7000
- Southwest Region 360-407-6300

Puget Soundkeeper Alliance 206-286-1309
Puget Sound Water Quality Auth.
....360-493-9300 or 1-800-54SOUND
Reporting Oil Spills 1-800-OILS-911
Seattle Harbor Patrol 206-684-4071
Shellfish Advisory:
- Department of Health 360-753-5992
- Red Tide Hotline.. 1-800-562-5632

U.S. Coast Guard 206-217-6232
Washington State Parks and Recreation Commission:
- Boating Safety Program 360-902-8851
- Clean Vessel Act Pumpout Program 360-902-8551
- Boating Environmental Education 360-902-8551

Wildlife Services:
- Marine Animal Resource Center (MARC)
- Marine mammal strandings .360-285-SEAL or 360-775-1311
- Department of Fish & Wildlife:
  - Fish Kill Reports.. 360-902-2534
  - 24 hour Hotlines 360-753-6618
  - Emergencies, oiled birds, etc 360-902-2537

Pre-Cruise Planning for the Family's Needs

Jo: Any cruise starts long before leaving the dock. It begins with a general idea of an intended destination, whether it's Puget Sound, or anywhere in the world. Plan with alternate passages and layovers in mind. The suggestions below are not limited to cruising in South Puget Sound, but are applicable to any trips.

Safety: If you can't read charts, tide and current tables, learn. Take a Power Squadron or Coast Guard class. Education is essential for safety. Anybody can get in a boat, turn a key and make it go. But to go and return safely no matter what the conditions, you MUST know what you're doing.

Be sure to include C.G. approved PFD's (personal flotation devices) for everyone aboard, and a couple of extra floating cushions, "just in case." Make sure little kids and nonswimmers wear life jackets at all times on deck. Get a Lifesling or good man-overboard device and learn to use it. Practice man-overboard drills. Have a dinghy with built-in flotation or rubber raft, stowed on deck or towed behind.

"Gear": In our early days of sailing in the 1960s, "B.C." (before Carl), our family had a 29' wooden sailboat, the *Sea Witch.* With five kids, cat and dog, we were obviously crowded.

Everyone in the family wanted to take everything each owned. To avoid hassles, I made canvas duffel bags for each of us. They were all the same size, but each was a different color for easy identification. Everyone could stuff jeans, shirts, shorts, sweaters and "unders" in their own bag. Rain gear, extra jackets, shoes and boots were stowed in the tiny hanging locker.

A couple of other duffel bags held sheets and blankets to make up the one "double" bunk in the main cabin (actually a fairly narrow single-bed size, but larger than anything else). The bags doubled as bolsters during the day.

We had a spare duffel bag for laundry. I made canvas bags to carry groceries, and for tools. Now, we use back packs.

From leftover canvas I made the "all bag," a small version of a duffel bag with pockets all around the outside for toothbrushes, toothpaste, combs, etc. The bag was large enough to hold soap (in plastic bags or boxes) powders, deodorants, etc., for a family. It hung on a hook in our tiny head.

Sleeping Arrangements: Where did seven people sleep on this 29 foot boat? Two adults in the "double" in the main cabin. Two oldest daughters in the coveted forward V-berths; next two kids on the cockpit benches under a boom tent. The youngest had a choice. He could sleep on the cabin sole and risk being stepped on when someone got up during the night to check the anchor or use the head, or he could sleep on the cockpit sole, where one of the other two kids would probably roll onto him during the night. He switched between both places and survived being stepped on and nearly suffocated by siblings.

Son Bill, who slept on the cabin or cockpit sole, has been sailing around the South Pacific in his Herreshoff 28' ketch, *Noctiluca,* since the late 1980s with wife Lisa. They're now in Tonga where he's manager and she's assistant manager of Moorings Charters in Va va'u', so it didn't deter him from a sailing life.

Son John, who slept on a cockpit bench, sailed around the South Pacific with wife Ann in their 43' foot yawl, *Iris,* for nearly five years.

Youngest daughter Debi, who also slept in the cockpit, is happy living in a house, but is great crew on the rest of the family's sailboats.

Daughter Megan, who slept in one of the forward bunks, lives aboard her 32' Alden cutter, *Timshel.* Daughter Robin, who also slept up forward, is hunting for a sailboat, and is great crew.

Medical Supplies: *Check with a doctor, nurse or druggist, regarding medical supplies and for a first aid kit.*

Galley—"KISS"—Keep it Simple Sailor

Plan supplies as though you won't be making any supply stops, which takes more organizing to begin with, but pays off in the long run.

Take enough canned and packaged food so no one has to work hard to make meals. **Everyone** is on vacation.

Paper plates or china dishes? Depends. If garbage is a problem, go with china or plastic. If dishwashing water is a problem, use disposable stuff.

If your boat has an ice chest and not refrigeration, consider forgetting about ice, especially if you go very far north. It's expensive to buy—as much as $3 to $4 a bag. We cruised without ice for nearly two months when we sailed north in *Scheherazade.* We take canned meats, vegetables, rice, pastas, fruits, powdered and packaged milk and other items that don't need refrigeration. Canned fruit juice and sodas keep cool in the bilge.

Some fresh foods keep well for as much as a week or more. Among these are potatoes, carrots, onions, cabbage, squashes. Mushrooms, celery and tomatoes keep for several days. Leafy vegies and lettuces don't do too well so use those up first. Citrus fruits and apples keep for quite a while. Take unripe bananas and eat them as they ripen.

Grow sprouts on board; you'll have fresh greens for sandwiches. Buy seeds at the local health food store where they'll give directions on growing and storing.

We had simple, one dish fill-'em-up meals, canned spaghetti, beans, stews, chili, etc., which I'd liven up with other things. On three Hawaii crossings when I crewed and cooked, the farther from shore we were, the more creative I was.

With a family, take a ton of peanut butter and jam, crackers and breads for lunches. Have instant oatmeal with raisins for breakfast as long as you can get away with it. Pancake and biscuit mixes are indispensable—it means you can always have a meal. I carry flour and yeast and bake muffins and breads. It's better, healthier and cheaper than anything we could buy—and fun to do. Freshly baked bread smells so good. I also take a huge box of Grape-Nuts. They're good to eat and I use them in place of nuts in breads and muffins.

Snacks: crackers, cheese, raisins, dried fruits, fresh fruits and vegetables when you can get them, candy and cookies for a treat now and then. Hot tea and a square of chocolate mid-morning does wonders.

I didn't have an oven in the wood stove aboard the *Sea Witch,* so I did stove-top baking in cast iron pans. *Scheherazade* has a three burner gimballed propane stove with an oven and I can do just about anything. On our 19 foot sailboat, *Winsome,* I cooked non-gourmet, filling, one-dish meals for seven on a Sterno stove.

Keep an inventory of what's on board, especially in the galley, and where supplies are stowed. It helps you know what you have and what you need, and others can find stuff. Makes shopping and meal planning infinitely easier.

Games, etc.: *If you have kids you need games.* Scrabble, Pictionary, cards, dominoes, crayons, paper, toys, are wonderful—anything that keeps them occupied when they're not actually helping run the boat—which of course they should be doing. Kids love to learn to tie knots.

Have oodles of books, especially about whales, birds, and other outdoor stuff. Read *Curve of Time* aloud. Use Elmer's glue to make driftwood and sea shell collages. Kites are fun to fly from boat or beach, especially plastic collapsible ones. Magnets are fun to play with—keep them away from the compass. Legos are great for a rainy day when you're stuck down below.

Have cassette tapes or CD players with favorite music and recorded books. You may be sailing out of reach of AM or FM radio stations. Even 12 volt or battery operated TV sets or laptop computers complete with games can be stowed safely. Does anybody play music? Take your guitar, harmonica, tin whistle or bongo drums. We had great fun the year we took my fiddle and ended up with impromptu sing-alongs on the beach. A word of warning: after we got home I found it had come totally unglued and I had to take it to a violin maker for repair! He told me it hadn't been built to keep in a damp saltwater environment.

We tried not to be underway for too long each day so we could anchor and swim, walk, beach comb and play for part of every day. A volleyball with net, soccer ball, softball and bat are great to stash somewhere. If you have kids you can get some good games going if you're anywhere with fairly level ground, especially if there are other families around.

Fishing: If the family loves fresh-caught fish, be equipped with whatever gear you need; get the proper licenses for both fish and shellfish. Let the kids fish while underway, if possible. Clams and oysters make wonderful meals. Do fill in clam holes and shuck oysters on the beach so shells, which may have spat (oyster seed) on them, can continue to be a home for the babies.

Check by VHF radio or phone for information on beaches closed to harvesting shellfish by pollution or paralytic shellfish poisoning (PSP), sometimes called "red tide." Dangerous stuff. PSP does not affect crabs or fin fish, only some shellfish. Call the PSP Hotline at 1-800-562-5632 for current information.

Discipline: We had a wonderful system of discipline on *Sea Witch*, but it backfired. If one of the five kids got too obstreperous, he or she was "isolated," from the rest. The "isolation chamber" was the dinghy we towed. That person had to stay in the dinghy until agreeing to behave. (We only used it on calm days, but those were the days they got bored and antsy.)

Whoever was banished sat there, trying different positions until they figured out a way to steer the dinghy on a zigzag course by shifting body weight. Obviously it was great fun, judging from the ear-to-ear grin on the "prisoner." For a while there was a contest to see who could misbehave the most and end up in the dinghy. Time to change rules, and we reversed the procedure. Only the BEST behaved got to be skipper of the dinghy after that, which worked fairly well. In fact, I sometimes wished I could get away from the group and ride in the dinghy myself.

Water: Every person needs about 1/2 gallon of water daily for drinking purposes. If you have a 50 gallon tank and four people on board that means you have enough water for 25 days, supposedly. But if you can make that work you're remarkable. If you have a pressure water system, it goes fast. Don't leave the water running while brushing your teeth.

When we cruised with the family—and a 20 gallon water tank—I always said we could go close to a week without having to stop for water or supplies. Before sun showers were invented, we swam every day after we anchored—we ALL dived in. We created quite a sensation in crowded moorages when we put on our "aquacade" show, ending up by soaping down with a floating Ivory soap bar.

We saved our water for drinking and cooking purposes—much to the dismay of the teenage daughters who hadn't lived without washing their hair daily until then. We washed dishes in sea water if far enough from civilization for it to be clean.

If you have an onboard shower, let's hope there's plenty of fresh water for it, or that you can stop often enough to refill your tanks. A sun shower hung from halyard or boom works wonders and it's amazing how clean you get on a couple of gallons.

Laundry: We did laundry in salt water. Haul up a bucket of water on deck, add bio-degradable detergent, slosh the clothes around in it and rinse the same way. Farther north you can often find a stream near the shore for laundry. Lifelines and shrouds make great drying lines. Don't forget clothespins. They're handy for a lot more than just hanging out the laundry.

Miscellaneous: Have a pet? Take shot records, licenses, food, litter box, and leash. Take turns with shore duty. Kids usually love the several times a day visits to the beach with a dog. So did I. A chance to be alone now and then.

On the *Sea Witch* I took small containers of paint, varnish, sandpaper, brushes, thinner and #4 glazing putty. If there was a scrape, bruise or gouge I could fix it before it got bad.

Garbage disposal can be a problem, especially since most Washington State Marine Parks and B.C. Provincial Parks have no garbage collection. When buying necessities for the boat keep this in mind and discard packaging before leaving home. It's not legal to throw anything, even food, over the side within three miles of a shoreline. Smash cans as flat as possible, keep recycling garbage separate from disposable stuff.

Stow toilet paper and paper towels in plastic bags to keep from getting damp; the bags can later be used for garbage.

We always keep a calendar in the cabin in addition to our running log, and jot down where we spend each night. It's an easy recap of the trip, and handy for instant recall.

Plastic bags of varying sizes are invaluable for storing for left overs, small tools, nails, screws, and other small items. Film canisters are handy for storing tiny things.

For cleaning ourselves and the boat, we carry a large plastic jug of bio-degradable detergent, floating Ivory soap for salt water bathing, sponges and various size brushes.

And of course, there's much, much more, but boaters come up with their own ideas as they cruise.

Going Ashore

We enjoy going ashore and hiking, whether it be in a state park or on local roads, or wherever we can find a good spot to stretch our legs. Over the years we've come up with our own list of necessities, some of which vary depending on where we're going and for how long, which can often be a half day if we feel like exploring. Perhaps our ideas will spark some of your own:

Daypacks, knife, compass, Washington State Lands quad map for the area, Band-aids, aspirin, etc., bee sting kit if necessary, matches in watertight container, extra shirt or jacket, camera and film, sunglasses, mosquito or bug repellent, food and water/fruit juice, plastic bags, bathing suit (unless you find a place to skinny dip) and towel.

Planning an Extended Northwest cruise— for Vessel

Carl: Before departing, purchase and stow onboard the total inventory for all supplies and spares, including emergency supplies and equipment. When confronted with emergency situations, there is a much better chance of saving the boat and lives if prepared.

Once underway in less populated areas, options become fewer, prices increase substantially, previously known or remote suppliers may be out of stock or out of business. When something fails in an uninhabited area, and if you can't sail or power out, you may have to be towed, or have parts flown in by seaplane—expensive alternatives.

An inventory control method is vital so anyone on board can determine where items are. We use a 3-ring binder and a single sheet for each separate item, with dividers to file sheets by item name and category. A full description, model and part number, size, supplier and instructions help a lot.

Annual Haulout: Check condition of, replace or repair:

- **Electrolysis control**—Look for reddish tinge or ragged edges on brass/bronze and corrosion on steel items:
  propeller and shaft, rudder stock, pipe and thru-hull fittings exposed to salt water.
  Inspect zinc plates on hull and pencil-type zincs in seawater piping systems and bonding to vessel ground system.
- **Propeller pitch and attachment,** shaft bearing for wear—consider a spare if exposure to damage is probable
- **Rudder attachment fittings** (See page 318)
- **Depth sounder transducer,** water speed indicator impeller
- **Hull condition:** sand and paint if necessary (especially a wooden hull)
- **Attachment of keel and/or skeg or propeller brackets to hull**

Engine Fuel Tank and Piping:

- Check attachment, condition, purge water and debris from the tank to the engine. Water sometimes comes aboard with fuel pumped into the tank. Moisture condenses inside empty tanks.
- If diesel, strainers and filters can be plugged by diesel bacteria.
- Fuel filter housing must be accessible and able to drain.
- Have at least one spare fuel filter with gasket.
- Fuel water-inhibitor treatment can be mixed with gas or diesel which enables some moisture to be absorbed into the fuel and burned in the engine. Have the quantity needed to treat the total fuel for the cruise. For a diesel engine, the bacteria treatment would be similar to that for gas/water treatment. Discuss this with a qualified diesel mechanic.
- Engine fuel: Top off tanks before departure.
- Sticking valves treatment: Certain engines seem to progressively develop erratic operation caused by sticky valves after extended use. If not treated the engine can eventually quit or fail to start. Make provisions for this treatment before departure. Several "top-cylinder-lubrication" fuel and oil additives are available. We use "Marvel Mystery Oil." At the time of each normal oil, change we add one quart in the crankcase, and one quart to every 100 gallons of gas when filling our tanks.

Engine oil:

- Make a complete engine oil change before departure. Carry the following quantity of engine oil onboard:
  - Quantity to keep oil level at dip stick mark for cruise
  - Quantity anticipated for all normal complete oil changes on the cruise
  - Quantity for at least three complete unscheduled emergency oil changes

Why three oil changes?
(Twice *Zade's* emergency oil reserve allowed us to survive bilge and crankcase floodings without distress calls, damage to engine or loss of vessel or loss of life. It takes about three consecutive oil changes to purge all contaminated oil from the system, running the engine only a few minutes after each oil change.

Engine oil filter: Install a new filter with each oil change; carry one new filter for each of the above complete oil changes.

Crankcase sump pump with hose and/or tube assembly *must be onboard* to enable making all complete normal or emergency oil changes at sea or in remote locations with no support facilities.

Engine "Waste Oil" containers: Label "waste oil" in the quantity equal to at least 150% of normal crankcase oil capacity.
- Stow below until needed and then fill and cap without having to transport or transfer waste oil from an open pail. Stow full waste oil containers below until taking to a recycle disposal site.

Buckets with strong wire handles: Two or more for serious bailing. Also use to hold waste oil containers while filling until capped, to control spills and other uses.

Paper towels: Reserve ample quantity to clean up after oil changes, in addition to the quantity anticipated for galley and other situations.

Bio-degradable detergent: Works well for clean up of onboard oil spills. Carry the total quantity expected for cruise. **Don't use it** to cover up overboard discharge of oil or fuel, which is subject to heavy fines.

General engine spares: Discuss all spares with your engine mechanic.
- Engine seawater cooling pump (including spare V-belt if used)
- Engine freshwater cooling pump (including spare V-belt if used)
- Engine thermostat
- Engine fuel pump assembly, including gaskets, rebuild kit
- Engine electric starter, at least one tested spare

Engine spares if gasoline powered:
- Complete tested distributor assembly including cap, points, condenser, and stem
- Ignition coil, tested, spares
- Set of resistor spark plugs and ignition cables

Engine spares if diesel powered: Glow plugs, fuel pump, and injectors

Engine alignment: Needs to be checked. If neglected, will cause excessive wear and accelerated failure of engine oil seal, thrust bearings, propeller shaft bearings and seawater seal

- **Bilge blower:** Required to remove explosive gasoline, propane, carbon monoxide, battery, diesel fumes, gasses and other odors from the bilge; must be properly vented to allow entry of fresh air. If accessible, an occasional sniff of the bilge blower exhaust tells what is happening below. Have tested spare bilge blower on board at time of departure.
- **Bilge hand pump:** Large capacity pump should be installed

within reaching distance of the steering station. Steering and pumping can be done by the same person, essential if single-handing or to make best use of available crew in emergency situations. Clean out bilge and sump strainer area, overhaul pump. Have onboard spare manual pump repair/replacement kit—or good bucket.

- **Electric bilge pumps and alarms:** Provides a degree of assurance, assistance and safety, depending on condition of batteries. Pump float switch and alarm should be cleaned and checked carefully.
- **Ship's batteries:** Well before departure, add steam-distilled water as needed, but don't overfill; fully charge, then disconnect batteries from system. Note voltage and hydrometer readings of each cell. Leave disconnected for a week then check and compare voltage and hydrometer with previous readings. If 12 volts or less, or if there are differences between the hydrometer cell readings, consider getting new batteries. Batteries must be fastened down to prevent being thrown about or tipping over in heavy weather, and should be contained in acid-resisting enclosures. Carry hydrometer for testing, filling batteries.
- **Steam distilled water:** We use one gallon plastic containers for batteries and emergency drinking water. Save empty containers for transporting water to vessel from streams on shore, if necessary in remote locations. Stow containers below in little used or unhandy lockers.
- **Baking soda:** Needed to neutralize sulfuric acid around batteries, on skin and clothing, or in the event a battery is dropped or leaks. Useful as a cleaning agent and other purposes, including brushing teeth. We carry 5 pounds in a capped plastic container (we brush a lot).
- **Engine 12 volt alternator/generator spare:** Tested and with belt and voltage regulator.

Shore Power and 115 volt a.c. On-Board Systems
- **115 volt a.c. 60 hz. /800 watt 12 volt d.c. portable gas generator** can be used to charge batteries if they are so low that main engine cannot be started.
- **Inverter/charger** converts any 115 volt a.c. source to charge and maintain the 12 volt d.c. battery electric system. Without shore power the inverter can convert the 12 volt d.c. battery power to energize the onboard 115 volt a.c. system, which enables operation of 115 volt a.c. hand tools, computers and small appliances within the capacity of the system.
- **Electric extension cord:** 100' long, 14 gauge 2 conductor cord with ground and multiple outlet receptacle for 115 volt a.c. shore or onboard electric needs. Also have assortment of cord adapters to accommodate various types of shore power outlets if and when needed.
- **Clip-on trouble light** fixture with extension cord with at least three 115 volt a.c. spare bulbs.
- **Spare light bulbs** for each type and size of bulb used on board, two or more of each.
- **Spare fuses,** four or more, for each type and size used onboard.
- **Volt-ohm meter** to check status of electrical system and components.

Miscellaneous Needs
- **Standby navigation lights, kerosene anchor light**
- **Portable spotlights and flashlights.** Carry ample dry cell batteries of proper sizes for all these lights.

- **Kerosene lamps** or candles as backup or in place of electric lights
- **Kerosene lamp fuel**
- **Propane:** Stoves, water heaters, tanks and piping require special attention. Installation must be made in approved manner. Check system carefully for leaks and operation and fill tanks. Consider portable propane torch and lanterns with disposable tanks

Ground Tackle
- **Anchors:** We carry three. In extreme cases we may set two in series. In other situations we may use bow and stern anchors. We have lost or left an anchor when unable to retrieve.

  Anchor weight and design need to be adequate for the size, weight and windage characteristics of the vessel. Stow spare anchors and chain below if possible. Some anchors can be disassembled for stowage.

  Zade's working anchor is a 35# Danforth swiveled to 50 feet of 5/16" chain, swiveled to 300 feet of 7/8" nylon, with the end tied off in the chain locker. We use a vertical electric capstan, but need a chain wildcat and roller chock before Jo is willing to trade this job for my cooking breakfast. We stow additional chain and anchor below the cabin sole. As backup for the electric anchor winch we lead the anchor line aft to either the port or starboard 2-speed manual sheet winches when we can't break the anchor out or raise it by hand.

  Farther north, anchoring may be in much deeper water—60 to 90 feet or more—because shorelines may be steep rock.
- Have enough line to make up at least two extra anchor lines, especially if cruising in remote areas.
- **Safety wire all screw shackle pins** on ground tackle before departure or after re-rigging. Otherwise they may unscrew and you will pull up an anchorless chain—if you don't blow aground first. (See Chapter 1, *Winsome* story)

Safety Considerations and Equipment
- **Distress flares and signals:** Check dates, quantity, how to use and condition. See Coast Guard regulations. Update before departure and stow in a convenient location.
- **Boarding ladder and Lifesling:** Check condition and installation options for use in boarding under adverse conditions. Stow in acceptable location for immediate use
- **Carry 300 feet of 1/2" yellow polypropylene line** for dual purpose stern tie and emergency overboard rescue line. Polypro floats and is very visible, but does not hold knots well. It will slip through a single half hitch on a cleat. Extra turns and hitches, or opening and tucking the bitter end between the strands, are necessary.

  As a stern tie line to shore, after the anchor is set, tie one end of polypro to the stern and row the other end ashore, pass it around a tree trunk and take it back out to the boat. Don't have any knots or spliced eyes in the end, so when ready to leave one end can be turned loose and the line pulled back aboard without jamming.
- **For emergency over board rescue** use the same line, tied to horseshoe life ring, dingy or other suitable object towed astern, proceed to circle around a conscious alert person in the water until the line is within their grasp, so they can be brought along side, and helped aboard. There are classes in rescue

procedures, and we suggest practicing with your own boat and crew.

General Concerns

- **Have adequate lines** for bow and stern mooring lines, spring lines, and 50 foot bow and stern lines necessary for the locks.
- **Rigging and sails:** Inspect every thing from chain plates to masthead and mast step, from shackle pins to winches and deckpads. Make a detailed inspection of roller furling bearings on the jib to be certain they are lubricated and working as intended.

    Inspect sails for wear and chafe, check out stitching. If you find flaws or weak areas in sails, or loose patches, check with your sailmaker. Make certain grommets are all in order and not pulling out. If you have jiffy reefing, be sure to have extra line for tying down reef points. Practice reefing at the dock or in light airs, before you need it.

    Carry spare rigging blocks, shackles, battens, emergency sail tape, sail stops, slides, etc. Cover sails when not using to prevent UV damage.

- **Dinghy:** Painter should be checked for chafe and wear and replaced if needed. In heavy weather a swamped dinghy needs a very strong painter. Flotation should be tested and sufficient to float the dinghy full of water, possibly with an outboard. Inspect oars and oarlocks, replace or repair. Oars and a good sized bailer should be tied in the dinghy, preferably under the thwart, so that if swamped they will stay in.
- **Steering gear:** Before departure, inspect steering gear and/or tiller, rudder and all parts and fittings to determine what if any work is required—and get it done. Before heading north to Nakwakto, Anchor Jensen and I realized *Zade's* rudder required installation of reinforcing straps. Where there is wheel steering, a backup method is advisable. *Zade* has an emergency pipe tiller that is awkward but effective.
- **Water hose and nozzle:** We carry two 50 foot lengths plus assorted hose hook-up adapters for filling tanks at wharves where fittings are nonstandard but water is available.

Miscellaneous:

- **Mechanic's tool box** with metric and U.S. wrenches and tools, hacksaws, drills, screwdrivers, etc., needed to service all equipment onboard.
- **Electrical tool box** with miscellaneous fittings including connectors, spare wire, tape, soldering iron, flux, solder, and specialty tools to service electrical equipment on board.
- **Bos'ns tool box** with specialty tools and supplies unique to rigging work, fids, shackles, clevis and cotter pins, palms, needles, beeswax, spools of waxed and heavy threads, assorted twines, etc.
- **Fastening spares**—nuts, bolts, wood screws, nails, etc., stowed in separate containers.
- **Plumbing spares**—pipe, hose and tube fittings, hose-clamps and other fittings.
- **Navigation Needs**
    Compass: Should be checked and compensated. If it hasn't been compensated, establish a 360 degree table of degrees and note visual bearing and compass courses actually steered in relation to courses plotted on the chart for the same destination during clear weather.

    A female crew member with an underwire bra standing too close to the compass can fog your glasses and affect your deviation in more ways than one.

    A spare hand-bearing compass can also be used while hiking on shore.

    Radar: We find it very useful with or without fog and during day and night travel. What we see on radar requires a lot of imagination and is not always what we get. Its usefulness comes with local knowledge, experience and constant reference to charts.

Navigation Instruments

There are many navigational gadgets available. Check with your favorite marine store.

Dividers, parallel rules are basic
Barometer—very necessary for noting weather patterns
Chronometer or accurate watch
Knotmeter—in its absence or its failure, use chip log
Fathometer or a calibrated (marked) leadline of 10 fathoms or more is vital to continued flotation. Today's depth sounders are almost indispensable. A calibrated mop handle is not quite adequate.

Publications

- **Charts, Tide and Current tables**

    Obtain all latest edition large and small scale navigation charts for the area to be visited from a nautical chart house. Road maps and place mats just don't work.

    - *U.S. Coast Pilot* and *Canadian Sailing Directions*, and other publications including chart symbol book
    - U.S. and Canadian *Tide Tables* and *Current Tables,* or *Reed's Nautical Almanac* and *Reed's Nautical Companion, Current Charts, Washburn's Current Charts*

        Study them carefully in planning—and during—a cruise.

- **Vessel licensing**

    Be certain all licensing, registration, taxes and use fees are up to date and you have proper documentation onboard for local harbor police, US Coast Guard, US customs, Canadian Coast Guard and Canadian Customs.

    Have on board a copy of Rules of the Road, including VTS regulations.

- **VHF marine radio:** Regulations for use and weather forecasting procedures need to be studied. Make sure license is valid and onboard and equipment working properly.

Have a wonderful time cruising—we can't think of a better pastime for family and friends. For us it's a way of life, and we wouldn't have it any other way.

* * *

Kids' Stuff—from our (combined) 8 kids

Growing up on Puget Sound's waterfront is the cause of it all. Having parents whose main interest was to be on the water didn't help matters. At 40 something, I'm basically worthless when confronted by anything landlocked.

I swim with great zeal, snorkel and dive with enthusiasm, and sail for my salvation. I've held only one shore-based job—the rest have been at sea.

And it's their fault. Bless their hearts, I can't imagine a better life.

John Bailey, *S/V Iris,* Port Townsend

I never realized how lucky I was to have Puget Sound as my

backyard playground. As with most children, I lacked the basis of comparison to recognize how unique it was to have endless stretches of beach and waterways at my disposal.

The beach was magical and I went there almost daily, never coming home empty-handed. The beach became my solace as well ... where I could be alone and just BE. The solitude and comforting sound of the soft wash of waves often seemed to carry my problems away on the outbound tide.

High tide would find us swimming, fishing, boating and playing in the waves with the whole family.

Puget Sound. Home. Ever-changing, yet always constant. Certain sights, smells and sounds still take me back in an instant to that familiar place—a place that now transcends time and sensory experience. Puget Sound has been such a part of my life that it has shaped, forever, who I am and its essence resides in my soul.

Debi Bailey, Olympia

* * *

... Falling! "I'm falling, Mom!"

I jerk awake. Our little runabout has encountered chop. Exhausted from play, my dreams have become mingled with the change in the boat's motion. An acknowledgment from mom sends me securely back to sleep, wedged between my two brothers and two sisters, all of us in bulky orange life jackets.

We're traveling back home to Olympia from a weekend of camping/boating at Harstine Island. I'm so excited to "discover" an uninhabited island (I thought) close to home that you can only reach by boat.

This was over 35 years ago and one of many trips exploring Puget Sound, beginning in a small outboard and graduating to slightly larger sailboats for our "cramping" trips. Fortunately for us kids, sharing the small spaces with the heaps of gear required for seven people, there were lots of places to explore close to home.

There were no cruising books, we just used local charts and shared knowledge with fellow boaters.

This book will be a welcome addition for people who want to "explore" close to home.

Megan Bailey, *S/V Timshel*, Port Townsend
Bill Bailey, *S/V Noctiluca*, Kingdom of Tonga

* * *

Sailing as a youngster in South Sound had so many advantages. I learned to sail in the protective waters of Budd Inlet, later venturing out into more open waters. Weekday sailing was a treat, though we seldom went far. Once past the old mothball fleet in Olympia, we were truly going somewhere. Overnights at Squaxin Island, Boston Harbor, Jarrell's Cove, Longbranch and Gig Harbor were easy weekend trips.

And my favorite time of night ... when the sun had gone behind the trees and they looked like they were cut out of construction paper with an ever changing background in the twilight. I was truly a lucky kid.

Robin Bailey, Gig Harbor

* * *

It's very early in the morning, have to get up before the fish, ya know, damp, dark, and a little chilly. Here I am, about 7 years old, heading out from Portage Bay to Puget Sound on one of our family fishing trips.

We've already gone through fun parts, like Mom and Dad

reminding each other to bring everything but the kitchen sink. We've also gone through the locks where you hear husbands and wives screaming at one another trying to compete for position of captain, while the lock tenders are trying to stop them from running into something.

I'm not sure when I first discovered the wonderful comfort in my life jacket straps. They became an odd kind of pacifier for me. They were always flavored with saltwater. At times like this they were the most comforting thing a kid could have.

Growing up on the water we had a number of strictly enforced rules, the most important was, "The only piece of clothing required at all times is a **life jacket**." Any other clothes were optional.

My sister Barb and I agree that **if Dad was in the boat we never worried**. We could go anywhere in any kind of boat or raft in any kind of weather and there was absolutely nothing we could not survive if he was there.

Gale Anne Nyberg, *S/V Camille,* Seattle

* * *

My fondest memory was the annual "Easter Chasc" of Port Madison Yacht Club when we lived on Bainbridge Island. Balloons were broadcast all over Port Madison. Sailing prams filled with kids and an "adult" gatherered as many as possible without popping them, beating the clock back to the dock. The folks on the other teams didn't want to see Carl Nyberg and his two daughters in the same pram—together we were unbeatable. Dad and Gale were the excellent sailors, and I was the retriever.

Grabbing balloons wasn't easy, requiring great sailing skills as early spring winds blew them all over the bay. My self-appointed job was to get the balloons in the boat, no matter what. I'm sure mom was horrified when she saw her "baby" jump overboard to get an elusive balloon—I took my job very seriously.

The boats raced back to the docks and we'd carry sailbags stuffed with balloons to be counted at the clubhouse. The kites each member of the winning team received were like trophies of gold to us kids. The Nyberg team won several years, naturally!

Barbara Nyberg Hanna, *M/V Yot,* Ashford, WA

* * *

Memories afloat started early for me, a fishnet playpen on deck and my focs'le bunk below, rocked to sleep gently by waves brushing the bow. Awakened, briefly airborne and flung about in my bunk. Winds roaring aloft, *Winsome* heeling deeply, plunging and thrashing to weather.

Older, I hauled sheets and halyards and steered courses.

Later, on a neighbor's grid, *Winsome's* nine foot draft dad and I scrubbed as the tide went down and, racing its rise, the bottom paint we applied.

We came upon *Grey Gull,* Bill and Kay Watts, with sons aboard, both boats broad reaching, to Ludlow we sailed to the annual New Year rendezvous, and rafted with friends. At midnight, eight bells were rung, whistles blew and a cannon salute was fired.

The perfect boat is the one being used. Mine have ranged from a 8' Sea Scout sailing pram to a 24' Blanchard sloop, and now my 18' "sled," *Jus' Think'n.*

The fun of sailing–the energy rush when slicing a curve while downhill skiing is the same rush I feel when sailing rail down.

John Cole, *M/V Jus' Think'n,* Seattle

SERIAL No. 696

TIDAL CURRENT CHARTS, PUGET SOUND, NORTHERN PART

THIRD EDITION 1973

These current charts show the direction and speed of the tidal current for each hour of the current at Admiralty Inlet (off Bush Point). They present a comprehensive view of the tidal current movement in the waterways which comprise the northern part of the sound and also supply a means of readily determining for any time the direction and speed of the current at numerous locations throughout those waterways.

The charts, which may be used for any year, are referred to the times of "Maximum flood" and "Maximum ebb" at Admiralty Inlet (off Bush Point), daily predictions for which are included in the Pacific Coast Current Tables published annually by the National Ocean Survey.

The directions of the current are indicated by arrows and the speeds by figures. The speeds, which are expressed in knots, are tropic speeds, that is, the greater flood and greater ebb speeds at the time of the moon's maximum declination. Factors for obtaining the speeds for any time are given below.

Nontidal currents.—These charts depict the flow of the tidal currents under normal weather conditions. Winds and freshets, however, bring about nontidal currents which may modify considerably the speeds and directions shown on the charts.

Use of charts.—There are 12 charts, 6 being referred to "Maximum flood" and 6 to "Maximum ebb." The chart to be used for a given time is determined by obtaining the difference between that time and the time of the nearest "Maximum flood" or "Maximum ebb" for Admiralty Inlet (off Bush Point) as given in the Pacific Coast Current Tables. The chart with the legend that agrees most nearly with this difference is the one to be used.

Having selected the proper chart, the direction and the tropic speed of the current throughout the area are shown by the arrows and figures on that chart.

The tidal current varies from day to day principally in accordance with the phase, distance and declination of the moon; and to obtain the speed for a particular day and hour the speed given on the chart should be modified as follows: Note whether the speed on the chart is accompanied by solid arrows or by dashed arrows. If the arrows are solid, obtain from the current tables the predicted speed of the "Maximum flood" nearest to the time for which the information is sought. If the arrows are dashed, obtain the predicted speed of the nearest "Maximum ebb." With the predicted speed enter the following table and obtain the corresponding correction factor. The speed of the current for the particular day and hour is then determined by multiplying the speed indicated on the chart by this factor.

In taking a flood factor from the table, note that the special factor in the third column of the table is to be used only when the speed on the chart is followed by the letter "a."

The asterisk (*) in the first column of the table corresponds to the asterisk which appears in the "Maximum flood" speed column of the predictions for Admiralty Inlet (off Bush Point).

The complexity of the current in Puget Sound, particularly the change in the character of the diurnal inequality from place to place, renders it impossible to devise a set of current charts which through a simple method of procedure always gives precise results. Some differences between current-chart values and actual currents encountered are, therefore, to be expected.

The large diurnal inequality usually exhibited by the Puget Sound current makes it very undesirable, except in the case of Port Townsend Canal, to use the speeds given on these charts without correcting them by means of the table of factors.

Off Bush Point, a "Maximum ebb" sometimes precedes a "Maximum flood" by a time interval as small as 5 hours. Consequently a time which is 3 hours after a predicted "Maximum ebb" may be very nearly the same as a time which is 2 hours before a predicted "Maximum flood." If current information is desired for such a time, it is usually advisable to obtain it from the chart designated "THREE HOURS AFTER MAXIMUM EBB OFF BUSH POINT."

The current in Port Townsend Canal differs from the current elsewhere in Puget Sound in that it is hydraulic, depending upon tidal differences in water level at the two ends of the canal. It exhibits much less diurnal inequality and has less variation in velocity from day to day than the usual Puget Sound current. The speed for Port Townsend Canal given on each chart therefore is an average (not tropic) speed which requires no correction factor. A notation to that effect appears on each chart.

Example.—Suppose the direction and speed of the current in midchannel off Point Wilson are desired for 5 a.m. on a day when the predictions for Admiralty Inlet (off Bush Point) are as follows:

SLACK WATER TIME H.M.	TIME H.M.	MAXIMUM CURRENT VEL. KNOTS
0101	0354	2.3 F
0657	1024	2.8 E
1405	1610	1.2 F
1824	2214	2.8 E

The desired time, 5 a.m., is $1^h 06^m$ after the "Maximum flood" at $3^h 54^m$, this being the nearest predicted maximum strength of current. The data desired will therefore be found on the chart designated "ONE HOUR AFTER MAXIMUM FLOOD OFF BUSH POINT." This chart shows that the current in midchannel off Point Wilson is setting east-southeastward. The number (3.3) at that location is the tropic speed of the current in knots. To determine the speed of the current for the particular day and hour, this tropic speed must be modified by a factor given in the table, "Factors for correcting speeds." Since the arrows accompanying this speed are solid arrows the proper factor will be found under the heading "Flood factors," and since the letter "a" follows the speed on the chart the factor is in the "Special factor" column. The predicted maximum flood nearest to $5^h 00^m$ occurs at $3^h 54^m$ and its speed is 2.3 knots. For a maximum flood speed of 2.3 knots the table gives a "Special factor" of 0.9 to be applied to the speed of the current in midchannel off Point Wilson is then $3.3 \times 0.9 = 3.0$ knots.

As the time $5^h 00^m$ is more than one hour after the nearest predicted maximum current, which occurs at $3^h 54^m$, a more precise value may be obtained by interpolating between values obtained from the two charts designated "ONE HOUR AFTER MAXIMUM FLOOD OFF BUSH POINT" and "TWO HOURS AFTER MAXIMUM FLOOD OFF BUSH POINT."

The corrected speed as obtained above from the chart for one hour after maximum flood is 3.0 knots setting east-southeastward, while a corrected speed similarly obtained from the chart for two hours after maximum flood is 1.8 knots setting approximately in the same direction. Interpolating between these values, the current in midchannel off Point Wilson at 5 a.m. is found to set east-southeastward with a velocity of 2.9 knots.

Factors for correcting speeds

Flood factors			Ebb factors	
For use with speeds accompanied by solid arrows			For use with speeds accompanied by dashed arrows	
When predicted "Maximum flood" speed (knots) off Bush Point is—	Multiply speed on chart by—		When predicted "Maximum ebb" speed (knots) off Bush Point is—	Multiply speed on chart by—
	Usual factor	Special factor "a"		Factor
(*)	0.0	0.2	0.3–0.4	0.1
0.3	0.1	0.3	0.5–0.8	0.2
0.4–0.6	0.2	0.4	0.9–1.1	0.3
0.7–0.8	0.3	0.5	1.2–1.4	0.4
0.9–1.1	0.4	0.6	1.5–1.8	0.5
1.2–1.3	0.5	0.6		
			1.9–2.1	0.6
1.4–1.6	0.6	0.6	2.2–2.4	0.7
1.7–1.8	0.7	0.7	2.5–2.8	0.8
1.9–2.1	0.8	0.8	2.9–3.1	0.9
2.2–2.3	0.9	0.9	3.2–3.4	1.0
2.4–2.6	1.0	1.0		
			3.5–3.7	1.1
2.7–2.8	1.1	1.1	3.8–4.1	1.2
2.9–3.1	1.2	1.2	4.2–4.4	1.3
3.2–3.3	1.3	1.3	4.5–4.7	1.4
3.4–3.6	1.4	1.4		
3.7–3.8	1.5	1.5		

(Text scanned in from the front cover of Tidal Current Charts, Puget Sound, Northern Part)

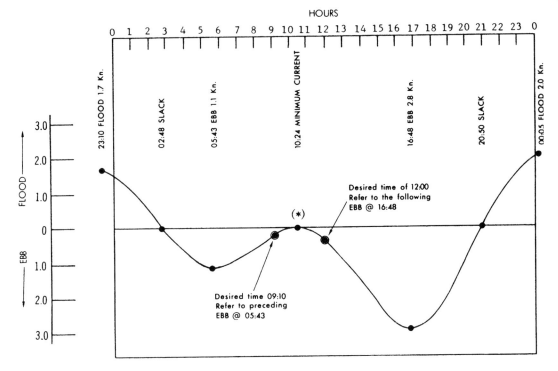

HOURS

The asterisk (*) indicates the current to be weak and variable and possibly ebbing. In these cases use the Tidal Current Charts that are referred to maximum ebb.
The chart to be used is determined in the following manner. When the desired time falls before the perdicted minimum current (*), then refer to the preceding maximum ebb. When the desired time falls after the predicted minimum current (*), refer to the following maximum ebb.

Admiralty Inlet off Bush Point, Washington

Day	Slack Water Time H.M.	Maximum Time H.M.	Current Velocity Knots
9	0142	0433	0.9E
W		*0912	(*)
		1547	2.6E
	2004	2310	1.7F
10	0248	0543	1.1E
TH		*1024	(*)
		1648	2.8E
	2050		
11		0005	2.0F
F	0337	0636	1.4E
		*1129	(*)
		1739	3.0E
	2134		

Above information is from the back cover of Tidal Current Charts, Puget Sound, Northern Part. Please note we have placed instructions contained in the NOAA publications here. The 12 hourly current charts are on the following pages.

(F-1)
One hour before Max flood at Bush Point

(F-2)
Two hours before Max flood at Bush Point

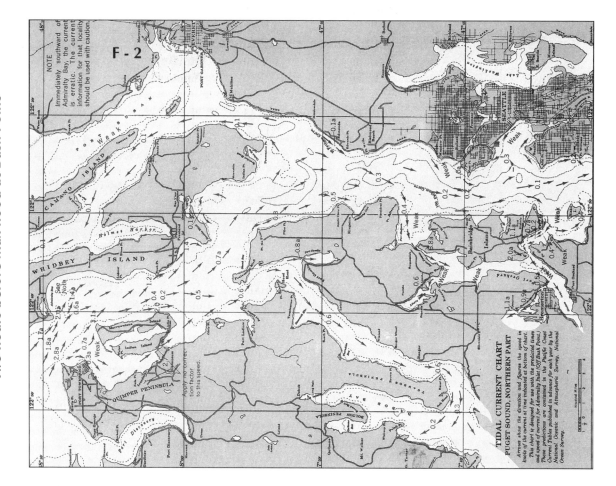

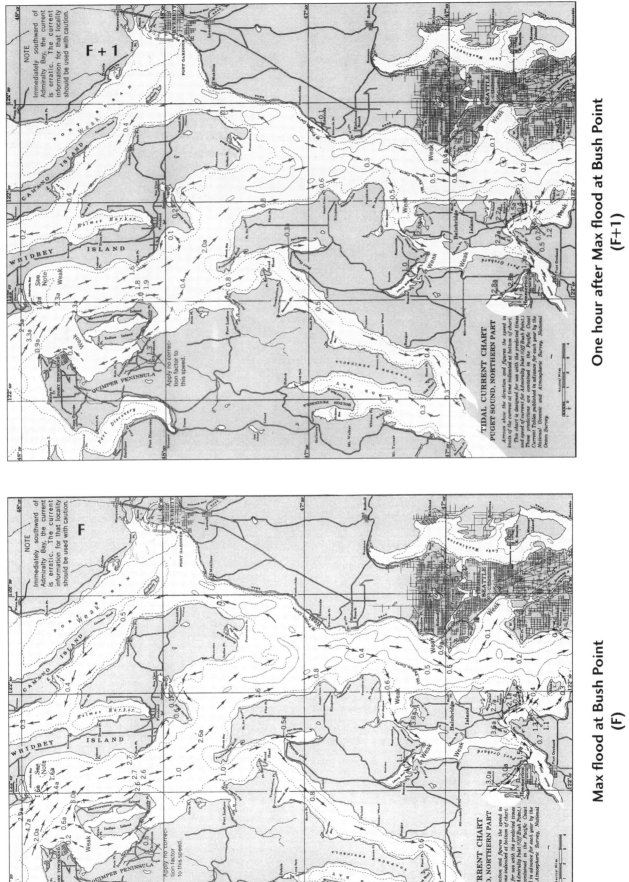

One hour after Max flood at Bush Point
(F+1)

Max flood at Bush Point
(F)

(F+3)
Three Hours After Max Flood at Bush Point

(F+2)
Two hours after Max Flood at Bush Point

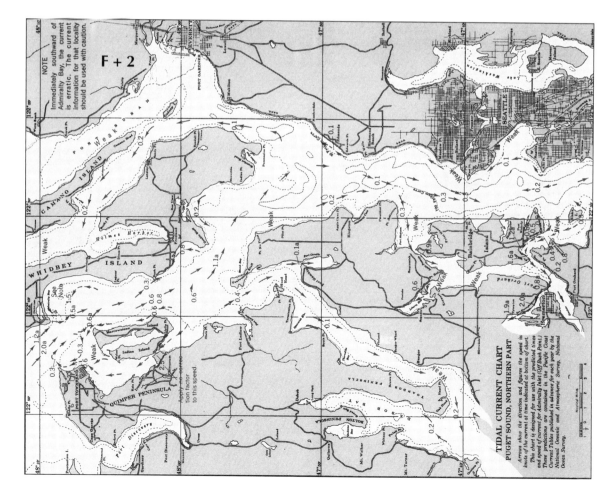

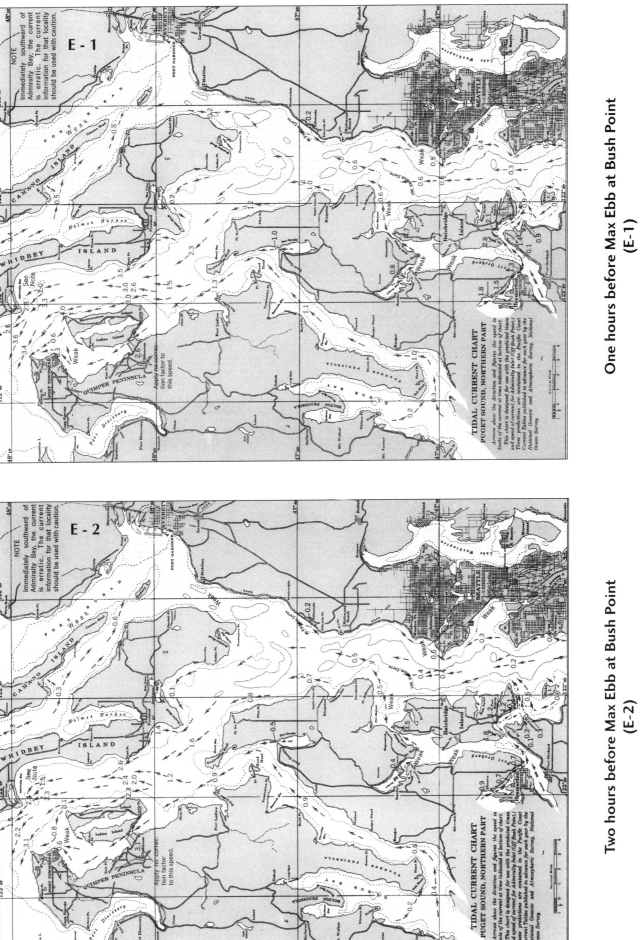

One hours before Max Ebb at Bush Point (E-1)

Two hours before Max Ebb at Bush Point (E-2)

(E+1)
Two hours before Max Flood at Bush Point

(E)
Max Ebb at Bush Point

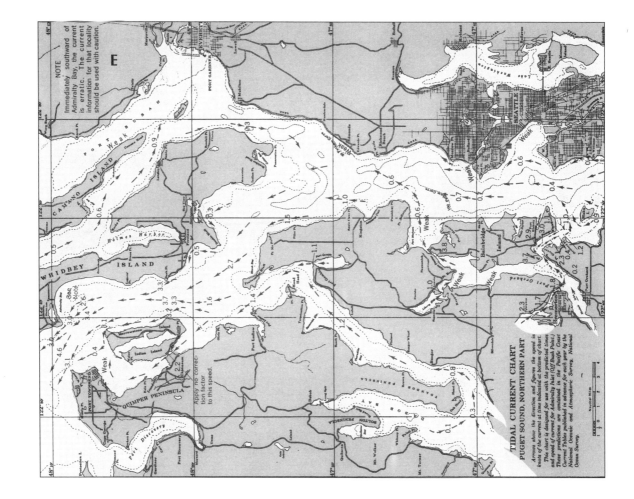

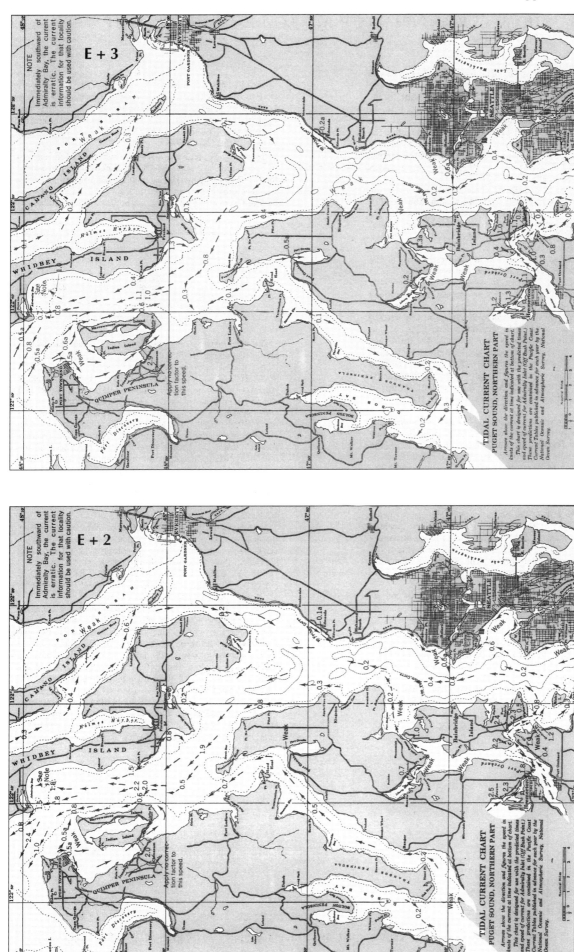

**Three hours after Max Ebb at Bush Point
(E+3)**

**Two hours after Max Ebb at Bush Point
(E+2)**

TIDAL CURRENT CHARTS, PUGET SOUND, SOUTHERN PART
Third Edition, 1973

These current charts show the hourly directions and speeds of the tidal current in Puget Sound)southern part). They present a comprehensive view of the tidal current in the entire area and also provide a means for readily determining for any time the direction and speed of the current at various locations throughout many of the inlets and passages of the sound. The directions of the current are indicated by arrows and speeds in knots by figures. Observations of the current from the surface to a maximum depth of 20 feet were used in compiling these charts.

The charts may be used for any year and are referred to the times of "Maximum Flood" and "Maximum Ebb" at The Narrows (north end), Puget Sound. Daily predictions for this station are included in the publication "Tidal Current Tables, Pacific Coast of North America and Asia", published annually by the National Ocean Survey.

Non-tidal currents—These charts picture the flow of the tidal currents under normal weather conditions. Strong winds and freshets, however, bring about nontidal currents which may modify considerably by speeds and directions shown on the charts.

Use of charts—There are twelve charts; six are referred to "Maximum Flood" and six to "Maximum Ebb". The chart to be used for a desired time is determined by the difference between that time and the predicted time of the nearest "Maximum Flood" or "Maximum Ebb" for the Narrows (north end), as published in "Tidal Current Tables, Pacific Coast of North America and Asia". The chart with the legend that agrees most nearly with that difference is the one to be used.

Factors for correcting velocities:—The speeds shown on the charts represent the current at the time of tropic tides. They are the greater flood and greater ebb speeds at the time of the moon's maximum declination. However, the tidal current varies from day to day, principally in accordance with the phase, distance and declination of the moon. Therefore to obtain speeds for the particular day and hour, the plotted speeds on the chart must be modified accordingly. This is done by selecting from the tidal current tables the predicted speed of the "Maximum Flood" or "Maximum Ebb" to which the chart is referred. With this predicted speed enter the appropriate column of the following table and obtain the corresponding correction factor. The speeds on the tidal current chart are then multiplied by this factor to obtain the required speeds.

For the west end of Hale Passage and the north end of Peale Passage, the given average speeds of the current should not be modified by the use of the factors from the table.

The complexity of the current in Puget Sound, particularly the difference in speed between the two flood currents or the two ebb currents of each day, renders it impossible to construct a set of current charts which, through a simple procedure, always give accurate predictions. Some differences between the current as derived from these charts and actually encountered are, therefore, to be expected.

Factors for Correcting Speeds

When the predicted speed in The Narrows (north end) is—	Multiply speed on chart by—
Knots:	Factor
0.2—0.5	0.1
0.6—0.9	0.2
1.0—1.3	0.3
1.4—1.7	0.4
1.8—2.1	0.5
2.2—2.5	0.6
2.6—2.9	0.7
3.0—3.3	0.8
3.4—3.7	0.9
3.8—4.1	1.0
4.2—4.5	1.1
4.6—4.9	1.2
5.0—5.3	1.3
5.4—5.7	1.4
5.8—6.1	1.5

CAUTION NOTE: In The Narrows a "Maximum Ebb" often precedes a "Maximum Flood" by a time interval much shorter than the average interval of about 6 hours. When this interval becomes as short as 4 or 5 hours, two different charts may apply to the same times, and a different result for the current at these times will be obtained from each chart. (See instructions on inside back cover).

Example.—Suppose the direction and speed of the current in midchannel east of the south end of Fox Island are desired for 1:00 P.M. (1300 hrs.) on a day when the predictions for The Narrows (north end) as given in the "Tidal Current Tables, Pacific Coast of North America and Asia" are as follows:

SLACK WATER		MAXIMUM CURRENT
TIME	TIME	VEL.
H.M.	H.M.	KNOTS
01 18	04 12	4.4F
07 33	10 38	3.3E
13 52	16 31	3.5F
19 32	22 46	3.6E

The desired time 1300 hrs., is 2^h 22^m after the nearest predicted maximum ebb at 10^h 38^m. Therefore the chart to be used is the one designated "TWO HOURS AFTER MAXIMUM EBB AT THE NARROWS" (E+2). This chart indicates that the current in midchannel east of the south end of Fox Island is setting north-northeastward (ebbing) with a tropic speed of 1.6 knots. To determine the speed of the current for the particular day and hour, this tropic speed must be modified by a factor given in the table "Factors for correcting speeds". From the Tidal Current Tables the speed of the current at 1038 (time of maximum current used as reference) is 3.3 knots. For a predicted maximum speed of 3.3 knots, the table gives a factor of 0.8 to be applied to the speed on the chart. The approximate speed of the current in midchannel east of the south end of Fox Island is therefore 1.6 × 0.8 = 1.3 knots.

As the time 13^h 00^m is somewhat more than two hours after the nearest maximum current, which occurs at 10^h 38^m, a more precise prediction may be obtained by interpolating between values obtained from the two charts designated "TWO HOURS AFTER MAXIMUM EBB AT THE NARROWS" (E+2) and "THREE HOURS AFTER MAXIMUM EBB AT THE NARROWS" (E+3).

The corrected speed as obtained above from the chart for two hours after maximum ebb is 1.3 knots setting north-north-eastward, while a corrected speed similarly obtained from the chart for three hours after maximum ebb is 0.6 knot setting approximately in the same direction. Interpolating between these values, the current in midchannel east of the south end of Fox Island at 1 p.m. is found to be setting north-northeast-ward with a speed of 1.0 knot.

All persons using these charts are invited to send information or suggestions for increasing their usefulness to the Director, National Ocean Survey, NOAA, U.S. Department of Commerce, Rockville, Maryland 20852.

(Text scanned in from the front cover of Tidal Current Charts, Puget Sound, Southern Part)

For sale by National Ocean Survey, NOAA, Rockville Maryland 20852 or from authorized sales agents.

EFFECT OF THE MOON'S DECLINATION ON THE USE OF TIDAL CURRENT CHARTS

The Puget Sound, Southern Part Tidal Current Charts are calculated using the average flood duration is 6^h19^m and the yearly average ebb duration is 6^h06^m as tabulated in Table 1. The speeds were calculated using the average tropic speeds.

These charts are calculated for conditions when the tidal cycles are divided into six hourly intervals as shown in Figure 1. Each hourly chart is referred to the time of maximum current.

The duration of flood and ebb varies throughout the month in accordance with the moon's phases (see Figure 2). Equatorial currents occur semimonthly as a result of the moon's being over the equator. At these times the tendency of the moon to produce a diurnal inequality in the current is at a minimum. There are no problems during these periods when the floods and ebbs have durations that allow the selection of the normal six hourly charts. At tropic tides when the moon is in its maximum north or south declination the current exhibits a maximum diurnal inequality. At these times the lesser flood and ebb durations do not permit the selection of the proper chart.

Caution must be taken to insure that the chart selected will be referred to the predicted maximum current.

EXAMPLE: The speed and direction of the current are required east of Munson Pt. in Hammersley Inlet for 13^h20^m on a day when the predictions for The Narrows (North End) Puget Sound as given in the "Tidal Current Tables, Pacific Coast of North America and Asia" are as follows:

Slack Water Time	Maximum Time	Current Velocity
H M	H M	Knots
0226	0444	1.1E
0744	1020	1.9F
1240	1629	3.5E
2024	2328	3.8F

(See figure 3)

INSTRUCTIONS: Even though the desired time of 13^h20^m is closer to the maximum flood (10^h20^m) than the maximum ebb (1629), we note that the current at The Narrows (North End) is ebbing (Figure 3). The chart to use is E−2. More precise results may be obtained by interpolating between the two charts designated E−2 and F−2.

(E−2) 0.6 x f0.9 = 0.54 knots flooding @ 14^h20^m
(F−2) 1.9 x F0.5 = 0.95 knots flooding @ 12^h20^m

The approximate speed of the current east of Munson Pt. at 13^h20^m is 0.8 knots, flooding.

Note that the short duration of the two lesser flood and ebb phases did not permit the division of six hourly intervals as shown in Figure 3. At these times of short duration the tidal current charts should not be used.

TABLE 1
GREENWICH Intervals

Slack	Flood	Flood Duration	Slack	Ebb	Ebb Duration
H M	H M	H M	H M	H M	H M
07:32	10:17	06:19	01:26	04:14	06:06

Average Tropic Speed (Knots)

Flood	Ebb
4.1	3.8

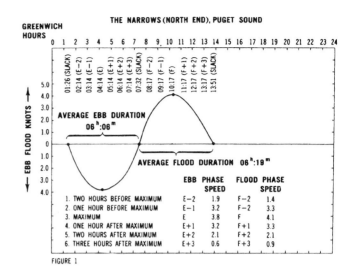

FIGURE 1

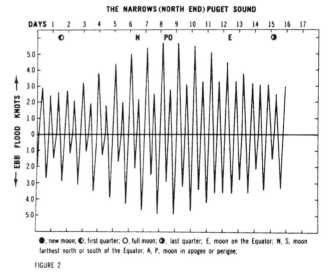

●, new moon; ◐, first quarter; ○, full moon; ◑, last quarter; E, moon on the Equator; N, S, moon farthest north or south of the Equator; A, P, moon in apogee or perigee;

FIGURE 2

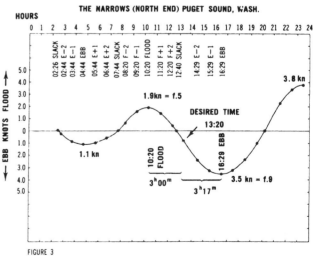

FIGURE 3

Text scanned from the front cover of Tidal Current Charts, Puget Sound, Southern Part. Please note we have placed instructions contained in the NOAA publications here. The 12 hourly current charts are on the following pages.

(F-2)
Two hours
before
Max flood at
The Narrows

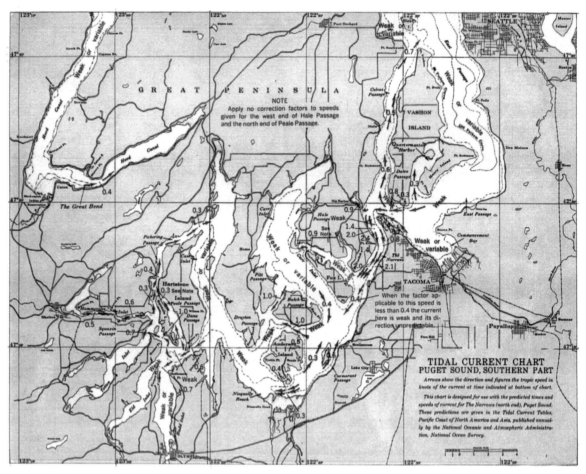

(F-1)
One hour
before
Max flood at
The Narrows

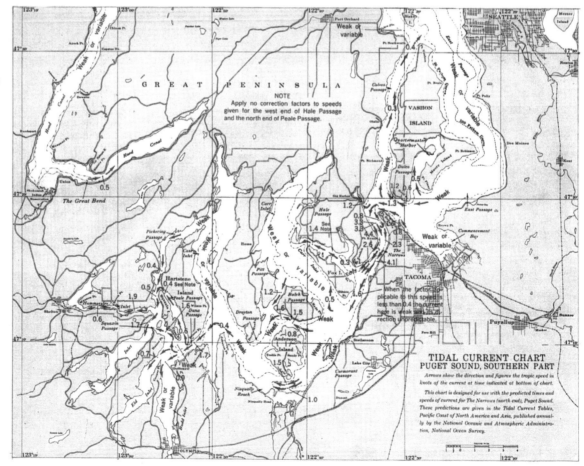

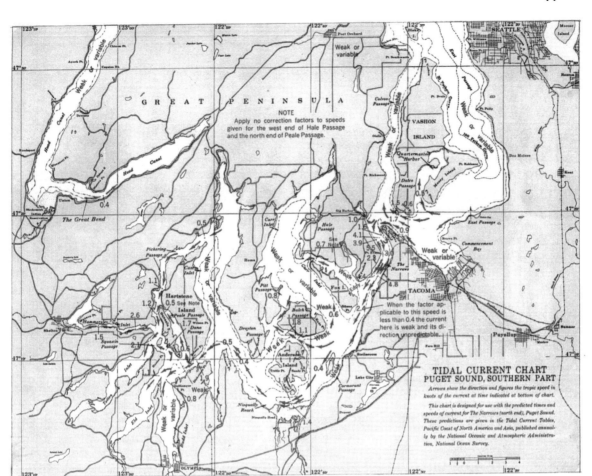

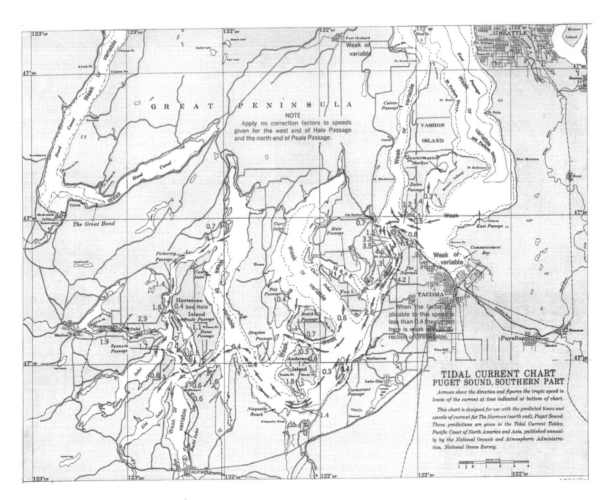

(F+2)
Two hours
before
Max flood at
The Narrows

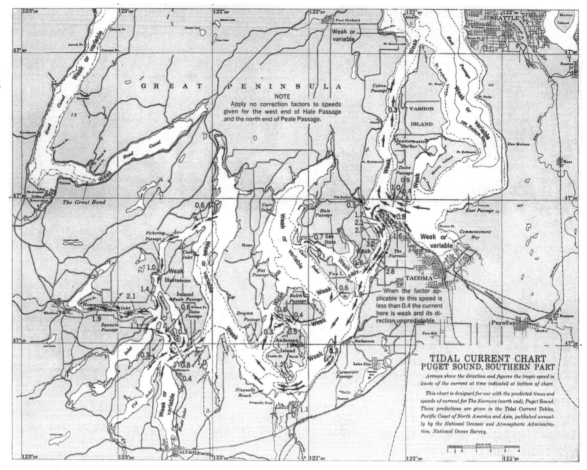

(F+3)
Three hours
before
Max flood at
The Narrows

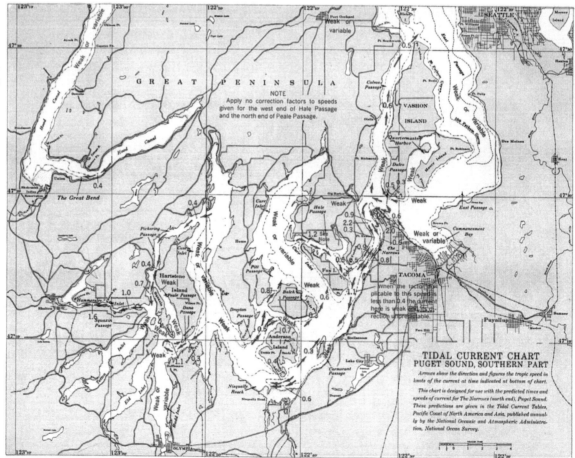

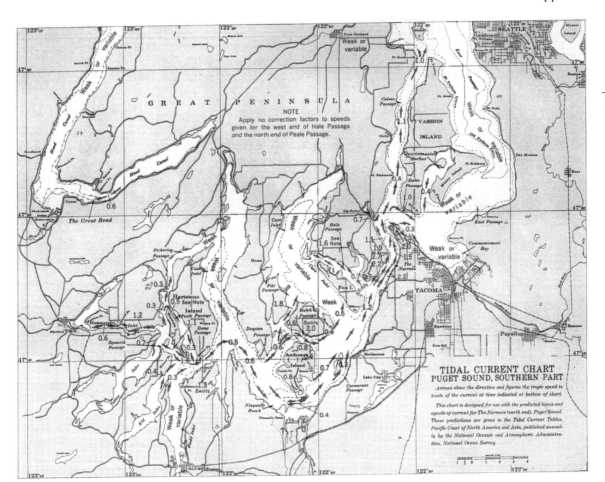

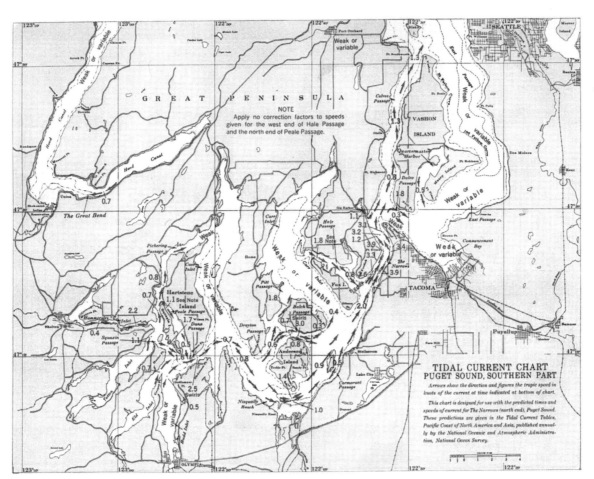

(E)
Max Ebb at
The Narrows

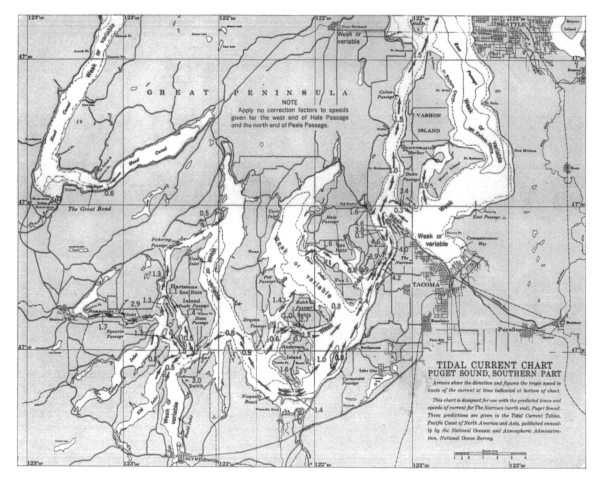

(E+1)
One hour
After
Max Ebb at
The Narrows

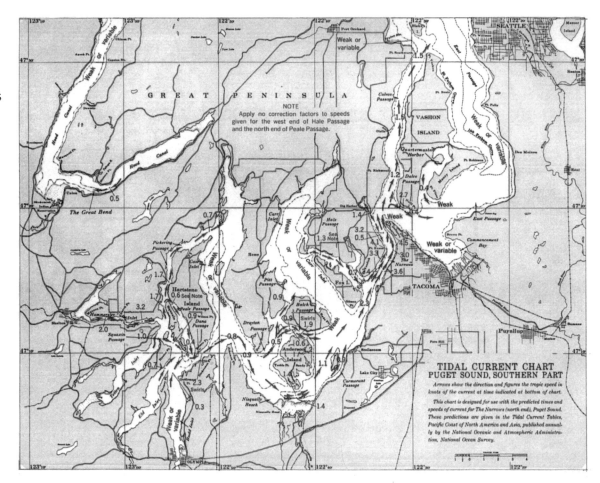

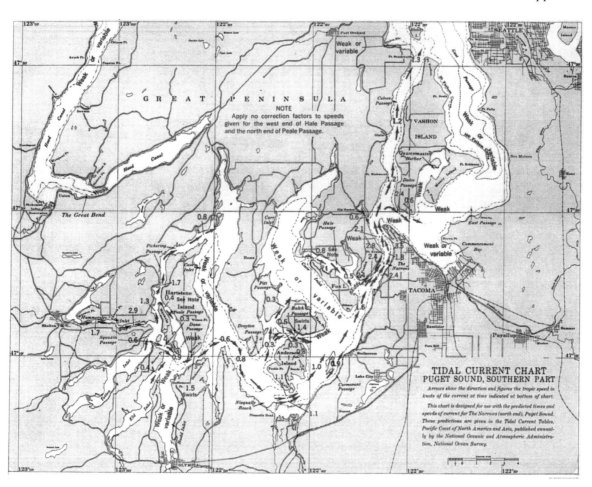

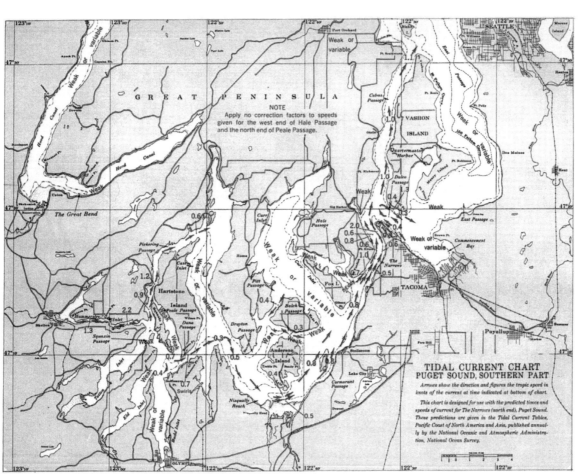

Bibliography

Barkan, Frances B. *The Wilkes Expedition: Puget Sound and the Oregon Country.* Washington State Capital Museum, 1987. Olympia, WA.

Cammon, Betsey Johnson. *Island Memoir, A Personal History of Anderson and McNeil Islands.* The Valley Press, Inc., 1969. Puyallup, WA.

Chapman, Charles F. *Piloting, Seamanship and Small Boat Handling.* Hearst Corporation, New York, N.Y.10019. 51st Ed. 1975.

Current and Tide Tables for Puget Sound, 1992. Bainbridge Island, WA. Island Canoe, Inc., 1991.

Dorpat, Paul. *Seattle Now and Then.* Seattle, WA. Tartu Publications, 1984.

Evans, Jack R. *Little History of Gig Harbor, Washington.* Seattle, WA. SCW Publications, 1988.

Ficken, Robert E. and LeWarne, Charles P. *Washington, A Centennial History.* Seattle, WA. University of Washington Press, 1988.

Fuller, George W. *A History of the Pacific Northwest.* New York, NY. Alfred A. Knopf, 1938.

Goodman Middle School Students. *Along the Waterfront: A History of the Gig Harbor and Key Peninsula Areas.* Gig Harbor, WA. Peninsula School District No. 401, Mostly Books & The Peninsula Historical Society, 1979.

Gotchy, Joe. *Bridging the Narrows.* Gig Harbor, WA. The Peninsula Historical Society, 1990.

Heckman, Hazel. *Island in the Sound.* Seattle, WA. University of Washington Press, 1967.

Hilson, Stephen E. *Exploring Puget Sound & British Columbia.* Holland, MN. Van Winkle Publishing Co., 1975.

Hitchcock, Beulah and Wingert, Helen. *The Island Remembers—A History of Harstine Island and Its People.* Harstine, WA. Harstine Island Women's Club, 1979.

Keve, Paul W. *The McNeil Century: The Life and Times of an Island Prison.* Chicago, Ill. Nelson-Hall, 1984.

Kirk, Ruth, and Alexander, Carmela. *Exploring Washington's Past, A Road Guide to History.* Seattle, WA. University of Washington Press, 1990.

Kitsap County Historical Society Book Committee. *Kitsap County History: A Story of Kitsap County and its Pioneers.* Silverdale, WA. Kitsap County Historical Society, 1977.

Kutz, David. *The Burgee, Premier Marina Guidebook, Second Edition.* Kingston, WA. Pierside Publishing, 1996.

Light List, Volume VI, Pacific Coast and Pacific Islands, 1995. U.S. Government Printing Office, Washington, D.C., 1995.

Meacham, Eva Pickrell. *A Chronicle of Indianola.* Silver Anniversary Edition 1993. Indianola, WA. Indianola Beach Improvement Club, 1995.

Meany, Edmond S. *Vancouver's Discovery of Puget Sound.* Portland, OR. Binfords & Mort, 1957.

Meeker, Ezra. *Pioneer Reminiscences of Puget Sound.* Seattle, WA. Lowman & Hanford Stationary & Printing Co., 1905. New materials copyright by Historical Society of Seattle & King County, WA., 1980.

Morgan, Murray and Rosa. *South on the Sound: An Illustrated History of Tacoma and Pierce County.* Woodland Hills, CA. Windsor Publications, Inc., 1984.

Morgan, Murray. *Puget's Sound. A Narrative of Early Tacoma and the Southern Sound.* Seattle, WA. & London, England. University of Washington Press, 1979.

Morgan, Murray. *Skid Road: Seattle—Her First Hundred Years.* New York, NY. Ballantine Books, 1974.

Mueller, Marge and Ted. *South Puget Sound, Afoot and Afloat.* Seattle, WA. The Mountaineers, 1996.

Pacific NW Quarterly, XXX#2, April 1939. *Notes and Documents of the Vancouver Expedition: Peter Puget's Journal of the Exploration of Puget Sound, May 7-June 11, 1792.*

Phillips, James W. *Washington State Place Names.* Seattle, WA. University of Washington Press, 1972.

Puget Sound Public Shellfish Sites. Washington State Department of Fisheries, June 1989.

Readings in Pacific Northwest History, Washington, 1790-1895, edited by Charles Marvin Gates. Published by the University Bookstore, Seattle, WA., 1941.

Reed's Nautical Almanac, North American West Coast 1996. Thomas Reed Publications, Inc., Boston, MA., 1995.

Reed's Nautical Companion, North American edition, The Handbook to Complement Reed's Almanacs. Thomas Reed Publications, Inc., London, England, Boston, MA., 1993.

Renner, Jeff. *Northwest Marine Weather.* Seattle, WA. The Mountaineers, 1993.

Sagerson, Mary and Robinson, Duane. *Grapeview, the Detroit of the West. A Narrative History of the Early Years, 1872 to 1923.* Shelton, WA. Mason County Historical Society, 1992.

Scherer, Migael. *A Cruising Guide to Puget Sound.* Camden, ME. International Marine, 1995.

Scott, James W. and Reuling, Melly A. *Washington Public Shore Guide.* Seattle, WA. University of Washington Press, 1986.

Wing, Robert C., with Gordon Newell. *Peter Puget.* Seattle, WA. Gray Beard Publishing, 1979.

Winthrop, Theodore. *Canoe and Saddle: Nisqually Edition.* Portland, OR. Binfords & Mort.

Wood, Bryce. *San Juan Island: Coastal Place Names and Cartographic Nomenclature.* Ann Arbor, MI. University Microfilms International, 1980.

Your Public Beaches: South Puget Sound. Washington State Department of Natural Resources.

Glossary of Abbreviations from Navigation Charts & the Light List

AERO ...... aeronautical
Al, Alt ...... Alternating
Auth ...... Authorized
B ...... Black
Bkw ...... Breakwater
Bl ...... Blast
BM ...... Benchmark
Bn ...... Beacon
Bn TR ...... Beacon Tower
C ...... Can
Ch. ...... Church
Chy ...... Chimney
CL ...... Clearance
Cup, Cup. Cupola
DIA, Dia ...... Diaphone
DN, Dol ...... Dolphin
E ...... East
E Int ...... Equal interval, isophase
Ed ...... Existence doubtful
ELW ...... Extreme low water
Entr ...... Entrance
F ...... Fixed
F Fl ...... Fixed and flashing
Fl ...... Flashing
fm, fms ...... Fathom(s)
FP ...... Flagpole
ft ...... foot/feet
G ...... Green
Gp Fl ...... Group flashing
Gp Occ ...... Group occulting
Int Qk Fl .... Interrupted quick flashing
IQ ...... Interrupted quick
Iso ...... Isophase
kn ...... Knot(s)
Lag ...... Lagoon
Lt Ho ...... Lighthouse
Lt. ...... Light
m ...... Minutes
M ...... Nautical mile(s)
mag ...... Magnetic
Maintd ...... Maintained
MHHW ...... Mean higher high water
MHLW ...... Mean higher low water
MHW ...... Mean high water
MLLW ...... Mean lower low water
MLW ...... Mean low water
Mo ...... Morse
N ...... Nun
N ...... North
NE ...... Northeast
NM ...... Nautical mile(s)
NW ...... Northwest
Obsc ...... Obscured
Obstn ...... Obstruction

Obstr	Obstruction	SE	Southeast	**Bottom Characteristics**		
Occ	Occulting	SEC	Sector	Bk	Broken	
Or	Orange	Shl	Shoal	Blds	Boulders	
PA	Position approximate	Sk	Strikes	Cl, Cy	Clay	
PD	Position Doubtful	st	Stones	G	Gravel	
Priv	Private	St M	Statue miles	Grs	Grass	
PROHIB	Prohibited	Subm	Submerged	gy	Gray	
Q	Quick	Subm piles	Submerged piles	h	hard	
R	Red	Subm ruins	Submerged ruins	M	Mud, muddy	
R	Rock or Rocky	SW	Southwest	Oys	Oysters	
R Bn	Circular radiobeacon	Tr	Tower	Rk,rky	Rocky	
R TR	Radio tower	VQ	Very quick	S	Sand	
Ra Ref	Radar Reflector	W	West	Sft	Soft	
Radome	Radar dome	W	White	Sh	Shells	
Rep	Reported	W Or	White orange	so	soft	
Ru	Ruins	WHIS	Whistle	stk	Sticky	
S	South, southern	Wk	Wreck	sy	Sticky	
s, sec	Second(s)	Y	Yellow			

We welcome you to our Gunkholing family. We're delighted you have joined us ***Gunkholing in South Puget Sound.*** We'd like to have you participate in revisions of this book or other Gunkholing books.

Please mail or fax the coupon below, and we'll add you to our mailing list, updating you on changes, new editions of our books, or other interesting information. (We do not distribute the mailing list.)

We also encourage you to send us anything of interest you have noticed in your cruising that would enhance our books— or heaven forbid !— any changes, omissions or errors you may have found. Thanks for your help. Jo and Carl

Mailing Address: San Juan Enterprises, Inc.   **TEL:** 206-323-1315
                       3218 Portage Bay Place East   **FAX:** 206-328-0067
                       Seattle, WA 98102

— —

Name: _____

Address: _____City: _____ State: _____ Zip: _____

Tel: _____   Fax: _____

Remarks: _____

_____

_____